RESOURCES FOR THE FUTURE LIBRARY COLLECTION
GLOBAL ENVIRONMENT AND DEVELOPMENT

Volume 6

Population and Development
The Search for Selective Interventions

Full list of titles in the set
GLOBAL ENVIRONMENT AND DEVELOPMENT

Volume 1: Rural Women at Work
Volume 2: Natural Resource Information for Economic Development
Volume 3: Foreign Investment in the Petroleum and Mineral Industries
Volume 4: The Development of Tropical Lands
Volume 5: Economic Equality and Fertility in Developing Countries
Volume 6: Population and Development
Volume 7: The Seventh Continent

Population and Development
The Search for Selective Interventions

Ronald G. Ridker

RFF PRESS
RESOURCES FOR THE FUTURE

Washington, DC • London

First published in 1976 by The Johns Hopkins University Press for Resources for the Future

This edition first published in 2011 by RFF Press, an imprint of Earthscan

Earthscan LLC, 1616 P Street, NW, Washington, DC 20036, USA
Earthscan Ltd, Dunstan House, 14a St Cross Street, London EC1N 8XA, UK
Earthscan publishes in association with the International Institute for Environment and Development

For more information on RFF Press and Earthscan publications, see www. rffpress.org and www.earthscan.co.uk or write to earthinfo@earthscan.co.uk

ISBN: 978-1-61726-046-9 (Volume 6)
ISBN: 978-1-61726-005-6 (Global Environment and Development set)
ISBN: 978-1-61726-000-1 (Resources for the Future Library Collection)

A catalogue record for this book is available from the British Library

Publisher's note

The publisher has made every effort to ensure the quality of this reprint, but points out that some imperfections in the original copies may be apparent.

At Earthscan we strive to minimize our environmental impacts and carbon footprint through reducing waste, recycling and offsetting our CO_2 emissions, including those created through publication of this book. For more details of our environmental policy, see www.earthscan.co.uk.

Population and Development

Population and Development

The Search for Selective Interventions

RONALD G. RIDKER, EDITOR

Published for Resources for the Future
By The Johns Hopkins University Press, Baltimore and London

Manufactured in the United States of America

Library of Congress Catalog Card Number 76-16806

ISBN 0-8018-1884-2

Library of Congress Cataloging in Publication Data will be found on the last printed page of this book.

RESOURCES FOR THE FUTURE, INC.
1775 Massachusetts Avenue, N.W., Washington, D.C. 20036

This book is one of RFF's studies on institutions and public decisions, which are prepared under the direction of Clifford S. Russell. Ronald G. Ridker is a fellow in RFF's Institutions and Public Decisions Division. Figures 2-9, 4-1, 4-2, and 5-1 were prepared by Federal Graphics.

RFF editors: Herbert C. Morton, Joan R. Tron, Ruth B. Haas, Jo Hinkel, Sally A. Skillings

Contents

Tables

Figures

Preface

This book grew out of a project initiated by Resources for the Future to search for selective interventions into the development process that in turn might speed the course of fertility decline in developing countries. The authors were asked to review what is known about the linkages between fertility and those determinants of fertility that might be amenable to policy manipulation, to consider policies that might move these determinants in a favorable direction, and to discuss research needs and ways of satisfying them. The authors were selected not because of discipline or nationality, but because they had something to contribute, appreciated the goals of the assignment and the seriousness of the effort we wished to make, and yet were close enough to each other to work together whenever necessary. During the year devoted to this task, the authors met three times: twice to review outlines, coordinate plans, and exchange information, and finally, to discuss their findings with critical reviewers at a conference. The final papers, written after this 1975 conference and incorporating the reviewers' comments, are presented in this volume along with a summary and interpretation of these materials.

The result is a volume that we hope will find wide use, not only by researchers and serious students of population problems, but also by administrators and policy makers. The latter may feel that their immediate needs have been slighted somewhat, despite my effort to speak to their concerns in chapter 1. But there is no sense in pretending that we have adequate answers to policy questions when most authors feel a desperate need for better data and sharper research tools. On the other hand, it makes no sense for the policy maker to ignore the modest insights that researchers can offer; but to make proper use of these insights, he will have to understand the possibilities and limitations inherent in the methodology and data used to derive them.

A special vote of thanks must be reserved for the discussants, the unsung but often important contributors to every chapter of this volume.

Unfortunately, the length of this volume precluded inclusion of their formal comments. A list of the discussants, along with authors and their affiliations, appears as an appendix. I also want to express our gratitude to the Rockefeller Foundation, which provided financial support for this endeavor.

Washington, D.C.
February 1976

Ronald G. Ridker

Population and Development

1.

Perspectives on Population Policy and Research

RONALD G. RIDKER

Within the broad spectrum of proposals aired at the Bucharest World Population Conference in 1974, the two policies most commonly advocated for reducing population growth in poor countries were more rapid economic growth and more effective family-planning programs. The former, it is believed, creates the desire for smaller families and the latter provide the means. There is evidence to support both positions. No country has ever achieved a high standard of living without experiencing a significant decline in its birth rate. Nor has any sizable country in modern times experienced low birth rates over sustained periods in the absence of significant economic growth. One can argue about the degree to which these generalizations apply to this country, or that, and can find historical counterexamples.[1] Moreover, some hopeful signs in one or two of the developing countries indicate that birth rates may fall in the next few decades before general economic development occurs. But as generalizations go in this field these two are better than most.

There is also growing evidence from a variety of countries which suggests that easier access to the information, services, and supplies provided by modern family-planning programs is effective in reducing the gap between desired and actual family size (Berelson 1974; IBRD 1974, ch. 5; Mauldin 1975). The extent of the effect in relation to the

[1] New evidence on the demographic transition in nineteenth-century Europe indicates that in some areas birth rates began declining before the spread of a number of important aspects of development, such as rising standards of living, industrialization, urbanization, and declines in mortality. This fact, plus the substantial differences between nineteenth-century Europe and today's less developed countries, should make us pause before assuming that development today is either a necessary or a sufficient condition for a decline in birth rates, despite the high correlation between the two. For an excellent summary of this viewpoint, see Teitelbaum (1975).

effort involved is difficult to judge because of substitutions between methods, simultaneously occurring social and economic changes that also influence family size, and difficulties in measuring levels and quality of effort. But there is no reason to doubt that such programs are capable of reaching and influencing those persons who are already motivated or easily encouraged to have small families.

For countries with good prospects for rapid socioeconomic development and reasonably good administrative infrastructures, sustained efforts in both these directions may indeed prove to be sufficient, though the time lags involved could be substantial. The most difficult problem arises in those countries that cannot achieve adequate rates of development in the near future, just because of rapid population growth. In such cases, the number of persons desiring small families may not grow fast enough to give even the best-run family-planning program enough to work on. If population growth is to be curbed reasonably soon, such countries must search for a third approach. This volume is dedicated to that search.

Each of the essays presented here focuses on one hypothesized socioeconomic determinant of fertility believed to be amenable to policy manipulation. The authors were asked to review what is known about the linkages between these determinants and fertility, to consider policies that might affect these determinants in a direction favorable to a decline in fertility, and to discuss research needs and possibilities to fill gaps in our understanding of these linkages and the efficacy of possible policies. Not all determinants and policy choices have been discussed. In general, we have limited ourselves to possibilities of changing the environment within which marital and parental decisions are made so as to increase the costs and decrease the benefits, broadly defined, that are perceived to be associated with the bearing and rearing of children, focusing on those that seem compatible with other goals, such as economic development, political stability, and individual freedom of choice. Within this set the choice has been further limited by a number of practical considerations, including the availability of information and hunches about promising possibilities. For example, legal and legislative changes pertaining to such factors as the age of marriage, school attendance, and child labor were set aside on grounds that while they do reinforce and sanction changes in attitudinal and behavioral patterns that are already under way, they cannot in general *initiate* such changes in an environment that is not ripe for it. In contrast, we have given substantial, though far from exclusive, emphasis to economic variables, since much of the business of government is to manipulate these variables. While many of them seem to be less strongly associated with fertility than some psychological and sociological variables, the policy emphasis of this volume makes us much less interested in explanatory power than in the "instrumental" capacity of a possible determinant of fertility.

Our focus is on poor countries that believe they have a population problem and are actively trying to do something about it. Because of the paucity of data on any one country, however, we must utilize evidence wherever it can be found. This problem—as well as the proclivities of some of the authors—has led to a greater emphasis on research needs and findings than on policy. Stronger emphasis on matters of policy would require getting into specific cultural, economic, institutional, and political issues within a particular country or even a region of a country—which it would have been highly inappropriate for us to attempt at the distance from which our observations were made. The governments involved must take the responsibility for utilizing the available evidence and sponsoring the additional studies necessary to turn general suggestions of the type presented in this volume into specific sets of policies that make sense in each locale. We shall be satisfied if the volume contributes to that process. Indeed, one indicator of success will be the rapidity with which this volume is made obsolete by more detailed, policy-oriented studies in specific countries.

Income and Its Distribution

A wide array of results are found in studies that attempt to relate income to fertility. Some find a positive, others a negative, and still others a curvilinear relationship as family income rises from low levels; and in a few studies no relationship at all is found. Part of the reason for these mixed results is the poor quality of the available data. *Income,* for example, should mean the full family income a couple expects to receive over their lifetimes, not the money income received in a particular year and certainly not some per capita regional or national average. But the most important reason is a failure to separate statistically the demographic effects of income from those of other variables. Practically all socioeconomic variables that might be important in explaining fertility are correlated with income; unless these variables are identified and measured and adjustments are made for their effects, one cannot properly assess the pure effect of income, however carefully defined and measured it may be.

Julian Simon tries to make sense of these studies by dividing them in two groups: those that are more or less appropriate for measuring what he calls the short-run, direct effects of income and those that come closer to measuring the long-run, total effects. The latter include the effects on fertility that operate indirectly through such variables as education and health, which are also influenced by the change in income. Since the immediate effect of an increase in income is to make it easier to finance marriage and support children, one would expect that the short-run, direct effect is positive: more income encourages larger families. This is just what Simon finds. In contrast, he finds that the long-run, total effect tends to be negative, at least above the lowest income levels. While a number of hypotheses have been put forward to explain these long-run results—and we shall come back to some of them in other sections—statistical problems make it difficult to put forward any explanation in which great confidence can be placed.

Unfortunately, these findings are of little help in making policy recommendations. The short-run effect is positive rather than negative, and to take full advantage of the long-run effect requires general economic development, which presumably is being pushed as fast as it can be in any case. But more to the point, these findings are too general and unspecific to be useful for policy. The effect of a change in income is likely to vary depending on whose income is being changed (which socioeconomic groups and which family members), how it is changed (through transfers, changes in the labor market such as increased wages or opportunities for more work, or changes in the ownership of wealth, for example), whether the change is considered transitory or permanent, and whether it is provided without reference to fertility behavior or is offered upon the condition of a change in such behavior (that is, as an incentive). It is at this level of detail that we are likely to find useful policy suggestions. For example, while the short-run effects on fertility of an increase in adult male earnings and opportunities for child labor are likely to be positive, both the short-run and the long-run effects of an increase in female wages or opportunities for work outside the home could well be strongly negative.[2] Similarly, there is good reason to believe that a conditional transfer of income will have a strong negative effect on fertility, even if the underlying pure income effect is positive.

Such issues are discussed later in this chapter. In the remainder of this section we concentrate on the question of which family incomes are being raised. Specifically, what difference would a change in income distribution have on fertility rates?

Recent thinking about economic development has shifted somewhat away from an exclusive emphasis on general economic development

[2] Such results are found in a number of U.S. studies. See De Tray (1972), Cain and Weininger (1973), and Lindert (forthcoming, ch. 5). But also see chapter 10 in this volume for a contrary view.

toward a concern for the poorest segments of the population. Frustrated attempts to raise national growth rates to acceptable levels in some countries, growing evidence that the poor often do not participate in whatever national growth there is, and recent concerns that the rural poor may *have* to be enlisted in the development process if adequate supplies of food and agricultural raw materials are to be forthcoming for other segments of the population have all come together to explain this new emphasis. Parallel with this shift in focus of development programs have come suggestions that redistribution of income might also encourage a more rapid rate of decline in the birth rate.[3] Typically, the poorer 60 percent of households receive 30 percent of the income but have fertility rates some 50 percent higher than the richer 40 percent of households. If socioeconomic development were concentrated here, perhaps the birth rate could be reduced by a larger amount per dollar of investment than it could by means of an across-the-board approach.

The little evidence that is available is certainly encouraging, as Simon's review indicates. But several questions can be raised about this approach. First, why *should* a redistribution of income in favor of the poor be effective in lowering their birth rates? If the argument is based on the assumption of emulation of upper-income-class norms, it is not at all certain which way completed family size would be affected. Is it the desire of lower-income groups to emulate the consumption patterns or the completed family size of the rich? If the former, the poor should now be having *fewer* children than do the rich, since larger shares of their incomes must be laid out in attempting to achieve those expenditure norms per child, and in this case an increase in their income would raise their fertility. If the latter, fertility would fall with an increase in income as the poor acquired the knowledge and means to purchase modern contraceptives. But if inadequate knowledge and contraceptive supplies are the principal reasons that the poor have more children than the rich, surely a cheaper way to close this gap is through a focused program of family planning. If the argument is based on the long-run, total effects of the change in absolute level of income, as Simon suggests, we must ask whether these total effects are likely to occur as a consequence of income redistribution alone; that is, without concomitant changes in the provision of social overhead capital and other structural changes—perhaps even including urbanization and occupational changes—which are normally associated with modernization and development.

[3] See chapter 2 in this volume for references to the literature. In addition, the World Bank has recently added a strong voice to this chorus. See IBRD (1974, ch. 5).

Second, the evidence is based on data that do not permit us to answer such questions. It is virtually impossible to hold cultural and institutional variables constant in cross-country comparisons, and data from the national level, while suggestive, provide little basis for indicating whether it is the relative or the absolute income effect of the redistribution that is important or which of the many variables normally correlated with income have also to be changed to bring about the desired effect.[4]

Third, as Simon demonstrates, the specific measures utilized to implement the redistribution are likely to be more important than the redistribution itself. For example, on the basis of survey data indicating that family size among peasants increases with landholdings, he suggests that the net effect of land reform could be an increase in aggregate fertility. This finding is, of course, very shaky, and as Eva Mueller points out, uniformly small holdings, as they exist in Taiwan, would reduce both the need and the opportunities for employment of children in peasant societies. The most promising approach, Simon believes, is redistribution of educational facilities, providing in particular more primary- and secondary-level facilities in rural areas.

Such redistributions, however, are difficult to implement, and their effects on fertility could take several decades to be felt. For these reasons, but even more important because redistributions involve political acts of profound dimensions, it is unrealistic to believe that they will ever be proposed for the primary purpose of reducing fertility.

The overall impression with which one is left is that unconditional transfers of income, while they could well be effective in lowering fertility in the long run, operate through a wide variety of other variables associated with modernization and development. If one is to speed up the process, either these other variables must be identified and the most critical ones changed as a package along with income (or the capacity to produce income), or the transfer must be made conditional upon an appropriate fertility response. This is a theme to which we will return after reviewing the possible impact of a number of these other variables.

Economic Value of Children

No one would claim that children are desired solely or even primarily because of their value as productive economic assets, but it would be a

[4] An exception to this statement may be a recently completed (but not yet published) study by Robert G. Repetto of households in Puerto Rico in which he tries to separate the relative from the absolute income effect and finds that the latter is more important.

rare case in which this consideration was entirely absent. And so long as it is present to some degree, the economic benefits and costs of children are worth investigating, for they are far more capable of being influenced by policy than are most of the noneconomic benefits and costs associated with children.

Given the broad view of their field often taken by economists, practically everything to be discussed in this volume affects the economic value of children. But here we consider just two principal components: the net contribution that children make to the family's income through their work (that is, their production minus their consumption) and the contribution they make later in life to the support of aging parents. Unfortunately, the available evidence is not only spotty and scarce, it is also ill suited for policy analysis. It is most useful for answering questions on the extent of the economic contributions and costs of children, while the fundamental need, as Repetto points out, is for information on how fertility changes when these economic benefits and costs change, no matter what the extent or even the sign of the net contribution. Still, an understanding of the economic role played by children may provide some hints about the feasibility of different policy alternatives and about the likely value of additional research to generate the more appropriate kinds of data.

Attitude surveys, anecdotal evidence, and even some a priori reasoning suggest that raising children provides some net economic benefits to parents, at least in peasant societies. But after carefully sifting through the evidence Mueller finds that children are usually a heavy economic burden. Up to some age between fifteen and nineteen they produce substantially less than they consume; indeed, aggregate production does not equal aggregate consumption, even by a male, until some time in his twenties, when he begins to have his own children to support. This finding is particularly significant because, first, Mueller makes an extreme effort to find positive asset values for children at birth (for example, by choice of assumptions on hours of work, wages, and consumption, and by not discounting) and, second, because if such values are negative in peasant societies, they are surely negative for the rest of society, in particular for urban areas where the costs of child rearing tend to be higher and the possibilities for contributing to family income at early ages tend to be lower.

This conclusion is supported by evidence indicating that in developing countries children under the age of fifteen do little economic work (that is, work contributing to marketable output) and that their productivity when working, even during peak seasons, tends to be low (productivity being judged according to the wages that would be received for the same work in the marketplace). It can be argued that this definition of productivity excludes housework by children, freeing the mother for additional economic work. But since children also create the need for additional housework, a correction for this factor is unlikely to change the overall result significantly. It can also be pointed out that the use of wages, even during peak seasons, represents an underestimation of the importance of having children available to fill in when needed. But it is difficult to believe that day labor hired during peak seasons would be more expensive than children who have to be supported throughout the year. School attendance by children under the age of fifteen certainly provides part of the explanation for low labor-participation rates by children; but low attendance rates and the possibility of fitting farm work in around school work suggest that this is not the principal reason. The most likely and obvious explanation for these findings of low child labor-participation rates is, simply, that labor in general is in excess supply in the countrysides of the developing countries with which we are dealing. If this analysis is correct, we must reckon with the likelihood that efforts to increase agricultural output through providing the necessary capital and modern inputs, unless accompanied by other offsetting changes, will result in increased employment opportunities for children as well as for labor in general.

Combining this evidence with that reviewed by Repetto on the extent to which changes in the demand for child labor might be expected to change fertility, we must conclude that the scope for policy intervention at this point is quite limited. Few studies deal with the change in demand for child labor per se (as opposed to changes in child labor-participation rates which are influenced by supply as well as demand); most researchers, moreover, fail to isolate the effects of other variables such as school participation and family income (thereby leading to incorrect inferences about lines of causation). As a consequence, Repetto has little to work with. But the relevant bits and pieces of econometric, historical, and sociological materials combine to suggest that while a decline in demand for child labor will lead to a decline in fertility, the effect is likely to be small and the time lags involved quite long. Given Mueller's findings that child labor-participation rates are already low, plus the likelihood that investments in the agricultural sector may increase the demand for child labor, there is little room for manipulating this variable by itself.

The evidence with respect to old-age support is mostly qualitative and indirect. As Repetto points out, it emerges strongly in attitude surveys in countries where strong family ties are traditional, but little is known about the actual extent of the transfers. Mueller finds that older rural males continue working on family farms until very close to the age of death and thus may not be receiving substantial transfers from their children. But little is known about the kind and productivity of the work involved or whether this finding is applicable to those without the opportunity to work on family farms. Moreover, labor-participation rates for older women are considerably lower than for elderly men, suggesting that some transfers must be forthcoming at least for them.

Perhaps more to the point, one can ask whether investments in children are the best way to provide for one's needs in old age. A plausible case can be made that they are not: there is no certainty of a child's surviving and being willing and able to provide support; there are periods during the life cycle when surpluses are easier to accumulate; and there are mechanisms available to transfer these surpluses to later stages in life. With respect to the last point, Repetto argues that markets for the transfer of capital and land exist, that rates of return in these markets are high, and that methods are available by which even those with relatively small amounts of savings can take advantage of these opportunities. Land could be purchased in small increments; small additional amounts of agricultural output could be set aside for sale in the peak price season; and even those in debt could increase their uncommitted income significantly simply by reducing their indebtedness.

On the other hand, there are substantial risks involved in attempting to save and transfer surpluses from one period to another over one's lifetime. Farm investments are illiquid; money and jewelry can depreciate or be stolen; commercial institutions can go bankrupt. Indeed, because of inflation and the risks of theft, fire, floods, confiscation, and other calamities, the perceived, long-run rate of return on many possible investments may well be negative. At least the peasant may feel that the situation is too dangerous to rely on any one approach, that a better course of action for him may be to save *and* to have children in case one of these approaches fails. In fact, the best plan may be to try to have a son when the father is between the ages of forty and forty-five, for at that point the probability of the father's surviving to ripe old age is high, and the probability of the child's surviving long enough to help his parents (that is, until he marries and has his own children to support) is fairly good. In addition, the cost of bringing children into the world is not very high, and the costs of supporting them are spread over at least ten to fifteen years. Accordingly, even if the economic return for having a child is negative, it may be less negative than alternative investments.

But all such arguments may be overshadowed by the fact of long widowhood in societies where women have little economic power and even less knowledge of economics. To them, children, especially sons, may appear to be all that will save them from destitution after their husbands are dead, no matter what the economic facts may be.

This area should be a fruitful one for research, and both Repetto and Mueller provide good suggestions for further work. In addition, the findings that have already been made have several interesting policy implications that do not depend on the results of further research. Efforts to improve access to savings institutions and to reduce the risks and improve the returns from such investments would be helpful in reducing the pension value of children as well as being useful for general economic development. So, too, would the promotion of life insurance, private pension plans, and other contractual savings arrangements, since they tend to bring about a net increase in the average rate of savings. Life insurance for children, or at least for the oldest son, would have an even more direct effect on the pension value of children. Government-sponsored social security programs would also make sense, but they could be quite costly unless they were made conditional on the number of children a couple had.[5]

Education

The linkage between education and fertility poses a paradox for both researcher and policy maker. On the one hand, probably no other socioeconomic variable has a stronger negative association with fertility. Parents with more education have smaller families and parents whose children have more education also have smaller families. These relationships hold in both cross-sectional and time-series studies at both the national and the family levels and whether or not other important variables, such as income and place of residence are controlled. While in some studies it has been found that the relationship is positive for families with only a few years of primary education—suggesting the possibility that it is necessary to achieve a certain threshold before the negative impact takes hold—these are exceptions to the general impression to be derived from reviews of the literature. On the other hand, research has not provided

[5] Mueller argues that the cost need not be great, since men continue working until close to the age of death. But it is likely that they do so out of necessity, and that if social security were provided to them, they would retire somewhat earlier. Moreover, if the effect on the birth rate were not significant, it would be difficult for the government to accumulate the surplus to pay the pensions. This problem could be overcome if the size of the pension varied inversely with the number of surviving children. Some suggested ways to do so are provided by Ridker and Muscat (1973).

adequate explanations for these correlations, with the consequence that most policy recommendations in this area remain on uncertain ground. Do the correlations imply causation or are other factors—such as industrialization and urbanization—at work to induce parents both to want fewer children and to give each a better education? Is the effect direct, or does it operate through other variables, such as female labor-force participation and wages, that might be influenced by policy more easily and quickly? Does education operate through changes in attitude, through changes in lifetime earnings potential, or both? Does its effect arise only when other factors are present, so that a number of policies—for example, education and jobs—must be combined for any to have a significant effect?

This volume presents two major attempts to answer these and related questions: the contribution by Donald B. Holsinger and John D. Kasarda, written from a sociological point of view, and the chapter by Dennis N. De Tray, written from the vantage point of an economist. In addition, a number of other contributions—in particular those of Robert G. Repetto, Eva Mueller, and Ruth B. Dixon—touch on educational policies in significant ways. It is difficult to summarize these diverse and sometimes conflicting contributions. I will try to do so by organizing the material in the following way. If parents could be persuaded to keep their children in school longer, what would be the likely effects, first, on the parents' desire for additional children and, second, on the children's desire for offspring when they reached reproductive age?[6] Third, to what extent are these effects associated with quantity of schooling and to what extent are they, or can they be, influenced by changes in the content? Fourth, how can parents be induced to keep their children in school longer or to provide them with a better education? In answering the first two questions, we divide the effects into three categories, the effects of changes in tastes and preferences induced by the education, income and wealth effects, and the effect on relative prices and costs.

The Effect on Parents' Desire for Additional Children

It is difficult to see what kinds of effects on parents' tastes and preferences might arise solely by providing more education to their children,

[6] An additional question pertains to the possible effects of providing more education for parents. But since there was general agreement that such a policy would not be as effective as providing additional education for their children, it is not discussed here. De Tray, however, does include a brief discussion of adult education policies in chapter 6.

except on subtle levels that can probably be ignored. But there are several income and price effects that could be important. First, the additional years of schooling place two burdens on the family budget: they reduce the income which children would otherwise contribute to the family and, depending on the way in which the costs of education are divided between private and public budgets, they increase the direct cost of rearing children. Second, the additional schooling increases the parents' expectations of receiving larger income transfers from a given child later in life, reducing the number of children needed to help with old-age security. And third, if the effective price of schooling were reduced, it would become more profitable for parents to invest more in fewer children, substituting "quality" for "quantity," along the lines suggested by Repetto and De Tray.

Doubts can be raised about the importance of these effects, especially in peasant societies. Mueller, for example, argues that up to the age of fifteen the work contribution of children is small and can be fitted in after school and during vacations and that beyond that age it is not feasible in poor peasant societies to consider significant extensions of universal education. The direct costs of sending children to public schools, especially in primary years, is typically small and in any case is offset by the baby-sitting function served by schools (although the value of this service is undoubtedly small where older children are available to care for younger). Moreover, economic transfers from better-educated children later in life are far from certain, not only because of high death rates but also because educated children are more likely to leave the extended family network of ties and obligations. Unless death rates fall and the net returns to education are increased significantly, parents may not be willing to give up security in numbers for improvements in quality. In any event, the time lags involved in trying to persuade them to do so are likely to be substantial. Nevertheless, even small changes add up over time. Since, as discussed below, the cumulative effects could be quite substantial after some decades, policies that might induce such shifts should not be ignored.

The Effect on Children's Subsequent Fertility

Here we can be somewhat more confident of finding a significant negative effect on fertility. First, there are a number of attitudinal changes associated with the acquisition of education that are likely to reduce the desire for a large number of offspring, independent of any effects induced by changes in income and prices. Education, according to Holsinger and Kasarda, increases exposure to appeals in the communications media aimed at encouraging family planning; increases aspirations for upward mobility and the accumulation of wealth, making one less interested in—or at least more desirous of postponing—the rearing of a large family; imparts a sense of ability to control one's own life and environment, thereby making family planning and the use of contraceptives appear less foreign; and encourages one to think about nontraditional ways of living one's life.

Working in the opposite direction is the income or wealth effect of education, which, independent of all other effects, makes it possible for the better educated to afford large families. But as De Tray points out in reviewing studies attempting to separate and measure the income and relative-price effects, the latter are all negative and appear to be sufficiently important quantitatively to offset the positive effects of income on fertility. These relative-price or cost effects are thought to be of the following types: education of women enhances opportunities for employment that are competitive with having and rearing children, thereby increasing the opportunity cost of children. Education of both parents tends to raise the educational norm that they are expected to provide to their children, thereby raising the cost of child rearing. It also seems to increase the capacity for effective use of contraceptive devices and for communication between husband and wife about such sensitive matters as family size and the use of contraceptives, thereby lowering the effective cost of achieving a given family-size norm. Since school and marriage are generally considered incompatible, the provision of more education tends to delay the age of marriage. Education helps parents reduce child mortality, thereby lowering the number of births required to achieve a given family-size norm and encouraging investments in quality rather than quantity, as discussed below. Finally, as a consequence of increased education, parents are more likely to be able to take care of themselves in their old age, thereby needing children for this purpose to a lesser extent.

As can be seen from the authors' valiant efforts to find quantitative information on the magnitude of these effects, empirical data are scarce and generally of poor quality. For example, as Holsinger and Kasarda have pointed out, years of schooling completed, rather than school days attended, is almost invariably used as a proxy for quantity of schooling, even though there is likely to be a low correlation between the two, especially across country and regional observations. Nevertheless, it appears likely that all these effects acting in concert could have a sizable effect on the fertility behavior of those receiving additional schooling. The time lag, of course, is quite long.

Content Versus Quantity of Schooling

An additional difficulty with the work on education and fertility is the nearly universal emphasis on quantity (however measured) as opposed to content. This is the emphasis of the authors in this volume as it is of other writers on the subject. De Tray mentions the importance of type of education and curriculum only as a caveat, and Holsinger and Kasarda delve into these issues only with respect to what has been termed *population education.* As reasons for not doing so to any greater extent, they point to the dearth of research on the topic in developing countries and to the suggestions to be found in the few relevant studies which do exist that quantity is more important than content. For certain of the effects discussed above—for example, the babysitting services provided, earnings forgone, and the postponement of marriage while attending school—time spent in school is clearly more important. But it is difficult to believe that it is so—or that it needs to be so—with respect to any of the other effects that operate through changes in attitude, self-perception, and the productivity of human capital. Negative findings about the effects of educational content in this area are more likely to be explained by inadequate measuring devices, lack of variation in content between schools, and the difficulty in linking content imparted at one point in the life cycle to behavior in another.

Two types of change in content have at times been suggested: the introduction of population education and literacy programs. The first, according to Holsinger and Kasarda, holds some promise, though it has not yet been tried to any significant extent, but they find no indication that literacy per se—that is, apart from the general effects of more schooling—has any significance. It can be argued that literacy makes contraceptive information more accessible and enhances the status of women, but it probably has to be part of a broader program the other components of which are necessary for literacy to be useful.

Apart from such specific components of educational programs, a number of more general changes in content could be considered, both for their value in achieving other societal goals as well as for their effects on fertility. It goes without saying that educational programs could be geared more toward advancing the productivity of human capital. Female labor-force participation could be fostered by setting up specific programs and training schools for girls and more subtly by portraying women in productive, nontraditional roles. The sense of being able to control one's own life can be fostered by improving the individual's problem-solving capacity (as opposed to emphasizing rote learning and memorization) and by projects emphasizing doing and making and then observing the consequences (as opposed to passive absorption of information). People can be encouraged to think about nontraditional ways of living by learning about the variety of ways that people in other cultures both within and beyond the borders of their own country handle common human problems. These examples are meant only as illustrations. More specific analyses are necessary to determine appropriate interventions in given contexts. All we can do here is point out that this is a neglected and difficult, but challenging and potentially fruitful, area for further work.

School Attendance

While the problem of inducing parents to provide their children with more and better education is discussed in both chapters on education, we will give only brief space to it here, not because of its lack of importance but because, once again, we cannot move far beyond generalities without digging deeply into specific cases.

Perhaps the principal need everywhere is for more and better facilities and teachers, but given the budgetary constraints that exist in low-income countries with rapidly growing populations, these deficits will not be made up quickly. Under the circumstances, any additional resources made available to the education sector must be allocated with care. There was general agreement that highest priority should be given to primary education in poor rural areas where birth rates are highest. One objection to such an allocation policy is that it seems to reward high fertility rates. While this is true in one sense, it is difficult to believe that parents would decide to have more children in order to influence the geographic distribution of educational facilities. Nevertheless, this objection could be eliminated and an immediate antinatalist effect introduced by allocating facilities within this high-priority area on a conditional or incentive basis—that is, to those rural villages meeting certain family-planning targets.

But lack of facilities is not the only problem. One important indication of this is the observation that available facilities are frequently underutilized. There are four possible ways to ameliorate this situation. The first, compulsory attendance laws, can be set aside as unworkable. The second, subsidies or monetary incentives for attendance, does not seem promising in view of budgetary stringencies, plus the possibility of a significant positive income effect on fertility in poor areas. Here again, however, these problems could be overcome in large measure by providing the subsidy as an incentive, given only to those families with fewer than a certain number of children, as is being tried experimentally in Taiwan (Finnegan and Sun 1972, Wang and Chen 1973). A third possibility is to improve the quality of the education provided and increase its relevance to the individual's daily life. A peasant has little incentive to keep his child in school if he believes that the child is not receiving much of value. But there is another way to enhance the value of education, namely, to change the environment in ways that increase the *need* for education. An education is of little value to a girl who will never take a job; even literacy is of little value unless there is some need to read. In a broad sense, urbanization and industrialization serve this purpose. So do reductions in infant and child mortality since, as discussed below, they have the effect of increasing the rate of return on investments in human capital. But it may be possible to affect the situation in more specific, deliberate ways. Suppose, for example, that jobs in the education and health sectors requiring a certain number of years of schooling were made available to girls. Such a change could make the difference between sending and not sending a daughter to school. Undoubtedly other possibilities for specific interventions of this type can be found. The principal point, however, is that one must look outside as well as inside the education sector to find ways of inducing parents to provide more education for their children.

Unfortunately, there is little or no evidence available to support all these presumptions and suggestions. As indicated at the outset, while we know that educational attainment is strongly correlated, inversely, with family size, we know precious little more; this information is of little help in formulating policies within this sector. All the suggestions made above, therefore, should be taken as hypotheses to be tested, and research priorities in this area should be developed accordingly.

Mortality, Morbidity, and Nutrition

It is frequently alleged that a fall in child death rates and better health and nutrition are necessary preconditions for a fall in fertility.[7] Cross-country and historical evidence tend to support this proposition. But what role do these health-related factors play independent of changes in income, education, and social structure? How much effect can policies aimed at reducing mortality and morbidity and improving nutrition levels be expected to have on fertility, and with what time lags?

It is clear that pure biological linkages cannot explain the positive correlation between morbidity and mortality on the one side and fertility on the other. They might even suggest the opposite, that improve-

[7] On the relation with nutrition, a somewhat less well-known argument, see Berg (1973).

ments in health, while not directly increasing the number of births, do increase the *capacity* to have more children. There is good evidence that raising the nutrition level of females results in earlier menarche, later menopause, and shorter periods of postpartum amenorrhea in nursing mothers. The linkage between male fertility and morbidity probably works in the same direction, although William P. Butz did not find any evidence to this effect. Reductions in adult mortality, because they decrease the number of widows and widowers of reproductive ages, also increase the potential for more births. Only reductions in deaths among nursing infants point in the opposite direction, since the period of lactation and postpartum amenorrhea are thereby made longer; but the contraceptive effect of this change is far from sufficient to account for the observed declines in birth rates as infant death rates have fallen. Another biological linkage is that between lower birth rates and improvements in health, both for the mother and her children. While this direction of causation also helps explain the positive correlation found in cross-sectional studies, our emphasis here is on causal linkages running in the opposite direction that might be useful for policy making. If the correlation between morbidity, mortality, and fertility is to be explained, one must look for behavioral changes. Four in particular have been emphasized in the literature reviewed by Butz and Jean-Pierre Habicht and by T. Paul Schultz.

First, setting aside responses to uncertainty for the moment, a decline in child mortality can be expected to increase desired family size, since the expected cost of rearing a survivor is thereby reduced and the benefits increased. An improvement in general health would work in the same direction.

Second, a decline in child mortality means that fewer births are required to achieve a given number of survivors. Schultz shows that, given plausible assumptions about response elasticities, the net effect of these first two factors is to reduce births. But this decline in births is unlikely to be sufficient to offset the increase in population growth resulting from the decline in mortality unless additional behavioral factors are brought into play.

One such additional factor is the response of parents to uncertainty. A plausible response is overcompensation: parents may well prefer to have too many rather than too few surviving children. If this is the case, a reduction in child mortality, which is generally accompanied by a reduction in uncertainty as well, would reduce births by somewhat more than is implied by the first two factors alone.

Fourth, and perhaps most important, improvements in the rates of mortality and morbidity and in nutrition at all ages increase the returns on investments in human capital in relation to investments in nonhuman capital and on investments with long gestation periods in relation to those with shorter ones. These effects should encourage parents to invest more in both their own and their children's education and health and make them willing to have fewer children in order to finance such expenditures. They could also make it somewhat more attractive to postpone marriage to the extent that marriage and early child rearing are incompatible with investments in education.

Other possible effects mentioned by these authors include the need to save more for old age and a more rapid rate of increase in family income and wealth in the course of time. These conditions might also reduce fertility, the former because it increases the need to conserve on current consumption and the latter because it is akin to Simon's long-run effects of income (in this case increasing child-expenditure norms, thereby inducing an even greater shift from quantity to quality).

While all these effects are plausible and more or less consistent with the evidence, there is very little information on their quantitative magnitude and none that adequately separates the various effects and lines of causation, including the biological, from each other. It is typical in less developed countries to find that the decline in child death rates precedes the decline in birth rates by at least a decade and that the decline in the latter compensates for less than the total decline in the former, leaving family size and the growth rate of population somewhat larger. But the variance around this average is sizable—Schultz, for example, finding that in about half the studies he reviewed response rates in excess of unity are implied—and an explanation for these differences is lacking. One cannot go further than this with the data, virtually all of which are cross-sectional, and methods available at present. With these difficulties in mind, Schultz and Butz and Habicht devote considerable space to the development of theoretical models for statistical analysis that define what data are necessary and how they should be utilized.

At one level the policy implications of these authors' materials are relatively straightforward. It seems reasonably certain that improvements in medical and health care will eventually encourage some decline in fertility. Beyond this statement, however, lie many unanswered questions, particularly concerning the extent and speed of the decline, the resulting effect on the population growth rate, and the overall cost-effectiveness of alternative methods of improving medical and health care. The authors address these questions only peripherally, Butz and Habicht reviewing the reasons for integrating health, nutrition, and family-planning services and Schultz surveying the reasons for the decline in mortality in less developed countries and concluding that future declines will depend more heavily on improvements in general economic conditions for the mass of the population.

The last issue is a particularly interesting one because it seems to lead us full circle back to the need for general economic development. It has two principal bases: First, there are studies indicating that declines in mortality in less developed countries have not occurred independent of economic development, as has often been suggested, and second, there is the argument that the major remaining causes of child mortality are gastroenteritis and diarrheal diseases associated with nutritional deficiencies, diseases that have resisted the efforts of medical researchers and appear to be related primarily to the level of private physical wealth and educational attainment. These judgments may be somewhat harsh. First, studies indicating the extent to which general economic development is associated with declines in mortality typically fail to hold constant investments in public health facilities such as potable water, sewage, and sanitation works that could be, and sometimes are, made independently. Second, diarrheal diseases are associated with contaminated water and with habits of personal hygiene; public health investments in providing potable water and sanitary waste-disposal systems in rural areas, plus education campaigns directed specifically at this problem, should have a high rate of return independent of general advances in economic welfare.[8] Here as in other areas there appear to be possibilities of finding specific interventions that might make it unnecessary to wait for general economic development.

Female Roles and Labor-force Participation

The next two chapters, those by Ruth B. Dixon and by James L. McCabe and Mark R. Rosenzweig, while different in subject matter and especially in methodology, conclude with similar implications for policy and research. Dixon, a sociologist, argues that high fertility rates

[8] It is sometimes alleged that such investments are so expensive that general economic development is necessary to create the surpluses required for the task. In large part, the level of expense arises from the assumption that international standards and capital-intensive methods of treatment will be used. But recent research by Richard Frankel has demonstrated that high levels of treatment can be obtained using inexpensive local materials for the filtration medium (for example, shredded cocoanut husks) and storage (ceramic crocks) and transport (bamboo). By obviating the need for chemicals, cast metal parts, and machinery, he has brought the cost down to a small fraction of what Western treatment facilities require, significantly reducing the dependence on foreign assistance or general economic development (see Frankel 1973).

in many developing countries are related importantly to the social and economic roles assigned to women and that the best way to change this situation is through changes in female employment. McCabe and Rosenzweig take an econometric approach, questioning the extent to which changes in female wages and job opportunities do in fact lead to changes in fertility. Since in the end both recommend experiments involving the manipulation of the female labor market, they are most conveniently discussed together at this point.

Women in a large number of developing countries, and especially in the rural sectors of these countries, are described by Dixon as powerless, economically and socially dependent, and isolated from the mainstream of life outside the immediate family circle. In Moslem societies, on which she concentrates, this situation is related to the practice of female seclusion, typically justified as an assurance of chastity before marriage and faithfulness thereafter. Among other things, it leads to limitations on economic activities outside the home. This makes daughters a greater economic burden on their parents, resulting in their receiving less education and leaving them with fewer ways to attain status and security besides early marriage and the production of children. While arising for different reasons and in different guises in non-Moslem societies, the more general features of this situation are not unfamiliar in large parts of Latin America and Africa.

The possibility that provision of better wages and jobs for women outside the home could change this situation and lead to a decline in fertility arises for two reasons: The roles of worker and mother tend to be incompatible, and a job and an independent source of earnings may give a woman a greater voice in family decision making.

The first factor has been stated most rigorously by economists in the following way: an increase in the wife's market wage rate will have two economic effects. First, it will increase household income, making it possible for the couple to afford a larger family. Second, it will increase the opportunity cost of the wife's time spent in nonmarket activities, inducing her to reallocate her time in favor of market activities. If child rearing is more time-intensive for the wife than are other nonmarket activities, the opportunity cost for children will increase by more than will that for other demands on her time, encouraging a decrease in desired family size. While the net effect of these offsetting tendencies cannot be judged entirely by reasoning a priori, studies in developed countries indicating a negative relationship between female work hours and fertility have led to a general presumption that the second effect, the substitution or price effect, tends to outweigh the income effect. But studies in less developed countries have not always indicated a negative relationship, and in the empirical work presented in their chapter, McCabe and Rosenzweig obtain strong positive associations between female wages and fertility. While this finding may be explained by the unconventional way they have specified their statistical models for testing, a topic to which we shall return, there can be no doubt that they have effectively questioned the automatic applicability of results from developed countries to the conditions of less developed countries.

There are several reasons that a positive relationship between female labor-force participation and fertility may occur in developing countries. First, the income effect could be much stronger at low levels of income. Indeed, it was argued by one of the discussants that poverty forces many women into the labor market even when it means a reduction in the quality of the care their children get; this is equivalent to saying that, for these women, an increase in their wages could well permit them to work *less,* increasing the amount of time they would have available to bear and rear children. Second, large families and extended families make it easier to find substitutes for the mother's time in child rearing. Finally, the jobs set aside for women in developing countries often permit caring for children while working, or at least they make the two roles less incompatible than they tend to be in industrial countries. These last two factors are stressed by McCabe and Rosenzweig, who feel that they could even be strong enough to lead to a positive substitution effect; whether that is true or not, however, they certainly lead to a reduction in the magnitude of the negative effect. Role incompatibility, therefore, cannot automatically be assumed in conditions prevailing in developing countries. To ensure a negative effect on fertility, the additional jobs provided for women must be deliberately chosen or designed to be for the most part incompatible with child rearing.

The second factor presumed to lead to a decline in fertility, the greater voice in family decision making resulting from a job, is stressed by Dixon. There can be little doubt that girls with an independent source of income are in a better position to resist pressures to marry than are those without jobs. Moreover, evidence suggests that there is a positive correlation between the extent of the wife's involvement in family decision making and use of contraceptives. But once again, whether the provision of jobs per se under conditions prevailing in poor rural areas would be sufficient to encourage a greater role in decision making, and whether that in turn—independent of other changes—would lead to a decline in fertility, is open to question. It is more likely that a number of changes together—the provision of certain kinds of jobs and conditions of employment and pay, possibly combined with a self-help organization to provide educational, legal, and psychological support—would be required for a significant, sustained effect to be observed. A good deal of Dixon's chapter is devoted to the search for the appropriate set of changes.

The authors appear to recognize these problems and try to take them into account in their proposals for both research and policy. This is particularly true of Dixon, whose carefully worked-out suggestions are centered around the establishment of rural industrial cooperatives employing only women. Her suggestions, as well as those of Aziz Bindary (1975) and others, to establish special workshops or industries for women, are attractive in many ways. At the very least a specific number of jobs will in fact be created. But several arguments can be raised against this approach. First, all such proposals involving the development of new institutions and special projects are difficult to establish, replicate, and operate on a large scale, and the history of efforts to do so (to develop rural producer cooperatives, for example) provides few success stories. Second, investments in such special projects are often expensive on a per-person basis and could run counter to the goal of maximizing total output. Third, such efforts may fail if the male unemployment rate is too high, because men will either preempt the jobs or demand that the investments be made in directions more directly useful to them. If the projects are conceived as self-financing and involve work in areas where women have a comparative advantage (whether it be natural or culturally imposed), the last two points may be less important. A case in point is provided by recent investments in electronic assembly plants in Malaysia in which most of those employed are women despite high urban male unemployment rates. But such opportunities are likely to be difficult to find on a large scale.

These problems with the special project approach have led some to argue that it is more effective to concentrate efforts on reducing the general unemployment rate (through across-the-board policies such as increasing the artificially low price of capital in relation to labor) and allowing the demand for female labor to increase as a natural consequence. Such a trickle-down approach seems to account in part for the increase in female employment in Pakistan, where, according to one commentator, women began to be employed in traditionally male jobs when better-paying jobs for men opened up elsewhere. But there are problems with an exclusive reliance on this approach as well. The immediate impact of such policies could well be pronatalist since they imply an increase in male earnings before female employment increases. Indeed, it could even result in some reduction in the supply of female labor as women, no longer forced by poverty into the labor market, withdrew to devote more time to child rearing. Moreover, while it is true that special projects are difficult to set up on a large scale, it has proved equally difficult to reduce general unemployment rates. To do so often requires a correction of factor-price distortions and an increase in the general rate of economic growth, and there have been few success stories here also. But most important, such across-the-board efforts to increase the demand for female labor do not provide the package of changes that Dixon suggests is necessary to obtain a commensurate increase in the *supply* of female labor.

Fortunately, however, these two approaches are not mutually exclusive. While everything should be done to lower the general unemployment rate, there is no need to wait until it is reduced to acceptable levels to begin experimenting with different institutional forms and interventions in the female labor market. Such experimentation will be needed in any case and can proceed on a sufficiently small scale so that it does not threaten male employment. It is only when some success has been achieved and attempts are made to expand the scale of operations that a conflict between these two approaches may arise. We are far from that point now.

Preferences and Tastes

Up to this point the possibilities of influencing preferences, or tastes, in relation to fertility have been discussed only in passing—that is, as they might be affected incidentally or indirectly through other variables. Now we want to consider such possibilities more explicitly. While very little in the way of a theory of taste formation is available, it seems plausible that preferences can be influenced in the following three ways. First, education might directly or indirectly alter tastes—directly by inculcation of new attitudes and indirectly by helping to place a person in a new socioeconomic or occupational reference group with different fertility norms. Second, a person's desire for goods and services, in competition with bearing and rearing children, might be stimulated by mass media, advertising, or the increased supply of attractive consumer goods. Third, a person's norms regarding appropriate age of marriage and family size can change as a consequence of exposure to different life-styles. Such exposure can occur through direct contact with new acquaintances, often as a result of migration, or less directly through mass media (and education) in which different life-styles and different ways of handling common problems are portrayed. We have already discussed education and its possible effects on tastes. Here we consider the second and third possibilities.

Deborah S. Freedman reviews the literature and evidence pertaining to possibilities involving the use of mass media and modern consumption goods in her chapter. Apparently, no evidence exists that mass-media programs aimed directly at promoting family planning increase rates of acceptance or change basic attitudes about family-size norms; the best that can be said for them is that they increase awareness, information, and willingness to listen to other appeals. There are serious methodological problems involved in trying to judge the indirect effects of mass media, and data are very scarce. From what little there are, however—in particular an extensive survey of Taiwanese husbands—Freedman finds evidence indicating that even after eliminating the effects of income, education, literacy, and ownership of modern objects, increased exposure to mass media is associated with increased use of contraceptives, higher consumption aspirations, lessened fears of child mortality, increased awareness of the financial costs of children, and so on. The effects are small, but not much smaller than those of such variables as education and income. She also finds from the same data that both aspirations for and ownership of modern consumer durables are associated with the use of contraceptives, other things being held constant.

From these findings, she concludes with three interesting suggestions for research. The first is to make television available to inhabitants of rural and urban sample sites and compare the inhabitants' behavioral and attitudinal responses over a five-year period with those of inhabitants of control sites (making family-planning services equally accessible to both groups). The second is a survey to determine what are modern consumption items in a given context, who buys them, whether their ownership is in fact competitive with having children, how work effort and savings are affected, and the extent to which marketing and production activities are found in communities with high levels of ownership, adjusting for the effects of income. If the second study shows a potential market for modern consumer goods, a favorable fertility impact, and no offsetting negative impacts (on work effort or savings, for example), a third study would be recommended: an experiment involving subsidies for the marketing or production, or both, of certain kinds of goods in sample areas. While her suggestions for field experiments would have to be worked out in much more detail, Freedman goes far enough to indicate that they are likely to be feasible.

An objection to these proposals can be raised on grounds that they might encourage socially unacceptable cultural values, in particular the consumption of luxury goods at the expense of investment in essential commodities. This objection can be answered on a number of levels. First, mass media can carry any message desired: it is not necessary that they encourage profligate styles of living. Second, the package of goods that constitutes an appropriate set of "modern consumption goods" is not the same everywhere; it will vary greatly depending on the specific cultural and economic context being considered. In poor peasant societies, it is more likely to include sewing machines, bicycles, power pumps, water taps, tubing for wells, and improved farm implements rather than phonographs, air conditioners, and aids to personal beauty. Third, one should not automatically assume that the consumption of such goods is always a deterrent to savings. Freedman's Taiwan data suggest that both aspirations for and ownership of what are appropriately defined as modern consumption goods in that context are *positively* correlated with savings, with income, education, and duration of marriage held constant. But finally, a good many of her research suggestions are designed specifically to determine whether there would be any negative effects from the policy suggestions she proposes investigating. Especially in this area, where data are so poor and where policies must be designed within the specifics of a given setting, such fact-finding research is an obvious first step.

David Goldberg's chapter raises another possibility for population policy, one that has been largely overlooked. From sample surveys that include information on respondents' residential locations within two metropolitan areas, Ankara and Mexico City, he finds that a significant proportion of fertility-related behavior is explained by residential location, over and above the effects of respondents' income, education, and place of birth. It is not possible to determine from his data whether this association is the result of a self-selection process—persons with similar attitudes tending to live in the same area—or whether people tend to take on the characteristics of those around them. Most likely, as Goldberg suggests, both effects are present, but to the extent that the second explanation is correct an appealing possibility for influencing fertility patterns presents itself.

Within limits the settlement patterns of rural migrants in urban areas can be influenced by public policy. The layout of vehicular access roads, sewage lines, and piped water are important determinants of the attractiveness of given locations. So too are renewal, rehabilitation, and public housing programs. To a large extent, this influence is negative, the poor migrant locating in areas where urban infrastructure and rehabilitation programs are not present, since only there are land values likely to be low enough for him. This fact tends to make migrants cluster together in urban slum areas, where many rural attitudes and behavior patterns are reinforced. If planners were to locate urban infrastructure and renewal programs in such a way as to encourage small rather than large migrant clusters and to encourage less segregation between older and newer migrants, perhaps the new migrants would become urbanized—and in the process give up their high fertility patterns—more rapidly.

At this stage, these ideas, plus the likelihood of their being politically feasible, must be presented in a very tentative way. But given the data presented by Goldberg, the possibilities appear sufficiently promising that further testing and exploration are warranted. He suggests a number of ways in which this might be done, including extensions of the techniques used in his Ankara and Mexico City studies and careful monitoring of experiments or quasi experiments already under way. Rapidly growing cities, where significant locational decisions will have to be made in the next few years in any case, are attractive candidates.

Overall Research Implications

The individual chapters in this volume are too rich in research suggestions for summarization here. There are, however, two broad issues that can be usefully raised at this point. One is the problem of specifying statistical models for testing and the other the pros and cons of social experimentation as a technique of data collection.

Insights into the determinants of fertility and policies for influencing them can come from many sources, including personal observation, a priori reasoning, and—perhaps most promising but least utilized to date—the application of anthropological methods. But in the last analysis, hypotheses so derived must be tested by means of statistical techniques. To do this properly is no easy task. A large number of variables influence decisions involving marriage and procreation. These variables are linked together in complex ways, since some are simultaneously determined and many are explanatory in one relationship and dependent in another. Often these variables move together over time making it difficult to isolate their independent effects. Time lags of unknown length are involved in many of the relationships. Measurement of these variables is often indirect, using proxies for what is really desired. And there are reasons to believe that some of the relationships are temporally and spatially unstable. While there is no single best way to cope with this situation, it helps enormously if the unit of observation is the individual decision maker, rather than some average across a geographic region, if these persons can be followed over a period of time rather than being interviewed only once, and if at least some variables can be held constant while others are manipulated specifically, as it might be possible to do in a field experiment (or in a quasi-experimental setting in which a new policy is being introduced in part of the universe to be studied), or where the size of the sample is sufficiently large that it can be partitioned into homogeneous groups. If the data are of this quality, it then pays to utilize sophisticated statistical methods, often involving, for example, simultaneous equations, as opposed to single-equation techniques, even if the latter are multivariate in nature. It is almost never the case that all these conditions are fulfilled. Usually researchers must pick up data collected for other purposes when and where they can, data that are often not suitable for careful and elaborate statistical analysis. The resulting studies must be interpreted with considerable caution to avoid incorrect or misleading implications.

While several of the chapters in this volume exemplify problems of this type, the empirical portion of the chapter by McCabe and Rosenzweig is especially useful to illustrate some of these points. To obtain an indication of the likely effect of wage subsidy for women workers on female labor-force participation and on completed family size, they set up a series of regression equations utilizing data from the Puerto Rican census for 3,000 married women between the ages of thirty-five and forty-four with spouses present. In one of these equations, children ever born is the dependent variable and the wife's *potential* wage, her age and education level, the husband's education and wages, and the nonlabor incomes of both are the independent variables. In another equation, hours worked is the dependent variable, and the set of independent variables is the same. The results indicate that women with higher potential wages work more hours and have a *larger* number of children. Should we conclude that in Puerto Rico, at least, a wage subsidy would be pronatalist?

Before drawing any such conclusion, one must look further into the methods used by these authors, particularly at their concept of potential wages. They argue, quite rightly, that the wages actually received by the women in the sample are affected by the numbers of children they have: the more children the less work experience and seniority they have and hence the lower their wages. What is needed is an indication of the wages a woman could have received if this effect of children on wages were not present. To obtain such an indication in the absence of work histories, the authors introduce a new variable—potential wage, which is derived from a subsidiary regression equation on unmarried women between the ages of eighteen and forty-four—in which wages are the dependent variable and age and education are the independent variables. By substituting this new variable, the authors are in effect saying that married women would have received the same wage as do unmarried women of the same ages and with the same education had they not married—that is, that there are no other differences between them. Since the wages offered to married women can be expected to move in the same way as potential wages, movements in the latter can serve as a good proxy for what is really wanted, the effect of an exogenous change in wages without the feedback effects of independent changes in fertility.

Apart from other questions that can be raised about this procedure,[9] the validity of this interpretation depends on what is assumed about self-selection. To what extent do women marry and have more children over their lifetimes because their market opportunities are restricted, and to what extent do preferences for marriage and children determine whether women enter the labor market and, if they do, what conditions of work they will accept? Indeed, it can be argued, as did one commentator on this chapter, that the difference between potential and actual wage (roughly equivalent to income forgone) is a proxy for tastes or preferences for children, in which case a positive coefficient is to be expected, since such a coefficient merely says that women with higher preferences for children have more children.[10]

Because of the absence of work histories, there is no way to obtain a good answer to these questions from McCabe and Rosenzweig's data. Their finding is useful, therefore, mainly as a warning that an across-the-board wage subsidy may not always work and that it may be necessary to apply such a policy to a limited range of jobs, those that are more clearly competitive with child rearing. It cannot be used, as the authors acknowledge, as firm evidence to argue against experiments with or trials of such policies. McCabe and Rosenzweig go on to analyze data from a cross section of countries in which an attempt is made to look at the effect of jobs with different characteristics (degree of compatibility with child rearing) and which supports the hypothesis that the type of job is important. Another set of problems and doubts can be raised about this analysis, however, in particular the lack of adequate wage data.

[9] Why use women between the ages of thirty-five and forty-four, many of whom have not yet completed their reproductive period; why compare them with women between eighteen and forty-four; and why include some of the determinants of wages in the same equation as wages itself? The authors have answers for these questions, some of which are included in their chapter.

[10] In the version of the paper appearing in this book, the authors test this hypothesis and conclude by rejecting it.

This discussion leads directly into the question of social experimentation, for in the last analysis it is difficult to believe that any body of nonexperimental data, no matter how good, can provide answers acceptable to policy makers about the long-run quantitative effect on fertility of specific policies to improve labor-market conditions for women. Can social experiments provide the data necessary to obtain more useful answers?

There is much to be said for social experimentation as a research tool for studying population policy. First, if the changes that policy is designed to bring about have never been experienced before, nonexperimental data obviously cannot be very helpful. The effects of an increase in wages beyond the range previously experienced, an incentive never before offered, and a new housing policy are cases in point. Second, if it is possible to assign a large number of treatment and control areas on a random basis, it is not necessary to know as much about all the variables that could influence the situation as it is if nonexperimental data are used. While an ideal situation is seldom found in practice, the closer it can be approximated the more confidence one can have in the results of testing simple or partial models. Third, social experimentation can turn up unexpected side effects that might be important in deciding whether to implement a policy. Even if it is known that women will have fewer children if job opportunities become available to them, policy makers will also want to know what the effects will be on male labor markets and attitudes. Finally, whether they deserve to be or not, analyses derived from social experiments are more easily understood by policy makers than are those derived from the manipulation of nonexperimental data. The former are more like trial runs, whereas the latter, at best, can only simulate the situation and then only under a number of limiting assumptions.

But social experimentation has its problems as well. It is a more costly way of acquiring information (that is, assuming that the noninformational benefits—the births prevented by the experiment and the additional quality of information obtained, for example—are not subtracted from the costs, as they should be). It may be unacceptable on political or ethical grounds because treatment and control groups must be treated differently. It may be difficult to avoid "contamination"—that is, spillover effects between treatment and control groups that distort the outcome. [It is of interest to note that neither of these last two problems proved to be serious in the large-scale experiments involving the negative income tax conducted in the United States between 1968 and 1972 (Kershaw and Fair 1975, Kershaw 1972). Such problems could be serious in other contexts, however.] It is often impossible in practice to set up and monitor more than one or two treatment and control groups, although the classic experimental design calls for a large number spread at random through the population. The seriousness of this failing depends on the nature of the information one wishes to obtain and on the alternatives available (in particular on the weaknesses likely to be present in nonexperimental data concerning the same phenomenon). Finally, to obtain useful information, it may be necessary to run a fertility experiment for a long time, longer than is feasible (although, of course, no longer than is necessary to obtain useful nonexperimental time-series data).

Clearly, there is a need for both experimental and nonexperimental studies. But, when all is said and done, neither method is likely to provide adequate answers to some questions within a reasonable period of time. To illustrate the latter conclusion, consider the problem of determining the effect of different educational programs on completed family size. The problem of following the recipients through a number of years and eliminating the effects of other influences along the way places an almost insuperable burden on any method of gathering data. In such cases decisions about policy will have to be made a priori. If the policy appears reasonable and has other more general advantages—is beneficial for general economic development, for example—it would be best to proceed directly to implementation without trying first to reduce uncertainty through additional research. The suggestions made by Mueller to improve access by rural families to lending and savings institutions are a case in point. Research may never adequately prove that such a change is useful in reducing births, even though it is reasonable to believe that it does have that effect. In view of the seriousness of the population problem in many developing countries, moreover, it makes no sense to demand a greater degree of certainty in this area than is present in others in which policy makers are forced to proceed without any stronger factual underpinning.

Some Broader Policy Implications

It is now time to take up several policy issues that cut across all aspects of the subject under study. The first issue is that of incentives—that is, changes that are conditional upon a favorable change in fertility-related behavior. While Simon, in his chapter on income, is the principal author to discuss them, incentives could as well be considered in conjunction with education, public health, housing, or the provision of employment opportunities for women. The second issue is the need for a group of closely related and mutually reinforcing changes. Finally, we must consider the question of priorities: given all the possibilities we have surveyed, can we say anything about which is likely to have the highest benefit–cost ratio, defining benefits and costs to include more than just the economic magnitudes involved?

Incentives

A wide variety of incentives has been suggested and a number are being tried. They can be positive (payments for acceptance of a vasectomy, for example, as in India) or negative (increased hospital and maternity fees and lower priority for public housing for parents with larger families, for example, as in Singapore). The incentive can be provided to the couple themselves (the only kind to be discussed here), to "motivators," or to the community at large (funds for public works projects dependent on achievement by a village of certain targets, for example, as once proposed for use in Maharashtra). They can be provided for changes in behavior ranging from the use of a particular method of family planning, changes in the age of marriage, increased spacing, or smaller completed family size. They can involve transfers of cash, goods, or services (the Taiwan education bond and the Pakistan proposal to offer life insurance for the oldest son, for example). Such transfers can be immediate or deferred (as in the case of the tea-estate experiment in India, in which payment at the time of retirement varies inversely with the number of children). While evidence on the effects of such schemes is sparse at present, it is likely to improve substantially in the next few years as the schemes under way mature to the point at which evaluation becomes feasible.[11]

Whatever their nature, there are five principal arguments in favor of incentives. First, they are known to work in other fields. Price incentives to induce farmers to shift to new varieties and differential tax rates to encourage investments in some fields and discourage investments in others are cases in point. Second, the conditional nature of the offer is useful in overcoming the positive income effect associated with many social changes. In addition this factor reduces the social cost and risk involved in policy changes that would otherwise be difficult to reverse if the expected fertility effect is not forthcoming. These last two points can be explained by reference to an old-age security scheme: if the pension varied inversely with the number of children a couple had, the

[11] For a description of these schemes, plus discussion of their pros and cons, see Pohlman (1971), Hickman (1972), IBRD (1974, ch. 6), and works cited in these publications and in chapter 2 of this volume.

pronatalist effect of the higher lifetime income would be counteracted, and the scheme could be set up in such a way that no pensions would be provided unless fertility actually fell. Fourth, incentives can help to overcome the time lags inherent in many forms of social change. The principal effect of providing additional schooling to rural youths is likely to be felt only after they become adults, but if this schooling were offered on the condition that their parents limited family size, at least some of the effect would be shifted to the present generation.

Finally, and most important, the use of incentives obviates the need for knowing in detail the nature and strength of the principal determinants of fertility. Incentives should work so long as something considered to be of value by the recipient is provided, whether or not it compensates him in kind for the loss he incurs from having fewer children. It is likely to be more socially acceptable if it does provide such a compensation; but it is the perceived, not the real, value of children that counts in gaining such acceptability and that is easier to discover through research.

This point can be pushed further by considering the three main views held about the general nature of the population problem in less developed countries. Some argue that people want to limit fertility but do not have effective means. Others assert that individuals have reason to limit fertility but are not sufficiently motivated because of lack of knowledge and the persistence of old attitudes and values. Still others argue that given the present environment within which parents in less developed countries live, they do not have good reason to lower their fertility and cannot be motivated to do so in the absence of substantial social, economic, or political change. Incentives can be effective no matter which of these explanations is correct. If the first is correct, the incentive will induce people to find effective methods or demand that they be given them. If the second proves to be correct, the incentive will help speed up the adjustment process, just as high "incentive" prices for food grains in India and Pakistan in 1967–68 increased the rate of adoption of the new hybrid seeds. If the third explanation is correct, the incentive serves as a substitute for the social change that has not yet occurred. At a minimum it will change behavior without affecting attitudes in any fundamental way, but given normal dynamics of attitude formation, changes in attitude will follow the changed behavior in order to justify and rationalize the latter, thereby reinforcing the behavioral change.

There are, of course, a number of arguments on the other side. If used by itself, the incentive may have to be quite large, causing budgetary and possibly also political problems. In any event, some types of incentives may be considered distasteful, despite the fact that they are openly and blatantly used in other walks of life. Third, implementation of incentive programs sometimes poses difficult administrative problems, among which are possibilities for the misuse of funds. Fourth, a number of persons might receive payments who would have behaved as they did in any case; where such a problem exists, special efforts must be made in the design of the scheme to minimize this consequence.

Whatever stand one may take with respect to incentives, they do appear to be an excellent instrument for social experimentation. Indeed, the doubts and questions about incentives can probably not be answered otherwise. How else, for example, can one determine how large the incentive must be or whether the administrative problems can be solved and whether favorable or unfavorable changes in attitudes are likely to occur as a result of their use?

A Package Approach

Up to this point we have considered policy possibilities one at a time, as if they were alternatives. This was done for convenience in discussion and presentation, even though we know that a group of closely related and mutually reinforcing changes are likely to be much more effective than a piecemeal approach. An incentive for girls to postpone marriage will be far more effective if combined with increased opportunities for them to use their time constructively. The provision of increased educational opportunities may not be taken advantage of unless it is clear that the education is useful and needed and that it opens up additional job opportunities. Mass media may stimulate the desire for a higher standard of living, but the result will be frustration unless opportunities are provided for improving the standard of living.

This point can be carried further. To induce parents to value "quality" over "quantity" will require opportunities to increase lifetime income, better training to take advantage of these opportunities, reduced mortality to increase the expected returns from long-term investments, and, quite possibly, some kind of community or peer-group support to encourage the individual to break with tradition and bear the uncertainties involved in a new approach to lifetime planning.

The situation is similar to that encountered in efforts to modernize traditional agriculture, in which planners have concluded after many frustrating years of effort that there is no single touchstone, that it is not sufficient to provide extension services or new credit institutions, better marketing and storage facilities, adequate supplies of new seeds, fertilizer, and water, or even land reform and consolidation, separately, that some combination of these incentives plus adequate prices appears necessary to break traditional patterns. But agricultural planners have also discovered that it is easy to overload local officials and the production capabilities of complementary sectors. The problem is to choose just the right set of changes, sufficient to induce the proper behavioral response yet not so comprehensive as to be infeasible. In the last analysis the determination of the appropriate package probably involves more art and intuition than it does science. And so it is and must be in the planning of population policy. We can say that a package of changes is necessary and identify some of its ingredients; we can warn planners not to overload the system; but the right balance and mixture cannot be specified without adding to the studies reviewed in this volume a large measure of intuition and judgment about specific local circumstances.

Toward a Priority List

After this review it should be clear that it is impossible to provide anything like a ranking of the various approaches to population policy according to their likely benefit–cost ratios. Educated guesses could be useful if additional information about specific countries were added but are of little value at a more general level. A first step in this direction can be taken, however, by considering the appropriateness of broad classes of policy options depending on the seriousness of the population problem in different countries.

In all cases, of course, countries should start with vigorous programs of family planning. In countries that do not anticipate any serious problems associated with population growth, such a supply-oriented approach may be sufficient. But if population pressure is expected to be severe in the future, even though it is not today, and if there are good prospects for growth and modernization in the meantime, it would be useful to add a demand-oriented approach that tries to influence the economic-development program in ways that speed up a country's transition to a low-fertility regime. The provision of more and better primary and secondary education in rural areas, especially coupled with an attempt to attract girls into the schools, the correction of factor-price distortions that dampen the demand for labor (including, of course, female labor), the elimination of discrimination against women in labor markets, and the movement of people out of traditional agricultural areas into more modern sectors as quickly as development permits are all cases in point. It is at least as difficult to establish priorities within this area as it is to indicate how to get general development going. But it is likely that placing an emphasis on such high demographic-impact programs would alter the style and composition of development in significant ways.

As we have seen, a number of the programs that would be included in such an approach can have positive income effects in the short run; indeed, it could take several decades before the long-run negative effects gathered sufficient strength to offset them. If the population problem is more immediately pressing or is likely to become so before this approach has time to work, more emphasis should be placed on the use of incentives, deliberate efforts to alter preferences (using mass media and other approaches), and institutional and organizational changes (for example, of the type suggested by Dixon) that represent somewhat more direct intervention into the determinants of the family's decision-making process.

If, however, the population problem is more urgent yet, creating severe short-term pressures and threatening to swamp the development program altogether, more coercive measures, such as prolonged separation of the sexes through drafts for military and work-camp service and compulsory sterilization after the bearing of a certain number of children, may be called for. We have deliberately not considered such measures in this volume. If we get on quickly enough with the tasks of developing and testing less draconian policies, we may hope that the number of cases in which they have to be used will be few and far between.

2.

Income, Wealth, and Their Distribution as Policy Tools in Fertility Control

JULIAN L. SIMON

The aim of this chapter is to evaluate various policies intended to reduce fertility in less developed countries by means of changing peoples' income and wealth. Income and wealth invite consideration as social control variables because economic status always matters. They seem to be related to almost every aspect of a society—its patterns of production and consumption, its attitudes, and its health and mortality, as well as its fertility. But just how income and wealth are related to fertility is exceedingly complex.[1] After an analysis of the income–fertility relationship, the ways in which countries might intervene in the relationship in order to influence fertility will be considered.

The plan of the chapter is as follows: In the second section, a selection of data that shows the main themes of the income–fertility relationship in less developed countries is presented. These data demonstrate that income is indeed strongly related to fertility. However, a country cannot reasonably think of its average income level (or more precisely, its gross national product) as a variable that it can manipulate in order to influence fertility. Hence, the general descriptive material in this section is relevant principally as scientific background.

The likely fertility effects of unconditional income redistributions are discussed in the third section. Recently there has been discussion about the relationship of income distribution to fertility, along with the suggestion that an equalizing redistribution policy might be an effective way of

I appreciate useful suggestions from members of the conference, especially Ronald G. Ridker and David Goldberg. Much of this chapter is drawn from my earlier monograph on income and fertility (1974a).

[1] From here on only the term *income* will be used, for two reasons: Data on and studies of the relationship of wealth on fertility are very sparse, and the distribution of income is often easier to manipulate than is the distribution of wealth.

reducing fertility. In this section the conclusion is reached that no sort of redistribution of income by itself is likely to reduce fertility in the short run, but in the long run, a more nearly equal distribution of income is likely to be associated with a considerably lower fertility than is a less equal income distribution.

In the fourth section, conditional transfers of income—that is, "incentive" bonuses and taxes that are conditional upon a family's having given numbers of children—are studied as a method of reducing fertility. The conclusion is that incentives might well speed a decline in fertility. Indeed, aside from contraceptive-distribution programs, such conditional transfers seem more promising than any other sort of fertility-reduction program, though the possibility of effectiveness for incentives surely depends upon the underlying conditions in the country. But we still lack good knowledge of just how great the effect is likely to be in a particular set of conditions.

An experiment to improve knowledge about the effects of incentive payments would require several years and considerable tolerance by one or more governments. But until a well-controlled experiment is finally done, no country will be in a good position to undertake a massive program of incentives.

The Relationship of Income to Fertility in Less Developed Countries

There are two main objectives of a study of the effects of income—its levels and its changes—upon fertility: the first is a forecast of what will happen to fertility in any given country as its income and economic conditions change. This includes such illustrative questions as: What pattern will fertility follow in a poor African or South American country as the country develops? What will happen to fertility in rich industrialized countries as their economies continue to change? The second objective is an evaluation of income as a possible social control variable. Among questions that may be asked are: Is economic development, with its consequent rise in income levels, an effective instrument for lowering fertility? Can redistribution of income influence fertility patterns? Are incentive payments in money or kind an effective way of inducing people to have fewer or more children, if one or the other is desired?

Figures 2-1, 2-2, and 2-3 show—in different ways, using different sorts of data—that the connection between income and fertility is strong. It can be useful, therefore, to explore the extent and the nature of the effect, which is the subject of this section.

FIG. 2-1. Cycles of harvest index and marriage rates in Sweden, 1753–83. *Source:* From Simon (1974a, p. 10, fig. 2), based on Thomas (1941, p. 82).

After a brief review of the relevant theory comes a discussion of the necessary underpinning for a direct relationship to hold between income and fertility, and then follows a sampling of the evidence on the short-run direct and long-run indirect effects of income on fertility.

The Theory of the Effect of Income on Fertility

A set of factors that I think useful in understanding the effect of income on fertility is compiled in figure 2-4. Change in economic conditions is here the central exogenous variable. One might argue that a congeries of psychological and sociological conditions commonly called "the beginning of modernization" precedes and causes changes in income level. Perhaps so. But for the purposes of this analysis it matters not whether it is change in technology or politics or markets or other conditions that is a "first cause." What matters here is that once the growth process is in motion, changes in economic conditions cause further changes in technology, social organization, and other conditions, which then feed back to the level of living. Hence it can be meaningful for a study to focus on the level-of-living variable and its effects on fertility.

The economic theory of the effect of income on fertility has usually concentrated on the microeconomic family-decision-making aspects. The theory has gone through several stages.

The first stage was simply to assume that a child is a good like most consumer goods. As income rises people buy more of most goods, and

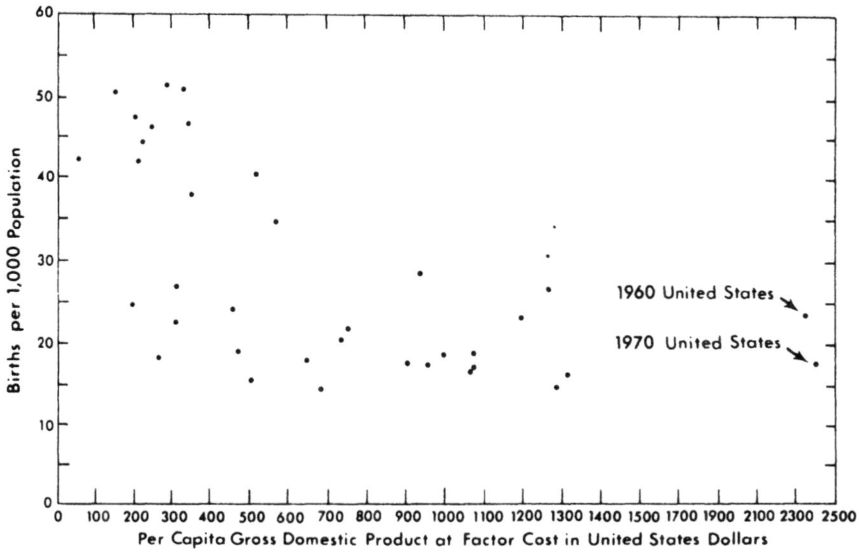

FIG. 2-2. Scattergram of per capita gross domestic product plotted against the crude birth rate for selected nations of the world, 1960. *Source:* From Simon (1974a, p. 110, fig. 20), based on Bogue (1969, p. 85) and *Population Index,* various issues.

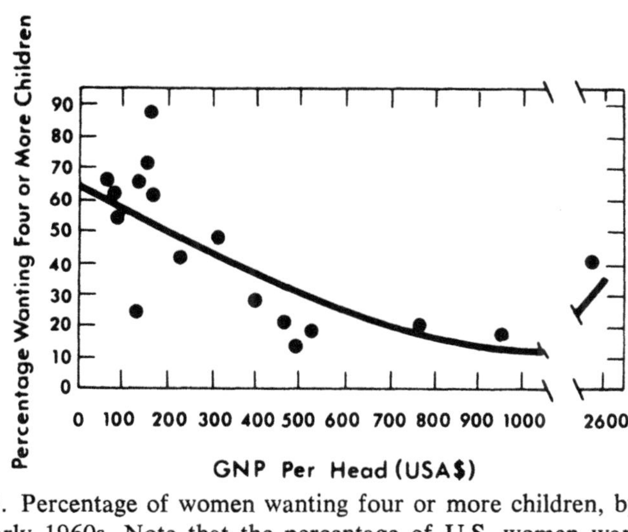

FIG. 2-3. Percentage of women wanting four or more children, by income, in the early 1960s. Note that the percentage of U.S. women wanting four or more children fell sharply from the early 1960s to 1970 (Easterlin 1973, p. 77), which greatly affects the right-hand end of the diagram. *Source:* From Simon (1974a, p. 133, fig. 22), based on Berelson (1966, p. 663).

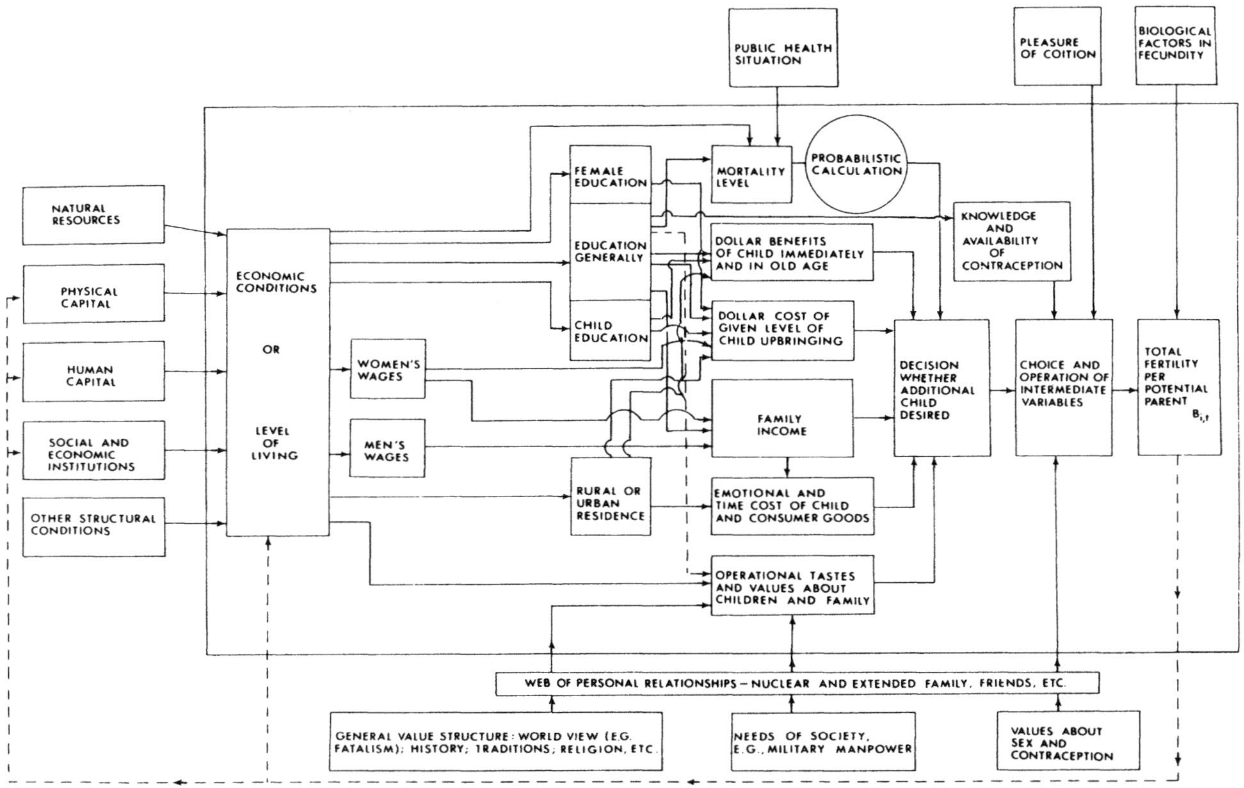

FIG. 2-4. The relationships between income and fertility. *Source:* From Simon (1974a, pp. 5–6, fig. 1).

it was assumed that they would then have more babies, too. Early theorists also assumed, however, that a rise in income affects tastes and values in such a manner as to reduce the number of children wanted. In the Dumont–Banks variation (Banks 1954) a rise in average income was said to increase aspirations for social advancement, which may be thought of as an increased desire for other goods that compete with children for family resources. This desire would act to reduce the number of children people would have. In this theoretical tradition, as in some subsequent stages of economic theorizing, a rise in income has effects on fertility in both directions, and there is no way of determining in advance which force will dominate. Hence there can be no purely theoretical prediction of the overall effect on fertility.

Next came the idea that with a change in family income come changes in the economic benefits from a child, in terms of the child's expected contribution to the family economy, and the costs of a child, in terms of the family's expected expenditures in raising the child. This view was spelled out most fully for less developed countries by Harvey Leibenstein (1957).

Then Gary S. Becker (1960) formalized the notion of the demand for children as "consumption" goods. He distinguished between two dimensions of a family's fertility decisions, the "quantity" (number) of children a family "purchases" and the "quality" (education, for example) per child it decides to purchase. Central to Becker's argument was that economic analysis of fertility should proceed on the assumption that tastes and values are unchanged by changes in income. Becker's is very much a microeconomic and short-run theory; Becker does not take up such matters as increases in education and urbanization that result from increased average income and their subsequent effects on fertility.

Next came the focus of Jacob Mincer (1963) on the woman's work decision, emphasizing the fact that children represent an opportunity cost in wages forgone, because additional children reduce the capacity of women to work in the market.

Recently there has been considerable sophisticated formal theoretical exploration by Yoram Ben-Porath (1973a), Dennis De Tray (1970), Robert T. Michael (1970a), and Robert J. Willis (1969) of the wider place of an additional child in the family's time budget as well as in the income budget, time and money being related in a manner analyzed by Becker (1965). Another aspect of this work tradition is a shift from thinking of commodities being consumed to thinking of the services—including "child services"—yielded to consumers by the objects of the expenditure of time and money. Perhaps the most provocative theoretical outcome of this "household utility maximization" school has been that an increase in income might immediately be translated into a decrease in fertility by way of an increase in the purchase of other goods whose enjoyment requires time and therefore competes with the time the family might spend with children.

Because the elaborated economic theory tells of income-produced forces that act on fertility in opposite directions, pure economic theory by itself cannot predict whether the effect of additional national or individual income will on balance be lower or higher fertility. If one also makes limiting assumptions appropriate to a particular situation, however, one can deduce the direction of the effect of income on fertility. The value of this theorizing at this stage is that it directs attention to the search for operational proxies for some of the various influences mentioned in the theory, in order to measure whether they behave as expected.

Distinction Between Short-run Partial Effects and Long-run Total Effects of Income on Fertility

The influences on family fertility decisions that originally stem from changes in national income may conveniently be classified into two groups. One group consists of the forces that flow immediately from changes in the family's current income opportunities. These forces directly affect the family's resources in time and money. They include an increase in the husband's earnings (assuming that he continues to work the same amount of time each year), an increase in other goods that the family buys from its increased income, changes in the wife's earning opportunities as well as in her felt need to earn income because of the increase in the husband's earnings, and so on. These effects, which can take place in a period as short as a year or two and hence are here labeled "short-run," have been the special focus of economic theorizing about fertility decisions in more developed countries, though of course these forces can be expected to be important in less developed countries, too. When important structural forces are held constant, these forces can, for the most part, be captured empirically by a single variable for the husband's income.

The other group of forces triggered by a change in national income are those that affect the structural aspects of people's life situations. Examples include increases in education, population shifts from country to city, and improved health. Partly because these effects are structural, they take a relatively long time to operate. An increase in children's education, for example, affects resources of time and money only after ten or twenty years. Such forces are here referred to as "long-run" and "total," and no single variable comes close to capturing all of them empirically.

This distinction between the short-run and the long-run effects of income on fertility reconciles the apparent contradiction between the negative relationship usually observed in simple cross-sectional analyses and the positive relationship observed in time series. Higher family income a decade or so earlier leads to more education and other fertility-reducing effects in the present. But higher education in earlier years is correlated with higher income now. So it is reasonable that cross sections—which embody long-run effects—indicate a negative relationship because of the lagged (indirect) effect of income in earlier years. In short time series, education and other indirect effects of income are held fairly constant, and hence they wash out; the positive short-run direct effect of income can therefore show itself in short time-series analyses.

The Necessary Conditions for an Income–Fertility Relationship: Rational Decision Making

The factors shown in figure 2-4—especially income—can affect fertility only if rational self-conscious thought affects the course of sexual passion. Therefore we must ponder briefly the extent to which reason and reasoning are at work in the actions of individual people in various societies at different periods in their histories. To put the matter bluntly, we must inquire into the notion that poor people in poor countries tend to breed without thought, foresight, or conscious control. We shall not, however, inquire into "collective rationality." To judge whether a community acts rationally one must know what its goals are and whether given behavior will attain those goals—both of which concepts are far beyond the scope of this chapter.

For most couples in most parts of the world, marriage is antecedent to births. It is therefore clearly relevant to a judgment about the amount of reasoning involved in "breeding" that marriages are, in most "primitive" societies, contracted after a great deal of careful thought, especially with reference to the economic effects of the marriage. Conrad M. Arensberg's description of a match being made in rural Ireland makes clear the importance of economic factors:

> "The young lady's father asks the speaker what fortune do he want. He asks him the place of how many cows, sheep, and horses is it? He asks what makings of a garden are in it; is there plenty of water or spring wells? Is it far in from the road, he won't take it. Backward places don't grow big fortunes. And he asks, too, is it near a chapel and the school or near town?"

The Inagh countryman could pause here; he had summarized a very long and important negotiation.

"Well," he went on, getting to the heart of the matter, "if it is a nice place, near the road, and the place of eight cows, they are sure to ask £350 fortune. Then the young lady's father offers £250. Then maybe the boy's father throws off £50. If the young lad's father still has £250 on it, the speaker divides the £50 between them. So now it's £275. Then the young man says he is not willing to marry without £300—but if she's a nice girl and a good housekeeper, he'll think of it. So there's another drink by the young man, and then another by the young lady's father, and so on with every second drink till they're near drunk. The speaker gets plenty and has a good day." [Arensberg 1937]

Economic conditions acting through rational self-conscious control are also seen to affect the marriage decision in a vignette recorded by Edward Banfield in a southern Italian town that then was "as poor as any place in the western world" (Banfield 1958, p. 45). The young man whose account is given had a total yearly cash and computed income of $482, as of 1955, for his four-person family, not much higher than the income of a peasant family in India. He described his courtship and marriage decision as follows:

In 1935 I was old enough to marry. My sisters wanted me to take a wife because they had no time to do services for me.

At that time there was a law that anyone who was 25 years old and not married had to pay a "celibacy" tax of 125 lire. That amount was much, if we recall that to earn it you had to work 25 days. I thought it over and finally decided to marry.

My present wife was at that time working with relatives of my employer. Once I stopped her and asked her to marry me, and she liked the idea too, but I had to tell it before her father. He was happy to accept me, and we talked about what she had to bring as dowry and what I had to do.

He asked me to bring my mother to call so that everything would be fine. The next time I brought my mother, and we had a nice feast. When I wanted to meet my fiancee I had to ask the boss' permission.

In 1937 I asked the girl and her family to hasten the marriage before I was 25 years old. The father told me that she was not ready with the dowry. I asked him if at least we couldn't have the civil ceremony on February 6, 1938, two months late, so that I had to pay the tax for that year.

Once my mother and I went to Addo to visit my father-in-law in order to discuss and establish definitely what they were going to give us [in the dowry]. My mother wanted everything to be conveyed through a notary.

> My father-in-law gave us one tomolo of land and my mother gave the little house, but she reserved for herself the right to use it. Everything was written on official taxstamp paper by the notary. As soon as my wife was ready with the dowry the church marriage was set for August 25, 1938. [Banfield 1958, pp. 111–112]

The effect of the harvest on nuptiality in eighteenth-century Sweden, which was then a backward agricultural country (but one that happened to have good vital statistics), is further evidence that people's sexual behavior is sensibly responsive to objective circumstances. When the harvest was poor, people did not marry, as shown in figure 2-1. Birth rates were also responsive to the harvest, as will be seen later. Even unmarried fertility was affected by objective economic conditions.

As to reason and thought about fertility after marriage, even among the most "primitive" and "backward" of people, fertility is subject to some degree of both personal and social control. For a single example, here is Firth's summary of the situation on the Polynesian island of Tikopia:

> Strong social conventions enforce celibacy upon some people and cause others to limit the number of their offspring. [Firth 1939, pp. 36–37]
>
> The motive of a married pair is the avoidance of the extra economic liability which a child brings. In this small but flourishing community there is a conscious recognition of the need for correlating the size of population with that of the available land. Consequently it is from this point of view that limitation of families is mainly practiced. The position is expressed very clearly by the people themselves. Here is a typical statement: "Families by Tikopia custom are made corresponding to orchards in the woods. If children are produced in plenty, then they go and steal because their orchards are few. So families in our land are not made large in truth; they are made small. If the family groups are large and they go and steal, they eat from the orchards, and if this goes on they kill each other." [Firth 1936, p. 491]

After an extensive study of the anthropological literature A. M. Carr-Saunders concluded, "The evidence so far adduced shows that the mechanism whereby numbers may be kept near to the desirable level is everywhere present" (Carr-Saunders 1922, p. 230), the particular mechanisms being "prolonged abstention from intercourse, abortion, and infanticide" (p. 214). And as a result of a study of "data on 200 societies from all over the world from tropic to arctic from sea level to altitudes of more than 10,000 feet," Clellan S. Ford (1952) concluded that "both abortion and infanticide are universally known. It is extremely common to

Table 2-1. Fertility of Women in Tribal Cultures

Race	*No. of children born*		*No. of children left to be reared, or actually reared*
Australians	4.8–5.0		2.7–3.2
Other savage peoples		2.5–3.5	
Eskimo and Northern people		2.1–2.8	
North American Indians		3.0–4.0	
Negroes	3.7–4.3		2.8–3.3
	(3.1–3.8)		(2.4–3.0)

Source: Krzywicki (1934, p. 217). (Designations of racial groups are from the original table.)

find a taboo on sexual intercourse during the period when the mother is nursing. In nearly every instance, the justification for this abstinence is the prevention of conception" (Carr-Saunders 1922, p. 773). Carr-Saunders also found instances of many kinds of contraceptive practices. Some are "clearly magical." Others "are relatively effective mechanical devices (for example) inserting a pad of bark cloth or a rag in the vagina (or) attempts to flush out the seminal fluid with water after intercourse" (Carr-Saunders 1922, pp. 765–766).

Physical evidence to confirm the anthropologists' findings about customs and norms comes from actual fertility itself; in practically no observed society (except, paradoxically, the very modern Hutterites and a few other groups) does fertility seem to come anywhere near to women's total fecundity, and in many very "primitive" (that is, tribal) societies fertility is quite low. Ludwik Krzywicki ransacked the anthropological accounts to obtain estimates of the number of children born and raised in hundreds of tribes and groups. Table 2-1 shows the averages among various tribes in various parts of the world. And despite the fact that "Every one of the [individual tribal estimates], taken apart from the others, is open to serious doubt . . . they mutually confirm each other by the unanimity of their purport: all unanimously indicate that, at the lower stages of culture, the number of (living) children is smaller than that to which prewar European conditions have accustomed us" (Krzywicki 1934, p. 216).

A more recent surveyor of the anthropological evidence, Moni Nag, reached conclusions somewhat different from those of Carr-Saunders and Krzywicki, however:

> Of sixty-one societies thirty-five have been rated as high, sixteen as low, and ten are very low on the (fertility) scale used in this study. These

> results do not agree with Carr-Saunders' [1922, p. 98] and Krzywicki's [1936, p. 256] findings that the fertility levels of "primitive" societies are generally quite low. All the societies in the present selection cannot be termed "primitive," but most of them can be classed as such. The data used in evaluating the fertility levels of these societies are not very satisfactory, but they are better than those used by Carr-Saunders and Krzywicki.
>
> On the other hand, it is not correct to assume that all non-industrial societies have uniformly high fertility. The statement by Davis and Blake [1956, p. 1], "A striking feature of underdeveloped areas is that virtually all of them exhibit a much higher fertility than do urban-industrial societies," seems to be too strong. The range of the value of total maternity ratio in my selection is 2.6–10.4. The total maternity ratio for United States Whites in 1950 by considering ever-married women aged 50–54 years was 2.7. [Nag 1962, p. 142]

Nag's classification of "high," "low," and "very low" was an overall judgment based on several measures of fertility. The figures corresponding to this classification for children ever born to women at the end of child bearing ("total maternity ratio") were 5.5, 3.01–5.5, and 2–3, respectively.

Additional evidence that income and economic circumstances are important in poor people's thinking about fertility is found in answers about advantages and disadvantages of large families in Africa. A summary of surveys in Ghana, Nigeria, and Kenya (Caldwell 1968a, pp. 601, 603) shows that the two advantages most frequently given are help in the household and on the farm and security in sickness and old age, while the two disadvantages most frequently given are the general economic burden and the burden of educating children.

On balance, this preliminary evidence—which I believe that the rest of the section confirms—shows that in all societies people do indeed give much thought to sex, marriage, and child bearing. To repeat, fertility is everywhere clearly subject to at least some rational control, though the degree to which the family size achieved matches desired family size varies somewhat from group to group. Families in some countries plan more carefully than families in other countries and are better able to carry such plans to fruition, because of differences in available contraceptive technology, infant mortality, and intracouple patterns of communication. But there is certainly strong evidence that people think rationally about fertility, and hence other objective forces influence fertility behavior to a significant degree, everywhere and always. Therefore it can be useful to explore the extent and the nature of the effect, which task is the subject of this chapter.

Evidence on the Short-run Effect of Income on Fertility in Less Developed Countries

TIME-SERIES EVIDENCE. Let us begin the quantitative evidence with some time-series data. Apparently fertility did indeed increase at the beginning of the economic development of the European countries. The same effect has been observed in the less developed countries in the twentieth century. "While the data are not so good as to give decisive evidence, it seems very likely that natality has risen over the past generation—certainly in the West Indies, very likely in tropical America, and probably in a number of countries of Africa and Asia" (Kirk 1969, p. 79). This rise may result partly from physical factors, such as a reduction in venereal disease; it may also partly result, however, from direct income effects, as Carl E. Taylor, a close observer of an Indian village, reports:

> In the early 1950s, conditions were distinctly unfavorable. The large influx of refugees from Pakistan was accompanied by severe disruption of economic and social stability. We were repeatedly told by village leaders on the panchayat, or elected village council, that important as all of their other problems were, "the biggest problem is that there are just too many of us." By the end of the study period in 1960, a remarkable change had occurred. With the introduction of more irrigation canals and with rural electrification from the Bhakra-Nangal Dam, and with better roads to transport produce to markets, improved seed and other benefits of community development, and especially because there were increasing employment opportunities for Punjabi boys in the cities, a general feeling of optimism had developed. A common response of the same village leaders now was, "Why should we limit our families? India needs all the Punjabis she can get." During this transitional period an important reason for the failure of education in family planning was the favorable pace of economic development. Children were no longer a handicap. [Taylor 1965, pp. 482–483]

The data for marriages and harvests in eighteenth-century Sweden, which was very much one of the less developed countries at that time, were shown in figure 2-1. Figure 2-5 shows all the relevant rates—harvest, death, marriage, and birth. They are evidence of the strength of the short-run direct effect of income on family size decisions.

In a study of eighteenth-century Flanders, Franklin Mendels (1970) found that the marriage rate in agricultural areas moved directly with the prices of rye, implying that a rise in farm income caused more marriages. In cities where the linen trade was important, the marriage rate moved together with the ratio of rye prices to linen prices. This suggests that

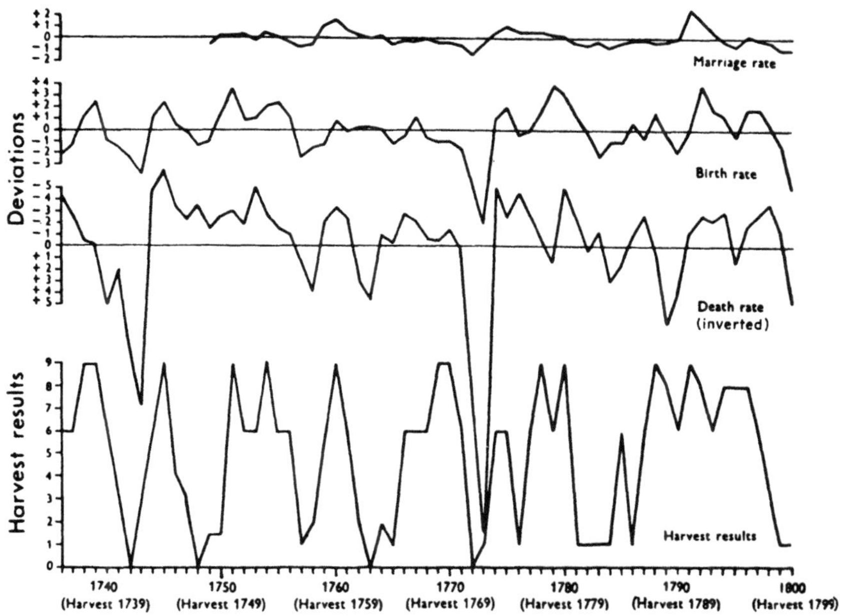

FIG. 2-5. Harvest results and deviations of marriage, birth, and death rates from their respective trends in Sweden. *Source:* From Gille (1949, p. 45).

lower rye prices and higher linen prices (both of which imply higher income to people in the linen trade) produced more marriages.

Ronald Lee (1971) considered the long-run trends of population size, mortality, and real wages in England from 1250 to 1750. He formulated a simultaneous-equation model in which fertility is a function of the real wage, the real wage is a function of population size, and population size is a function of fertility and mortality, with mortality being an exogenous variable. The resulting estimate for the elasticity of fertility with respect to the real wage is a substantial 0.4.

RURAL FAMILY CROSS-SECTIONAL EVIDENCE. For subsistence-farming rural societies the best study is that of W. Stys (1957) for rural Poland in 1948. It can be seen from table 2-2 that, for all those age groups of women that had reached forty-five at the time of the study, the fertility of women who lived on bigger farms was higher. There are variations in the data, to be sure, but Stys's least-squares-regression analysis showed positive slopes for each age group. The detailed data for Polish farm women born from 1855 to 1880, shown in table 2-3, are especially valuable for our purposes. First, consider line 10, which indicates that during those years between the first and last child fertility was much the same on farms of all sizes and was in fact almost as high as has been

Table 2-2. Children Born by Mothers of Different Ages (Actual Numbers)

Mother born in	Landless	0–0.5	0.5–1	1–2	2–3	3–4	4–5	5–7	7–10	10–15	Over 15
	Average no. of children born										
1855–1880	3.89	5.46	5.30	6.10	6.57	6.40	7.54	7.83	9.08	9.00	10.00
1881–1885	3.50	3.50	4.94	5.38	5.84	7.23	7.30	8.09	8.17	6.00	—
1886–1890	6.00	3.55	3.75	5.15	5.39	6.26	6.00	6.67	7.00	9.80	—
1891–1894	4.33	4.31	5.16	4.43	4.83	4.81	6.12	5.56	5.40	7.00	—
1895–1897	2.00	4.28	3.74	4.54	4.77	5.29	4.53	5.00	3.75	5.50	—
1898–1900	4.50	3.71	3.20	3.49	4.07	4.57	4.84	3.88	7.17	6.50	—
1901–1902	—	4.40	2.85	3.80	4.02	4.27	4.60	5.14	4.75	7.50	—
1903–1904	4.00	3.64	2.94	3.42	3.72	3.72	3.64	2.67	4.40	—	—

Farms by size in hectares

Source: Stys (1957, p. 140).

observed in the societies with the highest fertility known. This suggests that fertility was not controlled during that period, and it suggests also that physical health was excellent. Line 3 shows that the poorer the prospective couple, the later the marriage; this suggests an economic check on fertility. Furthermore, poorer couples ceased having children at earlier ages of the mothers (line 5), and physical infirmity was not a likely cause. Together, a later start and an earlier stop to fertility in poorer families had a substantial effect, as shown by comparison of lines 10 and 11.[2] [A. V. Chayanov (1966) suggested a reason to question the meaning of such a relationship, however, and offered supporting data. A farmer may increase by rental the amount of land that he farms when the size of his family makes greater output necessary. This factor was more likely to be important in Russia or Poland during the late nineteenth and early twentieth centuries than in Asia, however, especially at present.]

GEOGRAPHICAL CROSS-SECTIONAL STUDIES. Geographical cross sections of countries tell us little about the "pure" direct effect of income because fuller specification and better data would almost surely make the sign of the coefficient more positive. And specification is particularly difficult in the study of income and fertility, because the variables stand at different

[2] Davis (1963, p. 357) and Clark (1967, p. 190) interpret these data as showing "little limitation *within* marriage" and "little restriction on fertility *in* marriage," respectively (italics mine). But I calculate that if the poorer groups had continued to bear children as late as did the 7+ hectare group, the fertility of the poorer groups would have been 20 percent higher than it was; for example, an eighteen-year fertility period as compared with the observed fifteen-year period for the 0–1 hectare group. Hence, even within marriage, income affects fertility significantly.

Table 2-3. Fertility of Polish Peasant Mothers Born Between 1855 and 1880

	Size of peasant farms in hectares								
Item	*Land-less*	*0–0.5*	*0.5–1*	*1–2*	*2–3*	*3–4*	*4–5*	*5–7*	*7+*
Number of mothers	9	13	23	47	53	10	13	18	15
Average year of birth	1872	1875	1875	1876	1875	1875	1873	1875	1874
Average age at marriage (years)	31	25	25	25	24	23	23	22	20
Average period of actual fertility (years)	9	15	15	17	18	19	19	20	23
Average age of mother at birth of her last child	40	40	40	42	41	42	42	42	43
Average number of children born	3.9	5.8	5.3	6.1	6.6	6.4	7.5	7.8	8.1
Average number of children deceased	1.00	1.31	1.22	1.21	1.57	1.00	2.08	1.55	1.2
Average number of children surviving	2.9	4.1	4.1	4.9	5.0	5.4	5.5	6.3	8.0
Child mortality per 1,000	257	239	230	199	238	156	275	200	127
Average number of children born per year of potential fertility, from marriage to age 45	0.28	0.27	0.26	0.30	0.31	0.29	0.34	0.35	0.37
Average number of children born per year of actual fertility	0.43	0.36	0.34	0.35	0.37	0.33	0.40	0.39	0.40

Sources: Stys (1957, p. 139) and Davis (1963, p. 357).

stages of causation with respect to the dependent variable; for example, average income is itself a variable in the regression as well as a fundamental cause of change in other regression variables such as education. Hence, though regressions such as these can be useful for informing us about the partial effects of other variables, such as infant mortality and urban–rural residence, we should not look to them for information about the direct partial effect of income.

Another important difficulty with the cross-national and intranational geographical regression studies is that while the regressions are linear, the key underlying relationship may well be curvilinear; it may well be that fertility rises and then falls as income rises in less developed countries (for example, in Philippines data, see Encarnacion 1972). If so, it may be inappropriate to lump together less developed countries at the very lowest levels of per capita income with higher-income countries.

Yasukichi Yasuba (1962) conducted a study of the United States in the nineteenth-century—a period in which it should be considered a less developed country—which is distinguished by the fact that he examined the data both cross-sectionally and over a period of time. He worked with statistics of the amount of easily accessible land, which certainly is related to the prospects for income in a rural society. In those states where there was more accessible land per family, the birth rate was higher, and as the amount of accessible land diminished in the course of time, so did the birth rate. These results became apparent after such factors as land quality, urbanization, and average income are allowed for. (See also McInnis 1972.)

POPULATION TRAP MODELS. The short-run direct effect of rises in income in less developed countries has primary theoretical interest in the context of the so-called low-level equilibrium trap. Leibenstein's trap model (Leibenstein 1957, pp. 170–173) is a rigorous contemporary statement of Malthus's doctrine. The key idea is that under some conditions in less developed countries, as income rises, population will rise just as much in response. For example, in Leibenstein's model a 2 percent increase in total income immediately induces a 2 percent increase in population. This response would leave per capita income unchanged and hence block the growth of economic development. In Leibenstein's model the rise in population may be due—in various unspecified proportions—to a decrease in the *death* rate as well as an increase in the birth rate. In Richard R. Nelson's trap model (Nelson 1956), the *entire* effect is through the death rate.

But in the twentieth century, a very large part of the observed drop in death rates in less developed countries seems to have occurred independent of rises in income. That is, much of the increase in population growth that is accounted for by a drop in the death rate is not caused by a rise in income; for example, the expectation of life at birth is now in the sixties in Albania, Ceylon, Costa Rica, Cuba, Dominican Republic, El Salvador, Guyana, Hong Kong, Jamaica, Korea, Malaysia, Mexico, Panama, Philippines, Portugal, Taiwan, Venezuela, and in some other countries where birth rates are still high and where per capita income is far below the average of Europe or North America. And with respect to the inverse proposition, the effect of income on mortality, Simon Kuznets (1965, pp. 8–9) observes that, historically, "economically significant rises in per capita income were not followed invariably by significant and perceptible declines in birth rates. . . . Death rates may remain stable for decades, while per capita income rises, or decline sharply while per capita income barely moves, as [death rates] did recently in many underdeveloped countries."

After a reasonably short series of such decreases in mortality, a plateau must be reached at which further major reductions are unlikely. This means that if a rise in income is to cause a fully counterbalancing growth in population, it must be *fertility* that responds positively to the rise in income. If mortality does not take up any of the effect, then the elasticity of fertility with respect to income must be +33! For example, if the birth rate were 30 per thousand, and if there were a 1 percent increase in income inducing a 1 percent incremental increase in population, the birth rate would have to rise to about 40 per thousand to accomplish the offset. This would mean a 33 percent increase in the birth rate in response to the 1 percent population growth rate. Needless to say, there is no evidence that the short-run income elasticity approaches such a level. Hence the idea of a population trap is unrelated to the real situation in the less developed countries.

SUMMARY OF SHORT-RUN EFFECTS. To summarize the evidence on the partial direct short-run effect of a rise in average income in less developed countries: The immediate effect of a rise in income at the beginning of a secular rise in a traditional subsistence-agriculture setting is to increase fertility. This is the classic case in economic theory of the effect of income on fertility, tastes in the short run remaining unchanged while people find they can afford to raise more children. This effect may be expected in the less developed countries today just as it was found over a long period in Western Europe and was confirmed by the cyclical harvest fluctuations in Scandinavia in the eighteenth century.

The cross-sectional evidence seems consistent with the following proposition: before the agricultural sector is much affected by modernization, the education and outlook of richer and poorer farmers may be much the same. Therefore, the relationship of family size and income or wealth (usually measured by size of farm) may be interpreted as showing the direct partial effect of income. Such cross sections in both Europe and Asia show that richer peasants for the most part have more children. There is, however, some evidence that such empirical relationships are at least partly attributable to the pressure of more children stimulating farmers to acquire more land for cultivation, but the relative importance of the latter factor is not known.

Malthus thought that when there is a rise in income, fertility rises in response in sufficient measure to wipe out the gain in income. But the sum of the evidence suggests that the likely rise in fertility in direct response to a rise in income is, at most, a tiny fraction of what would be required to offset a growth in income in less developed countries.

The short-run effect by itself is not likely to have policy significance in less developed countries, unless the change in income is offered as a transfer payment conditional upon a change in fertility. Such incentive payments are discussed later in this chapter. The foregoing discussion, then, should be viewed primarily as an exercise contributing to our general understanding of fertility behavior. Perhaps it should also be seen as an argument against worrying about trap effects.

Evidence of the Long-run Indirect Effect of Income on Fertility in Less Developed Countries

The cross-sectional data in figure 2-2 show that there is a long-run negative relationship between income and fertility across the range of less developed countries and beyond. These data trace out what is called "the demographic transition."

Concerning the overall long-run effect of income changes in less developed countries, the history of present-day more developed countries also makes it clear that falls in mortality, falls in fertility, and rises in income (which we call "economic development") go together, after the initial rise in fertility. There is, moreover, enough evidence in hand from the vital statistics of countries that have more recently begun the process of economic development to show that a decline in fertility is already taking place or may soon be expected in those countries. Statements about desired family size are in accord with the vital statistics. These declines in fertility occur despite the high-fertility value systems with which less developed countries enter into economic development. Such value systems apparently change in the face of the new needs and opportunities presented by economic development, though the change may be sufficiently slow so that the fertility response to economic development is slower than it would be otherwise.

But just how do increases in income reduce fertility as economic development takes place? Is income really the causal force? The linkages between rises in income and declines in fertility are much less clear than is the observed overall empirical relationship. Rises in income and economic development imply such changes as increases in education, shifts from rural to city employment and living, increases in child health and life expectancy, and increased availability of contraceptive information. Each of these phenomena is by itself related to lower fertility. But for two reasons this complex cannot be broken down into separate parts: All of these correlates of rises in income are closely associated statistically, which makes it impossible to learn their separate effects by statistical analysis, and these forces are all interacting constituent parts of economic development, all linked together and working hand in hand. Hence it is not even sensible to try to separate their effects.

The relationships between fertility and some of the intermediate variables are not directly economic or income-related: for example, a drop in infant mortality probably reduces fertility because people's basic desires for children can then be met with fewer births. And an increase in knowledge about and availability of contraceptives increases the possibility that couples will achieve the family sizes they desire. But others of the variables are clearly income-related. An increase in education for women increases the wages forgone in the cases of women who choose not to work in order to have more children. A move from farm to city reduces the earnings of children that adults can count upon while raising the out-of-pocket costs of children. And by raising standards of education, the whole of the economic-development process raises the amounts that many parents aspire to spend on their children's educations. The best statement would seem to be that income is indeed a causal force in any long-run decline in fertility, but one that operates through a variety of other factors such as increased education, decreased mortality, improved health, and so on. Elsewhere (Simon 1974a) I have discussed these factors at length. But in the end it is the entire nexus of forces that we call economic development—of which the increase in income is both an indicator and a driving force—that causes fertility to fall in the long run as economic development takes place.

Certainly, increased income is desirable for less developed countries for itself as well as because of its effect on fertility. But income will not be raised in order to reduce fertility. That is, the overall income level is not a control variable in this context. So the subject may be left here.

Summary of the Empirical Relationships Between Income and Fertility

Concerning the partial direct short-run effect of rises in income in less developed countries: the immediate effect of a rise in income in a traditional subsistence agriculture setting is to increase fertility. This has been found to be true at the beginning of the present secular rise in income in less developed countries and in the earlier history of Western Europe, as it was also true of the cyclical harvest fluctuations in Scandinavia in the eighteenth century. As to an income-fertility trap, the sum of the evidence suggests that the likely rise in fertility in direct response to a rise in fertility is at most a tiny fraction of what would be required to offset a growth in income in less developed countries.

Concerning the overall long-run effect of income changes in less developed countries, the history of present-day more developed countries has made it clear that falls in fertility and rises in income (which we call economic development) go together, after the initial rise in fertility. And there is enough evidence in hand from the vital statistics of countries that have more recently begun the economic-development process to show that a decline in fertility is already happening or may soon be expected in those countries.

The long-run linkages between rises in income and declines in fertility are, however, much less clear than is the observed overall empirical relationship. Income clearly is a causal force, but it operates through a variety of other forces the nexus of which we call economic development.

The Fertility Effects of the Redistribution of Income

Recently several writers—James E. Kocher (1973) and William Rich (1973), for example—have suggested that fertility is lower where the income distribution is more nearly even, other things being equal,[3] and they imply that countries ought to consider redistribution of income in order to reduce fertility (in addition to whatever other effects it might have).

Before considering whether income distribution of some sort is a feasible policy tool for influencing fertility, let us consider the theory and the facts of the relationship of income distribution to fertility.

There are two ways in which income distribution might affect fertility. First, there may be a relative income effect. That is, a family's fertility may be a function of the neighbors' income as well as the family's own. Deborah S. Freedman (1963) presented some evidence for the operation of such a relative effect in more developed countries. But no data of this sort exist for less developed countries. (It should be noted that if there is such an effect, it is likely to be related to the distribution of income within occupations or areas, rather than the income distribution of

[3] Jim B. Marshall of the U.S. State Department also had this thought and commissioned me to do a feasibility study of the subject. Much of this section is drawn from the report of that study.

the nation as a whole; in fact, Freedman's data refer to the distribution within occupations.) Relative income may indeed affect fertility in less developed countries, but our knowledge about the matter is nonexistent. Second, redistribution of income also changes the *absolute* incomes of the people affected. Therefore, a redistribution of income may influence fertility through the absolute relationship of income to fertility. It seems to me that this absolute effect is likely to be more important than a relative income effect.

Evidence About the Relationship of Income Distribution and Fertility

As to the facts, Kocher and Rich offered anecdotal comparisons apparently showing that narrower income distributions are associated with lower fertility:

> The per capita income in Taiwan was approximately $246, or similar to that of the Philippines, which was $235. There was, however, a considerable discrepancy between the distributions of income in the two countries. The highest 10 percent of the population in the Philippines was significantly wealthier than the same group in Taiwan, but the lowest 20 percent was more than twice as well off in Taiwan. Moreover, there also is evidence that in Taiwan, income distribution has improved markedly over time, whereas in the Philippines it has become more and more concentrated among the wealthiest 20 percent of the population. These two factors help to explain why a much greater share of the population appears to have reached the socio-economic level conducive to reduced fertility in Taiwan than in the Philippines. Comparisons similar to that between Taiwan and the Philippines can also be made between Barbados, Argentina, South Korea, Singapore, Uruguay, Cuba, Costa Rica, or China on the one hand, and Venezuela, Mexico, Brazil, and many of the other Latin American countries on the other. [Rich 1973, p. 24]

Rich also calculates that the correlation between birth rates in the less developed countries and the per capita incomes of the poorest 60 percent of populations is stronger ($R^2 = .64$) than between the birth rate and the overall per capita income ($R^2 = .46$). But what we would like to know is just how different the birth rate would be in a country if its distribution of income were different.

Robert G. Repetto regressed the gross reproduction ratio, and separately, a measure similar to the general fertility rate, on income per capita, newspapers per capita, and the distribution of income as measured by the Gini coefficient. The elasticities of fertility with respect to distribution of income are 0.39 and 0.47 for the two fertility measures, respectively. To the extent that the relationship is causal, these estimates suggest that a change of 10 percent in the income distribution measure is associated with a change of 3.9 percent in fertility. It is important and impressive that the elasticities appear to be even higher than those just cited when Repetto takes account of the effects of fertility on distribution of income, as well as on the converse, with a simultaneous-equation-estimation method. This reinforces our belief that the estimated effect of distribution of income upon fertility is indeed causal. On the other hand, the absolute effect of a change of 10 percent in distribution of income (a large change) upon the fertility of a country is not great—a reduction of only 0.21 in the gross reproduction ratio.

So the data suggest that an aggregate redistribution might reduce fertility. Nevertheless, it would be unreasonable to assume that a country might undertake an aggregate redistribution for the purpose of reducing fertility, for at least two reasons: first, the likely reasons for undertaking a redistribution of income would include social justice, diminution of economic power blocs, increased agricultural productivity, general economic and social invigoration, and increased savings.

Second and more important, "redistribution of income" does not describe a concrete policy that a government might undertake. Rather, a government might seek to alter the distribution of income with land reform, educational redistribution, alteration in the terms of trade, or others among the sorts of policies to be discussed shortly. Different policies that might alter the overall distribution in the same direction, moreover, may well have quite different effects upon fertility. For example, a land redistribution scheme might have fertility effects quite different from those of an increase in the progression of the money income tax. Therefore, it is necessary to inquire about the effect on fertility of each of the concrete possible specific redistributions that might be undertaken by one of the less developed countries, rather than discussing income redistribution in the aggregate.

Not only are these specific redistribution policies sharper and more meaningful than aggregate redistribution of income from a scientific point of view, they are also capable of enough variation in a reasonably short length of time to exert a significant effect on fertility. That is, a redistribution of land may really alter the distribution of land ownership in ten years. But the income distribution for a country as a whole is likely to be much more glacial; one important reason is that the distribution of education and skills, which influences the distribution of income heavily, cannot be altered rapidly.[4]

[4] One might point to China as an example of rapid overall redistribution of income, but we certainly have no easy access to statistics with which to assess the

Still another reason for specificity in discussing distribution of income is that policy makers actually discuss policies at this more specific level rather than discussing policies for redistribution of income in general.

Here are some of the considerations that must be applied to each sort of income redistribution policy under discussion:

- Each ex ante income class must have its fertility response estimated separately. The sizes of the income classes must be assessed, and then the aggregate fertility effect of the policy may then be estimated.
- The short-run fertility effects of income change, before education and tastes have a chance to change, must be evaluated apart from the long-run effects that are caused by the changes in those background factors.
- The purely economic effects of income redistribution through the family budget, both directly on fertility and indirectly through such intermediate variables as education, must be considered separately from such noneconomic variables as a sense of national élan or increases in social mobility that may accompany a redistribution policy. Such distinctions need not be made if the study is empirical at an aggregate level; one then does not care which intermediate variables are responsible for the internal changes. But if the information is to be obtained from more analytic techniques, at a lower level of aggregation, then such problems must indeed be considered.

Fertility Effects of Some Redistribution Policies

Let us consider some specific mechanisms for redistribution of income that a country might undertake with reducing fertility as one of the objects.

LAND REFORM. In a land-reform redistribution, the smaller landholders, and perhaps the landless, have their holdings (and hence their wealth and income) increased, while the larger owners lose land and wealth. Some possible examples may be found in the history of nineteenth-century Europe; in twentieth-century India, Mexico, and Colombia; in the White Revolution in Iran in 1963; and in the Agrarian Reform of 1952 in Egypt. In principle, examinations of fertility before and after these reforms would tell about their effects upon fertility.

There is probably no feasible way at present to relate historical land reforms to fertility empirically. We may, however, try to estimate the

---

extent of the redistribution. Furthermore, the other social changes accompanying the Chinese redistribution have been so large that it would be quite impossible to determine what portion of the change in fertility is attributable to the redistribution of income alone.

effect of such a land reform by analysis. First, we can probably ignore the effects on the people who lose land, who are relatively rich anyway. For example, in Egypt, where only about 10 percent of the land was expropriated in 1952, more than a third belonged to "the King and other members of the royal family" (Warriner 1957, p. 34). Landowners could retain up to 300 acres (giving 50 acres to each of two children), which is still an enormous farm in a country where 72 percent of the landowners had 1 acre or less, 22 percent had 1–5 acres, and 0.1 percent (2,100 owners) had 200 acres or more (Warriner 1957, p. 24). Furthermore, the owners whose land was expropriated received bonds in compensation for land taken away from them. To the extent that the Egyptian reform is typical—and it probably is, in this respect—there will be no significant aggregate fertility effect on those who lose in the redistribution.

The gainers from the redistribution are likely to include both the landless families and the smallest landholders. Let us assume that the rural sector will continue in much the same way as in the past, with a slow rate of change in modernization—which would seem to be a good assumption in the case of India (though probably not in the case of China). On that assumption, the effect of a redistribution of income would simply be a shift in the numbers of families in the different categories of farm size and fertility. But the people within each category would be the same sort of people observed in contemporary surveys, and the gist of these surveys is that families with larger holdings have more children, as was discussed earlier.

These facts suggest the conclusion that the initial impact of a land redistribution policy in a poor country is likely to cause an increase in fertility in the short run, because many more peasants will have their landholdings increased than will have them decreased.[5]

The longer run is another story, of course. To the extent that the increase in income causes increases in education, mobility, urbanization, and the process of modernization generally, the long-run effect of the increase in income to the small landholders resulting from land reform

[5] Of course this inference assumes that there is no relative wealth effect involved; that is, it assumes that the operative factor is not whether a man is relatively well off, but rather what his absolute wealth is. If such a relative wealth effect is in fact the main determinant of fertility differentials by income, then the land redistribution would not be expected to change aggregate fertility. But the observed fact that the first surge of increased income tends to raise fertility in the aggregate in less developed countries makes me doubt that relative income is such a strong factor here, and hence I would expect an increase in fertility to follow immediately upon land reform.

will be to reduce their fertility. But for this to happen the land reform must really lead into economic development. Hence land reform is far from a surefire quick-acting policy tool for reducing fertility.

REDISTRIBUTION OF ACCESS TO EDUCATION. This sort of redistribution has apparently happened in many parts of Asia and Africa in the last two decades. Direct evidence on the effects of redistributions of educational access are not available, however, so that we must make inferences based on existing educational differentials.

Increased parental education in less developed countries reduces parents' fertility. This is clear from both the cross-national and intra-country cross sections. In fact, the negative relationship between education and fertility is stronger and more consistent over the observed ranges than is the relationship of fertility to any other single variable (Simon 1974a, chapter 4).

The nature of the causal connection between education and fertility is more complex. The woman's opportunity-cost effect is clear, but there is no apparently strong, direct reason other than contraceptive education that an increase in the father's education should decrease family fertility. It may be that the effect of education on the parents' fertility is through their children. If educational facilities are available, parents may choose to invest their purchasing power (and loss of children's labor) in more education for fewer children. This may be a good economic choice for the parents, as John C. Caldwell found in Ghana. And for Colombia and Taiwan, T. Paul Schultz (1969b, p. 23) found that "the enrollment rate is powerfully inversely associated with fertility."

Of even greater relevance for redistribution, however, is the fact that an increase of only one more year of education has more of a negative effect on fertility at low than at higher levels of education. (See, for example, Ben-Porath 1973a.) This implies that a transfer in the direction of educational equality will reduce *aggregate* fertility, and the magnitude of the effect is likely to be large.[6] An educational policy such as that which President Nyerere proposes for Tanzania would probably

[6] It should be noted that some countries have decided on the wisdom of a policy of purposefully *non*equalized access to education—for example, Tanzania: "Instead of expanding the number of standard I classes (first grade), the government decided to increase rapidly the number of classes at standards V–VII (grades 5–7) so that every child entering primary school could receive a full seven years of education. In supporting this position, President Nyerere argued as follows: 'We have made this decision because we believe it is better that money should be spent on providing one child with a seven-year education which may help him or her to become a useful member of society, rather than divide the same amount of money and staff between two children, neither of whom is likely to get any permanent benefit' " (Harbison 1973, p. 58).

result in higher fertility than would an egalitarian program and is not consistent with a policy of fertility reduction.

REDISTRIBUTION OF MEDICAL CARE. In less developed countries—and more developed countries, too—medical services are concentrated in urban areas and are disproportionately available to those people who are well off economically. A government might choose to redistribute access to health care (China has done so). This would reduce infant mortality, raise life expectancy at all ages, and increase total population, because the returns on health care surely are a decreasing function of the amount of health care, and hence more nearly even distribution raises total health output. The impacts on fertility would seem to be downward, however, judging from the results of J. E. Knodel (1968), Schultz (1969b) and his co-workers (Schultz and DaVanzo 1970b), and Ben-Porath (1974a). See also chapter 8 in this volume.

REDISTRIBUTION OF JOB OPPORTUNITIES. A government might attempt to increase job opportunities to the poorest people at the expense of those better off, as India has done in favor of the untouchables. But the number of jobs that a government might redistribute in one of the less developed countries is unlikely to be large enough to have much effect on aggregate fertility.

REDISTRIBUTION OF MONEY INCOMES BY CHANGES IN TAXATION AMONG THE URBAN POPULATION RECEIVING INCOMES IN MONEY. A traditional method of changing the distribution of income in the more developed countries is by taking a higher proportion of the incomes of the rich than of the poor. But the dispersion of family sizes in more developed countries is not too small for any likely redistribution of income to have any observable effect on aggregate fertility.

With respect to less developed countries now, on the basis of the sort of evidence adduced in the paragraph on land reform, I would deduce a mild increase in fertility at the very outset. But as the added income leads into the cumulative process of modernization (assuming that it does), fertility would be expected to be lower than it was before the redistribution of income. Myrdal notes that redistributions of taxation have not been successfully executed or even attempted with vigor. This may well be because most of the poorer countries do not possess the preconditions for effective progressive income taxation (Myrdal 1968, appendix 9, section 9). Much of the product is not monetized, the institutions cannot enforce tax collection and prevent corruption, and the social will is not consistent with sharp taxation of incomes.

There would seem to be no practical way at present to assess empirically the effects of such a redistribution on fertility in less developed countries.

REDISTRIBUTION OF CONSUMPTION AMONG SECTORS OF THE ECONOMY BY A SHIFT IN INDUSTRIAL–AGRICULTURAL TERMS OF TRADE. Such a policy seems to have been undertaken by the Soviet Union in the 1920s, though whether the terms of trade were really influenced is open to some doubt, I believe. The effect of this sort of redistribution toward (or away from) agriculture is to reduce (increase) the real incomes of farmers, assuming that the government's share does not change. An equal change would seem to have less effect on a city dweller, however, than on a farm family, because the urban family is already exposed to much of the force of modernization, and its fertility is already lower than in the farm family (Kuznets 1974; but see Robinson 1963). Hence one might expect, if the redistribution affected equal numbers of people with equal income in the two sectors, that the farm sector would show greater change in fertility than would the city sector—that is, the rise in farm income would in the short run result in a bigger rise in fertility than the resulting drop in fertility in the city. But in the long run one would expect a drop in fertility in the farm sector bigger than the rise (if any occurred) in the urban sector.

REDISTRIBUTION OF PUBLIC INVESTMENTS. The government can influence the distribution of incomes with its public-investment budget. For example, the government might decide to invest in infrastructure or industry in the western rather than the eastern part of a country; this would raise western incomes in relation to eastern incomes, and if western incomes had been lower to start with, the distribution of income would thereby be equalized. Or, the government might tilt the budget toward (or away from) labor-intensive industries and practices. Or, investment might be oriented toward (or away from) industries and occupations that would employ more women. And so on. Each of these redistributions of public investment would have main effects similar to redistributions discussed earlier in this section.

WHOSE FERTILITY WILL BE ALTERED? So far the discussion has not distinguished among additional children. But any policy that affects fertility must consider which kind of babies will be born in larger or smaller quantities. From the economic planning point of view (though not so easily from an ethical point of view) it matters whether an Edison or Einstein or Ghandi will be born, or whether the additional child will be a person who never leaves his village. Policy makers might (or might not) want to consider this when income-redistribution policies are considered.

SUMMARY. The aggregate evidence suggests that redistribution of income might have a very substantial effect upon fertility. But the fertility-reducing effect would come through indirect effects of additional income such as education and urbanization. And such indirect effects must lag at least a decade behind the redistribution of income.

Redistribution toward equalization of access to education is likely to be the most effective and most attractive fertility-reducing sort of redistribution. (In addition, it is likely to be relatively effective in equalizing the distribution of income.) Land reform may increase aggregate fertility in the short run.

Conditional Transfers of Income—Incentive Bonuses and Taxes

Monetary Incentives

Money and other payments that are made *if* a couple has a particular number of children are dealt with in this section.[7] That is, the incentives that are the subject of this section are made conditional upon having or not having children of given parities. These transfers are indeed redistributions of income, but they have a quite different behavioral meaning from that of unconditional redistributions of income, in which the transfers take place independent of the number of children the couple has. It is quite clear that a payment to a couple for not having a third child, say, is more likely to have a strong antinatalist effect than is a transfer of the same size that does not depend on having or not having the third child.[8]

Anecdotal evidence suggests that small payments to acceptors, such as time off from work, can boost the sterilization rate in India (Repetto 1968, p. 9). (But of course a high level of official and public interest in family planning could account for both the activity in incentive programs and high rates of sterilization in a given state.) More impressive evidence comes from several vasectomy campaigns in Ernakulam District in India in 1970 and 1971 (Rogers 1972) and in 1971–72 (*Population Chronicle,* July 1972). Payments of 86 and 114 rupees (U.S.$11.45 and U.S.$15.20) to acceptors, and of 10 rupees (U.S.$1.33) to promoters, produced large jumps in the number of vasectomies performed as compared with previous periods, when incentives to acceptors were 21 rupees (U.S.$2.80) and 2 rupees (U.S.$0.27) to promoters, as seen in figure 2-6. There is no doubt that the increased incentives were the major cause, over and above the special promotion and atmosphere.

[7] Pohlman (1971) offers a useful review of this subject and its background. See especially chapter 6 on some Indian evidence. Gillespie (n.d.) is also valuable. Rogers (1972) is an up-to-date review of past and future field research on incentives.

[8] Enke (1960a, 1960b; 1961; 1962; 1963; 1966, ch. 20); Demeny (1965); Simon (1968); and many recent general articles.

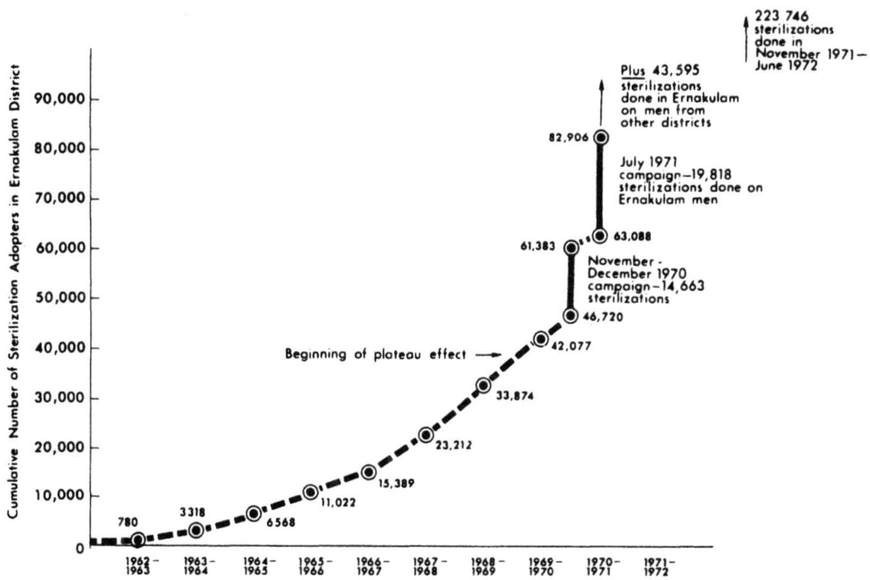

FIG. 2-6. Sterilizations in Ernakulam. *Source:* From Simon (1974a, p. 101, fig. 16), based on Rogers (1972) and *Population Chronicle* (July 1972).

Starting in September 1967, a total of 3,988 workers in four Tata factories in India were offered incentives of 210–220 rupees (about U.S.$27). A total of 3,872 workers in five other nearby factories were offered small incentives of 10–20 rupees (three factories) and 35–55 rupees (two factories). For the lowest-paid Tata workers, the incentive of 210–220 rupees represented well more than a month's pay. Figure 2-7 would seem to indicate that the incentives had a sizable effect. But by the end of the observation period, the relative effect is much smaller than at the beginning. The difference between the high-incentive and low-incentive program is only a little over 3 percent of all workers by the end of the observation period, and it is not increasing rapidly. This suggests that this incentive only induced a total of about 3 percent of all men to be sterilized, not very large in relationship to any population policy, though this figure has to be translated into nonbirths to be meaningful.[9]

[9] (Research and Marketing Services 1970, described in Rogers 1971.) Ronald G. Ridker has kindly provided the information that the results from the three areas differed greatly, and the data described in figures 2-6 and 2-7 combine data from the three areas. In one area, the incentives have a strong positive effect, in another area, the effect was insignificant, and in the third area, the effect was apparently negative. These results were not investigated by the original research organization, and it has not been possible for others to get access to the raw data. These results, together with other facts, suggest lack of care in the analyses which might vitiate it altogether.

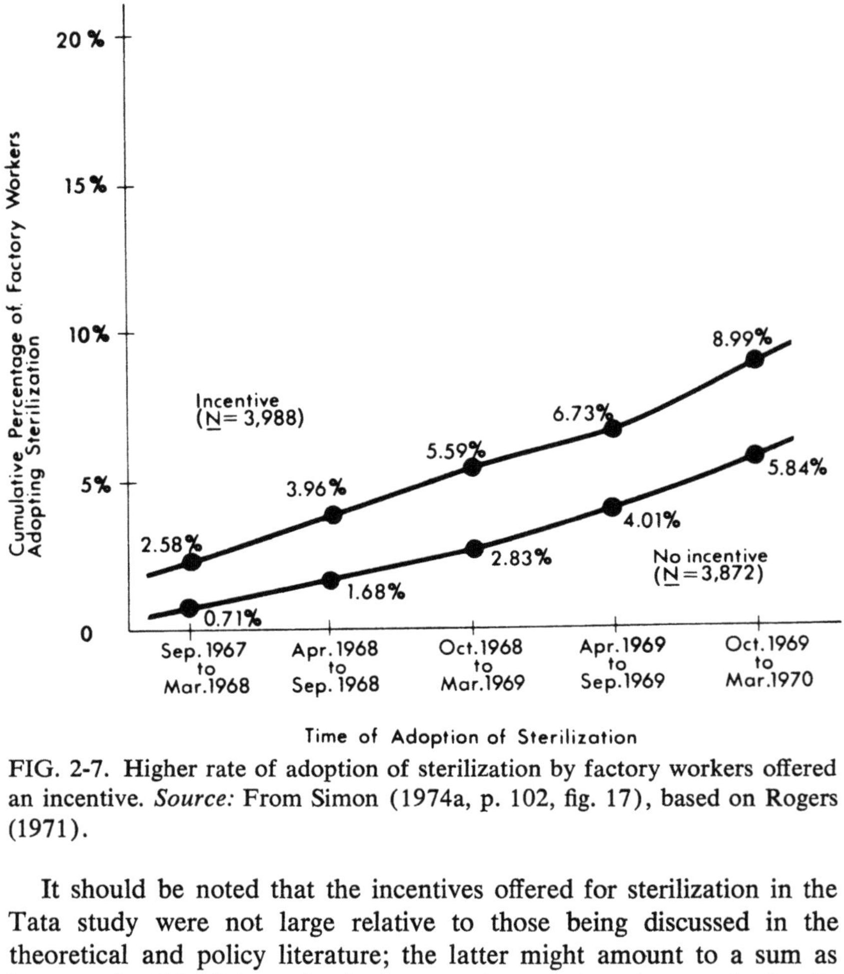

FIG. 2-7. Higher rate of adoption of sterilization by factory workers offered an incentive. *Source:* From Simon (1974a, p. 102, fig. 17), based on Rogers (1971).

It should be noted that the incentives offered for sterilization in the Tata study were not large relative to those being discussed in the theoretical and policy literature; the latter might amount to a sum as large as the "high" incentive in the experiment being given to the family every year rather than just once.

As one would expect, the 210–220 rupee incentive had its strongest effect upon the poorer workers. Figure 2-8 shows that 10.6 percent of the poorest workers accepted sterilization in the high-incentive program while only 3.3 percent in the lowest-income class accepted it, the difference representing 7.3 percent of the total workers in the poorest group. This proportion of the workers in the lowest-income group—which also have the most children on the average—might be important for population policy purposes.

In brief, small incentives to couples in India (10–30 rupees, about U.S.$1.33–U.S.$4.00) apparently have some effect, and incentives of

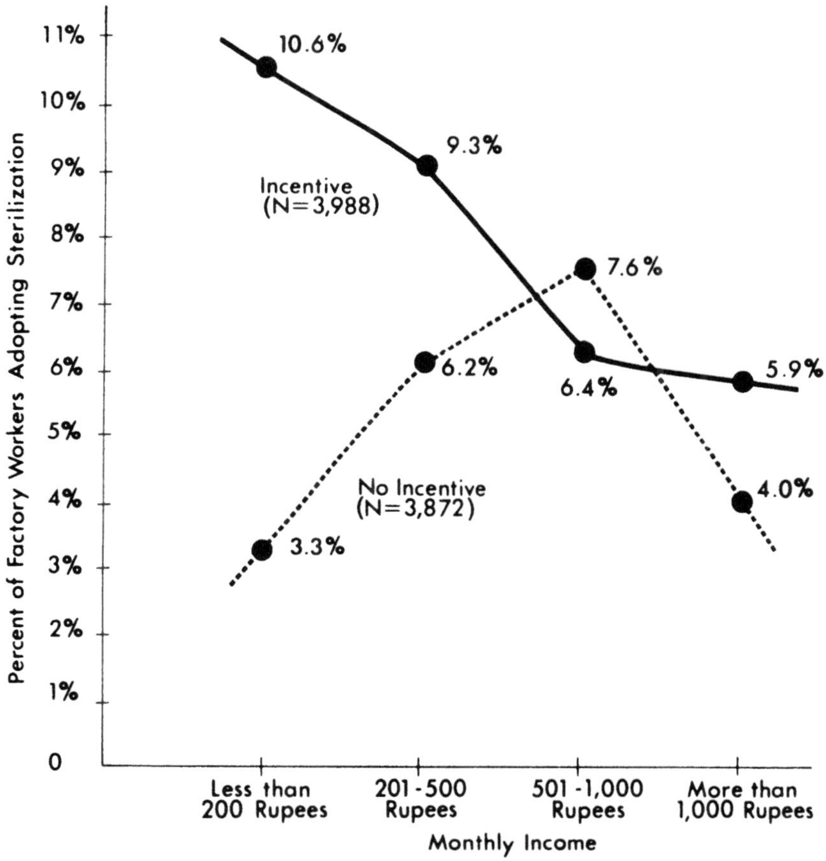

FIG. 2-8. Adoption of sterilization by lower-income factory workers encouraged by incentives. *Source:* From Simon (1974a, p. 103, fig. 18), based on Rogers (1971).

U.S.$10 to U.S.$27 apparently have had sizable effects. The overall magnitude of the response to incentives of this size is probably not large enough to have a substantial effect on India's birth rate, but the appropriate reckonings are still to be done. Payments of this size are far smaller than are many judgments of the size of the benefits of averting the births. Whether really large incentives—of the order of, say, $25 for each year that fertile couples do not produce a child—would have a major effect is still quite unknown.

In Taiwan, a certificate for children's education that "can total U.S.$385 after fourteen years for couples with two or fewer children or U.S.$192 for couples with three children" was offered in a rural township starting in 1971. As of a year after the beginning of the program, administrators had the impression that the offer had affected fertility, but the lack of scientific controls makes quantitative evaluation impossible (Wang and Chen 1973).

In view of the fact that evidence about the effect of incentives on fertility in less developed countries is in short supply, the following evidence from more developed countries may be relevant. For the United States, Rita J. Simon and I (1974–75) have completed a preliminary survey using hypothetical questions. The basic question was as follows, with appropriate changes for families that were planning to have more children, for "projective" questions about other people's behavior, and for incentives to have children rather than not have them:

> Now let's talk about your family. You said you do not plan to have any more children. If the government were to give you a payment of $50 a month for each child beyond the second until the child is 18 years old—that is, $600 per year for each child after the second until the child is 18 years old—do you think that you would have a bigger family than you now have? To make this a little clearer, under this scheme if you had three children the government would pay you $50 each month, if you had four children the government would pay you $100 each month, and so on. If the government had such a plan, do you think you would have more than you do?

Results are shown in table 2-4 and figure 2-9. The data suggest that money incentives could have a significant effect in inducing people to have more or fewer children, especially people with low incomes. Money incentives would seem to be more effective for reducing family size than for increasing the number of children a family would have. People are more likely to say that their neighbors will respond to money incentives than that they themselves will respond. That is, the projective questions indicate a greater responsiveness to incentive payments, especially in the upward direction, than do the direct questions. One may only guess whether the "truth" is closer to the direct or to the projective question results.

A conclusive answer about the effects of incentives in less developed countries will not be available until a well-controlled experiment with varying levels of incentives is actually carried out and completed.[10] One of the criticisms leveled against a controlled-incentive experiment is that it would take a long time—say, three or four years—to obtain reasonably conclusive results. But if that criticism comes to your mind, please reflect upon this: controlled experiments have been urged since at least 1962 (Balfour 1962). If the original suggestions had been tried out, the de-

[10] An ongoing experiment on the Indian tea estates may yield important data.

Table 2-4. Percentage of Respondents Who Say They Would Have More or Fewer Children: Direct and Projective Questions

Amount of payment per month per child (U.S. dollars)	*Direct form of question*				*Projective form of question*			
	National	*National*	*Illinois*	*National*	*National*	*National*	*Illinois*	*National*
	Percentage who say they would have more children							
25	7 (10)	—	—	—	26 (36)	—	—	—
50	9 (13)	14 (18)	5 (10)	—	34 (47)	27 (36)	15 (33)	—
75	—	—	—	12 (17)	—	—	—	32 (43)
100	15 (21)	18 (24)	7 (15)	—	53 (74)	47 (61)	28 (60)	—
150	—	—	—	19 (26)	—	—	—	51 (69)
200	—	22 (29)	10 (22)	—	—	57 (76)	39 (84)	—
300	—	—	—	26 (36)	—	—	—	62 (83)
	Percentage who say they would have fewer children[a]							
25	33 (39)	—	—	—	46 (54)	—	—	—
50	43 (51)	38 (39)	35 (49)	—	60 (70)	45 (53)	68 (119)	—
75	—	—	—	33 (43)	—	—	—	50 (57)
100	53 (61)	42 (55)	41 (59)	—	69 (81)	66 (78)	76 (133)	—
150	—	—	—	50 (57)	—	—	—	63 (72)
200	—	45 (59)	44 (61)	—	—	73 (86)	79 (139)	—
300	—	—	—	53 (61)	—	—	—	68 (77)

Source: Simon and Simon (1974–75).

Note: The number in a cell indicates the proportion of people in the subsample who say that they would change their fertility behavior in response to that particular money incentive (or a smaller one). The number in parentheses gives the absolute number of people giving that positive answer. The four subsamples in the table include the single Illinois subsample and the three groups within the national sample that were given different incentive schedules.

[a] Responses are based on families that have three or more children.

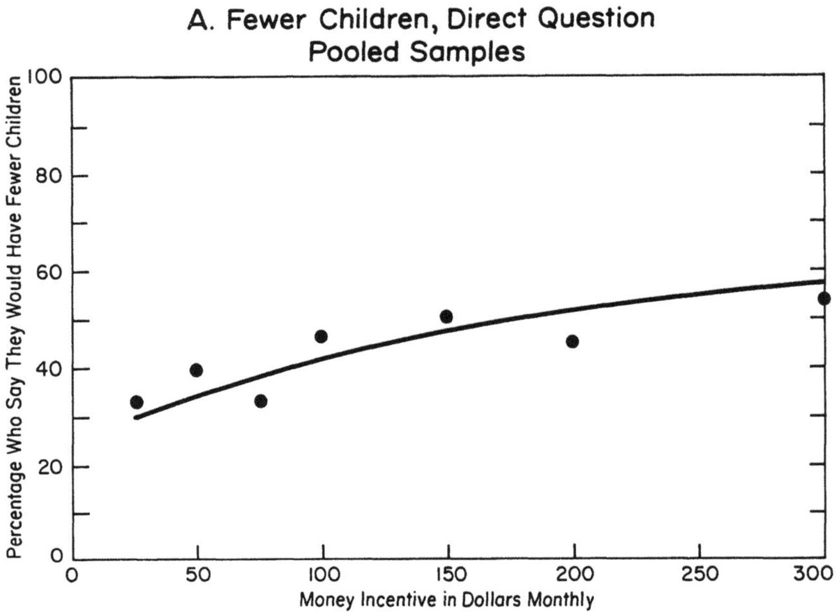
A. Fewer Children, Direct Question
Pooled Samples
Percentage Who Say They Would Have Fewer Children
0
20
40
60
80
100
0
50
100
150
200
250
300
Money Incentive in Dollars Monthly

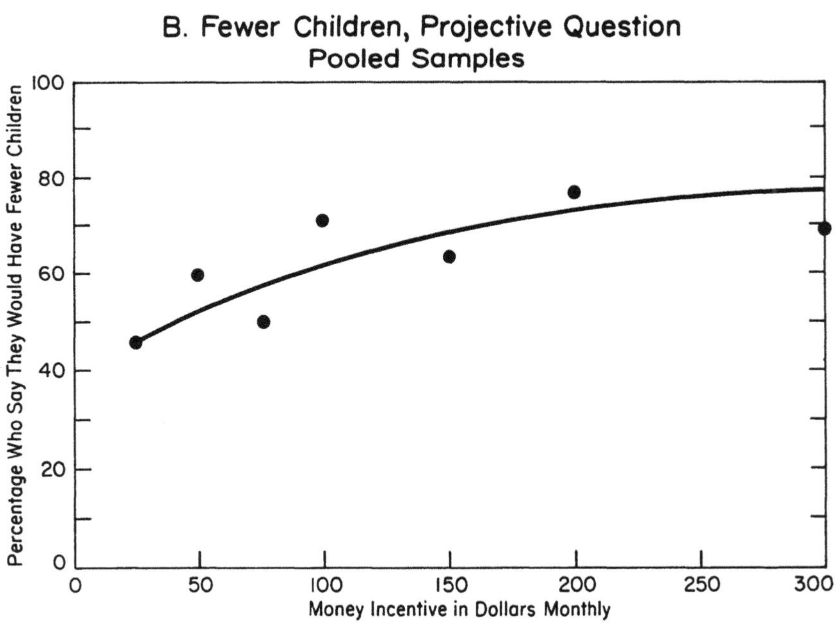
B. Fewer Children, Projective Question
Pooled Samples
Percentage Who Say They Would Have Fewer Children
0
20
40
60
80
100
0
50
100
150
200
250
300
Money Incentive in Dollars Monthly

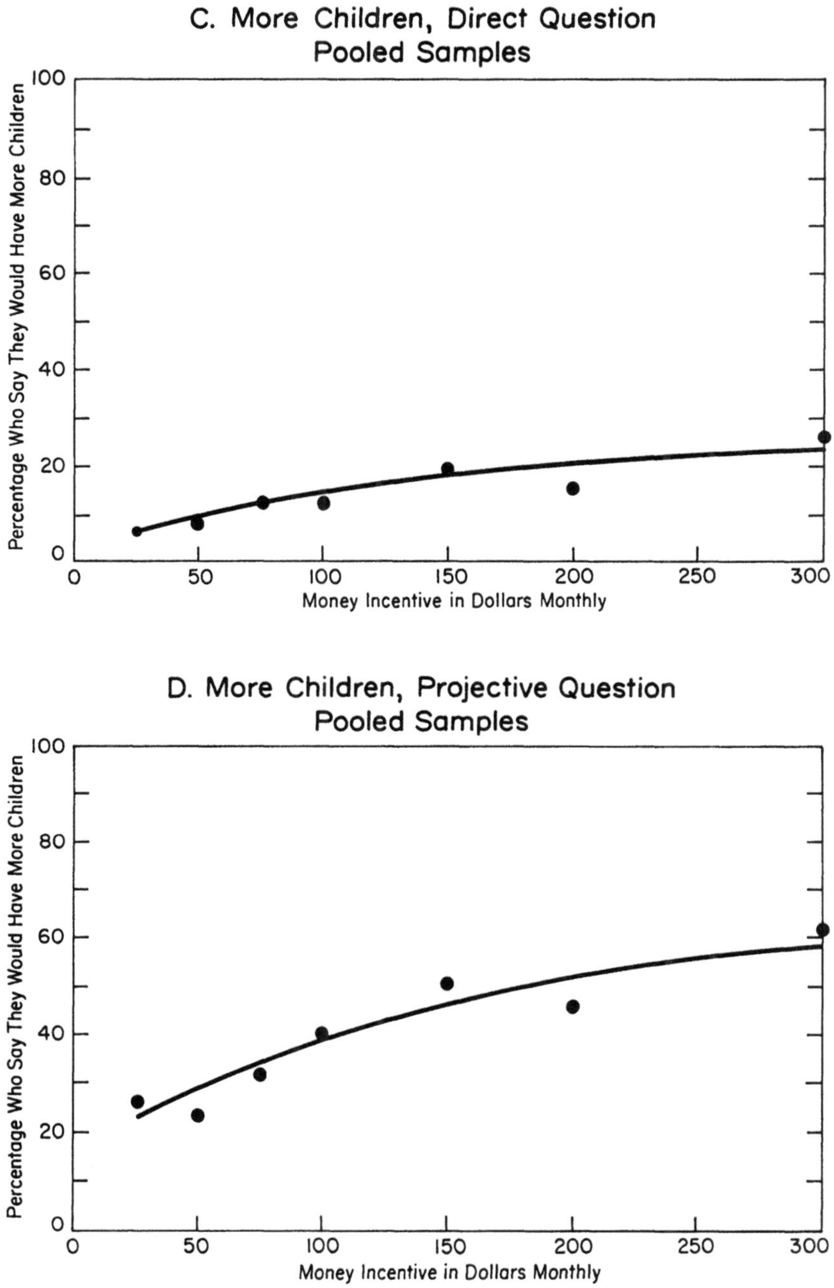

FIG. 2-9. Percentage of respondents who say they would have more or fewer children: direct and projective questions. *Source:* table 2-4, p. 69.

sired information would be available to us now. And if we again heed the criticism that the results will be too long in coming, five and ten years from now we will still be in the state of ignorance in which we now find ourselves.

By now a great many plans for various sorts of experiments in various places have been written and published; these are listed analytically in table 2-5 (IBRD 1974). Hence it is not necessary to give details of an experiment here.

Another promising—certainly much quicker and cheaper—method of obtaining fuller information on the effects of incentives would be studies in less developed countries using the hypothetical question method used in the U.S. study by Simon and Simon.

Nonmonetary Incentives

Governmental policy with respect to housing may be an important in-kind influence upon fertility. The price of living space surely has an important effect upon a family's decision to have more or fewer children, especially for apartment dwellers. By making living space more or less expensive in relation to other goods, therefore, the government can push fertility down or up. Such a policy may be implemented administratively by taxes (or subsidies) on land and on the components of housing construction, or by influencing the rate at which money is lent for home purchases, or by changes in the price of government-owned housing where this is an important factor. Where government housing is important, the government may influence fertility by making the family's apartment size contingent on its family size.

Some evidence on the importance of the influence of housing upon fertility comes from experience in a Columbian housing project (Felson and Solaun 1974). Families that received apartments subsequently had lower fertility than families that received houses—houses which the families could enlarge though they were originally no larger than the apartments. Additional evidence comes from Israel, where in a survey almost half the parents said that they might have had more children if their apartments had been larger (Peled 1969).

Unintended Incentives

The discussion so far has referred to policies that are explicitly related to the number of children. But in all countries there are various social and economic policies that are related to family size and that may act as incentives to have more or fewer children though they are not so intended and labeled. An example is the provision in the income tax law of the United States that allows a $750 deduction for each dependent. This works in a pronatalist direction, though it is not likely to be very important for many Americans. (If a family is poor, the tax deduction does not reduce their taxes much because they pay at a low rate; if they are rich, the total saving is small in relation to their total income.)

More important is the cost of public schooling, much of which is free in the sense that the parents pay the same amount of taxes no matter how many children they have. If parents had to pay the full cost of public schooling for their children, the sum might be great enough to influence fertility downward to a significant degree. Numerous surveys in poor and rich countries have shown that the cost of education is an important consideration to parents in the decision as to how many children to have. Laws that provide additional public education or otherwise subsidize education can have a pronatal effect. This poses a real dilemma for countries that wish to reduce population growth: Education is crucial for economic development, but increasing the availability of education by lowering its price to families may increase fertility. I have heard informally that some countries have tried to get around this by subsidizing education only up to three or four for children. But such a policy raises additional ethical problems. In any case there seems to be no evidence on the strength of the effect of education subsidies in any country.

On the other hand, legislation that requires children to attend school can have the same effect as child labor laws, which it often accompanies. Such policies can reduce the economic value to parents of additional children. The only national experience of this sort that has been studied is the English experience in the nineteenth century, and the results of the research (Branson 1968, West 1968, Becker 1960) seem to be inconclusive as to whether the effect of the compulsory schooling and child-labor laws was significant. (Many parents were already sending their children to school voluntarily at the time that the laws were passed.)

The law of inheritance may affect fertility unintentionally. This idea dates back to Malthus, who attributed the difference in fertility in France and England to differences in their laws of inheritance. But present notions of equity suggest that no country would opt for a change to a more unequal inheritance system as a way of reducing fertility, even if it were thought to be important. The matter can thus be ignored, for the most part, in this context.

Social security laws may have an unintended effect upon fertility by reducing old people's dependence upon the support of their children, thereby lessening the economic value of children. But in most of the

Table 2-5. Some Proposed Incentive Schemes

	Incentive payments			Deferred payments[a]		
Purpose	*Author*	*How checked*	*Amount (U.S. dollars)*	*Author*	*Deferred until*	*How checked*
Nonpregnancy	1. Sirageldin and Hopkins (1972)	4 months exam	Graduated with length of enrollment up to $11 per year	1. Enke (1960a)	Economic value of averted birth accumulated	4 months pregnancy check
				2. Ridker (1971)[e]	Women's age 45	3 months check
				3. Ridker and Muscat (1973)	Age 50	6 months check
Nonbirths	2. Simon (1969)	Birth registration local knowledge	25–50 percent annual per capita income	4. Balfour (1962)	3 yr or later	Certification local authority
				5. Chow (1971)	3 yr or later	Annual inquiry
				6. Finnigan (1972)	Not specified[b]	Affidavit and birth registration
				7. Finnigan and Sun (1972)[e]	10–14 yr[c]	Affidavit and birth registration

			8. Chow and Sirageldin (1972)	One year or later	Annual visit clinic
			9. Ridker and Muscat (1973)	Age 50	Annual visit clinic
			10. Kavalsky (1973)	Age 50	Registered participation, school records
Sterilization	3. Enke (1960a)	Graduated up to Rs 700 ($147)	11. Ridker (1969)	20 yr[d]	Proof of number of children at time of acceptance and payment
	4. Tata Scheme (1967)[e]	Rs 200 ($27)			
	5. India mass-vasectomy camps (1970–73)[e]	Rs 60–100 ($8–$13)			

Source: IBRD (1974).

[a] The method of payment for all of these is a lump sum deposit in an interest-earning savings account, except where some other method is indicated.

[b] Scholarship certificate.

[c] Voucher for educational expenses.

[d] Alternatives include lump sum payment, old-age pension, life insurance.

[e] Schemes which are being or have been put into operation.

more developed countries the parents rely little on the support of their children—a strong shift in this direction occurred after World War II, even in Japan—and a major social security program is beyond the financial capacity of most of the less developed countries. Decisions concerning social security legislation are therefore not likely to affect fertility decisions very much.

In brief, incentives to reduce fertility may well have an important effect in the appropriate circumstances. But the size of the effect will not be known with confidence until a well-controlled experiment is carried out.

Conclusions

Redistribution of income could affect fertility significantly. The qualifications are: The fertility-reducing effects would probably come about only after a decade or more, and governments are not likely to undertake redistribution of income just to reduce fertility. But the time span is not long in comparison with other "structural" socioeconomic change that may be fundamental in determination of fertility. And even if governments may not undertake redistribution for fertility reduction alone, the added factor that redistribution could influence fertility significantly might make redistributions more likely. Furthermore, some particular sorts of redistributional policies are likely to be more effective than others. For example, redistribution which increases access to education among poorer people may be expected to reduce fertility directly by way of the education and indirectly by way of the economic development which education speeds up.

Concerning the likely effects of incentive payments to raise births, the experience of more developed countries that have tried to raise fertility by child-allowance programs provides almost no guidance about the efficiency of such programs; the payments have been sufficiently small relative to other changes in income so that, in the absence of a controlled experimental design, the possible effects cannot be detected. Questionnaire study shows that people in the United States *say* that they and their neighbors would have families of different size, larger or smaller, in response to relatively large financial incentives to do so. But hard evidence will continue to be lacking until some controlled experiments are undertaken—research that would raise difficult ethical questions. I would guess, however, that incentives would have to be of substantial size relative to income for there to be a good chance that they would have a significant effect.

3.

Direct Economic Costs and Value of Children

ROBERT G. REPETTO

The purpose of this chapter is to explore the current state of knowledge regarding the effects on fertility decisions of changes in the direct economic costs and value of children; to identify, if possible, promising means of policy intervention, exploiting these effects, that would reduce fertility in the less developed countries through government action; and to devise, at least tentatively, experimental and other research that would test the efficacy and feasibility of such policies.

The chapter is narrowly circumscribed. In the discussion of the direct economic contribution of children, the focus is on the value of the children's earnings and nonmarket household labor services and on transfers to the parents later in life. The direct economic costs of children denote only the relative prices of the commodity inputs into children's consumption. The opportunity cost of the mother's time devoted to child care—her present and future earnings forgone—are excluded from this chapter but are discussed in detail in the chapter by James L. McCabe and Mark R. Rosenzweig. To confine a study of the topic in this way is somewhat artificial. Changes in the costs of child raising and in the economic opportunities for children in the labor force are closely bound up with changes in household income, the labor-force participation of women, and other economic variables. It is nearly impossible to treat one of these aspects of economic change in complete isolation from all others. Nonetheless, the topic is even further circumscribed by de-emphasis of the smallholding agriculture sector, which is unquestionably the largest employer of children in the less developed countries. That sector is also given separate treatment in the chapter by Eva Mueller. In this chapter I do present, however, a different approach from that of the authors who cover related topics, both in the range of evidence surveyed and in the possibilities for policy and research considered.

Within the common model of the economic influences on fertility behavior used by most of the participants in this conference (one developed by Gary S. Becker, Harvey Leibenstein, Robert J. Willis, T. Paul Schultz, and others, which has come to be known as "the economic theory of fertility"), the role of changes in the relative value or cost of children is comparatively unambiguous. A reduction in the effective demand for child labor tends to result in a negative wealth effect for the household, along with an increase in the opportunity cost of raising a child. The income and substitution effects operate in the same direction. Similarly, an increase in the relative price of inputs used intensively in child rearing generates reinforcing income and substitution effects. Consequently, there is a stronger presumption that the consequences for desired fertility will be predictable in the case of changes in the parameters governing the effective price of child rearing than in the cases of some other exogenous shifts. Increases in the relative price of children are expected to result in lower desired fertility, other things being equal.

This statement of the hypothesis deserves elaboration on at least two counts. First, it brings out the point that the hypothesis deals with changes, or differences, in the effective price of children, not with the absolute level of the price. Specifically, although much attention has been devoted to the problem of estimating the economic asset value of children to parents in the less developed countries, a problem discussed thoroughly in the chapter by Mueller, the question is largely peripheral to the issues explored in this chapter. Whether the discounted value of the marginal product of a child's labor services as a contributor to the household economy does or does not exceed the discounted value of the time and commodity expenditures attributable to his existence is not the point. Whether the marginal child happens to be an asset or a liability, the hypothesis which follows from the economic model of fertility behavior is that, other things being equal, desired fertility will be higher if the additional child is *more* of an asset (or less of a liability). It is the comparison of alternative situations which is relevant.

Second, the distinction between the price of children and their cost is important. Household decisions governing the allocation of time and income to child rearing are determined jointly with decisions on family size, patterns of labor-force participation, investments in human capital, and other expenditures. Therefore, the total cost of each child is endogenous to the decision model. It is only the price of inputs used intensively in child rearing, in relation to prices of other items of household consumption, which can legitimately be regarded as exogenous parameters, largely independent of individual household actions. Even this is not true in the important case of time inputs, since the mother's marginal wage rate depends on work experience and prior investments in education and training. That problem is dealt with in another chapter. The prices of commodity inputs into child rearing can be thought of as exogenous, along with the marginal value of child-labor services, which are typically used in unskilled jobs requiring little prior training. It is legitimate to explore the response of desired fertility and other household decisions to externally caused shifts in these parameters.

Methodological Problems

Investigations of the response of fertility to changes in the value or relative price of children have been confronted with tough methodological problems. Some of the main ones are inventoried at this point, as a preliminary to a survey of available research results. The excellent methodological discussion in the chapters by William P. Butz and Jean-Pierre Habicht, Schultz, and Dennis N. De Tray are equally applicable here, of course. There are problems of correct specification of the relevant model: for example, the relation between family size and child labor-force participation is undoubtedly a simultaneous one. For a household at a low income level, high fertility probably induces low school-attendance rates and high child labor-force participation rates because of income constraints. At the same time, the availability of ample employment opportunities for children and the lack of educational opportunities may induce families to have a higher fertility level. Care must be taken in attributing causality to any observed association.

This is the more true because incomplete specification may lead to a violation of *ceteris paribus* assumptions in the research design and to the observation of spurious correlation between variables under discussion. For example, if two households or populations were observed with different subjective valuations of education, or future over present income, the one with the higher valuation of education would probably be observed to have higher school-attendance rates, lower child labor-force participation, and lower fertility. Without controls on household "tastes," the influence of this underlying factor might be overlooked and causality attributed to the observed negative correlation between school attendance and fertility.

Another specification problem involves the correct description of the lags involved in the interaction of the variables of interest. This problem is bound up with the correct description of the mechanisms and channels of influence. For example, if much of the influence of changes in the effective price of children operates through changes in shared community norms concerning appropriate family size, and individual household fertility depends largely on these community norms, then the lag structure may be quite a long one. An inappropriate research design focused on short-term fertility responses within the household to short-term changes in the immediate economic environment of the household might fail to capture the true association, or capture quite a different phenomenon altogether, such as a shift in the timing of births.

A quite different, but no less intractable, problem is that of multicollinearity among the relevant explanatory variables. Changes in educational enrollment, income per capita, labor-force participation rates, and the like tend to be quite gradual and to have a strong intercorrelation structure. Especially in historical research, all these variables tend to be changing in the same broad sweep, and finding enough divergent motion in the variables of interest is a major problem. Unless the movement of the variables can be separately distinguished, it is impossible to tell which of them are moving the system or to break down the total fertility response among them. For example, it is generally true that, as income per capita rises, the relative price of inputs used intensively in child rearing also rises. This positive correlation makes it that much more difficult to distinguish income from price effects. Of course, these problems of correct specification, multicollinearity, simultaneity, lag structure, and sufficient controls for the maintenance of *ceteris paribus* assumptions are traditional ones in econometric research and not special to investigations of fertility behavior. They, together with the problem of insufficient data, are the problems which limit the existing state of knowledge in this as well as other research areas.

The Direct Economic Contribution of Children

With regard to the effect on fertility of differences or changes in the opportunities for children to contribute labor services to the household economy, or their propensity to transfer resources to their parents in later adult life, I have distinguished three sorts of evidence: the historical, the attitudinal, and the econometric. The available evidence is shaky, but it is at least compatible with the idea that greater economic value of children is a stimulant to fertility.

As an illustration of the historical evidence, there are the writings of a considerable number of economic historians of eighteenth- and nineteenth-century England in which notice is taken of the fact that, until a hundred years or so ago, children made a considerable contribution to their own support and to household income and that child labor-force participation rates were high by contemporary standards (Marshall 1929, for example). These historians have also noted that, typically, at about the time child labor-force participation rates were declining, fertility was also declining. This association, buttressed by a selection of quotations and other qualitative evidence, is about the extent of the historical evidence. There is evidence that fertility rose in late eighteenth- and early nineteenth-century England, and some attempts have been made to associate this increase with the broader employment opportunities for children in the early industrialization of England. Critics have pointed out that child employment was normal in agriculture and may have reached its zenith in domestic industry before the spread of factory organization. In the words of one specialist who has recently surveyed this area of research, "At best (or worst) children were not earning assets until at least the age of five, or possibly later, and no evidence is forthcoming yet to show that opportunity for children's employment really did raise fertility. . . . Nor can there be any certainty that the industrial changes of the period really did increase the overall demand for child labor that had always been a feature of the predominant forms of organization of earlier periods" (Flinn 1970). William Branson has attempted to use econometric techniques to associate the subsequent decline in the birth rate with the passage of child-labor and compulsory-schooling legislation in the decades after 1830, but his evidence is less than compelling (Branson 1968). The main obstacle, beyond the fundamental methodological problems already described, is the weakness of the link between the passage of legislation and actual changes in rates of labor-force participation or school enrollment. Legislation, especially at the beginning, was limited in coverage, and enforcement was inadequate. To a large extent, social legislation of this kind tends to ratify underlying social trends, sometimes with a lag, so that it is misleading to attribute the social changes in question entirely or even perhaps predominantly to the effects of legislation.

Also quantitatively oriented and set within the conceptual framework of an economic theory of fertility is a study of fertility and income inequality in the United States, during the nineteenth century, by Peter H. Lindert (1973). Among other interesting findings, he is able to show that, as the participation rates and relative wage rates of children fell in comparison with those of adult males, and as the impact of children in the home on female labor-force participation rates increased, from the last quarter of the nineteenth century onward, there came to be a basic change in the effect on the household economy of additional children in the family. In earlier periods, an additional child would imply an increase in the household's export of labor services, since the child's work contribution would more than offset the reduction in the mother's outside work occasioned by the child's arrival. In later periods, the reverse was true, and an increase in family size implied a reduction in the household's market labor supply, as it still does. From this he concluded that sometime during this period the response of the relative price of children to increases in market wage rates changed significantly, from negative to positive, and has become increasingly positive since then.

This is an interesting and suggestive finding, but it doesn't seem possible yet to assess its implications for the history of fertility in the United States. For instance, Stanley Lebergott (1960) has shown that in the United States the decline in fertility substantially preceded the decline in the child labor-force participation rate. In fact, for a number of decades the fall in the number of child workers in relation to the size of the labor force could be attributed mostly to the fall in the number of children in the population.

On the other hand, several historians have pointed out that fertility was higher in regions of the United States where labor was relatively scarce (Easterlin 1971; Yasuba 1962). This finding is paralleled in many other countries and populations, including many of the low-income countries such as India and Indonesia (Kleinman 1973). Especially on the frontier, where land was freely available and hired labor difficult to obtain, households had little incentive to attempt to limit their fertility and probably did not.

To summarize, one cannot do better than to quote Lindert's words, since his is the most careful study to date of trends in the relative price of children and their influence on fertility in the United States. He concludes:

> Limits have clearly been placed on the relevance of movements in relative child costs for explaining past fertility trends and swings, especially those before 1917. To account for the impressive decline in American fertility, both urban and rural, in the nineteenth century, one must turn from the cost variable back to tastes and income.
>
> What is true of the past, on the other hand, is probably less true of the postwar years and near future. It would appear that the relative cost variable is becoming increasingly relevant. This trend seems assured by the clear upward trend in wage rates for married women and in their labor force participation. [Lindert, 1973, p. 40]

Somewhat peripheral but an interesting sidelight on this historical issue is the evidence provided in the recent economic history of slavery in the United States, *Time on the Cross,* by R. W. Fogel and S. L. Engerman (1974). With respect to the magnitude of the economic contribution of children, this can, for several reasons, be considered a study of the limiting case. It deals with an institution which, unlike the family, was explicitly designed to maximize the economic rent extracted from the labor force. Fogel and Engerman showed that the value of the average slave's marginal product was higher than that of the free farm laborer, both because the slave worker worked with more complementary inputs and because slave agriculture was more efficient in the use of resources. They showed that mortality rates and life expectancies were virtually the same for slave and free laborers. They showed that participation rates for slaves were extremely high, especially for women, children, and the elderly. Thereafter, they presented evidence that the price of slaves, at birth, was barely positive on the average; that the owner managed to extract a surplus which amounted to no more than about 12 percent of the slave's total marginal product over his lifetime; and that the break-even point for a slave owner, when the expected discounted rents to be extracted from the slave's labor equaled the accumulated net investments, occurred when the slave reached his twenty-seventh birthday.

If these figures are even approximately correct, they imply that the asset value of children to free parents must have been significantly negative, even before the Civil War, when child labor-force participation rates and wages for children were relatively high. This inference is supported by several arguments. The household as an economic unit was probably less exploitative and less efficient in the use of child labor than was slavery. Participation rates in the free economy were lower, and the investments probably higher in children of free parents than in children of slave parents. Most important, most free children had left home by their early twenties and thenceforward made quite limited economic contributions to their parents. Parents were unable to obtain the returns from the adult labor of their children, as slaveowners were able to do of their unfree labor force.

The probability that the economic asset value of children was negative in U.S. agriculture in the antebellum period is interesting only as a benchmark for other populations and periods, not as evidence for or against the influence of such economic factors on fertility. Still, it is useful to have this sort of benchmark. It suggests that the asset value of children in the urban economy at comparable periods must a fortiori have been negative also, since child participation rates are lower in urban than in rural areas. It suggests, moreover, that in contemporary Asian agriculture, in which the man–land ratio is much higher and labor is anything but scarce, and where the marginal productivity of labor is much lower because of inefficient methods and the lack of complementary inputs, the asset value of children ought to be substantially less, unless Asian standards of consumption are lower by an even greater margin than labor productivity. Indeed, the broad sweep of the evidence for the less developed countries, as surveyed by Eva Mueller, supports this inference. She concludes that the asset value of a child at birth in peasant economies is probably negative.

This stands in contrast to a large body of attitudinal evidence from survey data generated in the less developed countries, which indicates that parents are aware of, and are to some degree sensitive to, the contribution that children can make to household labor or to the support of parents later in life (Caldwell 1967). It is certainly true that children do contribute substantially in agricultural work, domestic chores, and household enterprises. These contributions are often cited by respondents as reasons for wanting children or as advantages of larger families. There have been moderately successful attempts to relate indexes of these perceived benefits to desired fertility and, to a lesser extent, to actual fertility and contraceptive practice (Mueller 1972; Poffenburger and Poffenburger 1973; Anker 1973), while holding constant the socioeconomic characteristics of the respondents. However, indexes of perceived benefits seem to relate less closely to fertility variables than do indexes of perceived costs of children (Mueller 1972a), and measures of perceived benefits and costs both seem more closely related to such other attitudinal variables as desired family size than to actual fertility or contraceptive performance. There are well-known problems of interpretation of responses to attitude surveys: those of ex post rationalization of behavior and of accommodation to the imagined or actual expectations of the interviewer are two that stand out. Nonetheless, this extensive body of survey evidence and the underlying sociological literature certainly suggest that the economic security which has traditionally been believed to stem from large families, especially in peasant agriculture, has been a support for large family norms in the less developed countries. In long-term perspective, the gradual erosion of the objective basis for these beliefs may well have contributed to the change in family-size norms and consequently to declines in fertility. This impact of the changing economic environment on fertility norms, and thereby on fertility, would involve considerable lags and would be difficult for any tightly organized econometric research design to encompass. However, as such economists as Richard A. Easterlin (1969) and J. J. Spengler (1966) have pointed out, it is not for that reason properly ignored.

There have been numerous cross-sectional studies of fertility in which some proxy for the economic value or relative price of children has been included in the list of explanatory variables. However, at this stage only those in which some attempt has been made to deal with the difficult problem of causality will be considered. When fertility, child schooling, and child labor-force participation rates are related, it seems almost essential to take into account the plausible hypothesis that in low-income households with many children, a smaller proportion will be in school and a larger proportion in the labor force because of the income constraint on investment in the children's education. This is as plausible as the reverse hypothesis that fertility will be higher *because* more employment opportunities and fewer educational opportunities exist. Using simultaneous-equation techniques, T. Paul Schultz and his colleagues at the Rand Corporation have obtained a fairly consistent pattern of significant positive regression coefficients for child labor-force participation rates and negative regression coefficients for child school-enrollment rates, with various measures of fertility as dependent variables. In particular, A. J. Harman (1970) and DaVanzo (1972), with Philippine and Chilean data, respectively, showed these results in carefully specified and estimated econometric models. These findings reinforce the more suggestive historical and sociological evidence that the loss of a productive role for children in the household economy has contributed to the decline in desired and actual fertility. However, there is little evidence at this stage that this influence on fertility is a particularly tight or strong one. De Tray, in his contribution to this volume, also concludes that the evidence from less developed countries on this point is modest. There seems to be little reason to expect that, if government policies were somehow initiated in the less developed countries to reduce the demand for child labor, a decline in fertility of appreciable magnitude would follow within a span of, say, five to ten years. In other words, the relevant elasticity may be low and the lag structure quite long.

The evidence bearing on the pension motive for high fertility—the desire to have a number of children, especially sons, to rely on in old age—is almost all qualitative. This motive often emerges in attitude surveys and is strong in many countries in which multigenerational family structures and strong family bonds are traditional. Yet little is known about the actual extent of economic transfers from grown children to aged parents. Doubt has been cast on the extent to which children are a good "investment" for the long term (Robinson 1972; Ohlin 1969). Certainly in countries in which population is growing rapidly and the supply of land is limited, one would expect that the returns from labor would tend to fall in relation to the return from land, which is the most important asset available to the majority of households in the less developed countries. This was certainly the opinion of the classic economists, and it seems equally plausible today. Economic historians, such as Douglass C. North and Robert Paul Thomas (1973), have associated changes in the ratio of rents to wages with rises and declines in the rate of population growth in preindustrial Europe. Comparable data for Taiwan indicate a sharp rise in rents in relation to wage rates during periods of rapid population growth (T. H. Lee 1971). Over a twenty-five-year span, it seems likely that households in the densely populated low-income countries would do better to invest their savings in land than they would in expending those savings in raising children, even under the assumption that the expected old-age support would actually materialize. It may be that large families are analagous to "forced savings" or contractual savings arrangements in reinforcing weak savings motivations, or that imperfections in capital markets prohibit the mass of people from arranging long-term financing for the acquisition of small plots of land. To base the pension motive for large families on such phenomena, however, is to place it on quite a narrow foundation. Although capital markets in rural areas in the less developed countries are undoubtedly imperfect, they do exist, and a substantial volume of capital transactions takes place. Both firsthand observers and survey researchers report that a substantial fraction, perhaps a majority, of peasants have debts. Most of this indebtedness is to noninstitutional lenders, and interest rates usually range from 2 to 4 percent a month. What are these debts, if not capital transactions? Certainly, one feasible and attractive investment opportunity for at least one-half the households, the half which are in debt, is to reduce the level of indebtedness and thereby to earn a reward of 2 to 4 percent a month.

As any investor knows, if the long-term investment opportunities appear unattractive, it is always possible to roll over short-term investments. Innumerable studies have shown that, for the average peasant with a typical holding, the following sequence of investments, repeated year by year, would return an appreciable surplus: after the harvest, *hold* the crop until the seasonal price increase peaks, or until the next planting season; then, sell the surplus, using the proceeds to purchase improved inputs of seed, fertilizer, and pesticides for the next crop. In most years, these operations would yield returns in excess of 20 percent and perhaps as high as 50 percent. The magnitude of these returns is largely a reflection of the scarcity of capital in low-income rural areas. It is this scarcity that provides investment opportunities for those who have any capital, in petty trade and in small-scale production as in noninstitutional lending and the acquisition of physical assets.

It is a mistake to confuse the absence of a number and variety of financial institutions in such areas with the absence of any savings or investment opportunities. Given the prevalence of family enterprises that provide intrahousehold investment opportunities, the small scale of many transactions, and the importance of local knowledge in investment decisions, the absence of financial institutions can probably be attributed to their inefficiency in serving those savers and investors. The relatively high overhead costs of financial institutions require a volume of specialized financial transactions that is unavailable in rural, low-income areas and a local knowledge that would be expensive for such institutions to maintain. This is probably why those financial institutions that do exist in rural areas are generally subsidized considerably by the government.

On a closely related hypothesis, that the desire for a minimum number of sons provides a floor under fertility under conditions of high infant mortality, the evidence is mixed. The bulk of the evidence having to do with actual fertility in the less developed countries seems to contradict the hypothesis, despite simulation exercises demonstrating its plausibility. Data for rural populations in India, Bangladesh, and Morocco failed to reveal a tendency for households in which the early parities included all or mostly sons to have fewer subsequent births than households in which the early births were mostly female. In populations in which contraceptive practice is already widespread, however, and in which son preference is strong—for example, Taiwan—it does appear that households in which the early births fulfilled the desire for sons subsequently reduced their fertility more than did other households (Repetto 1972, Ronald Freedman 1975b). This finding reinforces earlier findings from a number of areas which show that the adoption of modern contraceptive practices was more widespread in households to which sons had previously been born.

The Direct Economic Costs of Children

In this section only the relative prices of the commodity inputs used intensively in the consumption pattern of the child are examined in association with variations in fertility. The opportunity cost of the mother's time, which has been shown to represent the largest single cost component, is excluded, because it is discussed fully in the context of labor-force participation by women. In the less developed countries, the time cost to the household indeed assumes less importance, because there are many other family members to share child-care duties and because the price of time is low in relation to the price of commodities.

The appropriate composition of the price index of children's consumption naturally varies with income. The lower the income, the greater the weight of food and clothing in the index (Espenshade 1973). This stands to reason. With fixed money income, an additional child lowers income per capita and results in a greater concentration of expenditure on income-inelastic items. Even more simply, at the low levels of income per capita prevailing in the less developed countries, a very large fraction of total expenditures for most households, whether they have children or not, goes for these basic necessities. Using a wide variety of evidence, Lindert has shown that food is the dominant item of direct cost, with clothing second. Poor households actually spend no more on housing as family size increases, even though space requirements rise. Typically, families cram themselves into less space per person and trade quality of housing for additional space (Lindert 1973).

One of the more difficult problems involved in investigating the proposition that differences in the relative price of children affect fertility is that of isolating price differences while maintaining other relevant things constant. For example, the usual way of getting at this issue is by examining rural–urban fertility differentials, on the plausible assumption that the relative price of children is lower in rural areas. It may well be, but that is by no means the only difference between rural and urban areas, and control over income, educational attainment, and other usual variables are not completely convincing indications that the residual fertility differentials represent the effects of price differences only. On the same theme, Bela Balassa's reappraisal of the purchasing-power-parity doctrine in the quite different area of international economics demonstrated that income and price effects are likely to be confounded both in cross-sectional and time-series studies of fertility (Balassa 1964). The reason for this is straightforward. Children tend to be relatively intensive consumers of nontraded goods, and there is a systematic tendency for the prices of these to rise in relative terms as income per capita increases, primarily because productivity in many services tends to lag behind productivity in manufacturing. It follows that the appropriate price index for children will tend to be positively correlated with income per capita, making it difficult to isolate the price effect alone.

There is also a small study of families who moved into a housing complex in Bogotá, which illustrates a similar problem (Felson and Solaun 1974). Those who moved into houses with room for expansion subsequently had more children than families that moved into apartments without room for expansion, even when the effects of age and socioeconomic characteristics were controlled. Although the quasi-experimental situation indicates that marginal housing costs were less for families in houses, failure to control for intentions to have additional children in the two groups undermines the results of this isolated study.

Governmental policies bearing on the costs of children, including tax provisions, family allowances and related child benefits, income maintenance schemes, and the like have been subjected to extensive analysis (Cain 1973; Glass 1940; Lloyd 1972; McIntyre 1974; Commission on Population Growth and the American Future 1972). No investigator has been able to demonstrate any very substantial effect on fertility of any of these programs, even those in the Eastern European countries where the total value of the child subsidies reaches a considerable fraction of average adult earnings. Cynthia Lloyd (1972) found a possible small pronatalist effect of child subsidies in the Scandinavian countries, and in Eastern Europe an effect on the timing of births is not ruled out by the data (McIntyre 1974). It is clear, however, that if any of these pronatalist incentives had any impact, it was relatively small.

Of the small number of antinatalist schemes under way in the less developed areas, very early results indicate that incentive schemes are capable of influencing at least the timing of births, and perhaps completed fertility as well. Enrollment in the Taiwan Education Bond Scheme and participation in the scheme of the United Planters of South India has been high, and the number of pregnancies among participating women has been much lower in the first year or two than demographic models would have predicted (Ridker 1971; Wang and Chen 1973; Rogers 1972). These schemes, although limited in extent and involving special populations, are clearly of great interest as possible sources of illumination of the effectiveness of tax-subsidy intervention in the less developed countries.

In summary, there is only sketchy evidence that variations in the relative price of commodity inputs to child consumption influence variations in fertility. Because of the difficulty involved in isolating price variations while controlling income and other differences among households, the evidence is perhaps even sparser than that on the effect of opportunities for child employment. The evidence of direct incentive experiments in the less developed countries is limited both in time and extent, but it certainly suggests the conclusion that households are sensitive to policy interventions that act through the relative price of children. The fact that incentive payments themselves represent both income and price effects, however, does nothing to clarify the situation.

Prospects for Policy Intervention

If the general drift of this survey is fairly accurate, then there is not a solid body of knowledge on which to base antinatalist policies operating through the economic price or value of children. The final section suggests some research possibilities. This section summarizes the results of an attempt to step back and think practically about policy prospects.

With regard to the economic value and labor-force participation of children, one relevant fact is the small size of the organized labor force under ready government influence. Large and medium industry, government services, plantation agriculture, large-scale trade, transport, and services occupy no more than 15 or 20 percent of the labor force in most of the less developed countries. These sectors are not large employers of children. Children are generally employed in small-scale and family enterprises, smallholder agriculture, petty trade, and services. By and large, government regulation, either of wages or conditions of work, does not extend to these sectors, nor do taxes on output or on factor inputs generally reach them. Without a time-consuming and costly extension of the administrative apparatus, which is not likely to take place, it is difficult to imagine that prohibitions, restrictions, or taxes on child labor would be broadly enforceable, at least in such large countries as India, Pakistan, Bangladesh, or Indonesia.

Also, it is generally true that for any occupational group, child labor-force participation rates decline as the economic status of the household rises. This seems to be true even in smallholder agriculture, although higher economic status there is usually associated with larger holdings and hence greater demand for family labor inputs. Consequently, any attempt to restrict child labor would affect most seriously those relatively poor households most difficult to reach with governmental programs and most in need of the supplemental income that child labor provides. Historically, writers on social change during the Industrial Revolution remark that poor working-class households were among the strongest defenders of the employment of children in factories (Hartwell 1971, p. 397; Collier 1964).

The history of child-labor legislation in the presently industrialized countries testifies to the importance of these problems. Real restrictions on the use of child labor were very slow in spreading, both because enforcement was gradual and because the coverage of regulations was broadened only one step at a time. In both England and the United States, the prohibition of child labor was a process that consumed about half a century, during which time, of course, substantial gains in living standards were achieved.

While it would be highly desirable from the standpoint of population policy to get children out of the labor force and to replace them with women, and while the elasticity of substitution between these two inputs should be quite high, it seems unlikely, for the reasons mentioned above, that this could be accomplished on a significant scale by means of labor legislation. The coverage of labor legislation in the less developed countries is too narrow, and it is likely to remain so for some time to come. On the other hand, every little bit helps, and so it would certainly be beneficial to restrict child labor and to remove obstacles facing women workers in the large-scale and organized sectors that are already or potentially subject to effective regulation. Measures aimed at accomplishing this, if not already on the books in most countries, could probably be enacted without lengthy prior experimentation or even rationalization on the basis of demographic considerations to recommend them to policy makers. The prevailing emphasis in most of the less developed countries on welfare objectives in the course of economic growth provides a favorable climate of opinion for regulations of this kind, and international agencies, particularly the International Labor Organization (ILO), have long stood ready to provide any needed assistance in their design and enactment.

On the cost side, the main stumbling block before policy interventions to raise the relative price of children is the composition of the aggregation of commodity inputs to children's consumption. Children are intensive users of the basic necessities of life—food, clothing, and shelter. Attempts to raise the relative prices of these would have widespread and extremely regressive welfare implications, and even "modest" experimental explorations would undoubtedly be completely unacceptable. In addition to the obvious objections to any proposal from an outside source in a fundamental area of policy such as this one is, it is unthinkable that one should suggest to a responsible official in a developing country that he try, on an experimental basis, raising the price of food grains to find out whether that would induce families to have fewer children!

To combat the pension motive for large families, governments in the less developed countries have often been advised to broaden social security schemes or to open avenues to the acquisition of real assets by low-income households. Widespread social security schemes are not likely to be adopted by the larger countries in the Third World for some time, largely because of financial and administrative constraints. At present, a very small fraction of the labor force is covered, mostly employees in the public sector and workers in large industry. Small-scale savings schemes involving some input of public-sector resources have been expanded in a number of countries, and in some—Korea and Indonesia, for example—have been successful in gathering fairly large deposits. Policies having to do with land reform also broaden access to alternative real assets. With respect to security of land tenure and redistribution of agricultural land, there are constant stirrings of policy, but there are a long history and extensive literature in this field, most of it discouraging. Even with strong political backing, nonrevolutionary land-reform programs are extremely time-consuming. Registration of title, investigation of tenurial rights, settlement of boundary and title disputes, and negotiation of compensation are involved. These take several years to complete within a single local area. Nevertheless, there are other strong policy grounds favoring the large-scale adoption of such programs: greater efficiency in land use, especially if leveling, consolidation, and drainage are carried out at the same time; greater incentive for on-farm investment by cultivators; redistribution of income; and improvement of the revenue base. All are primary motivations for such programs. The demographic dividend, should it exist, would be a by-product.

The policies concerning costs and economic value of children that at this time seem most promising are those affecting primary-school enrollment. More widespread school attendance is associated with lower child labor-force participation in the ten to fourteen age group. At the same time, maintenance of children in primary school, even if school attendance is "free," involves households in substantial additional direct and indirect costs. Clothing, school supplies, books, and incidentals are a significant expense for households. Moreover, the reduction in child labor contributions implied by school attendance is an important indirect cost. Policies increasing enrollment rates, therefore, should substantially raise the net economic price of children.

What kind of policies? One's first impulse is to think of compulsory school attendance. That would surely raise the price of child rearing. Yet on reflection it appears relatively unattractive as an approach. The history of compulsory school-attendance laws both in presently developed and underdeveloped countries teaches that they are not, and cannot be, enforced until the preconditions for nearly universal primary-school attendance are met. A careful history of the development of such laws in the United States during the nineteenth and early twentieth centuries indicates that the truancy laws were never enforced (Ensign 1969; Stigler 1950). Indeed, they are still not enforced if a situation arises in which community feeling turns against school attendance. What compels school attendance is a powerful and widespread norm that children of school age should be in school.

An informative study of the Indian experience with compulsory school-attendance laws tells the other half of the story (Saiyidain et al. 1952). In the Third World as a whole, perhaps about half the children of primary-school age are actually attending school. There are not enough teachers to increase that figure substantially in the face of rising population, nor are there enough classrooms, books, supervisors, or funds. Moreover, sheer quantitative expansion would be wasteful, because the existing system operates inefficiently, with high drop-out rates, low levels of educational achievement, low teaching standards and morale, outmoded and largely irrelevant academic curricula, and poor supervision and management. On the demand side, a great many students drop out of the school system because of poverty even before attaining functional literacy. In these circumstances, the passage of a law compelling attendance for four or six years would be, as it proved to be in India, an irrelevancy. Had the parents responded and sent their children, the educational facilities for them and the funds to create those facilities would have been absent. In fact, the parents did not respond, and there was nobody to compel them. Local leaders would not, and the school authorities were unable even to maintain effective supervision over the existing school activities, let alone investigate and prosecute truancy. In the middle 1950s UNESCO commissioned a set of country studies on compulsory school-attendance legislation which demonstrated the futility of those early legislative efforts (UNESCO 1954). That was an experience which should not be repeated.

Instead, substantial investment in primary education is required, to adapt the curriculum to the needs of the students, to improve the quality of the instruction, and to expand the number of places. At the same time, in countries in which it has not yet become normal for children to complete primary school, the burden of educational finance should be shifted to higher levels of government, reducing the effective price to parents. Both of these are necessary elements of a program to stimulate primary education in such countries. Even at zero price, there is little point in sending children off to sit in groups of fifty or sixty to a bare classroom repeating the rote lessons of a teacher who is only a primary-school graduate working in near isolation with little idea of what to teach or how. And whatever the improvement in the educational system, it will be irrelevant if the poorer half of the population cannot afford to send their children or keep them in school long enough to obtain a basic education.

That sort of program would reduce the price of child quality in relation to quantity and would stimulate parents to substitute investments in human capital for their offspring for larger families. Although there is little conclusive evidence on the point, there are reasons to believe that the demand for primary-school education among the relatively poor in the less developed countries is price-elastic. For one thing, a great many such households are purchasing little or no primary education for their children. For another, the demand is known to be income-elastic at low-income levels. Consequently, it is likely that total household expenditure on primary education would increase in response to a price reduction, necessitating a shift in expenditures away from other items. If numbers and quality of children are close substitutes, then desired fertility might decline. To the extent that an upward shift in school attendance leads to an adjustment in community norms or in the competitive requirements for employment in the organized sector, there is a kind of multiplier effect which operates on households that become motivated, not so much by the change in price itself as by the fact that other people's children are more likely to be attending school than in the past. John C. Caldwell (1968a) has described the strength of this social pressure in modernizing communities in West Africa.

Such a program can scarcely fail to yield important benefits. At least in comparison with other governmental expenditures on education, the yield from primary education is generally found to be high, and it represents a reasonable use of public funds. Widespread primary education would be expected to reduce the dispersion of the human capital stock and subsequently to reduce income inequalities. Also, many of the additional pupils would be female, and the evidence is strong that the school experience would contribute to reduced fertility in their adult lives. Therefore, even if the immediate demographic results were not forthcoming—if parents of school-age children did not reduce fertility in response to the lowered effective price of child quality—there would still be substantial benefits.

This certainty that such programs would be worthwhile whatever the immediate demographic response is one reason to prefer an action program to an experimental or pilot program. The higher the probability a priori that a proposed program will be a success (or a failure) the less the value of experimentation. There is, in addition, a practical reason. There are large economies of scale in programs of educational development. Curricula must be devised and tested. Manuscripts must be written and published. Teacher-training programs must be devised. The cost of all this "software" is virtually invariant with respect to the number of students to be enrolled. Also, if the return on investment in primary education is inframarginal, the time required to mount the program is a heavy fixed cost. Since many of the developmental activities are sequential, a reduction in scale does not imply a reduction in development time. Experimental research to test the effects of a primary-school development program on fertility would be time-consuming and expensive. There are many countries with sufficient resources to be able to invest substantially in this area. In the present intellectual climate, some might be disposed to do so in the name of social justice. Demographic, economic, and political arguments strengthen the case.

Research Approaches

It would be desirable to investigate the responsiveness of fertility to changes in the effective price of primary-school education. To do this in an experimental fashion, along the policy lines suggested above, would entail the need for lengthy, difficult, and politically sensitive efforts to raise the quality and lower the price of education in the experimental areas while maintaining it unchanged in control areas. A better scheme might be to try to "hitch a ride" with an ongoing educational experiment, adding on features designed to capture any effects on fertility or other variables of interest. This would put the research into the marginal cost category, eliminating the need to convince administrators that an elaborate educational enrichment project tied to different patterns of financing should be devised solely for the sake of a fertility experiment.

In almost every country, either as model schools for teacher training, experimental schools for curriculum development, or pilot schools for educational development programs, there exist schools and school districts that receive better education at lower cost to the parents than do the rest. Many of these experimental or model schools attain quite respectable ages. Indeed, there is a quip among educational administrators: "The trouble with educational experiments is, they never fail." In Indonesia, to illustrate the longevity of such programs, both model schools attached to the teacher-training colleges and experimental schools associated with various programs of curriculum development exist and have existed for five years or more. Many of these are located in villages, and there is generally one school to a village. Since these schools receive funding from central government projects for the training of teachers or the testing of curricula and teaching materials, the students get more educational inputs at the same prices, or at lower prices, than do pupils elsewhere.

Perhaps some such situation could be exploited to conduct a fertility experiment or quasi experiment, the essence of which would be the attempt to ascertain whether, as a consequence of a lower effective price of primary school education, enrollment rates are higher, households spend more on education (other things being equal), child labor-force participation rates are lower, and desired and actual fertility are lower. The experimental areas would be the villages and urban neighborhoods in which the experimental schools are located. Control areas would be matched villages and neighborhoods in which only the unaided, typical schools are available. Thus, the exogenous variable would be measured in terms of the educational inputs per student, expenditures per student, and tuition and other fees per student, leading to a calculation of variations in effective costs of primary schooling. The underlying model assumes that this effective price, along with household income, the educational attainment of the adult population, and the strength of demand for educated labor, determines the enrollment rate. The enrollment rate, in turn, is assumed to influence the composition of household expenditure, the child labor-force participation rate, and consequently, the level of household income. These last mentioned, along with the usual demographic and social variables, are assumed to influence desired and actual fertility. Therefore, subsidiary questions to be investigated include, Are enrollment ratios greater in the areas with the lower effective price, other things being equal? Do parents spend more on education from a given income when the effective price is lower, holding age, spacing, and numbers of children constant? Are child labor-force participation rates lower under these circumstances? Finally, the research would explore differences in desired family size, actual fertility, and contraceptive usage among experimental and control areas, with suitable consideration of other relevant variables.

One way in which to carry out such a program would be to do baseline surveys in the experimental and control areas, to ascertain population rates in terms of the specified community characteristics. After the influence of other factors had been eliminated through a standardization procedure, a difference between experimental and control areas in fertility and other related variables might be discernible, because of the effect of the educational price difference. Thereafter, a longitudinal perspective could be obtained by monitoring changes in these rates, along with changes in the explanatory or associated factors in the two areas.

If such research could be added to some ongoing educational program, it might be feasible. Its costs in administration, time, and money would be marginal. It would appeal to ministries of education, which like to feel that they are contributing to national development in some way. Such organizations as UNESCO would be enthusiastic, since universal literacy as a solution to the population problem is to educationalists what improved maternal and child health is to public health specialists or what incentives are to economists.

In searching for locations for such research, special attention might be given to the oil-exporting countries. If ever there were populations that have been catapulted from social backwardness into the modern world, such are the masses of people in the Arab Middle East. Free education, medical services, widespread employment, and contact with modern goods, are all becoming available to large segments of these populations within a comparatively short period. Since theirs is a special case, but is one that illustrates the changes that might ensue were adequate resources available, it would be interesting to monitor the demographic changes in those areas with particular attention.

There may also be quasi-experimental ways in which to investigate the pension motive for large families. For most households, the main alternative asset to children is land, and it should be possible to ascertain whether easier access to land reduces the desire for children. There have been a number of programs in various developing countries to grant cultivators security of tenure where they had none before, or to vest proprietary rights in the cultivators. It might be worthwhile looking into these situations, especially those in which there were no actual redistribution of holdings or accompanying programs of consolidation or agricultural credit, to see whether there was any subsequent change in the fertility pattern.

There is another quasi-experimental way of getting at the pension motive for large families, reminiscent of past research on the permanent-income hypothesis. In a country such as India there are many occupations which, although they are low-paying and relatively unskilled, nonetheless afford the jobholder considerable long-term security. Low-level government employees, railway workers, and the large contingent of peons and chuprassies on one or another public payroll are never discharged, are never promoted, get regular pay increments over the years, are often housed, are eligible for health care in the clinics, and may be covered by some sort of pension and insurance plan. They are found employed in urban and fairly rural areas. Yet, in income, educational background, socioeconomic status, caste, and other characteristics, they are not unrepresentative of the broader population. Families in these occupations could be matched against others in occupations much more subject to risk and variations in income—agriculturalists, casual laborers, and construction workers, for example. One would hypothesize that if security is an important motivation for high fertility, then, with suitable controls those in relatively secure occupations would be found to have fewer children.

Experimental research into variations in the direct commodity price of children would not be feasible. However, it would be possible to do more along econometric lines than to use rural–urban residence as a proxy for child costs. Food costs vary within rural areas between surplus and deficit areas, and oftentimes these price differentials are exacerbated by official or unofficial impediments to movement. Long-standing differentials in food costs are one source of variation in the cost of children. Similarly, the cost of alternatives to children, particularly modern durable consumer goods, may often be cheaper in ports or free-trade zones, and these price differentials might also generate an areal cross-sectional study. Such studies, although they would be faced with all the methodological problems enumerated at the outset of this survey, would be more practical than experimental research where the impact of variations in the relative commodity price of children is concerned.

4.

The Economic Value of Children in Peasant Agriculture

EVA MUELLER

One major barrier to the acceptance of family limitation in peasant agriculture[1] is purported to be the positive economic value of children. At least, the idea that raising children has some net economic benefit to parents (aside from their value as consumer goods) seems to be widely held among the peasants themselves. Many apparently view children as making a contribution to production while they grow up and, probably more important, as a source of support later in life. The thesis that a large family is an asset to peasants has recently been advanced rather forcefully by Mahmoud Mamdani (1972) and was advanced earlier by Colin Clark (1967) and Ester Boserup (1965). Mamdani's evidence is largely anecdotal and hence bears little weight. Clark and Boserup provide some a priori justification and some historical examples. Yet their work is far from a systematic examination of the data and assumptions which have a bearing on the value of children in peasant agriculture.

Studies by economists, concerned with the value of children to society as a whole rather than to their own parents, challenge the belief that large families entail some economic advantage. Attempts to estimate the value of a prevented birth in less developed countries have almost uniformly led to the conclusion that to the national economy the value of a marginal human life is negative at birth. Examples are the well-known studies by A. J. Coale and E. M. Hoover (1958), Goran Ohlin (1969),

The author is grateful for useful suggestions received from Ronald Lee, Deborah Freedman, Karen Mason, and George Simmons.

[1] The term *peasant agriculture* refers to agricultural systems which utilize largely traditional *methods* of cultivation, although cropping patterns may be affected by economic incentives and some commercial crops may be grown. The term further implies that because of small landholdings, the stagnant technology, and low capital inputs, cultivators for the most part have low incomes. South and Southeast Asia are the main regions I have in mind.

Stephen Enke (1966), and G. B. Simmons (1971). None of these studies deals explicitly with the agricultural sector. All deal with discounted values, which are heavily dependent on arbitrarily chosen discount rates. The analysis is not disaggregated by age and sex in such a way that one can study the separate economic role of children, women, and the aged. Thus we are uncertain whether and how the conventional wisdom of peasant families and the conclusions of economists can be reconciled.

Needless to say, the value of children to parents has a large social and psychological component (Fawcett et al. 1974). Indeed, the reasons for having large families may be largely noneconomic. Still, the strictly *economic* value of children deserves separate study because of its bearing on the pace of economic development. Since the economists' findings that high-parity children have negative economic value (and hence slow the development process) have recently come under attack from Mamdani and others, it is important to reexamine these findings carefully, especially as they relate to rural areas. In so doing, we shall distinguish between the value of children in the aggregate (that is, to the rural society as a whole) and their perceived private value to the peasant household.

For the analysis which follows, one should know to what extent in peasant agriculture male and female children contribute to household expenses, earnings, and savings at various ages and for various family sizes. Further, one should relate the economic role of children to the economic position of adult men, women, and the aged. Once the economic role of children is better understood, policy measures to modify that role should become more feasible. Unfortunately the age- and sex-specific data on consumption, production, and time use which are needed are acutely inadequate. We shall have to rely on bits and pieces of information to estimate "profiles" of consumption and production over the life cycle. To make these estimates as realistic as possible, the scattered pieces of empirical evidence about differentials in consumption and production by age and sex are reviewed. In the second section the available data are used to develop two alternative consumption profiles, and in the third section two production profiles are developed.

The terms *production profile* and *consumption profile* require clarification. Figure 4-1 depicts hypothetical curves of consumption and production for a rural male, figure 4-2 for a rural female. The unit of account is the amount of consumption by an adult male per unit of time. We call this one consumption unit (1.0 CU). A male's consumption requirement is an increasing fraction of 1 CU as he grows up, and it reaches 1.0 CU in his middle or late teens. It will decline to some frac-

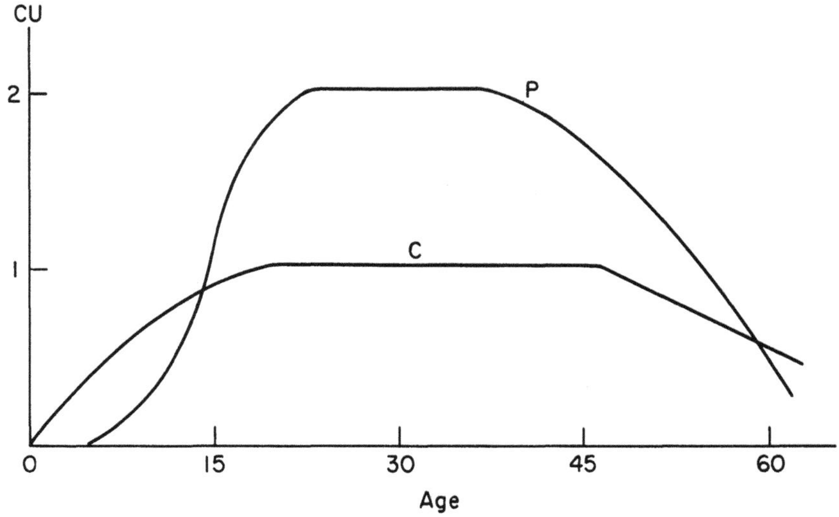

FIG. 4-1. Hypothetical male production and consumption profiles.

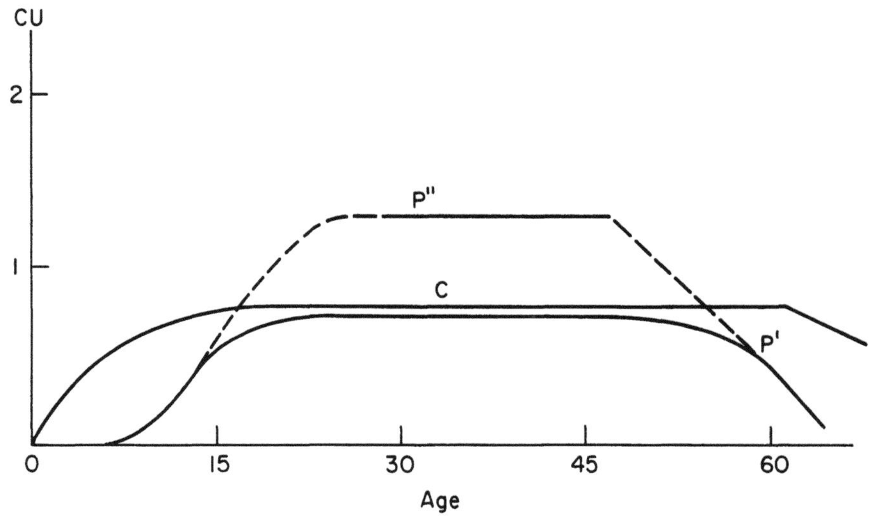

FIG. 4-2. Hypothetical female production and consumption profiles.

tion of 1.0 CU as he grows old. Line C in figure 4-1 illustrates a male consumption profile. Production (P) is below consumption at very young ages but then must rise above it by a considerable margin. In old age production may fall below consumption again. The consumption curve for females should be somewhat lower than the male curve after age 10 or so but should have a similar shape (figure 4-2). In most peasant societies the female production curve is lower and flatter than the male one. Two alternative production profiles are shown in figure 4-2 in order to call attention to the fact that the amount of market work done by women differs greatly among various societies.[2]

There is no presumption that the consumption and production profiles are independent of one another. Subsistence means different things in different societies. Peasant societies with relatively high production per capita also have relatively high consumption per capita and vice versa. In other words, the absolute magnitudes of C and P differ among peasant societies; their pattern over the life span and their relation to each other are of interest here.

The empirically derived consumption and production profiles are used later for aggregate analysis.[3] Equation 4-1 describes the analytical framework which organizes the available facts (or estimates):

$$\frac{\sum_{i=0}^{i=1} \sum_{j=0-4}^{j>65} a_{ij}(b_{ij}P - c_{ij}CU)}{\sum_{i=0}^{i=1} \sum_{j=0-4}^{j>65} a_{ij}b_{ij}P} = \text{rate of saving} \tag{4-1}$$

In this equation, a is the proportion of the population in the various age-sex groups, b represents the production profile, c the consumption profile. The subscript i refers to sex (where 0 = male, 1 = female); and j refers to the various age categories. CU and P are constants. CU is, as indicated earlier, the amount consumed by an adult male. P is the number of CU produced by a male in his peak working years, for example, 2.2 CU per unit of time. For an adult male in his peak working years b and c are both 1.0; for women, children, and the aged, b and c are various fractions of 1.0 as specified by the empirically based consumption and production profiles.

The sum of the $a_{ij}b_{ij}P$ is total production; the sum of the $a_{ij}c_{ij}CU$ is total consumption. The difference between the areas under the two curves is the amount saved or dissaved. If the savings rate is known and a, b, and c can be determined empirically, the equation can be solved for P, the number of CU produced by a male in his peak working years. This is useful since P is particularly difficult to determine empirically. We shall assume that in peasant agriculture the savings rate tends to be in the neighborhood of 5 percent; for peasant economies traditionally

[2] Production is here defined in the traditional way to include only activities that contribute to GNP. Such activities as housework, child rearing, and going to school are not considered to be production.

[3] Some of the ideas underlying the aggregate model were suggested by Ohlin (1969).

have experienced slow rates of capital deepening, if any.[4] Under this assumption, a realistic estimate of P can be derived.

A limitation of our approach is the fixed consumption and production profiles. This limitation is overcome in part by varying the assumptions about the shape of these profiles. Ideally, one should employ a multi-equation model which could estimate the b's and c's on the basis of economic, demographic, and cultural conditions rather than treating them as fixed, exogenously determined weights. The available data do not permit us to go that far, as will become amply clear to the reader in later sections, where the empirical evidence is reviewed.

The "aggregate model" provides a means of analyzing the way in which different assumptions regarding production profiles, consumption profiles, and demographic conditions affect the share of each age-sex group in total production, consumption, and savings or dissaving. The aggregate model refers to society as a whole with unequal numbers of people at various ages, depending on birth and death rates.

The "life-cycle model" has a different meaning and purpose. It represents an attempt to estimate production and consumption over the life span of a peasant couple as the couple would be likely to view its own future production and consumption streams.[5] The influence of family size is examined by comparing couples with two, four, and six children to see how the balance of production and consumption would vary over the course of their lives.

In the life-cycle model the figures for consumption and production by children are multiplied by the probability of their survival, in the belief that parents are aware of the possibility of child mortality. In contrast, the parents themselves are assumed to be concerned about their consumption and production stream, in the event that they should live to a ripe old age. That is, it would be imprudent of them to manage their resources on the assumption that they will merely attain their mean life expectancy. The life-cycle model, therefore, traces a couple's production and consumption balance until the husband reaches seventy-three and the wife seventy-five, presumably the terminal point of their time horizon.[6] Obviously, if peasant couples found it wise to act as if they

[4] If population growth were 2–3 percent and the marginal capital output ratio in agriculture 1.5–2.0, a 5 percent rate of saving would leave little room for increasing capital intensity.

[5] The concept of the life-cycle model was suggested by Lorimer (1965).

[6] A man who reaches the age of thirty (a time when marginal fertility decisions are made) has about a one-third chance of living to the age of seventy under mortality conditions prevailing today in many peasant societies.

would survive into their seventies, old-age support would require much more resources *in their view* than in our aggregate model, with its low proportion of persons living beyond their peak working years.

The reader should note that the difficult problem of finding an appropriate rate for discounting future returns is circumvented in both models. The aggregate model depicts a cross section of society (or a number of societies with different demographic characteristics) at one point in time; discounting is thus unnecessary. The life-cycle model attempts to represent a peasant's view of lifetime production and consumption. It is assumed that peasants would not be conscious of a difference in value between present and future goods. Indeed, in traditional societies many peasants may not be aware of reasonably safe opportunities to earn interest on savings,[7] so that the decision not to discount future returns may be reasonably consistent with the realities of peasant life. If a positive discount rate were applied to future production and consumption, the value of children would of course be lower than it appears to be in the calculations on pages 140–142.

The aggregate model suggests that under most plausible assumptions, the net worth of children in peasant societies is negative. The life-cycle model indicates, however, that from the viewpoint of the individual couple, a large family may offer economic benefits at certain stages of the life cycle. The discussion on pages 146–153 is addressed to the policy implications of these findings. The aim there is to identify policies that may bring about a closer correspondence between the value of children to society as a whole and their perceived value to individual parents. Often it is possible to develop new policies by making experiments and evaluating them carefully. In the area with which this chapter is concerned, policy experiments are hardly feasible. Some experiments which might reduce the net value of children could have negative welfare consequences in the short run. Other policies are likely to involve long time lags—in recognition, understanding, and behavioral response on the part of parents. Moreover, experiments to modify the value of children will alter fertility only if they are regarded as sufficiently permanent to reduce benefits from children fifteen or more years hence (when children about to be conceived begin to become a source of potential income to the family). I have therefore relied upon fact finding and economic analysis to chart a course.

[7] Ohlin (1969) even suggests that because of inflation and the risk of losing assets (by theft, fire, floods, and other calamities) some people in less developed countries may perceive the rate of return on savings as being negative.

Consumption Differentials by Age and Sex

In table 4-1 consumption differentials are summarized by age and sex, as they have appeared in the literature. The lack of uniformity in these estimates is worrisome. The available data relate to different countries in different periods of time. The source of the data, the population covered, and the definition of consumption are often not clearly specified. There are no controls for income or parity in most of the studies. If income is correlated with number of living children or with age of parents, the differences in consumption expenditures observed among couples with differing numbers and ages of children may be due partly to income effects. There may be economies of scale, and probably more important, parents may cut back their own consumption as family size and age of children rise. The difference in consumption between a couple, say, with one child between the ages of ten and fourteen and another couple with one child between five and nine plus another child between ten and fourteen, may therefore not reflect the true cost of the younger child.

There is no way of extracting the "true" differentials from this inadequate information. For our purpose, estimates relating to less developed societies are most appropriate. In these societies food expenditures, which vary more with age than do other expenditures, constitute a relatively large part of the budget. Accordingly, we disregard the 1950 U.S. Bureau of Labor Statistics estimate and more recent U.S. data. We disregard the Coale and Hoover figures since they appear to have no empirical foundation. The Wold estimates are the lowest available for children and provide a low-consumption profile.[8] The UN estimate, which has been widely used, represents a high-consumption profile. It is somewhat higher for children than the Prais and Houthaker estimates which relate to food consumption in England and Wales in 1937–39. The Lorimer estimates yield a medium-consumption profile for children. Being interested in peasant societies, where food expenditures dominate the budget, this study will follow Wold and Lorimer in assuming that adult women consume only 0.80 CU. The rationale is that women probably eat less, since they do less heavy physical labor than men.

Most of the sources cited in table 4-1 do not consider the possibility of a decrease in consumption with advancing age. In the more affluent

[8] The low-consumption profile becomes more plausible if one interprets the data as representing marginal additions to family expenditures resulting from the presence of an additional child in the household rather than as average consumption by children (that is, parents may be forced to cut their own consumption and there may be economies of scale).

Table 4-1. Consumption Unit Scales Found in the Literature

Age	*Coale and Hoover*[a]	*BLS*[b]	*Wold*[c]	*Lorimer*[d]	*Bils-borrow*[e]	*UN*[f]	*Prais and Houthaker*[g]	*Engel*[h]	*Epstein*[i]
Male									
0–4	0.5	0.42	0.12	0.32	0.42	0.45	0.48	0.34	0.50[j]
5–9	0.5	0.56	0.26	0.52	0.42	0.65	0.57	0.49	0.70
10–14	1.0	0.70	0.44	0.82	0.80	0.85	0.73	0.63	0.83
15–19	1.0	1.00	0.84	1.00	1.00	1.00	0.89	0.77	1.00
20–24	1.0	1.00	1.00	1.00	1.00	1.00	1.00	0.91	1.00
25+	1.0	1.00	1.00	1.00	1.00	1.00	1.00	1.00	1.00
Female									
0–4	0.5	0.42	0.12	0.32	0.42	0.45	0.48	0.34	0.50[j]
5–9	0.5	0.56	0.26	0.48	0.42	0.65	0.57	0.49	0.70
10–14	0.9	0.70	0.44	0.68	0.80	0.75	0.70	0.63	0.83
15–19	0.9	1.00	0.68	0.80	1.00	1.00	0.74	0.77	0.83
20–24	0.9	1.00	0.80	0.80	1.00	1.00	0.88	0.86	0.83
25+	0.9	1.00	0.80	0.80	1.00	1.00	0.88	0.86	0.83

[a] Coale and Hoover (1958). Choice of scale seems to be intuitive.
[b] Bureau of Labor Statistics (1960). Based on U.S. consumption statistics for the 1950s.
[c] Wold (1953). Based on data for Germany–Austria, 1907–08.
[d] Lorimer (1965). Based on data from India (1950) and the United States (reference b above); meant to apply to less developed countries.
[e] Richard Bilsborrow (1973b). Seems to be based on references a–d above, plus some intuitive judgment.
[f] United Nations, Department of Economic and Social Affairs (1956). Based on census and sample survey data, but vague regarding specifics.
[g] Prais and Houthaker (1955). Based on food consumption data from England and Wales; 1937–39.
[h] Woodbury (1944). Reproduces Ernst Engel's scale from 1895, which refers to Belgian working-class families.
[i] Epstein (1967, p. 160), according to Lusk.
[j] Second through fourth years; first year equals zero.

societies the aged doubtless have many needs for goods and services that do not decline with age and some (medical care and other services) that increase. In the less developed countries, where food is the major item of expenditure, some decrease in consumption is likely. Here we shall follow a UN suggestion that consumption of males is 0.7 CU after age sixty-five. Specifically, we assume that the consumption of males is 1.0 CU from ages fifteen to fifty-four, falls to 0.9 at ages fifty-five to fifty-nine, 0.8 at sixty to sixty-four, and 0.7 at ages sixty-five and over. The consumption of older females is 80 percent of the male level in the same age group. This last assumption is in accord with the assumption for ages fifteen and fifty-four.

As suggested earlier, consumption by children in relation to that of adults may be influenced by such factors as income level, work participation, and family size. However, these influences have not been tested or quantified in available consumption studies for the less developed countries. Consumption profiles may vary between cultures, moreover, so that no single analysis of consumption can be definitive. For example, in some societies men and boys may eat first, while women, girls, and the aged have to make do with what is left. In other societies the adequate feeding of children may take precedence over adult consumption, or vice versa. Since so little is known about consumption patterns in the less developed countries, we shall use two alternative assumptions later—the medium- and low-consumption profiles (summarized in table 4-2). The UN high-consumption profile is not used, since we are making an extreme effort to identify situations in which children may have some economic value. Resorting to fixed consumption profiles (unaffected by family size and economic circumstances) is in some sense consistent with the permanent-income hypothesis.

Production Assumptions by Age and Sex

Production profiles by age and sex are even more difficult to estimate than consumption profiles. Since work contribution is a major determinant of the value of children, the available evidence is reviewed in some detail in this section, and two alternative sets of production profiles are arrived at. The average work contribution of each age-sex group in relation to that of adult males is estimated as the product of the average number of full-time equivalent working days (in relation to that of adult males) times the relative wage rate (assumed to reflect marginal productivity). This approach requires examination of the available data with respect to amount of labor-force participation by age and sex in

Table 4-2. Consumption of Children, Women, and the Elderly Compared with Peak Consumption of Men

Age	*Medium-consumption profile (in CU)*	*Low-consumption profile (in CU)*
Males		
0–4	0.32	0.12
5–9	0.52	0.26
10–14	0.82	0.44
15–19	1.00	0.84
20–54	1.00	1.00
55–59	0.90	0.90
60–64	0.80	0.80
65 and over	0.70	0.70
Females		
0–4	0.32	0.12
5–9	0.48	0.26
10–14	0.68	0.44
15–19	0.80	0.68
20–54	0.80	0.80
55–59	0.72	0.72
60–64	0.64	0.64
65 and over	0.56	0.56

rural areas and productivity or wage differentials for agricultural labor by age and sex.

Reliance on labor-force participation and wage data, while unavoidable, has a number of problematic aspects. One cannot readily derive quantitative measures of labor input from labor-force participation data.[9] Children and women in rural areas are largely unpaid family workers. They may work regularly anywhere from one to ten hours or more a day. Or they may work occasionally—that is, on some days, in some weeks, or during some seasons. One should know the number of hours worked per year, but such data have rarely been collected. If women and children work occasionally, some of these occasional workers will have been active during the statistical reference period, thus being counted as labor-force participants, others not. Unless the reference period coincides with a seasonal peak or trough in the working year, there should be no serious bias on that account. When children and women work, but put in fewer hours than the number which qualifies them as labor-force

[9] These data include unpaid family work of the type that contributes to the GNP.

participants (usually one-half or one-third time),[10] they are counted as being outside the labor force, and work input is understated. Conversely, when women and children work the minimum number of hours (or days) required for labor-force status, they may yet work fewer hours a week than do adult males. In that case work input is overstated by the labor-force approach. In the absence of adequate information, I have assumed that in the aggregate such understatements and overstatements more or less cancel one another for any age-sex group.

Uncertainty about the validity of labor-force participation data arises from the possibility that, for status reasons, some men may underreport the amount of work done by their wives and young children. (However, many investigators making labor-force studies interview any available adult.) Further, market work and housework are not sharply differentiated from one another. Such activities as gathering firewood, fetching water, herding and milking animals, tending a vegetable garden, and processing food may or may not be reported as market work. Additional difficulty in working with labor-force participation data from a number of countries is that labor-force participation is defined differently in various statistical inquiries. The definitions are not always clearly indicated; nor is it certain that interviewers always adhere closely to the intended definitions. John D. Durand (1975) has made some effort to correct for gross discrepancies in coverage between labor-force participation series for different countries, but many sources of noncomparability remain even when his data are used.

Relying on differentials in agricultural wages between adult males, women, and children as indicators of differentials in productivity has hazards of its own. Wage differentials between age and sex groups may be influenced as much by social customs and historical traditions as by marginal productivity. Women's and children's wages may be depressed by role segregation in the labor market. On the other hand, most women and children are not in wage employment but work in family enterprises, where they may perform some tasks which are of less economic value than the prevailing wage rate for their services. Still, for social and status reasons they would not work as wage laborers.

Productivity depends not only on work effort but also on access to land, capital, and other complementary inputs. Children, together with women and the elderly, constitute the marginal labor force in peasant agriculture. This is not the place to review the voluminous literature on

[10] The official suggestion of the International Labor Organization (ILO) is that a person who worked for the family (other than on household tasks) for more than one-third of the working day (during the reference period) be classified as a member of the labor force. This suggestion often is not followed.

Table 4-3. Labor-force Participation by Age and Sex

Age and sex	*UN estimate for less developed countries*[a]	*Rural Taiwan (1966)*[b]	*Rural India (1961)*[c]
	Percentage of each group in labor force		
Males			
5–9	n.a.	n.a.	2
10–14	24	22[d]	29
15–19	79	54	70
20–24	91	79	90
25–34	96	96	97
35–44	98	97	97
45–54	96	92	96
Females			
5–9	n.a.	n.a.	1
10–14	10	21	23
15–19	31	43	37
20–24	32	41	44
25–34	30	28	48
35–44	31	28	51
45–54	29	24	47

Note: n.a., not available.

[a] United Nations, Department of Economic and Social Affairs (1962). These data are derived from censuses and surveys conducted between 1946 and 1957. The male data are based on twenty-one countries, the female data on twelve.

[b] Srikantan (1973, pp. 206–207).

[c] Visaria (1973, pp. 10–11). The data are from the 1961 census and cover Bihar, Himachal Pradesh, Punjab, and West Bengal.

[d] Ages 12–14.

the question of zero marginal productivity in peasant agriculture. In the succeeding sections this problem is avoided by focusing on average productivity by age and sex. Later, a closer look will be taken at the problem of surplus labor in peasant agriculture. In the meantime the reader must keep in mind that marginal children (that is, higher-parity children) should be less productive than the average child of a given age, unless inputs of land and capital keep pace with incremental labor inputs.

Time-Input Assumptions for Children and Youths

Table 4-3 shows labor-force participation rates for boys and girls as well as adults in their peak working years. The first column is an average prepared by the United Nations for a number of less developed countries

Table 4-4. Frequency Distribution of Labor-force Participation Rates in Rural Areas of Twenty-seven Less Developed Countries, for Children Between the Ages of Ten and Fourteen

Percentage participating in labor force	*Number of countries*	
	Males	*Females*
50 and over	2	2
40–49	5	—
30–39	4	1
20–29	6	3
10–19	3	3
Under 10	7	18
All countries	27	27

Source: Based on census and survey data for twenty-seven less developed countries, as adjusted by Durand (1975).

in which 60 percent or more of the labor force is in agriculture. The second column pertains to districts in Taiwan in which more than 50 percent of the population is in agriculture. In the third column, figures for *rural* India, based on the 1961 census, are presented. The Indian data are of particular interest because they exclude urban populations and also because the 1961 census defined a person as an unpaid family worker, and hence a member of the labor force, if he or she worked regularly for at least *one* hour a day (other than doing housework). Even this liberal definition produced a low proportion of rural children in the labor force. Labor-force participation by children under ten is not measured in most countries or appears trivial, as in the Indian data. For boys in the age group ten to fourteen, the participation rates cluster in the 20–29 percent range, and for girls in the same age bracket, they are somewhat lower. Thus it would appear that in most of the less developed countries children under fifteen do relatively little market work.

This impression is reinforced by the data in table 4-4, in which frequency distributions of labor-force participation rates for males and females between the ages of ten and fourteen in rural areas of twenty-seven less developed countries for which the relevant data are available are presented. More than two-thirds of the countries show rates below 30 percent for males and rates below 10 percent for females, although there is considerable diversity (partly for definitional reasons). Some of the economic and social reasons for the low labor-force participation of children will be discussed below.

Our standard time-input assumption (column 1 of table 4-8) is intended to be a medium estimate, reflecting common conditions. It is based on the first three columns of table 4-3, as well as table 4-4. To be clear, the 0.25 figure for boys between the ages of ten and fourteen does not mean that only a quarter of all boys work. Rather it should be interpreted to mean that something like 50 percent of this group participate in market work, contributing on the average half as many hours a year as adult men (since the need for their work is often seasonal, half might have worked during the reference period, the other half not). A further assumption, based on the statistical evidence, is that girls between the ages of ten and fourteen do only about 60 percent as much market work as males of the same ages, presumably because they devote more time to housework and the care of siblings. Market work is defined in this study to include unpaid family labor which contributes to the gross national product (GNP)—that is, agricultural work, house construction, processing of food for sale, and the like—but excludes housework and child care.

Turning next to the fifteen to nineteen age group, we find that labor-force participation rates for males in that group are placed into the 70–80 percent range in both the UN estimates and the data from India (table 4-3). The rate in Taiwan is lower, doubtless because of the high level of schooling there. Labor-force participation of women between the ages of fifteen and nineteen varies widely from country to country, but usually is substantially below the male level.

It is useful to establish an alternative time-input assumption, just as we did in the case of consumption. The alternative high time-input assumption is based on data for Egypt. These data are unique in that the members of a sample of households were interviewed every fourth day for an entire year to obtain an accurate work record for every member of the family. Children who did any market work at all were considered members of the labor force, and hours of work input were compiled for them. These labor-force participation rates and average annual hours per labor-force participant are shown in columns 1 and 2 of table 4-5. In column 3, average working hours per labor-force member are expressed as a percentage of the peak male rate of 2,388 hours. Column 4 is the product of columns 1 and 3. It shows the work-input rate for each age bracket (for *all* persons in that age bracket) in relation to the peak male rate of 94–100 hours.

Comparing table 4-5 with table 4-3, we find rather large differences for young males between the high time-input assumption on the basis of Egyptian data and our standard assumption. Aside from the effect of variations in age groupings (ten to fourteen versus twelve to fifteen; fifteen to nineteen versus sixteen to nineteen), there are other considerations that lend plausibility to such large differences. Egyptian agriculture, and particularly the cultivation of cotton, is highly labor-intensive.

Table 4-5. Egypt: Rural Labor-force Participation Rates

Age	*Labor-force participation* (%)	*Working hours (annual)*	*Working hours as percentage of peak male rates*	*Work input rate as percentage of peak male rates*
	(1)	(2)	(3)	(4)
Males				
Under 6	2.5	—	—	—
6–11	47.6	706	29.6	14.1
12–15	87.9	1882	78.8	69.3
16–19	92.2			92.2
20–24	94.1			94.1
25–34	97.9	2388	100	97.9
35–44	99.6			99.6
45–54	99.3			99.3
55–59	98.3	1954	84	82
60–64	97.7	2076		
65–69	96.1	1894	81	78
70 and over	73.1	1984		59
Females				
Under 6	2.1	—	—	—
6–11	39.8	520	21.8	8.7
12–15	56.4	1508	58.9	33.2
16–19	54.9			
20–24	52.3			
25–34	66.3	888	37.2	22
35–44	72.5			
45–54	64.1			
55–59	45.1	510		11.3
60–64	48.0	510	24.3	
65–69	22.8	740		5.5
70 and over	22.6	92	4.0	1

Sources: Column 1: Institute of National Planning (1965, p. 22). Column 2: International Labour Office (1969, p. 154).

Cotton picking also may be a more suitable task for children than the kind of work connected with raising rice, wheat, or sugarcane. Even more important, the uncommonly low labor-force participation of adult Egyptian women should leave more work to be done by children.

Having specified two alternative time-input assumptions for young people, we turn now to the assumptions for the older age groups.

Time-Input Assumptions for Older Age Groups

Labor-force data for the less developed countries universally indicate that male labor-force participation is above 90 percent in rural areas from age twenty to at least age fifty-four. Table 4-6 is based on tabula-

Table 4-6. Frequency Distributions of Labor-force Participation Rates in Rural Areas of Less Developed Countries for Older Age Groups

Labor-force participation (%)	*Age*				
	55–59	*60–64*	*65–69*	*70–74*	*75+*
Males					
90 and over	23	16	6	2	1
80–89	4	6	10	5	1
70–79	—	4	6	8	2
60–69	—	1	3	6	8
50–59	—	—	1	3	5
40–49	—	—	1	1	4
30–39	—	—	—	1	3
Below 30	—	—	—	1	3
All countries	27	27	27	27	27
Females					
90 and over	—	—	—	—	—
80–89	2	1	1	1	—
70–79	1	—	—	—	1
60–69	2	2	1	—	—
50–59	—	1	—	—	—
40–49	3	1	1	1	—
30–39	2	4	2	1	—
20–29	—	—	4	3	2
10–19	9	9	7	8	5
Below 10	8	9	11	13	19
All countries	27	27	27	27	27

Note: See footnotes to table 4-4.
Source: Durand (1975).

tions prepared by John D. Durand (1975) on the basis of census and survey data from twenty-seven countries. It shows a frequency distribution of labor-force participation rates for rural males in twenty-seven less developed countries by five-year age brackets starting with age fifty-five. Even in the age group of sixty-five to sixty-nine more than half the countries show participation rates above 80 percent. The interesting point suggested by these data is that older rural males continue to work on the family farm and thus may require little old-age support from their children. Durand observes that generally labor-force participation rates for older males are higher in rural than in urban areas and decline in both kinds of areas as development proceeds. The main reason for these tendencies is, no doubt, the availability of employment opportunities for older men in family enterprises. Labor-force participation rates of older women contrast sharply with those of men, being almost uniformly very low (table 4-6). Durand finds that declining labor-force participation with development is not apparent among women whose employment patterns are much more diverse.

The Durand data in table 4-6 are consistent with a UN compilation of labor-force participation rates for older persons.[11]

Age	*Male rate (%)*	*Female rate (%)*
55–64	91.6	23.7
65 and over	70.1	14.3

These data do not relate specifically to rural areas but cover countries where at least 60 percent of the population is engaged in agriculture. It appears that the reported male labor-force participation rate is above 90 percent among males fifty-five to sixty-four and around 70 percent for older males. The participation rates for women are much lower. Participation rates for older persons in India convey a similar picture:

Age	*Male rate (%)*	*Female rate (%)*
55–59	94.0	38.7
60–65	88.1	27.9
65–69	83.1	22.5
70 and over	61.9	11.5

The reader should recall here that the definition of labor-force participation in the 1960 Indian census was one hour of work during the reference day.[12]

The data thus far presented give no information about hours of work and thus may understate the decline in work input with advancing age by persons engaged in family enterprises. The Egyptian data presented earlier (table 4-5) allow us to take account of hours worked. Hours show a decline of less than 20 percent between peak work input (taking the participation rate and hours into account) of adult males and work input of the groups between the ages of fifty-five and sixty-nine; the group over the age of seventy exhibits a decline of 40 percent from peak activity and thus continues to exhibit a remarkably high rate of work input. Among older Egyptian women the participation rates and the hours worked by participants are again very low.

One further piece of evidence may be cited which is consistent with these findings. R. W. Fogel and S. L. Engerman (1974, pp. 71–75), investigating the market value of slaves in the United States, conclude that not until they were in their late seventies did the average price of

[11] See footnote a, table 4-3.
[12] See footnote c, table 4-3.

male slaves turn negative. To be sure, above the age of sixty-five some slaves were a net loss, but on the average, net income remained positive to an advanced age. At the age of fifty, prices of females were equal to 60 percent of the prices of males, and they fell below 50 percent by the age of seventy. In a free labor market the aged may choose not to work or be unable to find work. The pressure of poverty, however, together with the option to work in a family enterprise, does seem to lead most able-bodied rural males in less developed countries to continue to perform a substantial amount of market work.

The alternate assumptions, to be used in the calculations later in this chapter, for work input by males over the age of fifty-four are summarized in columns 1 and 4 of table 4-8. They are derived from the data presented above. The standard assumption for women is based on the statistical observation that, on the average in the less developed countries, labor-force participation by women declines faster with rising age than does that of men. Thus it is assumed that, on the average at ages twenty to fifty-four, women put in 40 percent as many days of market work as men; at ages fifty-five to seventy-four they put in 30 percent as many days, and at ages over sixty-five only 20 percent as many days as men of the same age.

The Productivity Assumptions

The purpose of this section is to arrive at a set of comparative productivity figures by age and sex that can be combined with the time-input estimates to arrive at male and female production profiles. Table 4-7 represents a rare attempt to measure relative productivity in crop cultivation directly. It is based on data collected in Korea, in 1930, for 1,249 farms. Efficiency was measured by the area covered—that is, it shows how large an area a man, woman, or child weeded per hour on the average. Table 4-7 suggests that women are slightly more productive than young males, but the difference is small. Adult males, on the other hand, appear to be about twice as productive as women and children.

For more information we must rely on the assumption that wage differentials between age and sex groups measure, at least approximately, differences in productivity. In making wage comparisons among children, adult females, and adult males, one problem is that these three groups do not do exactly the same kinds of market work. For our purposes the differential that is owing to division of labor should *not* be eliminated by comparing wages for identical tasks. There are seasonal fluctuations in wages, moreover, varying in intensity between areas and types of agricultural activity. Since rural women and children tend to do a large propor-

Table 4-7. The Efficiency of Men Engaged in Farm Work, 1930

Kind of work			*Man* (*hour-tsubo*)[b]	*Woman* (*hour-tsubo*)[b]	*Juvenile*[a] *(male)* (*hour-tsubo*)[b]
Plowing	Paddy field	With cattle	145	—	—
		Without cattle	17	10	10
	Other field	With cattle	152	—	—
		Without cattle	28	10	11
Transplanting	Paddy field		23	12	12
	Field		25	15	11
Weeding	Paddy field		34	17	14
	Field		33	14	13
Harvesting	Paddy field		33	14	15
	Field		47	21	20

Source: Lee (1936)

[a] The juveniles were between the ages of twelve and eighteen years.

[b] The figures in the table indicate the average number of tsubo (6 ft²) on which work was done in an hour, that is, "hour-tsubo" working ability.

tion of their work during the seasons of peak labor demand, their average annual wages must be estimated to reflect this fact.

The Egyptian rural wage survey of 1964–65 covered cash wages only and distinguished between six provinces in Egypt. In these six provinces wage differentials among men, women, and children show a remarkable degree of similarity. Women's wages ranged from 52 to 67 percent of male wages, the average being 65 percent. Children's wages varied from 44 to 56 percent of male wages, averaging 48 percent. The report in which these data were published contains the following observation: "Women's daily wages are about two-thirds those of men, children about one-half. This is precisely the relationship generally considered the norm for rural workers and found in all rural wage studies as far back as before the Second World War (International Labour Office 1969, p. 17)." Data on wage rates in rural India from studies in the mid 1950s show almost the same differentials as the Egyptian data. The Agricultural Labor Enquiry obtained the following average wages for agricultural labor (all-India, in rupees per day):

	Plowing	*Sowing*	*Weeding*	*Harvesting*	*All tasks*
Men	1.00	—	0.88	0.93	0.96
Women	—	0.82	0.52	0.58	0.59
Children	—	0.83	0.51	0.55	0.53

Source: Labour Bureau, Government of India (1960, pp. 117–119, 296).

Data collected by the Indian Farm Management Studies show a similar pattern (in rupees per day):

	Madras		*Bombay*	
	Field laborers	*Herdsmen*	*Field laborers*	*Herdsmen*
Men	1.00	0.60	0.99	1.17
Women	0.50	0.40	0.51	0.39
Children	0.40	0.30	0.50	0.45

Sources: Zacharias (1960, p. 5); Driver and Desai (1962, p. 32).

More recent data on male-female agricultural wage differentials are available for a number of less developed countries in *The Yearbook of Labour Statistics* (ILO, n.d.). These data distinguish only between males and females; no separate data for children are published. The female-male wage differentials for rural areas derived from this source tend to be somewhat smaller, ranging from 0.50 for Guyana (1971) to 0.80 for Marocco and Barbados.

Benjamin White (1973, p. 7) reports the following differentials for agricultural labor in Java in 1972: male labor (ground preparation), 30–40 rupiah for a three- to four-hour period; and female labor (planting, weeding, harvesting), 15–25 rupiah for a three- to four-hour period.

The evidence presented so far suggests that the agricultural wage rates for women average about 60 percent of the male rate and those for children about 50 percent. However, these very rough estimates may not allow adequately for the fact that female and child labor are concentrated during the peak working season to a greater extent than is male labor. Indeed, the argument that the work of children is of great value depends heavily on the idea that at harvest time (or other peak seasons) their contribution is crucial.

The enhanced value of agricultural labor at harvest time should be reflected in seasonal wage differentials. A study by S. V. Sethuramen (1972, pp. 24–27) of seasonal variations in Indian agricultural wage rates for men and women indicates that in the Indian states, in the 1950s and 1960s, the difference between the peak-season wage rate and the slack-season wage rate was in the 25–40 percent range for both sexes. This is an all-India average; in some states the differentials were larger or smaller. The Rural Employment Survey in the United Arab Republic found larger seasonal differentials. The peak-season daily wage was about 50 percent above the seasonal low for men, while the corresponding figures were about 100 and 175 percent for women and children, respectively. Of course, women and children do not confine their work to the busy season, but we need to allow for the fact that a larger proportion of female and child labor than of male labor occurs during

Table 4-8. Work Contribution in Relation to That of Adult Males

	Standard assumptions			*(Egypt) High male production assumption*		
Age	*Time input*	*Productivity*	*Work contribution [(1) × (2)]*	*Time input*	*Productivity*	*Work contribution [(4) × (5)]*
	(1)	(2)	(3)	(4)	(5)	(6)
Males						
0–9	—	—	—	—	—	—
10–14	.25	.60	.15	.55	.60	.33
15–19	.75	1.00	.75	.90	1.00	.90
20–54	1.00	1.00	1.00	1.00	1.00	1.00
55–64	.8	.75	.60	.82	.75	.62
65 and over	.7	.50	.35	.73	.50	.36
Females						
0–9	—	—	—	—	—	—
10–14	.15	.60	.09	.27	.60	.16
15–19	.375	.75	.28	.25	.75	.19
20–54	.40	.75	.30	.22	.75	.17
55–64	.24	.56	.13	.11	.56	.06
65 and over	.14	.38	.05	.05	.38	.02

Source: Author's estimates.

seasons when labor is most productive. To some extent wage measures should reflect such differences in work patterns. To make certain that they are taken fully into account we raised our estimate of female productivity in relation to adult male productivity from 0.60 to 0.75 and our estimate of children's productivity from 0.50 to 0.60 of adult male productivity (table 4-8, columns 2 and 5).

Separate data on wage rates or productivity for older persons are not available. With advancing age men doubtless perform tasks that are less strenuous, though not necessarily less skilled. It is assumed (somewhat arbitrarily) that productivity of working males falls 25 percent below peak productivity at ages between fifty-five and sixty-four and 50 percent below peak productivity at ages above sixty-four. For women, the assumption is that above the age of fifty-four, just as at earlier ages, their productivity is 75 percent of male productivity in the same cohort (table 4-8, columns 2 and 5).

Production assumptions arrived at in this section so far are summarized in table 4-8. There are two major sets of assumptions—the standard assumption, which should resemble the average case, and the high-production assumption (based on the Egyptian data), which may represent the upper range of the values for the work contribution of young males. This high work participation by young males is, however, accompanied by low labor-force participation by women. No low-production assumption is presented, since even the standard and high assumptions suggest that the economic value of children is negative.

In contrast to the consumption profiles, the work-input data show a considerable degree of consistency. Despite the many weaknesses cited earlier, the work-input estimates from many countries and diverse sources have important similarities. This consistency justifies some confidence in the production profiles. Yet fixed production profiles represent a severe simplification of reality, only partly compensated for by examining alternative profiles that encompass a range of observed conditions. Ideally, production profiles should be derived endogenously in a simultaneous-equation model, where demographic and economic circumstances influence the decision of who works and how much. Moreover, as the situation in Egypt illustrates, work patterns of children are not independent of work patterns of other family members. Adult men may gain leisure by having large families, or the women may be freed from market work. In the limiting case, work by children may be merely a substitute for work by others in the household. In an intercountry analysis Bilsborrow (1973b) found indications of a negative correlation between labor-force participation by women and children in less developed countries as well as between youths and adults.

The problem of housework (including child care) has also been disregarded. Sometimes women may be kept out of the labor market by pregnancies and child care. At other times they may be relieved of housework and child care by older children. Investigators, such as Benjamin White (1973), who emphasize the contribution of children to nonmarket work seem to forget that the amounts of rice to be pounded, water to be carried, the clothes to be washed, and the number of small children to be cared for are functions of family size. Not knowing how the housework *caused* by children and the housework *performed* by children balance at different ages and parities, we are forced to ignore housework here. Detailed labor-force and time-use studies are needed to clarify this aspect of labor supply.

The data presented so far suggest that work input by children under the age of fifteen in peasant agriculture is quite limited. Where labor-force participation by children appeared to be relatively high (in Egypt), it was exceptionally low for women. Thus our findings are consistent with the observation that labor tends to be underutilized in peasant agriculture. Market work may be divided up differently among men, women, and children in different cultures, but there seem to be few peasant societies where men, women, *and* children show high rates of labor-force participation. Low labor-force participation need not imply zero marginal productivity, of course, but it does imply that productivity is too low to provide an incentive for use of all the available labor. If the potential labor force is indeed seriously underutilized, the notion that farmers in the less developed countries benefit from having large families loses plausibility.

The fact that the labor of children and women may be of great utility during peak seasons does not invalidate our inference that there seems to be excess labor in many peasant communities. The fewer children a farmer has, the more money he can put aside to purchase hired labor or other farm inputs. As long as children consume more than they produce, they deplete farm resources. The above estimates of production by children allow for the relatively high value of child labor during peak seasons, relying on the assumption that seasonal differentials in the value of labor are of the same order of magnitude as seasonal fluctuations in agricultural wages.[13]

Demand for Labor in Peasant Agriculture

It must be recognized that in peasant societies production profiles may depend more on demand for labor than on supply. Additional data on labor use in peasant agriculture throw some light on labor demand. In table 4-9, data for the Indian Punjab, which quantify average labor use on farms of various sizes, are presented in terms of full-time equivalent workers, with workers under fourteen and over sixty counting one-half and women counting three-fourths. Table 4-9 thus implies that husband and wife and one child working half-time constitute a sufficient labor supply for a farm of up to 5 acres, even at the peak season. A farm of 5 to 10 acres requires an additional adult male at harvest time or two additional children old enough to help. Larger farms require more labor. It must of course be kept in mind that extended families are common in India, especially on the larger landholdings, so that a farm of 5 to 10 acres could be operated by two brothers with part-time help from their wives. Children might assist in place of the women but would not be essential.

[13] To be sure, if there were fewer children, wages of hired labor—adult and child—would rise, particularly during peak seasons. Some substitution of capital for labor should then occur in the long run. Whether more or fewer farmers would want their children to do wage labor under these improved economic circumstances cannot be predicted a priori, since the per capita income effect and the wage-rate effect would work in opposite directions.

Table 4-9. Average Number of Workers on Selected Holdings and Sizes in Punjab–Haryana

Farm size (in acres)	Distribution of farms by size (%)	Labor source			Total required (at peak season)
		Family	Permanent	Casual	
0–5	37	2	—	—	2
5–10	25	2	—	1	3
10–30	31	3	1	3	7
30–50	5	3	2	7	12
50 or more	2	3–4	3	11	18

Source: 1964–65 Farm Accounts in Punjab: NSS, 17th Round and Census of India, 1961, vol. XIII, Punjab, part 1–A(II), general report.

Table 4-10. Size Distribution of Land Owned, Rural India

Amount of land owned (in hectares)[a]	Distribution of households (%)
Landless	32.4
Less than 1	24.5
1.1–2.5	22.9
2.6–4.5	10.7
4.6 and over	9.6
Total	100.0

Source: National Council of Applied Economic Research (1974, table 5).
[a] One hectare (ha) equals 2.5 acres.

Table 4-9 indicates that, in the Punjab, 62 percent of farms have fewer than 10 acres. In table 4-10 some data are presented for all of India on the distribution of farm households by the amount of land they own. Nearly a third of rural households are landless. Most of them consist of landless farm laborers, but some others are cultivating tenants, artisans, traders, and the like. Another 47 percent own less than 2.5 ha (6.25 acres). Only 20 percent of rural households own more than 2.5 ha of land and thus would have need for help from several children or hired laborers. India is by no means a unique case. A large majority of peasants in the less developed countries operate small holdings.

In Taiwan a random sample of farmers with wives below the age of forty-two were questioned about labor use on their farm. Conditions in Taiwan differ from those in India; farms are smaller in Taiwan but more intensively cultivated, and children go to school considerably longer. As many as 73 percent of farmers in Taiwan cultivated less than 2.5 acres, and most of them used less than 25 man-days of hired help a year. Only among the "larger" farmers did a majority hire more than 25 man-days of casual labor per year. Overall, 70 percent of Taiwanese farmers reported some help from their wives while only 22 percent reported any significant help from their children (including children above the age of fifteen).

One further study may be cited which suggests low labor requirements in peasant farming, this one having to do with Africa. John H. Cleave (1970) reviewed fifty surveys of labor utilization by African smallholders in various territories of tropical Africa that were formerly under British jurisdiction. Most of these surveys were anthropological or farm-management studies, and they used a variety of techniques in collecting data. These African studies show women devoting almost as much time to agricultural work as men. However, Cleave summarizes the situation as follows:

> Examination of the records shows that with quite remarkable consistency, adult members of farm families work in the fields for only 120 to 160 days in the year, and the working day tends to be 4 to 6 hours long. In some areas—particularly in West Africa—a further one, two, or even three hours are spent each working day simply walking between house and fields. Even with the growth which has taken place, in total about 1,000 hours per adult per year are spent on agricultural field work, and frequently less. [p. 269]

Cleave found further that, even in the month of peak demand for labor, it is common for adult family members to work only 20 to 40 hours a week on the land. Cleave discovered little material on hours worked by children. Where he did, he found wide variation, with a maximum of 800–900 hours a year for children ten to fourteen.

White (1973) observed much longer hours of work input in a Javanese village. The following figures represent total hours worked over an eight-day time span observed in his study. Work includes the gathering of firewood and the care of animals but excludes child care, food preparation, and other housework.

Sex	*Hours Worked by Various Age Groups During an Eight-Day Time Span*					
	7–9	*10–12*	*13–15*	*16–18*	*19–29*	*30 and over*
Male	18.9	36.6	40.4	60.7	73.2	72.5
Female	27.1	13.9	40.1	61.6	69.9	53.9

White's divergent results can be explained in a number of ways: His village is located only 25 miles from Jogjakarta, which probably means that the demand for vegetables, meat, handicraft products, and nonagricultural labor is greater there than in more remote areas. The season covered was, according to White, one of peak labor input. Earnings are so low in the village that in order to subsist women and children had to perform work of low marginal productivity.

Obviously there are great variations in the demand for labor in peasant agriculture. Some of the factors affecting labor demand may be considered briefly so that we can see the reasons for the prevalence of low labor utilization clearly.

First, the demand for labor depends on the stage of agricultural development of the society in question. The case of Taiwan is often cited. There, average labor input per hectare of land increased from 195 man-days a year in the period 1911–15 to 305 man-days a year in the period 1956–60. As a result the annual average working days per farm worker rose from 117 man-days in the years 1911–15 to 155 man-days in the years 1956–60. Agricultural output more than tripled. The preconditions for the more intensive application of labor, however, were advances in farming methods and a rapid growth of farm capital, particularly irrigation systems, farm implements, and working animals, as well as working capital in the form of fertilizer, purchased animal feed, and so forth. The improved technology, together with the additions to the capital stock, made possible the greater labor-intensity, especially double- and triple-cropping. There is no reason to assume that farmers in a country lacking the requisite capital—for example, India—would find it worthwhile to apply as much labor per hectare as is done in Taiwan, even if the country had unutilized manpower. In brief, there can be surplus labor in agriculture in countries which have a far lower labor–land ratio than has Taiwan.

Another reason for low labor input is the highly seasonal character of agricultural operations in the less developed countries. Women and children constitute the marginal labor force used to meet peak seasonal labor needs. Thus it is plausible that women or children, or both, put in a rather small number of working days, although their contribution may be valuable when they do work. As development proceeds, the seasonality of demand for agricultural labor tends to be attenuated, leading to increased labor intensity overall. Double- and triple-cropping become possible. Farmers may learn to plant different varieties of the same crop (rice, for example) which can be planted and harvested successively. Crop diversification tends to become more feasible. Often, however, these options are not available until farm technology and capital accumulation have reached a fairly advanced level. Until then, the demand for labor, especially that of women and children, is limited by the prevailing agricultural methods.

There are also considerable differences in demand for labor according to crops grown. Vegetables, cotton, and irrigated rice, for example, are much more labor-intensive than some other crops. The extent to which farmers can grow the more labor-intensive crops, however, depends on such factors as soil characteristics, water, transportation, and storage facilities. Also, in many areas farmers have learned by experience that they must grow subsistence crops to safeguard their food supply in case of adverse conditions, whether or not this choice of crops represents an optimal use of farm labor.

Farm-management studies show with some consistency that small farms are more productive per unit of land than large farms because of the intensive application of family labor (often perhaps with marginal productivity below the prevailing wage). It follows that the larger farmers do not make such full use of the women and children in their households as do the small farmers. The reasons are obvious, having to do with social status and with the tendency of the larger farmers to want more education for their children. Thus, the poorer farmers have a limited demand for the labor of women and children because their landholdings and their capital are small, while for the larger farmers it is because they do not want their women and children to spend too much time doing agricultural work.

Customs relating to agricultural work done by women and children vary greatly by country and by social class. Certain tasks may be considered inappropriate for women *and* children, especially heavy or dirty manual work. All but the smallest landowners, even though they may not utilize their family labor fully, tend to be reluctant to let their children do hired labor on other people's land. Thus, unless it is economically imperative, they do not supply surplus labor to the larger farmers. Gunnar Myrdal (1968, pp. 1083–91) suggests that such customs have an economic origin—low demand for labor creates a need to reserve some work for the landless labor force.

The foregoing discussion of the limits imposed on participation in agricultural work by women and children does not apply to the poorest stratum of the agricultural labor force, the landless or nearly landless households. This fact is documented by the Egyptian Labour Survey of 1963–64, the Indian Agricultural Labour Enquiries of 1956–57 and 1963–64, as well as White's work in Java. (See also Hansen 1969.) These studies indicate that households which depend heavily on wage labor for their livelihood cannot earn enough unless women and children are fully employed. While the labor of children and women supplements the family income, it also depresses the wage rate of adult males, as the Indian Agricultural Labour Enquiry rightly points out.

In sum, economic reasons account for the low utilization of child labor in less developed countries that we have seen in the available statistics. These reasons ultimately relate to the traditional technology, the low level of capital investment, and the small (often severely skewed) size of landholdings that characterize peasant agriculture. Because of the low level of complementary inputs, labor productivity is low, and the incentive to make use of every available hand the year around is missing. Clearly, the relation between fertility and the rate of savings is crucial. We shall return to this topic in the next section.

The Aggregate Model

Having constructed alternative consumption and production profiles for males and females, the next task is to combine them. In the aggregate models presented in this section, production and consumption rates for various age groups are weighted by the proportion of the population in those age groups. By varying the demographic assumptions (but holding constant the consumption and production profiles) we can isolate the impact of variations in birth and death rates on the economic role of children.

Assumptions

This section utilizes three alternative sets of assumptions developed earlier: the medium-consumption and standard production profiles for children, the medium-consumption profile together with the high Egyptian production assumptions, and the low-consumption profile together with the Egyptian production assumptions. This particular selection of assumptions reflects our search for conditions under which children may be an economic asset. The reader will see that the economic value of children in peasant agriculture appears negative, even when we assume relatively high-production and low-consumption values for them. Hence there is no need to look at production profiles that envisage children producing less (compared with adult males) than under our standard production assumption or consuming more than under our medium-consumption profile, although such assumptions would have some plausibility.

For the demographic assumptions, stable population model life tables are used, specifically the "West" set in the Princeton series (Coale and Demeny 1966). The calculations which follow are based on mortality level 14, implying an average expectation of life at birth of 49.5 years for males and 52.5 years for females. Level 14 was chosen because it provides an age distribution similar to those found in many less developed countries at present. In order to see the effect of variations in birth rates on the economic value of children, we use gross reproduction rates (GRR)—first of 3.0 and then of 2.0. At mortality level 14, if the GRR is 3.0, the birth rate is about forty-four per thousand, the death rate fifteen per thousand, and the population growth rate is 2.9 percent. With a GRR of only 2.0 the birth rate falls to thirty-one per thousand, the death rate is sixteen per thousand, and the population growth rate 1.5 percent.

As described at the beginning of this chapter, the ratio of production to consumption (P/C) for adult males is determined in the aggregate model, if the consumption and production profiles and a rate of savings are assumed. With the medium-consumption profile, the standard production profile, and a GRR of 3.0, a P/C of 2.2 yields an aggregate production estimate for males and females combined which exceeds aggregate consumption by 4.8 percent—that is, a savings rate of 4.8 percent. We chose the 2.2 ratio, since a savings rate of 4.8 percent appears to be of the appropriate order of magnitude for peasant agriculture. To be clear, a ratio of 2.2 implies that the average adult male produces 2.2 times as much as he consumes in the course of a year. This surplus is available to support children, adult women, and the aged.

The Model

Column 1 of table 4-11 is based on the standard production profile, as presented in column 3 of table 4-8. Each figure in column 3 of table 4-8 is multiplied by 2.2 in order to obtain production in terms of consumption units. Column 2 presents our medium-consumption profile (table 4-2). Column 3, showing the proportion of people in various age groups, reflects the demographic assumptions. Columns 4 and 5 present weighted production and consumption for each age group. These columns can be totaled to arrive at average production and consumption for the whole population. Finally, column 6 shows the surplus or deficit for each age group.

Three rather striking findings emerge from table 4-11. First, under the initial assumptions, children of either sex consume substantially more than they produce until they reach fifteen to nineteen years of age.[14]

[14] Fogel and Engerman (1974, pp. 153–155), estimate that, in the antebellum South, slave owners did not break even on their slaves until they reached the age of twenty-seven. The cost of capital required to raise young slaves is included in

Table 4-11. Aggregate Consumption and Production Model (medium consumption, standard production, GRR 3.0)

Age	*Production (in CU)*[a]	*Consumption (in CU)*[b]	*Proportion in age group*[c]	*Weighted production (1) × (3)*	*Weighted consumption (2) × (3)*	*Deficit or surplus (4) − (5)*
	(1)	(2)	(3)	(4)	(5)	(6)
Males						
0–4	0	0.32	0.178	0	0.057	−0.057
5–9	0	0.52	0.146	0	0.076	−0.076
10–14	0.33	0.82	0.124	0.041	0.102	−0.061
15–19	1.65	1.0	0.106	0.175	0.106	0.069
20–54	2.20	1.0	0.384	0.845	0.384	0.461
54–59	1.32	0.9	0.022	0.029	0.019	0.010
60–64	1.32	0.8	0.016	0.021	0.013	0.008
65 and over	0.77	0.7	0.024	0.018	0.017	0.001
Total			1.000	1.129	0.774	0.355
Females						
0–4	0	0.32	0.176	0	0.056	−0.056
5–9	0	0.48	0.145	0	0.069	−0.069
10–14	0.20	0.68	0.123	0.025	0.084	−0.059
15–19	0.62	0.80	0.104	0.065	0.084	−0.019
20–54	0.66	0.80	0.383	0.253	0.306	−0.053
55–59	0.29	0.72	0.023	0.007	0.016	−0.009
60–64	0.29	0.64	0.018	0.005	0.011	−0.006
65 and over	0.11	0.56	0.029	0.003	0.016	−0.013
Total			1.000	0.358	0.642	−0.284

[a] Table 4-8, column 3, times 2.2.
[b] Table 4-1, column 4.
[c] Coale and Demeny (1966), "West," mortality level 14, GRR 3.0.

Second, the aggregate cost of supporting people aged fifty-five and older is much lower than the cost of supporting children. This is true in part because children are much more numerous than older people, but also because of a fact which is less widely recognized—that older males still contribute appreciably to production. Third, males over fifteen produce about twice as much as they consume; women produce considerably less than they consume. Nearly a fifth of the economic surplus generated by males over fifteen is used to support females over fifteen. Needless to

their cost estimates, unlike ours. The death rate before the age of nineteen in the antebellum South was much higher than that assumed here, a factor which delays the break-even age. On the other hand, time input per worker and probably output per worker were higher than is the case today in many less developed countries.

Table 4-12. Aggregate Model with Medium Consumption and Standard Production

Age group	Proportion in age group (%)	Weighted production (in CU)			Weighted consumption (in CU)		
		Males	Females	Total	Males	Females	Total
	(1)	(2)	(3)	(4)	(5)	(6)	(7)
				GRR 3.0			
Under 15	44.6	4.1	2.5	6.6	23.5	20.9	44.4
15–19	10.5	17.5	6.5	24.0	10.6	8.4	19.0
20–54	38.3	84.5	25.3	109.8	38.4	30.6	60.0
55 and over	6.6	6.8	1.5	8.3	4.9	4.3	9.2
Total	100.0			148.7			141.6
				GRR 2.0			
Under 15	34.4	3.5	2.0	5.5	18.6	16.4	35.0
15–19	9.5	15.8	5.8	21.6	9.6	7.5	17.1
20–54	44.3	98.0	29.1	127.1	44.6	35.2	79.8
55 and over	11.8	12.0	2.6	14.6	8.8	8.0	16.8
Total	100.0			168.8			148.7

	Surpluses (+) and deficits (−) compared (Column 4 minus column 7, in CU)	
	At GRR 3.0	*At GRR 2.0*
Under 15	−37.8	−29.5
15–19	+5.0	+4.5
20–54	+40.8	+47.3
55 and over	−0.9	−2.2
Total	+7.1	+20.1

say, women perform household chores and may be just as useful as men.[15]

In the upper part of table 4-12 the results presented in table 4-11 are summarized. Age brackets are collapsed and the male and female data

[15] The available statistics indicate that in some geographic areas, notably in Africa and Southeast Asia, rural women do more market work than the standard production profile envisages. In others, especially the Moslem and Latin American countries, rural women work less. In our aggregate model one could compensate for such variations by adjusting the male ratio of production to consumption units so as to maintain a plausible savings rate. In this chapter I take only a peripheral interest in the economic role of women. Hence we will not recompute the aggregate model with alternative assumptions about women's work. The standard production assumptions for women reflect a medium level of work input by women.

are combined. Also, all figures are multiplied by 100 so that we can speak of one hundred pairs (one hundred males plus one hundred females) with a representative age distribution. These one hundred pairs produce 148.7 CU and consume 141.6 units, the difference of 7.1 units representing a savings rate of 4.8 percent. The 38 percent of pairs in the peak working years produce 109.8 units and consume 69.0 units, thus generating a surplus of 40.8 units. Young people aged fifteen to nineteen generate a further surplus of 5.0 units. Of this total surplus of 45.8 units, 37.8 are needed to support children under fifteen, 0.9 are needed to support the aged, and 7.1 are saved. Thus, if the assumptions underlying tables 4-11 and 4-12 are realistic, it follows that children are a heavy economic burden on society; the surplus generated by young people aged fifteen to nineteen is small in relation to the deficit generated by children under fifteen;[16] and raising a large number of children would seem to be an expensive method of providing for the relatively minor aggregate burden of old-age support.

The last point is substantiated by the calculations for GRR 2.0, also in table 4-12. All production and consumption assumptions are the same

[16] The finding that before the age of fifteen children do not earn enough on the average to cover the expense they cause to their parents is supported by findings from John C. Caldwell's Nigerian "Value of Children" survey (urban and rural). Caldwell distinguished between groups of children by age, sex, and education. He then asked about each group: "We want to know if children of this kind have to have more money spent on them than the value of their work or earnings (parents worse off) or if their work and earnings is worth more than the money spent on them (parents better off)." For all children going to school at present, regardless of age, the answer was overwhelmingly that costs exceed earnings. The following answers were received for groups not now in school (in percentages):

	Money spent greater	*Earnings or work greater*	*Same or uncertain*	*All*
Sons 11–14				
Past schooling	56.2	27.0	16.8	100
No schooling	43.4	38.3	18.3	100
Sons 15–18				
Past schooling	16.6	63.0	20.4	100
No schooling	10.8	70.3	18.9	100
Daughters 11–14				
Past schooling	54.2	29.9	15.9	100
No schooling	43.2	40.3	16.5	100
Daughters 15–18				
Past schooling	17.3	61.5	21.2	100
No schooling	11.6	65.9	22.5	100

Source: Caldwell, unpublished tabulations.

as those in the upper part of the table. Mortality remains at level 14. The age distribution corresponding to GRR 2.0 appears in column 1. The economic gains to society from having a higher proportion of people in the peak working years and from having to subsidize fewer children far outweigh the somewhat greater burden of the old-age deficit. As a result, 20.1 CU can be saved per one hundred pairs, compared with 7.0 at GRR 3.0—that is, the potential savings rate rises from 4.8 to 11.9 percent.[17] It appears that under the conditions specified here neither the work done by children nor the need to help the aged justifies high birth rates.

Next, we shall repeat our calculations with the higher Egyptian production assumptions for children (table 4-8, column 6), retaining the medium-consumption estimates. The assumption that adult males produce 2.2 CU is also retained. The question is to what extent the higher labor-force participation by children observed in Egypt alters the results of table 4-12. The detailed calculations, corresponding to table 4-11, are omitted for brevity's sake, and, in table 4-13, we proceed directly to a summary of results, corresponding to table 4-12. Starting again with a GRR of 3.0, table 4-13, when compared with table 4-12, shows a slight decline in aggregate production, and hence in the savings rate. The reason is the relatively low labor-force participation by adult Egyptian women. There is also a substantial shift in production between age groups. The productive contribution of children doubles, although the relative size of that age group is the same as in table 4-12. The group of fifteen to nineteen year olds show a slight increase in production; the older age groups produce less. Since consumption is by assumption unchanged, the deficit associated with the youngest age groups declines. The net cost of raising children (consumption minus production) is still substantial, however, and far outweighs the net cost of supporting the aged.

The lower part of table 4-13 reveals the effect of a decline in the GRR from 3.0 to 2.0 in the Egyptian setting. We find that a decline in the GRR from 3.0 to 2.0 generates a substantial increase in the net surplus of production over consumption despite the need for some additional old-age support.

Next, we shift to the low-consumption assumption for children. The consumption profile for the age groups above nineteen remains unchanged, but children are assigned the lowest number of consumption

[17] The potential savings rates are computed on the assumption that there are no induced behavioral or productivity changes when the birth rate declines. For a further discussion of savings rates, see pages 133–137.

Table 4-13. Aggregate Model with Medium Consumption and Egyptian Production

Age group	*Proportion in age group (%)*	*Weighted production (in CU)*			*Weighted consumption (in CU)*		
		Males	*Females*	*Total*	*Males*	*Females*	*Total*
	(1)	(2)	(3)	(4)	(5)	(6)	(7)
				GRR 3.0			
Under 15	44.6	9.1	4.3	13.4	23.5	20.9	44.4
15–19	10.5	20.9	4.4	25.3	10.6	8.4	19.0
20–54	38.3	84.5	14.2	98.7	38.4	30.6	69.0
55 and over	6.6	7.0	0.6	7.6	4.9	4.3	9.2
Total	100.0			145.0			141.6
				GRR 2.0			
Under 15	34.4	7.6	3.6	11.2	18.6	16.4	35.0
15–19	9.5	18.9	3.9	22.8	9.6	7.5	17.1
20–54	44.3	98.0	16.3	114.3	44.6	35.2	79.8
55 and over	11.8	12.4	1.1	13.5	8.8	8.0	16.8
Total	100.0			161.8			148.7

Surpluses (+) and Deficits (−) Compared (Column 4 minus column 7, in CU)

	At GRR 3.0	*At GRR 2.0*
Under 15	−31.0	−23.8
15–19	+6.3	+5.7
20–54	+29.7	+34.5
55 and over	−1.6	−3.3
Total	+3.4	+13.1

units in relation to consumption by adult males that was suggested in the literature. Since we want to see whether extreme assumptions will turn the deficit associated with the rearing of children into a surplus, we combine these low-consumption assumptions with the high Egyptian production assumptions. The result (not shown here) is that the deficit prior to the age of fifteen is nearly balanced by the surplus produced at ages fifteen to nineteen—that is, by the age of twenty (when they have children themselves) the consumption costs and productive contributions of children are almost equal.

Upon closer examination, however, it turns out that this extreme set of assumptions must be rejected as being unrealistic. First, boys between the ages of ten and fourteen are visualized as working 55 percent as

Table 4-14. Aggregate Model with Low Consumption and Egyptian Production

Age group	*Proportion in age group (%)*	*Weighted production (in CU)*			*Weighted consumption (in CU)*		
		Males	*Females*	*Total*	*Males*	*Females*	*Total*
	(1)	(2)	(3)	(4)	(5)	(6)	(7)
				GRR 3.0			
Under 15	44.6	7.5	3.7	11.2	11.4	11.3	22.7
15-19	10.5	17.6	3.6	21.2	8.9	7.1	16.0
20–54	38.3	71.3	12.2	83.5	38.4	30.6	69.0
55 and over	6.6	6.0	0.6	6.6	4.9	4.3	9.2
Total	100.0			122.5			116.9
				GRR 2.0			
Under 15	34.4	6.4	3.1	9.5	9.1	8.9	18.0
15–19	9.5	16.0	3.3	19.3	8.0	6.4	14.4
20–54	44.3	82.6	14.0	96.6	44.6	35.2	79.8
55 and over	11.8	10.4	0.9	11.3	8.8	8.0	16.8
Total	100.0			136.7			129.0

Surpluses (+) and Deficits (−) Compared (Column 4 minus column 7, in CU)

	At GRR 3.0	*At GRR 2.0*
Under 15	−11.5	−8.5
15–19	+5.2	+4.9
20–54	+14.5	+16.8
55 and over	−2.6	−5.5
Total	+5.6	+7.7

much as adult males (though at a lower level of productivity) but as consuming only 44 percent as much as adult males. If growing boys do work such a substantial number of hours, they surely need more food. More important, the lowering of the consumption coefficients in the younger age groups (other things being the same as in table 4-13) raises the savings rate to nearly 20 percent at GRR 3.0 and to nearly 25 percent at GRR 2.0. Such high rates of saving are clearly not characteristic of peasant societies. If children required so little support, adults could and would consume more in relation to what they produce. Thus the ratio of adult male production to consumption would have to be lower. Hence, in table 4-14, the ratio of male production to consumption is lowered to 1.85, resulting in a more realistic set of assumptions—a savings rate of

4.6 percent at GRR 3.0 and 5.7 percent at GRR 2.0. (The assumption remains that boys consume only 44 percent as much as adult males but work 55 percent as long, although its plausibility is questionable.) In table 4-14 children are shown as constituting a smaller, but still substantial, net cost to society than was shown in earlier tables.

In sum, the initial conclusions are not reversed when alternative assumptions are examined that are designed to enhance the estimated value of children up to, and probably beyond, plausible limits. The work contribution of children is not large enough to prevent their being an economic burden on peasant societies. In the aggregate, old-age support is a minor drain on the resources of these societies. Under all our assumptions a decline in the GRR from 3.0 to 2.0 would increase the surplus (aggregate production minus aggregate consumption) generated by these economies. Indeed, the rise in the potential surplus with falling birth rates would seem to be understated by our calculations. These calculations are based on average productivity for children in each age group. If it had been possible to take into account the diminishing marginal productivity of high-parity children, the surplus generated at GRR 2.0 would be larger relative to the surplus at GRR 3.0 than appears here.

We have called this surplus "potential saving," since it could be used to raise living standards or to decrease work effort, instead of being saved and invested. In any case, the larger the surplus generated, given the patterns of consumption and work input, the greater the growth potential or material welfare, or both, of the society. Since the rate of saving is a crucial variable in rural development and additional investments are a precondition for the more productive use of children's labor, we shall now examine savings rates generated by our model under a larger range of demographic assumptions.

The Demographic Transition and the Savings Rate

Demographic change may affect the savings rate in two ways: through its effect on age distribution and through induced behavioral and productivity changes. The aggregate model is helpful in isolating the pure demographic effects, which are essentially age-distribution effects. The expression "potential savings rate" is used in the first part of this analysis, since no allowance is made for behavioral and productivity adjustments which may accompany changes in birth rates. The second part contains a brief (and much more speculative) discussion of induced behavioral and productivity adjustments. That is, we first compute savings rates on the assumption that age- and sex-specific production

Table 4-15. Demographic Assumptions

Gross reproduction rate	*Female life expectancy at birth*	*Crude birth rate per 1,000*	*Crude death rate per 1,000*	*Population growth rate (%)*	*Percentage of population aged 20–54*
Mortality level 6					
GRR 3.0	32.5	47	32	1.5	42
GRR 2.0		32	32	0.0	48
Mortality level 14					
GRR 3.0	52.5	44	15	2.9	38
GRR 2.0		31	16	1.5	44
Mortality level 21					
GRR 3.0		43	6	3.7	36
GRR 2.0	70.0	30	8	2.2	42
GRR 1.5		22	10	1.2	45

Source: Coale and Demeny (1966).

and consumption differentials are given while demographic changes are taking place. Then the question is raised how demographic changes may alter the savings rate by way of changes in consumption and production behavior.

For the pure demographic analysis, seven different sets of demographic assumptions are compared: mortality levels 6, 14, and 21, in the Coale and Demeny *Regional Model Life Tables and Stable Populations* volume for "West," each with a crude reproduction rate of 3.0 and 2.0. For level 21, we also look at a crude reproduction rate of 1.5. The demographic implications of these seven assumptions are summarized in table 4-15. The first demographic assumption—female life expectancy of 32.5 years and a GRR of 3.0—may be unrealistic in that early deaths would make it difficult to reach a GRR of 3.0. The second demographic assumption—mortality level 6 and GRR 2.0—may represent a stage prior to the onset of the demographic transition, when death rates are high and in balance with birth rates. The seventh assumption—mortality level 21 and a GRR of 1.5—would represent a society that had completed the demographic transition, having attained relatively low birth and death rates. Societies would not necessarily pass through all the intermediate stages or pass through them in the order listed. The range of intermediate assumptions is useful, however, in that it clarifies the separate effects of declining birth rates and declining death rates.

It should be clear that stable population models are used here to obtain age distributions. Thus we disregard transitional movements of age distributions, as birth and death rates shift from one level to another. As an alternative, actual age distributions from countries at different

Table 4-16. Pure Demographic Effects on the Potential Savings Rate

Mortality level	*GRR 3.0*	*GRR 2.0*	*GRR 1.5*
	Standard production–medium consumption potential savings rate (%)		
6	9.0	15.2	—
14	4.8	11.9	—
21	2.1	10.2	13.9
	Egyptian production–medium consumption potential savings rate (%)		
6	6.0	11.0	—
14	2.3	8.9	—
21	0.1	6.6	9.5

stages of the demographic transition might have been used. Actual age distributions reflect the combined result of changing birth and death rates, while stable population models enable us to distinguish between the impact of fertility and mortality trends on savings rates.

In table 4-16, potential savings rates are shown for each of the seven demographic assumptions combined with the two production profiles and the medium-consumption profile. A clear pattern emerges within each set of production-consumption assumptions. A decline in mortality, given a constant GRR, lowers the potential savings rate. This occurs because the decline in death rates increases the proportion of children and old people in the population, thus reducing the proportion at peak working age (see the last column of table 4-15). On the other hand, a decline in GRR, given constant mortality levels, reduces the dependency burden because of the smaller proportion of children in the population. As a consequence, the potential savings rate rises. Thus the demographic transition has two effects on the potential savings rate, which work in opposite directions. When the demographic transition is completed, the countervailing influences on saving may more or less offset one another. However, in the less developed countries the decline in birth rates typically lags behind the decline in death rates. This lag depresses the potential savings rate and may slow economic development in the intervening period.[18]

[18] While the crudity of this method of estimating the impact of demographic change on savings rates must be acknowledged, it would seem to offer substantial advantages over previous attempts. See, for example, Kelley (1973). Kelley also attempts to distinguish between dissaving by the young and the aged, but he measures the savings impact of changes in age distribution by using the coefficients from Nathaniel Leff's intercountry regressions, which are hardly suitable (Leff 1969).

Parallel calculations (not shown here) using the low-consumption profile illustrate how the magnitude of the response of savings rates to demographic change depends on the size of the deficit (consumption minus production) associated with each dependent. As this deficit is reduced by assuming higher production or lower consumption by children, it becomes less important what proportion of the population is in the dependency age groups, thus lessening the effect of demographic change on savings rates.

There remains the question of whether falling birth rates could affect the savings rate further through induced behavioral or productivity changes. Turning first to consumption, we observe that large families may be forced to economize on food and other consumer outlays more than smaller families are. There also may be economies of scale in consumption. The diminishing dependency burden may thus be offset in part by an upward shift in per capita consumption that would reduce the positive effect of falling birth rates on the savings rate. However, if an increase in consumption outlays affects nutrition, health care, or education favorably, the development of human capital would be enhanced by declining birth rates.

On the production side, Scarlett Epstein has suggested that members of large families may be more productive than members of small families because of teamwork and the division of labor. However, it is difficult to accept the idea that on small landholdings either teamwork or a division of labor is really important. Some economists believe that large families may provide an incentive to hard work, to agricultural innovation, to the taking of new land under cultivation (where new land is still available), or to the making of labor-intensive agricultural investments, leading presumably to increased per capita income and savings. Indeed, Ester Boserup (1965) and Colin Clark (1967) base their case on this particular behavioral response, when they argue that population growth may stimulate agricultural development. However, quite the opposite may be true. First, it would seem that modern agricultural development is more dependent on purchased inputs (fertilizer, pump sets and other irrigation facilities, improved seeds, modern implements, chemical plant protection, and the like) than on additional labor inputs or labor-intensive investments. Farmers who are supporting small families would seem more likely to be able to acquire purchased inputs than farmers with higher consumption requirements.[19] Second, the production profiles are based on average labor-force participation and productivity. As indicated earlier, the productive contribution of women and children at

[19] This idea is developed further in Mueller (1975).

high birth rates are overestimated in our production calculations, since there is no specific allowance for the negative impact of frequent child bearing on the work contribution of mothers or the effect of diminishing returns on the productive contribution of children. On that account also, the increase in savings rates with declining birth rates may be understated.

In table 4-16, it is demonstrated that the pure demographic effect of a decline in the birth rate is to raise the savings rate. Induced behavioral and productivity changes appear to work in both directions. Hence one cannot be certain whether taken together they will accentuate or diminish the positive influence of declining family size on the savings rate. The case for arguing that induced behavioral and productivity adjustments will on balance offset the pure demographic effects is unconvincing a priori. Thus our analysis gives some support to the proposition that high birth rates reduce investment rates and hence interfere with economic development and more intensive utilization of the labor force.

The Life-Cycle Model

The life-cycle model, an analytical framework proposed by Frank Lorimer, traces the balance of production and consumption over the married life of a couple. That is, instead of aggregating age- and sex-specific production and consumption data for the society as a whole at one point of time, as was done in the preceding section, the data will now be aggregated over the life span of an individual couple. The life-cycle model reveals at what stages of the life cycle children create financial stress and at what stages they help to generate a potential surplus of production over consumption. By making the kinds of assumptions about earnings opportunities and demographic events that a typical peasant couple might make, one can get some idea of the perceived private, as opposed to the social, cost of bringing up varying numbers of children.

The following demographic assumptions are made in the calculations to be presented:

1. The wife marries at the age of eighteen and the husband at the age of twenty-one.
2. The first live birth occurs during the second year of marriage. Subsequent intervals between live births are three years up to the fifth live birth. The interval between the fifth and sixth live births is four years. This spacing pattern allows for some stillbirths.

3. Half of all children born are males, half females. The first, third, and fifth children are males; the second, fourth, and sixth are females.[20]

4. Mortality is at level 14 in the Coale and Demeny "West" series. Children are assumed to be subject to these mortality rates, and their production and consumption streams are multiplied by these survival probabilities.[21]

5. Parents are viewed as making decisions about economic matters and fertility on the cautious assumption that they will live to what is a rather advanced age in peasant societies—the husband to the age of seventy-three, the wife to the age of seventy-five.

6. Daughters get married and leave the parental home at age eighteen; at that point they cease to affect family finances. Sons marry at the age of twenty-one, and after one year of marriage begin to have children. The initial assumption here is that at that time they would find it difficult to contribute to the parents' household. It is often assumed that all grown sons can be counted on to help their parents. From the analysis to be presented below, however, it is suggested that married sons raising children are under serious financial pressure for a number of years. Whether or not they live in a joint family, sons are in a good position to generate a surplus that can support parents only before they have two or three children of their own and after their own children have become substantial earners.

The consumption and production assumptions parallel those made in the preceding sections. The consistency and reasonableness of the aggregate results gives one some confidence in these assumptions. However, for brevity's sake, two (rather than all three) sets of consumption-production profiles are considered here. In the first, the medium-consumption profile is combined with the standard production profile, and lifetime consumption, production, and savings streams are derived from these data. In the second, the Egyptian production profile is substituted for the standard production profile. In both, it is assumed that the adult male produces 2.2 CU, which is in accord with the calculations in the preceding section. Since the consumption and production estimates are based on observed averages for rural areas of less developed countries,

[20] Assumptions 1 through 3 are taken from Lorimer (1965). While they may have an arbitrary element, they reflect contemporary conditions in many peasant societies reasonably well.

[21] Coale and Demeny (1966). The life-cycle model is not very sensitive to mortality rates, since these are used only to reduce the expected consumption and production by children, but do not affect the life span of parents and hence their expected production and consumption.

the intended implication is that parents expect their children to consume and produce like the average child in the rural society.

The assumption of diminishing returns to high-parity children does not have a place in the life-cycle model. *In the aggregate,* assuming a rather stagnant technology in peasant agriculture and limited possibilities for bringing additional land under cultivation, we would expect population growth to be associated with diminishing returns from the land—that is, to depress real wages. By contrast, *at the micro level,* a couple would not see itself as depressing wages or marginal productivity by its fertility decisions. As is illustrated by table 4-17, under our assumptions there are very few years in a couple's life cycle when two sons are in the fifteen to twenty-two-year age range (the period when sons contribute substantially to production) and none when three are in that age range. By the time the second son reaches the age of fifteen, the first son is close to getting married and having children of his own. True, in real life births of boys and girls do not alternate so regularly as in our model. If a couple should have two or three closely spaced sons in succession, they might become aware of the phenomenon of diminishing returns from their own land. Even then, the second or third son might be expected to find outside work or to migrate.[22]

It was noted earlier that a zero discount rate is assumed, partly out of a desire to replicate the peasant point of view. In any case, this issue is not of fundamental concern since, as we shall see, children have a negative rate of return over the life cycle of the couple, even at a zero discount rate.

Consumption and production of a couple and its children are traced in full detail in table 4-17. This table illustrates for the reader the nature of the calculations made. Tables 4-18 and 4-19 are shorter summaries derived from this basic format. Table 4-17 is based on standard production and medium consumption, adjusted for child mortality of level 14. The results are summarized in table 4-18, comparing couples with two, four, and six children.

With the given assumptions, the net cost of a pair of children (one boy and one girl) is 6.86 CU. That is, over the period from birth to the time when they cease to contribute to (or derive support from) the

[22] In some families remittances from children who have migrated could add considerably to the value of children. The frequency and size of remittances depends on employment opportunities available to migrants, their age at marriage, and their own fertility. Very little empirical information on remittance patterns is available. There may be some "lottery effect," that is, a small probability of receiving a large remittance may have quite a large effect on the willingness of parents to incur the expense of another child.

Table 4-17. Production and Consumption over the Life Cycle: Standard Production and Medium Consumption (in CU)

	Father		Mother		*First child (M)*		*Second child (F)*		*Third child (M)*		*Fourth child (F)*		*Fifth child (M)*		*Sixth child (F)*		*Family of four children*		*Family of six children*	
Age of wife	*P*	*C*	*P*	*C*	*P*[a]	*C*[a]	*P*[a]	*C*[a]	*P*[a]	*C*[a]	*P*[a]	*C*[a]	*P*[a]	*C*[a]	*P*[a]	*C*[a]	*P*	*P-C*	*P*	*P-C*
18	2.20	1.0	0.62	0.8													2.82	+1.02	2.82	+1.02
19																				
20			0.66		0	0.27											2.86	+0.79	2.86	+0.79
21																				
22																				
23							0	0.28										+0.51		+0.51
24																				
25						0.42												+0.36		+0.36
26									0	0.27								+0.09		+0.09
27																				
28								0.40										−0.03		−0.03
29											0	0.28						−0.31		−0.31
30					0.26	0.66											3.12	−0.29	3.12	−0.29
31										0.42								−0.44		−0.44
32													0	0.27						−0.71
33							0.16	0.56									3.28		3.28	−0.71
34												0.40						−0.56		−0.83
35					1.30	0.79											4.32	+0.35	4.32	0.08
36									0.26	0.66					0	0.28	4.58	+0.37	4.58	−0.18
37														0.42						−0.33
38							0.50	0.64									4.92	+0.63	4.92	−0.07
39											0.16	0.56					5.08	+0.63	5.08	−0.07
40					1.70	0.77	↓	↓									5.48	+1.05	5.48	+0.35
41									1.30	0.79						0.40	6.02	+2.10	6.02	+1.28
42					↓	↓							0.26	0.66			4.32	+1.17	4.58	+0.37
43																		+1.17		
44											0.50	0.64					4.66	+1.43	4.92	+0.63
45																				
46									1.70	0.77					0.16	0.56	5.06	+1.85	5.48	+1.05
47									↓	↓	↓	↓	1.30	0.79			4.56	+1.99	6.02	+2.10

48									2.86	+1.06	4.32	+1.17
49												+1.17
50												+1.17
51							0.50	0.64			4.66	+1.43
52	1.32	0.90			1.70	0.77			1.98	+0.28	4.18	+1.07
53					↓	↓	↓	↓				+1.07
54											1.98	+0.28
55			0.29	0.72					1.61	−0.01	1.61	−0.01
56												
57		0.80								+0.09		+0.09
58												
59												
60				0.64						0.17		+0.17
61												
62	0.77	0.70							1.06	−0.28	1.06	−0.28
63												
64												
65			0.11	0.56					0.88	−0.38	0.88	−0.38
66												
67												
68												
69												
70	↓	↓										
71									0.11	−0.45	0.11	−0.45
72												
73												
74												
75			↓	↓					↓	↓	↓	↓

[a] P and C for children multiplied by survival probability at mortality level 14.

Table 4-18. Difference Between Production and Consumption over the Life Cycle: Standard Production and Medium Consumption
(in CU)

Age of wife	*Couple with two children*	*Couple with four children*	*Couple with six children*
18–27	+6.51	+5.97	+5.97
28–31	+1.00	−1.07	−1.07
32–34	+0.78	−1.44	−2.25
35–39	+6.37	+2.35	−0.57
40–46	+9.14	+10.20	+4.68
47–53	+5.86	+6.79	+9.18
54–61	+0.87	+0.87	+0.87
62 and over	−5.37	−5.37	−5.37
Total	+25.16	+18.30	+11.44
Potential savings rate (%)	18.4	12.2	7.0

Table 4-19. Difference Between Production and Consumption over the Life Cycle: Egyptian Production and Medium Consumption
(in CU)

Age of wife	*Couple with two children*	*Couple with four children*	*Couple with six children*
18–25	+3.65	+3.65	+3.65
26–31	+0.64	−1.97	−1.97
32–34	+1.16	−1.06	−1.87
35–46	+13.24	+13.40	+6.74
47–53	+3.91	+4.84	+8.57
54–61	−0.22	−0.22	−0.22
62 and over	−6.44	−6.44	−6.44
Total	+15.94	+12.20	+8.46
Potential savings rate (%)	12.5	8.5	5.3

parental household (at the ages of twenty-one and eighteen), a pair of children consume 6.86 CU more than they produce. This is not a very large deficit, considering that parents produce 2.86 CU a year, or about 100 CU, during their peak working years (ages twenty to fifty-four). Obviously, if the parents have three pairs of children, the deficit becomes more significant. It follows from the negative value of children that the savings rate declines as the number of children increases, as it did in the aggregate model. According to table 4-18, the household's savings rate over the life cycle would be 18.4 percent with two children, 12.2 percent with four children, and 7.0 percent with six children. These rates are higher than those derived from the corresponding aggregative model, primarily because parents are assumed to live through the entire period of their lives when production exceeds consumption.

Of course, the economic burden of raising children is not spread evenly over the life cycle. According to table 4-18, during the first ten years of marriage the couple produces a potential surplus of some size. If the couple had only two children, it would never suffer a deficit until the wife reached the age of sixty-two and the husband the age of sixty-five. Couples with four or six children do incur deficits after the tenth year of marriage. The next seven to ten years are the years of maximum financial strain. These should be the years when, for economic reasons, the couple would be most receptive to the idea of limiting family size. Once the oldest son approaches the age of fifteen, he produces a substantial surplus and thus should relieve the strain on family finances.

The figures in table 4-18 indicate that the surplus generated in the first ten years of marriage should be sufficient to cover deficits in the following years when child raising is most burdensome. However, the couple may have to use the initial surplus to invest in the farm, a business, a craft, or housing; they may have to share the surplus with parents or other relatives; they may have a short planning horizon and thus adopt a standard of living that cannot be sustained in the long run; or the couple may not know of a low-risk method of holding savings for a period of time without loss of purchasing power.

Once the eldest son starts to contribute significantly to production, as the second and third sons will do later, the couple enters its period of greatest financial ease, generating potential surpluses of considerable magnitude. At first, the fewer children the couple have, the greater these surpluses are, but when the parents are in their late forties to mid-fifties, the balance is reversed. The couples with six children still benefit from their third son, while the couples with only one or two sons (who are themselves burdened by family responsibilities) are less well off. The advantages to parents of late marriages by sons can also be inferred from table 4-17. The largest part of the economic benefit that parents derive from children accrues from sons aged about fifteen to twenty-two. If marriage were postponed until the age of twenty-five or twenty-seven, these benefits could be greatly enhanced. Indeed, one must wonder how far recent trends toward later marriages in such peasant societies as that of rural India are motivated by increasing financial pressure on parents.

Given the economic role of women, as reflected in the available data, it is not irrational for parents to prefer sons to daughters. Economically, sons are much more rewarding than daughters. It would probably be difficult to change the son preference of parents in the less developed countries [often regarded as contributing to high birth rates (Freedman and Coombs 1974)], unless the economic roles of the sexes first became less disparate.

There is a final stage in the life cycle when the parents no longer can support themselves. From table 4-18, it can be seen that if earlier surpluses had been saved, the parents would not require old-age support from their children or anyone else, no matter what the size of the family. The life-cycle model suggests, just as the aggregate model does, that the cost of old-age support is relatively small. For a variety of reasons (suggested earlier), potential surpluses may not have been set aside for old-age support. In that case help from children is needed. One of the older sons may be entering the period when he generates surpluses, having a working son of his own. Or the youngest son may delay marriage while he has financial obligations toward his parents. The more sons the couple has, and the younger the last-born son, the better are the chances of help.

Table 4-19 parallels table 4-18, except that the Egyptian production profile is substituted for the standard production profile. The results are not changed greatly. With the Egyptian production pattern, because of the high work participation of boys, the net deficit generated by a pair of children is only 3.74 CU. Nevertheless, because of the low labor-force participation of women, especially married women, it is somewhat more difficult for parents to make ends meet, and the potential savings rates are lower. The Egyptian couples generate a smaller surplus during the early years of marriage than do the couples with the standard production profile, and they incur a deficit after only the eighth year of marriage if they have more than two children. During the years of maximum strain, the Egyptian couples with six or more children incur deficits that exceed any surpluses accumulated in the early years of marriage. Only when the first son reaches the age of fifteen or so is the family again in a position to earn more than it needs for consumption. The larger the number of sons and the later they are born, the longer the period of potential surpluses will last. Finally, in the Egyptian case, old-age deficits are somewhat larger than in our standard case, again because of the low labor-force participation of women.

Comparison of the Egyptian case with the standard one again draws attention to the economic role of women. Whether or not the wife engages in market work is very important, since she could make a contribution during much of her married life. Sons, on the other hand, spend only a small part of the period when their production exceeds consumption in the parental household. Some might argue that daughters and wives are so burdened by housework, child care, and repeated pregnancies that they have little time or energy for market activities. In the almost complete absence of comprehensive time-use studies for the less developed countries, it is difficult to evaluate the validity of this argument. However, it must be recalled that the extent of female labor-force participation varies widely from country to country. In regions where female labor-force participation is relatively high, such as Southeast Asia and parts of Africa, peasant households *do* seem to manage satisfactorily without devoting so many woman-hours to housework and child care.

Low female labor-force participation in many less developed countries may reflect cultural barriers to the more extensive use of all labor. Gunnar Myrdal (1968, pp. 1083–91) views these cultural restrictions on labor use as being economic in origin. According to Myrdal, when there is surplus labor on the land, and the marginal productivity of labor is therefore low, the culture finds ways of restricting the effective labor force—by celebrating many holidays, making manual labor demeaning for the upper classes, making it socially unacceptable for all but the poorest women to work, and the like. The possibility that the culture may lead women to stay out of the labor force in order to enable the growing cohorts of young men to support themselves is of great relevance for this chapter. Where reasonably productive work is not available for wives *and* children, the economic burden of child raising is in a sense understated in our models. To be sure, the individual couple may not be aware that cultural restrictions on women's work may result in part from high birth rates. It only sees women as being confined to very limited market roles, while adolescent boys and young men have an opportunity to make substantial work contributions.

In sum, the aggregate model and the life-cycle model agree in showing that children have negative economic value in peasant agriculture. Up to the time that they become parents themselves, children consume more than they produce. Surveys conducted in less developed countries support this conclusion. They find many rural respondents of the opinion "Children are expensive" (Mueller 1972b, Fawcett et al. 1974). However, the individual point of view would seem to lead to a lower estimate of the net cost of children than does the social point of view. First, all individual parents must make some plans for old-age support in case they should live well beyond their normal life expectancy. True, parents living beyond their working years, and hence needing substantial help, constitute a small proportion of the population. At the individual level, however, once a parent reaches the age of thirty, he or she is more likely to survive beyond the age of sixty-five than to die earlier. The uncertain life expectancy combined with the threat of serious need, should parents become quite old (especially should the wife survive much longer than the husband), makes provision for old age an important motivation. Second, even though couples experience periods of significant surpluses that provide potential resources for deficit periods, such as old age, that are related to the life cycle, they may find it difficult to transfer potential reserves from one period of time to another. Therefore, it may be important to have a source of surplus (that is, a working son) at a fairly late stage in the life cycle. Third, individual parents are not likely to be aware of the law of diminishing returns. Fourth, individual parents may be faced with social pressures against the substitution of women's labor for that of children. Robert G. Repetto, in chapter 3, refers to other differences between social and private costs, such as publicly financed school or health systems.

It should be clear that the results obtained here depend heavily on two assumptions—that parents have an economic planning horizon extending into their early seventies and that they do not necessarily value current income or expenditures more highly than future ones. In his widely quoted article, Ohlin estimates that the cost of raising a child to the age of fifteen is 8.9 CU, while the consumption required from the ages of sixty to eighty-five is 13.4 CU. After adjusting these figures for survival probabilities *at birth* and discounting at 10 percent, the value of childhood consumption declines to 3.2 CU and that of old-age consumption to 0.02 CU. Thus Ohlin concludes that "investment in children is a costly way of securing old age support" (Ohlin 1969, pp. 1724–27; see also Robinson 1972). We have argued that in a household decision model it is not appropriate to use the Ohlin assumptions—that parents judge their need for old-age support in terms of their survival probability *at birth* and that they think in terms of a discount rate of 10 percent.

The finding that over the life cycle of a couple, periods of surplus alternate with periods of deficit points up an advantage of the joint family: one couple may have a deficit while another has a surplus. Pooling of several incomes is one way of adjusting fluctuating income to fluctuating needs. The larger the joint family, the more effective the pooling is likely to be. This is doubtless a motive for large families.

The Value of Children and Population Policy

The purpose of this concluding section is to focus on the policy implications of the analysis presented. One problem in deriving conclusions and policy recommendations from this analysis is the uncertainty surrounding the data base. While it is likely that the data used are of the correct order of magnitude, more precise information is needed that is specific to the country for which policies are to be formulated (or at least to a neighboring country with very similar conditions).

Because of the glaring inadequacy of pertinent data, the first policy recommendation must concern the collection of data. Data collection is urgently needed in three areas—consumption profiles, production profiles, and the intrafamily transfer system. The need for information in each of these areas will be described briefly.

CONSUMPTION PROFILES. The reader will recall the wide variations in the consumption profiles that have appeared in the literature. Yet a number of consumer-expenditure studies have been conducted in rural areas of less developed countries, for the most part quite detailed and based on fairly large samples. The problem is that the data (collected for other purposes) are hardly ever analyzed by family composition. To obtain significant consumption profiles specific as to age and sex, income has to be controlled, while consumption by farm families with varying numbers, as well as varying age and sex distributions, of children is compared. It would be desirable to have such an analysis, not only for aggregate consumption, but also for critical subcategories of consumption where substitution or economizing may occur when family size grows. Such studies are needed for rural societies at different levels of development and growing different kinds of crops (for example, subsistence versus commercial crops) to see whether recurring patterns of expenditure can be identified.

PRODUCTION PROFILES. To derive production profiles, age- and sex-specific data are needed on *hours worked*—during different seasons of the year, in different kinds of agriculture as well as outside agriculture, on farms in different-size classes. Except for the Egyptian study, there are no data which come near meeting these information needs. Children below the age of twelve, or even the age of fifteen, are often omitted from employment studies. Usually women and children are classified only as being or not being employees or family workers, without any indication of hours worked. As noted earlier, women and children often perform tasks which are on the borderline between housework and market work. Thus their reported labor-force status may depend on how such work is viewed. Moreover, it would be interesting to know how much time is spent on housework and by whom under different economic and demographic circumstances. In sum, time-use studies are needed, covering *all* activities and *all* members of the household above the age of six or eight. To be of real value, these studies must be repeated several times during the year to allow for seasonal and incidental variations in work patterns. Visiting sample couples every fourth day, as was done in the Egyptian study, minimizes recall error but is costly in money and survey personnel. Somewhat less frequent interviews could still provide better information than is now available.

Together with time-use data, one should have data on *wage rates* paid to men, women, and children. Variations in rates of pay at different stages of the annual agricultural cycle should receive special attention in view of the disproportionate amount of work done by women and children at harvest time and other peak seasons of labor demand. Since wage rates are not reliable measures of relative productivity, comparative (by age and sex) productivity studies would be useful (see table 4-7 as an example). Again, there is need for data covering enough countries so that diversities in production profiles and the reasons for them can be analyzed.

THE INTRAFAMILY TRANSFER SYSTEM. Couples produce potential surpluses during some stages of their life cycles and deficits during others. In modern societies savings and consumer credit enable couples to transfer purchasing power from periods of lesser need to periods of greater need. In peasant societies saving and borrowing are likewise commonly used to bring consumption flows into line with changing needs. Data on household savings have large margins for error. Nevertheless, it would be interesting to analyze the few available data sets by life-cycle stage, family size, and age of children—to see how consistent the data are with the indications of the life-cycle model. A second method of balancing temporary deficits and surpluses, much more common in peasant societies than in modern societies, is intrafamily transfer of income or assets. Indeed, much of the perceived economic value of children in less developed countries seems to stem from the expectation that children will help parents when the latter have deficits in old age, in periods of sickness, or in other emergencies.[23] Therefore it would be highly desirable to collect data on the frequency of intrafamily transfers (including dowries, bride price, large gifts, and so forth); the amounts involved; who makes and receives such transfers at various stages of the life cycle; and how this transfer pattern is affected by the economic circumstances of parents and children, and also by their migration status. Such data sets have rarely been collected in less developed countries, and the few available ones are rather limited in scope.

Turning now to substantive policy issues, the main conclusion of this chapter is that in peasant societies children—from birth to the time of their own marriages—tend to produce less than they consume. The higher the birth rate, the lower is the potential for saving and capital formation. Since labor utilization in these societies seems to be limited

[23] In this connection, see also Neher (1971).

by shortages of complementary inputs into agriculture, agricultural development should be facilitated by lower population growth. To be sure, raising children produces noneconomic satisfactions for parents. And, because of the felt need for old-age support, raising children is apt to look more advantageous from the viewpoint of the individual peasant couple than it does from the viewpoint of society as a whole. Yet the fact remains that countries eager to reduce rural poverty should find it advantageous to lower birth rates.

Some suggestions of ways in which this reduction might be achieved also grow out of this chapter. The joint family is one way of pooling the burden of old-age support. The larger the family, the smaller the risk of serious deprivation. Social insurance is a more efficient way of achieving the same end. An obvious implication of this chapter is that governments in peasant societies should develop social security systems for the aged. With such protection couples would not need numerous or late-born sons to be assured of support when they can no longer manage on their own. The data on production assumptions and on the aggregate model, presented earlier, indicate that in peasant societies men typically continue to make substantial work contributions beyond the age of fifty-five, and women sometimes do also; and only a small proportion of the population is above the age of fifty-five. As a result of these two facts, the old-age deficit—what is needed by persons aged fifty-five and older beyond what they can produce themselves—is very small. At GRR 3.0 and mortality level 14 this deficit varies from less than 1.0 to about 2.5 percent of aggregate production under the various sets of assumptions used with the aggregate model. At GRR 2.0 it would be about twice as large. True, if life expectancy rose to seventy years for women (mortality level 21), the deficit would be somewhat larger still. However, by the time such favorable demographic developments have occurred in a peasant society, the society's ability to finance a somewhat costlier old-age security system would presumably have grown. For the time being, while old-age support may loom as a large and threatening problem in the minds of individual couples, it would be a small problem if insurance principles were applied in the society as a whole.

This is not the place to consider in detail how such an old-age security system should be designed or administered (see Ridker 1971, Ridker and Muscat 1973). One possibility is to restrict old-age benefits to parents with fewer than two surviving sons. This option could reduce the cost of the system and might strengthen its incentive effect. On the other hand, in some countries such a system might be politically less acceptable than a more universal one. There are many ways of financing an old-age security system, depending on the nature of the economy, its existing revenue system, and its commitment to income redistribution or economic growth, or both. As an alternative to a government-operated system, one may conceive of an old-age support system administered by agricultural cooperatives or farmers' associations; members would contribute in their peak working years and thus become eligible for a kind of old-age pension. Needless to say, the development effort would be strengthened if the system could be financed out of new taxes or savings and if these new funds exceeded disbursements by the system in its early stages.

A related policy suggestion concerns the development of savings media and institutions accessible to rural people. Life insurance is an important means of old-age support in more developed countries and should be promoted more energetically in less developed countries, including the rural areas. Life insurance premiums, like contributions to old-age security pension systems, are contractual savings. People obligate themselves to make these payments regularly and thus come to view them as obligatory expenses rather than savings. Hence, in the United States, increases in contractual savings are only partly offset by decreases in noncontractual savings. A study conducted in urban India suggests that the same is true there, at least among the lower- and middle-income groups (National Council of Applied Economic Research 1963).

More generally, our analysis suggests that peasants need a method to safeguard surpluses until they are needed in old age or emergencies. Agricultural land tends to be a good investment, but in many less developed countries little additional land of reasonable quality is available for cultivation. Often in peasant communities there is no land market. Nor is it possible for the poorer peasants to acquire land in very small increments. Other farm investments are illiquid and may be unproductive at the margin when landholdings are small and modern farming methods unfamiliar. Money and jewelry hidden away may be stolen or may depreciate. Aside from an old-age security system and life insurance, such savings media as postal savings, savings banks, and government bonds should be made accessible and familiar to peasants and, of course, safe. These media should pay interest commensurate with returns from capital in its more productive uses, or they might be designed to compensate peasants for inflationary changes in the value of money.

Next, some courses of action related to the family-planning program are suggested by our analysis of the value of children. References to the economic burden of raising children should be of some value in persuading parents to practice contraception. However, timing is important. Couples are most likely to be receptive to such arguments during the period of maximum financial stress, roughly between the birth of the third child and the time the oldest son approaches the age of fifteen. Once substantial economic contributions from growing sons are forthcoming or have already materialized, the felt need to limit family size should diminish. Further, it is evident from our analysis that spacing not only may avoid the bunching of years of significant deficits; it may also provide parents with late-born sons, despite moderate family size. Perhaps parents could be interested in spacing by emphasizing these particular advantages.

A further policy goal, suggested by this chapter, concerns the economic role of women. This topic is dealt with elsewhere in this volume by Ruth B. Dixon. It suffices to point out here that in peasant societies it would probably be difficult to enhance the social status of women and their roles other than the mother role unless women participate more actively and productively in economic life. Indeed, an explicit policy objective should be to have children devote less time to market work and women more time, thereby increasing both the direct and the opportunity costs of children.

Another policy option which has been viewed as slowing down population growth is raising the age of marriage. Our analysis suggests that such a policy may have countervailing side effects. True, in noncontracepting populations couples that marry late have fewer children on the average than couples who marry earlier, although some catching up may occur. Further, women who marry relatively late, and perhaps work before marriage, may want fewer children than others. However, we have seen that sons make their major contribution to family finances between the age of fifteen and the time they have children of their own. If marriage were delayed, for example, from the age of twenty-one to the age of twenty-seven, the surplus generated by sons over fifteen would be roughly doubled. Family limitation might well become less attractive as a result. To be sure, when sons marry later, daughters are likely to marry later too. However, unmarried women over eighteen generate small deficits at most; they might even earn an additional surplus for the parents if the cultural and economic conditions permitted it.

Another policy which is sometimes looked upon as reducing the value of children to parents is longer schooling. While education has many benefits for population and development policy (discussed elsewhere in this volume) it is doubtful that it will reduce the economic gains which rural couples expect from their children. Hopes are bound to arise that children with more education will have more substantial incomes, perhaps after having migrated to urban areas, and will make large income transfers to parents. Moreover, schooling need not interfere appreciably with the work contribution of children while they are growing up. We have seen that children under fifteen do not produce large surpluses in peasant societies. The kinds of tasks they perform while under fifteen could probably be done after school or during vacations (presumably timed to coincide with peak agricultural labor demand). Only if compulsory education were extended beyond the age of fifteen or so, could it make substantial inroads into the work contribution of children. Few peasant societies are likely to raise educational requirements to that extent.

For similar reasons, reducing the value of children by passing laws against child labor is a doubtful proposition. It is hardly realistic to think of laws that would prohibit work by children over the age of fourteen or fifteen in peasant societies. Younger children not only make relatively small productive contributions; much of their work is on the borderline between house and market work and thus would be difficult to prevent. Finally, such laws might rightly be viewed as penalizing the poorest classes of peasants, the landless and nearly landless, whose wives and children work as hired laborers.

Another policy option is to make some labor-saving farm equipment available at concessional rentals to farmers—perhaps to those over the age of forty-five—with a small number of living children. The advantage of such a policy would be to help small families without directly hurting large families. The indirect consequence, however, would be a reduction in labor demand, and thus in agricultural wages, thereby again threatening the incomes of the lowest class.

Thus, some comments may be in order about the relationship between population policy and land-reform policy. If landholdings were made *uniformly* small, as they are in Taiwan, farms could be operated by husband and wife without substantial help from their children. The other side of the coin is that with the disappearance of large landholdings, children would have little chance to obtain work outside the parents' farm. As a result the economic value of children while they are growing up should diminish. In contrast, if permissible landholdings were linked to family size, the incentive to have large families would be maintained or even increased.

An aging couple without a son available to help with the farm work could theoretically share the farm work and proceeds with a tenant and acquire sufficient old-age support in that manner. In countries with an active land-reform movement such an arrangement often would give the tenant some right to the land. The typical peasant, however, attaches great importance to keeping the land in the family. This would seem to be a reason that help from a son is greatly preferred to help from a tenant. In the interest of population policy, perhaps special arrangements should be made for elderly couples with only one, or no, living son to facilitate temporary tenancy arrangements.

In all, while one can think of quite a few policies which might reduce the value of children, some have negative side effects, and for the others there is no evidence that any one of them would be highly effective. One must therefore think in terms of policy packages. The most promising candidate for such a package would seem to be an old-age security system, the further development of savings media suitable for farmers, greater involvement of women in market work, a subdivision of large and medium-sized landholdings. Other possibilities worth trying are economic appeals in family-planning programs at the time of maximum strain and as arguments for spacing.

5.

Education and Human Fertility: Sociological Perspectives

DONALD B. HOLSINGER AND JOHN D. KASARDA

Few scholars would take issue with the position that rising levels of education result in lower fertility rates. Belief in the universality and invariant nature of this relationship has invested formal education with substantial promise as the major social institution amenable to policy manipulation that can help solve the problem of rapid population growth in less developed nations. Yet we find it difficult to write definitively on the effect of education on fertility. Despite an abundance of studies showing negative zero-order and partial correlations between education and fertility, the causal mechanisms that link the two have yet to be specified adequately and submitted to systematic empirical testing. Some have divided the task into two parts; the *direct* effects of education, broadly defined, on fertility with other causal influences eliminated, and those influences of education thought to operate *indirectly* on fertility through other variables. The category involving direct effects is suspect on the grounds of imperfect conceptualization. Some argue that there simply can be no direct effects of education or schooling on fertility and that even such highly focused pedagogical activities as sex and contraceptive education must be regarded as indirect, owing to the complex and often tenuous link between the teaching act and the learning outcome and between these and behavior congruent with the original expectation, that is, low actual fertility. Since fertility is the condition of consummate interest, this line of reasoning holds that all influences of education bear at best indirectly. We reject this argument because we view fertility more broadly to include certain personal dispositions and preferences.

Nevertheless it does appear reasonable to assume that some effects of education are more direct than others and that not all are equally plausible. For example, some have preferred to view schooling as an investment alternative to children. According to this argument, after couples in less developed countries have had a number of children they are confronted with the choice between paying for the education of these children or having more children. The question is, shall we better educate the few we have or shall we continue to bear children knowing that we shall probably be unable to pay for educating them all as we wish? While this type of decision is not too challenging for cautious and highly educated couples in more developed regions of the world, the dilemma is much more difficult for those in the less developed countries. First, there is the likelihood that a couple has already had many children before even the first has reached school age. Second, there is the problem attending the efforts of many less developed countries to make basic education free and compulsory. This is to say nothing of the absence of any real evidence that couples in such places do make cost-accounting arguments for education. Such arguments presuppose quite an optimistic amount of rational decision making leading to contraceptive behavior.

There is a growing awareness among educational policy makers that equal access to education will be virtually impossible to achieve so long as it continues to mean formal schooling. From the cries of the deschooling critics to those of hard-nosed educational finance planners has emerged a strong interest in nonformal education. There is increasing recognition that universal educational opportunity will be impossible to achieve in the less developed countries while we are tied to the concept of formal schooling as its single expression. We shall try in this chapter to make a distinction between formal schooling and other forms of education as they relate to questions of fertility.

Studies on education and fertility have been conducted at both the macro (population) and micro (individual) levels and have treated education as an endogenous as well as an exogenous variable. The following questions are illustrative of the range of possibilities:

- To what extent does the number of years an individual spends acquiring a formal education affect his family-size preferences or actual fertility, or both?
- To what extent does large family size inhibit educational attainment and life chances of its members?
- To what extent do rising levels of aggregate educational attainment result in lower fertility rates among populations or population subgroups?
- To what extent do high fertility rates add to the cost of or impede the educational advancement of a population?

In our analysis we shall be concerned exclusively with schooling as an exogenous variable. Unlike most earlier studies, however, in which only elementary bivariate relationships between schooling and fertility have been examined, our study will emphasize the causal mechanisms through which schooling operates. In this respect we believe that schooling influences fertility in three fundamental ways. First, it operates independent of other causal variables, exerting a direct impact. Here, the influence of the environment, curriculum, and content of schooling in shaping attitudes, values, and beliefs toward preferences concerning family size will be explicated.

Second, schooling affects other variables that bear direct influence on fertility. Causal links of the second type to be explored include the effect of education on age at marriage, female labor-force participation, social mobility, husband-wife communication, exposure to contraceptive information and material, and mortality and morbidity of children. We believe that the major effect of formal education on fertility comes about in this indirect manner. Third, schooling may operate jointly with other independent variables to have an interaction effect on fertility. For example, Charles Westoff and his co-workers (Westoff, Potter, and Sagi 1973) found education related to fertility in opposite directions among active Catholics and Protestants. Their data showed that higher education in Catholic colleges may, in fact, promote rather than diminish values compatible with high fertility.

Where direct and indirect influences of education are thought to operate and key intervening variables have been specified, techniques of path analysis may be employed to decompose zero-order correlations between education and fertility into direct and indirect effects by way of each intervening variable. Where education interacts with another independent variable in such a way that its effect on fertility is a function of the level of the other independent variable, Goodman's log-linear modeling approach may be applied. The manner (or type of model) in which education influences fertility is extremely important for effective policy. As Robert O. Carleton (1967) observes, only if the influence of education on fertility were of the first type would it be practical for governments to concentrate solely upon a program of education expansion.

The Research Literature

From Malthus to the present day most Western thinkers writing on the relationship of fertility to several facets of social structure have placed great faith in mass education as the one sure hope of reducing population growth. That faith has been affirmed in the last decade by research evidence that has found schooling to exhibit a stronger and more consistent relationship to fertility than does any other single variable (Bogue

Table 5-1. Live Births per Thousand Married Women Aged Forty-five and Over, by Education and Residence, Puerto Rico, 1960

Years of school completed	*Puerto Rico*	*San Juan SMSA*[a]	*Other urban*	*Rural*
None	7,421	6,936	6,454	7,830
Primary				
1–4	6,896	5,962	5,865	7,626
5–6	5,836	5,078	4,942	6,886
7–8	4,288	3,924	4,106	5,271
Secondary				
1–3	3,367	3,032	3,295	4,454
4	2,453	2,386	2,525	2,648
College				
1+	1,920	1,909	1,938	1,931

Source: Stycos (1967), from special tabulations of the 1960 census of Puerto Rico.
[a] SMSA, Standard Metropolitan Statistical Area.

Table 5-2. Number of Children Ever Born per Thousand Women Ever Married, by Education, by Urban or Rural Residence (Standardized for Age), and for Total Kingdom of Thailand by Age, 1960

	Years of school completed			
Location of residence	*None*	*Primary 1–4 years*	*Secondary 1–6 years*	*University 1+ years*
Thailand (total)	4,368	4,127	3,297	2,280
Bangkok	3,635	3,357	3,389	1,695
Other urban, nonagricultural	4,232	3,810	3,314	2,729
Urban, agricultural	4,488	4,371	3,615	2,011
Rural, nonagricultural	3,870	3,872	3,642	1,871
Rural, agricultural	4,033	3,750	3,366	—

Source: Goldstein (1972, p. 434).

1969; Simon 1974a). Cross-tabular associations, presented in tables 5-1 and 5-2, illustrate the nature of the relationships frequently observed when large and representative samples are drawn in developing nations. Note that whether actual or desired family size is considered, fertility shows a steep negative gradient with rising levels of husbands' and wives' education.

Table 5-3. Number of Children Ever Born per Thousand Women Between the Ages of Fifteen and Forty-four Ever Married, by Education and Years Since First Marriage, United States, June 1973

		Years since first marriage			
Years of school completed	*Total*	*Less than two*	*Two–four*	*Five–nine*	*Ten or more*
Elementary					
Less than eight	3,416	1,388	1,551	2,743	4,136
Eight	3,015	824	1,439	2,651	3,617
High school					
One to three	2,744	783	1,370	2,322	3,538
Four	2,116	372	1,005	1,823	2,908
College					
One to three	1,802	242	827	1,653	2,821
Four or more	1,557	123	566	1,443	2,595

Source: U.S. Current Population Survey, June 1973.

The patterns exhibited in industrialized nations also typically show lower birth rates among those with higher levels of education, although a U-shaped relationship between socioeconomic status and fertility has emerged in some nations (cf. Freedman et al. 1959, Gille 1971). Data drawn from the 1973 U.S. Current Population Survey, however, indicate monotonically declining fertility for married women between the ages of fifteen and forty-four as the number of their years of schooling rises. The inverse relationship is particularly strong among women married for two years or less, reflecting the effect of their education on postponement of the first birth (table 5-3).

Multivariate analysis of the education–fertility relationship across nations yields strong negative correlations (Bogue 1969, Friedlander and Silver 1967, Heer 1966, Kasarda 1971). Bogue's analysis, for example, of the relative impact of nine indexes of modernization on fertility revealed that education and literacy have the largest effect in terms of explained variance. In this analysis, education alone accounted for 56 percent of the variance in the movement of nations from high to low fertility, whereas all other indexes of modernization combined accounted for only an additional 16 percent of the variance. On the basis of this analysis Bogue concluded that

> Rising education levels, increased school attendance, and elimination of early marriage are much more powerful in promoting fertility reduction than simple urbanization and rising levels of living. A major driving force behind fertility reduction appears to be education. . . . If this is true, *it should be comparatively easy to discover what aspect of rising literacy*

and educational attainment is most intimately related to lower fertility and then to "mass-produce" it on a large scale to hasten fertility decline in advance of other aspects of educational attainment. [pp. 676–677]

Few would argue that the italicized part of Bogue's conclusion is not a key to policy programs designed to reduce fertility in developing nations. At least when compared with the finding of a gross relationship between rising education levels and reduced fertility, however, discovering which aspects of schooling account for the relationship is not at all easy, as we shall make clear later. Furthermore, whether there are only one or a few specific mediating variables through which education operates in affecting fertility—and which governments can "mass-produce"—is at the least questionable. Education affects a wide variety of factors, each of which has been shown to have an influence on fertility. Some of these factors, such as age at marriage and infant mortality, may not be so easily manipulated by policy as others, such as female employment opportunities outside the home. Nevertheless an understanding of the manner in which education influences fertility requires considerable refinement in our conceptualization of the education variable and identification of the intervening variables and specification of their mediating function in the education–fertility relationship.

Indirect Effects of Schooling

Among the arguments that have been made for the indirect effects of schooling on fertility are the following, which we have categorized below.

Formal schooling delays age at marriage and thereby reduces the total possible number of child-bearing years of the wife. One of the most important effects of rising education on fertility is indirect, through its influence on age at marriage. To a large extent, size of family may be viewed as a function of the years of marital fertility and the spacing of children during those years. The former, of course, is predicated on age at marriage and the latter on knowledge and practice of contraception.

The bulk of research indicates that age at marriage increases with rising levels of education. Young men and women typically are not married when attending high school or college, and their postponement of marriage has actually been found to reduce the number of children ever born (Husain 1970a, Mandelbaum 1974, Mysore 1961, Yaukey 1961).

Education provides directly or facilitates the acquisition of information on modern contraceptive devices and use. Extended schooling beyond the primary grades exposes young men and women, both formally and informally, to contraceptive information and material not often available through familial or other channels. In India as well as other developing countries, knowledge and practice of contraception has been shown to be closely linked to the educational level of husbands and wives (Bhutnagar 1972, Dandekar 1967, Husain 1970b, Kripalani et al. 1971, Miró and Rath 1965, Sen and Sen 1967, Yaukey 1961).

Likewise, the Indianapolis and other fertility studies conducted in the United States demonstrate the importance of educational attainment in successful family planning. Most research supports the conclusion of Ronald Freedman and co-workers (1959), that "the more education a wife or husband has, the more likely it is that the couple has used contraception, that they began early in marriage, and that they planned their pregnancies and avoided more than they wanted" (p. 115).

Education increases exposure to mass media and printed materials concerning family planning. Of growing importance to fertility-control programs in developing nations is the use of mass media as an information device. Here, too, education (and corresponding literacy) indirectly affects fertility by increasing exposure to and understanding of newspapers, magazines, pamphlets, and other printed media for transmitting family-planning information. Though studies examining the empirical links between formal education and exposure to mass media are limited, one would expect a high positive correlation.

One extensive survey recently conducted in Taiwan documents the importance of schooling in exposure to the mass media (Cernada and Lu 1972). The survey examined the extent to which women between the ages of twenty and forty-four, by years of formal schooling, were reached through various types of mass media. Results showed that women with formal education were reached to a greater extent by all types of mass media. The gap in exposure to the media between those with and those without formal education was particularly large with respect to movies, newspapers, and magazines. Not surprisingly, less than 1 percent of wives without formal education were reached by newspapers and magazines, while 19 percent of the wives with formal education were reached by magazines and 29 percent by newspapers. It thus appears that literacy (a function almost entirely of schooling) will play an increasingly important role in the success of fertility-control programs as greater emphasis is placed on the mass media for disseminating family-planning information.

Education increases aspirations for upward mobility and the accumulation of wealth, which reduce the desirability of large families. In a field experiment conducted by Donald B. Holsinger (1974) among nonschool and third-, fourth-, and fifth-grade school children in Brasilia,

Brazil, schooling was found to be positively and significantly related to the ability to identify correctly the products of industrial society and to a desire to possess them. Conventional wisdom and astute businessmen have long maintained that the school is indeed a rich environment for the whetting of young appetites for the products of industrial society. Fashions and fads are nowhere more prevalent than in schools, which officially may do little to encourage them but unofficially—through "show and tell" hours and the like—contribute unwittingly to an atmosphere in which being different is odd and the pressure for uniformity is high, thereby creating an inducement to consumerism.

Schooling enhances a girl's prospects for obtaining employment outside the home that competes with bearing and raising children as a career. In many developing nations, the only career path open to the uneducated woman is that of mother and housewife; therefore, the basic way in which she can demonstrate her value is by producing children. The educated woman, on the other hand, can demonstrate her worth by such alternative means as obtaining employment in offices, factories, and other sectors of modern economies. Through well-paying jobs open to her because of her formal training, she may become self-sufficient and less inclined to early marriage. Furthermore, married and single women with better educations are more likely to find jobs that provide them with satisfactions alternative to children, such as companionship, recreation, and creative activity, or the means to such satisfactions in the form of financial remuneration (Blake 1965).

The strength of the education to female employment to fertility linkage has been demonstrated in a recent comparative study of forty-nine nations (Kasarda 1971). The level of education in each nation was found to have a large effect on the proportion of females employed for wages and salaries, which in turn had a strong negative association with fertility. There is no doubt that as the educational levels of women throughout the world rise, we may expect larger proportions of them to be employed outside the home, and we will then find correspondingly lower fertility rates.

Although we found no empirical support for the notion, it appears plausible that by increasing employment prospects, schooling will also contribute indirectly to reduced fertility by requiring that couples reconsider an equitable division of labor for household chores. Such realignment of traditionally female responsibility might be likely to convince couples that their joint personal resources are sufficient for only a small number of children.

Education reduces the perceived economic utility of children, thus lowering the demand of parents for them. Schooling reduces the economic utility of children in a number of ways (Becker 1960, Friedlaender and Silver 1967, Mueller 1972). The first is simply that while children are attending school, either by choice or by law, they are not contributing to the economic support of the family. The longer they remain in school, the more they become a short-run liability. John D. Kasarda's analysis (1971) of the relationship between the percentage of children between the ages of five and fourteen enrolled in school and the percentage under the age of fifteen who were economically active revealed a negative correlation of −.64 for forty-nine nations. Moreover, as had been anticipated, fertility rates were found to be substantially higher in nations where a larger proportion of the youth under the age of fifteen were economically active ($r=+.54$).

Second, by promoting social and economic mobility, rising education levels of parents enables them to reduce their dependence on children for economic assistance. The higher-paying jobs held by those with better educations provide them with a growing sense of self-reliance and feelings of security toward old age (Mueller 1972b). Decisions concerning family size among the better educated can thus be made without so much concern for later economic dependence.

Third, educated parents are better able to assess the relative costs and benefits of children under changing economic and social conditions. Parents with better education typically have higher educational aspirations for their children. Except perhaps for those of substantial wealth, most parents realize that if their educational aspirations for their children are to be attained, they must limit the size of their families.

Finally, the large majority of higher-educational facilities and jobs appropriate for those with greater education are found in the urban sections of developing nations. These factors serve to attract and hold those with better education in the urban centers, where the costs of raising children are higher and the economic benefits of children are less than in rural sectors. Furthermore, the urban milieu as the nucleus of change in developing nations restricts young couples less to traditional familial norms and makes contraceptive information and material more readily available.

Schooling affects communication between husbands and wives in ways that are conducive to lower fertility. Increased education has been found to have a strong impact on communication of family-size preferences between husbands and wives (Olusanya 1971). Those with schooling beyond minimal levels can better express and articulate their feelings concerning the often sensitive issues of contraception and family size (Carleton 1967). The effect of lack of education on fertility because of limited husband-wife communication can be quite important, as shown by J. Mayone Stycos (1955). His findings in Puerto Rico indicate that numerous couples with little or no formal education actually wanted fewer children, but they did not practice contraception because of the mistaken belief that their spouses desired additional children (see also Stycos et al. 1956).

Schooling affects fertility by reducing infant and child mortality. Often overlooked but nevertheless an important variation of the usual negative relationship between schooling and fertility is the influence of the former on the latter in a positive direction by means of increasing probabilities of life expectancy. As Dudley Kirk (1971) pointed out, the spectacular increases in population growth are in large measure the consequence of scientific and technological advances, focusing on a widespread reduction of death rates. Schools transmit these successes to students through the provision of preventive medical services, school lunch programs, nurses, and dental hygienists. One thorough study of elementary education in northeast Brazil (ATAC 1971, pp. 44–45) reported that "if we can rely on the experience and apparently unanimous judgment of teachers and school administrators, the most important motivation for school attendance is the school lunch programs." In the less developed countries the schooled citizen is more likely to be immunized, to live under improved sanitary conditions, and to buy antibiotics for the control of disease. Hence, infant and child mortality rates are much lower among families where formal education is present than where the parents and children are unschooled.

Evidence indicates that where infant and child mortality rates are low, birth rates are also low (Chandrasekhar 1972). Since infant and child mortality are lower among children of couples with more schooling, and those couples are cognizant of this fact, educated parents do not need—and are not likely to try—to have additional children simply for insurance (Mandelbaum 1974). Thus the overall negative association between schooling and fertility is preserved.

Schooling imparts a sense of self-efficacy, control over one's own fate, trust in science and technology, all of which promote the use of contraception as a rational means of controlling one's life and destiny. Despite years of frustrating and frequently ambiguous and contradictory research on the outcomes of schooling, there is one comparatively small effort to explore systematically the so-called noncognitive outcomes that has produced clear and consistent results. For reasons that are not entirely plain, most of the empirical effort to explore these outcomes has involved the notion of psychological modernity. Modernity as a concept related to human personality is fairly recent and has received its fullest expression in the work of Alex Inkeles (Inkeles 1969, 1974, and Smith and Inkeles 1966). The extent or level of individual modernity is typically measured by a series of attitude and value questions and in its ideal form describes a person competent to deal with the kind of life demands epitomized by factory work, urban residence, and industrial economy.

In the Inkeles formulation the modern man is distinguished from the traditional man principally on the basis of his informed contact with the outside world, his sense of personal efficacy, his openness to new experience, his readiness for change, his education, his occupational aspirations, and his relation to traditional authority. Other topics investigated in defining the modern personality are attitudes toward kinship and family, women's rights, and birth control or restriction of family size. Taken together these themes form a reasonably coherent portrait of a kind of person who has been found to be remarkably well suited to the exigencies of contemporary urban–industrial society.

In the present context of education and human fertility, the research on modernity is germane because of its direct overlap with attitudes and values favoring contraceptive practices and restriction of family size, the demonstrated susceptibility of modernity to influences stemming directly from the school experience, and the available research evidence on this topic from regions of the world where population problems are most pressing. In regard to points two and three, consider the following: "Taken all together, therefore, the evidence argues that the school in developing countries, for all its presumed defects, is surely one of the most powerful means for inculcating modern attitudes, values, and behavior" (Inkeles 1974b, p. 18).

In a recent publication focusing more directly on fertility-related questions, Karen A. Miller and Inkeles (1974) posited a model of population growth consisting of seven steps: (1) societal modernization; (2) individual experiences with modern institutions; (3) individual psychological modernity; (4) individual psychological acceptance of birth limitation; (5) individual practice of birth limitation; (6) number of children born to an individual woman; and (7) societal birth rates. Their concern focused on an explication of the relationship among items 2, 3, and 4, which they hypothesized as linear and positive. The study's relevance to ultimate birth rates is assumed on the strength of the argument that the psychological acceptance of birth control precedes its effective practice. They argued further that the acceptance by an individual of birth limitation is a function of holding modern attitudes and values that result from experiencing modern institutions, such as the school, the city, the factory, and mass media.

Using data from adult male factory workers in East Pakistan, India, Israel, and Nigeria, the writers reached the conclusion that the influence of experience with such institutions as the school and factory on acceptance of the principle of family-size limitation is mainly indirect through the influence of modernity of attitudes and values. "In short, our data indicate that structural change in institutions *without* intervening psychic change in individuals seems to have little or no effect on acceptance of birth limitation" (p. 21).

Because of the multifaceted character of psychological modernity the writers broke down the modernity scale into its major components and discovered that among them the valuation of science and technology made the greatest contribution to explaining variation in acceptance of birth limitation and did so consistently in all four countries. Elsewhere, Holsinger (1974) has shown that valuation of science and technology is one of the modernity themes tightly connected to the quantity of exposure to schooling, thus lending further credence to the proposition that one of the so-called unintended consequences of schooling may well be linked to lower fertility rates.

Direct Effects

In addition to the larger number of indirect effects of education on fertility, education has a substantial direct effect on individuals' attitudes, values, and beliefs toward small family size. Education has been found to affect a broad spectrum of psychological attributes, including freedom from tradition, heightened aspirations, views concerning ideal family size, contraception, and other modern values that motivate couples to restrict the size of their families (Caldwell 1968b, Chung et al. 1972, Carleton 1967, Jaffe 1959). It provides women with a feeling of control over the conditions of their lives and bodies. Mandelbaum's comment on the social components of fertility in India provides an apt characterization of this important consequence of education.

> An educated woman is usually less closely confined, physically and psychologically, with her husband's family and its narrow familial concerns than is the woman who is brought into their home as an uneducated girl. . . . She is more likely to feel that she can do something about the conditions of her life, including the condition of pregnancies in close succession or conceiving during her later reproduction years. Her horizons of information are wider, if only being able to read a newspaper; her network of communication is likely to be broader, if only to school friends beyond the confines of household and kin. These differences are not, of course, direct results of her having studied algebra or learned to read another language, but they are potent consequences that help shape her life and are (more) likely to induce her to limit her fertility. [Mandelbaum 1974, pp. 54–55]

Perhaps the largest body of research relating educational experiences to such natality attitudes as "approval of family planning" are the KAP (knowledge, attitudes, and practice) surveys. Nearly eighty countries have been surveyed, and the results have been well reviewed (Berelson 1966, Population Council 1970). Although many sources of influence on attitudes favorable to low fertility have been identified in the KAP surveys, the data lend prominence to the place of formal schooling as a determinant of such central attitudes as acceptance of birth control and small family size.

Attitudes and values are thought to be important to the discussion of the effects of schooling on fertility for two basic reasons. First, attitudes have shown susceptibility to the influence of the classroom, and second, people's attitudes toward birth control in general and contraceptive devices in particular are held to be predictive of their behavior. There is a large literature in psychology, sociology, education, and political science dealing with the construct of attitudes. While it is impossible here to discuss fully the variety of ways the term has been used by social scientists, we are using it broadly to mean the way people feel about an issue presented to them—that is, whether they like or dislike it, favor it or not. In our review of the fertility literature, attitudes are used in at least two other ways in addition to the affective way previously mentioned. Occasionally, for example, attitudes are taken to be cognitive in nature and pertain to an individual's information on the question, say, of birth-control techniques. Still others have referred to attitudes as essentially behavioral in character—for instance, the self-reported use of contraception.

Obviously the biggest question in this area is the extent to which the view that behavior follows attitude is a correct one, leading to more or less invariant relationships and high predictive efficiency. It is also important to ask in this connection which attitudes are germane to the prediction of actual behavior and, at the same time, which of these are amenable to influence by schooling.

Perhaps the most cogent summary statement of the attitude–behavior match is that of Thomas J. Crawford (1971). His argument, essentially a restatement of the "expectancy × value" theory, runs as follows. The strength of the association between attitudes and a future act congruent with it depends upon the expectancy that the behavior will be followed by a certain outcome and upon the value of the outcome to the actor. As Crawford puts it, "Respondents who perceive birth control as leading to positive goals and preventing negative consequences, will be . . . likely to use reliable methods of contraception" (p. 2).

What most researchers investigating the psychological bases for fertility have attempted to do is identify empirically those attitudes which distinguish reliably between users and nonusers of contraceptive techniques. Weak, ambiguous, and insignificant results in this research are commonplace, but the suspicion always seems to remain that either the wrong attitudes were selected and equivocal results thus obtained, or, more recently, that the level or intensity of the attitude was not measured and that if such were known, the weak relationship between attitudes and self-reported or observed behavior would be relatively stronger. One thing seems clear: the persistence with which researchers have pursued this veiled association results from the nature of most family-planning programs, that are essentially communicative—which are, in short, institutions whose only hope of success is pinned squarely on the possibility of changing attitudes and beliefs about birth control, ideal family size, and the like. But since it is the long-term intention of such programs to lower birth rates, the significance of changed attitudes for this process is of perennial interest.

There have, of course, been many excellent reviews of the KAP surveys. Since almost all of these surveys contain attitudinal items, they are a rich source of information about the range of attitudes that have been considered important in relation to population problems. In a concise review of this matter, Fawcett (1971) reports three broad categories of attitudinal coverage: desire for more children, views concerning ideal family size, and approval (or disapproval) of the practice of birth control. Fawcett says nothing of the relationship of these attitudes to fertility behavior on the one hand or to education on the other, but he does provide us with a good picture of the kinds of attitudes that have been investigated.

A persistent criticism of research embodying attempts to identify those attitudes that are significantly related to the use of contraception takes the form of a challenge to the assumption that the attitude is the cause of the behavior. For some (Kirk 1971), it has appeared more reasonable to argue that an attitude favoring contraception may be formed after such behavior has been adopted just as attitudes regarding the mysterious "ideal family size" questions may reliably be taken only after family size has been completed. Such reasoning argues that attitudes are rationalizations, formed in response to behavior in a manner to reinforce and support them. It seems undoubtedly true that some proposals for strict population-control programs stem from an underlying suspicion of the futility of family-planning programs designed to change the attitudes of the participants. It should be apparent here that insofar as education—that is, formal schooling—is thought to operate to reduce birth rates by imparting attitudes favorable to the reduction of birth rates, the assumption that attitudes cause behavior must be made.

Joint Effects

Along with its direct and indirect effects on fertility, schooling also operates jointly with other exogenous variables, such as urbanization and industralization, to affect the intervening variables as well. Schooling, in fact, is a vital engine of modernization and social change (cf. Anderson and Bowman 1965, Vaizey 1962). Numerous studies have documented the importance of the role of education in the modernization process and, hence, in bringing about lower fertility rates.

Urbanization has occupied a central position in discussions of societal development. Marion J. Levy, Jr. (1972, p. 96) spoke for many development theorists in saying, "Our research laboratories, our industrial plants, our training schools are largely urban, and what is done in them is critical for the productivity of the rural areas. It is no accident that so many of the social movements associated with modernization seem to pit rural versus urban peoples. Most of the nonmodernized people have lived very close to the margin of subsistence and, of course, most of them have been rural."

It is now prosaic to observe in most of the less developed countries an unequal distribution of schools favoring urban areas. But the problem is far more deep-seated than it is often imagined to be, since the realities of politics in educational policy are such as to militate against increasing the number of schooling places in areas remote from urban centers. And beyond the fact that such institutions as the mass media, schools, and factories are disproportionately located in cities there is little evidence to support a view that urbanization exerts an additional independent effect on fertility. So it is that we expect the main effects of urbanization to manifest themselves indirectly through the schooling variable or to operate interactively with education.

It is not easy to separate the effects of industrialization from those of urbanization, for where there are concentrations of industry there is invariably a high degree of urbanization—that is, there are large cities. Although we do not argue that it must be so, it seems convincing that the powerful forces of industrialism have a significant place in the creation of a common element of culture wherever these forces are found. Schools, we believe, follow industrialism, not simply in the literal sense of seeking a strong tax base to support them financially, but in spirit or ethos as well. If industry typifies the ability of mankind to subdue nature in his own behalf, schools imbibe this sense of efficacy and transmit it to their young charges in a way that increases their sense of efficacy and overcomes despair and passivity in the face of common predicaments (Inkeles and Holsinger 1974). Again, we expect schooling and industrialism to team up in affecting fertility and have designed our model to reflect this expectation.

The Content of Schooling

By and large, in research dealing with schooling effects, the school is viewed as a solitary, monolithic entity exerting its influence in a diffuse, undifferentiated way. Even if the precise form of the effect of schooling on an individual's fertility were known and could be specified under varying societal conditions, the question of how schooling performs this function would still be a very important one. To this point in our analysis we have focused attention on quantity or extent as the principal schooling variable. In so doing we have attempted to establish whether the institution of formal schooling is an important contributor in its own right and in concert with other social factors to declining rates of human fertility. In other words, given that for persons who have had at least a fundamental education in school there is a moderate negative association between the quantity of their schooling and a variety of fertility measures, what features of the school ambience broadly conceived are responsible for this social fact? Are there school environments that increase the probability that the association will occur or that strengthen the association? If so, how can they be identified?

In our perusal of the literature no attempt has been made to delineate the special features of the school ambience that lie behind its ability to affect fertility, with the obvious exception of those studies dealing with the explicit effects of the school curriculum. It is at this point that schooling, heretofore taken as formal education, must be separated from education more broadly conceived, for much of the curriculum specifically addressed to questions of population and fertility is written for nonformal settings in which adults are the consumers and the target clientele.

It appears to us that it is useful to think of the qualitative aspects of schooling as they may relate to fertility in two ways. First, there is the formal content or curriculum just mentioned. Here the population education movement is preeminent, and the distinction between formal schooling for adolescents and adult education is a crucial one. Second, but no less important in our judgment, is the so-called unwritten curriculum—that is, the social characteristics of a school that shape a student's daily experience and thereby the kinds of things he learns.

Population Education

The best example of the conscious and deliberate use of instructional programs in schools for the ultimate purpose of reducing fertility rates is the population education curriculum. Because of its completeness and clarity, Stephen Viederman's definition of the field is worth reproducing here:

> Population education may be defined as an educational process which assists persons (a) to learn the probable causes and consequences of population phenomena for themselves and their communities (including the world); (b) to define for themselves and their communities the nature of the problems associated with population processes and characteristics; and (c) to assess the possible effective means by which the society as a whole and he as an individual can respond to and influence these processes in order to enhance the quality of life now and in the future. [Viederman 1974, p. 319]

Our examination of the rapidly expanding number of instructional programs in this area has shown them to bear marked contrast to curricula dealing with sex, family, and environmental education. Not professing a value-free but a value-fair presentation of empirically verifiable population characteristics, population educators take as their object the creation of a climate in which students ostensibly can reach their own conclusions, but at the same time a climate in which the probability that the conclusions reached will favor preferences for lower fertility is greatly increased. Topics frequently encountered in these programs are the interconnections between population growth and natural resources, health and nutrition, and economic and societal development (Jayasuriya 1972).

The complete absence of population matters in public school curricula was first pointed out by Phillip M. Hauser (1962), who underscored the anomaly by drawing attention to the fact that schools were being hard hit by rapid population growth. Viederman (1972, 1974), who has written extensively on the development of population education, particularly in the United States, believes that the situation in American schools is not substantially unlike that which Hauser decried in 1962. Other energetic developers and apologists for population education are Sloan Wayland (1971a, 1971b), Noel-David Burleson (1969), and Byron Massialis (1972).

Unfortunately, we found little research evidence to substantiate the claims that population education does operate to reduce fertility. Advocates point out that there is similarly little research evidence regarding the efficacy of printing warnings of health hazards on cigarette packages or of posting highway safety signs and that the lack of evidence about the value of population education springs foremost from an absence of research and not from negative findings.

One noteworthy exception here is the research reported by Hyun Ki Paik (1973). The subjects were seventy-five fourth-year college students from the West Visayas State College in Iloilo City, the Philippines. The students were assigned at random to one of three groups; the first received prepared materials and in-class discussion of population-education issues. The second group were given only the written curriculum materials, which they studied individually. The third group of twenty-five was a control group and received neither written nor oral treatments. The pretest, posttest design represented an attempt to assess the effect of the population education curriculum on attitudes favorable to declining fertility in the Philippines. The difference in performance between the two experimental groups was slight, but the important finding emerging from this study was a change in the attitudes of the experimental groups toward ideal family size. The pretest groups chose five (children) as the mean size of the "ideal" Filipino family, whereas in the posttest the number chosen was three. The control group registered no change: the desired number of children remained constant at four. In addition, the desirable marriage age for Filipino men showed an upward change as a result of the population-education curriculum.

Although this is slim evidence in some respects, more experimental work of this sort is needed to evaluate the effectiveness of population-education programs at different levels of schooling. Longitudinal data, tracing the impact of changes initially attributable to population education, are also required in order to assess the staying power of attitudes and values favorable to limited fertility.

Schools as Social Organizations

The second item in our discussion on the content of schooling redirects attention to the school as a social organization and to the unwritten or hidden curriculum. In the discussion following his discovery that the amount of exposure to formal schooling surpassed all other variables as a predictor of psychological modernity, Inkeles (1969) contended that these effects "reside not mainly in [the school's] formal, explicit, self-conscious pedagogic activity, but rather are inherent in the school as an organization. The modernizing effects follow not from the school's curriculum, but rather from its informal, implicit and often unconscious program for dealing with its young charges" (p. 213).

The school is still something of a black box when it comes to identifying the special features which endow it with the ability to exercise its negative influence on fertility. In the absence of population education, whatever it is about the school that explains this capability is not obvious from an examination of the formal curricula. Furthermore, the Equality of Educational Opportunity Report (EEOR, Coleman 1966) and its several restatements by others have left many sociologists and other educational researchers with the conclusion that size and quality of the school, the availability of teaching materials, and the existence of the kinds of things characteristic of the typical classroom exert no significant influence on the "achievement" of children, at least as judged by their performance on a battery of standardized tests. Regardless, however, of where one stands on the adequacy of the EEOR as a measure of the effectiveness of schooling, when it comes to fertility attitudes, values, and related behavior we need to ask whether we have really tapped the full range of environmental conditions of interest with respect to this product of schooling. Recent work by Rudolph Moos (1974), Holsinger (1976), and Herbert J. Walberg (1971) has identified certain features of learning environments that contribute to the understanding of the mechanisms whereby those environments are able to accomplish a teaching task. Certainly more work is needed in this area to contribute to the precision of the causal models we advance elsewhere in this paper.

The Quantity of Schooling

We should now like to turn to the question of the nature of the relationship that has been reported between education and fertility by asking whether the relationship is constant and linear, or, contrariwise, whether it is irregular and nonlinear. To question the linearity of the relationship is simply to ask whether *x* years (or whatever unit) of exposure to schooling or nonformal education produces a constant level of depression in fertility rates or whether schooling below or beyond a certain level affects fertility at an exponential rate.

Here it should be clear that we are dealing exclusively with the quantity of schooling received. The kind of curriculum and the nature of the educational environment, including the social context, are for the moment put aside. In short, we are here analyzing the nature of the relationship between schooling and fertility, wherein schooling is assumed to be one vast undifferentiated mass whose influence is known and assumed to be similar across all levels and situations.

Even at this crude level of conceptualization and measurement, we have already shown that the mean quantity of schooling attained by a population appears in numerous studies to be a fair indicator of fertility, "idealized" family size, family-planning attitudes, and use of contraception. However, Robert M. Bjork, who reviewed a large number of studies relating education to fertility, offered a refinement of the general finding of an inverse relationship of education to fertility by observing that the normal association did not hold when fertility differentials for persons with no schooling were compared with those for persons with only a very few years of schooling. "Rarely does the difference in the number of children born differ by more than a fraction of a child, and in a surprising number of instances those with no schooling were less fertile than those with a modicum of elementary training" (Bjork 1971, p. 131).

Bjork's findings present a stark contrast to the familiar understanding of the role of formal education in lowering fertility in the less developed countries. In countries that are to some degree developed, such as Argentina, Bjork contends that educational advances can be expected to reduce fertility. In contrast, Bjork found in Bolivia, which is much less developed, a complete absence of the usual inverse relationship. From this he postulated, "As the process of educational development advances, the likelihood of inverse relationships, on a regional basis, between educational indices and fertility increases" (p. 129).

So it appears that the relationship between education and fertility is not always linear. No relationship, or even a positive one, may exist up to the first few grade levels, especially where the general social and economic setting in which this education is obtained is one in which schooling is not likely to alter one's general station in life in an appreciable manner. To the question of the precise amount of schooling required to reduce fertility Bjork argues that as many as ten to fourteen years may be the needed amount. He concludes:

> From the evidence we have available, it appears that Malthus was much too sanguine when he argued that a few years of education emphasizing prudence and economic understanding might be the major force in resolving the population dilemma. Only in those countries where the vast majority of youth stay in school for a considerable number of years does there appear to be some significant tie between controlled population growth and educational achievement per se. [pp. 140–141]

A different refinement of the concept of the quantity of schooling has been made by others (Wiley 1973 and Wiley and Harnischfeger 1974).

Taking issue with critics of schooling who advocate the elimination or reduction of exposure to schooling on the assumed basis of its negligible impact on "achievement," Wiley maintains not only that there are important effects of schooling but that if we measured schooling more precisely, these effects would be shown to be pronounced. In order to improve educational decision making Wiley reasons that we need precise assessments of the exact effect that is produced (in reading, for example) by a certain amount of schooling. To do this he urges that attendance, length of school day, and length of school year be used to quantify the schooling variable.

By reanalyzing the Detroit Equality of Educational Opportunity Survey data in this way he found variations in hours of schooling per year ranging from 710 to 1,150. Some students were receiving 50 percent more schooling than others, and he quite appropriately concludes that, if such enormous variations are not explicitly accounted for in school research, the consequences of the characteristics of teacher and school will be inaccurately measured and misunderstood. Wiley acknowledges that attendance is influenced by background variables in the home and community but insists that an appropriate causal model would have exposure to schooling as an intervening variable or a moderator of the effects of school characteristics for various outcomes.

It appears to us at least plausible that if Wiley is able to describe as enormous the differences in the amounts of formal public education offered to adolescents in the United States, variation in exposure to schooling more precisely quantified in the less developed countries must be noteworthy indeed. We would expect that the systematic application of this mediating variable would enable us to know with greater precision the influence of schooling on fertility-related characteristics and should therefore be a powerful input to policy concerning investment in education.

Recommendations for Empirical Assessment

We have observed that education may influence fertility *directly* by altering attitudes and behavioral patterns of individuals, *indirectly* by affecting such factors as age at marriage, and *jointly* by operating with other aspects of modernization, such as urbanization and industrialization. The crucial issue for policy research, however, is to determine the relative importance of each type of effect and to estimate the parameters of change necessary in schooling, as well as its interrelated variables, to produce a given change in fertility. Such a task requires a research design that incorporates sufficient data, models, and statistical procedures for generating and decomposing zero-order correlations among education, fertility, and related variables into the direct, indirect, and joint effects of education.

A useful first step in this methodology is to design a theoretical model (a path diagram, for example) which identifies all variables that mediate or otherwise influence the education–fertility relationship. This model should specify the nature and direction of each theorized causal path linking education to fertility. Given the acquisition of data from a representative sample that provides valid measures of the variables identified in the model, two techniques may then be used to assess the models and estimate the relative strengths of the effect parameters. Let us consider each briefly.

The first technique is the method of *path analysis* as developed by geneticist Sewell Wright (1934, 1960) and explicated more recently by sociologists Otis Dudley Duncan (1966), K. C. Land (1969), and H. M. Blalock (1969, 1971). In essence, path analysis is no more than conventional regression analysis with certain assumptions about linearity, additivity, and causality. Path analysis provides algorithms for decomposing zero-order correlations among variables in causal models into direct, indirect, and joint associations. For example, consider the semi-reduced-form recursive model presented in figure 5-1. (The full model would contain all other intervening variables mediating the education–fertility relationship discussed above such as female labor-force participation and economic utility of children.)

The unidirectional arrows between measured variables in the model represent postulated causal relationships. Double-headed, curved arrows represent unanalyzed correlations between variables not dependent on others in the model (that is, the exogenous factors). Also included in the model are residual terms (R_{1_w}, R_{2_u}, and R_{3_v}) which represent variables not included in the model, measurement error, and departures of true relationships from linearity and additivity. The symbols P_{ij} are the computed path coefficients that measure the proportion of the standard deviation of the endogenous variable (i) for which the designated variable (j) is *directly* responsible, while all other variables (including residual variables) are constant (Land 1969, pp. 8–9). Path coefficients are standardized partial regression coefficients obtained by regressing each endogenous variable in the model on all measured variables antecedent to it.

The zero-order correlations between each independent variable and fertility in figure 5-1 will be equivalent to its standardized partial regression coefficient (direct effect) plus the sum of the products of the re-

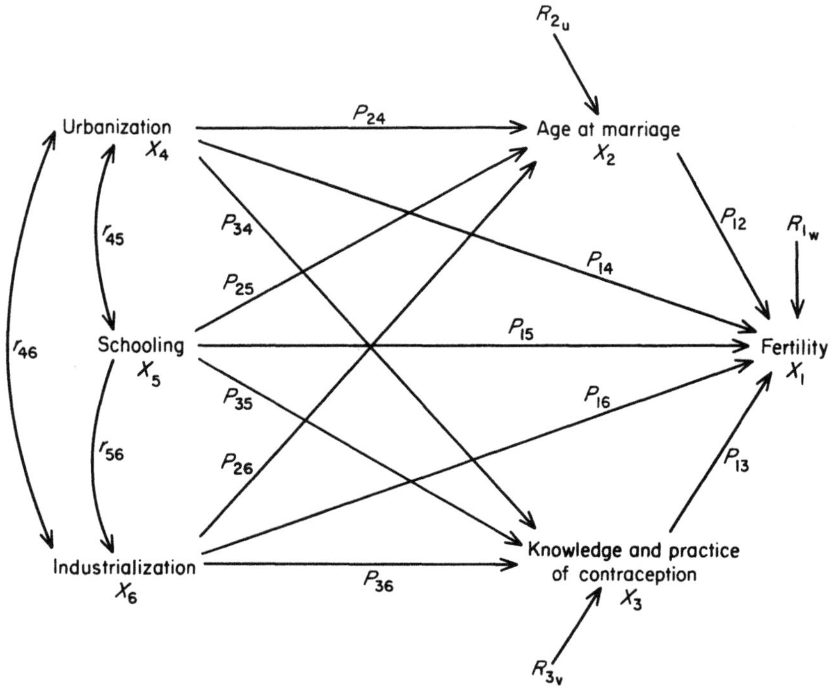

FIG. 5-1. Semireduced-form path model of education–fertility relationship.

gression coefficients along each unidirectional arrow tracing forward only (indirect effects) and an unspecified (possibly spurious) joint association attributable to the independent variable's association with other antecedent variables that also influences fertility (joint association). The decomposition of the zero-order correlation between schooling and fertility (P_{15}) for the recursive model in figure 5-1 would be: direct effect P_{15} plus indirect effect (via age at marriage $P_{12}P_{25}$, via contraception $P_{13}P_{35}$) plus residual joint association with other factors associated with urbanization and industrialization $r_{15} - (P_{15} + P_{12}P_{25} + P_{13}P_{35})$.

If measures are obtained for additional intervening variables, such as economic utility of children and female labor-force participation, their direct effects on fertility would be obtained in a similar manner, as well as the indirect effects of schooling operating through utility of children and female labor-force participation.

When policy researchers wish to estimate the absolute rather than the relative amount of change produced by a given change in schooling through its direct and indirect effects, unstandardized partial regression coefficients (that is, partial slopes) are substituted for the path coefficients in the algorithms for estimating direct and indirect effects.

Perhaps the major limitation of path analysis and other more sophisticated parametric techniques for decomposing the effects of schooling on fertility is that their use requires assumptions about the data that often are not met in fertility surveys. Not only are many variables of theoretical importance qualitative rather than quantitative, but heteroscedasticity, correlated error terms, and absence of linear additive relationships can significantly bias estimated parameters. With problems of causal inference from survey data in mind, a new technique has been introduced recently that could be of substantial importance to policy research on fertility. Since the technique developed by social statistician Leo A. Goodman (1971, 1972a, 1972b, 1973) has yet to be formally named, we shall simply call it Goodman's system.

Goodman's system is designed specifically for multivariate causal analysis of survey data that do not meet assumptions of measurement scale, additivity, homoscedasticity, and independence of error terms required in conventional regression analysis. In brief, the Goodman system analyzes relationships among cell frequencies of multilevel factorial designs and provides effect parameters analogous to path coefficients and measures of association analogous to the squares of zero-order, partial, multiple, and multiple-partial correlation coefficients of conventional regression analysis. The Goodman system also provides estimates of the magnitude of all interaction effects as well as their levels of statistical significance.

Initially, Goodman's system converts each cell frequency in an N-level cross-classification to logarithms. A procedure similar to analysis of variance on the logs of the cell frequencies is then carried out which generates main and interaction effect parameters. Standardized effect parameters (analogous to T-ratios) are obtained by computing the standard error of each effect parameter and dividing the effect parameters by their standard errors. With large samples, the effect parameters are normally distributed with a mean of zero and unit variance. Therefore, to determine statistical significance of a particular effect, one simply consults a table of areas under a normal curve.

Goodman's system should prove particularly useful for decomposing the influence of education on fertility when higher-order interaction exists among schooling and other variables such that the effect of schooling on fertility is predicated on the presence or level of other conditions. By means of Goodman's system one can estimate the main effect of schooling on fertility as well as each order of the interaction effects of schooling with other pertinent variables and can make causal inferences based on the direction, strength, and significance of each parameter.

Conclusions and Policy Recommendations

Because of the paucity of systematic empirical tests of models specifying the causal mechanisms by which schooling affects fertility, our comments are necessarily tentative. Nevertheless, sufficient evidence does exist to suggest that greater exposure to schooling will, in the main, ultimately result in declining fertility. However, compulsory education, while at first glance holding some appeal, is not a practical policy solution in the less developed countries. This is because educational places are so severely limited in much of the world that more than an elementary education may never be acquired by a majority of the people. To compel attendance, even if it were feasible—and we doubt that it is—would mean that the child's contact with the school would be assured for only some four to eight years, after which it would be lost. This situation is not only possible but very likely, since those countries most in need of population control are often the ones with the fewest schools.

Despite an already dramatic increase in the percentage of the GNP spent on education in the less developed countries a net loss in the number of children sent to school is anticipated (Jones 1971). Experts in international and comparative education predict that during the decade of the seventies the total school-age population in the less developed countries will rise roughly 25 percent. In South America, during the period 1955–65, the number of school children increased 75 percent, from 16 million to 28 million; the number *not* enrolled, however, was 35 million greater at the end of the period (Jones 1971).

The case of Thailand offers an even more compelling argument against compulsory education. Thailand passed a law in 1940 making literacy compulsory for Thai citizens but repealed it in 1969 because of adverse economic conditions. Although the percentage of the population that were illiterate decreased from 70 percent to approximately 33 percent during that period, many felt that progress toward general literacy had been retarded substantially because of very high population growth. With a growth rate of 3.3 percent a year Thailand's population, 27 million in 1960, will probably have doubled by 1980, when the next census will be taken. Such growth will strain the capacity of the educational system to keep abreast of even the present inadequate standards and could be accompanied by an increase in the absolute illiterate adult population.

In addition to being a vacuous exercise in lawmaking, compulsory-education statutes aimed at universal elementary education should be viewed in the light of the research evidence suggesting that the largest decreases in fertility occur starting somewhere near the completed primary level of schooling (Miró and Mertens 1968). We therefore urge a redoubled emphasis on expanding access to elementary schooling together with efforts to increase the actual time spent in school within the school year. Studies should be carried out to determine the range in amounts of schooling offered in target areas in the less developed countries. Compulsory-education laws have in some instances imposed a theoretical minimum amount of schooling but have fallen short of guaranteeing that equal amounts of schooling are offered to everyone.

Future research should simultaneously define the concept of schooling in both its qualitative and quantitative dimensions. While taking note of the many facets of the school environment, as they are related to personal dispositions toward low fertility, future research should at the same time refine the measurement of the quantity of exposure to the formal and informal curricula now shown to be important in learning basic skills and social norms.

The problem with moving from our observation of an empirical regularity to recommended public policy resides in the fact that where the desired quantity of schooling is available numerous other societal characteristics are very likely to be found competing with it as alternative explanations for falling birth rates. These are, to name but a few: high urbanization, industrial growth, alternative career options for women, and greater per capita income, which increases the capacity of the elderly to care for themselves or for the agencies of the state to do so. Since these factors are interwoven in the social and economic structure of a society, we expect that in the long run outlays for fertility control might bring greater returns if they were invested in general economic development, of which education is an important feature. We would emphatically urge this general approach in preference to more narrowly defined programs for the dissemination of contraceptive information.

Since it appears quite unlikely that many poor nations will soon be able to satisfy anything approaching universal demand for education, we would suggest that governments wishing lower fertility rates make a special effort to provide opportunities for women to attend school and, at the same time, increase opportunities for employment outside their households.

Indeed, it is under the general rubric to enhance the status of women that we believe that schooling could be a strong factor in the achievement of fertility goals. We do not suggest that social pressure and propaganda aimed at women will soon bring birth rates under control. Rather we expect that a decline in the birth rate will be a spontaneous result of the emancipation of women from traditional roles in developing societies. We do not believe that this can happen by simply increasing female enrollment ratios in formal educational institutions without concurrently providing jobs. But neither do we feel that, in the economic context we are here considering, simple expansion of jobs will matter much, since there is also a shortage of jobs for men. Only where the dignity and worth of women as workers for the common good is understood and is reinforced by increased access to schooling and employment will the birth rates decline.

In this regard we suggest that studies be initiated to explore ways whereby women can be employed. We must understand the cultural obstacles to this process and the roles that schools might be called on to play, in addition to the more or less obvious ones of curtailing expressions of sex-stereotyping of occupations in the formal curriculum. We should investigate ways to recruit women into teaching, where they are not already in that profession. Research is needed to investigate the possibility of incentives for parents to keep girls in school and to change local mores regarding the desirability of work outside the household for women. We realize that to achieve such ends would require major shifts in some economic structures from household-unit economies to the commercial-industrial type, so that women can be readily employed in offices, factories, and other nonresidential establishments. Boarding schools might be logical precursors of this kind of transformation. By adopting policies favorable to such changes not only would extrafamilial alternatives be provided to women but the economic necessity of children would also be lessened.

It has frequently been suggested that there is an important causal relationship between literacy and fertility. We have not been able to establish the special importance of literacy apart from its place as a very important outcome of schooling. In other words, our exposure-to-schooling variable is very much like literacy, and we would expect high but imperfect correlations between them under most circumstances.

This is not to deny that a certain minimum literacy makes contraceptive information more accessible or that adult literacy programs can be extremely efficacious. They might also have the effect of enhancing the overall status of women discussed above. We would very much like to see the development and proliferation of functional literacy courses, especially for women. But it is not so much the literacy per se that will affect fertility as it is the opportunity to bring together persons who already recognize a need for change in their lives and who are quite prepared to make the commitment required for accomplishing that change. By combining family-planning themes with instruction in reading and writing, the difficult connection between literacy and fertility can be established. While we do not generally endorse the now fashionable movement to study nonformal education, we acknowledge the potential of literacy instruction for affecting people in ways incidental to the formal objectives of these programs, and we recommend further study of this potential avenue to lower fertility levels.

6.

Population Growth and Educational Policies: An Economic Perspective

DENNIS N. DE TRAY

Social scientists have long been aware that as education levels rise, marital fertility declines. This relationship is statistically robust, is of sufficient magnitude to be empirically important, and holds cross-sectionally, over time, and across countries. Further, it holds for parent education and family size and for child schooling and the number of siblings that children have. Given the pervasiveness and apparent strength of these relationships, it is natural to consider schooling as a potential policy instrument to reduce fertility in areas of rapid population growth. However, before large-scale efforts to increase either parent or child schooling are undertaken, a number of issues must be settled. Among these issues are the following:

- Separating causation from correlation. It hardly need be said that a strong negative simple correlation between schooling and family size does not necessarily imply that public policy-induced increases in parent or child schooling will cause parents to want and to have fewer children.
- Isolating direct and indirect avenues of influence. Historically, education has played many conceptual and empirical roles in models of fertility determination. Several of these roles imply that the link between education and fertility is indirect, working through such intermediaries as wage rates. If the influence of education on fertility is mainly indirect, then it is possible that an alternative policy prescription directly affecting, say, wages, would be a more efficient and effective means of slowing population growth.

I would like to thank William P. Butz, Julie DaVanzo, and Ronald G. Ridker for useful comments on an earlier draft of this chapter. Many of my own ideas on the topics discussed herein were developed under a grant to the Rand Corporation from the Rockefeller Foundation. The views expressed in the chapter are my own and not those of any organization with which I am affiliated.

• Determining the type of schooling to promote. Faced by severely constrained resources, governments must know which policies will bring about greater reductions in family size, policies promoting adult education, or policies promoting child education. Similarly, curricula and types of training that are most effective in reducing family size must be identified.

• Determining the lag between policy implementation and fertility decline. Knowledge of this lag is essential if we are to assess the merits of education-related policies in relation to other potential policies for reducing family size.

• Determining whether educational policies aimed at reducing fertility complement or conflict with broader development goals.

A comprehensive analysis of each of the points listed above is beyond the scope of this paper and beyond the scope of my expertise. I have chosen, therefore, to concentrate on those areas in which my comparative advantage is greatest—that is, on assessing what the "new economics of fertility" and several recent econometric studies have to say about some of these points (much of which is not so new).

Although I have tried wherever possible to draw out the policy implications of the work I am reviewing, this chapter is considerably more academic than most other contributions to this conference. This emphasis is partly a reflection of my view that in deriving policy implications from research we have often tried to run when we should have been learning to walk or sometimes even to crawl. I recognize that we cannot always afford the luxury of a long and careful learning period, but this seems the kind of forum in which the immediacy of tomorrow's policy decisions can be played down, and we can turn to a careful review of the structure on which future policy may be based.

The plan of this chapter is roughly as follows: first, I discuss the major features, assumptions and criticisms of the so-called household production model and review the role that education plays when this model is used to study the determinants of family size. I then consider the transferability of this conceptual framework to a setting typical of conditions found in developing nations. The chapter concludes with a brief discussion of proposed research to explore the links between education and fertility and a summary of implications for future research, education, and population policies.

Before proceeding I would like to make two points, although once they have been made, I will ignore them. The first is that while this volume rests on the presumption that slowing population growth will increase a society's well-being, this presumption has never been adequately established either logically or empirically (see Blandy 1974,

Krueger and Sjaastad 1962, and Robinson and Horlacher 1971). The second is that even were we to know the *direction* in which governments should attempt to influence the demand for children, neither theory nor any foreseeable empirical work can supply us with a guide to the appropriate *magnitude* of government intervention. Without detailed information on individual preferences it is not possible to know whether government intervention increases or decreases social welfare, even when the appropriate direction of intervention is known.

Economic Theories of Fertility

> The [economic] theory of household choice does not claim that each individual goes through an explicit calculus of pleasure and pain as a guide to behavior and this is certainly true when it is applied to fertility. It is recognized that the process each individual goes through is very complicated and varies among individuals. The assumption is that one possible way of capturing and making sense out of common elements of behavior is to derive propositions as if people were acting according to a specific rule—maximizing a utility function subject to a budget constraint. There is no guarantee, of course, that this is a good strategy. [Ben-Porath 1974b, p. 303]

The Basic Framework

Traditionally, when studying individual behavior economists have concentrated on the interface between the marketplace and household activities; this is particularly true for the allocation of time between these sectors. For all its potential shortcomings, the household production model[1] has one major advantage: its very formulation recognizes and emphasizes that the word *leisure* is a poor description of much of the time that family members spend outside of market work. Although classic consumer theory can in many cases accommodate the study of the intrahousehold allocation of time and resources, the language of the household production model encourages economists to expand their analytical sphere once again beyond decisions on the amount of time to spend at market work and on which market goods and services to purchase.

[1] Extensive discussions of the household production model are available in a number of sources. See especially Gary S. Becker (1965), Robert T. Michael and Becker (1973), K. J. Lancaster (1966), Jacob Mincer (1963), and R. F. Muth (1966).

In this model the family is viewed as a firm engaged in the production of basic items of consumption usually called "household commodities."[2] Families are assumed to produce household commodities by combining their own time with purchased goods and services. They obtain these goods and services in exchange for market work and income from other (nonwage) sources. Because of the close link between the production and consumption of household commodities—the process can, in fact, be considered one and the same in many applications of the model—commodities are not traded in the marketplace and thus have no explicit market price. Since each uses up a certain portion of the household's scarce resources, however, each has an implicit shadow price that consists of the marginal resource requirements per unit (both time and market goods) valued at their opportunity cost. Finally, families are assumed, on an average, to allocate resources available to them in such a way as to maximize the satisfaction that they receive from those resources.

In models emphasizing fertility determination,[3] families are said to maximize a (lifetime) utility function of the form

$$U = U(c,s) \tag{6-1}$$

where c and s are, respectively, a measure of the services derived from children (both monetary and psychic),[4] and "standard of living," an aggregate bundle of all other items consumed by the household. For simplicity, parents are assumed to make all fertility and consumption decisions during a single period, although more recent applications of this model are beginning to incorporate the sequential nature of decisions on family size (Heckman and Willis 1974).

Commodities c and s are not directly available from the market, but must be produced within the household, using the resources and technology at the household's disposal. Production functions for c and s may be written as follows:

$$\begin{aligned} s &= s(t_{m,s},\ t_{f,s},\ x_s;\ E) \\ c &= c(t_{m,c},\ t_{f,c},\ x_c,\ n;\ E) \end{aligned} \tag{6-2}$$

[2] As an example, the commodity "good health" may require as inputs doctors' services, drugs, a nutritious diet, and a person's time.

[3] During the past decade economists have developed several models of fertility determination of the type discussed here. See, for example, the papers by Yoram Ben-Porath, De Tray, and Robert J. Willis in the March–April 1973 supplement of the *Journal of Political Economy*.

[4] The assumption that child services and not children enter parent utility functions is a major departure from many previous models of fertility determination. This assumption suggests that parents may produce a given level of child services

where t_{ij} is the time input of the ith family member [$f = m$ (husband's time), f (wife's time)] into the production of the jth commodity ($j = s,c$), x is an index of purchased inputs, n is the number of children a couple has, and E is a measure of the technology under which the household operates.

The model's emphasis on time as a productive resource in the household is, perhaps, its main departure from the traditional economic theory of consumer behavior. The production-consumption decisions of households at any given time, and throughout their life cycles, now depend not only on the prices of market goods and services that the household faces, but also on how "valuable" or scarce time is to the household.

A critical and often unstated tenet of this type of model is that "home time" (time of the husband and wife, and possibly of children) is a different input into the household production process from "hired time" (maids, cooks, tutors, babysitters, and so on). Technically, this means that male and female time hired in the marketplace as an input into household production never substitute perfectly for the husband's or the wife's time in that production.[5]

For many persons, one important factor determining the price or value of time is the market wage he or she forgoes when not engaged in market work. For persons who work, exogenous (unanticipated) increases in market wages thus carry with them two effects. On the one hand, family wealth is increased and the household's demand for commodities increases; on the other, the price of one of the inputs into household commodities, family members' time, has increased, making commodities more expensive to consume. This second price effect is especially important for time-intensive household commodities, that is, commodities which require large inputs of time in relation to other inputs. A traditional example of such time-intensive commodities is the "production" of children.

The concept of differing technologies (E) among households is partly an expression of ignorance about the internal workings of families, just as appeals to differing technologies among firms and to changes in technologies in the course of time are often expressions of ignorance of underlying market production and growth processes. Partly, however, the introduction of different technologies is a means of recognizing that some persons may be relatively more efficient at running their "firms" (households) than are others both in general and with respect to per-

---

with different combinations of births and other child-related inputs, a possibility that underlies much of the following discussion.

[5] If hired and own time did substitute perfectly, there would be no need to distinguish between them in household production; commodity production functions could then be written as a function of x only [for example, $c(x)$, $s(x)$].

formance of certain specific tasks. Efficiency in contraception and early investments in children are two important examples of this effect and are discussed in detail below.

The quantities of s and c produced will depend not only on production technologies and tastes as embodied in the utility function, but also on the scale at which households operate. The scale of household operation is defined by the "full wealth" available to families. Full wealth is a broader concept of income than the concept traditionally used in consumer demand theory and includes the value of all family resources whether they enter the marketplace or not. If we ignore the value of child time and assume further that the value of the husband's and the wife's time is constant over their life cycle, a family's full wealth (R) may be written as:

$$R = (w_m + w_f)T + V = w_m \sum_j t_{m,j} + w_f \sum_j t_{f,j} + p \sum_j x_j \tag{6-3}$$

where w_m and w_f represent the value (price) of husband's and wife's time, T is the total time available to each member of the household, V represents nonwage sources of income, and p is the price of market goods.

Although the concept of full wealth is straightforward in theory, it is often difficult to measure in practice. One of the major problems in arriving at an acceptable measure of full wealth in fertility-related studies involves the value of the wife's time. First, there is no simple way of measuring the value of the time of wives who do not work; second, even if a wife does work, her current wage is likely to depend on her previous experience in the labor market, which, in turn, will depend on the number and spacing of her children. Thus, causation flows both from the value of a woman's time to the number of children that she wants and from the number of children that she has to the value of her time. Recent advances have been made [see, for example, Cogan (1975), Hanock (forthcoming), Heckman (1974)] that show promise of eventually solving these problems, but for the moment they remain a serious obstacle along the path from economic theory to econometric modeling of fertility decisions.

The "demand" equations for child services and for standard of living [$c(\cdot)$ and $s(\cdot)$] derived from this model are of the usual form in which prices (of both market goods and of household time), income, and some measure of household technology determine the levels of these commodities. For example,

$$(6\text{-}4) \qquad \begin{aligned} s &= s(w_m, w_f, p_x; E) \\ c &= c(w_m, w_f, p_x; E) \end{aligned}$$

In this theory, as in many other economic theories, generality carries with it the price of ambiguity. In a sense, unless we already know something about the child-services production process, economic theory in itself produces little in the way of refutable hypotheses. Without further restrictions on the model, the predicted effect of, say, a rise in the value or price of the husband's or the wife's time is ambiguous and, therefore, in its most general form the model may not be rejectable.

The value of this unrestricted theory is that it supplies a convenient language in which to discuss issues of fertility determination, and to some extent it promotes a more careful and logical discussion of casual statements about these determinants. How one goes about restricting this general model depends critically on the subset of issues toward which a particular research effort is directed.

Detailed derivations and discussions of these derived demand curves (equation 6-4) have been presented elsewhere (De Tray 1973, Willis 1973), and to repeat them here would serve little purpose. To summarize, the effect of a change in a price variable, say, the wife's wage, depends on the following factors:

1. The (current) allocation of the wife's time between market work and home production
2. The relative importance of the wife's time in various household activities (*c* and *s* in our model)
3. The ease or difficulty with which other inputs available to the household can be substituted for the wife's time in the production of household commodities
4. And finally, how fixed or variable the family is in its consumption patterns.

The relative time intensity of different commodities determines the effect of an increase in the wife's wage on the marginal cost, and therefore the relative price, of each commodity. Time-intensive commodities, as children are thought to be, will exhibit relatively large price rises, which in themselves will cause parents to desire less of those commodities.

The current allocation of the wife's time determines the "income effect" associated with an increase in her wage. For those hours allocated to nonmarket activities, an increase in market wages has two offsetting effects. On one hand, the value of that time to the household has increased; on the other, the cost of household commodities using that time has risen. It can be shown that these two effects exactly offset each other and, therefore, that an increase in market wages affects a family's full wealth only to the extent that husbands and wives work in the marketplace (De Tray 1973).

The third point has to do with the production technology under which the household operates. In some household activities the husband's time, or purchased goods or services, may be very good technical substitutes for the wife's time, while in others there may be no reasonable alternative inputs to her time. An example of the first activity is dishwashing, of the second, breast-feeding. Those commodities in the production of which the wife's time has few good substitutes will tend to increase in price (marginal cost) relatively more than commodities with production processes in which the wife's time has many good substitutes.

The fourth point is a roundabout way of bringing tastes into the picture. If families have strong preferences for certain consumption activities (inelastic demands), changing prices will have relatively little effect on consumption levels; where preferences are not so strong (demand is more elastic), price changes will have larger effects on consumption levels.

Symbolically, the total effect of an increase in the wife's wage on, say, the consumption of child services (points 1 through 4), can be written in elasticity terms as:[6]

(6-5) $$\frac{w_f}{c}\frac{\partial c}{\partial w_f} \equiv \eta_{cw_f} = \eta_{cR}\frac{e_f}{R} + k_s\sigma_{sc}(k_{fs} - k_{fc})$$

where η_{ij} is the elasticity of i with respect to j, e_f/R is the share of the wife's market earnings (e_f) in full wealth, k_s is the share of family expenditures on s in full wealth, σ_{sc} is the elasticity of substitution between s and c in the utility function, and k_{ij} is the share of input i in total cost of output j. The first term on the right-hand side thus represents the pure wealth effect of increasing the wife's wage. Although some empirical evidence suggests otherwise, η_{cR} is usually assumed to be positive but small. The share of the wife's *market* earnings in full wealth is also not likely to be large on the average, in either developed or developing nations, so that the income effect associated with an increase in a wife's wage rate (point 1 above) is likely to be quantitatively small.

The second term captures both substitution in consumption and substitution in production effects (points 2, 3, and 4 above). The elasticity of substitution between s and c (σ_{sc}) will be positive if child services and standard of living are substitutes in consumption. The sign of this term will, therefore, depend on the sign of ($k_{fs} - k_{fc}$). If child services are relatively time-intensive, k_{fc} will exceed k_{fs}, and an increase in a wife's wage will reduce desired fertility. A numerical example of the

[6] See De Tray (1973) for the derivation of equation 6-5. The elasticity of i with respect to j is the percentage change in i divided by the percentage change in j.

offsetting influences of these income and substitution effects is given in the next section.

One of the most sophisticated and comprehensive extensions of this general model has been proposed by Robert J. Willis (1973). Two features distinguish the basic structure of Willis's model. First, the production relationship for child services is assumed to be homogeneous of degree 1.[7] Under this assumption, the production of child services can be characterized equally well by equation 6-2, or by:

$$c = n \cdot \hat{c}(t_{m,c}/n,\ t_{f,c}/n,\ x_c/n;\ E) \tag{6-6}$$

Child services may thus be thought of as numbers of children (n) times some transformation of average investments (inputs) per child ($\hat{c}$) or as $n \cdot q$ where q is quality per child ($= \hat{c}$).

A second feature of Willis's model is that, to permit differential effects of income on n and q, each component of child services enters the utility function directly, and equation 6-1 becomes

$$U = U(n,q,s) \tag{6-7}$$

Although the main purpose of the homogeneity assumption in economic models is often analytical tractableness, G. S. Becker and H. G. Lewis (1973) and Willis have suggested that if the assumption holds, it may have important implications for the estimation of the derived demand equation for numbers of children. Willis's model implies that parents will always want to invest equal amounts in each child they have.[8] One implication of this result is that under reasonable assumptions about relative income elasticities of n and q, the observed relationship between n and income (holding wages and the price of market goods and services constant) could be negative, even if the "true" or marginal-cost-constant income effects were positive.

Thus, the homogeneity assumption in the Willis model has the unusual effect of robbing us of what would otherwise be a fairly unambiguous prediction[9]—that the effect of income on children should be positive

[7] That is, an n percentage increase in all inputs will result in an n percentage increase in output.

[8] Other forms of this argument have been suggested by Harvey Leibenstein (1957) and James Duesenberry (1960), and in some respects the Becker and Lewis model is a formalization of these earlier discussions. W. C. Sanderson (1974) offers an interesting history of economists' efforts to analyze fertility, which links the earlier works of Leibenstein and Richard A. Easterlin to the models of Becker and Lewis and of Willis.

[9] For another example of the cost of assuming homogeneity of degree 1 production functions, see De Tray (1973). In that model, child services are assumed to be produced by a linear homogeneous production which has as arguments

(Ben-Porath 1975). It does, however, allow us to "accept" an economic model of fertility such as the one posited above, even in the face of a negative partial relationship between income and family size. It may also be worth noting that neither the Willis nor the Becker and Lewis model implies that the relevant effect of income on family size for policy or prediction purposes is any different from one calculated holding input prices (w_m, w_f, and p_x) constant; put another way, there is no real bias associated with measuring income effects using observed income if other "price effects" associated with changes in income are unavoidable.

Criticisms

"The main shortcoming of the 'new home economics' for the analysis of fertility decisions is that it assumes too little. The basic postulates . . . do not distinguish children from hi-fi sets!" (Griliches 1974, p. s220).

Economic models of fertility based on the household production model have been criticized on a number of fronts by economists (Griliches 1974, Leibenstein 1974, Nerlove 1974) and noneconomists (Blake 1965, Namboodiri 1972, Ryder 1973) alike.[10] For example, N. K. Namboodiri (1972) and Orley Ashenfelter (1973) have raised the question of whether economists' models of fertility are too general and too simple to be useful analytical tools. Zvi Griliches (1974) argues in a similar vein that in order to advance economic analysis of fertility we need to return to the basics, to try to understand the motives that families have for producing children. He suggests several (reciprocal caring, immortality through one's offspring, and so on) that may indeed be worthy of study in the future; few economists would argue, however, that a detailed knowledge of the utility-yielding characteristics of a good is essential to a study of the demand for that good.

Along the same lines, I suggest that we can contribute (and have contributed) significantly to the explanation of household fertility behavior without knowing explicitly why it is that parents have children. One of the important contributions economists have made to the study of fertility is that they have treated children exactly as they would any

numbers of children and total investments in children. An implication of this formulation of the model is that the income elasticity of investments per child is zero. That is, increases in income result in equiproportional increases in numbers of children and total child investments. Although aggregate data did not reject this form of the model, subsequent work using more appropriate individual level data did.

[10] I consider here only a subset of those criticisms, since many of them have been adequately and articulately discussed by Yoram Ben-Porath (1974b).

other household commodity. This has led to a theoretical model with few unambiguous predictions, but one that emphasizes the many important *empirical* questions that must be answered if we are to understand the socioeconomic determinants of fertility.

In their application of the household production model, economists have been accused of ignoring exactly what they are purporting to study: the family and family formation. Technically speaking, in applying the household production model to the study of such areas as the demand for health and family formation, economists have been criticized for assuming a single household utility function and therefore bypassing the issue of interdependent utility within the family (Ryder 1973, Nerlove 1974, Griliches 1974). Further, critics have pointed out that most applications of the household production model assume that production processes are strictly separable in the sense that joint production is not a factor in determining resource allocation and output levels (Nerlove 1974).

Problems that arise from the assumption of the single utility function are discussed in detail by Marc Nerlove (1974) and Griliches (1974) and center on whether children are arguments in some parental utility function or partial formulators of the family's overall utility function and just what it is about children that enters parents' utility functions, child utility or actual child behavior.

Regarding the first point, how far off we are in assuming a single utility function depends on two factors—the question being asked and the potential differences among individual utility functions within a family. If we are principally concerned with the *number* of children a family chooses to have, the prospect that children's preferences for siblings directly influence parental fertility decisions seems remote. On the other hand, parental *investments* in children clearly depend on child cooperation and to that extent on the child's own objective function.[11]

Whether children actually alter (shift) the family utility function or whether their actions (or utility) simply affect the level of parental utility is open to question; so, too, is the issue of whether these alternative hypotheses can be distinguished empirically. At least for now, I will continue with the assumptions that children affect utility levels, but not

[11] Griliches suggests the possibility that in the United States the potential for substantial differences in objectives led to current-generation parental disenchantment with children and hence to the rapid fall in birth rates in the 1960s and 1970s. This can be interpreted as a kind of extended Easterlin hypothesis (Easterlin 1968, 1973) whereby the current child-producing generation bases its expectations on the closeness with which parent and child objectives will match their own experience with their parents.

utility functions, and that, on the average, either parental expectations about future child behavior and cooperation are unbiased, or, if expectations are biased, the bias is unrelated to other variables of interest in the model (wages, income, education, and so forth).

Interdependent utility is considered by Gary S. Becker (1974) in his formulation of a marriage model. In that model he shows that "caring" between family members is a sufficient condition for assuming that the family behaves as if it has a single utility function. Griliches's objections to this formulation are along the lines considered above (whether or not children shift utility functions) and need not be discussed again.

The last of the criticisms mentioned above concerns joint production. Nerlove (1974) has argued that most applications of the household production model have ignored not only the possibility of common overhead inputs (that is, nonseparability of certain inputs), but the more important possibility of complementarity among different consumption outputs. Nerlove's particular example concerns investments in health which may increase the level of production of other dimensions of child quality—for example, education—with no additional expenditures on schooling. At a later point in this chapter, I argue that this may indeed be the case; if it is, a link can be drawn between early home investments in children and later public schooling investments, which may be useful in explaining the pattern of child investment adopted by parents in developing nations.

Education and Fertility

On the basis of the preceding discussion, one might well question the relationship between the title of this chapter and its contents. The reason for the omission of specific references to education up to this point is that education enters the picture as one begins the move from conceptual model to either empirical test or policy implementation. The value of an abstract discussion of "economic" influences on fertility is that it acts as a guide to direct our attention toward points in the process through which fertility is determined at which such policy-responsive variables as schooling may affect final outcomes. Although many of these points are not new either to demographers or to other social scientists, models like the one presented above do help clarify the potential complexity of the role of education in influencing family size. Economic models of fertility have also served to highlight one important role of education that has hitherto received only minimal attention in policy circles: the potential tradeoff between family size and child schooling.

Parent Education

Past studies have linked the education of parents, especially mothers, to the number of children they have and to other aspects of family behavior through many paths. Education, both in the narrow sense of formal schooling and in the broader sense of human capital, is thought to influence tastes by exposing people to alternative life styles and improving information on the set of choices available (Easterlin 1973, and others). It has been shown to affect the value of an individual's time in the marketplace; there is weaker evidence that it may also play a similar role in influencing the value of nonmarket time; and education may partially determine how well couples perform certain specific tasks—important examples in this context being contraception and early (preschool) investments in the human capital of children.

MARKET EFFECTS. Researchers have long recognized education or years of schooling as one of the primary inputs into the human capital earnings function (Ben-Porath 1973a, DaVanzo 1972, Easterlin 1973, Harman 1970, T. Paul Schultz 1969, 1972b, and others). In this capacity education is assumed to have two indirect effects on a couple's desired family size—one through its effect on the opportunity cost of the time required to have and rear children and the other through its effect on the total wealth that a couple has at its disposal. If children are time-intensive, the first of these effects is predicted to reduce a couple's desired fertility, while the second should increase desired fertility if children are in an economic sense normal goods.

One of the few low-income-country studies that contain the information necessary to assess the quantitative importance of education effects through the medium of market wages is Julie DaVanzo's 1972 work on family formation in Chile. She uses 1960 age-specific data on twenty-five provinces in Chile, subdivided into urban and rural areas, to estimate a simultaneous-equations model with female labor-force participation, female wages, marital status, fertility (children ever born), and child labor-force participation or school attendance as the endogenous variables in the system. These equations allow us to trace the effect on fertility of years of schooling through market wages and family income. To simplify matters, and because this example is primarily illustrative, I will restrict the discussion to effects of changes in female education.

Education's "price" effect on fertility through the wife's market wage can be conveniently expressed as the product of two elasticities, one measuring the responsiveness of market wages to changes in levels of schooling and the other the responsiveness of family size to changes in market wages. In DaVanzo's Chilean sample, the elasticity of wages with respect to schooling was approximately 1.1 for women between the ages of forty and forty-four in 1960.[12] At the mean schooling level of 4½ years for this group, this elasticity implies a rise in female wages of about 20 percent for each additional year of female schooling.

For the Chilean sample—the second elasticity—that of numbers of children ever born with respect to the wife's wage, is −0.36. Thus a 10 percent exogenous rise in a woman's market wage is projected to reduce births by 3.6 percent. To calculate the implied elasticity of family size with respect to the wife's education as it works through her market wage, we multiply together the two elasticities given above (1.1 and −0.36), thereby arriving at an elasticity of approximately −0.4.

The calculation of a wealth effect of a rise in female education is considerably more complicated, requiring a number of assumptions, since DaVanzo's fertility equation contains no direct measure of family income or wealth. In order to complete this example, I will assume that the husband's time generates only market income, and thus changes in his wage affects only family income (not relative prices of consumption) and that the husband's contribution to family full wealth is 0.5, and the wife's contribution through her *market* earnings is 0.2.[13]

DaVanzo finds that the elasticity of children ever born, with respect to the husband's wage, is 0.08; this figure can be interpreted as the income elasticity of children weighted by the share of the husband's earnings in full wealth, implying a full wealth elasticity of 0.16. The income effect of an increase in the wife's wage is this full-wealth elasticity weighted by the share of the wife's market earnings in full wealth, or 0.03 (= 0.16 × 0.2).

To summarize, if we consider only the effect of education on market earnings, a 10 percent increase in female schooling (approximately half a year in Chile in 1960) will have two partially offsetting effects on family size: a price effect that reduces children ever born (at mean levels of family size) by fifteen children per hundred couples; and an income effect that increase children ever born by 1.3 children per hundred couples. The net effect is thus a reduction in children ever born of about fourteen births per hundred couples, or a reduction in average family size of 3.8 percent (from 3.637 to 3.497 children ever born).

This example is oversimplified, but it does serve to identify *part* of the process necessary for a full evaluation of the influence of education on fertility. Whether the calculated effect should be considered big or small depends, of course, on the cost of increasing schooling and the costs and

[12] In addition to female wage rates, other variables included in the children-ever-born equation were marital status, child labor-force participation or child schooling, male wage rates, infant mortality, and an urban-residence dummy.

[13] This implies that the wife's nonmarket time and nonwage sources of income account for the remaining 30 percent of family full wealth.

fertility responses of alternative schemes for reducing family size. Since schooling may benefit development objectives in ways other than through its effects on family size, the process of evaluating the relative merits of plans to increase, say, female schooling levels as a fertility-reducing policy is indeed complex. Finally, it should be noted that while the Chilean data have some shortcomings for the study of family behavior, we will not be nearly so lucky when it comes to evaluating the quantitative effect of other avenues through which education is thought to affect decisions concerning family size.

NONMARKET EFFECTS. The effects of education on the productivity and allocation of nonmarket time and on household information levels have recently been stressed by several authors (De Tray 1973, forthcoming, Grossman 1972, Leibowitz 1974, Michael 1972, 1973a). The gist of these arguments is similar to the argument given for the relationship of education to market wages: increased schooling raises the level of effectiveness (efficiency) with which people use their nonmarket time in general and with which they perform certain specific tasks. In other words, just as education is thought to increase a person's marginal product in the marketplace, it may also increase the marginal productivity of time in nonmarket activities. For many issues, distinguishing this effect of education on family behavior from education-related effects that work through changes in tastes may not be possible. But there are at least two areas in which it is important to distinguish between hypotheses of taste and efficiency. These are the effect of education on the use of contraceptives and the relationship between levels of parent education and early investments of human capital in children.

The relationship between education and contraception has been explored in detail by Robert T. Michael (1973a) and Michael and R. J. Willis (1976).[14] Michael's discussion of education and fertility control provides a useful summary of both past studies in this area and generally accepted views:

> It has long been argued that more-educated couples have greater access to fertility-control information and are therefore more successful in pre-

[14] Recent comments of both Ronald Freedman and Marcelo Selowsky on this chapter bear directly on this issue. Freedman argued that, at least for Taiwan and Thailand, recent evidence does not support the view that the negative correlation between education and fertility is due entirely to more effective contraception by the better educated. His point that family planning is a complementary input into any scheme to reduce the demand for children is also well taken. Selowsky commented on the possibility that the relationship between observed fertility and parent education could be the result of "unwanted" births for poorly educated couples.

> venting unwanted pregnancies. Indeed, there is considerable evidence, from sociological surveys in the United States . . . that . . . more-educated couples do use contraceptive techniques more extensively, approve of their use more thoroughly, and adopt contraception at an earlier birth interval. . . .
>
> Similar findings are reported for other countries as well. [Michael 1973a, pp. S140–41]

As is the case with respect to any commodity, the observed amount of contraceptive knowledge and use depends on considerations of both supply and demand. If we ignore factors affecting the *demand* for children, the implication of the findings cited by Michael is that households with little education have a higher probability of producing "unwanted" children—that is, of having more children than they would have had with "perfect" contraception. A corollary to this is that if policy makers wish to reduce future population growth they need only increase the level of education in general and contraceptive knowledge in particular or subsidize the use of contraceptives.

At least in developing nations, this policy has not always worked as predicted. Although acceptance rates for new forms of contraception are often high when these forms are first introduced, the effect on birth rates was sometimes significantly less than the acceptance rates implied (T. Paul Schultz 1972b; see also Freedman et al. 1974, p. 275). One explanation for this result is that many acceptors are substituting one form of contraception for another rather than using the new forms of contraception to reduce fertility. If this is true, it raises the question of whether it is education itself or the correlation of education with knowledge and efficient use of birth control techniques that results in the observed negative relationship between education and fertility. [For a more detailed discussion, see De Tray (1973) and Gardner (1973).]

The major confusion in interpreting and assigning causation to the relationship between education and contraception lies in the fact that past studies have usually failed to control the *demand* for contraceptive knowledge adequately. How much contraceptive knowledge a couple wants should depend in part on how much use they plan to make of that knowledge. Put another way, a household's demand for contraceptive knowledge is derived in part from their desires for numbers of children (or to restrict those numbers).[15] The more children they want the less valuable contraceptive knowledge may be to them and the less they will demand. Therefore, before we can assess the role that education plays

[15] As Ronald Freedman pointed out, desires to regulate spacing may also affect the demand for contraception.

in determining the ability of families to control the number of children they have, we must have a theory of the demand for contraceptive knowledge that takes into account the fact that some families may want more knowledge and some families less. Even were such a theory available, few sources of data are rich enough to allow identification of both the supply of and the demand for contraception or contraceptive knowledge. The upshot of all this is that policy makers may have to wait some time before they have adequate information at their disposal to judge the relative merits of contraceptive-promoting schemes aimed at reducing population growth.

Michael and Willis (1976) offer some preliminary evidence on the link between contraception and education for the population of the United States. After first classifying contraception into good (pill, IUD, condom, and diaphragm), poor (all other types), and none, they find that when female education levels are held constant, the major effect of "better" contraception was to reduce *variances* in live births;[16] they conclude, however, that "contraception use had no significant effect on mean *numbers* of live births" (Michael and Willis 1976, p. 53) when the wife's education level is also included in the regression. The wife's education, on the other hand, is negatively related to both the level and variance of live births.

Similar results seem to hold for "unwanted" births: although results were erratic, higher female education (holding contraception constant) was generally associated with fewer births classified as unwanted [see also Ryder and Westoff (1971) on this point], whereas little systematic relationship existed between better methods of contraception and unwanted births (holding female education levels constant). Finally, female education was found to be positively associated with probability of adoption of the pill, but not as strongly as was the husband's predicted income.

How one interprets these scattered findings depends on the role one assigns to female education. I would argue that they point toward a couple's *demand* for children as a prime determinant of choice of contraceptive technique. The reason is, of course, that I consider female education to be an important determinant of a couple's desired family size, rather than a factor in the "production" of effective contraception. Others may argue that the results of Michael and Willis reflect either taste factors, such as willingness to accept and to use contraceptive devices, or as a measure of knowledge about alternative contraceptive techniques. While the case surely remains open, it seems to me that evidence is accumulating on the side of the demand hypothesis.

[16] Regression observations were cell means.

Does it matter, for policy makers in developing nations, whether female education works through wage rates and household efficiency on the demand for children or, say, through tastes? As usual, the answer depends on the context in which the question is asked. If we are interested in assessing the value of further investments in female schooling, one return that should enter the calculation is the reduced average family size that such an investment might bring about. This is a legitimate benefit whether education works through demand or through tastes. If, however, the objective of policy is directly to reduce population growth rates, matters become more complicated. Policy makers are faced with a number of options, and to choose among them requires knowledge about the link between education and contraception. For example, funds might be best spent subsidizing and promoting contraception if the tastes and knowledge hypotheses are correct; if demand considerations are at work, then policies affecting female schooling levels must be compared to alternative ways of reducing couples' demand for children.

Several authors, including myself, have argued that another major link between fertility and education is through the effect of parent education on the ability of couples to invest in their children. In its simplest form, the argument is that the more highly educated parents are, the more efficient and effective they are at investing in their children during preschool years. This increased efficiency reduces the relative price of early investments in children, which in turn increase the quantity of preschool human capital that parents instill in children. The picture may be extended by recognizing that early investments in children are likely to be complementary to later investments that the children themselves make; that is, we expect a positive association between early investments in children, such as health, and later investments, such as formal schooling or other types of training.

Although the language may be different, this relationship between certain characteristics of parents and the characteristics of their children is a relatively old one to both social scientists and policy makers. The well-known work of P. M. Blau, O. D. Duncan, Beverly Duncan, D. L. Featherman, and others on occupational mobility between generations is in this vein;[17] and, in the United States, the Headstart Program of the Office of Economic Opportunity reflected a recognition that some children arrive at the schoolhouse door with a considerable handicap in regard to their accumulated investments in human capital. The quantitative importance of this relationship for family size is not well established,

[17] For a complete bibliography of work on occupational mobility, see Otis Dudley Duncan, D. L. Featherman, and Beverly Duncan (1972) and the references contained therein.

but preliminary evidence, to be discussed in the next section, suggests that it may be among the most important avenues through which parent education works to influence fertility.

Child Education

Demographers have long recognized that parents may want, say, boy children more than girl children and that uncertainty in achieving this goal may affect family size. In several recent studies, economists have extended this theory and argued that one of the factors influencing family size is the characteristics that parents expect or want their children to have. If parents care about such things as sex of children and innate mental and physical health of children, deviations between expected and actual characteristics of progeny may affect the completed fertility of couples (Ben-Porath 1973, Ben-Porath and Welch 1972, and Welch 1974). Although this fact is of some interest to policy makers, since the not-too-distant future may bring a significant reduction in the uncertainty associated with the sex of unborn children, I want to concentrate here on the interplay between the number of children parents have and the human capital that they want to invest in their children.

Although possibly a poor choice of terms, this interaction between numbers of children and their characteristics is usually called the *quantity/quality tradeoff* (Becker 1960, De Tray 1973, Willis 1973). The argument proceeds roughly as follows: Parents first determine what level of family resources they want to devote to producing child services; they do this on the basis of the utility they expect to receive from the services (psychic and monetary) that children supply and on the cost of factors (time and purchased goods) that enter into the production of those services. Parents then decide how these resources are to be allocated between the number of children they have and the amount of resources they invest in each child.

Parents divide resources between numbers of children and investments in children on the basis of the relative expensiveness of producing numbers and quality and on the effectiveness of each component in generating child services (that is, the relative marginal products of quantity and quality). "Child services" is intentionally an abstract and loosely defined concept, but it is possible to approximate it in any of several related ways. For example, in the context of less developed nations, and even perhaps among the lower-income portion of the population of the United States, one could argue that parents, in producing and investing in children, want to maximize the *pool* of income produced by their children. Thus, for a given resource allocation, their alternatives are a large number of children with relatively low potential income (low investments per child) and fewer children with relatively high potential earnings. Depending on the rate of return to human capital, the value of "raw" labor, and the expected survival rate of each child (O'Hara 1972a), parents will determine optional levels of investment in both quantity and quality of children.

Although the evidence is preliminary, there has been some empirical confirmation of the hypothesis that parents may substitute investments in children for numbers of children. In general, higher rates of school enrollment for children or more years of schooling completed appear to be associated with lower completed fertility both in the United States (De Tray forthcoming) and in several developing nations (DaVanzo 1972, T. Paul Schultz 1969, 1971). If subsidizing investments in children would reduce the demand of parents for numbers of children, then exploiting that relationship is a particularly appealing policy option, since it should also have the effect of increasing per capita education and the earnings of future generations.

Application to Developing Nations

In this section, I consider the application of some of the concepts presented above to a typical developing nation. The severe constraint on public resources faced by developing nations dictates that we consider first the issue of the expected level and timing of the returns from various policy alternatives. In this context, it is useful to view policies affecting adult education and policies affecting child education as competitors for public funds. As we shall see, the environments in which these alternative policies are expected to work in the developing countries are critical in determining the anticipated results of each.

Adult Education Policies

Adult education policies are those policies that affect couples in the current child-bearing generation. These policies are presumed to take advantage of the negative association between parent education and fertility to effect a reduction in average family size. As the preceding discussion has indicated, the mechanisms through which adult education influences fertility are complex, and their quantitative importance is not well established for developing nations. Further, adult education may be too blunt a policy instrument in that policies aimed directly at, say, increasing female wages, may produce a larger reduction in population growth rates per unit expenditure than policies that increase female wages indirectly through improved opportunities for schooling.

A judgment as to whether these shortcomings are worse for adult education as a policy instrument than for child education would be only speculation at this point, but when we turn from the benefit (fertility-reducing) side of the picture to the production side (private and social) we are on firmer ground. The literature on human capital has stressed three aspects of the education investment process that are pertinent here: First, the principal private costs of acquiring schooling are the income-earning opportunities forgone; second, the value of a given unit of education depends on the number of years over which returns are received; and third, external capital markets in which investments in human capital can be financed seldom exist.

Each of these points suggests that adults may find it more costly, less rewarding, and more difficult to invest in themselves than to invest in their children. Parent time is worth more than child time; young children face a longer investment-recoupment period than do adults; and the only source of financing for human capital investments may be a couple's current market earnings. The last point is especially important in situations in which nonmarket sources of income and savings are minimal. (Extended families may alleviate this financing constraint somewhat, but the direction of the effect will be unchanged.) The net result is that governments may find that a substantially higher subsidy is required to induce parents to invest in themselves than is required to induce parents to invest in their children.

A final point on the riskiness of adult education policies concerns the lag between policy action and parent reaction. Although some progress has been made in determining fertility response lags (T. Paul Schultz 1972b), we know almost nothing about the length of time it would take for a policy-induced increase in adult education to filter through to a reduction in fertility. The requirements for data to supply this missing information are stringent, and we can only speculate that the process is unlikely to take place very rapidly. Such policies may therefore be untenable, because interim population growth rates would be unacceptably high.

Child Education Policies

Policies that increase the amount of schooling received by children may affect population growth rates in two ways, one through the effect of increased levels of child education on the size of the family desired by parents, and the other, a long-term effect working through children's desires for progeny when the children themselves become adults. Here I will concentrate more or less exclusively on the first of these effects because of its potential for a relatively short response lag and will mention considerations having to do with the second effect only briefly.

Policies affecting child education are one avenue through which governments can influence the decisions of parents as to desired levels of quantity and quality of children. There are, of course, other means of influencing this decision, and several recently suggested policy options and pilot programs have that implicit aim. Incentive schemes that penalize parents who have too many children (Ridker 1971, Finnigan and Sun 1972) raise the cost to parents of having an additional child in relation to the cost of investing more in existing children. I am sure that this statement would not come as news to the authors of these proposals, but viewing these efforts in the context of the more general model discussed above emphasizes the fact that couples have, in a technical sense, always had this option. That parents appear to have *chosen* many children and relatively low investments per child is a fact worthy of careful consideration. Ascertaining why parents make these choices may lead to policy prescriptions that could give considerable impetus to economic development in general and to the goal of reducing population growth rates in particular.

CHILDREN AS CAPITAL—A DIGRESSION. The issue of the "rationality" of low-income parents who have many children depends in part on answers to the following questions: What is it about low-income, traditional economies that might lead parents to use children as a means of transferring income from one period of time to another? In this same setting, what is it about child rearing that induces parents to have many children and invest little in each?[18]

In answer to the first question, I suggest that lack of market alternatives, poorly developed or nonexistent capital markets, and a set of factors associated with the relative riskiness of investment alternatives are conditions sufficient to make children an attractive form of capital in most developing nations. Developing nations are characterized by a limited set of long-term investment possibilities and old-age support programs, with land as perhaps the main alternative to children. Without substantial initial wealth, however, land purchases require a working long-term capital market. Children, on the other hand, require relatively low "down payments," and their full cost to parents is automatically and conveniently spread over a period of ten to fifteen years. Further,

[18] Although I am convinced that there are consumption benefits to having and rearing children even in developing nations, I will ignore them in this discussion.

in the relatively unsettled political climate of some developing countries, children represent an asset with a fairly low probability of confiscation, and, especially within the framework of an extended family, a fairly high probability of yielding returns.

But what of the negative rate of return to children that Stephen Enke (1960) and others claim to have found? In one important sense, this point by itself is immaterial. It is quite possible that the rate of return on children could be zero or negative and that children could still represent the best capital investment *in comparison with available alternatives*. The point is a simple one, but easily overlooked: children may be good capital investments because in comparison with alternative investments they yield the *least* negative return.

The second question raised above concerns the *type* of child capital in which parents invest. In the context of the model presented earlier, the basic determinants of this decision are the relative rates of return to human capital, especially schooling, and to "raw" labor. Several factors that may affect these rates of return were mentioned subsequently (parent education, for example); two issues remain, however, one concerning the role of inputs complementary to schooling and the other the quantitative importance of the so-called quantity/quality tradeoff.

In his excellent theoretical piece on infant mortality and family size, Donald J. O'Hara (1972a) found that without some knowledge of the underlying parameters, the theoretical relationship between infant mortality and births was ambiguous:[19] the model did, however, predict unambiguously the relationship between infant mortality and the desired level of investment per child. In regimes of high infant mortality, parents will tend to spread their child-related investments over many children because of the high risk associated with investing large amounts in any one child.[20] As mortality rates fall, parents shift from numbers-intensive portfolios to more investment-intensive portfolios.

Mortality levels depend partly on community factors and partly on such factors as hygiene and nutrition, over which parents have some

[19] That is, economic theory alone does not predict whether a decrease in infant mortality will increase or decrease birth rates.

[20] This risk factor and the fact that children come in discrete quantities could be responsible for the relatively high desired family sizes in less developed countries. Say that a couple wants to be 90 percent sure of having an economically successful *son*: if the probability of success for each son were in the range of 0.7, which does not seem unreasonable, two sons would be required to achieve the 0.9 probability of the successful son. This implies a mean number of living children on the order of four, and four living children per couple represents a rapidly expanding population.

control (see chapters 7 and 8 for detailed discussions of this point). O'Hara's work suggests a strong positive relationship between these investments in children's health and, later, school investments; it also suggests that parents may resist shifting their child-capital portfolio into schooling unless the requisite early investments in health have been made either privately or publicly. The returns on policies that recognize this complementarity may be considerably higher than returns on policies that concentrate action in one area or the other.

POLICY OPTIONS AND POTENTIAL EFFECTS. Let us assume that children are considered by parents as having good capital or asset characteristics. Given this assumption, the case for policy intervention to influence investments per child seems strong. Such policies take advantage of the superiority of children as investment goods; introducing new investment opportunities, on the other hand, might entail a considerable lag between government action and behavioral response during which couples would have to learn about the advantages and risks of the new options. With investments in children, policy makers face only the problem of how to influence the type of child parents want.

Policies related to public education and health services are an obvious source of influence. The unanswered questions concerning them are whether such policies, as they would probably have to be instituted in developing nations, might not be pronatalist rather than antinatalist, and whether these policies can be expected to have much quantitative effect on fertility levels.[21]

The potential for pronatal effects of public education results from the implicit income effect of these policies and the possibility for parents to increase their consumption of child services in relation to their current standard of living.[22] If desired numbers of children are affected only slightly by pure changes in income as scattered evidence seems to indicate (DaVanzo 1972, De Tray 1973, forthcoming; Michael 1971), then

[21] An *unrestricted* subsidy *could* be antinatalist because of the assumption that parents consume child services directly and numbers of children and investments in children only indirectly. Thus, if the demand by parents for child services were sufficiently unresponsive (inelastic) to changes in the price of child services, parents could end up having fewer children, investing more schooling in each child, and "producing" child services at relatively unchanged levels.

[22] Were it feasible to finance these investments through taxation, any positive income effects associated with these policies would be much reduced. However, this seems an unlikely source of funding in most of the less developed countries, especially from the income levels at which we are most interested in influencing fertility.

a policy that reduces the price of investing in children can induce parents to have fewer births and invest more in each child. Technically, this will occur if the substitution effect of a reduction in the price of child investments outweighs the concomitant income effect.[23]

Empirical work appropriate for calculating the net effect on fertility of an educational subsidy is not, to my knowledge, now available. There is, however, some indication of the degree to which parents appear to trade child schooling for numbers of children. In a forthcoming paper I estimate by means of U.S. household data the rate at which parents give up numbers of children for another year of schooling per child.[24] The results offer strong support for the tradeoff hypothesis, although the magnitudes themselves are not believable.[25] Holding constant income, parent wage rates, and schooling levels, and certain occupational information about the father, a 10 percent increase in average level of schooling per child is associated with a 30 percent decrease in family size. These results were highly significant statistically.

There was no obvious way in my data (the National Longitudinal Survey for men between the ages of forty-five and fifty-nine) to determine whether this tradeoff resulted from the relative price structure faced by couples in the sample, or whether it was a reflection of taste differences. The important point in the context of this volume, however, is that the quantity/quality tradeoff hypothesis passed its first direct test, and it did so in a manner that suggests that policies aimed at influencing levels of child schooling may have a quantitatively important secondary effect on population growth rates. The speculative nature of these results quite clearly underlines both the need for and the direction of future research to improve our assessment of the fertility-reducing potential of child schooling policies.

Research Guidelines

In designing an experiment to test and measure the effect of education on family size, it is important to keep certain basic considerations in mind. At the risk of oversimplifying, one could argue that plans attempt-

[23] There is a third dimension of the problem—the substitution that may take place between a couple's consumption of child services and their consumption of "standard of living," a factor that would work to increase family size. The final outcome of these forces is an empirical question of some complexity.

[24] The methodology for estimating these effects is complex because of the endogeneity of numbers of and investment in children, family income, and wife's wage.

[25] It appears likely that multicollinearity biased the estimated tradeoff coefficients, and possibly the t ratios, upward.

ing to influence the demand of couples for children must generally fall into one (or more) of the following types:

- Attempts to influence a couple's taste for children (a propaganda campaign)
- Policies that make children more expensive to produce (a poll tax or bonus scheme)
- Subsidization of close substitutes for the services that children supply to parents (farm implements or old-age security)
- Reduction of the uncertainty that accompanies demographic transition (insuring the survival of children).

I would, in general, advocate experiments that fall *directly* into one of these categories. Education-related experiments will tend to influence parents through more than one of these avenues and may have important side effects, both positive and negative. For these reasons, it may be difficult to assess the value of educational policies as they affect overall economic development.[26]

For the sake of argument I will assume that the use of education to influence population is a politically appealing policy option in most of the developing countries. I have argued above that, because of the lags and the costs involved, tests of the relationship between parent education and family size are probably best carried out directly on the individual avenues through which adult education is thought to affect fertility.[27] Because of this I will concentrate here on research proposals that would attempt to test the strength of the negative influence of child education on desired family size.

To design an effective experiment on the relationship between child education and fertility we must first have some notion as to why parents

[26] As an aside, I would hazard the guess that one of the potentially most fruitful and least costly ways of influencing fertility is through policies that fall into the fourth category listed above. While parents are likely both to be risk-averse and to consider too few children a far more costly mistake than too many children, governments will tend to view the situation neutrally and symmetrically. In a regime of rapidly declining mortality, the actuarial cost of insuring couples against having fewer than two surviving children should not be especially large. An alternative scheme is suggested by some of the work of Ethel Shanas et al. (1968) on old-age security in the United States. The Shanas study indicates that at least in the United States children most often help aged parents in time of transitory (unexpected) financial crisis. If this motive for having children is also at work in the less developed countries, governments—and social science researchers—may want to consider establishing some form of insurance against catastrophes as a substitute for insurance supplied to parents by their children.

[27] Obvious examples are experiments that change market wage rates, especially of women, and experiments that alter the supply of contraceptive techniques and contraceptive knowledge.

have many children and invest relatively little in each child rather than the other way around. Obvious possibilities are that parents are ignorant of the rate of return on investments in their children, that parents would like to invest more schooling in their children, but cannot because of constraints on the supply of schooling, and finally, that given prices, income, and an uncertain future, having many poorly educated children is, in fact, a sensible, well-informed investment decision.

The major analytical issue is to determine whether an *unconstrained* subsidy to the schooling that parents give their children would cause a net reduction in the demand for numbers of children. One might, for example, consider ways of either increasing the accessibility of schools to rural parents or of otherwise subsidizing investments in children. These would be unconditional subsidies aimed at measuring the net (income and substitution) effect of reducing the price of child schooling.

The basic plan could be very simple—for example, building a new or expanding an existing school facility where schooling is supply-constrained. Or, the Finnigan and Sun (1972) educational incentives project could be modified so that each newly married couple receives a certificate worth a certain number of years of child schooling beyond some socially determined minimum level of schooling. Parents could spend these certificates as they wished—all on one child or one year on each of *n* children. Schooling beyond the child years allocated to each family would presumably be supplied to parents at cost. Problems that might arise under this scheme are that it could be pronatalist for couples who desired very few children initially and that it would require a coordinated increase in the local supply of schooling, so that parents would believe in the value of the coupons. If parents are investing optimal amounts in their children (schooling is not supply-constrained), then a different form of subsidy may be required (free or subsidized meals while at school, for example).

In the simplest case of increasing the supply of schooling, problems of experimental design would be mainly operational and not conceptual. Determining what couples would have done had there been no experiment will be one of the major problems. Even if two similar villages could be isolated, one as a control and one in which to carry out the experiment, the effect of subsidizing schooling on the timing of children must still be resolved. If it could be determined that there were no major incentives in the program for parents to alter the timing of their children, then a year-by-year comparison of age-specific births between the experimental village and the control village could indicate in a relatively short period of time whether increased schooling would ultimately reduce completed family size.

Conclusions

In this chapter I have outlined a microeconomic model of population growth and have tried to consider, in a heuristic fashion, what this perspective on family behavior says about the relationship between education and fertility. The evidence I cite is generally incomplete, so that any conclusions drawn are highly tentative; with this caveat, I will venture the following recommendations:

- The policy return on fertility-related research is unlikely to be anywhere higher than on research on the relationship between both parent and child education and family size. The *potential* of education as a policy instrument to influence family size is great, but our ignorance of the mechanisms through which education may affect fertility is also great.
- Based on a priori considerations and some empirical findings, adult education policies may not be the most promising venture into which scarce public funds should be channeled. Costs will be high, and lags between policy action and fertility reduction may be long. Policies that more directly influence a wife's wages, a couple's contraceptive behavior, and the early health and nutrition of children may be a more effective and quicker means of reducing family size.
- The choice that parents appear to make between the number of children they want and the investments they make in each child may be the key to middle- and long-term population policy in developing nations. The evidence is tentative, but it suggests that this tradeoff may be quantitatively important and may be easily affected by public policy.

Finally, there is the issue of feasibility. A policy maker reading this chapter might well throw up his hands in despair since, of course, developing nations would like to increase the amount of schooling and health investments that reach children for reasons entirely independent of population growth and family size. But such policies are simply too expensive to be realistic possibilities nationally. This is a real and pressing problem, and it serves to underline the following point: when public resources are very scarce, it is imperative that policy makers have access to objective assessments of the relative returns on various policy options. In most cases, these assessments do not now exist, and only continued research can supply them.

7.

The Effects of Nutrition and Health on Fertility: Hypotheses, Evidence, and Interventions

WILLIAM P. BUTZ AND JEAN-PIERRE HABICHT

The health and nutritional status of a population generally improves and fertility rates fall during the process of socioeconomic development. Similarly, the nations of the world exhibit in cross section a strong negative association between health and nutrition, on the one hand, and fertility on the other.[1] Clearly, these three are part of the interrelated processes of household and societal changes that occur during socioeconomic development. In this chapter we shall look at the evidence to determine to what extent relations among them are directly or indirectly causal, so that alterations in nutrition or health or the factors that influence them might be expected to alter fertility in a predictable direction.

We first examine the presumed *biological effects* of health and nutrition on fecundity and fertility. We also examine *factors influencing individual and family decisions* about nutrition and health which in turn affect fecundity and fertility. This information is then integrated into a simple model to predict changes in fertility that result from changes in nutrition and health and to illustrate some statistical pitfalls in research. We then consider the implications of the available evidence for choosing among modes of delivering health, nutrition, and family-planning services and suggest research questions whose illumination would help governments to choose among alternative interventions.

The authors would like to acknowledge the helpful comments of Julie DaVanzo, Dennis N. De Tray, James J. Heckman, Ronald G. Ridker, Carl E. Taylor, and Charles Teller on an earlier version of this paper.

[1] We define fertility in this chapter as the bearing of children. This demographer's usage differs from the medical definition as the capacity of a woman to have children. The latter we call fecundity.

Review of the Evidence Concerning the Effects of Nutrition and Health Factors on Fertility

Nutrition and health may affect fertility directly through biological mechanisms in potential mothers or through behavioral linkages at the individual and family levels. Indirect linkages may also exist that have the effect of relating seemingly independent maternal characteristics or facets of behavior to fertility.

Biological Effects

Health and nutrition can affect a woman's fecundity by influencing the ages of menarche, menopause, and death, the success of each pregnancy, the duration of postpartum sterility, and her fecundity during the menstrual cycle.[2] There is no direct evidence at a population level that health or nutrition affects coital frequency or male fertility.

At the population level, maternal morbidity appears not to be a significant influence on fecundity.[3] Nevertheless, there are historical instances of disease that appear to have lowered fecundity.[4] A difficulty in

[2] In reviewing the biological evidence we concentrate on the association between nutrition and health and fertility, rather than on a discussion of the possible biological mechanisms underlying these associations. In addition, the effects of infant and child mortality on fertility and the causes of mortality are covered in chapter 8 and are only considered here insofar as they influence nutritional status and health. Furthermore, except where it is essential to do so, we do not discuss specific components of health and nutritional inputs and status or the way they are measured.

Finally, we are concerned with fertility as a dependent variable, not with its effects on health and nutrition outcomes. Joe D. Wray (1971a) affords the best survey of evidence on the effects of family size and spacing on children's mortality, morbidity, and physical and mental development. Wray (1975) indicates the possible effects of nutrition in these relationships in decreasing fertility. Samuel M. Wishik and Susan Van der Vynckt (1973, pp. 9–19), review the evidence concerning effects of birth spacing and family size on maternal and child nutritional status. Many studies reviewed in the three papers indicate substantial effects, but the relative importance of birth spacing, total number of pregnancies or births, and number of living children is rarely sorted out. Further, many of the statistical associations are laid to the presumption that a family with more children has less income (or food) per child than a similar family in the same community but with fewer children. This presumption ignores the productive value of children and the exclusion of that value from most statistics on family income in less developed countries.

[3] Dugald Baird (1965, pp. 357–361) reviews the literature to that time concerning health status effects on fecundity.

[4] R. H. Gray (1974) discusses possible effects of Ceylon's eradication of malaria on fertility. Peter Pirie (1972) discusses the relationship between disease and fecundity on some Pacific islands.

interpreting those results, however, lies in an inability to separate changes in fecundity from changes in fertility. In times of stress caused by widespread disease, fertility might fall because of economic or social factors quite apart from changes in the population's fecundity.[5]

On the nutrition side, substantial evidence from animal and human clinical studies, as well as from time trends in human populations, points to earlier menarche (Frisch 1974) and later menopause in females from better-nourished populations compared with those from malnourished populations. In acute severe malnutrition the menstrual cycle is suspended.[6] However, a more important amenorrhea is that occurring after pregnancy when ovulation is suspended for a period ranging from weeks to more than a year.[7] Postpartum amenorrhea can be lengthened for many months by lactation.[8] Better nutrition and health may also increase postpartum fertility, since better-nourished mothers appear to be slightly more fecund after menstruation begins again (Said, Johansson, and Gemzell 1974, Habicht and Delgado 1973). However, better maternal

[5] Maternal health status can, however, affect the mother's response to pregnancy, the outcome of pregnancy, and the development of the infant. See Earl Siegel and Naomi Morris (1970) and Wishik and Van der Vynckt (1973, pp. 7–9).

[6] In addition, Alan Berg (1973, pp. 38–39) and Wishik and Van der Vynckt (1973, p. 37) note the effects of nutritional anemias in some populations on IUD-retention rates and the potential role of nutritional supplements in supplying the additional vitamin A requirements of women taking oral contraceptives. The extent of contraceptive efficiency that might be gained through better nutrition is unknown, but it is likely that it is small in comparison to the effects on the use of contraceptives of alternative interventions discussed in this conference.

[7] See, for example, John B. Wyon and John E. Gordon (1971), R. G. Potter et al. (1965), Alfredo Perez et al. (1971, 1972), Anrudh K. Jain et al. (1970), Habicht and Behar (1974), and E. J. Salber, Manning Feinleib, and Brian MacMahon (1966).

[8] Over a range of lactation from several weeks to two years, three to five weeks of amenorrhea appear to result, on the average, from every two months of lactation. This relationship cannot be counted as reliable in individual cases, both because the variance of the estimated coefficient is large and also because a woman's first menstruation after a birth frequently follows ovulation: she can be fertile before she knows it. Nevertheless, in the aggregate, lactation appears to be a reasonably effective contraceptive for a year or so after birth. Beyond that time, its effectiveness diminishes rapidly. The biochemical mechanism responsible for this relationship is not known, but Habicht and Behar (1974) offer a hypothesis. Others [Jain et al. (1970), Perez et al. (1972), and Habicht and Behar (1974)] provide regression estimates of the effects of lactation on amenorrhea. Jain et al. and Perez et al. correct for age and parity. Still others (Salber, Feldman, and Hannigan 1968) report significant mother-specific components of amenorrhea from birth to birth, independent of the length of the period of lactation.

nutrition also extends the period of lactation, other things being equal, and does so to such a degree that the duration of postpartum infecundity may in fact be extended rather than shortened by improving maternal nutrition (Habicht and Behar 1974).

Nutrition during lactation, however, is a negligible factor in the fall of fertility rates in developing countries, because breast-feeding, and therefore periods of postpartum infecundity, decreases rapidly with socio-economic development. In fact, in early stages of development, the rapid declines in breast-feeding that have occurred in many societies may have resulted in higher fertility.[9] These declines have in some cases undoubtedly contributed to infant and child mortality and reduced physical (and perhaps mental) development as well.

Finally, it is often hypothesized that malnutrition decreases the probability of a successful pregnancy by increasing the chances of early or late abortion. There is as yet no direct evidence in human beings of such a relationship.

The above evidence indicates that the reproductive function is well protected from nutritional insults and poor health. Hence, though fecundity generally increases with betterment of nutrition and health from dangerously low levels, the movement from moderate malnutrition and chronic morbidity to adequate nutritional and health levels is nearly always accompanied, or followed, by decreasing fertility.

Behavioral Effects

Since the biological links that are reasonably well substantiated generally point to a *positive* relationship between maternal health and nutrition and fertility, it is to behavioral factors that we must look to understand the *negative* relationship that is, in fact, observed. Certain of the biological relationships mentioned above can be presumed to be strongly influenced by behavioral factors. However, there is virtually no direct empirical evidence about these behavioral links.

Looking at the biological influences on intervals between births, we have concluded that maternal health and nutrition have little influence at the usual levels found in most populations. Lactation does affect the renewed onset of ovulation, however, and lactation will presumably be affected by the degree of a mother's desire and opportunities to be doing something else, or in economic terms, by the opportunity cost of her

[9] To the extent that other contraceptive practices were substituted for lactation, fertility will not have increased. Alan Berg (1973, pp. 230–232) documents the recent decline in breast-feeding in Singapore and the Philippines. For most parts of the world, information comes mainly from anthropological observation.

time spent in breast-feeding.[10] There are no estimates of the effect of this opportunity cost of time on breast-feeding behavior; there are several clues, however. Sara B. Nerlove (1974) finds in a cross-sectional study of primitive cultures that the time between birth and the introduction of supplementary infant food has significant negative correlation with the participation of women in subsistence activities contributing to the food supply. This is an important clue but an indirect one, since no adjustment was possible for other economic and sociological variables probably correlated with work participation, occupation, and breast-feeding. Anrudh K. Jain (1968) and his associates (Jain et al. 1970) report estimates of the direct association between level of education and length of the lactation period and the association between these two variables and postpartum amenorrhea. In their sample of married Taiwanese women they find, after adjustment for age and parity differences, that more highly schooled women lactate less. In addition, size of community of residence is negatively associated with length of the lactation period in gross and partial regression analyses. The partial regression coefficients for the sample of all women are -0.204 for education and -0.167 for residence.

Although level of schooling and size of place of residence bear an uncertain relationship with opportunity cost of time in this sample, they are probably correlated positively. There is generally a larger supply of jobs outside the home in the labor markets in larger communities, and there is reason to think that the wages paid to educated workers in these jobs exceed the value of their marginal product in work at home. However, education and size of place of residence are generally correlated with many things other than the opportunity cost of a person's time—components of modernity, for example. The problems of isolating the causal effects of education conceptually and empirically are not so difficult here as in recent analyses of these effects on fertility, but the problems are nevertheless substantial.[11]

The sparse evidence is thus consistent with the presumption of a negative relationship between lactation and the opportunity cost of the mother's time, but it fails to discriminate at all between this relationship and a host of associated possibilities. Since breast-feeding in this connection is a use of time, however, evidence concerning relationships between

[10] This cost may include both economic and social components. The opportunity cost of time may be high because jobs are available that cannot easily be performed with an accompanying child or because enjoyable social activities are available with the same characteristic. In general, more jobs than social activities are probably incompatible with child care in the less developed countries.

[11] See chapters 5 and 6 of this volume.

cost of time and other kinds of time use is pertinent. There is no doubt that, in many developing countries, higher wages paid for work outside the home induce higher rates of participation in those jobs and fewer hours spent at home by women.[12] On the average, higher wages should therefore induce less time spent in many particular home activities, since the total amount of time at home is reduced. Unless the income elasticity of derived demand for breast-feeding and the share of women's earnings in family income are large, a reduction of breast-feeding time in response to offers of higher wages outside the home is implied by this evidence on labor-force participation and hours of work. More direct evidence is lacking.

Just as a mother must decide whether to breast-feed or engage in another activity, she may also decide between lactation as a means of postponing the next pregnancy and other methods of family planning. It is known that mothers in many low-income cultures are aware, in general terms, of the contraceptive function of lactation.[13] To the extent that they breast-feed in order to delay their next pregnancies, it is reasonable to expect them to substitute cheaper or more effective goods or services for their own time when such substitutes become available. The extent to which they do so is not known.

Similarly, mothers may decide between breast milk and other foods on the basis of their value to their children's health and development. The mother's decision to substitute other infant foods for her milk may depend on the cost of the substitute foods in relation to the cost of her time (Habicht, Delgado et al. 1973). The decision may also depend on the quality of the alternative food and upon the parent's evaluation of the importance of the child's health.

Most parents everywhere value the health of their children for non-economic reasons, but it is reasonable to expect parents to devote more time and money to good nutrition and health care for their children in settings where such care is also expected to pay off economically—because healthier children do better in school and therefore earn more, or because high-paying jobs exist that require persons with strength or good mental development. Understanding the role of economic returns on investments in health and nutrition is important, not because these returns are more important quantitatively than noneconomic values (they probably are not) or necessarily because economic returns con-

[12] See chapter 10.

[13] For example, Habicht and Robert Klein (1972) report that more than three-quarters of the mothers in four traditional rural Guatemalan villages believe that lactation postpones a new conception. In the absence of modern contraceptive devices, lactation is probably the main child-spacing mechanism.

tribute to national income and economic growth. The reason is rather that many of the important determinants of the *economic* returns on health and nutrition can be affected by public policies aimed at increasing the incentives for care of health and nutrition and removing the stumbling blocks to popular participation in supply-oriented public programs. Alternatively, there is little theoretical or empirical guidance available concerning the way in which the level of parents' *affective* valuation of child health, or of any other child quality, can be systematically influenced by public policy.

Although we have no direct evidence concerning the nature of parental *responses* to changes in the value of investments in health and nutrition, there are scattered indications that the economic returns on these investments can be large. In an important paper, Marcelo Selowsky and Lance Taylor (1973) used two sets of data from Chile and one from the United States to estimate the effect of investment in childhood nutrition on adult earnings. Using weight (at different ages) of Chilean children as proxies for nutritional status, Selowsky and Taylor related this to the children's IQ. They then estimated the effect of adult IQs on earnings in a sample of Chilean workers and unemployed persons and predicted the IQs of adults from their IQs as children.[14] Their results suggest that an increase of 10 percent in a child's weight generates an increase in measured child IQ of 5 to 6.5 points and that this effect remains when a rather comprehensive index of socioeconomic status is included in the regression. Further, a change of 10 percent in measured adult IQ is associated with a 6 to 7 percent increase in earnings.

In spite of the inclusion of a socioeconomic status index in the regressions, it is possible, as Selowsky and Taylor recognize, that the estimated associations may be due to some underlying common factor that influences nutrition and IQ test results separately. If this is the case, changes in nutrition alone may have no effect on IQ test results. However, this is the only study we know of to attempt to link child health or nutritional status all the way to adult earnings. A number of other researchers have investigated the strength of particular links in this chain, though rarely with close attention to probable biases introduced by the nature of their data and statistical methods. Many of these studies also suffer from not correcting for nonnutritional or nonhealth differences that are probably systematically related to both nutrition and health inputs and to the output measures of interest. To attempt a summary of this diverse litera-

[14] The relationship between child and adult IQs was estimated from a U.S. sample. On the basis of an assumption about the effect of milk consumption on birth weight, Selowsky and Taylor then computed the rate of return on a milk supplementation program.

ture, we can say that chronic mild to moderate malnutrition in infancy and childhood can stunt physical growth (Habicht et al. 1974), and small stature of women appears associated with low birth weight of their children (Habicht, Yarbrough et al. 1973); hence, malnutrition can have intergenerational effects. Severe malnutrition in infancy and childhood has more severe physical and morbidity effects and also harms mental development, which seems usually to escape permanent damage from mild to moderate malnutrition (Scrimshaw and Gordon 1968, Latham and Cobos 1971). The effect of malnutrition and illness of children on their subsequent adult absenteeism, agricultural productivity and earnings is not known (Oelhaf 1971, pp. 10–14; Weisbrod et al. 1973). Even the association of adult moderate malnutrition and illness with indexes of adult work performance is unstable from study to study.[15]

Finally, there is the possibility that many parents see the number of children they have and the health and development status of their children as substitutes for one another in yielding that which they value about children. We know nothing about the empirical strength of this tradeoff. It is known, however, that parents in many cultures act as if years of schooling per child and number of children were substitutes (see chapter 6). Good health, nutrition, and development are, like schooling, components of the "quality" of children. The presumption is that parents also trade these more difficult-to-measure attributes against numbers of children. If so, and if the tradeoff is substantial, public programs aimed at increasing the supply of inputs to health and nutrition could have considerable effectiveness in reducing fertility, as parents learn that their children live longer and are stronger, healthier, and perhaps more intelligent.

Research designed to estimate the magnitude of behavioral responses discussed in this section should take account of the existence of customs and social norms. The rapidity with which people change their behavioral patterns with respect to food and health depends on the strength of these norms as well as upon the amount of personal benefit or absence of loss that they stand to experience by changing. Indeed, in several

[15] See James C. Knowles (1969) and D. H. Griffith, D. V. Ramana, and H. Mashaal (1971). Several studies have utilized cross-national aggregate data to evaluate the contribution of health to national income and economic growth. These studies suffer from the usual debilitating inadequacies of aggregate national data of these types from less developed countries. For example, see Walter Galenson and Graham Pyatt (1964), Wilfred Malenbaum (1970), Irma Adelman and Cynthia Taft Morris (1968), and Hector Correa and Gaylord Cummins (1970).

studies, norms appear to exert independent influence on fertility behavior after personal and family characteristics are accounted for.[16] As such, their nature and strength should be taken into account by investigators researching the lags that characterize behavioral adjustments to disequilibria.

In the course of time, however, norms are surely not independent of the factors that created the disequilibria. As adjustment occurs and families approach a different pattern of behavior related to food and health, the regularities that characterize their new behavior will again begin to take on a social life of their own in the form of new traditions and norms. If conditions continually change, new norms may not have a chance to form, unless they concern the process of adjustment to change itself. But where they do form, they are a result of objective factors in families' environments, even as they modify personal responses to changes in that environment. Hence the inclusion of community averages as proxies for norms in path or regression analysis may produce underestimates of the long-run effects of particular environmental changes on health, nutrition, or fertility behavior. However, in studying short-run effects—that is, the dynamics of adjustment—consideration of norms may be an important way of identifying lag structures.

A Simple Integrated Model of Household Interactions Among Nutrition, Health, and Intervals Between Births

In this section, we develop a model that includes the causal links indicated by the available evidence summarized in the previous section as most important.[17] This exercise has the purposes of integrating this evidence and of illustrating the problems that arise from clinical or statistical research that neglects consideration of multivariate influences and jointly determined variables. The model is focused on determinants of closed intervals between births, having nothing to say directly about the age at onset of coitus or the total length of a woman's fecund period. Hence, we do not discuss here influences on the timing of the first birth or on completed family size. Alternative methods exist for measuring the variables in the model; some of these alternatives are discussed briefly at a later point. The basic symbols used are as follows: *C*, price of al-

[16] Deborah Freedman (1963) found this phenomenon in a U.S. sample, and Richard Bruce Anker (1973) demonstrates it quite convincingly in rural India.

[17] J. E. Austin and F. J. Levinson (1974) propose a conceptualization of relationships between nutrition and fertility that includes some of the links discussed below as well as several others.

ternative contraceptive methods; H, health and development status of children; I, interval between births; L, length of lactation period; M, amount of health and medical care received; N_1, current and past nutritional intake of the mother; N_2, infant's nutritional intake from foods other than breast milk; F, length of time after birth before mother's next ovulation—that is, before she becomes fecund again; T, cost of time spent in child care; V, value of a healthy surviving child.

Let us assume, in equation 7-1, that within a maternal age-parity group the length of the current interval between births depends positively on the length of time between the previous birth and first subsequent ovulation: the longer the infertile period, the longer the interval, other

$$I = \delta(F, T, C, V, H) \tag{7-1}$$

things being equal. In addition, the higher the opportunity cost of the mother's time spent in child care, the more expensive to her is another child; hence, higher opportunity cost of the mother's time induces a longer interval between births, other things being equal.[18] A high price of contraceptive methods and materials induces less use and therefore a shorter interval.[19] And if the value of a surviving child is high, parents will have a child more quickly, other things being equal. In addition, if parents consider child health a substitute for numbers of children, the interval may also depend positively on the baby's health: other things being equal, a decision to invest more in the health of the child may imply a decision to invest less in additional children by delaying or omitting the next birth.[20]

[18] The assumption of a positive partial relation between the wife's opportunity cost of time and birth spacing in this model assumes that the income effect of the wife's earnings on desired birth spacing is relatively unimportant compared with the substitution effect. It also ignores the role of differential availability of substitutes for the mother's time—older children, other relatives, industrial child-care facilities—in conditioning the fertility effect of a change in the mother's opportunity cost. Further, it omits consideration of possible economies of scale in child care. If another baby means little additional work to the mother of a two-year-old, the mother may have the second baby in the presence of an opportunity outside the home that would otherwise induce her to delay. Empirical analyses of birth spacing should account for these additional effects. The last two, concerning availability of child-care substitutes and scale economics in child rearing, would become central in a dynamic model of birth spacing.

[19] The concept of "price" includes such factors as inaccessibility, inconvenience, and ineffectiveness. A contraceptive method obtainable no closer than 10 miles that produces inconvenient and unreliable protection has a high price in this framework. The prices of other goods and services in this model are defined in similarly broad terms.

[20] The conditions for such a tradeoff in a model of parental decisions about the quality and quantity of their children are discussed in chapter 6.

The sign of these hypothesized causal dependencies can be simply indicated by partial derivatives. For example, the partial derivative of length of interval between births with respect to length of postpartum infecundity, $\frac{\partial I}{\partial F} \equiv \delta_F > 0$. Similarly, $\delta_T > 0$, $\delta_C < 0$, $\delta_V < 0$, and $\delta_H > 0$.

The baby's health and development status, H, depends, in equation 7-2, upon how long it is breast-fed, L; how much nutritional intake it receives from other sources, N_2; the value of a healthy surviving child, V (the higher the value, the more parents will decide to invest in their child's health); and the amount of health and medical care it receives, M.

(7-2) $$H = \beta(L, N_2, V, M)$$

where $\beta_L > 0$, $\beta_{N_2} > 0$, $\beta_V > 0$, and $\beta_M > 0$.

In addition, the length of time a mother lactates during the current interval, L, depends, in equation 7-3, on her current and past nutritional intake, N_1; her baby's nutritional intake from other foods than breast milk, N_2; the opportunity cost of her time spent in child care, T; the value to the couple of a healthy surviving child, V; and the price of alternative contraceptive methods, C.[21]

(7-3) $$L = \alpha(N_1, N_2, T, V, C)$$

The partial effect of the mother's nutritional intake on the length of her period of lactation, $\frac{\partial L}{\partial N_1} \equiv \alpha_{N_1}$, is expected to be positive. On the other hand, the amount of other food the baby eats substitutes for mother's milk, so that $\alpha_{N_2} < 0$. The higher the opportunity cost of the mother's time in child care, that is, the more she values her time spent in other ways, the less time she chooses to breast-feed, so that $\alpha_T < 0$. The partial effect of the value of a healthy surviving child on the parents' desired length of the period of breast-feeding is positive, $\alpha_V > 0$, since the higher the value the greater is their incentive to contribute to the child's health. Other things being equal, a couple having inexpensive access to alternative effective methods of contraception will choose a shorter lactation period, $\alpha_C > 0$.[22]

[21] In a fuller treatment, a variable indicating the death of a nursing child would be included as a determinant of lactation. However, this variable is treated in chapter 8.

[22] Lactation is a physiological process while breast-feeding is a behavioral phenomenon. While it is possible for a woman to continue lactating without feeding the milk to her child, in our example we may consider lengths of the periods of lactation and breast-feeding to be equivalent.

Finally, the length of time after the baby's birth before the mother has her first ovulation and becomes fertile again, F, depends positively, in equation 7-4, on the length of time she breast-feeds, L, and negatively on her current and past nutritional intake, N_1.

(7-4) $$F = \gamma(L, N_1)$$

where $\gamma_L > 0$, and $\gamma_{N_1} < 0$, since better nutrition speeds the return of ovulation, holding length of breast-feeding constant.

These four equations constitute a simple model of biological and behavioral influences on intervals between births.

By differentiating the equations totally and substituting the expressions for left-hand-side variables into the right-hand sides of other equations, a set of expressions relating changes in each of the model's left-hand-side variables *dL, dH, dF,* and *dI,* to changes in the other variables results. For our purposes, the equations explaining changes in length of postpartum sterility, lactation, and child's health are of less interest than the one characterizing changes in length of the interval between births:

(7-5) $$\begin{aligned} dI = {} & (\delta_F\gamma_L\alpha_{N_1} + \delta_F\gamma_{N_1} + \delta_H\beta_L\alpha_{N_1})\, dN_1 \\ & + (\delta_H\beta_{N_2} + \delta_H\beta_L\alpha_{N_2} + \delta_F\gamma_L\alpha_{N_2})\, dN_2 \\ & + (\delta_H\beta_V + \delta_H\beta_L\alpha_V + \delta_F\gamma_L\alpha_V + \delta_V)\, dV \\ & + (\delta_F\gamma_L\alpha_C + \delta_H\beta_L\alpha_C + \delta_C)\, dC \\ & + (\delta_T + \delta_H\beta_L\alpha_T + \delta_F\gamma_L\alpha_T)\, dT \\ & + \delta_H\beta_M\, dM \end{aligned}$$

The behavioral and biological relationships specified in equations 7-1 through 7-4 are obviously extremely simplified. On the behavioral side, family wealth and income are not factors, and the opportunity cost of the mother's time is assumed to be unimportant in affecting her baby's health and development. Among the potential biological links omitted are effects of mother's health and development status on her lactation and the characteristics of the baby's environment *in utero* on its health status. However, even in this simple specification only one variable, medical and health care (*dM* in the last line of the equation), has an unambiguous effect on the interval between births in equation 7-5—the derivative is positive. The effects of changes in all other variables are ambiguous, a priori, depending on the relative magnitude of direct and indirect effects throughout the system. As an example, from the second line of equation 7-5, consider the effect of an increase in the baby's nutritional intake from sources other than breast milk:

$$\frac{dI}{dN_2} = \delta_H(\beta_{N_2} + \beta_L\alpha_{N_2}) + \delta_F\gamma_L\alpha_{N_2} \tag{7-6}$$

The first term on the right side of the equation, δ_H, reflects the tendency of the couple to want fewer children and longer intervals between them if their existing baby is healthier. Whether the baby is healthier or not as a result of the feeding change is uncertain, however. On the one hand, β_{N_2} is positive, representing the healthful effect of additional nutrients in the baby's diet, other things being held constant. On the other hand, $\beta_L\alpha_{N_2}$ is negative, reflecting the diminution of health that results from the lessened breast-feeding that accompanies increased volume elsewhere in the baby's diet. The last term, $\delta_F\gamma_L\alpha_{N_2}$, represents the shortened interval between births induced by reduced lactation as the baby substitutes other food for mother's milk.

Considering all factors together, the interval between births is shortened because of supplemental feeding if the supplement has little or negative value in promoting the baby's health and development, as might be the case with water or contaminated animal milk. For in this case, β_{N_2} is small, zero, or negative, reflecting the supplement's low value, but α_{N_2} within the parentheses remains at nearly the same level regardless of the nutritional and hygienic quality of the supplement, since the substitution of other food for breast milk depends mainly on the quantity of other food rather than its quality. Hence with small β_{N_2}, the entire first term is negative. Since this substitution effect embodied in α_{N_2} also shortens the period of sterility and thereby shortens the interval between births, as represented in the last term on the right side of equation 7-6, the smaller the health- and development-producing effect of the supplement in relation to its effect in shortening the period of lactation, the more reduction is expected in the interval between births in response to supplementary feeding. On the contrary, of course, a hygienic and highly nutritious supplement may lengthen the interval if it increases child health and development sufficiently (β_{N_2}), and if parents are satisfied in this situation to have fewer children, and thereby delay (or omit entirely) their next pregnancy (δ_H).

To carry this example a bit further, the relative importance of the terms in equation 7-6 also depends on the child's age when the supplement is begun. After four to six months of age, β_L declines if there are any other foods with protein and caloric content in the diet. After twelve months or so, the child's nutritional requirements have outgrown the ingredients of mother's milk sufficiently so that β_L may be quite small indeed, with β_{N_2} having grown correspondingly. At the same time, γ_L decreases as the marginal capacity of lactation to delay ovulation declines after eighteen to twenty-four months of lactation. Hence, as the child grows older, failure to feed it food other than breast milk may induce shorter intervals between births as parents rush to have another child to supplement (or possibly replace) their sickly baby even as the sterility effects of lactation come to an end.

Consideration of the effects of another variable in equation 7-5 will lay sufficient groundwork for our later discussion of the difficulties of measuring the variables. The effect of an increase in the opportunity cost of the mother's time in child care, T, on the interval between births is also ambiguous a priori. From the fifth line of equation 7-5,

$$\frac{dI}{dT} = \delta_T + \delta_H \beta_L \alpha_T + \delta_F \gamma_L \alpha_T \tag{7-7}$$

The first term on the right side of equation 7-7, δ_T, is positive, representing the longer spacing between births that the couple is expected to choose in response to the increased price of an important input in child rearing, the mother's time. The second term on the right side, $\delta_H \beta_L \alpha_T$, is negative, since the mother's lessened lactation in response to an increased opportunity cost of her time results in a less healthy child and a consequent desire to have another child sooner. The third term on the right side, $\delta_F \gamma_L \alpha_T$, is negative, reflecting the fecundity effect of the mother's lessened lactation. In sum, therefore, an increase in opportunity cost might lengthen or shorten the interval between births. The net effect depends on the relative strength of behavioral factors and the biological effects that they induce.

The model we have considered is simple and illustrative, necessarily omitting some variables and interactions of potential significance. One such variable is family income, and the interaction is intergenerational. Equation 7-4 in our model embodies a hypothesis that parents consider child health and development to be a substitute for having another child quickly. In addition to this substitution effect, child health may also have an intergenerational influence on the spacing of births and on completed fertility by affecting the future market income and home productivity of the next generation. If early investment in a child's health and nutrition produces a stronger or more intelligent person who performs better in school and earns a higher lifetime income than he might otherwise, his higher income may induce a fertility effect. In addition, if early investments in the nutrition and health of girls increase their productivity in caring for their own children, other kinds of fertility effects may result.[23]

An Approach to Understanding Poor People's Health and Nutritional Behavior

Theodore W. Schultz (1964) has suggested that the investment behavior of persons in traditional agriculture corresponds closely to what economic theory would predict for producing units in long-run economic equilibrium. With little change for generations in available tools, seed, and other types of productive capital, traditional farmers have learned through trial and error the optimal allocation, through space and time, of human and other resources to yield maximum income. The present values of all investments are equated at zero; opportunities for producing more with the resources at hand are exhausted. The studies cited by Schultz and the econometric evidence accumulated since then constitute a convincing case for the hypothesis.

Among policy implications that Schultz drew from this hypothesis is the proposition that technical assistance concerning cropping patterns, land management, and care of animals will not succeed. Generations of experience under unchanged conditions have produced more expertise in the fields than in the colleges, at home or abroad. In addition, increasing the flow of information about where and when to buy the traditional inputs and how to use them will have no effect. It is already known. Instead, Schultz suggested, *new* inputs must be supplied. If the new inputs were profitable when used in conjunction with the farmer's existing human and physical resources, and if their profitability were demonstrated to farmers, then farmers would adopt them. The creation of disequilibria, therefore, is the key to agricultural growth.

Similarly, we suggest that the patterns of disposition and consumption of food actually observed in many rural, traditionally low-income environments may correspond closely to the pattern predicted by economic theory under the following conditions: Available jobs for children and adults require little intellectual activity, since optimal production allocations have long since become community traditions known to all; an underdeveloped capital market makes relatively attractive the buying

[23] These productivity effects are formally analogous to the home-productivity effects of education analyzed by Robert T. Michael (1973b). Discussion of the effects of income on fertility is in chapter 2, while chapters 9 and 10 deal with issues related to women's work and time use and their fertility.

and selling of animals as noncash stores of value from harvest to planting; productive requirements for physical strength are highly seasonal, peaking perhaps two or three times a year, but at a low level otherwise.

Under these conditions an optimal allocation of resources gives much food to persons having the highest value of marginal product in production, generally the men, and little to persons having the lowest marginal product, children. This procedure maximizes production and general purchasing power; in the process it may reduce the future health and development of children somewhat, but the return on these investments is small. Further, this optimal allocation of resources gives an even larger share of the available food to the most productive workers during seasonal peaks in labor requirements. This allocation is most striking when it is coupled with food scarcity before the harvest, when it causes some members of the family to go hungry. Throughout the year, some nutritious food, even corn and tomatoes, is fed to the hogs or the bullocks instead of to the children, since keeping the animals healthy assures next season's seed money, perhaps with capital gains, while keeping the children healthy brings only long-term dividends and perhaps not large ones at that.[24]

The policy implications of this approach are very different from those associated with the contending approach at the other extreme, the "backward peasant" model. In the final section of the chapter we shall outline the differences.

Implications for Programs

To this point we have examined evidence and hypotheses largely concerning linkages at the family level between health and nutrition factors, on the one hand, and fertility outcomes on the other. Perhaps equally important are issues concerning economic, institutional, and bureaucratic factors that affect the relative desirability of alternative modes of delivering health and nutrition services to families. The issue here on the supply side that has received most attention concerns program-level integration of either nutrition and family-planning services or health and family-planning services, or of all three. Such integration has been called for since World War II by influential researchers, planners, and

[24] This picture is quite consistent with parental love for children. Children need housing, clothing, and other things as well as food, and these things can be produced or purchased in greater amounts if resources, including food, are allocated so as to produce a higher family income.

international institutions.[25] We review here the arguments for such integration and the weight of scientific evidence, such as it is.

The arguments often advanced for such integration include the following:[26]

1. If modern family planning methods are the first nontraditional input introduced into the community, reluctance to try them and continue their use might be overcome by delivering at the same time health care, the results of which can be quickly seen (Taylor 1965, p. 478; Taylor and Hall 1967, p. 655; Berg 1973, pp. 35–37).
2. If the family planning methods being supplied require continuing health or nutrition services, delivery of the first without the second is inefficient.
3. Since the spacing of births can affect both maternal health and child morbidity and mortality, a family-planning component can contribute to the success of health and nutrition programs.
4. Since good child nutrition and health tend through behavioral responses to lengthen the intervals between births, nutrition and health components can contribute to the success of a family-planning program.
5. Since the primary target populations—pregnant and lactating women with young children—are the same, there are economies of scale in delivering all desired services in as few visits as possible.
6. The personnel who deliver health, nutrition, and family-planning services require similar training and attributes; there are thus economies to be realized from having the same person do more than one job.
7. There are other economies of joint production at the local or national level arising from bulk purchasing or joint administration.
8. In some situations, one program cannot be approved at the national level without justification in terms of a separate but related goal. In these cases, as perhaps when there is a Ministry of Health but none of family planning, program integration may be a solution.

The first four reasons depend on assumptions about the nature and strength of biological and behavioral interactions. If the characterization of the family discussed in the preceding section and the role of norms outlined earlier are useful conceptualizations, the first reason in this list makes sense. The crucial assumption is that parents *want* their children

[25] The World Health Organization and Pan American Health Organization are among the institutions. See Pan American Health Organization (1970).

[26] Others [Wishik (1972, pp. 5–8), Wishik, Thomson, and Habicht (1972, pp. 23–25), Austin and Levinson (1974), and the National Academy of Sciences (1975)] discuss many of these points in more detail.

spaced or want fewer children. The second reason is true in the case of the IUD and the pill. The truth of the assumption underlying the third reason has not been strongly demonstrated, in our opinion. Research has not been successful in separating effects on health of the spacing of births from the effects of total number of pregnancies and children and from the effects of other factors associated with maternal age, fertility patterns, and health. The correlations are strong, but causality is much less certain. The evidence concerning the fourth presumption is weak but suggests that it is a quantitatively important phenomenon. The fifth reason rests on an obviously true presumption, while the last three reasons are important wherever they apply. Only evidence bearing on reasons one and four is reviewed in this chapter. The evidence on these points is sparse and largely circumstantial, but it tends to support the arguments.

Nevertheless there are cases where family planning has apparently been successfully offered without nutrition and health services, just as successful cases of integrated delivery exist (Taylor and Hall 1967, pp. 655–656; but see Wishik and Van der Vynckt 1973, pp. 28, 30–32). Several large demonstration projects—one in Narangwal, Punjab, India (Oelhaf 1971, pp. 37ff.), and one in Danfa in Africa (UCLA School of Public Health 1972)—that feature treatment communities with various combinations of family-planning materials, family-planning information, and health services, have been operating for more than four years. These projects have considerable promise in sorting out the importance of the various effects hypothesized to justify joint program delivery. To achieve this goal, however, will require more attention than biomedical research has heretofore devoted to the role of *behavioral* relationships linking health, nutrition, and fertility behavior in the family. Otherwise, inferences from correlations to causality may not be possible, and the identification of particular causal factors that should be considered or replicated in other settings will be hindered.

Required Research for Selecting Intervention Points

The available evidence is insufficient in most settings for choosing among alternative interventions on grounds of cost and effectiveness. The costs of some interventions—particularly programs of public health and nutrition—have been carefully measured, but estimates of their benefits are often flawed. For most others, the order of magnitude of neither costs nor benefits is known.[27] Ranking the alternatives in terms of political

[27] However, Schlomo Reutlinger and Marcelo Selowsky (1975, pp. 27–44) developed formulas to measure the cost and effectiveness of food price sub-

feasibility is an easier job and has of course been done in countries in which particular policies were being considered (Berg 1973, pp. 241–247).

In the area of nutrition, the public and private *supply* systems that link together agricultural production, transportation, and marketing are ill understood in most of the less developed countries. Potential bottlenecks have rarely been identified.[28] For both nutrition and health, even the most basic parameters that characterize family *demand* for foods and health care and the allocation of these goods among family members have only rarely been estimated for the less developed countries. Yet it is these behavioral relationships that transform public policy changes in other areas into often unintended health and nutrition effects and that may constrain the effectiveness of many public programs.[29]

The gains from additional understanding of pertinent economic and social relationships on the supply and demand sides appear to be much greater than the gains from additional biomedical research on biological links in the system. This conclusion need be based on only one fact: the biological effects of better health and nutrition are primarily to increase fecundity and therefore fertility. Yet except in states of severe morbidity or malnutrition, higher levels of health and nutrition of a population are accompanied by lower fertility (often with a lag). Nonbiological links predominate. In spite of these clear gross relationships, it was demonstrated earlier that considerably more systematic knowledge has been accumulated concerning biological linkages than concerning behavioral ones.[30] This imbalance results partly from the fact that biological systems appear more regular and less complex than socioeconomic systems, in the light of the knowledge available at present. But it is also because

---

sidies, income transfers, and food stamp programs. Simulation of their formulas with alternative values of elasticities of demand and supply of food strongly suggests that programs oriented toward target groups are considerably more cost-effective than a general price subsidy. This important paper contains a number of other conceptual and empirical insights concerning the distribution of nutrition in less developed countries and the returns on alternative policy approaches.

[28] Work undertaken by nutritionists, economists, and operations researchers in the Applied Nutrition Division of the Institute for Nutrition of Central America and Panama (INCAP) shows promise in developing appropriate methodologies for studying supply systems in Central America.

[29] A principal conclusion of a PAHO working conference on the economics of malnutrition was that "the major unfilled data and methodological limitations are in the household system. Preferred intervention points depend heavily on knowledge of the determinants of individual behavior" Popkin (1972, p. 6).

[30] Wishik and Van der Vynckt (1973, pp. 49–50), outline needed physiological and biological research on nutrition-health linkages.

relatively little research money has gone to social scientists interested in studying health–nutrition–fertility relationships, and of that, almost nothing has gone for the study of the crucially important demand factors.

If more money *will* be spent in these areas, how should it be allocated? The following research subjects focus, in our opinion, on the crucial links in the supply and demand networks that determine the level and distribution among persons and families of stocks of nutrition and health and the effects of these stocks on fertility outcomes:

- Determinants of the earnings and agricultural productivity effects of investments in the health and nutrition of children. This basic quantitative knowledge about V, the value of a healthy surviving child, is necessary for estimating family demand for health and nutrition inputs and for studying parental tradeoffs between numbers of children and "quality" of children (equation 7-1).
- Economic and social determinants of intrafamily patterns of food distribution. These patterns are the proximate determinants of N_1 and N_2, the nutritional intake of mother and child, respectively. Descriptive data on these patterns are needed to investigate the explanatory power of the approach suggested earlier.
- Determinants of the income and price elasticities of demand for preventative and curative health care among disadvantaged groups. These elasticities are the basic parameters characterizing the demand for health care, M. Knowing their magnitude permits prediction of the effects on health care of changing prices and family income. Understanding their determinants shows intervention points at which family demand can be raised.
- Determinants of the income and price elasticities of demand for nutritious foods among disadvantaged groups.[31] Knowledge about these elasticities of demand for nutrition, N_1 and N_2, is important for the same reasons as in the case of health care, above.
- Determinants of patterns of parental substitution between numbers of children and "high-quality" children of superior health and nutritional status. This knowledge of the sign and magnitude of the coefficient of H, in equation 7-1, is important for understanding parents' fertility responses to changing incentives for health care and nutrition.

[31] The high share of expenditure going to food and relatively high income elasticities of demand for most kinds of food among poor people generally give increased income a strong effect on the amount and type of food consumed. Yet the foods subject to highest income elasticities are not necessarily the most nutritious, since food can have taste-satisfying and status-augmenting functions as well. Therefore, higher family income does not necessarily lead to better nutrition.

• Economic and social determinants of the mother's breast-feeding behavior, characterized by the child's age at the first introduction of other food and the length of the lactation period. Having estimates of the parameters of equation 7-3 will facilitate understanding of the reasons for declines in breast-feeding during socioeconomic development and may point to interventions useful in stemming this decline.

None of these subjects approaches being a complete study of the potential cost and effectiveness of particular policies in influencing fertility, or health or nutrition. In general, understanding of the particular components of the relevant systems is still rudimentary and does not justify putting the pieces together and looking for internal tendencies and inconsistencies. First, we must know more about the signs and magnitudes of particular parameters. Most of these recommended research areas also deal with household demand phenomena, and therefore more with influences on the effectiveness of public programs than with their costs. This bias comes from a presumption that ranking effectiveness is a prior task. Policy makers can then select among those environmental changes that will work, on the basis of cost considerations.

Some of these research areas could undoubtedly be illuminated with existing nutrition and health surveys.[32] Others will require household-level data that describe a wider range of family members' activities.[33] Nearly all could be profitably investigated through the vehicle of demonstration experiments that alter particular features of the environment in order to study patterns of direct and indirect effects.[34]

Aspects of Estimation, Inference, and Measurement

Research in the biological and social sciences related to health, nutrition, and fertility has frequently produced results with misleading implica-

[32] This process is needlessly hindered when bodies of survey data are impounded for years by their collectors, or by the agencies that supported the collection. After a reasonable period of exclusive use to ensure incentives for competent researchers to collect data, all survey data gathered at the expense of public institutions should be released into the public domain, where social returns from additional research can accrue.

[33] Two such data sets are being collected by the Rand Corporation and the Division of Human Development, Institute for Nutrition of Central America and Panama (INCAP), in Guatemala, and by Rand and the Department of Statistics, Government of Malaysia, in Peninsular Malaysia. General characteristics of the required data are summarized in Butz (1972, pp. 40–46). Wishik and Van der Vynckt (1973) also discuss desirable features of survey data sets in this area.

[34] Only long-run and intergenerational responses are impossible to investigate in a short-run experiment. In the absence of intergenerational panel data, these effects must be studied in cross-sectional data sets.

tions, if any, for policy makers. Analysis of the particular research topics listed above and of other related topics would benefit from consideration of several methodological points.

For example, in the problem addressed in this chapter, the relationship between the length of the lactation period and the duration of postpartum amenorrhea or sterility has been examined in a number of clinical and field studies.[35] We can investigate the implications of a common approach to this problem by looking at equation 7-8, derived from equations 7-1 through 7-4, which relates a change in the period of sterility to a change in the length of the period of lactation.

$$dF = \gamma_L dL + \gamma_{N_1} dN_1 \tag{7-8}$$

where

$$\gamma_L dL = \gamma_L \alpha_{N_1} dN_1 + \gamma_L \alpha_{N_2} dN_2 + \gamma_L \alpha_T dT + \gamma_L \alpha_V dV + \gamma_L \alpha_C dC$$

The most common analytic procedure in these studies is to compute the gross correlation between the length of the period of lactation and the period of amenorrhea or sterility.[36] The analogues in our model are a correlation between changes in these variables, or an estimation of the coefficient γ_L in a regression of dF on dL. If the model of equations 7-1 through 7-4 is specified correctly, this simple procedure leads to an underestimate of the direct causal relationship between lactation and amenorrhea as long as $dN_1 \neq 0$. For, in this case, there is a direct determinant of amenorrhea, namely, the mother's nutritional intake, that independently and negatively ($\gamma_{N_1} < 0$) affects the length of the period of postpartum sterility.

Neglecting to take statistical account of this part of the relationship causes the gross correlation between L and F to include the negative direct effect of dN_1 in addition to the positive effect, α_{N_1}, operating indirectly through lactation. Therefore, the simple correlation between F and L is an underestimate of the true causal relationship between lactation and postpartum sterility.[37]

The relationships in this simple example are purely biological. The problems would be compounded by estimating a gross correlation be-

[35] Ovulation need not begin prior to the first postpartum menstruation; anovulatory cycles are possible. Hence the interval between a birth and the mother's first subsequent menstruation may be shorter or a little longer than her period of postpartum sterility.

[36] The model in our example is deterministic. The simplest stochastic specification would add random error terms to equations 7-5 and 7-8 and other estimating equations.

[37] For a general treatment of omitted-variable bias, see Theil (1971, pp. 548–550).

tween the length of the period of lactation and the interval between births. Isolating the terms in equation 7-5 that involve lactation responses gives

$$(7\text{-}9) \qquad dI = (\delta_F\gamma_L + \delta_H\beta_L)\, dL + \delta_F\gamma_{N_1} dN_1 + \delta_H\beta_{N_2} dN_2 + (\delta_V + \delta_H\beta_V)\, dV + \delta_C dC + \delta_T dT + \delta_H\beta_M dM$$

where $(\delta_F\gamma_L + \delta_H\beta_L)\, dL$ is the collection of effects that operate through the lactation variable,

$$(7\text{-}10) \qquad (\delta_F\gamma_L + \delta_H\beta_L)\, dL = (\delta_F\gamma_L\alpha_{N_1} + \delta_H\beta_L\alpha_{N_1})\, dN_1 + (\delta_F\gamma_L\alpha_{N_2} + \delta_H\beta_L\alpha_{N_2})\, dN_2 + (\delta_F\gamma_L\alpha_V + \delta_H\beta_L\alpha_V)\, dV + (\delta_F\gamma_L\alpha_C + \delta_H\beta_L\alpha_C)\, dC + (\delta_F\gamma_L\alpha_T + \delta_H\beta_L\alpha_T)\, dT$$

The simplest relationship that can be estimated is the gross correlation between L and I, or between changes in L and changes in I. The latter, or estimation of the reduced-form coefficient $(\delta_F\gamma_L + \delta_H\beta_L)$ in a regression of dI on dL, is more conveniently discussed in the framework of our model. From equation 7-9 it is apparent that this procedure yields a biased estimate of the true causal relationship.[38]

These two examples illustrate the importance of prior conceptual modeling and appropriate statistical methodology in estimating the magnitude of causal links between health, nutrition, and fertility variables at the family level.[39] Beyond these considerations, a researcher interested in deriving information useful for the formulation of policy would presumably seek to sort out the causal effects of variables in equation 7-5 that are amenable to policy manipulation aimed at changing fertility. Among these might be N_1, N_2, V, C, and T, depending on the social, economic, and political characteristics of the setting. The length of the lactation period itself is a less likely candidate, since the institutional and political tools required to influence women's behavior in this sphere directly are generally lacking.

[38] Components of this bias disappear if any of the coefficients on the right side of equation 7-10 are zero or if any of the coefficients on the right side of equation 7-9, except the coefficient of dL, are zero. Health and medical care, M, is not a component of dL, so that ignoring it does not bias the simple correlation or regression coefficient.

[39] These examples do not take up the common and important problem of joint determination resulting in simultaneous-equation bias. For discussion of this topic related specifically to economic and demographic household models, see Butz (1972, pp. 11–25), and T. Paul Schultz (1974, pp. 22–31).

Faced with this policy-oriented task, the researcher would err in running a regression, based on equation 7-9, that included lactation time explicitly as an explanatory variable. This procedure would bias the coefficient estimates corresponding to the other variables, in some cases causing them to overestimate the true causal influence. This means, for example, that the estimated coefficient δ_C, in equation 7-9, is less than the total reduced-form coefficient $(\delta_C + \delta_F \gamma_L \alpha_C + \delta_H \beta_L \alpha_C)$, reflecting all effects of the price of contraceptives on the length of the interval between births. If the price of an ineffectual contraceptive were to be lowered, intervals between births could actually become shorter if women reduced their lactation periods as a result—especially if shorter breast-feeding significantly hindered the health and development of their children. Yet the partial effect, δ_C, is all one would catch by regressing dI on both dC and dL in such an equation as 7-9. More generally, a regression based on equation 7-9 would yield estimates of the effects on the interval between births of changes in the value of children and the price of contraceptives that are biased in a negative direction from the true total effects to be expected. A policy effecting a reduction in the value of children or the price of contraceptives would not actually engender so large an increase in the interval between births as the estimated regression coefficients would indicate. Similarly, an estimate in equation 7-9 of the relation between changes in the opportunity cost of the mother's time and changes in her interval between births would appear more positive than the total association actually is.

In the case of maternal and child nutrition, their causal influences on intervals between births can be consistently estimated in the framework of equation 7-5. Even if estimates of this kind existed, however, they might not be useful in many policy situations. To change maternal and child nutrition themselves is a complex task, about which far too little is known, in spite of much research.[40] The required research for policy purposes should be based on models of food intake as a function of determining factors *amenable to public policy*. A simple economic model for constructing such an analysis might be $N_1 = \varepsilon$ (prices of available foods with high nutritive content;[41] prices of available foods with low nutritive content; the productive value of good nutritional status in agricultural and labor-market work; household income; mother's level of schooling; characteristics of advertising or other information inputs about the nutritive values of different foods).

[40] Wishik (1972) has pointed out that "the implications of intimacy and depth of affect associated with one's sexuality are probably exceeded only by one's protectiveness about food likes and preferences. Nutritionists can well believe that sex behavior may be easier to change than eating habits."

[41] Recall our broad definition of "price," in footnote 19.

Such an input-demand function could be derived from a structural model of behavioral-biological interactions, such as equations 7-1 through 7-4, with the addition of a utility function and another equation representing the couple's budgetary constraint. Alternatively, sociological and social-psychological theory would suggest other specifications. The important thing, in any case, is to concentrate on those explanatory variables amenable to change by instruments of policy.

Joint estimation of specifications based on equation 7-5 and the relationship determining N_1 would yield predictive relationships connecting the prices and availabilities of nutritious foods, perhaps supplements, to the length of intervals between births. Such a grand scheme can well await careful estimation of the magnitudes of separate crucial links in that long chain, however, since several may be extremely weak in many settings. Little of this groundwork has been laid.

A related methodological consideration concerns evaluation of public health programs that change environmental factors requiring no individual behavioral responses in order to affect health and nutrition but in which behavior can affect the outcome. Cleaning up the public water supply or adding fluoride, giving free inoculations at school, and instituting mosquito control against malaria have been common examples in low-income countries. Two virtues of these programs are that they can be administered directly as part of public policy and that their effects occur without response (or even necessarily knowledge) on the part of the target population. Furthermore, their effects are relatively easily evaluated with simple control-group designs. The only difficulty, and one not frequently recognized, is that evaluation should account for changes in composition of the target populations. The in-migrant group will in general contain a disproportionate number of persons who value the public health input and substitute it for goods and services that they purchased previously. Their posttreatment health status is high, but it may also have been high before the treatment began. These in-migrants will also tend to use the nutrition and health services more, so that the amount of services provided will also rise, again with no improvement in actual health, nutrition, or fertility. A solution to these biases lies in identifying cohorts which can be followed for the duration of the study.

It should be obvious that direct measures of health, nutrition, and fertility are more significant than measures of health services given, gallons distributed, or contraceptive pills dispensed. It is also evident that better health and nutrition inputs will not improve the health and nutrition of the healthy and well fed. Nevertheless, these obvious facts are neglected in the design and interpretation of many studies.

As pointed out above, we deal with interactive systems when we deal with health, nutrition, and fertility—the human body as a biological system, the family and community as economic and social systems. Changes in one part of a biological or economic system have, in general, both direct and indirect effects in other parts. Estimates of the effect of a change in one variable upon the value of another variable may be biased if important indirect links connecting the two variables are improperly handled or if other factors that change simultaneously are not accounted for in the analysis. In general the complexity of biological and social systems precludes a complete accounting of these links in theory or estimation, but it is incumbent upon researchers to utilize conceptual models of the most important suspected links in guiding experimental and statistical work, in order to minimize the bias of estimates. Within the conceptual models the definition and measurement of variables as proxies for the previously discussed conceptual variables are of critical research importance. Among the biological variables that characterize health and nutrition inputs and status, those that have a likely causal relationship to fertility are the ones in which we are interested. The validity and reliability of alternative measures of nutritional and health status are the subjects of a vast literature and are beyond the scope of this paper. Likely candidates for measures of health and development status in most of the developing countries, however, are birth weight, mortality rates, weight by age, and simple anthropometric ratios based on height, head circumference, chest circumference, and circumference of upper arm. Different measures are best for children of different ages. For many evaluative purposes, neonatal, perinatal, infant, and child mortality rates (or mortality experience, in the case of individual families) are the best measures of health and nutritional status. Mortality can be measured and surveyed with relative ease and reliability, even retrospectively, and is highly correlated with morbidity and malnutrition. One drawback of mortality rates, however, is that they may fail to distinguish adequately among different levels of health, development, and nutrition in populations not suffering from severe malnutrition and morbidity. Another drawback is that both biological and behavioral mechanisms triggered by the death of a child can differ from the mechanisms arising from child morbidity and poor development. The death of a breast-feeding child may hasten the return of the mother's fecundity, while the death of any child may induce a shorter interval between births from replacement motives (see chapter 7).

Concerning lactation, both its duration and its intensity appear to be related to the length of the period of postpartum sterility. Therefore, the measurement of lactation should ideally include not only length but also simultaneous infant ingestion of other foods and frequency of suckling (Habicht and Behar 1974). The length of the period of lactation, however, is by far the most easily and reliably measured. The best empirical proxy for I, the interval between births, in the model of this paper would be the number of months between the outcome of a pregnancy and the next conception. The actual interval between births, measured from one pregnancy outcome to the next, is less satisfactory because its length depends on determinants of the next baby's survival in utero, as well as upon biological and behavioral factors associated with the previous child.

With regard to the behavioral variables of interest in these relationships, there is space here only to warn that empirical proxies that suffice in developed countries may be inadequate in less developed settings. For example, family income in less developed rural settings properly includes not only the value of agricultural and cottage-industry products, whether sold or consumed at home, but also the value of household production of goods and services for which markets are poorly developed, if they exist at all. Such services as child care, cooking, cleaning house, and cutting and carrying wood have value; they are often purchased in urban settings in the form of appliances and maid service. To disregard their existence in rural families biases statistics on rural income downward in relation to urban income. Further, the transfers of money, goods, and services that commonly occur among households and generations in societies lacking developed capital markets and institutionalized insurance and old-age security can make a family's annual disposable income quite different from its annual earnings.

Another behavioral concept difficult to measure accurately is the opportunity cost of a mother's time in child care. In many rural communities, work opportunities exist at home and elsewhere that interfere very little with child-care duties. Women desiring children will tend to choose these jobs, if any, while their children are young. The concepts of earnings, labor-force participation, and hours worked that have served economists and sociologists studying developed countries, therefore, require rethinking in the context of less developed countries.

General Conclusions

Of the known or suspected relationships among health and nutrition factors on the one hand and fertility outcomes on the other, considerably more is understood about biological links than about behavioral ones. For particular individuals, the biological dependencies of fecundity and fertility on nutrition, health, and lactation can vary a great deal. For groups of individuals, however, a negative relationship between health and nutritional status, and fertility measures clearly emerges. It is therefore clear that the behavioral factors are considerably more important at the population level.

Outlined earlier was an approach to understanding the health and nutrition behavior of poor people that emphasizes the reasonableness or rationality of their observed behavior and points to real changes in their economic incentives and constraints regarding health care and nutrition as the means to altering their behavior. Though the responses that people are hypothesized to make ultimately affect their health and nutrition, and therefore their fertility, largely through biological mechanisms, it is behavioral factors that bring these mechanisms into play.

If this picture is correct, technical assistance to families concerning the storing, preserving, and cooking of food may not succeed. In this case, the community has honed these techniques to perfection over the generations. In their own setting, the people know all the tricks that work. Likewise, instructing people in the nutritional needs of infants and children will contribute little. After generations of experiencing child mortality and morbidity, parents probably perceive these relationships in reasonably accurate terms, and allocative decisions are made accordingly. Similarly, decrying the feeding of nutritious crops to animals will not help. A family that made these suggested changes, if it had been in long-run equilibrium, would afterward be worse off in terms of its own preferences.

Instead, if this picture is correct, the solution is to introduce real changes in the environment in which allocative decisions are made. These may include new job opportunities that require a higher level of intelligence and physical stamina; a more efficient capital market supplying short-term credit at competitive rates; chemical fertilizers and agricultural technology that substitute for human labor and require instead allocative intelligence and schooling; and a local school in which well-nourished intelligent children perform better. Introducing these changes creates disequilibria, which in themselves place a premium on intelligence and schooling, and thereby on investments in childhood nutrition.[42] Finding the points of effective intervention is the important task, and understanding the determinants of couples' *demand* for health- and nutrition-producing inputs and for children is the key. A "balanced approach," influencing many aspects of the environment simultaneously, is not likely to be as cost-effective as concentrating resources on particular crucial points of intervention.

The policy implications of this model obviously differ strikingly from those of the contender at the opposite extreme, the backward peasant model. Not only would the latter's recommendations not work in the world we have sketched; neither would the recommendations that we

[42] Theodore W. Schultz (1964) emphasized the important role of education in dynamic settings. Finis Welch (1970) formalized this concept in a model of the allocative function of education and tested it.

have outlined work in the other world, for people there are either too lazy, too ignorant, or too much bound by social norms and tradition to accept a good thing if it is new.

The evidence concerning adoption of new agricultural inputs and reallocation of land among crops in response to changing prices of inputs and outputs indicates clearly, by now, that peasant farmers in Asia, Latin America, and Africa can adjust quickly. There is a presumption that these same families would also adjust their allocation of food and other goods if their environments changed so as to make a response worthwhile, and if they were convinced that this was true. But the presumption remains untested, except that broad trends in patterns of food consumption during economic development seem consistent with it.

8.

Interrelationships Between Mortality and Fertility

T. PAUL SCHULTZ

Life expectancy has probably increased by one-half since 1940 in most low-income countries.[1] This extraordinary extension of life occurred in high-income countries more gradually at a later stage in their economic development. Such an important modification in man's environment creates widespread opportunities for improved welfare but at the same time necessitates modifications in individual behavior and social institutions to exploit these new opportunities fully.

Given the speed and magnitude of this achievement in the low-income world, various disequilibria are likely to emerge in the wake of the reduced incidence of death and disease. These disequilibria arise precisely because social institutions and individual behavior adapt, for many reasons, with a substantial lag to new and unanticipated developments. Rapid social and economic changes in response to disequilibria appear to be an essential feature of development, and Simon Kuznets (1973) has argued that the "decline in death is an indispensable prerequisite for [this pattern of] modern economic growth." Nonetheless, the reallocation of resources required to utilize the increased length of life may not

This chapter is based on research on determinants of fertility and economic development that was facilitated by a grant from the Rockefeller Foundation and a 211d grant from the Agency for International Development to the Economic Development Center of the University of Minnesota. I am indebted to J. A. Brown, Jr., J. J. Heckman, J. L. McCabe, G. B. Rodgers, T. W. Schultz, and C. E. Taylor for helpful comments on an earlier draft, although they are, of course, not responsible for errors or interpretation. I appreciate the able research assistance of H. Shimamura and G. Tauchen in preparing the chapter.

[1] For a review of mortality trends see G. J. Stolnitz (1955, 1956, 1965), D. V. Glass and E. Grebenik (1966), UN Department of Economic and Social Affairs (1953, 1963), and, by cause, see S. H. Preston and V. E. Nelson (1974), and in perspective, H. L. Browning (1968).

automatically take place with desired efficiency and equity. Public policy may play an important role by disseminating information and appropriate technologies to facilitate private and social adaptation to this change.

I am primarily concerned with the implications of mortality for desired and actual levels of fertility. Ignoring migration, I have undertaken to appraise the way in which the decline in mortality in the low-income world is likely to affect population growth rates and whether the underlying relationships suggest opportunities for policy to hasten the decline in fertility. What is known about the links from policy instruments to fertility that operate through their effect on infant, child, and adult mortality? How can nonexperimental and experimental research close gaps in our knowledge about these behavioral relationships, on the one hand, and about the economic administrative capacities of the public sector to reduce mortality, and hence fertility, on the other? This chapter is a tentative effort to develop an analytical framework that will focus discussion on empirical issues that might be important for policy.

First, I shall examine conceptually how child and adult mortality might influence household behavior, including fertility, by means of both biological feedback mechanisms and self-interested behavioral responses. Methods and models for the empirical study of the relationship between mortality and fertility are discussed in the next section, though the subsequent review of the empirical literature reveals that existing evidence rarely illuminates the parameters of the proposed stock or flow models of fertility determination directly. For this reason, it may be helpful to indicate ways in which future statistical analysis of this relationship could be designed in order to yield more information on these mechanisms underlying the "demographic transition." The relationship between the determinants of health and death rates also is considered briefly. In the final section, I assess the way in which policies to reduce mortality might be evaluated through the study of both experimental data sources and, more important, "natural experiments" that have already altered radically the prevailing class and regional patterns of morbidity and mortality in the world.

Mortality as a Determinant of Fertility

For the policy maker, factors affecting fertility are more interesting if they can be influenced by administratively and politically feasible means. Unfortunately, determinants of fertility that are linked to policy are often poorly understood; how policy affects nutritional habits, the age at marriage, or child mortality, for instance, remains for the most part a mystery. Though any manageable representation of the intricate biological-behavioral process determining fertility must neglect many facets of the problem, several interacting aspects of the household's environment are essential. Statistical theory leads one to expect that when nonexperimental data are analyzed for evidence on the determinants of fertility, an integrated treatment of at least these several factors is probably necessary if the independent effect of any single factor is to be adequately evaluated. Moreover, mortality is an unusual determinant of fertility, because in certain situations it can influence both the *biological* capacity to bear children and the *behavioral* desire to bear them. Separating the biological or *supply effects* of mortality from its behavioral or *demand effects* is one of the more challenging problems in the study of fertility.

Biological Supply Effects

In contemporary societies most parents can have the number of children they want without being constrained by fecundity, or the capacity to bear enough children. Although the relative effectiveness of various individual and societal means of reproductive control are difficult to measure, it is widely agreed that biological constraints on fecundity are relatively unimportant today in accounting for systematic differences in the average level of fertility, except perhaps across societies with very different standards of living and endemic disease (Freedman 1963, Ryder 1967).

At the individual level, however, where biological constraints are potentially important, it is hard to distinguish empirically between the biological and behavioral components of the process regulating reproduction. The onset of sterility and the natural spacing of births (anovulation) may be influenced by diet, general health, prevalence of specific diseases, and earlier child-bearing and breast-feeding practices. It is widely believed that the time between birth and the return of ovulation depends on the duration and intensity of breast-feeding.[2] Since some of these "biological" processes can be influenced behaviorally by social custom or individual choice, differences in fecundity associated with, for example, breast-feeding might to some extent reflect differences in desired fertility. Thus, except where the conditioning variable is clearly outside the control of the parents (that is, exogenous to the fertility

[2] For a survey of evidence see Jeroen K. van Ginneken (1974). Later it is observed that evidence presented in many studies is likely to overstate the biological effects of breast-feeding on fecundity because a potential role for behavioral factors is denied.

decision), it is difficult to infer that the association between a seemingly biological variable, such as breast-feeding, and fertility is in fact a purely autonomous biological feedback mechanism and not a reflection of the reproductive preferences of the parents.

The death of a young child may, according to the same logic, activate a biological feedback mechanism, for the cessation of lactation hormones may increase the mother's fecundity in subsequent periods. This biological effect should be greater the more dependent the child is on breast-feeding before its death and should be less the older the child is after six to nine months.[3] This biological effect would appear to be independent of the mother's age and parity and, of course, is unaffected by the sex of the child that dies.[4]

Behavioral Determinants of Demand: The Simple Model

A couple's choice of final consumption during their married life is limited by their time and nonhuman capital resources. Typically, market-determined wage opportunities for husband and wife in high-income countries provide exchange rates between the two scarce inputs into family consumption—own time and market goods and services (or home-produced substitutes). Because children can absorb a substantial share of a couple's available time and market income, it is likely that market prices, levels of spouses' wages, and nonhuman wealth exert substantial effects on the number of children parents want. This demand framework for understanding individual differences in fertility was conceptualized by Gary S. Becker (1960), implemented empirically by Jacob Mincer (1963), and has of late led to a number of investigations of reproductive behavior in various societies (T. Paul Schultz 1974).

Given plausible assumptions concerning the time intensity of child rearing for wives and husbands and alternative opportunities for the use of their time, the household demand framework predicts that a relative increase in the value of the wife's time will exert a more negative effect on the demand for children than will a relative increase in the value of the husband's time. The effect of nonhuman wealth is assumed to increase the demand for children, for it would contain no offsetting price-

[3] This pattern of effect would, of course, depend on many characteristics of the specific population illustrated by the extremes of the American Hutterites (Eaton and Mayer 1954) and rural Senegalese (Cantrelle and Leridon 1971).

[4] Empirical evidence of the relationship between child mortality and subsequent fertility by age of mother, parity of mother, and age and sex of the deceased child will be examined in a later section in order to determine the extent to which this association is caused by purely involuntary biological mechanisms and the extent to which behavioral mechanisms are in evidence.

of-time effect. These differential value-of-time (or education) and physical-wealth effects on completed fertility behavior have been confirmed in most empirical studies that appropriately exclude other endogenous variables in the prediction equation (T. Paul Schultz 1974).[5]

It is in the context of this simple demand model of fertility that I wish to explore the consequences of infant, child, and adult mortality on the demand for numbers of births per woman.

If we assume that parents want children in order to obtain economic and other benefits, infant and child mortality exert two offsetting effects on fertility. First, a reduction in child mortality increases the number of survivors demanded by decreasing the expected "cost" (including monetary, opportunity, and psychic costs) to parents of bearing and rearing enough offspring to obtain a survivor. Second, it decreases the derived demand for births for a fixed surviving family-size goal of parents by decreasing the number of births required to obtain, on average, a survivor. The former price effect of decreased child mortality on demand should induce parents to want more surviving offspring, but fewer births will be required for any desired number of surviving children, because of the latter supply effect.

A couple's response to decreases in child mortality may be characterized, in this sense, as "demographically stabilizing" if they reduce their desired number of births. If the elasticity of costs of a survivor with respect to the probability of child survival were -1—that is, if these quantities changed proportionally, but, of course, in opposite directions—then demographically stabilizing reproductive behavior would require that the demand for surviving children is *price inelastic*.[6] A relative change in the price of children would then induce a relatively smaller opposite adjustment in parental demand for numbers of surviving off-

[5] For example, including closely related choice variables such as age at marriage or female labor-force status or attitudes toward family size, the value of children, contraception, etc., implies that ordinary regression analyses are likely to be biased.

[6] The elasticity of demand for births, B, with respect to the probability of a child's survival to maturity, P, can be expressed as follows: $\eta_{BP} = \eta_{SC}\eta_{CP} - 1$, where S is the number of births that survive from which parents are assumed to derive utility under risk-neutral assumptions, and C is the expected cost of a surviving child, which is assumed to depend inversely on P and be independent of family size. Since it is known that η_{SC} and η_{CP} are both less than zero, if their product is less than unity, the elasticity of demand for births with respect to the probability of survival will be negative. Yoram Ben-Porath and Finis Welch (1972) illustratively assume that $\eta_{CP} = -1$, whereas Donald J. O'Hara (1972a) indicates why it might exceed unity in absolute value. The positive relationship observed between child mortality and fertility is therefore suggestive of an inelastic demand for surviving children, that is, $|\eta_{SC}| < 1$.

spring. Where evidence suggests a positive association between child mortality and fertility, and thus price-inelastic demand for surviving children, the surviving family-size goals of parents may be assumed to be relatively insensitive to changes in the relative price of children, despite the paradoxical responsiveness of fertility to declining mortality.

It may be instructive to consider also what stronger conditions would be required to induce a couple to reduce its fertility sufficiently in response to a decline in child mortality so that its number of mature children did not increase.[7] Holding to our prior assumption that child survival rates proportionately affect the expected cost of rearing a child to maturity, the price elasticity of demand for survivors would have to be zero (that is, perfectly inelastic) to prevent surviving family size from increasing. Thus, this simple two-good demand framework, without uncertainty, implies only under implausible assumptions a fully offsetting or overcompensating demand response on the part of parents to a decline in child mortality. But many assumptions underlying this approach require modification in a more realistic model.

Uncertainty and the Demand for Births

Parenthood is, undoubtedly, subject to many risks. The simple demand approach to fertility determination, as outlined above, assumes that parents are risk-neutral—that is, that parents behave as though they considered only the expected value of family outcomes and ignored the variance (and higher moments) of the anticipated distribution of family-size outcomes. Loss or utility functions of parents may also be assumed to be symmetric with regard to having more or fewer than the desired number of surviving children. Moreover, the mechanism by which parents form expectations about probable future child deaths is rarely given explicit attention, and perfect foresight is implicitly assumed. This rudimentary single-period demand framework, therefore, neglects risk and uncertainty and provides few direct insights into the dynamic process determining the way in which expectations and behavior adapt in the course of time to changes in mortality.

A simple but plausible characterization of the way in which parents view these risks and this uncertainty suggests that in low-income agrarian societies, these risks increase birth rates, other things being equal. But the magnitude of the "risk and uncertainty effect" of child

[7] This would imply no long-run increase in population growth associated with a reduction in child mortality if the mean age of child bearing remained unchanged. In fact, the mean age of child bearing may decline with development, increasing slightly the population growth rate. See the definition of "length of generation" in Coale (1972).

mortality may be attenuated by the sequential nature of family formation.

More specifically, it seems reasonable to assume that the direct and opportunity costs of an additional child do not increase abruptly after three to five children, particularly in a poor agricultural setting. A strong asymmetry, therefore, may emerge in the parents' preferences for having more or fewer than the number of children they might seek under a predictable regime of birth and death rates. This would occur if parents wanted *no fewer* than a specific number of children (or sons) and did not regard additional children as a substantial economic or psychic liability. Variance in expected surviving family-size outcomes will tend to increase the desired birth rate under these conditions (T. Paul Schultz 1967, pp. 11–14, appendix B).[8]

This does not imply that parents would adapt their fertility to compensate throughout their marriage for "expected" child mortality in order to be confident (95 percent sure, for example) of having the desired number of surviving children (or sons) when they reached retirement age. In such a single-period model of reproductive choice (Heer and Smith 1968, May and Heer 1968), the biological facts that reproduction extends over a considerable number of years in a woman's life and that child mortality is concentrated in the first years of a child's life are ignored. Parents are likely, in fact, to respond largely to the actual, not expected, incidence of mortality among their own children, having sufficient time thereafter to replace losses as they are incurred (T. Paul Schultz 1967, p. 12). A sequential model of reproductive choice, as shown by Donald J. O'Hara (1972b) implies that for the same decision rule, the excess of births caused by the "uncertainty" of child mortality is much less than that implied by a single-period model.[9]

[8] If new methods of contraception reduce this variance in family-size outcomes without raising the "costs" of obtaining this control, child mortality may become the major remaining source of family-size uncertainty in most low-income societies.

[9] For this reason, models which emphasize the way parents form their future expectations are not likely to clarify the relationship between fertility and child mortality, because information about actual mortality experience is available to parents relatively soon after marriage. Improved theories of the process of expectation formation in sequential decision-making situations may have more promise where mature skills of children are the "uncertain traits" that affect parental preferences for more children and more investments per child (Ben-Porath and Welch 1972). In this case, the long lags in obtaining information would require parents to rely more heavily on subjective expectations. How many parents wished they knew what their first children were going to grow into (as teenagers) before they had to make subsequent reproductive choices? In a low-fertility society this opportunity does not present itself often.

Returns on Human Capital and Relative Price Effects

Reduction in child mortality also affects relative prices of all consumption or investment activities that have an intertemporal dimension. If these affected activities are substitutes or complements for children, cross-price (substitution) effects on fertility might be an important indirect consequence of a decline in mortality. For example, reduced death rates at all ages increase the returns on all forms of investment in human agents, either as a producer or consumer, in any generation.[10]

Parents are confronted with two joint decisions in forming their family: how many children to have and how much they want to commit in both time and resources to the rearing of each offspring (Becker 1960, De Tray 1973). A reduction in the regime of mortality makes both more attractive—that is, both having an additional child and investing more in each child. But a longer-gestating investment, such as increasing the child's schooling, is enhanced more than the investment in having a larger number of (surviving) children (O'Hara 1972a). Hence the relative price effect of a reduction in mortality rates at all ages favors increased investment in the quality of the younger generation in relation to investment in its size. Both margins, nonetheless, become more attractive as investments in comparison with nonhuman capital, as human life becomes more certain and longer.

If the quality and quantity dimensions of offspring are sufficiently good substitutes for one another, the number of surviving children wanted by parents will decrease as the expected length of life increases (O'Hara 1972a). Since school-enrollment rates have increased in virtually all low-income countries in recent decades, the reduction in mortality may have contributed to the shift of resources by parents from increases in family size to increases in their children's schooling, training, migration, and other investments that enhance the productivity and welfare of their offspring. To my knowledge there is unfortunately little firm evidence on the existence or size of this hypothetical relationship between mortality and the composition of investments in children.

Parents may also invest more in themselves, either before or after marriage, through extended schooling, vocational training, occupational mobility, and interregional migration.[11] The spread of adolescent school-

[10] Since the decline in mortality increases the incentive to invest in human rather than physical capital, it may be partially responsible for the puzzling decline in the (physical) ratio of capital to output and the rise in labor's share of national income in this century.

[11] The proportion of males surviving from the age of twenty-five to fifty-five, the age of mature repayment of investments in human capital, has increased from probably little more than a third in the high-mortality regimes in low-income countries at the turn of the century to about 94 percent today (Browning 1968).

ing and more extensive enrollment in vocational training activities is often associated with a delay in marriage, with women therefore beginning to bear children at a later age. Migration from rural to urban areas tends to be selective of the better-educated, unmarried youth or married couples with few or no children. Labor markets and nonmarket productive opportunities for women in urban areas are different from those available in traditional rural societies. Jobs are frequently less compatible with child rearing in the urban setting and may also be less rewarding in combination with other nonmarket tasks and productive activities than in the rural setting. Though evidence is meager and contradictory, it appears that migrants to the large cities in many parts of the low-income world, such as Latin America, have distinctly lower fertility than nonmigrants that stay in the rural sector. In some instances, the urban migrant actually exhibits lower fertility than native city-born residents of similar age and education (Macisco, Bouvier, and Renzi 1969). Consequently, the decline in mortality tends to increase the returns on many forms of investment in adult human capital which appears, on balance, to facilitate structural changes such as migration from rural to urban areas and declines in fertility (Nelson, Schultz, and Slighton 1971).

Finally, advances in life expectancy could affect the time path and equilibrium level of personal savings. In the long run, the returns one can expect to realize in one's lifetime from the postponement of current consumption increase as mortality declines or the effective social rate of discount falls, other things being equal. Also, in the short run, the extension of life requires persons to modify their savings behavior to accommodate an increased period of retirement, with the probable consequence of increasing current savings within a youthful population. As was the case in mortality's effect on the relative returns on child schooling and numbers of children, returns from longer-gestating investments would probably be enhanced in relation to those from short-run investments, other things being equal, after a decline in mortality at all ages.[12]

The Value of Life: The Wealth Effect

A reduction in mortality influences the tradeoffs among many intertemporal activities by changing their relative prices. It also increases welfare, holding relative prices constant, a result referred to as the

[12] With the decline in mortality there may also be a substantial reduction in morbidity with consequent increases in labor productivity. But the magnitude of this effect is not well documented (Malenbaum 1970, Knowles 1970, Weisbrod et al. 1973). Jere Behrman (1968) makes the only convincing case I know of in which the eradication of malaria is related to productivity of Thai peasants in a comprehensive framework.

"wealth effect," associated with increased life expectancy. It is obvious that this gain is widely valued, yet it eludes measurement. In principle, the value of life should include the individual's own valuation plus the gains (and losses) incurred by others. Perhaps the simplest examples, in economic terms, arise when the person surviving is a "dependent," such as a child or slave whose welfare need not directly enter the utility function of the decision maker—the parent or slaveholder. But even here, economics is not yet well equipped to measure the advance in human welfare or its productive attributes. As with other changes in man's environment that are not bought or sold in the marketplace, economists disagree on the appropriate conception or an empirical estimate of value.[13] A summary of the issues and magnitudes involved may be useful, nonetheless.

Three general approaches to evaluating life can be distinguished. The first is to calculate the earnings of a "representative" person over his lifetime. Discounting these streams of earnings back to any specific age, adjusted for mortality, one obtains an estimate of the stock of human capital that would be "lost" by society by a random death within that age cohort (Dublin and Lotka 1946, among others). Economic logic does not clearly prescribe the way the individual's own consumption in this human-capital approach should be treated.[14]

A second approach is the attempt to infer from differences in individual behavior a revealed preference for one's own life by observing how much one pays or is paid to modify the riskiness of life. This scheme of estimating compensating variations in consumer behavior requires unusual data and has not been applied, to my knowledge, to materials from low-income countries. Using U.S. occupation-specific mortality and wage data, it has been estimated that the revealed value of an adult male life was in the neighborhood of $200,000 in 1967, or about twenty-three times the average earnings of men over the age of twenty-five who were employed full time throughout that year (Thaler and Rosen 1974).

[13] For reviews of the conceptual issues, see E. J. Mishan (1971) and T. C. Schelling (1968). For estimates of human life involving good discussions of the related problems, strong assumptions, and unusual data, see Richard Thaler and Sherwin Rosen (1974) and, in particular, Dan Usher (1973). As it applies to the U.S. slave population, see R. W. Fogel and S. L. Engerman (1974).

[14] Should consumption be deducted to obtain "net earnings," and if so, how is own consumption to be singled out of the family system of expenditures? If own consumption is deducted as a net cost and interrelated family utilities are ignored, it is possible to draw grossly misleading conclusions, such as that an infant at birth and an adult at retirement are large liabilities to their family and to society (Enke 1960b, Ohlin 1967, Nelson, Schultz, and Slighton 1971, Blandy 1974).

The third approach is to specify individual and social utility functions, in terms of a social discount rate (r) and a scale parameter of consumption in each period (β). Usher (1973) assumes that individuals maximize expected utility and have intertemporal separable utility functions. Without considering distributional issues—that is, assuming that persons are not embedded in families and all receive average shares of national income—the growth in individual average utility is shown to be a sum of the growth in per capita income (or the usual measure of progress) and the ratio of the growth of life expectancy to the consumption scale parameter, β. If β, or the elasticity of utility with respect to consumption, were 1, individuals would maximize expected wealth without regard to the timing of consumption. In this case, individual utility increases at a rate equal to growth in per capita national income plus the full growth in life expectancy.[15]

Usher's approach is essentially one of valuing stocks in human capital as we do stocks in physical capital. Depreciation in a machine, for example, erodes the present value of such a physical asset by undermining its future income streams and hence is deducted from current income. Conversely, the decline in mortality extrapolated to the future implies increased expected earnings for the existing stock in human capital, and hence an appreciation in its present value which can be viewed as current income. Some procedure, such as that proposed by Usher, is required to treat human and physical capital symmetrically and capture the present productive implications of the decline in human mortality. If the appropriate adjustment in personal welfare is of the magnitude suggested by Usher's exercise, it is clear that the wealth effect of the increases in life expectancy in low-income countries has been substantial.

Summary

Mortality exerts many effects on the process of family formation and related intertemporal incentives to save and invest. Predictable conse-

[15] Applied to Canadian data for the period 1926–68, the growth in per capita national income was 2.25 percent, but utility would have risen 26 percent faster if we assume that the social discount rate was 3 percent and the consumption scale parameter, β, was 0.3, which implies an average capital value of $182,000 of a life in 1961. In contrast, given the more rapid recent rates of growth in life expectancy in low-income countries the understatement of welfare gains is more dramatic. For example, Ceylon has sustained a 1.65 percent growth per annum in per capita national income throughout the period 1946–63, but including increased life expectancy with the same assumptions, welfare would have grown one and one-half times faster than national income, namely, at 4.22 percent per annum. Even a country

quences of mortality on desired fertility can be deduced only when the household demand framework is severely restricted. This restricted framework suggests that a positive relationship will emerge between fertility and child mortality if the demand for surviving children is price inelastic.

For fertility to respond fully—or, in other words, for the elasticity of fertility with respect to the reciprocal of the probability of child survival to equal or exceed 1—demand functions within this simplified framework must be perfectly inelastic. However, considerations of risk and uncertainty, the sequential nature of the process of family formation, and the strong probability that resource-intensive investments in children substitute in part for more surviving children, provide grounds for expecting that fertility might overcompensate for declines in child mortality, and ultimately for declines in general mortality. The measurement and consequences of wealth effects linked to increased life expectancy are even more problematic. More precise predictions of the way in which man's increased length of life influences his behavior must await more extensive theoretical and empirical research on an integrated life-cycle model of family formation and behavior.

Methods for the Analysis of Empirical Evidence on the Relationship Between Fertility and Mortality

At the crux of the demographic-transition hypothesis is the presumption that historical declines in mortality set into motion forces that lead to an eventual decline in fertility of a sufficient magnitude to offset the effect of lower mortality on the overall growth rate of the population. Though demographers frequently study the behavior of birth and death rates, the basic components of natural increase in a closed population, it is somewhat surprising that there does not appear to be any accepted characterization of the general features of the *relationship* between fertility and mortality. This might be due either to the lack of a common analytical framework within which to view and accumulate evidence on the possible relationship or to the lack of a relationship exhibited consistently across similar investigations.

It is not possible here to review the large and widely scattered literature that is addressed to these issues.[16] A selective survey, however, is

such as Taiwan, that has experienced rapid growth in income of 4.15 percent a year in the period 1952–66, would adjust upward by one-fourth its estimate of growth in welfare to incorporate the reduction in mortality (Usher 1973, table 3).

[16] Not only have I undoubtedly neglected many investigations of the fertility–mortality relationship, I am unable to cite even the preeminent contributions in

attempted in the next section, with emphasis given to empirical studies in which an attempt has been made to control the principal exogenous determinants of the demand for children, as identified earlier.[17] In this section a statistical framework within which to interpret empirical evidence will be developed.

Toward a Common Statistical Framework

There are many sources of evidence on the qualitative and quantitative nature of the relationship between fertility and mortality. It may serve a purpose, therefore, to propose a simplified model for statistical estimation and compare it with the methodology used in the empirical literature.

From a complete characterization of the process determining reproductive behavior, it should be possible to derive stochastic relationships for either the number of children born to women at any point in time, or the rate at which women will bear children over a period of time. In other words, given the correct specification of reproduction as a stochastic process, information on either the accumulated *stock* of children born or the *flow* of births should enable one to measure parameters to the underlying process generating both aspects of fertility (Heckman and Willis 1974).

But unfortunately, we lack as yet a comprehensive dynamic model of reproduction. The demand approach to determination of fertility, which emphasizes wealth and value-of-time effects, is explicitly formulated in terms of a single-period choice of a desired *stock* of children (or surviving children). The timing or spacing of those births has been treated in only a constant-flow formulation (over the reproductive years) that bears little resemblance to actual behavior. Dynamic models of reproductive behavior have not yet clarified the determinants of the optimal time path by which parents should arrive at their desired stock of children.

Consequently, the demand approach to fertility is appropriate in explaining stocks of children toward the end of the reproductive period. When this model is used to account for birth rates, birth probabilities,

---

languages other than English, such as French. A comprehensive survey is provided in several UN Department of Economic and Social Affairs publications (1953, 1963).

[17] Multiple regression or nonlinear regression techniques are typically used to control or hold constant various exogenous determinants of parental demand for children in order to evaluate the effect of child mortality or overall mortality on fertility. In the case of individual data, nonlinear maximum-likelihood methods would seem useful for the study of dichotomous dependent variables (for example, birth or no birth in a year). See T. Paul Schultz (1974).

or their inverse, intervals between births, interpretation of findings is least ambiguous among older cohorts of women for whom current births are frequently marginal increments to completed family size and hence reasonable proxies for differences in completed fertility. Since the stock and flow dimensions of fertility should both be examined for evidence of the relationship with mortality, two regrettably disjointed models are presented below. It would be desirable in the future to view both the stock and flow formulations as but different aspects of the same process.

The immediate objective is to estimate three possible effects of mortality: how the prior levels of community and family mortality affect child mortality expectations of parents and thereby influence the number of births they want; how the actual death of own children influences the voluntary demand for births; and how the actual death of breast-feeding infants affects, involuntarily, the supply of births.

Define the probability of a child surviving from birth at time t to maturity, equal to age m, as

$$P_t = \prod_{i=0}^{i=m} (1 - {}_1q_i(t + i))$$

where ${}_1q_i(t)$ is the probability of dying from age i to $i + 1$ at time t. If the survival probability anticipated by parents for the community, P_t^c, were a weighted average of past death rates, with the weights declining exponentially, their expected value could be expressed

$$P_t^{c*} = L \sum_{i=0}^{\infty} (1 - \lambda)^i P_{t-i}^c$$

where $0 < \lambda < 1$, and

$$L = 1/\left(\sum_{i=0}^{\infty} (1 - \lambda)^i\right)$$

Family mortality experience, P_t^f, is expressed as a ratio of the number of children alive, A_t, to the number ever born, B_t; $P_t^f = A_t/B_t$.

Parental expectations for the mortality of all of their offspring, P_t^*, are based presumably on a weighted average of community and family experience.

$$P_t^* = \alpha P_t^f + (1 - \alpha)P_t^{c*} \tag{8-1}$$

where $0 < \alpha < 1$.

The number of surviving children that parents desire is denoted F_t^* (z, u), which depends on a set of socioeconomic factors, z, as well as tastes distributed at random, u. The number of births parents want, B_t^*, can be expressed as a product of the reciprocal of the expected child survival probability raised to some exponent γ, and this surviving family-size goal:

$$B_t^* = (1/P_t^*)^\gamma F_t^*(z, u) \tag{8-2}$$

Suppose that $\alpha = 1$, or that parents consider only the mortality among their own offspring in forming their expectations regarding future child mortality. Assume also that $\gamma = 1$, or that parents maintain their surviving family-size goal, regardless of changes in child mortality. Given the age structure of improvements in mortality that are heavily concentrated among children in low-income countries, one might anticipate that the compensating decline in fertility would offset 50 to 75 percent of the declines in overall mortality in the long run.[18]

It is not unreasonable to expect that at the community level the average P_t^f and P_t^{c*} would be of similar magnitude, depending of course on when the existing population of parents had their children and how rapidly they disregarded the past (that is, how large λ is). Consequently, the relationship between earlier levels of child mortality and current completed fertility may not be sensitive at the community level to the actual value of α. Also, earlier child mortality can probably be measured by either a weighted average of past period-specific rates of child survival, or cohort-specific rates of child survival without serious distortion.[19]

Unfortunately, as the discussion in the preceding section indicated, the modeling problem is more complicated. Mortality probably also affects the number of surviving children that parents want and the number

[18] If the dynamics of adjustment implied by changes in the age structure that affect crude vital rates but not intrinsic rates are neglected, assuming that the net (surviving) reproduction rate of women is held constant implies that half to three-fourths of the increment to the natural rate of increase of the population attributable to declines in mortality are offset by the corresponding decline in fertility.

[19] If recent past period-specific rates of child survival are used as a proxy for cohort rates it may be safely assumed that they approximate with greater error the mortality actually expected or experienced by older cohorts of parents. The secular decline in the level and variability of period-specific child mortality will, on the other hand, tend to bias upward the response coefficients estimated contemporaneously for older parents. The errors-in-variables argument would suggest that parameter estimates of the reproductive response to mortality would be biased downward for the older cohorts of parents. However, if interregional differences in child mortality were strongly correlated serially over time, as tends to be the case, but relative differences declined over time, then small relative differences in current levels of child mortality between regions would reflect a larger relative (and absolute) difference in the past. This source of systematic bias in measured child mortality would contribute to an *increase* in the estimated response estimates of older parents. How the two sources of bias balance out is not known.

that are supplied, given their capacities to regulate fertility. First, the absolute price effect of a decline in child mortality encourages higher fertility. Second, the reduction in uncertainty of family outcomes probably contributes to a reduction in desired fertility. Third, the relative price effect adds to the attractions of increasing child investments, such as schooling, with a possible substitution effect on the desire for more children. Finally, the bias in returns toward all forms of human capital may induce parents to invest more in themselves, to delay marriage, to migrate from rural to urban areas, and to displace extended family networks that are oriented toward nonmarket activities by nuclear family arrangements that are more responsive to market incentives. All but the first effect of a decline in mortality seem to contribute to reducing the number of surviving children that parents want.

The desired number of births now becomes a product of the "expected" level of child mortality and an implicit function of child and adult mortality and other socioeconomic determinants of the number of surviving children that parents want:

$$B_t^* = (1/P_t^*)^\gamma F^*(P_t^c, P_t^f, e_m^o, z, u) \tag{8-3}$$

where e_m^o is the life expectancy of parents at age m, when they are assumed to take responsibility of their own consumption-investment decisions. Desired fertility can be achieved only with a considerable lag, subject to fecundity, and control technology and the like. Thus, observed completed fertility becomes some form of distributed lag function of B_t^* and A_t in earlier years, subject, of course, to a large random error.

On the basis of the demand framework, completed fertility is a relatively complex function of the reciprocal of child survival rates experienced by the parents and their immediate community and, in addition, a function of adult mortality. Long-run response elasticities should tend to exceed short-run responses, but errors in measuring mortality in the more distant past make it difficult to test this conjecture. As noted earlier, one anticipates that older mothers with nearly completed families will weigh more heavily the recent death of offspring in their decision to have further children than will younger mothers who have, for the most part, not yet reached their surviving family-size goal.[20]

[20] If the demand framework is a satisfactory characterization of parental response to child mortality, current birth rates should not only be more responsive to recent death rates among older women—say, over the age of thirty—but these period-specific birth rates may be more responsive to male child deaths than to female child deaths, if cultural preferences for the sexual composition of offspring favor sons.

Analysis of Time Series on Family Formation

Whereas the *behavioral demand framework* implies a relationship among completed fertility, surviving offspring, socioeconomic conditions of the couple, and their expectations for the future, the *biological supply framework* implies a relationship among the probability of birth, the time interval between births, and past and present conditioning "biological" variables. Renewal theory has been applied to model the reproductive process and disaggregate the expected value of intervals between births into component periods required for ovulation to begin again after a previous birth, for conception to occur, for the fetus to survive, and for a live birth to occur. There is a presumption in the demographic and medical literature that observed associations between (behaviorally influenced) biological changes and subsequent intervals between births are unbiased measures of the purely biological (supply) effect of the particular event on a woman's fecundity.[21]

There are two problems with this interpretation. First, the behavioral outcome, such as the death of an infant, may induce not only a biological change (that is, the cessation of lactation) but also may induce a shift in parental demands for further births. An association, in this case, between the infant's death and subsequent fertility will be the sum of a biological effect and any resulting behavioral effect.[22] Second, if the

[21] The mathematical models presume a noncontracepting population for simplicity, but, in fact, the empirical estimates of the relevant parameters are rarely obtained from a model that explicity deals with both the biological and behavioral side. Exceptions are as yet quite crude (T. Paul Schultz and DaVanzo 1970a, Welch 1974). But the traditional view persists that direct associations among breast-feeding, infant mortality, and intervals between births are useful estimates of the biological effect of the former two events on fecundity. For example, L. C. Chen and W. H. Mosley (1974) criticize the behavioral approach that stresses the surviving-family-size hypothesis because it is clear to them that the relationship between fertility and prior mortality of offspring is essentially a biological relationship. They are only following the traditional literature in presuming that their measures of the "effect" of lactation on fertility (components of the interval between births) contain only biological and not behavioral influences on the reproductive process.

[22] Research has also indicated that U.S. fetal mortality (loss of a pregnancy other than by induced abortion) may be dependent on the psychological status of parents, and in particular on whether the pregnancy was desired before conception (Ronald Freedman, Coombs, and Friedman 1966). It is not unlikely that the desire for an offspring continues to have a bearing on its later survival. Infanticide is no longer common throughout the world, but the allocation of limited family resources among members and the mother's time to care for them cannot help but reflect family priorities and influence chances for survival in a statistical sense. The traditional sex ratio of infant mortality that favors females is notably reversed in South Asia in those areas where girls require large dowries and are permitted to contribute in only

behavioral outcome is in any way subject to individual control, such as is the age at which an infant is weaned from its mother's breast, the mother may modify other aspects of her behavior in a coordinated fashion to reinforce the widely recognized effect of breast-feeding practices on her subsequent fertility.[23] Consequently, there is a statistical tendency for both sources of bias to overstate the biological effect of these events on a woman's fecundity, because behavioral aspects of the reproductive process have been neglected.

The traditional method for demonstrating the effect of an infant's death on its mother's fertility is to tabulate the length of the intervals between birth by the survival status of the previous birth and its age at death, if it is deceased.[24] As noted above, the task of differentiating between the two causal mechanisms that might explain this association requires a different method of analysis, although such tabulations do provide a satisfactory estimate of the short-run *sum* of both effects of infant mortality on fertility if it is assumed that all other determinants of fertility, both biological and behavioral, are uncorrelated with child mortality.[25]

---

limited ways to production outside of the home (Boserup 1970). Evidence is even available from Bangladesh suggesting that at the individual family level the survival probabilities for an infant depend on its sex and the sexual balance among its siblings (Welch 1974). All of this evidence should lead one to be cautious in interpreting even child mortality as an exogenous event that parents are unlikely to influence.

[23] This is an example of the way in which the omission of a relevant variable (behavioral changes) that tends to be positively correlated with the fertility determinant that is included (duration of weaning) biases upward the estimated effect of weaning on fecundity (see Kmenta 1971, pp. 393–395). It is also widely noted that breast-feeding is terminated in many societies when the mother becomes pregnant again. This additional feedback linkage adds further complexity to any interpretation of the usually cited evidence of the relationship between duration of breast-feeding and length of intervals between births. See Jeroen van Ginneken (1974) for a traditional review of the evidence.

[24] In the first example of such an exercise that I know of, the resulting relationship was interpreted as a behavioral response to the child's death (Sanders 1931, table 47). More recent investigators have tended to view the linkage as biological in origin. See, for example, J. E. Knodel (1968, table 6; 1970, table 13), R. G. Potter et al. (1965), T. E. Smith (1960), Pierre Cantrelle and Henri Leridon (1971), and John B. Wyon and John E. Gordon (1971).

[25] This assumption is of course unlikely to be satisfied. If child mortality is higher in lower socioeconomic classes and desired surviving fertility is higher, the correlation between childhood deaths and subsequently shorter intervals between births would overstate the *independent* effect of the childhood death, *holding* socioeconomic class constant. [See omitted-variable bias, for example, Kmenta (1971, pp. 392–395).] From the biological side one might imagine that the unusually fecund

Though it is beyond the scope of this paper to propose a rigorous statistical framework for the study of the determinants of birth probabilities or intervals between births, a simplified linear regression model may heuristically illustrate an initial approach to the problem. To identify and measure the supply and demand effects on fertility requires time-series information on the process of family formation such as is typically collected in retrospective pregnancy rosters. Prospective data have their obvious attractions in comparison with retrospective data sources, but the collection of prospective data is costly and time-consuming. For the sake of simplicity I shall neglect the censorship bias that arises because some intervals between births for a given group of women remain open and are, therefore, undefined.[26] It is also assumed that behavioral factors that exert a systematic effect on the number of surviving children that parents want exert a comparable inverse effect on *all* intervals between births, or, in other words, it is assumed that the level of desired lifetime fertility does not influence the desired spacing of those births over the mother's reproductive lifetime. Both of these assumptions are clearly unrealistic.

The length of the intervals between births might then be expressed as an approximately linear function of the duration of breast-feeding that is terminated by voluntary weaning; the duration of breast-feeding that is terminated by the (involuntary) death of the infant; the age at death if it occurs after weaning; the sex of the deceased child; socioeconomic determinants of the number of additional children sought before the interval being studied. Since the first three factors need not influence the spacing of births proportionately, a series of dummy variables is used to allow for nonlinear but additive effects on the length of the intervals between births.

---

woman has shorter-than-average intervals between births, other things being equal. If these closely spaced births contribute to early weaning of her children and consequently higher child mortality, the association between child mortality and shorter intervals between births may reflect the reverse causation, from fecundity (or fertility) to child mortality. Again, the simple correlation would overstate the causal effect of childhood deaths on fertility. All such examples only illustrate that since the system of biological and behavioral factors determining fertility and mortality is quite complex, a more complete specification of the underlying causal system is likely to imply very different parameter estimates from those obtained from simple single-way tabulations of the sort cited in the demographic and medical literatures.

[26] The censorship of intervals between births presents complications for estimating the probability of birth and using empirical evidence to derive parameters to renewal theory models of the reproductive process. See, for example, Sheps and Menken (1973).

The regression equation that might be estimated from the individual data for women of a specific age and with the same initial number of surviving children would be as follows:

$$(8\text{-}4) \quad BI = a + \sum_{i=0}^{m} b_i w_i + \sum_{i=0}^{m} c_i D_i + \sum_{i=n} d_j A_j + eS + f(z) + u$$

where BI is the number of months between births; w_i is 1 if the child immediately preceding is weaned after exactly i months and zero otherwise, for $i = 1, 2, \ldots 36$; D_i is 1 if the preceding child dies before being weaned at exactly age i months, and so on; A_j is 1 if any older child dies at exactly age j, where j exceeds the relevant i; S is 1 if the deceased child is male;[27] $f(z)$ is a function of the socioeconomic determinants of desired additional births; u is a random error which is assumed to be normally distributed with constant variance. The a's, b's, c's, d's, and e are estimated parameters obtained by minimizing the sum of squared errors. If the expected value of the probability of birth within a group of women did not decline as the time since their last preceding birth increased,[28] the estimated values of d_j would probably be approximately constant with respect to age of the older child at death or, $d \simeq d_j$ for all j. In this case, $c_i - d$ might be viewed as an estimate of the autonomous biological feedback (supply) effect of an infant's death on his mother's subsequent fecundity. Similarly, $b_i - d$ would reflect a combination of the biological (supply) effect and the effect of unmeasured behavioral patterns that were related to weaning practices across mothers. The former biological effect is widely thought to emerge after the minimum period of postpartum sterility of, say, six to twelve months, but to augment the interval between births at a diminishing rate. Eventually, the additional effect upon the interval between births of

[27] For ingenious additional variables to capture the effect of sex composition of earlier living children in the family, see the study by Finis Welch (1974).

[28] This assumption conceals many problems of interpreting intervals between births and the directly estimated probability of birth based on a parity group over time. Essentially any behavioral or biological factor will introduce a serial correlation in the residual disturbance that will bias parameter estimates unless directly incorporated into the model's specification and its estimation. When any unobserved factor on either the supply (fecundity) or demand (behavioral) side of the reproductive process exerts a systematic and persistent effect on fertility, the real birth probability for a given parity group will tend to decline as the more fertile members in the group progress to the next parity. This may be interpreted as a selectivity bias or serial correlation component in the disturbances to the equation determining the probability of birth. For a maximum-likelihood estimator for this class of problem, see James J. Heckman and R. J. Willis (1974).

prolonged breast-feeding is exhausted after twenty-four to thirty-six months.[29]

Further Complications and Qualifications

Estimation of the parameters in regression equation 8-4 is more difficult than it would appear. Demand determinants of fertility influence reproductive performance principally by affecting the age at which childbearing starts (and hence the age at marriage in many societies) and stops and is less notably related to the tempo of reproduction before family-size norms are achieved. Thus, intervals from marriage to first birth and subsequent early intervals between births are not always good indicators of completed fertility. For the most part, the demand theory is relevant to an understanding of the determinants of intervals between births at the "margin" when parents already have approximately their desired number of surviving children. But these later intervals are open for many women, and simply excluding observations with open intervals can contribute to a substantial truncation or selectivity bias in estimating the parameters to equation 8-4. To avoid this source of parameter bias, either some information is sacrificed or a substantially more sophisticated reformulation of the model is required (Heckman and Willis 1974).

One simplification is to define the dependent variable as a dichotomous birth "probability" within x months of entering status group n. The status group might be defined in terms of the age of the mother (a proxy for fecundity) and the number of surviving children she has, rather than parity. Since the dependent variable is now dichotomous or binary, the equation might be estimated using a logit or probit model.[30]

[29] For example, in a recent study of a contemporary rural Senegalese population evidence is found that if the first child dies after eighteen to twenty months, the average interval between births (where the second conception occurred after the death) is about thirty-five months, whereas the average interval for mothers whose first child died during the first two months of life is twenty months. If the first child survived to the end of the prospective study period, or at least forty-two months, the average interval was thirty-four months (Cantrelle and Leridon 1971, table 12).

[30] Maximum-likelihood estimators to a transformed nonlinear model such as that implied by the logit or probit framework are preferable to ordinary least-squares or direct-regression estimates of a linear-probability function. The linear-regression model can predict for outliers a negative or greater-than-1 probability of birth, which may be difficult to interpret. Ordinary regression estimates are less efficient because they neglect heteroscedasticity in the disturbances. Finally, standard errors of the linear-regression parameters are not consistent, and conventional t tests are consequently suspect, whereas asymptotic efficiency and consistency are properties of maximum-likelihood estimators of the nonlinear formulations of the model.

Combining in a single equation information on the occurrence of births in various periods since the last birth (or change in status), X, the time pattern of selectivity bias could be estimated by the inclusion of period-specific dummy variables.

Another difficulty of inferring from data the magnitude of mortality's effect on fertility is the possibility that mortality also depends, to some degree, on fertility. If causal relations work in both directions, and both are positive, the direct association between these variables will represent the sum of these two causal effects. In this case, reducing mortality by some policy intervention will operate on only one side of this two-way system of relationships. The direct association between mortality and fertility will, consequently, overstate the policy leverage of mortality-reducing programs on the subsequent level of fertility. Two questions arise in this context: How large is the reverse effect of fertility on mortality, and how can one eliminate this reverse effect from response parameters obtained when estimating models such as those proposed in equations 8-3 and 8-4?

The conjecture is made in numerous studies that an infant's survival and physical and mental development depend on such variables as the size of family he is born into, the length of the interval before and after his birth, and his mother's parity and age (Wray 1971b, Williams 1974). This large body of evidence is to some degree misleading, for it has long been recognized that socioeconomic class and environmental variables are highly correlated with *both* fertility and mortality (see, for example, Verijn-Stuart 1902). Since the majority of these investigations report only simple tabulations and make no effort to hold constant the socioeconomic determinants of both fertility and mortality or disentangle the two causal effects, the observed association between child mortality and family size probably overstates both independent causal effects.[31]

I am not aware of substantial evidence on the magnitude of this potentially important effect of fertility on child mortality in low-income

[31] It is not obvious to me that cross-sectional aggregate data will permit one to identify confidently the two simultaneous relations linking fertility and child mortality. Even time series on aggregates from low-income countries would probably exhibit sufficiently strong serial correlation that the results would probably be very fragile. For example, Robert G. Repetto (1974) ingeniously derives from a cross-sectional sample of forty-five countries simultaneous-equation estimates of both relationships. He concludes that fertility influences infant mortality more strongly than infant mortality affects fertility. But his identifying restrictions and specifications are on the whole arbitrary, and the use of income-distribution variables in the mortality equation (Rodgers 1974) might have reversed his interesting results. The research technique implicit in Repetto's investigations is admirable, but I suspect that only individual survey data will permit one to disentangle the two causal relations.

countries. A. D. Williams did not find evidence of such an effect on child mortality in the 1965 U.S. National Fertility Survey. She noted weak evidence that neonatal mortality is lower and postneonatal and preschool mortality (between the ages of one and four) somewhat higher the more live births there were in the family, holding constant the mother's education, age, and husband's income (Williams 1974, tables IV.3 and IV.4). Without being able to include any socioeconomic status variables, Finis Welch (1974, table 7), in survey data collected in Bangladesh in 1960, found evidence that child survival was positively related to length of interval since preceding birth but negatively related to the length of the subsequent interval. On the other hand, Pierre Cantrelle and Henri Leridon (1971, table 13) found no evidence that the length of the interval since preceding birth affected an infant's chances of survival in a rural Senegalese population.

If one shifts from child mortality to other measures of child development, educational attainment, and intelligence, several recent studies in high-income countries confirm the role of family size and birth order on these later measures of performance.[32] What causes these relationships, however, is not yet clear; do less-than-adequate parents tend to have larger families, or does the sheer size of large families lead to deprivation in terms of material goods and maternal time available per child? Peter H. Lindert (1974) has suggested for the United States that a mother's time inputs per child vary in roughly the same fashion by family size and birth order as does educational performance of the offspring. Direct evidence on the effect of fertility on child and maternal mortality and the cause of this effect must await more precise and rigorous statistical analysis of family histories from low-income settings.

[32] In a careful analysis of several bodies of data collected in the United States, Lindert (1974) estimates family-size and birth-order effects on a child's educational attainment, holding constant other socioeconomic characteristics of his parents. He is also able to show that there is a corresponding variation in the mother's input of her own and others' time into each child by family size and birth order of the child. Although the mother's time input per child declines somewhat if she is in the labor force, substitute child care more than offsets this decline, neglecting any quality differences. L. Belmont and F. A. Marolla (1973) show that males in the Netherlands from a single birth cohort exhibit family-size and birth-order effects on intelligence, measured by a standard armed forces examination. Both of these effects are measured simultaneously by tabulation of IQ within three socioeconomic classes defined by the child's father's occupation. More directly relevant to this study, child mortality is linked to social class in a classic series of studies (Morris 1964) performed in England. Exploratory models based on international cross-sectional data suggest that fertility is associated with mortality. But improved measures of both variables and careful choice of identifying restrictions will be required to transform these models into convincing evidence of child mortality's effect on fertility (Repetto 1974).

If there are no satisfactory estimates of the effect of fertility on child mortality, how is one to minimize or correct for this source of simultaneous-equation bias in estimating the converse relationship? One approach is to analyze the time sequence of vital events for individual families (equation 8-4), holding constant determinants of demand, z, such as the husband's wage and the wife's education. Alternatively, if units of observation are aggregated over a period of time, as study shifts to completed fertility, or aggregated over a number of couples, as study turns to average birth rates, the tendency will be for the measured association between child mortality and fertility to overstate the single-direction causal effect.[33]

Summary

Two general approaches to measuring the effect of mortality on fertility may be distinguished. In the first the relationship between completed lifetime numbers of children born by women (stock) as a function of the reciprocal of the expected and actual child-survival rate is examined. In addition there are plausible, if not theoretically strong, reasons to anticipate that desired fertility will diminish as life expectancy of adults and older children increases. Estimates of the lifetime reproductive response of parents to the survival status of their offspring will embody both the effects of shifts in supply (biological) and demand (behavioral), as well as possible secondary effects emanating from fertility to child and maternal mortality. To the extent that increasing child-survival rates extends the period of postpartum sterility and reduces the *supply* of births, less modification of behavior will be required to control fertility to correspond with the parents' diminished *demand* for births. To disentangle these alternative and reinforcing explanations for the association between lifetime reproductive performance and child mortality, it is useful to examine the process of family formation over a period of time and to develop a statistical framework for interpreting the rate of reproduction.

The second general approach is to estimate an equation similar to equation 8-4, in which the dependent variable is a fertility-flow variable, such as an interval between births or its reciprocal, a birth probability. Since demand factors are thought to operate by limiting reproduction at the margin of the surviving family-size norm, analysis of early or infra-

[33] Methods for analysis of time series of cross sections also hold promise of distinguishing between the one-way, short-run dynamic effects of mortality on fertility and the long-run, persistent two-way association between the average community levels of mortality and fertility (T. Paul Schultz 1967, 1973, Nerlove and Schultz 1970).

marginal intervals between births may illuminate the role of biological factors. Analysis of later intervals between births, on the other hand, should be useful for approximating both biological and behavioral factors. To avoid complications associated with truncation bias, short-period birth probabilities might be studied using the logit or probit model for women of the same age, "surviving" parity (that is, having the same number of children alive), and time since last birth. With these two compatible statistical frameworks in mind for the study of fertility as a stock or flow phenomenon, it is now possible to review the empirical literature critically.

A Selective Review of the Empirical Evidence

The relationship between fertility and mortality can be analyzed with data collected at several levels of aggregation—for example, the nation-state, the subnational unit, and the individual couple or woman. Models of fertility are formulated, for the most part, in terms of an individual family decision-making unit. But with conventional assumptions regarding the functional form of the relationship and the nature of statistical disturbances, the parameters obtained from higher levels of aggregation should equal those obtained at the individual family level. Explanatory variables applicable to the region, of course, may have a plausible role in explaining individual behavior, for as observed earlier, individual expectations regarding the future state of mortality may be based on what has occurred in the local community. For some purposes, therefore, the small community or peer group may represent an ideal observational unit for estimating the response of fertility to aggregate trends in mortality.[34]

Intercountry Comparisons

Comparisons of fertility and mortality across countries have not yet made a notable contribution to our understanding of the determinants of fertility and the causal relationship between fertility and mortality.[35] The encyclopedic UN survey, *The Determinants and Consequences of Popu-*

[34] Many studies of the relationship between child survival and fertility are summarized in a background working paper (no. 8) for the 1974 World Population Conference by Carl E. Taylor, J. S. Newman, and N. U. Kelly (1974). Their second table is particularly helpful as a summary of the literature. They also refer to several doctoral dissertations that were not available to me.

[35] Cross-country comparisons of fertility and its determinants are hazardous. Not only do the usual problems of relative prices and inconvertible exchange rates make international comparisons of income levels treacherous, but also most

lation Trends, mentions, almost as an afterthought in concluding its section on the socioeconomic determinants of fertility, that "the decline in mortality among infants and young children has been advanced as a factor responsible for the decline in family size" (UN, Department of Economic and Social Affairs, 1953, p. 81). Regressions of birth rates on infant and child death rates have been reported on several occasions. The failure to replicate findings across these studies may be attributed to the lack of an explicit analytical framework which would help to specify a common estimation equation and to the hazards of using international demographic data, where the errors in measurement are large and anything but random. Moreover, intercountry comparisons have generally been based on period-specific measures of fertility, such as crude or age-adjusted birth rates.

Robert Weintraub (1962) found a positive partial correlation between infant mortality and crude birth rates in the 1950s across a sample of thirty countries. Warren C. Robinson (1963), using census fertility ratios and registered infant mortality rates, found an inverse relationship among some thirty-two low-income countries. Stanley Friedlander and Morris Silver (1967) compiled data for eighty-two countries and found no consistent relationship between infant mortality and crude birth rates or general fertility rates, but they did discover a positive partial correlation when they replaced the UN infant mortality series by a child death rate (deaths, age 0–14 per thousand persons 0–14) obtained from another source. Anker (1974) examined age-adjusted birth rates for the late 1960s across a sample of seventy-six low-income countries and found no indication of a statistically significant (0.1 level or better) partial association between his period-specific measure of fertility and life expectancy at birth (his measure of mortality). Robert G. Repetto (1974), using data for forty-five countries, estimates an equation pre-

---

of the additional data required to test the central propositions discussed here are not available from standard international compendiums in a satisfactory form. For example, few demographers would accept official registered birth and death rates as satisfactory evidence of the level of completed fertility and life expectancy in low- or high-income countries, yet official or registered vital rates are the basis of several such cross-sectional regression studies. Statistics on infant and child mortality are notoriously underreported, particularly in those populations for which true rates are very high. One of the first regression studies of population statistics was that by Irma Adelman. Although accepting the possibility that infant and child mortality might belong in the birth-rate equation she discovered that "since infant mortality is highly correlated with per capita income, the partial regression coefficient of age-specific birth rates upon infant mortality was not statistically significant and fluctuated in direction. This variable was therefore eliminated from the ultimate set of equations" (Adelman 1963, pp. 318–319).

dicting the age-adjusted birth rates as a function of infant mortality and another equation explaining infant mortality as a function of fertility. Both partial regression coefficients are positive but not particularly significant statistically. None of these exercises, unfortunately, examines the data specified in either equation 8-3 or 8-4, and, given the importance of age-composition effects on the crude birth rate and underregistration of official figures on infant mortality, these disappointing results are not a sufficient reason to reject the hypothesis that mortality affects fertility.[36]

In another effort to use country aggregates, Carl E. Taylor, J. S. Newman, and N. U. Kelly (1974, table 1) compare the postwar decline in infant mortality rates and crude birth rates across fifty-three low-income countries. In contrast to the view that birth rates are unaffected by child death rates, they find that, in all but one case, uninterrupted declines in infant mortality preceded the decline in birth rates, with a median interval of 11.7 years. In only three of the fifty-three countries have birth rates not yet begun to decline. Although no relationship between the rates of decline is reported, the tabulated results suggest strongly that the more rapid the postwar rate of decline in infant mortality the more rapid the postwar rate of decline in crude birth rates. Clearly, the next step is to refine the measures of mortality to reflect a broader age span of childhood and replace the crude birth rate by either a measure of completed cohort fertility or a birth rate for women of specific older ages—thirty or over, for example—or later parities.

Registered or official birth and death rates are notoriously unreliable for intercountry comparisons, but tabulations of completed fertility and number of living children by age of women are published in various censuses and surveys. A few of these results are shown in table 8-1, including all the instances I could locate readily in which populations residing in urban and rural areas were tabulated separately. Retrospective data of this kind are undoubtedly prone to serious errors also, particularly in

[36] Robert Weintraub (1962) held constant per capita income and the agricultural share of the labor force, neither of which was strongly related to crude birth rates. Warren C. Robinson (1963) controlled urban share of population and ever married share of women over the age of fifteen. In both of these cases the only statistically significant partial correlation was between infant mortality and fertility, though the signs of the relationship differed. Stanley Friedlander and Morris Silver (1967) included numerous other variables in one regression or another, such as literacy or agricultural and self-employed share of labor force. Infant mortality was inversely related to fertility in the least-developed sample of countries, but in all samples fertility was directly related to child mortality. This implausible reversal when infant mortality constitutes the majority of child deaths raises doubts about the comparability of the sources of data, and in particular, the data on infant mortality registered in the UN *Demographic Yearbook*. The main objective of Robert G. Repetto (1974) is to isolate the effect of income level and personal income inequality on fertility.

Table 8-1. Average Number of Children Ever Born and the Number Living, by Age of Woman and Urban or Rural Current Residence Where Available

Ages of mothers	*Liberia 1970*		*Tanzania 1967*		*Bulgaria 1965*	
	Urban	*Rural*	*Urban*	*Rural*	*Urban*	*Rural*
			Children ever born			
30–34	3.69	3.86	2.87	4.12	1.644	2.138
35–39	4.29	4.21	3.16	4.73	1.830	2.357
40–44 45–49	4.54	4.59	3.19	5.04	2.075	2.602
50+	3.59	3.89	3.27	4.97	2.213	2.796
			Children alive			
30–34	3.24	3.27	2.42	3.06	1.566	1.957
35–39	3.67	3.41	2.61	3.37	1.699	2.076
40–44 45–49	3.70	3.58	2.52	3.33	1.832	2.192
50+	2.75	2.81	2.20	2.90	1.789	2.242
			Survival rate			
30–34	0.88	0.84	0.84	0.74	0.953	0.915
35–39	0.86	0.81	0.83	0.71	0.928	0.881
40–44 45–49	0.81	0.78	0.79	0.66	0.883	0.842
50+	0.77	0.72	0.67	0.58	0.808	0.802

(continued)

underreporting of births and early child deaths that occurred in the more distant past. But these data are at least more appropriate than many to obtain some insight into the relationship represented by equation 8-3. The following relationship is, therefore, estimated by ordinary least squares:

$$CEB_{ij} = F_i(1/P_{ij})^{\gamma_i}u_{ij} \tag{8-5}$$

where *CEB* is the number of children ever born per woman,[37] *P* is the proportion of *CEB* still living at the time of the census, *F* is the desired number of surviving children, γ is the own-cohort child-mortality adjustment elasticity, and *u* is a random, log-normally distributed disturbance term. Within each age group, subscripted *i*, the observation on *CEB*

[37] The underlying data are often reported as children per married woman or per woman with children. All observations were converted to the comparable base of all women in the respective age group. It may be argued, however, that the notion of replacement reproductive response could also be evaluated on the basis of the restricted population of women *with children*. This has not been done for lack of data on most countries.

Table 8-1 (*continued*).

	Republic of Korea (South) 1970			Jordan 1961		Taiwan 1967[a]	
Ages of mothers	*Cities (Sis)*	*Towns (Eubs)*	*Country-side (Myeons)*	*Urban*	*Rural*	*Five cities*	*Other areas*
			Children ever born				
30–34	3.004	3.588	3.950	5.83	6.03	3.525	3.994
35–39	3.914	4.540	5.026			4.286	5.016
40–44	4.618	5.397	5.758	7.14	7.61	4.577	5.579
45–49	5.010	5.712	6.019			4.712	5.869
50–54	5.167	5.693	5.915			4.739	5.847
55–59	5.052	5.422	5.615	6.52	7.08	4.906	5.849
60+	4.747	5.040	5.147			4.639	5.444
			Children alive				
30–34	2.839	3.350	3.654	4.53	4.41	3.394	3.793
35–39	3.605	4.222	4.509			4.045	4.657
40–44	4.066	4.701	4.925	4.98	5.17	4.187	5.000
45–49	4.191	4.751	4.895			4.144	5.057
50–54	4.161	4.552	4.630			4.015	4.832
55–59	3.907	4.131	4.228	3.76	4.04	4.013	4.667
60+	3.370	3.549	3.616			3.579	4.095
			Survival rate				
30–34	0.945	0.933	0.925	0.777	0.731	0.963	0.930
35–39	0.921	0.929	0.897			0.944	0.928
40–44	0.880	0.871	0.855	0.698	0.680	0.915	0.896
45–49	0.836	0.831	0.813			0.879	0.861
50–54	0.805	0.799	0.782			0.847	0.820
55–59	0.773	0.761	0.752	0.576	0.570	0.181	0.798
60+	0.709	0.704	0.702			0.772	0.753

(continued)

and P for a sample of j populations imply estimates of the parameters F and γ, which are assumed to be constant within an age group across the sample. Undoubtedly, F actually differs across the sample, even if γ is constant. If the regression equation could have included appropriate and accurately measured socioeconomic determinants of the demand for surviving children, I would have had greater confidence in the utility of the exercise.[38] Nonetheless, the overall pattern is of some interest simply because all other cross-country studies of fertility have relied on less-

[38] Unfortunately, to include any age- and sex-specific variables that would appear to have a place in such a fertility equation requires dropping most of the observations on fertility and child mortality. Data on education and income were sought by age and sex, and even in the case of literacy only about thirty observations survive. Also, more stringent tests of the consistency and plausibility

Table 8-1 (*continued*).

Ages of mothers	El Salvador 1971 Urban	El Salvador 1971 Rural	Syria 1970 Urban	Syria 1970 Rural	Malaysia, Sabah 1970 Urban	Malaysia, Sabah 1970 Rural	Malaysia, Sarawak 1970 Urban	Malaysia, Sarawak 1970 Rural
				Children ever born				
30–34	3.63	5.06	4.99	3.22	3.63	4.74	3.50	4.20
35–39	4.65	6.22	6.29	6.75	4.64	5.36	4.72	5.05
40–44, 45–49	5.22	7.16	7.20	7.77	5.21	5.28	5.37	5.83
50+	4.85	6.74	6.62	7.20	4.30	4.49	4.46	4.23
				Children alive				
30–34	3.04	4.13	4.29	4.20	3.46	4.05	3.51	3.76
35–39	3.74	4.93	5.23	5.24	4.44	4.50	4.58	4.44
40–44, 45–49	4.02	5.37	5.62	5.60	4.92	4.26	5.18	4.34
50+	3.22	4.49	4.25	4.28	3.84	3.28	4.18	3.41
				Survival rate				
30–34	0.837	0.816	0.859	0.805	0.955	0.854	0.961	0.894
35–39	0.804	0.792	0.831	0.776	0.958	0.841	0.970	0.879
40–44, 45–49	0.770	0.750	0.780	0.721	0.946	0.807	0.964	0.859
50+	0.664	0.666	0.642	0.595	0.892	0.730	0.933	0.807

(*continued*)

appropriate period-specific measures of fertility. Frequently they have even interpreted registered vital rates or official estimates thereof. In table 8-2 the logarithm of the number of children born per woman is regressed on the logarithm of the reciprocal of the cohort's child survival probability. In table 8-3 the regression also includes a time trend (the last two digits of the calendar year of the census or survey; sample and data sources are available from the author).[39] Table 8-4 reports the

of the data might have reduced the size but improved the quality of the sample analyzed here. For example, the Liberian survey-census of 1970 reported a larger number of children alive than ever born. No explanation for this anomaly was provided, but clearly different populations were tabulated in the two tables in the UN *Demographic Yearbook*, 1971.

[39] James McCabe pointed out an additional bias in this stock formulation that would occur if a response error, e_l, occurred because women forgot some of their children who had died but not those who were still living. In the stock model, one can then rewrite the estimation equation 8-5 as follows:

$$ln(CEB_{ij} + e_{lij}) = \alpha_i + \hat{\gamma}_i \, ln\,[(CEB_{ij} + e_{lij})/CA_{ij}] + ln(u_{ij})$$

Table 8-1 (*continued*).

Ages of mothers	Poland 1970 Urban	Poland 1970 Rural	Brazil 1940	Brazil 1970	Indonesia 1965	Central African Republic
			Children ever born			
30–34	1.649	2.538	4.329	4.15	3.863	3.20
35–39	2.032	3.003			4.555	3.44
40–44, 45–49	2.273	3.355	5.910	5.26	4.697	3.94
50+	1.643	2.575	6.220	5.49	4.498	4.22
			Children alive			
30–34	1.579	2.408	3.339	3.62	3.011	2.13
35–39	1.920	2.810			3.477	2.16
40–44, 45–49	2.093	3.035	4.390	4.40	3.360	2.22
50+	1.394	2.144	4.127	4.29	2.943	2.15
			Survival rate			
30–34	0.957	0.948	0.782	0.87	0.779	0.67
35–39	0.944	0.938			0.747	0.63
40–44, 45–49	0.930	0.904	0.742	0.84	0.715	0.56
50+	0.848	0.832	0.683	0.78	0.634	0.51

Source: Liberia, Tanzania, Bulgaria, Poland, Brazil, Indonesia, Zanzibar, Central African Republic: UN *Demographic Yearbook*, 1971, tables 21 and 22. Data without rural/urban breakdown available for an additional sixty countries. Taiwan, Republic of Korea, Jordan: Derived from respective national census publications.

[a] Urban areas of Taiwan are defined as the five largest cities—Taipei, Keeling, Taichung, Tainan, and Kaoshiung—whereas the remainder of the country is not uniformly "rural."

where CA is the number of children living, and α_i is an estimate of $ln(F_i)$ and $\hat{\gamma}_i$ of γ_i. Since this error in the measurement of the dependent variable recurs in the numerator of the right-hand variable (that is, $1/P_{ij}$), this specific source of errors in variables would bias the estimate of $\hat{\gamma}$ toward $+1$. Including other variables determining desired surviving family size (zs) that might be correlated with e_1 could presumably reduce this source of bias. One might have anticipated that if this source of response bias had decreased over time, it would have been negatively correlated with the time trend, and the inclusion of the time trend in table 8-3 would have decreased the estimate of γ below 1. But such is not the case. Considering a smaller sample of countries where data are available on literacy by age and sex, the inclusion of these literacy variables as proxies for the "value of time" (determinants of desired surviving family size) the resulting estimates of γ stabilize at slightly lower levels than those reported in table 8-3.

Table 8-2. Regressions of Children Ever Born on Reciprocal of Child Survival Experience

Ages of mothers	*Size of sample*	*Constant term (ln F)*	*Elasticity of reciprocal of child survival probability (γ)*	R^2	*F (df)*
13–19	96	−2.56	5.27	0.16	18.3
		(14.2)	(4.28)		(1.93)
20–24	94	−0.21	2.10	0.19	21.3
		(2.79)	(4.62)		(1,92)
25–29	97	0.70	0.97	0.11	11.9
		(12.9)	(3.45)		(1,95)
30–34	97	1.13	0.56	0.04	4.31
		(19.3)	(2.07)		(1,95)
35–39	98	1.29	0.60	0.04	5.10
		(20.1)	(2.26)		(1,96)
40–49	94	1.35	0.67	0.07	6.97
		(18.8)	(2.64)		(1,92)
50 or more	99	1.23	0.70	0.16	20.1
		(18.9)	(4.48)		(1,97)

Source: See table 8-4 for variable means and standard deviations. Sample and data sources are available from the author.

Note: *t* ratios reported beneath regression coefficients are in parentheses.

Rural and urban populations shown in table 8-1 are treated as separate observations. Country censuses are from a wide and not obviously unrepresentative sample of countries, of which perhaps ten are developed countries. The first observation is from the 1930 Hungarian census, and the last relate to the 1971 censuses.

arithmetic means and standard deviations of the variables used in the regressions.

Child survival rates alone account for between 4 and 19 percent of the intercountry relative variance in completed fertility (table 8-2). Adding the secular time trend boosts the R^2 to between 0.18 and 0.31 (table 8-3). The number of children that parents appear to want in the absence of child mortality (solving for F) increases in the expected fashion from 0.1 among teenaged women, to an average in excess of three children among women over the age of thirty.[40] Estimates of the elasticity of fertility with respect to cohort child mortality are positive in

[40] Taking the antilog (natural base) of the constant terms in table 8-3 implies that F rises from 0.12 to 0.81, 2.01, 3.10, 3.63, 3.86, and 3.42 over the cohorts by age. From table 8-3, the antilog of the constant term must be increased by the time trend to obtain similar estimates of F in, say, 1960, for example, for the ages thirty-five to thirty-nine: $.017*60+$ antilog $(.17) = 2.21$.

Table 8-3. Regressions of Children Ever Born on Reciprocal of Child Survival Experience and Time Trend

Ages of mothers	*Size of sample*	*Constant term (ln F)*	*Elasticity of reciprocal of child survival probability (γ)*	*Time trend (last 2 digits of year)*	R^2	*F (df)*
15–19	95	−3.65	6.00	0.016	0.18	10.1
		(4.24)	(4.44)	(1.29)		(2,93)
20–24	94	−1.51	2.91	0.020	0.32	21.6
		(4.78)	(6.32)	(4.23)		(2,91)
25–29	97	−0.45	1.57	0.017	0.31	21.5
		(2.01)	(5.76)	(5.27)		(2,94)
30–34	95	−0.05	1.10	0.018	0.28	17.6
		(0.24)	(4.29)	(5.44)		(2,92)
35–39	98	0.17	1.06	0.017	0.24	15.0
		(0.70)	(4.14)	(4.88)		(2,95)
40–49	94	0.40	0.98	0.014	0.21	11.8
		(1.59)	(3.96)	(3.95)		(2,91)
50 or more	99	0.89	0.77	0.005	0.18	11.4
		(3.97)	(4.78)	(1.58)		(2,96)

Source: See table 8-4 for variable means and standard deviations. Sample and data sources are available from the author.

Note: *t* ratios reported beneath regression coefficients are in parentheses.

Rural and urban populations, shown in table 8-1, are treated as separate observations. Country censuses are from a wide and not obviously unrepresentative sample of countries, of which perhaps ten are developed countries. The first observation is from the 1930 Hungarian census and the last relate to the 1971 censuses.

every regression; in the restricted-demand framework this finding suggests that demand for surviving children is price inelastic. These elasticity estimates are "significantly" different from zero at confidence levels exceeding the conventional 0.025 level. The magnitude of point estimates of the elasticity of fertility with respect to cohort child mortality fluctuates considerably by age group, however, and is sensitive to whether or not a time trend is included in the specification of the regression equation. Among women over the age of thirty, when most lifetime fertility has occurred, the elasticity estimates are on the order of 0.6 without allowing for a time trend, and they approach 1.0 when a time trend is admitted. Neglecting differences in desired surviving family size, cohorts exhibit the tendency to vary fertility between 60 and 100 percent of the amount required to compensate fully for intercountry differences in child mortality. This may be an upward-biased estimate

Table 8-4. Mean and Standard Deviations of Variables Used in Intercountry Regression

Age group	*Children ever born*	*Children living*	*Proportion surviving*
15–19	0.27 (0.32)	0.21 (0.22)	0.89 (0.11)
20–24	1.18 (0.46)	1.02 (0.38)	0.88 (0.08)
25–29	2.45 (0.68)	2.08 (0.57)	0.86 (0.09)
30–34	3.58 (0.99)	2.99 (0.84)	0.84 (0.10)
35–39	4.34 (1.25)	3.52 (1.04)	0.83 (0.10)
40–49	4.82 (1.42)	3.75 (1.12)	0.79 (0.10)
50 and over	4.64 (1.28)	3.17 (0.86)	0.70 (0.12)

Numbers in parentheses are the standard deviations.

of the responsiveness of fertility to child mortality because the omission from the regression of socioeconomic determinants of surviving fertility demands that are plausibly correlated with mortality.

There are also a few instances in which it is possible to follow both fertility and surviving fertility over a period of time within a given country. In Brazil, from 1940 to 1970 (see table 8-1), there has been a 40 to 60 percent reduction in the rates of child mortality to mothers of a specific age. With no adjustment in the numbers of children born, Brazilian women in 1970 would have had 10–15 percent more living children than in 1940. Indeed, among women under the age of thirty, the numbers of living children increased substantially. But at later ages, reproductive adjustment is evident; fertility fell among women between the ages of thirty and thirty-nine, between forty and forty-nine, and over fifty by 40, 98, and 78 percent, respectively, of the amount required to keep surviving family sizes at the levels recorded in 1940. This represented a decline in numbers of children ever born of 4, 10, and 11 percent in comparison with those of their "parents" generation enumerated at these ages in the 1940 census. Many changes in Brazil have undoubtedly worked to increase and decrease fertility in this thirty-year period, but whatever the cause it appears that the combined effects of these changes have been sufficient to approximately maintain the surviving family size despite the dramatic decrease in child mortality.

Table 8-5. Ratio of Child Mortality in Rural Areas to That in Urban Areas by Ages of Mothers

Country and year of survey or census	*Ages of mothers*			
	30–34	*35–39*	*40–49*	*50 or more*
Liberia 1970	1.17	1.36	1.16	1.22
Tanzania 1967	1.63	1.71	1.62	1.27
Bulgaria 1965	1.81	1.65	1.35	1.03
Poland 1970	1.21	1.11	1.12	1.11
South Korea 1970[a]	1.36	1.30	1.18	1.10
Taiwan 1967[b]	1.35	1.29	1.19	1.11
Jordan 1961	1.21	1.21	1.06	1.01
El Salvador 1971	1.13	1.06	1.09	0.99
Syria 1970	1.38	1.33	1.27	1.13
Sabah 1970	3.24	3.79	3.57	2.50
Sarawak 1970	5.58	4.03	3.91	2.88

[a] Korean comparison is ratio of mortality in Myeons (rural) to that in Si's (larger cities).

[b] Ratio of mortality in noncity regions to that in five major city areas. See note a, table 8-1.

Rural–Urban Comparisons

Until at least the turn of the twentieth century, the expectation of life at birth was higher and infant and child mortality was lower among rural than among urban populations in Europe and North America (UN, Department of Economic and Social Affairs 1953). Even after World War II, registered crude death rates were often higher in major cities than they were elsewhere in a country, regardless of the country's stage of development (WHO 1950). Warren C. Robinson (1963, tables 2 and 3) concludes from his survey of the evidence that infant and child mortality rates are as high in urban areas as in rural areas of nonwestern countries or higher. It is not clear, however, whether these registration figures reflect anything more than the greater margin of underreporting of vital events (Arriaga 1967a) in rural areas, particularly in low-income countries, where the costs to parents in time of birth and infant death registration can be substantial and the anticipated penalty for noncompliance inconsequential.

Where rural and urban data are readily available on children ever born and children now living by age of mother (table 8-1), child death rates for the two populations are compared in table 8-5. In every instance, except among women of the age of fifty and over in El Salvador, rural child death rates exceed urban. Relative differentials have not markedly narrowed with time (among younger parents), although the existence of such a trend could be masked by many factors.[41] Whatever interpretation one attaches to time trends, this retrospective evidence from a small and possibly unrepresentative group of eleven countries is not consistent with Robinson's conclusion.[42]

With the exceptions of Liberia and Sarawak, the number of children ever born per woman is greater at each age in the rural populations than in the urban (table 8-6).[43] On an average across these countries, rural fertility exceeds urban by 20 to 24 percent. But by the age of thirty-five or over, the greater incidence of child mortality among rural populations than among urban has narrowed the difference in *surviving* fertility by one-third. These retrospective data again challenge Robinson's evidence of higher child–woman ratios in urban than in rural areas of many nonwestern countries. There are, undoubtedly, urban areas where both fertility and child mortality are higher than in surrounding rural areas, but as a generalization for nonwestern countries it would seem appropriate to rely more on retrospective and prospective survey and census materials and use vital registration data with caution.[44] Contemporary retrospective evidence indicates that a substantial share of the observed excess of rural fertility over urban might arise because of the greater incidence of child mortality in rural areas than in urban.[45]

[41] For example, more frequent underreporting of early child deaths (and probably also births) among the less literate, *older* rural populations and the increasing share of younger urban residents that have migrated to the city and report, to some degree, the child-mortality rate they experienced in rural areas before migrating.

[42] It also conflicts with the presumption of the UN Department of Economic and Social Affairs survey (1953) and subsequent reviews of the evidence (see Johnson 1968). Simon Kuznets (1974) expresses the judgment that probably in many areas rural death rates are higher than urban, but the evidence he cites is evenly divided on the direction of the differential.

[43] The 1970 Liberian survey was noted earlier for its inconsistencies and discrepancies among the younger cohorts and would have been excluded had it not conflicted with the point I wanted to make.

[44] Other isolated studies of mortality based on census and survey materials have confirmed higher mortality (and fertility) among rural than urban segments of the population; for example, see F. C. Shorter (1968, table 3) on Turkey, T. Paul Schultz (1972, p. 419) on Bangladesh, and S. K. Gaisie (1975) on Ghana.

[45] Simon Kuznets (1974) has proceeded in the reverse fashion with a larger number of countries. Working backward from the number of children under five per 1,000 population, he adjusts for the fertility-weighted proportion of women in the rural and urban populations and estimates that the child–woman ratio is 20 percent larger in the rural than in the urban areas of forty-seven less developed countries and 31 percent larger in fourteen developed countries (see table 11, col. 7). Adjusting for greater infant mortality in rural than urban areas of less developed countries (assumption 1), he estimates that birth rates are 25

Table 8-6. Ratio of Children Ever Born (CEB) and Children Alive (CA) in Rural and Urban Areas by Ages of Mothers

Country and year of survey or census		*Ages of mothers*			
		30–34	*35–39*	*40–49*	*50 or more*
Liberia 1970	CEB:	1.05	0.98	1.01	1.08
	CA:	1.01	0.93	0.97	1.02
Tanzania 1967	CEB:	1.44	1.50	1.58	1.52
	CA:	1.26	1.29	1.32	1.32
Bulgaria 1965	CEB:	1.30	1.29	1.25	1.26
	CA:	1.25	1.22	1.20	1.25
Poland 1970	CEB:	1.54	1.48	1.48	1.57
	CA:	1.53	1.46	1.45	1.54
Korea 1970[a]	CEB:	1.32	1.28	1.22	1.13
	CA:	1.29	1.25	1.19	1.10
Taiwan 1967[b]	CEB:	1.13	1.17	1.23	1.19
	CA:	1.12	1.15	1.21	1.16
Jordan 1961	CEB:	1.03	1.03	1.07	1.09
	CA:	0.97	0.97	1.04	1.07
El Salvador 1971	CEB:	1.39	1.34	1.37	1.39
	CA:	1.36	1.32	1.34	1.39
Syria 1970	CEB:	1.05	1.07	1.08	1.09
	CA:	1.02	1.00	1.00	1.01
Sabah 1970	CEB:	1.31	1.16	1.01	1.04
	CA:	1.17	1.01	0.87	0.85
Sarawak 1970	CEB:	1.17	1.07	0.94	0.94
	CA:	1.07	0.97	0.84	0.82

[a] Korean comparison is ratio of mortality in Myeons (rural) to that in Si's (larger cities).

[b] Ratio of mortality in noncity regions to that in five major city areas. See note a, table 8-1.

Interregional Comparisons

Since vital statistics are collected and often published according to civil administrative units, these subnational regions are frequently the unit of observation in empirical research on the determinants of, and trends in,

percent greater in the rural than in the urban populations (table 12, col. 3) of less developed countries. He thus obtains an estimate that one-fifth of the differences in fertility between rural and urban areas is offset by early child mortality, under his first assumption regarding differential child mortality under the age of five.

demographic phenomena.[46] In early studies in Germany (Geissler 1885) and the Netherlands (Verijn-Stuart 1902) the fact that birth and death rates varied together across regions is documented. Verijn-Stuart, in his Dutch study, attempted to hold personal income level constant by grouping twenty rural communities without industrial employments into four wealth classes. Comparing the poorest and richest rural areas, the (live) birth rate was 26 percent greater in the former than in the latter. According to the mortality figures reported, the number of children reaching the age of five would have been only 11 percent greater in the poor community than in the rich community. This evidence suggests that socioeconomic differentials in fertility might be due in part to class differences in mortality.[47] Evidence for regions of Amsterdam also conformed to this pattern.

A number of recent investigators have also sought to explain interregional differences in fertility in terms of mortality and socioeconomic factors. Birth rates in Puerto Rico across municipalities in 1894–97 and 1951–57 are positively associated with earlier death rates (T. Paul Schultz 1967). In the more recent period, for which registration of vital events is virtually complete, death rates lagged one and two years help to explain birth rates; the magnitude of this time-series cross-sectional relationship indicates that birth rates are sufficiently depressed in locali-

[46] It is beyond my competence to survey the complicated and rapidly growing literature on interregional patterns of fertility decline in Western Europe. In such a broad area there are probably instances where interregional differences in child mortality do not parallel fertility differences, as may be the case for Belgium or Hungary from 1850 to 1910 (Coale 1973). But child mortality is only one among many factors that could provide a comprehensive explanation for the timing and magnitude of the secular decline in fertility. Simple correlations or one-way tabulations will not settle the question. In other areas, such as France (van de Walle 1974) and Germany (Knodel 1974), the interregional variation and even turning points of child mortality and fertility appear to be highly correlated. This is still weak evidence of causality, for other socioeconomic changes may have produced both outcomes. The coincidence of the declines in child mortality and fertility in Germany is noted by Knodel as casting doubt on the causal relation from mortality to fertility. Within the five-year average that he examines, this coincidence may only indicate the speed with which older parents can be expected to respond to changes in their child mortality experience. The historical record of Western Europe may yet contribute significantly to the formulation of a model of the demographic transition which will be partially applicable to the experience of low-income countries. But for this contribution to materialize, the potentially rich time series on interregional developments in Europe will have to be analyzed with sophisticated statistical techniques.

[47] Relatively few studies of socioeconomic differentials in mortality can be cited, since mortality statistics typically contain less information on the deceased than fertility statistics contain on parents. See A. J. Mayer and P. M. Hauser (1953), E. M. Kitagawa and P. M. Hauser (1968), and the classic series of articles on child mortality by J. Morris and J. Heady (1955).

ties where death rates are low to yield lower rates of natural population increase.[48, 49]

In studies of Taiwan that are based on meticulously collected registration statistics for 361 administrative units of the island, a positive relationship between age-specific birth rates, particularly among women over the age of thirty, and the reciprocal of the child survival rate to the age of fifteen is confirmed (T. Paul Schultz 1973). Holding educational characteristics of the population constant, as in the Puerto Rican study, the relationship to child mortality is statistically most significant if the child mortality variable is lagged two to four years. The length of the replacement lag varies with the age of the mother as does, presumably, fecundity. The magnitude of the reproductive response of older women is sufficiently large that surviving-family size may be held in check as child mortality declines.

Simple cross-sectional estimates of the response elasticity of birth rates to child mortality in Taiwan diminish when an error-components model is estimated on the basis of both time-series and cross-sectional information or on the basis of variables that are expressed as changes over time. Even with these more restrictive short-run dynamic formulations, the response coefficients are robust and large in magnitude among women over the age of thirty (see table 8-7), and the reproductive response is found to be stronger when the deceased child is a boy than when it is a girl.[50]

Analysis of completed fertility by age of woman across fifty rural and urban areas of Chile on the basis of the 1960 census reveals a similar positive relationship to infant mortality (DaVanzo 1972). Though mortality is not measured by the cohort's actual child mortality, as pre-

48 This study held constant the local population's educational characteristics and children's and women's labor-force participation rates. As in the Taiwan study reported next, both cross sections and the time-series data are combined in an error-components model, and the resulting response parameters appear to be less than is implied from a straightforward cross-sectional regression.

49 From a simultaneous-equation model estimated for Puerto Rican municipalities for the 1950–60 period it can be inferred that some of the effect of mortality on fertility is associated with other forms of intervening household behavior, such as marriage and women's labor-force roles (Nerlove and Schultz 1970). In this simultaneous-equation study an attempt was made to account for marriage patterns, family income levels, women's labor-force participation, and the birth rate. In this later period only two-fifths of the decline in crude death rates was offset by a decline in birth rates. Both of these studies of Puerto Rico are limited by their analysis of crude birth and death rates, and they are unable to adequately adjust indirectly for age composition effects. They do not clearly provide the information needed to test equations 8-3 and 8-4.

50 See the Jordanian census of population 1961, table 4.3, for example, as reported in Schultz (1970, table 7).

Table 8-7. Estimates of Reproductive Response to Child Mortality Expressed as a Percentage of That Required to Maintain a Constant Number of Children Reaching the Age of Fifteen per Woman

	Taiwan 1964–69 age-specific birth rates[a]			*Chile 1960 children ever born*[b]	*Bangladesh birth probability*[c]		*Philippines 1968 children ever born and infant mortality*[d]		*Sierra Leone 1966–68 children ever born*[e]
Ages of mothers and size of sample	*Pooled cross-sectional time series*	*Difference 1969–64*	*Error-components cross section of time series*	*Regional cross section*	*1957–61*	*1955–56*	*Own experience of mortality*	*Community level of mortality*	
15–19	479	−62	−5	116	61	54	—	—	117[f]
	(12.3)	(−0.80)	(−0.19)	(1.04)	(5.73)	(4.30)	—	—	(5.72)
20–24	118	36	1	94	38	24	104	474	123[f]
	(9.03)	(0.95)	(0.04)	(1.38)	(4.02)	(2.78)	(2.6)	(2.7)	(7.63)
25–29	72	32	45	133	20	17	NS	NS	—
	(8.22)	(1.30)	(4.76)	(2.52)	(2.54)	(2.13)	(−0.27)	(−0.01)	
30–34	231	161	109	169	54	29	NS	NS	117[f]
	(14.5)	(4.05)	(7.79)	(2.69)	(5.44)	(2.50)	(−0.79)	(0.86)	(5.46)
35–39	510	389	204	191	40	38	103	266	112[f]
	(17.9)	(5.33)	(8.19)	(2.72)	(4.92)	(3.80)	(3.3)	(2.4)	(3.95)
40–44	659	477	264	172	—	—	NS	NS	92[f]
	(16.6)	(4.08)	(7.33)	(1.98)			(0.80)	(−0.64)	(2.12)
45–49	449	96	300	201	—	—	0.92	268	—
	(4.97)	(0.28)	(3.02)	(1.97)			(2.4)	(1.8)	
	Total fertility rate								
15–49	201	105	61	—	—	—	—	—	—
	(20.7)	(5.14)	(9.83)						
Age 12 and over	—	—	—	121	—	—	—	—	1.15
				(1.78)					(10.6)
Size of sample	361 × 6	361	361 × 6	50	700–900	600–900	150–250	150–250	50–233

[a] Age-specific birth rates are regressed on the reciprocal of the child-survival rate from birth to the age of fifteen, derived from the current period, holding education and occupational structure of the population constant (Schultz 1973, tables 4A, 4C, and 5A). The mean child death rate to the age of fifteen is 56 per 1,000 live births.

[b] The study of Chile regresses the infant mortality rate on numbers of children ever born to women of different ages as well as on children–women ratios. The sample mean infant-mortality rate was 124 per 1,000 live births, and it is estimated that about 170 children born alive died before reaching the age of fifteen in 1959–61 in Chile. The percentage reduction in births associated with a percentage reduction in infant mortality is related to the percentage decline presumed to extend uniformly to later child deaths up to the age of fifteen (DaVanzo, 1972, table 4, pp. 47–48, and table 11, pp. 78–79).

[c] See Schultz and DaVanzo (1970a), tables 8 and 11. These estimates are based on the linear probability formulation. Reestimation using the logit model and maximum likelihood procedures obtained slightly larger partial derivatives of the birth probability with respect to a child death (about 15 percent) and larger *t* statistics (about 10 percent). The age ranking of coefficients and their statistical significance did not change between the two formulations of equation 8-4.

[d] Harman (1970) constructs three child-mortality variables, each defined as the reciprocal of the child-survival rate (tables 1, 2, and 3 and p. 33). The first is defined in terms of the woman's own infant-survival rate (i.e., survival for the first year of life). The second is defined in terms of the same measure of mortality averaged within the relevant residential area of which 112 were sampled in the Philippine National Demographic Survey (NDS) of 1968, or a community infant-mortality variable. The third is defined as the proportion of pregnancies of the women that resulted in children still living at the time of the survey. Although this last variable seemingly incorporates relevant information on later child mortality, it also includes information on fetal wastage that tends to be unreliable. The survey implies infant- and child-mortality rates that are too low, and these rates do not systematically increase for births in earlier years. Thus it seems reasonable to conclude that the NDS measures of child mortality are less reliable than those used in other studies cited in this table. To calculate the response rates, I used the third regression (Harman 1970, table 2) that included both the mother's own infant-mortality experience and that of her residential community. NS indicates that the corresponding coefficient is not statistically significant and that no elasticity was reported by Harman (1970, table 3).

[e] Derived from Snyder (1974, tables 5 and 6). The mortality variable is defined as the reciprocal of the child-survival rate. The education of the husband and of the wife are held constant among other socioeconomic variables.

[f] The age groups are different from those in the stub of the table; they are 15–21, 22–28, 29–35, 36–42, and 43–49.

scribed in equation 8-3, current differences in infant mortality by region appear to be a useful proxy for regional variation in the previous child mortality experience. Again, it is noteworthy that the estimates of reproductive response are relatively larger and more statistically significant among the older cohorts of women (table 8-7). Since the biological (supply) effect should be comparable across ages, the more pronounced reproductive response among women over the age of thirty suggests that behavioral (demand) factors are predominantly responsible for the observed positive relationship between child mortality and fertility at these ages.

Individual Differences in Fertility

Contingency-table analysis has often been applied to fertility data tabulated by various socioeconomic and demographic characteristics. Although it is often found that more fertile women have experienced more frequent child mortality, this empirical association may reflect, for the most part, a tendency for underlying socioeconomic variables to affect fertility and child mortality in the same direction. To interpret such findings, therefore, one must at a minimum hold constant such socioeconomic characteristics as the woman's education, and in order to disentangle channels of causation it may be necessary to examine information on the timing of child mortality and fertility over the individual's life cycle.

As noted earlier, Sanders (1931), using data for Rotterdam from 1870 to 1920, tabulated the length of intervals between births by the woman's initial parity and according to whether and when the first child died. The evidence that child mortality hastened the arrival of the subsequent birth was interpreted by Sanders as "proof" of a substitution or replacement motivation on the part of parents that helped him to account for the twentieth-century decline in fertility. Historical demographers have more recently studied the effect of infant mortality on intervals between births and viewed it as proof of the biological effect of lactation on fecundity. No one, to my knowledge, has yet estimated, according to equation 8-4, the separate fertility effects of a child's death attributable to behavioral and biological factors, while holding constant the more important socioeconomic determinants of reproductive demands. But several investigations based on individual retrospective histories have estimated the overall magnitude of the compensating response of fertility to child mortality.

A sample of 4,200 married women in Central Bangladesh collected in 1960–61 was used to estimate a birth-probability function similar to equation 8-4, but without controls for socioeconomic determinants of desired surviving family size (T. Paul Schultz and DaVanzo 1970a). The effect of a child's death on the mother's subsequent probabilities of birth are shown in table 8-7, holding constant the postpartum sterility effect of a birth in the previous year (or two). The magnitude of the response to child death is greatest among the youngest and oldest women, even though the mean probability of birth is greater among women between the ages of twenty and twenty-nine. Also, the reproductive response is greater, as noted in Taiwan, when the deceased child is a boy than when it is a girl.

The Philippine National Demographic Survey, collected in 1968, was used by Harman to estimate the fertility effects of infant mortality among a couple's own children and community levels of infant mortality. Though the survey's retrospective information on fertility and mortality is not entirely consistent with national time trends, associations at the individual level generally support the hypothesis that young and older mothers respond positively to both their own reported infant mortality and the average infant mortality rate for their residential region (see table 8-7).

From a 1966–68 sample of 717 married women between the ages of fifteen and forty-nine in Sierra Leone, Snyder (1974) estimated by cohort the elasticity of completed fertility with respect to own child mortality, measured by the reciprocal of the survival rate, holding education of husband and wife constant. Estimates of elasticity average greater than 1, and they are highly significant in a conventional statistical sense (table 8-7). In this African population, the replacement response is fully compensating and is apparently not delayed until the process of family formation is more or less complete at the age of thirty-five, as it evidently is in Taiwan, Chile, and Bangladesh.

From a 1963 survey of 2,700 Egyptian mothers, S. Hassan (1966) confirmed that the death of a child influenced the tendency for a mother of a given parity to have an additional birth, holding educational attainment and religion constant. The larger the number of children that died, the larger the ultimate family size. His evidence, however, is not readily converted into behavioral response coefficients, as shown in table 8-7.

Shea O. Rutstein (1971, 1974) found evidence among Taiwanese women sampled in 1967–68 that reproductive performance compensated partially for child mortality, holding wife's education, husband's occupation, and family income constant. The probability of a wife's progressing from one parity to the next tends to be an increasing function of the number of children lost earlier. But the replacement response, in his sample, is not quite sufficient to assure that women with greater-than-average child losses would, on an average, have an equal or greater-than-average number of surviving children.

Yoram Ben-Porath (1975) examined the fertility and child-mortality experience of immigrants to Israel before and after immigration, according to their region of origin (Europe and America or Asia and Africa) and time of immigration (before or after 1948). The derivative of births abroad before migration with respect to child deaths abroad is approximately unity in the twelve age, origin, and time-of-immigration groups. Additional births in Israel respond inversely to the number of previous births and positively to the number of child deaths, but total replacement before and after immigration is somewhat greater among the Western than among the Eastern immigrants. Summing the reproductive replacement response both before and after immigration, the response of Eastern immigrants is two-thirds to three-fourths that required to maintain the average numbers of surviving children, holding husband's and wife's education constant. Among the Western immigrants from Europe and America, the total reproductive response to child mortality exceeds replacement, suggesting that, on an average, they ultimately have one-sixth to one-fourth more surviving children (Ben-Porath 1975, table 14) than otherwise.

David M. Heer (1972) undertook the more ambitious task in Taiwan of attempting to measure the reproductive response to child mortality *and* to determine how well people were able to quantify their observations about the local time trends and the levels of child mortality. On the average, the fertility of a mother in his sample compensated for about 60 to 70 percent of her child losses.[51]

Finally, A. D. Williams (1974), in her analysis of the 1965 National Fertility Study of 5,600 currently married U.S. women, was unable to find evidence of replacement-reproductive behavior in a population in which infant mortality was relatively low—about 36 per thousand live births.[52]

Summary of the Evidence

There are undoubtedly many other investigations of the relationship between mortality and fertility that have escaped my attention. But from

[51] Although subjective evaluations of child mortality and attitudinal questions in general were not reliably replicated for the same person upon reinterview, behavioral outcomes and characteristics were. Regional differences in the actual level of child mortality and past trends were quite accurately perceived by the population, *on an average,* in different regions of Taiwan, even though there was substantial variability in individual responses. Heer is engaged in further work on the perception of changes in mortality and its effect on fertility in several other low-income countries.

[52] Holding wife's and husband's education constant, she finds a tendency for the number of births to respond positively to child mortality (age one to four years) but negatively to neonatal mortality (age birth to twenty-seven days),

those surveyed here the evidence is qualitatively strong though quantitatively imprecise regarding the underlying biological and behavioral processes. It cannot be said with assurance that the reproductive response of parents in the course of time to the declining incidence of child mortality is likely to compensate fully for the increased number of their offspring that today reach maturity. The evidence, nonetheless, uniformly suggests that in low-income countries the response is likely to exceed one-half of the amount required to achieve a constant surviving family-size target. Moreover, about half the studies of aggregate and individual data imply response rates in excess of unity; increased research seems warranted to determine under what conditions a reduction in child mortality induces a more than offsetting decline in fertility, leading directly to a decline in the size of surviving family. Since adult mortality tends to decrease along with child mortality, though proportionately less, it should be noted that a reproductive response coefficient of about 1.3 would be necessary for the decrease in fertility to offset entirely the tendency of advances in life expectancy to increase the intrinsic rate of population growth.[53]

Because empirical analysis of family histories has not taken the form of estimating the parameters to an equation such as equation 8-4, only highly tentative conclusions can be advanced as to the roles of biological and behavioral factors in the positive relation between child mortality and fertility. Response coefficients for period-specific birth rates and birth probabilities appear to be frequently larger for women over the age of thirty. This age pattern of response is consistent with the sequential adaptive view of the adjustment of fertility to child mortality (T. Paul Schultz 1967). In a few cases it would appear that very young mothers also respond strongly to replace a deceased child, perhaps in instances in which it is a firstborn or firstborn male that dies, and the wife's status depends significantly on the presence of a male heir. The general age pattern of response coefficients and evidence of sex preference found in several studies does not seem, on the surface, consistent with an explanation for the association between child mortality and fertility that stresses the predominance of an autonomous biological mechanism.

---

with little net effect exhibited for the sum of all preschool child mortality (table IV.5).

[53] A far more complex model must be specified to make more precise statements about the effects of mortality decline on cohort fertility and period-specific fertility. The simulations reported by J. C. Ridley et al. (1967) demonstrate the way in which the decline in mortality may influence natality by its positive effect on the prevalence of intact marriages, but no behavioral adaptation is introduced explicitly into their simulation exercise.

The Determinants of Mortality and the Opportunities for Policy Intervention

Much has been written about why mortality declined. For simplicity, these explanations are grouped here under two headings: developments associated with increased levels of private material well-being and developments that either depend on public investments or derive from new medical knowledge and technology that reduce the cost of effective health measures. In economic terms, the first class of factors is linked to individual wealth effects and the second to social-policy interventions and changes in relative prices.

It is widely believed that differences in mortality in Western countries during the early stages of industrialization were directly related to levels of personal wealth and that they resulted from class differences in quality of housing, nature of work place, diet, education, and place (rural or urban) of residence (Wrigley 1969). The gradual decline in mortality in Western Europe during the eighteenth and nineteenth centuries is seen as the net consequence of two offsetting trends: rising average levels of real wealth, on the one hand, and the redistribution of the population toward less healthy urban areas, on the other. Personal inequality in the distribution of incomes may have also increased in this period, but in this respect the data are not robust. With the exception of control of smallpox, the role of improved knowledge of medicine and public health was relatively unimportant in the decline in mortality until the last years of the nineteenth century and became significant only later in this century (Glass and Grebenik 1966, p. 73).

Once Western societies had ceased to be primarily rural and agricultural and had become primarily urban and industrial, personal wealth and residential location became the primary determinants of mortality differentials, since medical knowledge was not yet of much value. The diffusion of valuable medical innovations in the early twentieth century contributed to the rapid control of many infectious and pneumonial diseases. One might have expected to find stronger evidence that health care and the ability to buy it mattered in this period of rapid change, but such is not clearly the case. As degenerative diseases, such as cancer and those of the heart, became an increasingly important cause of death in high-income countries, the risk of mortality, with notable exceptions, may have become less strongly associated with socioeconomic class.[54]

[54] It should be noted, however, that infant and early childhood mortality continue to be linked to socioeconomic class and wealth level. It is believed that this is due to the fact that the lowest-income classes in a country such as the United States do not receive adequate prenatal medical care. See also J. Morris and J. Heady (1955).

Some investigators argue that today educational attainment and consumption patterns are becoming more highly correlated with mortality than material wealth and accessibility to and use of medical services (Fuchs 1973). But evidence is still woefully inadequate for such generalizations with regard to the United States or other high-income societies (Kitagawa and Hauser 1973, Reid 1975).

In low-income countries the decline in mortality is often interpreted quite differently. G. J. Stolnitz (1955, 1956, 1965) has concluded that innovations in public health and sanitation were the direct and proximate cause of contemporary mortality trends in the low-income world and not increases in overall income levels. Mortality trends are "remarkably neutral with respect to economic events. . . . Economic misery as such is no longer an effective barrier to the vast upsurge in survival opportunities in the underdeveloped areas" (Stolnitz 1965, p. 117). Other scholars interpret events in similar terms but stress the catalytic role of international agencies and outside assistance in reducing death rates without increasing material levels of living correspondingly (Glass and Grebenik 1966, pp. 86–89, Coale 1973, Berelson 1973). Consequently, it is frequently asserted that levels of private wealth and resulting opportunities for consumption are much less relevant to the secular trends and differentials in mortality in low-income countries today than they were in high-income countries at a similar stage in their demographic or economic development. Furthermore, great importance is attached to investments in public health, organizational capacity, and new medical technology in increasing survival rates in low-income countries in the last several decades.

Although this widely accepted view may be plausible, it has not been rigorously inferred from quantitative analysis of mortality trends and differentials. The possible exception may be programs for the eradication of malaria in a few countries (Newman 1965, 1970, Meegama 1967, Newman and Meegama 1969, Frederiksen 1960, 1961, Barlow 1967). But even in the most dramatic instance of Ceylon, only a quarter of the postwar decline in mortality is attributable to control of malaria, and the remainder is *not* associated at the district level with various public health services or their utilization (Gray 1974). Socioeconomic development and redistribution of income would appear to be responsible for a large part of the unexplained decline in Ceylon's death rate.

Vital statistics on mortality and information on health inputs have not been widely analyzed, holding socioeconomic factors associated with income and nonmedical price effects constant. In order to estimate with confidence the causes for past trends in mortality and thereby to provide a basis for evaluating the probable effects on future levels of mortality of changes in public-sector priorities, more sophisticated quantitative studies of this type are going to be needed. Evidence has been accumulating, meanwhile, that levels of private wealth and patterns of consumption do exert pronounced effects on the speed and timing of declines in mortality in both middle- and low-income countries—Italy from 1870 to 1930, for example (Newell 1972).

There is also evidence in low-income countries that further declines in mortality will depend increasingly upon improved economic conditions for the mass of the population. Field research shows that high levels of childhood mortality found in low-income countries are primarily due to gastroenteritis and diarrheal disease, which are on the whole immune to Western modern medical technology (McDermott 1966, Gordon et al. 1964, Preston and Nelson 1974, Sullivan 1973), and which are likely to be the cause of death only in an already malnourished population (Scrimshaw et al. 1968, Scrimshaw and Gordon 1968, Kallen 1972, Puffer and Serrano 1973). In many low-income societies this remaining major cause of childhood mortality is intimately related to nutritional deficiencies that are in turn closely linked to private physical wealth of families and educational attainment of mothers (Sloan 1971).

Investigations of differences in death rates across countries also cast doubt on the common view that declines in mortality have occurred independently of economic development in low-income countries. In an exploratory study based on data from fifty-six countries, Gerry Rodgers (1974) sought to account for differences in expectation of life at birth, in terms of per capita income and its distribution.[55] Rodgers found an implied maximum life expectancy, as the level of income rises, of about seventy-five years among his sample of low-income countries, and a robust negative partial correlation between his measure of inequality of personal income (that is, a Gini coefficient) and life expectancy, holding constant the nonlinear effect of income level. Other investigations have also confirmed that in an international cross section, per capita income levels are negatively associated with age-specific death rates, even when a number of additional socioeconomic variables are included in regression equations (Adelman 1963).

An international comparison of cause-specific mortality rates (Preston and Nelson 1974) is also consistent with fragmentary field and survey evidence.[56] The relative structure of cause-specific mortality has changed

[55] Income levels were assumed to affect life expectancy in a nonlinear fashion. The level of income was therefore introduced in various transformations to permit the marginal effect of equal increments to income to diminish as the level of income rose. If the individual relationship between income level and life expectancy were nonlinear, then the personal distribution of income would be relevant in determining a country's average life expectancy.

[56] See J. M. Sullivan (1973) for an analysis of cause-specific mortality in Taiwan in which he arrives at the same conclusion.

in the course of time with infectious and parasitic diseases and respiratory tuberculosis declining and being replaced in low-income countries by diarrheal disease. "Western and nonwestern populations shared to approximately the same extent in the accelerating progress against infectious diseases, and developments during the postwar period are more appropriately viewed as an extension of prior trends rather than as radical departures therefrom" (Preston and Nelson 1974, p. 2). The increasing "rate of medical and public health progress against infectious diseases" contrasts with the "disappointing rate of progress against diarrhoeal disease," specifically in nonwestern populations (Preston and Nelson 1974, p. 2). To the extent that diarrheal disease responds mainly to increases in levels of living, educational expenditures and consequent improvements in nutrition and home hygiene (category one), nontraditional "health" policies may be needed to reduce child mortality further. It would be premature, however, to conclude that the evidence collected to date is sufficiently convincing to use for most public-policy purposes in low-income countries (Taylor, Newman, and Kelly 1974).

In sum, there are strong indications that a large part of the decline in mortality in this century, in both high- and low-income countries, is due to control of infectious and parasitic diseases and respiratory tuberculosis. Some persons believe that further reduction in the incidence of the remaining degenerative diseases in high-income countries will be less responsive to increased levels of wealth or increased per capita medical inputs, at least as they are currently distributed. Conversely, the persisting high levels of diarrheal disease and resulting mortality among children in low-income countries are not readily linked to the provision of modern medical services, but to the provision of better nutrition and living conditions that depend, for the most part, on increases in levels of private income and their more nearly equal distribution among persons. In these low-income countries, the further decline in childhood mortality increasingly depends on improved levels of living, particularly among the poor, and perhaps also the increased educational attainment of women. These nontraditional interventions of policy to reduce mortality warrant increased quantitative study. Only when they are analyzed together with the relationship between fertility and mortality (discussed in earlier sections of this chapter) will we obtain a clear picture of the way in which economic development has contributed to, and been influenced by, the recent changes in death and birth rates.

Conclusions

Parents seem to respond to the decline in child mortality by having fewer births, perhaps to some extent because of the biological effect of an infant's death, which interrupts lactation and shortens the mother's sterile period following a birth. But this association also appears to reflect strong behavioral preferences of parents to replace an infant who dies. This replacement motivation cannot be derived from a simple economic model: many related economic effects of a child's death on family wealth, prices, risks, and returns on human capital might contribute to a positive behavioral relationship between fertility and mortality. Declines in mortality increase the real value of income streams, and in particular they raise the relative value of human versus physical capital goods for accomplishing intertemporal life-cycle transfers. Since these human assets are less unequally distributed among persons than are physical assets, such as land and reproducible physical capital, the decline in mortality also has an equalizing effect on the personal distribution of wealth, at least in the short run.

Existing empirical evidence does not permit a precise attribution of the response of fertility to mortality between biological and behavioral factors, yet the noticeable pattern of reproductive response coefficients obtained for women of different ages and according to the sex of the deceased child indicate that behavioral aspects of this relationship should not be underrated. Future investigations of pregnancy histories should estimate the biological and behavioral effects separately, which would be possible with the use of equation 8-4.

Fortunately, the sum of the biological and behavioral effects is of principal interest for policy or the *total* reproductive response to child mortality. With all their deficiencies, about half the studies contain evidence that the reproductive response of mothers is sufficient to maintain a nearly constant or even diminishing surviving family size while adjusting to lower child mortality. In the other half of the cases, the response in the time horizon studied (often two to five years) was sufficient to compensate only partially for the observed differences in child mortality.

It would be worthwhile to estimate the coefficients of comparable fertility models from a variety of surveys (using the standard survey pregnancy roster format) to ascertain under what conditions demographic equilibrium within the family (implicit in the demographic-transition hypothesis) reasserts itself most rapidly. What social conditions, such as perhaps a national family-planning program, are associated with larger and more rapid reproductive responses? Are there threshold values below which steady declines in child mortality elicit an increasing response? These are clearly topics that are tractable to analysis but are not studied within a common conceptual framework. Empirical evidence from many different sources has, therefore, not yet added up to much firm knowledge about these relationships.

Extending human life is viewed as an indisputable good, requiring no justification. But I suspect that a consequence of this attitude has been a certain demotion in the claims to public resources of public health programs in low-income countries. Without serious efforts to measure the effects of development policies on mortality, and an equally diligent effort to quantify the consequences of mortality on fertility, child schooling, labor productivity, and personal welfare, policy interventions to reduce mortality are likely to continue to lose out in the competition for funds.

Research on this topic will rely mainly on nonexperimental data. It will, therefore, be very important what is being held constant in such a study and in what manner it is being held constant when partial associations among fertility, mortality, and policy variables are being evaluated. The most serious barrier to an experimental approach is the ethical one of administering "treatments" that are thought to influence the risks of human mortality. Also, any prospective framework will be costly because of the infrequency of mortality in most contemporary populations and because of the consequently large size of the samples that will be required to obtain statistically precise results. Selective migration, which is taking place at unprecedented rates in most low-income countries, further complicates the use of prospective data even where it would otherwise be justified.

Consequently, increased effort may be directed to improving retrospective survey instruments that would compile life histories of demographic events and temporally related socioeconomic aspects of the family's environment and behavior. With such improved sources of data many of the questions posed, but left unanswered, in this chapter could be settled. There is no reason to expect, however, that identical answers would be forthcoming from different groups. One may entertain the working hypothesis that with sufficient study the biological mechanisms regulating fecundity could be generalized to all populations. But it would be premature to anticipate, in the foreseeable future, that social science research on such a complex and poorly understood process as the determination of fertility would yield a common behavioral model for the world's many populations. Country- and culture-specific investigations will be required for the design of sound local policy.

9.

The Roles of Rural Women: Female Seclusion, Economic Production, and Reproductive Choice

RUTH B. DIXON

In a broad sweep of land extending across North Africa through the Middle East into South Central Asia, one finds a number of countries that share certain economic and cultural characteristics relevant to the issue of female roles and reproductive behavior. In most of these Moslem and Hindu countries—from Morocco to India—rural women, on the average, marry while still in their teens, some into polygamous households; bear children at rates among the highest in the world; are unable to read or write; and, with few exceptions, are not engaged in what is officially defined as "gainful economic activity" (see table 9-1).

With authority vested in the hands of their elders and individual wishes subordinated to the needs of the larger family unit, young people in these rural areas tend to have little, if any, control over the major events of their own lives. Decisions regarding their schooling, marriage, place of residence, vocation, and day-to-day activities are largely out of their hands. For women, early and frequent pregnancies are a way of life. Sharing the hardships of poverty with male members of the household, many girls and women endure, in addition, the consequences of cultural systems and religious beliefs incorporating the practice of female seclusion.

All societies develop techniques for dealing with the potentially explosive aspects of girls' sexual coming-of-age. In Moslem societies (with the exception of Indonesia) and among higher-caste Hindus, one finds in some classes a variously expressed, complex system of beliefs and

I would like to express my great appreciation to Cathy Holden, Judith Justice, Emily Moore, Hanna Papanek, John Ratcliffe, Ronald G. Ridker, John Stoeckel, and Caroline Strout for their helpful comments on an earlier draft of this paper.

practices in which girls approaching marriageable age, as well as married women, are secluded within the home in order to protect both the chastity of the females and the honor of the entire kin group (Papanek 1971, Youssef 1974). Even in rural village communities, female participation in economic production outside the home or in other public activities (except those that are segregated by sex) is frequently forbidden.

The central argument of this chapter is that the practice of female seclusion, by depriving girls and women of direct access to material and social resources in the community at large, creates in them a condition of extreme economic and social dependence that not only compels their early marriage but also militates against the effective practice of birth control within the marital union. From a policy perspective the question is whether the cluster of social, economic, and cultural motives governing these marital and reproductive decisions could be substantially altered. Certainly the possibility of changing decision-making patterns within the family *directly* seems rather remote. What a policy *can* do, however, is to change the external variables that are likely to lead to internal change (Goode 1963, p. 145). As social and economic opportunities for girls and women in the community begin to undermine old bases of authority within the family, and as traditional patterns of early marriage and frequent child bearing become less easy to justify, a more "desirable" form of demographic behavior may emerge. It is toward this goal of influencing reproduction indirectly, through changing the socioeconomic environment in which the relevant decisions are made (either explicitly or implicitly), that the proposals in this chapter are directed.

The Influence of Female Economic Dependence on Nuptiality and Fertility

The theme of premarital chastity for girls pervades the literature on marriage in regions of Moslem and Hindu influence. Quite simply, "virginity is revered" (Omran 1973, p. 108). When this reverence coexists with the belief that, without close supervision, women's strong sexual drives know no restraint, the result is inevitable. "A social system in which the security of a man's honor lies in the sexual virtue of his womenfolk is bound to engender within its very structure rules controlling the relationship between the sexes. . . . It is, therefore, to be expected that concern with sexual purity and the high cultural value placed on virginity would lead to the practice of early and parentally supervised marriage and the relative seclusion of adolescent girls before that event" (Youssef 1974, p. 85).

Table 9-1. Demographic and Labor-force Data by Sex for Countries in North Africa, the Middle East, and South Central Asia, Based on Recent Censuses in Countries with Populations of One Million or More

Region and country	Percentage never married: Females 15–19 (1)	Percentage never married: Females 40–44 (2)	Percentage never married: Males 20–24 (3)	Percentage never married: Males 45–49 (4)	Mean age at first marriage[a] Female (5)	Mean age at first marriage[a] Male (6)	Mean age at first marriage[a] Gap (7)	1973 crude birth rate (8)	Percentage females 15–19 literate (9)	Literacy ratio F/M (10)	Percentage females 20–24 enrolled (11)	Percentage females 20–24 economically active (12)	Percentage females 15+ in non-agricultural (13)	Non-agricultural ratio F/M (14)
North Africa														
Libya 1964	25.7[b]	0.7	69.4[b]	2.4	18.8[b]	25.1[b]	6.3	46	15.3	22	13.5	4.4	4.2	8
Morocco 1960	45.0	1.7	59.0	2.5	17.5	23.9	6.4	50	14.0	43	n.a.	7.6	8.3	23
Algeria 1966	53.5	1.4	54.4	2.3	18.3	23.6	5.3	50	23.8	44	n.a.	3.6	2.4	8
Egypt 1960[c]	66.9	1.8	75.5	2.2	19.7	25.9	6.1	37	18.1	50	n.a.	7.3	3.0	13
Tunisia 1966	81.1	1.8	82.3	3.8	20.8	26.8	6.0	38	34.6	49	15.9	8.7	4.5	10
Middle East[d]														
Iran 1966[e]	53.9	1.0	69.0	1.5	18.5	25.0	6.5	45	27.8	50	13.9	14.2	10.8	25
Syria 1960	58.9[f]	3.0	72.3[b]	4.6	20.4[f]	25.6[b]	5.2	48	16.8[g]	31[g]	n.a.	10.0	5.4	12
Iraq 1965	67.9	4.4	65.0	6.4	20.6	25.2	4.6	49	26.8	41	n.a.	n.a.	n.a.	n.a.
Jordan 1961[h]	72.0	2.8	64.2	3.6	20.3	24.6	4.2	48	34.0	45	11.8	6.9	1.9	6
Turkey 1965	72.3	1.6	56.2	2.3	19.3	23.3	4.0	40	51.5	64	n.a.	61.1	n.a.	n.a.
South Central Asia[i]														
Bangladesh, Pakistan 1961	25.5	1.0	51.2	2.8	16.6	23.2	6.5	51	13.4	36	2.5	14.2	1.7	10
Nepal 1961	26.2	0.7	26.8	1.6	16.6	20.0	3.4	45	n.a.	n.a.	n.a.	69.3	1.9	24
India 1961	29.2	0.6	43.9	3.3	16.8	21.8	5.0	42	23.8	46	n.a.	43.6	3.6	13
Sri Lanka 1963	85.0	4.3	84.8	7.4	22.1	27.6	5.5	30	82.0	91	n.a.	29.3	8.2	21

Sources: Columns (1)–(4) UN *Demographic Yearbook*, 1971, table 12; 1968, table 7. (5)–(7) Calculated from Hajnal (1953, p. 130). Figures are singulate mean ages at first marriage calculated from census data with the assumption that the percentages of males and females defined as never married at the census date represent the experience of real cohorts passing through their marriageable years. (8) 1973 crude birth rate; Population Reference Bureau, Inc., 1973 World Population Data Sheet. (9)–(10) Percentage of females between the ages of fifteen and nineteen, defined as literate, and female literacy rates as a percentage of male rates; calculated from UN *Demographic Yearbook*, 1971, table 18; 1964, table 33; 1963, tables 12 and 13. (11) Percentage of females currently enrolled in school; UN *Demographic Yearbook*, 1971, table 20; 1964, table 36; 1963, table 15. (12) Percentage of females between the ages of twenty and twenty-four defined as economically active; International Labour Organisation (1972, table 1; 1971, table 1). (13–(14) Percentage of females fifteen years old and over in nonagricultural employment, female nonagricultural employment rates as a percentage of male rates; International Labour Organisation (1973, table 2A/1; 1972, table 2A/1).

n.a., Not available.

[a] Calculated on the assumption that no one is married before the age of fifteen, which may overestimate the mean marriage ages for some countries.

[b] Percentage between the ages of eighteen and nineteen never married. Singulate mean age at marriage calculated on the assumption that no one is married before the age of eighteen, which will overestimate the mean marriage age, especially for females.

[c] Excluding aliens and population in frontier districts.

[d] Excluding Lebanon, Saudi Arabia, Yemen Arab Republic, and People's Republic of Yemen, for which no information is available.

[e] Settled population only.

[f] Percentage between the ages of sixteen and nineteen never married. Singulate mean age at marriage calculated on the assumption that no one is married before the age of sixteen, which may overestimate the mean marriage age for females.

[g] Percentage literate aged ten and over.

[h] Including Palestinian refugees.

[i] Excluding Afghanistan, for which no information is available.

Although the ideal of seclusion is possibly more difficult to fulfill in rural districts where women's work is often needed for agricultural labor or other outside chores such as carrying wood or water, in towns and villages the practice may be more easily enforced. Indeed, it is frequently considered a mark of high social status for a man to keep his women confined to the home, concealed from the eyes of strangers. Consequently, among many caste and class groupings the participation of girls and women in economically productive activities outside the home is severely limited. The low percentages of females between the ages of twenty and twenty-four who are defined as "economically active" in recent censuses (as shown in table 9-1)—well under 10 percent in North Africa and in some Middle Eastern countries—speak directly to this point.[1] In Egypt, even where girls and women do participate to some extent in agricultural labor, their participation rates and hours worked fall far below those of males (see chapter 4). The discrepancy is probably typical of the North African, Middle Eastern, and South Central Asian regions as a whole, with the possible exception of the poorest classes of rural peasants.

Effects on the Timing of Nuptiality

While the economic dependence of girls and women on the men of their household undoubtedly strengthens male control over female activities, the men must bear the economic burden of maintaining the entire family. This support includes daughters of marriageable age who, unlike daughters-in-law residing in the household, do not offer the "saving grace" of producing sons. Among poor families, early marriage of non-income-producing daughters thus appears an ideal solution to their economic pressures, and the daughters themselves have little voice in the matter. In Iran, for example,

> Poverty is one of the main reasons for inducing children to leave their parents' home, as parents begin searching for ways acceptable to the norms of the society to reduce the burden of too many children for too

[1] It is important to note at the outset that census figures on women's economic activity in the countries under discussion here frequently exclude large numbers of agricultural workers who labor regularly in the fields but are not counted as "economically active" or "gainfully employed." The economic contribution of women's labor in the home is, of course, also excluded from official figures. The focus in this paper on women's low levels of economic productivity is not meant to imply that females are in any way economically "inactive," but only that the activities in which females commonly engage are far less likely to be directly rewarded than are male activities.

> little food and space. The most widely accepted way of relieving the burden is to marry off the girls as soon as possible. Thus, as soon as *Sar Bezeer* (a man who has some income and has no bad habits such as drinking, gambling, etc.) is found, the family council will immediately approve of the marriage, and the girls have no part in making the decision. [Momeni 1972, p. 548]

But unmarried daughters are not economic burdens in all rural societies. Parents in rural and urban Nigeria, for example, were equally likely to consider their out-of-school daughters (between the ages of fifteen and eighteen) as their sons more than "worth their keep" in the earnings or work they contributed to the household (more than 60 percent of parents believed this for both daughters and sons; see chapter 4). In sub-Saharan Africa, in Burma, Malaysia, and Laos, and in parts of Sri Lanka, India, and Indonesia, girls and women of some classes and castes perform a major portion of the agricultural work (Boserup 1970, Ward 1963). The work may be wage labor on plantations or estates producing a direct cash income; elsewhere it is unpaid work on family holdings. Even communities normally practicing female seclusion may mobilize their young girls and womenfolk for seasonal tasks such as planting, weeding, or harvesting.

Adolescent girls, whether secluded or not, are also frequently productive in other ways: they may take on the major burden of running the household and caring for younger siblings, or they may produce handicrafts or other goods for household consumption or for sale. Their value to the family is such that the loss of their contribution at the peak productive ages of early adulthood would be keenly felt—particularly so if there were no marriageable sons to bring young brides into the family.

If daughters do perform an important productive role, is it not possible that parents will be less eager to marry them off when it means losing the benefit of their labor or earnings and that the daughters, if their work produces income or property over which they have some control, will be more assertive in decisions regarding the choice of a mate (perhaps postponing the marriage itself)?

Regarding the first point, entire families among the Achutas in the rural Punjab, who perform agricultural labor, contract to harvest land by sharecropping (Mamdani 1972, p. 94). Since girls and women now share agricultural labor with their husbands and brothers, these low-caste families are said to look upon the birth of females with much less disfavor than formerly and are reluctant to see their daughters marry and move away to another village precisely when they have reached the age of greatest productivity.[2] Similarly, among the Jats, or higher-caste farmers, the intensification of agriculture has increased the work load of girls and women who remain secluded in the home but who must prepare food for the wage laborers. "The longer the daughter stays unmarried, the more assistance she can lend her family" (Mamdani 1972, p. 102). Grown daughters among the Jats also earn their dowries by sewing, spinning, and weaving. Some of these products are sold for cash; others accrue to the household. Mueller suggests that the desire to capitalize on the economic benefits of grown sons may be partially responsible for recent trends toward delayed male marriages in agrarian societies such as rural India (see chapter 4). If parents could be induced to take a more "instrumental" (that is, material) and less "moral" view of their daughters' nuptials (Blake 1967), and if daughters were economically productive, is it not possible that female marriages could be considerably delayed as well?[3]

To consider the second point, although researchers have explored in different cultures the effects of wives' income on family decision-making patterns, there are few studies that show the effects of children's income on these patterns. In Hong Kong the contribution to the household income "has elevated the unmarried working-class daughter to a position of unprecedented authority," although she is still hampered by the traditional ideology of age stratification (Salaff 1972b, p. 15). This authority presumably gives her greater say in the choice of a husband and the timing of her nuptials, which she may then delay while she follows her vocation. In contrast, Youssef believes of Moslem cultures that "whereas in other societies an unmarried working girl enjoys economic independence, emancipation from parental control, and a more favorable bargaining position in the marriage market, in Middle Eastern countries she has none of these advantages" (Youssef 1974, p. 106). The difference may

[2] Increasing the economic contribution of girls could be a potent force in reducing the strong preference for sons that is thought to contribute to high birth rates in many developing countries (see chapter 4). I am arguing that rather than having a pronatalist effect, reducing the discrepancy between the value of girls and the value of boys could have a substitution effect. It is important that the economic returns on having daughters be delayed insofar as possible to their otherwise marriageable years, however.

[3] In late nineteenth-century Japan, for example, unmarried daughters often left home to work in city factories or shops or households, sending home earnings to their rural families who invested the much-needed cash in improving agricultural productivity. By delaying their daughters' marriages, parents not only maintained the benefit of the additional income but postponed payment of a dowry as well (Davis 1963, p. 355). Janet W. Salaff reports of Hong Kong that parents of working daughters who are contributing heavily to the household expenses are not at all anxious to see them leave home (Salaff 1972b, p. 17).

be due to the Moslem working girls' higher class backgrounds, in which parents are especially concerned to maintain their privileged status by arranging financially and socially desirable marriages for their daughters. It is doubtful that working daughters of poor rural peasants or landless laborers would be quite so constricted.

Influence on Desired and Actual Fertility

In most of the Hindu and Moslem countries under discussion here, marital fertility in rural areas remains extremely high. Table 9-1 shows crude birth rates in the forties and low fifties for all but three countries in the region. In Bangladesh, "on an average a rural woman has eleven to twelve pregnancies. She might have one or two miscarriages, two or three of her children might die young and she might have six or seven surviving children. . . . She has little control over her body, the decision to have children is totally her husband's. Rarely would a rural woman practice any form of birth control" (Jahan 1973, pp. 11–12). Although Jahan's observations are largely subjective, numerous family-planning surveys confirm, with few exceptions, the low level of deliberate birth control throughout the rural regions.[4]

If married women in rural villages were economically active in agricultural wage labor or were producing goods for sale or exchange, and if they had some control over the money they earned, would their reproductive ideals and practices be altered? Discussions of the relation between female employment and fertility usually focus on the argument of role incompatibility: where mother and worker roles are most incompatible, it is argued, an inverse association between female employment and fertility is most likely to appear. (For a review of theory and findings in this area see Dixon 1975, Frejka 1971, Hass 1972, McGreevey et al. 1974, Piepmeier and Adkins 1973, Stycos and Weller 1967, and Weller 1968, among others, and chapter 10 in this volume.) The evidence holds primarily for nonagricultural work in the modern sectors of towns and cities—exactly the type of work that is extremely rare in the countries under discussion here. It can be seen from the data in table 9-1 that even where relatively high proportions of males engage in nonagricultural work, females are virtually absent from this sphere. In Libya, Algeria, Tunisia, Jordan, and Pakistan (including Bangladesh), for example, fewer than 5 percent of adult women were involved in non-

[4] This is not to suggest that child bearing approaches the maximum biological limits. Many practices, such as extended periods of lactation or postpartum taboos on sexual intercourse, limit total fertility whether or not they are intended to do so.

agricultural occupations in recent censuses, less than one-tenth the percentage of males.

These census figures include urban employment; opportunities for nonagricultural work in the rural villages are of course even scarcer. Most studies show that the type of economic activity in which women commonly engage in rural areas may encourage them to have *more* children, not fewer. Women (and men) who labor in the fields may wish for more children, especially sons, to lessen their burden (Bindary et al. 1973, Goldstein 1972, Mamdani 1972). Women engaged in handicraft work at home, confined as they are to the domestic sphere, bear children at rates similar to those of housewives not otherwise engaged (Jaffe and Azumi 1960). Indeed, the isolation of home-based handicraft production has been viewed as a conservative influence on attempts to change family roles and to organize production on a larger scale in northern and central China (Salaff 1972a, p. 250). Only when agricultural wage labor takes women away from the home for long hours on a more-or-less permanent basis—thus approximating the conditions of nonagricultural employment (Pinnelli 1971)—or when handicraft production is organized around a central work setting where women are placed in active contact with one another, does the "expected" negative relationship between female employment and fertility in rural areas begin to appear.

The role-incompatability argument is too narrow by itself, however. Women's gainful employment outside the home may reduce fertility not only by motivating women to want fewer children, but also by enabling them to express their intentions more effectively. Access to birth control is a crucial factor. Unskilled women hospital workers in Old Delhi, for example, were more likely to adopt family planning than were similarly unskilled women factory workers because the former had access to family-planning information and services on the job (Minkler 1970). Women who earn their own money and contribute to household expenses are also likely to participate more actively in family decision making, including decisions about family size and family planning, than are women who are totally dependent financially on their husbands or on other male household members (Oppong 1970, Khalifa 1973). Their greater role in decision making is associated, in turn, with a higher probability that the couple is practicing some form of contraception and practicing it effectively [see Goldberg (1974) on Turkey and Mexico; Mitchell (1972) on Hong Kong; Mukherjee (1973) on India; United Nations ECAFE (1973) on Iran, India, Singapore, and the Philippines]. Policies aimed at creating a socioeconomic environment favorable to aspirations toward smaller families in rural areas must clearly take the particular conditions of women's employment into account to maximize their potential impact on reproductive behavior. Home-based handicrafts and subsistence agricultural labor are simply not enough.

The Effects of Social Dependence and Individual Powerlessness

The practice of seclusion, aside from producing a condition of economic dependence in females by impeding their access to income-producing activities in the public sphere, can create simultaneously a condition of extreme social and psychological dependence deriving from their physical and social isolation in the home. There are, however, important differences in the observance of purdah between Moslems and Hindus as well as across regions, classes, and castes within the religious groupings.

Although the purdah system everywhere limits interaction between males and females outside certain categories, among Moslems the excluded categories are males outside the kin unit, whereas among Hindus the restrictions apply primarily to a woman's interaction with the males in her husband's family (Papanek 1973, pp. 289, 302). In several (Hindu) Agarwal communities in India, for example, only 16 percent of the adult women said they felt free to discuss important decisions with the person in authority in their husband's household, and most observed purdah in the presence of older males (including their husbands) by keeping to separate quarters, standing while males were present, and eating only after the men had finished (Gore 1968, pp. 153–170).

The degree of physical isolation of women observing purdah also varies considerably: some may remain confined strictly to their household compounds while others are able to move more freely through public areas by wearing their *burqas* or to visit in one another's homes. Again, the variation by religion, region, class, and caste is enough to warrant Papanek's conclusion that it is "impossible to make any categorical statements about its extent or even its distribution" (Papanek 1973, p. 296). The practice is integrally related to the maintenance of status, the sexual division of labor, rules of endogamy and exogamy in the selection of marriage partners, and attitudes toward female sexuality, among other factors. In addition, the combination of deference to male authority, personal powerlessness, and narrow world view engendered by the severely constricted social and spatial environment of girls and women observing purdah probably constitutes a major determinant—or at least a major correlate—of their early marriages and frequent child bearing.

Influence on the Timing of Nuptiality

In the rural areas of the countries under discussion, the arranged match remains very much the rule.[5] Although we have suggested that parental control over the timing of nuptiality may not necessarily result in early marriage if elders stand to benefit in other ways by keeping unmarried daughters at home, we are speaking here of cultures in which adolescent girls are viewed as being highly vulnerable to their own and others' volatile sexual impulses (Papanek 1971, p. 519, Youssef 1974, p. 85). Control over sexuality is maintained through strict segregation of the sexes, close supervision of unmarried girls, and the arrangement of early marriages.

Considering that the arranged match is also intended to create and maintain essential social, economic, and political alliances among families, tribes, or villages, it is clear that one cannot talk of reducing parental control without recognizing the extreme resistance that such an idea would encounter. Although many countries legally require the consent of the young woman to her marriage, such "consent" is often a pro forma, passive acquiescence on the girl's part. Under current conditions in rural Bangladesh, for example, "a girl would not dream of going against the wishes of her elders" (Jahan 1973, pp. 20–22; see also Goode 1963, pp. 92–93). But the arranged-match system does tend to break down naturally under the impact of urbanization and industrialization, as processes of individual geographical and social mobility undermine old patterns of social control (Mitchell 1971). *Within* rural communities, increasing the access of girls and young women to material resources, such as income-producing labor, and to social resources, such as schooling and the open exchange of ideas with other people in the community, could also enable them to exercise their right to marry only with free and full consent.

Levels of schooling are strongly correlated with the timing of female nuptiality. Among thirty-three East European, Middle Eastern, and Asian countries, the percentages of girls between the ages of fifteen and nineteen who were defined as illiterate in censuses around 1960 explained 55 percent of the variance across countries in the proportions of females between the ages of twenty and twenty-four never married (Dixon 1971,

[5] The preferred age at marriage for boys expressed by adults in M. S. Gore's study of Agarwal families averaged 20.9 years and for girls 16.2 years. Only 2 percent of the sample thought that marriages should be decided by the boy and girl concerned. Fifty-six percent declared that elders should initiate the arrangements and make the sole decisions, and 42 percent felt that elders should consult with the boy or girl before making the final decision (Gore 1968, pp. 201, 207).

p. 226). Extremely low levels of literacy among girls between the ages of fifteen and nineteen in most countries of North Africa, the Middle East and South Central Asia are shown in table 9-1, the highest levels of literacy being found in Sri Lanka (82 percent) and in Turkey (52 percent). In rural areas girls are even less likely to be able to read or write. Note that with the exception of those in Sri Lanka and Turkey, girls are less than half as likely as boys of the same age to be literate.

The literacy differentials between females and males mean that girls and women frequently depend entirely on their menfolk for even the simplest transactions involving reading, writing, or basic arithmetic.[6] These educational inequalities translate into lower levels of communication between husbands and wives that impede the practice of family planning, as we shall see. But the inequalities also encourage the early marriage of girls, whose parents frequently take them out of school—if they attend at all—on the grounds that "too much" schooling makes a girl unmarriageable (Jahan 1973, p. 6). Or perhaps it is more accurate to say that early female marriage exacerbates the educational inequalities. Among social classes in which it is considered appropriate for girls to have at least some elementary skills to attract more highly educated husbands, parents may keep their daughters in school longer. As males in India postponed marriage in order to obtain education for better employment, girls also had to wait longer to find eligible husbands and, in the interim, were often kept in school (Gore 1968, p. 53). In rural villages, however, the combination of either no schooling for girls or only five or six years of schooling at most, with the absence of gainful employment once they leave school, is highly conducive to early nuptiality. And how can a young girl refuse, when she has no other options?

Social Dependence and Family Size

Upon marriage, the young Moslem or Hindu bride—once totally dependent upon her own family for her economic survival and social identity—shifts her primary expectations for support onto her husband and his kin.[7] In patrilineal societies in which the bride goes to live in her

[6] An anecdotal report from Nepal tells of one girl: "She is 21 years old and completely dependent on her seven-year-old brother for every transaction made outside the home because she is illiterate and does not even know how to count adequately. So, she is ashamed to go out alone." Of a widow who lives in the village of Batlichauer, "She is fighting with her brother-in-law over property. She knows that she is being cheated but since she is illiterate she has little recourse except to weep and scream" (Kankalil 1973, p. 19).

[7] Her natal family may still be obligated for her support if she is later divorced, however. [For a discussion of the respective responsibilities of the two

husband's household, the groom's family naturally wishes for a young girl who is healthy, compliant, and hard-working, with many years of potential fertility before her. "At no point in this ideal extension of kin was the husband–wife relationship a central focus. The extreme fragility of the marriage bond undermined still further the importance of the conjugal relationship. Economically and socially the man remained secure in his familial network. *Women came and went.* . . . A marriage brought in a female to produce more family members, to adjust to the larger family, to create wealth for it by her work, but not to found an independent nuclear household with her husband" (Goode 1963, p. 89; italics added).

Not only is the girl disadvantaged by her youth, she is also physically isolated from the security of her own family. For the Hindu bride, her husband's village might be several days' journey from her own. Set suddenly in the midst of strangers, frequently treated as a servant with little or no emotional support from her new husband or his family, the young bride has little choice but to prove her worth by producing children—specifically sons—as soon and as frequently as possible. Moreover, having children is, for the isolated young bride, a way to "build her own intimate social world in which to find recognition and self expression" (Ryan 1952, p. 378). Similar emotional needs were fulfilled by an early first birth in traditionally patrilocal Taiwan and China (Salaff 1972a, p. 246).

In what ways would the social powerlessness of the young bride affect her reproductive behavior? Studies of the distribution of decision-making power between husbands and wives show that the greater the influence the wife has in decision making, the more likely it is that husbands and wives communicate with one another about sex, family size desires, and family planning and the more likely they are to practice effective birth control. (For a review and critique of sociological studies of household decision making, see Safilios-Rothschild 1970.) To cite a few examples:[8] Robert E. Mitchell found in Hong Kong that women are more likely to practice family planning if they have high levels of influence over family

families at divorce or widowhood, see Afzal, Bean, and Husain (1973); Goode (1963), *passim;* Matras (1973), pp. 262–263.]

[8] For additional studies of decision making and reproductive attitudes and behavior among predominantly urban samples in both industrialized and developing countries, see John C. Caldwell (1968c); E. Garcia and A. Ramirez (1971); Reuben Hill, J. Mayone Stycos, and K. W. Back (1959); Attiya Inayatullah (1963); Lee Rainwater (1965); R. Ramakumar and Y. S. Gopal (1972); Florangel Z. Rosario (1970); Bernard C. Rosen and Allan B. Simmons (1971); Constantina Safilios-Rothschild (1969); Robert H. Weller (1968).

decision making, but if husbands and wives differ in their attitudes toward family limitation, the husband's preferences are most likely to predominate (Mitchell 1972). A 1972 UN survey of couples in urban India, Iran, the Philippines, and Singapore found that males dominated family decision making in all four countries, but more so in the first three than in Singapore (UN, ECAFE 1973, p. 10). In all four societies, couples whose decision-making patterns were most dominated by the male were less likely to practice birth control and less likely to talk to one another about sex and family planning than were couples who shared decisions.

Married women interviewed in 1972 in urban and rural areas of three Indian states (Haryana, Tamil Nadu, and Meghalaya) were most likely to know about and practice contraception if they participated in joint decision making in the home and reported their status within the household to be high (Mukherjee 1973, pp. 6–8). In addition, evidence from Mexico City and from Ankara, Turkey, suggests that couples among whom husbands make most decisions about social contacts, household budgets, and other family matters have more live births, expect more children ultimately, and are far less likely ever to have used contraception than are couples among whom both decide or among whom the wife usually or always makes the decisions (the latter a rare event indeed) (Goldberg 1974).

If a greater degree of communication and equality between husbands and wives in household decision making facilitates the adoption of family planning and smaller family-size ideals, is it possible to specify the conditions under which joint decision making is most likely to occur? Although we referred above to the positive influence of the wife's income, some studies suggest that control over economic resources may not always result in greater decision-making power for the woman in those cases where a strong ideology of male dominance prevails (Safilios-Rothschild 1970). Two additional potentially relevant social resources that appear to contribute to joint decision making within the home, and which are subject to manipulation through policy measures, are female schooling and freedom of movement outside the home.

The education of the woman, both in absolute numbers of years and in relation to that of her husband, correlated significantly with patterns of reported joint decision making in studies in Hong Kong (Mitchell 1972); India, Iran, the Philippines, and Singapore (UN, ECAFE 1973); India (Mukherjee 1973); the United States (Rainwater 1965); Greece (Safilios-Rothschild 1969); Brazil (Rosen and Simmons 1971); and Ghana (Oppong 1970), among others. A 1972 survey of 1,200 married women in several urban and rural communities in Upper and Lower

Egypt found that the wife's education was the most important factor determining her status in the family and in the community. Illiterate women—the majority of the rural sample—were particularly disadvantaged. Women who could not read or write were the least likely to have been consulted by their families regarding the choice of their future husbands (fewer than half, while among women with secondary or higher education more than 90 percent had been consulted). Moreover, illiterate wives were more likely than literate wives to say they should "accept their lot in life" or "accept for the children's sake" if their husbands treated them badly; more likely to say that the husband should decide in matters of household management; less likely to go out of the house alone; and less likely to agree that a wife should use contraceptives even if her husband disapproves (Khalifa 1973, pp. 169–179, 220).[9] In the Ankara and Mexico City surveys, the wife's education was a better predictor of her decision-making power, her attitudes toward role segregation, and the extent of her husband's restrictions on her movements than were the husband's income or the wife's urban or rural origins (Goldberg 1974).

The freedom to move about in the community and to interact with others can also be considered an important social resource, yet many women in cultures practicing female seclusion are deprived of even this basic right. In an Egyptian survey, for example, 84 percent of the married women said that they had to get their husbands' permission every time they went out—75 percent in urban areas and 91 percent in the rural communities studied (Khalifa 1973, p. 151). Forty percent were not permitted to go out alone at all to buy things from the market, and 17 percent were not permitted to visit relatives alone (Khalifa 1973, p. 150). Yet women who *were* permitted more freedom of movement by their husbands were more likely to agree that wives should use contraceptives, even if their husbands disapprove, and were more likely actually to attend a family-planning clinic if they knew about its existence than were women who were strictly confined to the home (Khalifa 1973, pp. 221–223, 246). In Ankara 37 percent of the wives were forbidden to go shopping by themselves (Goldberg 1974). Indexes constructed from a number of questions regarding the husbands' control over their wives' movements were strong predictors of actual and expected family size and of contraceptive practice, with husband-dominant couples being most fertile.

[9] A surprisingly high proportion of the Egyptian women said yes when asked, "Do you agree that a woman should go ahead and use a contraceptive even if her husband disagrees?" About 30 percent of the total sample agreed, ranging from 11 percent in rural Kena Governate to 37 percent in rural Sharkia and 38 percent in the urban areas (Khalifa 1973, p. 219).

In sum, a strong argument could be made that the condition of economic and social dependence engendered among women observing strict seclusion has highly disadvantageous consequences for the individual, the family, and the community. Those women who are most dependent are most likely to have been married without their consent, most likely to be unaware of birth control methods or to practice them, and most likely to accept their lot in life with resignation. Moreover, the social and economic development of the community in which they live may in turn be impeded by women's lack of schooling, their low level of participation in gainful economic activity, and their resistance to change. Male workers are weighted down by the heavy dependency burden of their women as well as their young children. Women themselves become active participants in their own oppression, hoping for sons to relieve their burdens and greeting the birth of daughters with indifference or despair. Birth rates remain unacceptably high, a drain on the woman's health and on the carrying capacity of the village community. Can population policies be designed to alter these social, economic, and cultural conditions fundamentally?

From Seclusion to Production: The Rural Cooperative

A holistic approach is required to generate change in the socioeconomic conditions of rural villages, particularly when the goal is to reduce the social and economic dependence of women, thereby altering reproductive attitudes and practices. The proposal that follows takes on greater significance when considered as an integral part of larger rural development programs to include land reform, sanitation, health care, functional literacy training, and the generation of new employment opportunities for men as well as women (see Kocher 1973 and Rich 1973 for discussions of the demographic implications of land reform and the redistribution of wealth and social services).

What would happen if small-scale, labor-intensive light industries *employing only women* were established in rural villages and towns? What if, in conjunction with the establishment of these workshops, other innovations were introduced, such as simple living quarters constructed for young unmarried girls living away from home (even in the same village) while earning an independent income, on-the-job functional literacy classes and exposure to mass media as well as vocational training and health care, and the provision of child-care and family-planning services for married women? And what if these centers were not simply imposed on the community by outsiders, with profits extracted from already poor rural districts, but were locally planned and organized according to local resources and needs? What if they were cooperatively owned and run—by the women themselves?

I am suggesting that the establishment of small-scale, collective light industries employing women only would draw females effectively out of the home while removing one of the central obstacles to female employment among Hindu and Moslem groups practicing female seclusion—the fear of indiscriminate association with men. The economic incentives would offer a powerful inducement for the participation of both unmarried girls and married women in poor families. Aside from contributing to the general development and diversification of rural economies, such cooperative workshops would also have other influences on marital and reproductive patterns.

By offering unmarried girls an opportunity for the acquisition of skills and paid employment, they could reduce the economic pressure on parents to marry off their daughters at an early age. If working daughters were to send part of their wages home, they could become highly valued contributors to the family's economic resources. Traditional norms may demand that all incomes of family members be pooled and that expenditures be allocated by the eldest male (Gore 1968, p. 17). If the girl or woman is to have an economic incentive to participate in the program, however, she must be able to keep part of her income for herself or at least have some control over the way in which it is spent. A proposal for working-women's cooperatives in Bangladesh specifies that a fixed percentage of the earnings of each worker be deposited in a savings account for meeting her future needs (National Board of Bangladesh Women's Rehabilitation Programme 1974, p. 31). This could be one way for women to counter the pressures to contribute all of their earnings to the larger family unit. On the other hand, both custom and necessity might require that a method be sought to ensure that the family does receive some immediate economic benefit from the gainful employment of their female members.

If simple residential quarters were constructed in the cooperative workshops for unmarried girls, daughters would no longer be a drain on the limited spatial or economic resources of their families. Close supervision of living quarters and workshops to maintain high moral standards should alleviate parental fears of dishonor.[10] The residences would also

[10] In Puerto Rico, for example, the high moral standards of the textile factories had first to be established before suspicious parents and husbands could be persuaded to permit their daughters and wives to go to work (Boserup 1970, p. 116). The advantages of home employment for women in avoiding contact with males are frequently mentioned in Latin American and African countries as well as in India and in Moslem societies (Boserup 1970, p. 115).

provide places for girls or women who might come into the program from surrounding villages to stay. Half the trainees in a women's polytechnic training institute in Dacca, for example, dropped out before finishing the program because they were unable to find adequate accommodations in the city (National Board of Bangladesh 1974, p. 18). It seems likely that the economic independence of unmarried girls would increase their bargaining power in choosing a husband, timing the marriage, and perhaps even in deciding whether to marry. And in addition to a place to live, girls would have an alternative source of support should they refuse to abide by the wishes of their elders.[11]

Sexually segregated employment, although highly conservative from a Western perspective, can offer truly revolutionary opportunities to women in countries and locales where the prevailing mode is absolute exclusion from public life and isolation within the domestic sphere. It should be considered as a transitional stage on the road to full equality. One writer describes the plan as "a sort of wedge" which could break through cultural resistance to change (Bindary 1972, p. 6). Segregation of the sexes provides channels of upward mobility (supervisory positions in cooperatives or schools, for example) that would otherwise be foreclosed if women were to compete directly with men for these positions (Boserup 1970, p. 129, Papanek 1971, Youssef 1974). Employing and training girls and women under female supervisors should also provide role models to challenge the unquestioned acceptance of male authority in public and private life. Production centers cooperatively owned and run would offer women the means to acquire decision-making and managerial skills of crucial importance to themselves and to the future course of political mobilization in the larger community. Leaders of women's trade organizations in many parts of Africa, for example, have come to play a major role in the politics of their communities.

Girls and women who work with one another on a regular, cooperative basis may well develop strong bonds of solidarity. The cooperative form of social organization offers a genuine alternative to total depen-

[11] Anecdotal evidence is offered in a report of a new training program for female teachers in the town of Pokhara, Nepal. Married women away from their own villages for the first time gave vent to rebellious feelings. " 'I don't care for my husband—let him take another wife,' says one young woman. 'I do not want to work in my husband's home,' another complains. And yet another cries: 'Let my parents give me some property and I will look after myself' " (Kankalil 1973, p. 20). The author continues, "A streak of toughness can be seen in the girls of Nepal. Take Shak Maya who resisted marriage. Her father had chosen a husband for her and one day he came to the hostel to claim her. Shak Maya did not want to marry, so the girls of the hostel rallied around and actually drove the would-be bridegroom and his supporters from the hostel gates."

dence on the family for fulfilling the needs or representing the interests of the individual—perhaps the first such alternative if the girls have not attended school. K. B. Piepmeier and T. S. Adkins (1973, p. 518) stress that Westerners are likely to overlook the potential of traditionally strong bonds between women and of women's organizations in non-Western societies for raising the status of women and encouraging the spread of family planning. In Africa, women's mutual benefit societies not only create networks of social contacts and information, but also give social or financial support to women in times of crisis. Although female seclusion has tended to militate against the formation of strong women's organizations in the rural areas of Moslem and Hindu communities, active women's groups have grown among the educated urban elite in Egypt, India, and Indonesia, as well as in other countries (Tharpar 1963).

The development of solidarity with fellow workers may be especially significant for unmarried girls who work together. In China, for example, the unmarried girls of the "iron women's brigades" in the Ta-Chai collective are said to be reluctant to leave this highly valued heavy agricultural labor for marriage and the bearing of children, once they have acquired productive and leadership skills and a commitment to collective work in preference to domesticity (Salaff 1971). For Hindu girls who generally must move to another village when they marry, the disinclination to leave their fellow workers could induce them to delay their marriages. For Moslem girls who remain in the same village, the requirement that they leave their former work setting and join a different cooperative for married women could also motivate them to delay marriage.

It is essential that unmarried girls be included in these projects. A women's chicken-raising cooperative in Comilla, Bangladesh, apparently rejected local unmarried girls on the assumption that they would marry and leave the area; in contrast, a project in Daulatkhan encourages unmarried girls to become managers (Lindenbaum 1974, p. 21). The latter approach should have far-reaching implications for the status of the women in question and for their marital and reproductive behavior.

By gathering women together in one central work place, the cooperatives provide an opportunity not only for the development of vocational and leadership skills but for the transmission of concurrent programs in functional literacy, more advanced reading or writing, elementary arithmetic, health care, nutrition, legal advice, exposure to mass media, and family planning. Where women are dispersed and isolated, many of these services are almost impossible to deliver adequately. Vocational and professional training programs for women in Bangladesh strongly emphasize the importance of adult literacy: in each center of one program, for example, about 30 percent of the time each day is devoted to language and mathematical skills taught by qualified teachers (National Board of Bangladesh 1974, p. 15).

Child-care facilities at the place of work would permit married women to participate in the program without having to depend on their daughters or other family members to care for young children. Child-care centers would also offer opportunities for training girls as teachers—another important avenue of employment in rural villages—while seeing to it that children who are otherwise not attending school receive some basic educational and health services. Although it is frequently argued that providing child care and other maternity benefits encourages child bearing by reducing the incompatibility between employment and motherhood, we have little concrete evidence to support this assertion. From a policy viewpoint it would seem more important to *facilitate* female labor-force participation, not to impede it. Few women in any country can be expected to forgo child bearing entirely in order to work outside the home, particularly in the countries under discussion here. For a mother, then, the choice (if there is one) could be among *not* working if there is no one to care for her children, working if child care is available, or working to the neglect of the children. If she can choose employment freely, one could argue that she is far more likely to be exposed to antinatalist influences outside the home than if she were to remain in the domestic sphere (see Piepmeier and Adkins 1973, p. 516, for additional arguments to this effect).

The example of China is illuminating. An economic policy of the Cultural Revolution stressing the self-sufficiency of local communities in manufactured products and social services, as well as in agriculture, has gradually created a corps of rural-based nonagricultural workers (Salaff 1972a, p. 253). These new jobs attract women who operate light machinery, work in experimental agricultural stations, or become semiskilled barefoot doctors and veterinarians. According to Janet W. Salaff, the new rural semiindustrial and service jobs for women, unlike traditional agricultural activities or housework, do establish alternatives to child bearing. The work time competes with domestic responsibilities, *the work is highly valued,* leadership and responsibility are shared among the workers, and peers exert strong pressure on their co-workers to stay on the job (Salaff 1972a, p. 254). Young women will frequently delay their marriages and first pregnancies to retain these desirable assignments. In addition, the jobs remove young women, to some extent, from the more conservative influence of their parents, placing them in coeducational (in the Chinese example) peer groups based on an egalitarian ethos.

In brief, the policy proposed here for rural women consists of a cluster of factors operating together: nonagricultural employment; living quarters for unmarried women; money incomes; shared responsibility and leadership; cooperative ownership; the acquisition of vocational skills; training in functional literacy; the provision of family-planning and child-care services for married women on the job; peer-group support and solidarity from co-workers; and a source of pride and prestige apart from marriage and child bearing. Each of these factors is hypothesized as independently incorporating antinuptial and antinatalist effects. No attempt will be made to isolate the variables, however: what I am proposing here is a "package deal" to maximize the potential for radical change. The expectation is that these projects would become self-generating, with long-term potential for rural development. They should change both the attitudes of women toward themselves and their roles, and, given time, the attitudes of men as well.

Obstacles to the Implementation of a Rural Cooperative Program for Women

A number of obstacles are likely to impede the successful implementation of a rural cooperative plan for women: Some of these have been encountered in existing male cooperatives; others are probably unique to a women's program. Because this chapter is designed to emphasize the potential demographic effects of a women's program, I do not outline in it procedures for setting up a series of cooperatives, with all of the attendant financial and administrative problems. Several particularly relevant potential obstacles are mentioned briefly here, however. The first is the resistance that such a program might encounter among *both* women and men. The second is the lack of a cooperative spirit that some writers have observed in some communities. The third is the administrative difficulty of finding raw materials, marketing finished goods, and so forth. Where it is possible to do so, we suggest ways in which some of these obstacles might be overcome.

Resistance to Change

Male resistance to such a scheme could well be expected—even with sexually segregated employment—for several reasons. Great care must be taken to ensure that female employment is not viewed as taking jobs away from men, especially where male unemployment and underemployment are high. Aziz Bindary (1972, p. 5) suggests designing light industries around functions already performed by women. Defined culturally as "women's work," these tasks would not be seen as competing directly with male income-producing activities. The particular tasks would vary considerably from one community to another according to the unique division of labor in each place. For example, women in a Bangladesh cooperative raised chickens, but elsewhere chicken raising may be considered "men's work," and considerable resentment would arise if women were to take over such a task, especially for profit. Possibilities for noncompetitive production include food processing, weaving, garment manufacturing, handicraft production, pottery, and carpet making. The range of activities undertaken in women's training programs and workshops in some of the countries under discussion here is quite extensive.[12] Initially it might be wise to introduce women's cooperatives either simultaneously with men's cooperatives or in villages where men's programs already exist.

Husbands may also resent their wives' working if it means a new independence for the women along with their new income. Fears about the potential of female employment for undermining male authority in the home are a common theme in the literature (Dube 1963, p. 195, Ward 1963, p. 48). Male opposition to the women's agricultural cooperative in Comilla is said to have been based on claims that the women involved were gaining too much independence and leading "immoral" lives (Lindenbaum 1974, p. 28; see Boserup 1970 for other examples). In Mexico the wife's employment is reported to be "the fiercest and most overt battleground in the decision-making struggle" (Cromwell et al. 1973, p. 188). In Egypt, 33 percent of unemployed married women in rural Sharkia Governate and 12 percent in rural Kena said they would like to work if offered the chance, but approximately half of these said their husbands would not agree to their working. What proved to be binding on female employment was "not the opinion of the community but rather of the husband. . . . The wife will rarely work without her husband's consent but will rather try to convince him and in case of failure, stays home" (Khalifa 1973, p. 163).

[12] To give a few examples: women's workshops in Bangladesh produce food items such as chickens and ducks, spices, jams, and jellies; clothing items such as silk, hand-printed and woven cloth, embroidery, wool knits, bedcovers; cosmetic items; other home consumption items such as mats, pottery, toys, leather goods, jute products (Lindenbaum 1974, National Board of Bangladesh 1974). Government rural cooperatives for women in Iran, Madagascar, and Syria emphasize carpet weaving (UN, ECOSOC 1973).

Would fathers fear for their daughters' employment as strongly as husbands for their wives'? We have little evidence. Twenty-five percent of parents of daughters with the master's degree in Lahore and 11 percent in Karachi said they would not permit their daughter to work *under any circumstances;* an additional 67 and 52 percent, respectively, would permit it only under the condition that she worked solely with other women (Papanek 1971, p. 527). Once again, this may be a class phenomenon pertaining to the maintenance of high status, as mentioned earlier. Where economic pressures are more severe, we might find a different view. In at least one work-training program in Bangladesh, for example, there is a waiting list of applicants from among the local population of unmarried girls about fifteen or sixteen years of age. The People's Health Centre in Savar pay their trainees a small salary; the girls in turn live at the center and receive six months of practical and theoretical training, much of it in family planning. Of particular interest for its demographic implications is Shirley Lindenbaum's (1974) comment that "the ability of the Centre to attract unmarried girls from all the religious groups puts to rest the assumption that young women in this 'dangerous' age group would not be permitted to come forth." "Indeed," she continues, "apart from the financial reward, employment at the Centre may even relieve the girls' parents from the social pressure of neighbors who comment on unoccupied and therefore presumably unmarriageable young women living at home." The young paramedics gain considerable prestige in the eyes of the community because they can assure villagers of access to hospital treatment for their illnesses. The *value* of their work as an alternative to staying at home is clearly visible.

Of course, girls and women themselves may resist the innovation of work outside the home, fearing the loss of protection and security this may initially represent. Some young women in a teacher-training program in Pokhara, Nepal, are said to have returned to their villages because they were lonely.[13] When the new marriage law was promulgated in China, in 1950, specifying for the first time free choice of marital partners, the abolition of polygamy, the right of widows to remarry, and an end to child betrothals and bride prices, women as well as men initially resisted these changes and clung in fear to the old ways (Wolf 1974, p. 170). However, assuming that younger women in general are more easily motivated to change, recruitment of women to the cooperatives could be limited to those under thirty years of age (National Board of Bangladesh 1974, p. 13). This limitation is also important if the pro-

[13] John Stoeckel, communication to Ronald G. Ridker.

gram is to influence the age at marriage and the child-bearing patterns of its participants.

If the domestic burdens of women are not reduced in any way, women might also resist participating in the new program because it would only add to their labors. Most rural women spend many hours each day on time-consuming, repetitive household chores—fetching water, washing clothes, preparing food, caring for children, tending gardens or small animals, spinning and weaving, and so on. Because the goal of the cooperatives is to *improve* the status of women, great care must be taken that women are not further exploited. The need to lighten the domestic burden by means of labor-saving devices (water pumps, small stoves, and the like) in conjunction with expanded productivity outside the home is heavily emphasized in a Food and Agricultural Organization report on rural women. They point out that in Zaïre, for example, "Poultry schemes which are introduced into a rural community, but are not accompanied by a water supply, result in increasing the burden on the women. It is estimated that 100 chickens need approximately 25 litres of clean water per day. The task of fetching extra water falls on the shoulders of the women" (UN, ECOSOC 1973, p. 22). As a consequence, women often resist these so-called innovations. "They may revolt or adopt an indifferent, if not hostile, attitude toward everything labelled as 'development' or 'progress.' They may lose confidence in all projects aimed at improving their own condition, the family's and the community's wellbeing. But who can blame them?" (p. 23).[14]

If care is taken to protect women's interests, one should find in most rural communities a substantial number of women who want to work outside the home. The Egyptian study quoted above is one example. In India, too, 34 percent of the women in several Agarwal communities accepted without qualification the statement that "women may work for money if they so choose," although none was employed at the time (Gore 1968, p. 160). It is noteworthy that rural women were more likely to agree without qualification (50 percent) than were women living in urban fringe areas (37 percent) or in Delhi (30 percent). (In contrast, only 11 percent of the men interviewed accepted this idea.) In Bangladesh, too, women are demanding entry into vocational training programs in numbers far greater than the current capacity of the women's programs to absorb them (National Board of Bangladesh 1974).

[14] The same argument is used when compulsory education of children is introduced without concomitant improvement in living conditions, leaving women with an additional amount of work to be done at home which was formerly shared by the children (UN, ECOSOC 1973).

Lack of a Cooperative Ethic

Is it possible to overcome class, religious, or caste differences—or to transcend fierce family loyalties—within a single cooperative venture? Some sceptics have claimed that the collective spirit is so weakly developed in many communities that it is virtually meaningless to base programs on appeals to the common good. However, the plan here does not require that immediate sacrifices be made on the promise of future benefits; it does require a spirit of cooperation in the management of the enterprise and the sharing of earnings on an equitable basis. Presumably this can be considered a skill to be learned along with all the others. Women from different communities in Saudi Arabia are now organized into small handicraft-marketing cooperatives; their societies are said to "constitute one of the best educational methods designed to accustom women to working together and to give them a knowledge of commerce and management" (UN, ECOSOC 1973, p. 8).

I do not want to venture here into the delicate issue of whether women are "inherently" more cooperative and less competitive than are men, although one could argue that in most societies, compliance and cooperation are more likely to be rewarded among women than among men (with the opposite being true of competition and aggression). Much would depend on the extent to which women have been previously isolated from women outside their own kin group. A little investigation could easily uncover in many communities informal mutual aid, savings, or informational networks among women who, to the casual observer, appear to have few contacts beyond the household. In any case, women's ability to work cooperatively with one another could easily be studied under varied conditions in existing programs. The International Labour Organisation reports that "at times, women exhibit a greater co-operative spirit than do men. That is borne out by the example of a co-operative credit society set up in a village in Sierra Leone: at first it was open to both men and women, but the women later withdrew and set up their own co-operative because of the mediocre results achieved by the men" (p. 9). The successful acquisition of collective behavioral skills cutting across kinship groupings could have important implications for political decision making in the larger community.

Administrative and Economic Problems

Unavailability of raw materials, lack of capital, unskilled management, marketing problems, and political interference seem to pervade ventures such as the many male agricultural cooperatives in India and Bangladesh. There is no reason to believe that women's cooperatives would be exempt from these difficulties; indeed, problems of lack of skills and capital are likely to be exacerbated. Reports by Shirley Lindenbaum (1974), the National Board of Bangladesh Women's Rehabilitation Programme (1974), and the FAO and ILO (UN, ECOSOC 1973) attest to this point.

It is not possible to discuss here the many administrative problems that might be encountered. Two could be singled out, however. First, how are goods to be effectively marketed if women are to observe purdah? Although women account for half or more of the labor force in trade in many African countries, they are virtually absent from the markets both as buyers and sellers in most Hindu and Moslem cultures, accounting for less than 1 percent of the labor force in trade (Boserup 1970, p. 87). Even in countries where women engage in animal husbandry, grow cash crops, or make goods for sale, the requirements of purdah often force them to leave the marketing of their wares to men, who gain control over the money and frequently over other matters as well (Boserup 1970, pp. 106–118; Lindenbaum 1974, p. 28).

In Sri Lanka the government provides outlets for the sale of cooperatively produced women's goods in state stores, and private shops also take their wares (UN, ECOSOC 1973, p. 7). Women's organizations from the cities might also undertake to set up distribution centers. Eventually, however, rural women engaged in production will appear in the marketplace themselves. Women from cooperatives in Daulatkhan, Bangladesh, a highly conservative area, have begun to attend fairs exhibiting their handicrafts (Lindenbaum 1974). This is a significant breakthrough deriving naturally from their increasing participation in nondomestic spheres. The additional economic activity so generated, including the increased effective demand for goods and services engendered by women's incomes, should be a powerful force toward rural community development.

Shortage of capital is a second, more severe problem. Male cooperatives are usually favored for loans, the modest allocation for funds for training rural women being justified on the basis that women's participation in development programs is relatively unimportant (Lindenbaum 1974; UN, ECOSOC 1973b, p. 11). Successful ventures appear frequently to depend on the efforts of a single powerful person who can provide or negotiate for the necessary capital. Organizations of educated urban women are likely to be too distant from the concerns of rural women, both geographically and socially, to be able to set up training programs, and they lack funds in any case. Strong ideological and financial support from governments would consequently appear to be crucial to the success of such programs.

If a government is committed to the idea of genuine rural development, placing high priority on the redistribution of wealth and on the equal rights of women, the outlook for rural women's cooperatives is optimistic. If governments are indifferent or antagonistic to such efforts, the outlook is bleak. For this reason it is essential that an experimental pilot program for testing the demographic impact of women's cooperatives be undertaken in a country in which the national government, as well as the local villagers, support the project enthusiastically.

Research and Implementation

Investigating Existing Projects

Training programs of various types, or production workshops for rural women, or both, have been undertaken in a number of countries in North Africa, the Middle East, and South Central Asia—in Tunisia, Syria, Iran, Saudi Arabia, Democratic Yemen, Nepal, Pakistan, Bangladesh, and Sri Lanka, to name a few. The programs have been designed primarily for the purpose of encouraging the development and diversification of rural economies while improving the standard of living of participating villagers. Some programs cite improvements in the status of women as a specific goal. One of the aims of the Integrated Rural Development Programme in Bangladesh, for example, is to enable women to become "economically productive and ultimately self-reliant" (quoted in Lindenbaum 1974, p. 28).

None has been developed with the explicit intention of influencing reproductive attitudes and behavior, although Bindary (1972) has outlined such a proposal for Egypt. Nor do most programs fulfill the cluster of conditions spelled out in this chapter. Some cooperatives do not provide a central workplace—which is essential to the demographic argument—but serve only to market handicrafts produced by women at home. The teacher-training program in Nepal (Kankalil 1973) and the People's Health Centre in Bangladesh (Lindenbaum 1974) house trainees and workers in group living quarters, but production workshops generally do not. Many cooperatives are not yet able to pay regular incomes to their participants. Nevertheless, existing programs might fruitfully be studied before a full-scale experimental project is undertaken. I would propose taking advantage of existing programs as noted below.

An inventory should be taken in the countries under discussion of income-producing programs for rural women that approach the model of cooperative ownership and management, a centralized workplace, and an all-female work setting. Vocational training programs, privately rather than cooperatively owned workshops, and other forms of cooperative marketing ventures among women could also be investigated. Urban women's production cooperatives and male agricultural cooperatives would provide a comparative perspective on different organizational structures, goals, and processes. The purpose at this preliminary stage is to analyze the basic social, economic, cultural and political determinants of the success or failure of such programs—*success* being roughly defined as the ability to become financially and organizationally self-sustaining in the space of, say, three years.

Complete histories (a case-study approach) should be taken of these projects by interviewing key persons responsible for instituting and maintaining them, paying special attention to problems of administration, marketing, finance, political opposition, and so forth and to ways in which these problems might be overcome. Reactions of villagers and workers to the program, both retrospective and current, should also be recorded.

For a preliminary investigation of the demographic effect of women's cooperatives, two or three existing programs most closely adhering to the criteria outline in this chapter could be selected for analysis. Girls and women of reproductive age who are directly involved in the training programs or workshops could be matched by family income, current age, number of years of schooling, and religion or caste (if relevant) with girls and women who remain confined to the domestic sphere. The latter may be engaged in handicrafts or some other home-based production but differ from the former in being generally cut off from public social interaction. The precise organizational structure of the activities in which women in each group are engaged, and the perceived value of these activities, should be carefully defined.

The question then becomes one of establishing the connections between the types of activity in which the women are regularly engaged and their reproductive aspirations and behavior. How do the two groups differ in their demographic characteristics—current marital status, number and ages of children, family-planning knowledge, attitudes, and practice (KAP)—and in their marital and reproductive desires—age at marriage for themselves if unmarried, degree of freedom desired in the choice of a husband, feelings about the possibility of not marrying, the number and timing of children wanted? Do girls and women involved in the women's projects have greater influence over their elders or their spouses, or both, in family decisions, and do they participate more substantially in decisions regarding their own marital, sexual, and reproductive behavior than the matched sample of girls and women engaged in traditional activities within the home? Both the women themselves and other adults in the household should be interviewed regarding their perceptions of who makes the decisions on key issues, given that discrepancies are likely to appear (Gore 1968, Safilios-Rothschild 1970). How do the groups differ in their attitudes about appropriate roles for women and men in the community and in the family?

Matched samples of girls and women, along with relevant household members, could also be interviewed in neighboring villages without women's projects that share the general social and economic characteristics of villages in which women's projects are located.

This type of evaluation suffers from a major defect, however: it leaves the question of causality unanswered. Indeed, most research on factors associated with the timing and quantity of nuptiality and fertility utilizes a cross-sectional approach [see Weller (1973) for a critique]. Age at marriage, children ever born, current use of contraceptives, and other demographic variables are correlated with the number of years of schooling of the husband and wife, their current employment status, the husband's current income, the couple's place of residence, and so on. Yet, tempting as it may be to do so, valid causal inferences cannot be drawn from these cross-sectional data. Longitudinal studies following individuals and cohorts through a sequence of major life-cycle events would point more accurately to the particular motivations underlying each transition at the time that it occurs. Such studies would be particularly helpful in understanding the *process* of decision making that results in relationships such as those between the number of years of schooling a girl receives and the timing of her marriage, or between the employment of wives outside the home and the number and timing of their children. For this reason, once the observations of current programs have been completed, an experimental project should be set up to trace the dynamics of the process from the beginning.

An Experimental Model

A fuller test would follow the progress of one or more vocational training or cooperative programs, incorporating from their inception all of the qualities specified in this proposal. Deciding on an appropriate experimental procedure is of course a highly complicated matter that cannot possibly be spelled out in detail in the abstract, without reference to the concrete cultural and structural conditions of the communities in question. Nevertheless, a few guidelines might be proposed.

• A cluster of three to six villages of approximately 1,000 persons each, sharing a network of social interaction and economic exchange (perhaps around a central market town), could be specified as an experimental setting. Male unemployment in these villages should be relatively low; if possible, male agricultural cooperatives should already be in operation. The large majority of women should be observing purdah.

Politically influential officials and village leaders themselves must be amenable to the initiation of such a project.

• Careful analysis of the current division of labor by sex in the experimental villages is needed to uncover tasks that are currently performed by women, or that probably would be defined as "women's work" if undertaken. Before deciding on a suitable task for the cooperative workshops, we need also to know about the availability of raw materials, the distribution of local or regional market outlets, the range of existing skills among women, and the local need for goods of various types that could be produced. To avoid flooding the market at this initial stage, each cooperative should ideally produce a different product or set of products. Fulfilling local needs for foodstuffs, household goods, or items of clothing might be more desirable than producing luxury goods such as jewelry or embroidered clothing for regional markets or for export, although the question of effective demand for these goods should be paramount if the venture is to become economically sound.

• A house-to-house census should be taken to determine the number of eligible females in each village. Eligibility for the cooperatives should be limited to women between the ages of fifteen and thirty—that is, prime marriageable and prime child-bearing ages. If possible, separate cooperatives should be set up for unmarried and married women—the former with attached living quarters, the latter with child-care and family-planning services. Aside from these differences, the structures and activities of the two cooperatives would be similar.

In villages of 1,000 persons, one would expect to find approximately 100 to 120 women between the ages of fifteen and thirty.[15] About 40 or 50 of these would be between the ages of fifteen and twenty. Workers would be recruited from this group. It might be possible to build on an existing informal network of women involved in a credit society or other joint venture.

Assuming that about half the eligible unmarried girls could be recruited and about one-quarter of the eligible married women, two workshops could be set up in each village for about ten to fifteen and twenty to twenty-five women, respectively. A small financial inducement should be offered to women and to their families to encourage their initial participation in the program. Once training and production got under way the workers would be paid a regular salary, which would be shared with their families.

[15] These estimates are derived from 1951 age-sex structures of rural Indian villages, from Wyon and Gordon (1971, p. 88). There were 500,000 villages in India, according to the census, with a mean population size of 529. Half of the rural population lived in villages of under 1,000 persons, with a mean household size of 5.5 persons.

It is highly probable that girls and women who already have some say in household decisions, who are less isolated socially and spatially, and whose families are less traditional in their sex-role ideologies, would be the first to take advantage of the new opportunities. From a practical point of view this selectivity is valuable in producing highly motivated, active role models for the larger community. From a research point of view, however, it biases the outcome toward showing that participation in cooperatives encourages "modern" sex-role and reproductive ideas. With adequate baseline data, however, *changes* in attitudes and practices among participants in the program and their families could be compared with changes among nonparticipating women and their families. In addition, the distribution of such attitudes could be compared at a later date with those in a control village.

- The basic research design would be similar to that outlined for the evaluation of existing projects, including the selection of experimental and control villages and the within-village comparisons of girls, women, and other household members according to the type of activity in which the females are regularly engaged. A cluster of control villages of approximately the same size, matched insofar as possible with the cluster of experimental villages but without frequent contact with them, would provide a means of evaluating the effect of the programs more precisely. Intensive observations in both experimental and control villages could be undertaken for approximately three years, with periodic follow-up measurements collected once a year thereafter.
- I believe that combining an intensive case-study approach, in which the villages themselves would be studied as they experience these new projects, with a series of detailed, intensive interviews with a relatively small sample of women and other adults in their households would elicit more informative data than would a large-scale survey. This approach is most appropriate in trying to uncover the delicate nuances of motivational factors at the major transitional points in the life cycle—at the timing of marriage, for example. How can a large survey adequately tap the richness of detail possible in longer, more exploratory, and more frequent interviews with the same people over a period of time?

Participant observation would be ideal. At least two observer-interviewers, one male and one female, should live in each village to take detailed, daily notes of the events surrounding all aspects of the projects and of community reactions to them. If the projects are to spread, films should be taken to impress upon the villagers the prestige of the undertaking and to show in other villages. The observers would also be able to conduct long interviews with female and male villagers by joining with them at their places of work or in their households in a natural, informal setting. Every attempt should be made to match the characteristics of the observers with those of the villagers as closely as possible, so that extremes of misunderstanding or misinterpretation can be avoided (cf. Mamdani 1972). Locally trained adults would be preferable to young city-bred college students, for example.

Although a wealth of information could be gathered as the cooperatives got under way, an evaluation of their initial demographic effects would probably require a minimum of five years. I expect that postponement of marriage among the young girls in the project would occur sooner than postponement or limitation of the number of births among married women—even with birth-control services as an essential ingredient of the program. The long-run prospects are probably more significant than short-term behavioral changes.

What effect might such a policy have on overall birth rates? The establishment of a few women's cooperatives scattered across the occasional village in Bangladesh or Iraq or Morocco would clearly have no effect: programs reaching a few hundred women in a region whose population totals 1 billion are simply too small in scale. Nevertheless, if they were viewed as an integral part of a massive development effort aimed at the diversification of rural economies, and if women were actively encouraged to participate fully in the development process in all village communities, the eventual results could be substantial.

Critics of current population policies and approaches (cf. Kocher 1973 and Rich 1973), as well as the majority of participants at the World Population Conference in Bucharest, have strongly emphasized the need for a more equitable distribution of wealth among and within nations as a prerequisite for authentic economic and social development—itself a prerequisite for significant declines in fertility. With the overwhelming majority of the population of North Africa, the Middle East, and South Central Asia living in rural areas, the bulk of the investment should be made in this sector. Recognizing the centrality of the role of rural girls and women to the success or failure of rural development efforts, moreover, it would seem clear that programs must benefit women equally with men. Indeed, the World Population Plan of Action declares that more moderate fertility levels could be achieved in developing countries through "the full integration of women into the development process, particularly by means of their greater participation in education, social, economic and political opportunities, and especially by means of the removal of obstacles to their employment in the non-agricultural sector wherever possible" (quoted in Mauldin et al. 1974, p. 386). Perhaps most important, improving the status of women is seen not simply as a possible means of reducing birth rates, but as a clear goal in itself, regardless of it demographic consequences.

10.

Female Employment Creation and Family Size

JAMES L. McCABE AND MARK R. ROSENZWEIG

Two important phenomena characterizing developed societies in the twentieth century are a decline in marital fertility rates and a rise in the labor-force participation of married women. These persistent trends, combined with a recognition of the importance of the mother in child rearing, suggest the possibility that one means of accelerating the adoption of goals leading to smaller family size in less developed countries might be to encourage the employment of women. Such a policy prescription, however, presupposes that the inverse association between female employment and fertility in industrial nations implies a causal relationship and that there exists a strong conflict between the economic employment of women and child rearing within less developed countries. To evaluate such a policy in the context of a developing country therefore requires extreme care.

The general lack of evidence pertaining to family behavior in less developed countries makes it difficult to formulate firm conclusions regarding the natalist impact of the creation of employment for women. However, it is important that a framework for investigating these issues be established before further empirical tests or the collection of data are undertaken. This chapter is primarily concerned with the formulation of such a framework and with methodological issues, although our analysis is tested on two sets of data from less developed countries. It is shown that family size and labor-force participation are among a number of endogenous choice variables of a family that are jointly influenced by a common set of exogenous parameters. Thus it is possible that despite a

An earlier draft of this chapter was presented at the Eastern Economic Association Meetings, October 1974. We are grateful for the comments and criticisms of Nancy Birdsall, James Heckman, T. Paul Schultz, and Donald Snyder. Jarlath Johnston and Katherine Norstrom provided extensive research assistance.

negative simple correlation between female labor-force participation and fertility, changes in some exogenous variables may have the same qualitative affect on the two variables. Moreover, it is argued that there are a number of important characteristics of developing countries which might reduce the effect of any general employment-creation policy on birth rates. Two important factors discussed are the availability of substitutes for mothers' time in household activities and the occupational distribution. For example, responsibilities for child care in less developed countries are often assumed by relatives and older children and, unlike the situation in the developed nations, a large portion of the female laborforce in less developed countries is employed in cottage industries and retail occupations in which on-the-job child care is commonplace.[1]

Theoretical Framework

The framework adopted here for examining the relationship between female labor-force participation and fertility is based on the one-period static model described by Yoram Ben-Porath (1973a) and Robert J. Willis (1973).[2] In this model of household choice it is assumed that there are two categories of service flows which provide satisfaction to the household: commodity services and child services adjusted for quality. These commodities are produced within the household from the application of the time inputs of the husband and wife and inputs purchasable in the market and are consumed only by the household itself and not traded in the market.

Part of the time of adult members of the household is assumed to be allocated to household and part to economic activity (formal employment, for example) which yields market goods. The money prices of the three factor inputs (the wages of employed adult men and women

[1] See Ester Boserup (1970) for information on the extent of this type of female employment in less developed countries. A. J. Jaffe and K. Azumi (1960) among others, have demonstrated that cottage industries are highly compatible with child rearing.

[2] The model described refers to the lifetime decisions of the family and specifically to completed fertility and "lifetime" labor-force participation. Models of sequential decision making have not as yet provided qualitative policy implications which differ from the static framework adopted here. For an example, see James L. McCabe and David S. Sibley (1974). Moreover, the econometric problems involved in testing these models, involving dichotomous dependent variables, are severe, particularly when using panel data in which serial correlation is important. See, for example, James J. Heckman and R. J. Willis (1976) and Marc Nerlove and S. James Press (1973).

and the price of market goods) are specified. Given household utility maximization and constant returns to scale, these specified factor prices will determine factor proportions in the two activities. The price of household-produced good *j* is equal to the sum of the money prices of the three factor inputs weighted by coefficients representing the amount of the respective factor input required to produce a unit output of good *j*. The "full" income of the household is equal to the "total" time of the wife (both market and household) multiplied by her money wage rate plus the "total" time of the husband multiplied by his money wage rate plus nonlabor income. Hence, in this model a rise in the wife's market wage rate has two effects: It increases (decreases) the price of children in relation to that of commodity services if children are more (less) intense in the wife's time than are commodity services,[3] and it increases the full income of the household. The first is essentially a substitution effect which may increase or decrease desired child services depending on the relative intensity of this good in the time of the wife. The second is an income effect which tends to increase the demand for children, assuming that the latter are normal goods.

The qualitative response of desired children to the wife's market wage rate thus depends on the relative intensity of the child services activity in the wife's time input. If child services are substantially more intense in the wife's time than are commodity services, there will be a substitution effect which will be opposite in sign to, and may outweigh, the income effect. On the other hand, if other commodities are more intense in the wife's time than child services, then an exogenous rise in the wife's wage rate will unequivocally increase desired child services.

The intensity of the wife's time in child rearing in relation to that in commodity services depends on a number of technical factors which may vary more among low-income countries than among more developed countries. Factors affecting the relative inputs of the wife's time include the following:

- The ability to substitute purchased inputs for the wife's time in child rearing in comparison with other activities
- The extent to which the rearing of younger children can be taken over by older children or adult relatives, or both
- The compatibility of a particular female occupation with child rearing.

These technical characteristics influencing the time-intensity of child rearing may differ among societies and to a certain extent reflect the

[3] Intensity is measured by the ratio of the particular factor input valued at its price to the price of the household commodity.

values and norms endemic to them. For instance, the length of the period of breast-feeding, which may be partially a cultural phenomenon, will influence the substitutability between the wife's time in child rearing and one purchased input, domestic help.[4] However, given the technology of household production within a society, described in part by the technical relations listed above, the relative amount of the wife's time consumed in the production of a unit of child and household commodity services will be influenced by the ratio of the price of the wife's time to the (imputed) price of market inputs. Thus if the substitutability between wife's and other person's time in child rearing is greater than that in the production of nonchild services, then the ready availability (low imputed wages) of domestic servants and adult relatives to care for children, a characteristic of many developing countries, could result in child rearing in these societies being relatively less intensive in the wife's time. In such cases, the net effect of a rise in female wage rates on desired child services will be small or even positive. (The demand for domestic servants' or relatives' time, however, will increase.)

The low rates of return on schooling and the low probability of market employment of older children, which characterize some less developed countries, may result in a significant substitution of older children's for the wife's time in child rearing. This substitution may also lead to child services becoming less time-intensive.

The intensity of child services in the wife's time in relation to that of commodity services will also tend to be less if the wife's occupation is somewhat compatible with child rearing. In the usual model, designed for industrialized countries, the occupation of the wife is assumed to be totally incompatible with child rearing. Once time allocated to commodity services has been determined, the wife's time available for child rearing is computed by subtracting time spent in economic activity from the total time remaining. Holding commodity service inputs constant, the partial derivative of the wife's time available for child rearing with respect to her time spent in economic activity is minus unity. Yet, in the case of some occupations, part of the time spent by the wife in market employment may be allocated to child care without significantly affecting productivity. For example, women in Africa frequently carry children on their backs while they are engaged in retail or agricultural activities (McCabe 1974, p. 18). In this case, at least at the margin, children may not be very intensive in the wife's time.

The relative time-intensity of child rearing and the compatibility of certain occupations with the household production of child services (the

[4] Factors affecting the age of weaning are examined by Moni Nag (1968).

extent to which joint production of money income and child services with respect to the wife's time is possible) are crucial determinants of the relationship between female labor-force participation and fertility. Both the quantity of child services and the amount of time spent in the market by women are household choice variables which are influenced by an identical set of parameters. The wage rate of women, for instance, has been shown to have a positive effect on female labor-force participation rates.[5] Whether a wage rise will have a similar influence on fertility—that is, whether the labor-force participation of women and family size move in the opposite or same directions—will depend on the relative time-intensities of the two types of household activities, which will in turn depend on the variety of societal and market characteristics identified broadly above. Thus it is not surprising to find in the literature that the simple relationship between female labor-force participation rates and fertility differs among countries.[6]

Empirical Testing

We have just shown that the household production model is perfectly consistent with a number of conditions prevalent in less developed countries which may tend to make child services less intensive in the wife's time than is the case in developed countries and to produce an ambiguous association between female employment and fertility. In this framework, it is clear that the wife's labor-force participation and her fertility are *jointly* determined by a common set of exogenous variables including the wife's and the husband's market wage rates. Such a system contrasts sharply with the models developed by Marc Nerlove and T. Paul Schultz (1970) in which somewhat different exogenous variables affect labor-force participation and fertility, and each of these endogenous variables enters the equation determining the other.

The impossibility of finding exogenous variables that influence female labor-force participation and do not influence fertility and vice versa means that the model suggested by Schultz is generally underidentified. For example, changes in the wife's market wage rate have a separate

[5] The empirical studies showing a positive association between the female wage rate and labor-force participation are reviewed by Ben-Porath (1973c).

[6] For example, Aziz Bindary, Colin B. Baxter, and T. H. Hollingsworth (1973) find a positive association between female employment and fertility in urban Egypt, whereas Andrew Collver and Eleanor Langlois (1967) find a negative association in urban areas for a number of countries.

effect on fertility other than through labor participation to the extent that fertility is sensitive to changes in the value of time and in the total income of the household. By the same token, even with completed fertility constant such wage-rate changes will influence female labor-force decisions. With no other exogenous variables, the influence of a change in the wife's wage rate with her labor-force participation held fixed cannot be separated from the total effect of this variable on fertility.

Exogenous estimates of the wife's market wage rate and the husband's wage rate are crucial to any empirical test of a joint determination model. Clearly, one cannot simply look at the relationship between actual current wages and labor-force participation rates in order to measure the effect of an exogenous increase in wage rates on female employment and fertility; how much one works (and family-size choice) influences the level of the wage. Thus, one might observe a negative relationship between women's wages and their fertility simply because the women who choose to have more children will work less, will have less experience in the labor force, and will thus have lower earnings currently than women who choose smaller families.[7]

One procedure, utilized later in this chapter, to correct for this simultaneity with a micro data set in which information on the actual work experience of married women is not available is the following: The log of the hourly wage rates of never-married women is regressed against a number of exogenous variables including age, age squared, and years of education. This provides an exogenous predicted value of the potential wage rate for married women (that is, the wages they would earn if they bore no children). Age and the labor-force experience of married women are not a simple linear transformation of each other so that a reliable predicting equation for married women's wages based solely on their age and schooling characteristics cannot usually be obtained. As Gronau has demonstrated, however, the estimated wage is affected by "selectivity bias," since the potential wage of nonworking women may not correspond to the actual wage rate of working women of similar characteristics. James J. Heckman (1974) has proposed a maximum-likelihood iterative method which yields consistent and asymptotically unbiased parameter estimates for computing the potential wage offers of nonemployed persons. Because of the expense of this technique, however, it is not applied in the next section. An exogenous predictor of the husband's wage rate may be obtained in a similar manner, but can be

[7] See Jacob Mincer and Solomon Polachek (1974) for empirical evidence on the depreciation of women's earning potential attributable to nonparticipation in the work force.

estimated from data pertaining to all males.[8] Thus in its simplest form our model may be depicted as follows:

$\hat{W}_f$ = The predicted wage rate of the wife
$\hat{W}_m$ = The predicted wage rate of the husband
I_m = Nonearnings income of the husband
I_f = Nonearnings income of the wife
E_m = Years of completed schooling of the husband
E_f = Years of completed schooling of the wife
N = Completed fertility
L_f = Labor-force participation of wife

In general, it is difficult to predict the signs of the individual coefficients in these equations.

$$N = a_{10} + a_{11}\hat{W}_f + a_{12}\hat{W}_m + a_{13}E_f + a_{14}E_m + a_{15}I_f + a_{16}I_m \quad (10\text{-}1)$$

$$L_f = a_{20} + a_{21}\hat{W}_f + a_{22}W_m + a_{23}E_f + a_{24}E_m + a_{25}I_f + a_{26}I_m \quad (10\text{-}2)$$

For instance, the sign of a_{11} will depend on the relative time-intensity of child rearing and the magnitude of the income effect. If the production of child services is female time-intensive and if the resulting negative substitution effect outweighs the (presumed) positive income effect of a wage change, then $a_{11} > 0$. Similarly, the sign of a_{21} depends on the magnitude of income and substitution effects. Education may also influence the wife's ability to utilize domestic servants and relatives for child-care purposes—her "efficiency" in the production of child services. To the extent that this is true, we would expect at least certain kinds of education to be positively associated with completed fertility and labor-force participation.

Given the importance of female occupational choice and the use of servants and relatives as surrogate mothers in the nexus between labor force and fertility, the number of endogenous variables in the system should be increased. A general system may be written:

$$\begin{bmatrix} N \\ L_f \\ CI \\ H \\ S \\ R \end{bmatrix} = \begin{bmatrix} a_{10}, a_{11}, \ldots, a_{16} \\ a_{20}, a_{21}, \ldots, a_{26} \\ \\ \\ \\ a_{60}, a_{61}, \ldots, a_{66} \end{bmatrix} \cdot \begin{bmatrix} 1 \\ \hat{W}_f \\ \hat{W}_m \\ E_f \\ E_m \\ I_f \\ I_m \end{bmatrix} + \begin{bmatrix} U_1 \\ \\ - \\ \\ U_6 \end{bmatrix} \quad (10\text{-}3)$$

[8] Selectivity bias is less severe for males, given their relatively high level of employment.

where *CI* (compatibility index) is the average completed fertility associated with the occupation chosen by the wife, *H* is a dichotomous variable having a value of 1 if the wife's occupation is carried on outside the home and 0 otherwise, *S* is the number of servants employed by the households, and *R* is the number of relatives living in the household; the U_1 are the relevant error terms. The exogenous variables included in the vector at the extreme right-hand side of equation 10-3 are those used in equations 10-1 and 10-2. Whether this list may be expanded depends on the comprehensiveness of the data that are available. In cases where a household sample encompasses a large number of different commodity and labor markets, experiments should be made with the wage rate of domestic servants, and the price of animal milk in relation to that of other commodities. These exogenous variables may well interact with those presently in the system. If, for example, the wage rate of domestic servants is low, the effect of an increase in the wife's wage rate on completed fertility is, under certain conditions, more likely to be positive. The same may be said about the relative price of milk—that is, the lower this relative price the more likely is a positive effect of the wife's wage rate on fertility and labor-force participation.

The enlargement of the model allows the specification of some a priori relationships between the qualitative responses of different endogenous variables to the same exogenous variable. Suppose that the wife's predicted wage rate is positively associated with both completed family size and labor-force participation; then it should be positively associated with at least one of the variables *CI, H, S,* or *R,* assuming that the household production activities have the property of constant returns to scale.[9] An increase in one of these variables represents a means by which the effective time available for household activities can be increased. This can be accomplished either by the wife seeking occupations more compatible with child rearing or by the purchase of time from relatives or servants.

The econometric methodology outlined, with the limitations noted, is suitable for the empirical analysis of the determinants of these family

[9] With increasing returns and nonhomotheticity in the production of child services, it is possible for the intensity in the wife's time of these services to decrease with output. It may not require twice as much of the wife's time to take care of $2n$ children as it does to take care of n. Under these conditions, the marginal intensity of child services in the wife's time will decrease more rapidly than the average. It can be shown that if, given nonhomothetic production functions, child services become less intense in the wife's services than do commodity services at the margin, then an increase in the wife's wage rate will unequivocally increase family size. Moreover, this can happen even though there has been no variation in the levels of inputs of servants and relatives into child care and even though the woman's choice of occupation has not become less competitive with child rearing.

behavior variables on the basis of cross-sectional data. The interpretation of the results obtained, especially with respect to policy conclusions, must however be modified by an awareness that cross-sectional parameter estimates do not necessarily provide accurate measures of the effects of exogenous changes that occur over time. Marc Nerlove (1974), for example, has pointed out that women who prefer to have few children and have a high taste for market work will tend to demand and receive more formal schooling than women with opposite preferences. Thus the estimated cross-sectional schooling coefficients obtained in fertility or labor-force-participation regression equations will in part reflect the distribution of tastes in the population and therefore do not provide unbiased estimates of the effect of increased female schooling on birth rates or female employment. Because of this limitation of cross-sectional data and the econometric problem of selectivity bias, mentioned previously, an alternative means of evaluating the natalist impact of the creation of female employment are suggested in the final section.

Existing Studies

Many empirical investigations of the relationship between female labor-force participation and fertility involve simple comparisons of the parity levels or age-specific fertility rates of active and nonactive women.[10] Sometimes these comparisons are made within socioeconomic groups designated by such variables as the education of the wife or the husband's income. These intracountry cross-sectional studies (Collver and Langlois 1967 and Gendell 1967, for example) generally show that economically active women have fewer children, according to the various criteria used, than do women who are not economically active. There are, however, some important exceptions. For example, the inverse association between female economic activity and fertility does not seem to be nearly so strong in rural areas as in urban areas (Gendell, Maraviglia, and Kreitner 1970, Miró and Mertens 1968). In fact, in some rural studies, birth rates are positively correlated with female economic activity (Bindary, Baxter, and Hollingsworth 1973, Goldstein 1972, Pinnelli 1971).

It should be clear from the foregoing discussion that this approach involving simple correlation has a number of serious drawbacks. In particular, classifying fertility measures by degree or presence of female economic activity can never support the following hypothesis conclusively: that an exogenous increase in the number or attractiveness of

[10] For an excellent review of the literature on female labor-force participation and fertility, see William P. McGreevey et al. (1974), especially pp. 20–23.

jobs for women will, other things being constant, decrease the birth rate. Even if women who have children are less able to work than women who do not, this opportunity cost of having children may not influence a woman's fertility decisions. At the same time, it is clear that, given some incompatibility between child bearing and work, either differences in the taste for children or simply random variation in parity across households will lead to an inverse association between birth rates and economic activity. Under these circumstances, the birth rate could be considered the exogenous variable and the female labor-force participation the endogenous. Thus, an increase in the number of female job vacancies or an increase in the female wage rate may well lead to a rise in female labor-force participation but not to a decrease in fertility.

There are two more sophisticated empirical studies which purport to isolate the effect of purely exogenous changes in female labor-force participation on fertility (Nerlove and Schultz 1970, Maurer, Ratajcyak, and Schultz 1973). These studies generally show a negative coefficient for predicted female labor-force participation in the fertility equation, although in the latter study of Thailand the female labor-force participation variable—that is, the ratio of urban economically active women to total adult population including rural—is not well defined. In the Nerlove and Schultz study of Puerto Rico, data for individual *municipios* are collected for a large number of variables including crude birth rates, death rates, and female labor-force participation rates. The sample involves a pooling of time series and cross-sectional data and, in the process of estimation, a correction was made for omitted variables which are serially correlated. A predicted value for the female labor-force participation rate in each *municipio* is obtained from three instruments: unemployment (male and female), adolescent schooling, and an index of the demand for female labor services based on output composition.

The crucial assumption embodied in this approach is that the instruments affect the crude birth rate only through female labor-force participation.[11] However, these variables either have a separate direct effect on fertility or are themselves affected by fertility and labor-force participation decisions. Consequently, one can not conclude from their results

[11] The level of unemployment influences the crude birth rate directly in a number of ways; it is a measure of total wage-income uncertainty, for example, which may well affect fertility decision even though labor-force participation rates remain constant. It remains to be seen, therefore, why Schultz and Nerlove did not include unemployment as a separate independent variable in the fertility regression. Further, the index of the demand for female labor based on industrial composition is not exogenous. The remaining "exogenous" instrument determining predicted female labor-force participation—adolescent schooling—also appears in the fertility equation. For these reasons, the system of Schultz and Nerlove is not really identified.

that an exogenous increase in female labor-force participation brought on by a previously unobserved policy will decrease fertility.

Implementation of the Proposed Methods

To show how the methodology proposed in the preceding section may alter existing results, we shall estimate equations for a number of household choice variables, using some readily available data sets. This exercise will involve both a large individual household sample for Puerto Rico and an intercountry, cross-sectional sample.

The Case of Puerto Rico

One of the better existing sources of micro data pertaining to a developing country is the 1970 1:100 Public Use Sample for Puerto Rico, which contains detailed characteristics on approximately 3,000 households with both spouses present (table 10-1). The empirical model described earlier is applied to this data set in order to illustrate the concepts discussed and to examine the nexus between female employment and fertility better in one less developed country.

Table 10-1. Female Occupations Ranked by Children Ever Born (CEB) to All Married Women over the Age of Thirty-five, Puerto Rico, 1970

Occupation	*Average CEB*	*Number in sample*
Typists	1.63	8
Telephone operators	1.67	3
Miscellaneous clerical workers	1.77	35
Bookkeepers	2.00	9
Secretaries	2.18	49
Hairdressers	2.20	10
Registered nurses	2.26	23
Private household workers	2.36	11
Secondary-school teachers	2.45	22
Dressmakers and seamstresses, except factory	2.50	22
School administrators, elementary and secondary	2.58	12
Restaurant and bar managers	2.60	10
Cashiers	2.64	11
Elementary-school teachers	2.66	58
College teachers	2.67	6
Personnel and labor relations workers	2.67	6
Professional, technical, and kindred workers	2.70	10
Foremen	2.76	21

(*continued*)

Table 10-1 (*continued*).

Occupation	*Average CEB*	*Number in sample*
Child-care workers	2.83	6
Sales clerks, retail trade	2.89	35
Managers and administrators, nonfarm	2.90	21
Social workers	3.10	10
Checkers, examiners, and inspectors	3.13	8
Miscellaneous sales workers	3.14	7
Other employed[a]	3.16	87
Chambermaids and maids, not private household	3.38	8
Practical nurses	3.44	9
Clothing ironers and pressers	3.47	17
Food-service workers	3.62	29
Sewers and stitchers	3.70	166
Child-care workers, not private household	3.86	7
Laundry and dry-cleaners workers	3.86	7
Machine operators	4.00	54
Packers and wrappers	4.10	10
Laundresses	4.14	7
Nursing aids and orderlies	4.33	9
Maids and servants	4.33	46
Service workers, not private household	5.05	20
Cooks, private household	5.17	52
Not employed	5.29	2,822
Housekeepers	5.33	6
Janitors	5.44	34
Miscellaneous laborers, nonfarm	5.83	6
Farm laborers and wage workers	7.00	10
Mean for employed women	3.43	982
Mean for all women	4.81	3,804

Source: 1970 Public Use Sample 1:100.
[a] Occupations in which sample numbers <6.

The dependent variables utilized are the number of children ever born (CEB), the number of annual hours worked (FHRS),[12] and the child-rearing compatibility of the occupation (OCC), as measured by the average CEB of all married women in the occupation over the age of thirty-five and, reported in table 10-1, of married, spouse-present, nonfarm women between the ages of thirty-five and forty-four along with

[12] The use of a lifetime labor-force participation variable rather than the available current one would be a more appropriate test of the theoretical model. However, Ben-Porath (1973c) provides evidence that there is a high positive correlation between the participation of women in the labor force at any two points in their life cycle—women who work more in any given period of time tend to be employed more throughout their lifetime.

the annual hours worked by their husbands (MHRS), the presence of adult relatives (REL) in the household and the location of employment (HOME) (1 if work is outside the home, 0 otherwise). The independent variables used in each equation are the predicted wages (PWAGEF) of married women, based on regression equation 10-4, involving all never-married working women over eighteen years of age, the predicted wage of the husband (PWAGEM), estimated from regression equation 10-5, which was run on all married men over eighteen, and the non-earnings income and number of years of schooling completed by the husband and the wife, respectively (NEIM, NEIF, EDM, EDF), as well as control variables including the wife's age (AGEF) and household location.

$$(10\text{-}4)\quad lnPWAGEF = -1.4054 + \underset{(.0088)^{***}}{.07641EDF} + \underset{(.0203)^{**}}{.04108AGEF} - \underset{(.0002)^{**}}{.00050AGEF^2}$$

$$R^2 = .146 \qquad F(3,477) = 27.23$$

$$(10\text{-}5)\quad lnPWAGEM = -1.0648 + \underset{(.0028)^{***}}{.06563EDM} + \underset{(.0078)^{***}}{.03685AGEM} - \underset{(.0001)^{***}}{.00036AGEM^2}$$

$$R^2 = .187 \qquad F(3,2622) = 200.47$$

** Significant at the 5 percent level (two-tailed test).
*** Significant at the 1 percent level (two-tailed test).

The log-linear specification for the predicted-wage equations was chosen because the distribution of wages tends to approach the log-normal density function in most societies. Elsewhere (McCabe and Rosenzweig 1976) we present estimates of more general earnings functions involving two additional independent variables, education squared and an interaction term, the product of age and education. The results of the second-stage equations were not sensitive to the alternative specification of the earnings functions. The predicted wages were introduced in the second-stage regressions in linear form, however, so that the schooling and age variables enter those equations both exponentially, through the wage, and linearly, as controls for demographic and educational influences. An exogenous prediction of the wage rate itself, not its natural log, is used as an explanatory variable in the equations determining children ever born, hours worked by the wife, and other endogenous dependent variables. The expected value of the predicted wage rate is given by the approximation formula

$$(10\text{-}6)\qquad E(\hat{wage}) = (1 + 1/2(SEE)^2)e^{(ln\hat{}wage)}$$

where (*ln^wage*) is the predicted value of the log of either the wage rate of unmarried working women over eighteen or the wage rate of married working men over eighteen, and *SEE* is the standard error residual in the relevant log wage prediction equation 10-4 or 10-5.

In addition, the age of the wife was set at forty in the wage-predicting equations, so the wage rate represents the expected opportunity wage of a married woman at the age of forty; the husband's age was set at forty plus the actual husband-wife age differential.

The second-stage household regressions are presented in table 10-2. The set of independent variables in each equation contributes significantly to an explanation of the variance of each dependent variable. More important, however, the female wage-and-schooling-attainment variable coefficients provide a consistent and informative picture of the relationship between female labor-force participation and fertility.

Equations 10-1, 10-2, and 10-3 indicate that an exogenous rise in the wage rates of women increases family size at the same time that it increases the amount of work performed both in total and outside the home. The positive fertility-wage effect appears to be an economic rather than a demographic phenomenon, since the age and the age squared of the wife are contained in the second-stage equations, and age does not influence the variance of the predicted wage. [Both the age variables contribute significantly to the exploratory power of the equations (5 percent level), but their coefficient variances are high because of the marked degree of collinearity between them.] This finding also appears consistent with the Puerto Rico results of Carlton (1965) on the basis of 1960 census data, in which he found that college-educated women had larger families than wives who had received only a secondary education, even though the latter group exhibited lower fertility than women who had not gone beyond the primary grades. The inclusion of the wife's predicted wages along with her level of schooling in the specification used here provides one possible explanation for Carlton's results: female educational attainment appears to have a direct negative linear effect on fertility, perhaps because of its association with contraceptive knowledge, but has an exponentially positive influence through the wife's wage. Thus at high levels of wife's education, the positive education (wage) effect on fertility would tend to dominate.

The positive relationships of the female wage with both completed fertility and labor-force participation is possible, according to the enlarged household production framework, if mothers can find substitutes for their time or engage in occupations that are more compatible with raising children when the value of their time increases. The *OCC* equation indicates that the latter is indeed the case in Puerto Rico—wives with high wages, and thus with high-fertility levels, tend to enter occupa-

Table 10-2. Household Regression Coefficients for Women Between the Ages of Thirty-five and Forty-four, Married, with Spouse Present, in Puerto Rico

Variable	*CEB*	*FEHRS*	*ATHOME*	*OCC*	*REL*	*MHRS*
PWAGEF	1.6500	653.839	0.26312	1.7021	0.83468	−206.1656
	(0.7085)**	(171.652)***	(0.09008)***	(1.8578)	(0.71828)	(242.875)
EDF	−0.32284	−43.829	−0.01450	−0.01740	−0.03111	43.381
	(0.0829)***	(20.019)**	(0.0105)	(0.0698)	(0.0219)	(28.39)*
AGEF	−0.42113	−28.013	0.04526	0.31545	0.05737	360.073
	(0.9059)	(219.430)	(0.1151)	(0.3565)	(0.1379)	(310.48)
$AGEF^2$	0.00592	0.20088	−0.00066	−0.00373	−0.00052	−4.5575
	(0.0115)	(2.781)	(0.0015)	(0.0045)	(0.0018)	(3.935)
PWAGEM	2.1746	−352.805	−0.21073	0.78483	0.04000	240.5388
	(0.5250)***	(127.169)***	(0.06669)***	(0.20678)***	(0.07992)	(179.9314)
EDM	−0.40367	49.119	0.02867	−0.11444	−0.00249	12.2584
	(0.0735)***	(17.800)***	(0.0093)***	(0.0289)	(0.0112)	(25.187)
NEIF	−0.00001	−0.28921	−0.00010	−0.01740	−0.00007	−0.09840
	(0.0005)	(0.1128)***	(0.00006)	(0.0698)	(0.00007)	(0.1595)
NEIM	−0.00003	−0.00474	−0.00001	0.00002	0.00001	−0.29515
	(0.0001)	(0.0240)	(0.00001)	(0.00004)	(0.00001)	(0.0339)
EDF^2				−0.01488	−0.00370	
				(0.0080)	(0.0031)	
R^2	0.231	0.324	0.458	0.372	0.028	0.198
F(11,964)	26.39	42.05	74.11	47.57	2.319	21.68

Other variables: metropolitan residence, residence five years earlier, location of work [in standard metropolitan statistical area (SMSA) or not].

* Significant at 5 percent level (one-tailed test).

** Significant at 5 percent level (two-tailed test).

*** Significant at 1 percent level (two-tailed test).

tions with higher-compatibility indexes. The positive wage coefficient in the *REL* equation is consistent with the notion that substitution of relatives' time for that of the mother also occurs when wages rise, but the effect is not significant by conventional standards. One important possible explanation for the insignificance of the *REL* wage effect is that an exogenous rise in all female wage rates raises both the potential wage of the mother and of adult (female) relatives, leaving unaltered the female relative–mother wage ratio.

The rationale for using the expected value of the predicted wage rate derived from equation 10-4 predicting the natural log of the wage rate for never-married working women, is that this variable is an unbiased estimate of the potential wage rate for married women having no children—that is, that the potential wage rate for married women does not differ from that for never-married women because of differences in the characteristics of the two groups not captured in the variables utilized. An additional interpretation of the positive predicted wage coefficient in the *CEB* equation, however, is that it represents a "taste-for-children" effect. Among women with identical characteristics, those who marry and bear children must have a greater preference for children. If married women with high potential wage rates must forgo a relatively greater amount of earnings through marriage and child rearing than women whose characteristics entail a lower potential wage, then preferences for children would be positively correlated with the potential wage.

Such an interpretation may be tested in the following way. Consider only that portion of the households in which wives are working. For this sample, let us estimate the *CEB* equation with the same independent variables, as presented in table 10-2, with the exception that the actual wage of working women has been added as an independent variable (residence and location variables included but not reported).

$$(10\text{-}7)\quad CEB = \underset{}{2.77423} + \underset{(1.1039)}{2.5904PWAGEF} + \underset{(.06798)}{.00401WAGEF} - \underset{(.15998)}{.45063EDF}$$

$$+ \underset{(1.36173)}{.04266AGE} - \underset{(.01735)}{.00061AGE^2} + \underset{(1.0451)}{2.0762PWAGEM} + \underset{(.06736)}{.02281WAGEM}$$

$$- \underset{(.11066)}{.41944EDM} - \underset{(.00691)}{.00607NEIF} + \underset{(.00015)}{.00006NEIM}$$

$$R^2 = .235 \qquad F(13{,}282) = 6.671$$

In this equation, the estimated coefficient for the predicted wage rate of the woman, assuming her to be single, and for her actual wage have two alternative interpretations. The equation may be written in the alternate forms $CEB - BV = b_1\ WAGEF + b_2\ PWAGEF = b_1\ (WAGEF - PWAGEF) + (b_2 + b_1)\ WAGEF$, where *WAGEF* is the actual wage rate for working women, *PWAGEF* is the predicted wage rate for these women, assuming that they are single, *B* is a diagonal matrix, and *V* is column vector of the other independent variables and a constant unity. If there is no significant taste effect, the coefficient $(b_2 + b_1)$ may be interpreted as the marginal effect of a change in the expected potential wage (which may be of either sign) and b_1 the effect of a random fluctuation around expected wage or "transitory" income effect. It is generally hypothesized that b_1 is zero or at least of the same sign as b_2. The interpretation that *WAGEF* is in part a proxy for differences in the relative desire for children implies that equation 10-7 should be interpreted in the following form: $CEB = b_2\ (WA\hat{G}EF - PWAGEF) + (b_1 + b_2)\ PWAGEF + BV$. The differential between the predicted wage for a single woman with the same characteristics as the married working woman and the latter's actual market wage, the sacrifice in income resulting from marriage and child bearing, captures the relative desire for children; b_2 is therefore hypothesized to be positive. The coefficient $(b_1 + b_2)$ represents a negatively biased estimate of the wife's wage effect.

In the differential taste version of the model, we would have no basis a priori; for expecting b_1 to be insignificant or of the same sign as b_2, and we would expect $(b_1 + b_2)$ to be significantly greater than zero. The estimated equation 10-7 is more consistent with the expected income model than it is with the differential taste model. As hypothesized in the expected income model, the actual wage rate of the wife is statistically insignificant. The sign of the coefficient for *PWAGEF* is positive and significantly greater than zero at the 5 percent level. Moreover, the sign of the coefficient for the actual wage is positive even though, as previously indicated, simultaneous equations bias would probably cause it to be negative, other things being equal. The same pattern may be observed in the case of the husband's wage rate in equation 10-7. Here the estimated coefficient for the predicted wage rate is highly significant and positive, and the coefficient for the actual wage rate is positive but insignificant, all of which is consistent with the expected income explanation for fertility determination.

The results, displayed in table 10-2, also provide information on the importance of the schooling of women in the relationship between fertility and female employment. Two important roles of female education in the context of fertility and employment determination are a positive association between education and contraceptive knowledge, which may tend to reduce desired and "excess" children, and the household efficiency effect of education, which may tend to increase the productivity of women's time in household production and thus decrease the time spent in the home. The set of equations shows that both these educational roles may be important. Female schooling is indeed negatively related to completed family size, for controlling the female wage, which is consistent with the birth-control hypothesis. The negative association between female schooling and hours worked is consistent with the household production efficiency argument: given the market productivity of women, as reflected in their wage rates, those with higher levels of schooling are more productive at home and thus tend to work less outside the household. This relationship also appears in the other equations—husbands work more when their wives are better educated, as more efficient women's time is substituted for that of their husbands in household production, fewer relatives are used in the household when women are more efficient at home, and better-educated women, who bear fewer children, enter occupations with lower child-bearing compatibility.

The policy implications of these results are not encouraging: inducing women to work by means of a general female wage subsidy may not lead to a reduction in family size so long as occupational mobility is relatively high, as in the Puerto Rico context. However, such a subsidy would not, at least in the context of Puerto Rico, significantly reduce the labor-force participation of males. A policy of encouraging female schooling has ambiguous effects on family size and female employment, since such a scheme will result in higher wages for women (pronatalist in Puerto Rico) as well as an increase in contraceptive knowledge (antinatalist) and will tend to increase nonmarket efficiency.

Intercountry Results

From an intercountry cross-sectional sample, additional evidence may be obtained that some exogenous variables are related to both female labor-force participation and fertility; but the main value of these data is that they indicate that factors affecting the composition, as well as the overall level, of female labor-force participation are crucial in determining urban—and to some extent aggregate—fertility. In table 10-3, data on the ratio of women to total persons in the labor force are shown by less developed region, along with aggregate crude birth rates. On the basis of the available intracountry household data, one would not expect the aggregate ratio of women to total persons in the labor force to be as important a determinant of the aggregate birth rate as the share of women in the nonagricultural labor force. Nonagricultural activities appear on the whole to be more competitive with child rearing than do

Table 10-3. Aggregate Crude Birth Rates and the Proportion of Women in the Total Labor Force of Major Less Developed Regions, 1960

Region	*Aggregate crude birth rate (per thousand)* (*1*)		*Proportion of women in total labor force* (*2*)	
Sub-Saharan Africa	46.5	(25)	0.32	(21)
North Africa	45.7	(4)	0.17	(5)
Middle East	36.7	(7)	0.14	(7)
Asia	38.2	(17)	0.30	(14)
Northern Latin America	40.6	(14)	0.23	(14)
Southern Latin America	39.1	(12)	0.23	(12)
Total	41.6	(79)	0.26	(73)

Source: All the underlying data are from IBRD (January 1973, table 2).

The ratios presented in columns 1 and 2 represent arithmetic means of the individual country rates.

The number of countries appears in parentheses beside each arithmetic mean. In some cases there are birth rate estimates for countries for which the *World Tables* do not offer female labor-participation estimates, and vice versa.

agricultural activities, as already indicated.[13] It is not particularly surprising, therefore, that sub-Saharan Africa, with a relatively high share of women in the overall labor force (mainly because of a high female agricultural participation rate), has the highest crude birth rate. (See table 10-3, columns 1 and 2.) What is surprising, however, is the situation that appears in table 10-4. Here northern Latin America has both the third-highest regional crude birth rate (above the fifty-eight-country mean) and the highest share of women in the nonagricultural labor force in a reduced sample of countries for which nonagricultural labor-force data are available.

While it has a slightly negative but insignificant simple correlation with the aggregate crude birth rate in this second sample of countries, the female share of the nonagricultural labor force is negatively correlated at the 1 percent level with the urban child–woman ratio. Thus, part of the anomalous behavior of northern Latin America is attributable to the high rural birth rate in relation to the urban birth rate in this region discussed by Simon Kuznets (1974) and Carmen A. Miró and Mertens (1968). But at the same time intercountry regressions, such as those presented in the paper, consistently underpredict urban child–woman ratios in this region when such variables as per capita GNP and the

[13] See footnote 10.

Table 10-4. Aggregate Crude Birth Rates, the Proportion of Women in the Nonagricultural and Agricultural Labor Forces, and the Ratio of Service to Total Female Nonagricultural Labor in Major Less Developed Regions (Reduced Sample), Late 1950s and Early 1960s

Region	*Aggregate crude birth rate (per thousand)* (1)		*Urban child–woman ratio* (2)		*Proportion of women in non-agricultural labor force* (3)		*Ratio of service to total female non-agricultural labor force* (4)	
Sub-Saharan Africa	44.5	(10)	0.66	(5)	0.19	(10)	0.48	(10)
North Africa	45.2	(6)	0.81	(4)	0.14	(6)	0.41	(6)
Middle East	40.8	(6)	0.70	(6)	0.12	(6)	0.44	(6)
Asia	41.2	(12)	0.65	(7)	0.24	(12)	0.34	(12)
Northern Latin America	42.5	(13)	0.60	(13)	0.35	(13)	0.56	(13)
Southern Latin America	38.8	(11)	0.59	(9)	0.29	(11)	0.55	(11)
Total	42.0	(58)	0.64	(44)	0.24	(58)	0.47	(58)

Numbers in parentheses represent the number of countries used to compute mean. For sources and countries, see the appendix to this chapter.

female literacy rate are used as independent variables, despite the low mean urban child–woman ratio shown in table 10-4. It should also be noted that many women living in rural areas in northern Latin America are employed in the nonagricultural sector, whereas relatively few women living in urban areas are employed in agriculture. The average ratio of women in the nonagricultural labor force to the urban adult female population is extremely high (.99), and in some countries—Guyana, Jamaica, Barbados, and Trinidad—it exceeds 1. The latter could only be true if the rural nonfarm female labor force exceeded the urban female labor force associated with agriculture. For this reason, we would expect the share of women in the nonagricultural labor force to affect both urban and rural birth rates. The high rural birth rate in northern Latin America, therefore, may be inconsistent with an inverse association between female nonagricultural labor-force participation and rural nonfarm birth rates.

There are several additional explanations for the northern Latin America case. One is that greater employment opportunities for women in urban areas have caused a disproportionate number of single women to migrate to the cities; this has inflated the general rural fertility rate directly and has also reduced the economic cost of female children to farm families. The size distribution of income is more uneven in northern Latin America than it is in other regions.[14] If fertility rises more than proportionally with decreases in household income, then we would expect a rise in aggregate income inequality to lead to a fall in the birth rate. Indeed, it has been shown, using a large cross-sample of both developed and developing countries, that there is a significant positive association between summary measures of income inequality and aggregate birth rates (IBRD 1974). Another explanation, not unrelated to income inequality, is that the relatively high availability of female domestic servants in urban areas in Latin America has meant, in effect, that some purchased inputs are highly and cheaply substitutable for the wife's time in household production (Youssef 1974). In addition, an increase in the ratio of servants and day-care workers to other female laborers may mean that the overall female occupational mix is more compatible with child rearing as evidenced in our Puerto Rican sample. (See table 10-1, particularly the categories "maids and servants" and "child-care workers, not private household".) But, since domestic servants have been shown to have relatively low fertility in some developing countries—Guatemala, for example [Gendell, Maraviglia, and Kreitner 1970]—we shall assume that this occupational composition effect, if it exists, is of a second order in comparison with the effect associated with changes in the relative cost of children for households employing servants.

It is impossible to obtain estimates of the number of female domestic servants for a significant sample of developing countries. An approximation as good as any is obtained from the sample used by Boserup (1970). She provides estimates of the number of female service workers, about two-thirds of whom are domestic servants, for a sample of twenty-nine developing countries.

The proportion of women employed as domestic servants both affects and is affected by birth rates. To get around this problem of two-way causality, we use instrumental-variable estimation. First, the ratio of female domestic servants to total women employed in the nonagricultural sector is regressed against three exogenous variables in addition to the other exogenous variables appearing in the fertility and employment equations (discussed below): the female share of the total agricultural labor force, *AGFM;* the ratio of the urban adult population not employed in industry to the total urban adult population, *POT;* and a

[14] See estimates of income inequality compiled by the World Bank in Shail Jain and Arthur E. Tiemann (1973).

dummy variable, *MOSLEM*. The first variable, which is determined by such exogenous factors as the prevalent customs and relative scarcity of land, represents an important "push" factor in female migration, expected to be negatively associated with the supply of female domestic servants in urban areas (Boserup 1970). The second exogenous variable indicates the proportion of the adult urban population potentially available for employment in the service sector. Finally, the dummy variable is a control for the preference on the part of husbands in Moslem countries against their wives being employed as domestic servants.

The regression equation predicting the proportion of women employed in services with the insignificant variables removed is shown below.

$$FMSERV = .20017 - \underset{(.11407)^{***}}{.42565AGFM} + \underset{(.17218)^{*}}{.29633POT} - \underset{(.011407)^{***}}{.042565MOSLEM} \qquad (10\text{-}8)$$

$$R^2 = .494 \qquad F(3,26) = 8.12$$

*Significant at 5 percent level (one-tailed test).
***Significant at 1 percent level (two-tailed test).

where

FMSERV = Proportion of service workers in female nonagricultural labor force (Boserup's data)
AGFM = Female proportion of total agricultural labor force
POT = Adult urban population less total industrial labor force per adult urban population
MOSLEM = Dummy variable with a value of 1 if the country is predominantly Moslem and 0 otherwise.

For sources of data and countries used in the regression, see the appendix to this chapter. Here all variables have the hypothesized sign and are significantly different from zero by conventional statistical standards.

The predicted values of the share of women employed in the service sector in total female nonagricultural employment are then used as an independent variable in second-stage regressions. These regression equations are intended to explain the urban child–woman ratio (a measure of urban fertility), the aggregate crude birth rate, and female nonagricultural labor-force participation, the latter being measured by the ratio of female to total nonagricultural workers.

It is hypothesized that the ratio of the wage rate of domestic servants to that of other female nonagricultural laborers is inversely associated with the exogenous prediction *FMSERV* and that, therefore, this exogenous prediction is positively associated with fertility. The predicted share of the nonagricultural female labor force employed in the service sector is being used as an independent variable *only because* under certain conditions it is a proxy for the relative wage rate of female domestic servants. If data on this wage rate were available, a far more appropriate technique would be to obtain an exogenous prediction of the relative wage rate of female domestic servants and use that as the independent variable, rather than the predicted employment share of service workers.

Aside from the predicted share of female service workers in the total nonagricultural labor force, we experimented with five other exogenous variables in these equations. These included per capita GNP, the total adult literacy rate, the female literacy rate, and a dummy variable representing whether or not a country was predominantly Moslem. These variables are used frequently to explain female labor-force participation or fertility, or both, in interregional cross-sectional samples, except possibly for the Moslem dummy, indicating a cultural preference against female employment (Adelman 1963, Simon 1974a). Thus, the hypothesized effect need not be explained. The regression results for the aggregate birth rate and urban child–woman ratio equations and the equation predicting the female share of nonagricultural labor force are presented in table 10-5. Only those variables that were statistically significant in at least one of the regression equations were used in the final runs shown in table 10-5.

The most significant result that the regressions in table 10-5 bring out is that the predicted ratio of service to total female nonagricultural laborers is a very important variable explaining differences in aggregate crude birth rates and urban child–woman ratios across countries. They have the hypothesized positive sign and are statistically significant at the same critical level in both the birth rate and child–woman ratio regressions. On the other hand, in the regressions explaining the share of women in the nonagricultural labor force, they do not have the hypothesized positive sign and are insignificant by conventional statistical standards. Here is an example of instruments (that is, those predicting the share of female service workers) that influence fertility through the composition of female employment without being associated with its overall level.

The variable involving the share of female service workers must be interpreted with extreme caution as a proxy for the relative wage rate of

Table 10-5. Labor-force Participation and Birth-rate Regressions

Independent variable	*Urban child–woman ratio* (1)	*Crude birth rate* (2)	*Female proportion of total nonagricultural labor force* (3)
	Dependent Variable		
Predicted proportion of service workers in the female nonagricultural labor force on the basis of Boserup data	0.50029 (0.22313)**	23.20979 (10.14450)**	−0.03582 (0.16940)
1960 per capita GNP at factor cost in 1964 U.S. dollars	−0.00010 (0.00011)	−0.01947 (0.00499)***	−0.00013 (0.00008)
Female adult literacy rate	−0.23595 (0.09424)**	−4.56112 (4.22505)	0.25661 (0.07055)***
Dummy variable indicating whether country is Moslem, with value of 1 if population is Moslem, 0 otherwise.	0.07228 (0.04791)	1.28824 (2.26847)	−0.05841 (0.03788)
R^2	0.481	0.406	0.512
F statistic	7.659	7.358	11.299
Number of observations	38	48	48

Standard errors appear in parentheses under coefficients.
For sources and countries, see the appendix to this chapter.
** Significant at 5 percent level (two-tailed test).
*** Significant at 1 percent level (two-tailed test).

domestic servants, not only because the qualitative association between relative factor prices and shares is not always the same but also because female domestic servants are not the only female workers in the service sector, though they do constitute a majority. Nonetheless, the negative association between the relative wage rate of female domestic servants and fertility suggested by our results is found in other studies where actual price data are available. Maurice Wilkinson (1973) finds a negative association between the aggregate wage rate of female domestic servants and the crude birth rate in Sweden for the period 1911–40. Glen G. Cain and Adriana Weininger (1973) find a significant negative association between the annual wage rate of domestic servants and average children ever born in different cohorts, using a cross section of urban areas taken from the 1960 U.S. Census.

Policy Implications

It has been suggested that policies designed to increase female employment in urban areas both reduce the urban birth rate and increase aggregate output. The latter conclusion is, according to Boserup (1970), based on the fact that the additional social infrastructure required to support employed wives already living in the city is practically nil. By contrast, the social infrastructure requirements of new urban plants employing mostly males is substantially higher because of the new family units that they attract.

The evidence presented in this chapter, however, by no means suggests that an overall increase in female employment in urban areas would involve less public capital costs than a comparable increase in male employment, to say nothing of natalist effects. To begin with, consider the following likely policies designed to increase overall female employment in urban areas: subsidized employment of women in existing industries and public investment in industries where mainly women rather than men would be willing to accept employment (sewing factories, for example). Even if these policies could be implemented so as to benefit only resident wives, there would still be substantial rural-urban migration. The total income (husband's and wife's) of an initial set of urban households would have increased even though employment opportunities for male migrants would have declined. Under these circumstances, the willingness of urban households to accept unemployed relatives might increase substantially, simply because the value of these relatives' time in household activities had risen. This is much more likely to be the case if the wage subsidies and factories oriented toward female employment were financed in a way that did not decrease the disposable income of urban males—by forgoing public investment in agriculture rather than increasing the tax on urban income, for example. Increases in the employment of women already living in urban areas, therefore, would not necessarily minimize the need for urban social infrastructure investment, as Boserup contends.

In order for such a policy to be successful in this sense, the female wage subsidy or the female industry investment would have to be financed by fiscal measures unfavorable to urban residents—a tax on urban income, for example. Such policies, designed to discourage migration, would result in a net decrease in the wage income of urban men, while the net wage income of women would increase. The political feasibility of policies having these effects does not seem great.

Irrespective of the way in which it is financed, however, an overall increase in urban female employment may well increase fertility. Increases in the female potential wage rate may be positively associated with female labor-force participation and completed fertility, other things being equal. This is not only supported by the Puerto Rican evidence discussed above, but by a positive association—despite a bias toward a negative one—between average wage rates for females and period fertility in a preliminary investigation of urban data from the 1970 U.S. public-use sample. Of course, it is by no means clear that these spatial relationships occur over time or what, if any, their lag structure is. Estimates based on different cohorts in different cities must be obtained before the pronatalist effect of a rise in the wife's wage can be substantiated for a given country.

One policy influencing female labor-force participation which may well have an antinatalist effect is that producing an exogenous change in the composition of female employment. For example, women working in jobs highly compatible with child rearing, such as self-employed retailing, could be shifted to jobs less compatible with child bearing, such as secretarial work. Also, greater occupational alternatives could be made available to women who would potentially enter domestic service. As suggested by our intercountry cross-sectional evidence, the availability of persons in this occupational class is inversely related to the opportunity cost of children, especially in households where the value of the parents' time is high. However, subsidized wages and retraining might be necessary in order for occupational changes to take place voluntarily. There is little existing empirical information on changes in the composition of female employment induced by such policies. Moreover, whether their combined effect on fertility through a positive pure income effect offsets that of the relative wage rate change remains ambiguous a priori. Finally, the evidence concerning the effects on fertility of changes in female employment composition is only suggestive, even in a partial-equilibrium context, let alone in a general-equilibrium one. Straight cross-sectional regressions, as already indicated, suffer from omitted-variable problems and therefore do not provide legitimate bases for evaluating associations between variables over time. Further, selectivity bias error is involved in using an earnings function estimated for working women to predict the potential wage rate for nonworking women.

While the general equilibrium problem is beyond the scope of this chapter, in the next section we outline further means of testing the partial-equilibrium effect of a policy designed to increase the relative wage rate of occupations incompatible with child rearing.

Experimental Design

It would require considerable time and expense to determine the partial effect on completed fertility of a change in the relative wage rates of female occupations through a controlled experiment. It is possible, however, to determine the partial impact of such a potential change in relative earnings on the probability of a household's having an additional child, though the effect of this change on completed fertility may only be of the second order. This may be accomplished by comparing two urban areas in which occupations largely incompatible with child rearing did not exist initially. In the first urban area, a factory whose female occupational mix was basically incompatible with child rearing would be built. In the second, there would be no policy intervention. The new factory would have an announced policy of hiring only women already living in the city, so as to minimize the possibility that migration of female labor would rapidly bring relative wage rates back to their original level. Panel data would be collected for a representative set of households in the two urban areas covering the several years immediately following the introduction of the factory in the first city. From these panel data, pooled over both cities, equations would be estimated explaining the probability that a woman would have an additional child, her annual hours worked, and an index of the compatibility of her occupation with child rearing.

Appearing as independent variables in these three separate equations would be exogenous predictions of both the husband's and the wife's potential wage rates, denoted by $\hat{w}(m)$ and $\hat{w}(f)$, respectively. Information on prior work histories would be obtained for both men and women in the sample. Although work experience up to a given date depends on children ever born, such experience within a household may be treated as exogenous to the probability of its having an additional child in the future. Our dependent fertility variable in the experiment is the annual probability of having an additional child within the same household, rather than simply children ever born across households. Therefore, given information on work experience in previous years (which is exogenous to a particular household's current birth probability, though not to its children ever born), earnings functions in this experiment will be estimated for working married, not single, women, as well as working married men. The system of earnings equations for household i in the year t will take the form shown below.

Variables:

$w_{it}(k)$ = Husband's wage rate, if m in parentheses, and wife's wage rate if f in parentheses
$e_{it}(k)$ = Husband's or wife's years of education
$x_{it}(k)$ = Husband's or wife's total years of employment experience prior to year t
δ_{it} = 1 in year t and 0 otherwise
δ'_{it} = 1 in year t if ith household in city of experimental plant and 0 otherwise.

Vectors:

$$Z_{it}(k) = \begin{bmatrix} 1 \\ e_{it}(k) \\ x_{it}(k)^2 \\ x_{it}(k) \\ \delta_t \\ \delta'_t \end{bmatrix}$$

and

$$C = [\alpha_{k0}, \alpha_{k1}, \alpha_{k2}, \alpha_{k3}, \alpha_{k4}, \alpha_{k5}]$$

Stochastic equations:

(10-9) $$\log w_{kit} = cZ_{it}(k) + \eta_{kit}$$

where η_{kit} is an error term.

There are important problems which may arise in estimating the set of two equations represented by equation 10-9. The first problem concerns the possible presence of selectivity bias in that wage-rate predictions based on households in which women work at least some of the time do not accurately predict the level or the change over time of the potential wage rates of nonworking women. The second concerns the fact that the disturbance term may have a component specific to individual households which is invariant over time. A possible representation may be

(10-10) $$\eta_{kt} = \rho_k \mu_k + \epsilon_{kit}$$

where ρ_k is a correlation coefficient, μ_k is a household specific, time-independent error component, and the ε_{kit}'s are mutually independent error components. If this is the appropriate error decomposition, then equation 10-9 may be estimated by the two-stage, generalized least-squares procedure outlined by Marc Nerlove and T. Paul Schultz (1970).

Once the equations for the predicted earnings of the husband and the wife have been estimated, a system of equations will be fitted determining the probability of a birth, P_{it}, hours that the wife works, h_{it}, and a compatibility measure of her occupational choice, O_{it}, in year t. Denote the wife's predicted wage rate by $\hat{w}_{if}(f)$ and her husband's predicted wage rate by $\hat{w}_{it}(m)$, and other exogenous variables by v_{jit}. Let

$$D_{it} = \begin{bmatrix} P_{it} \\ h_{it} \\ O_{it} \end{bmatrix}$$

$$Q_{it} = \begin{bmatrix} 1 \\ \hat{w}_{it}(f) \\ \hat{w}_{it}(m) \\ \delta_{it} \\ \delta_{it} \\ v_{lit} \\ \cdot \\ \cdot \\ \cdot \\ v_{nit} \end{bmatrix}$$

and

$$\beta = \begin{bmatrix} \beta_{1,0}, \beta_{1,1}, \ldots, \beta_{1,n} \\ \beta_{2,0}, \beta_{2,1}, \ldots, \beta_{2,n} \\ \beta_{3,0}, \beta_{3,1}, \ldots, \beta_{3,n} \end{bmatrix}$$

Then we may estimate a system of equations of the form

$$D_{it} = \beta Q_{it} + \gamma_{it} \tag{10-11}$$

where γ_{it} is a 3×1 vector of error terms.

The hours-worked variable h_i may involve a large number of zero observations but be continuously distributed otherwise. In estimating the equation for this variable, it may be appropriate to assume that the error term has a truncated normal distribution or one of a similar type. T. Amemiya (1973) has suggested an iterative maximum-likelihood estimation technique, which he demonstrates to yield strongly consistent and asymptotically normal parameter estimates when the dependent variable displays this property.

The error terms in the system are probably not mutually independent. If this is true, then estimating each equation separately by either a univariate probit modified for panel data in the case of birth probabilities or other single-equation procedures in the case of the other dependent variables will yield inefficient coefficient estimates. Though less is being explained, it may be more appropriate, therefore, to redefine the dependent variables k_{it} and O_{it} as dichotomous variables indicating respectively whether a wife is active in the labor force and employed in an occupation incompatible with child rearing in year t. In this case, the system of equations would involve three dichotomous dependent variables and could be estimated jointly, using the Nerlove and Press multivariate logit technique (Nerlove and Press 1973), adapted to panel data.

If, according to the likelihood ratio test, the coefficients for the time dummy variables specific to the city in which the factory was installed, δ'_t's, are significantly negative in the birth-probability equation, then the hypothesis that the factory had an antinatalist effect, holding wage rates constant, would be supported. The total effect can only be determined by taking into consideration the indirect effect on birth probabilities of these dummies as a result of their entering the expression for predicted wage rates.

The sign and significance of the coefficients for the δ'_t variable in equations explaining hours worked by the wife and her choice of occupation provide insight into the mechanism by which the new factory influences birth probabilities, if it actually does. However, unless the households are examined for a period of twenty years or more after the introduction and other variables influencing fertility remain relatively stable during this period, we cannot conclusively reject the hypothesis that the introduction of the factory has merely caused younger married women to postpone having their children without influencing their actual completed fertility. The effect of the experiment on the completed fertility of women close to the end of their child-bearing years can be determined. But we would expect the maximum potential magnitude of this effect to be relatively small in comparison with that on the completed fertility of younger women; younger women generally practice birth control less than do older women in developing countries. Moreover, even over a short span of time the present value of earnings from continuous employment in a job largely incompatible with child rearing is probably substantially higher for younger than for older women because of differential learning ability and the fact that these jobs almost by definition require extensive training and retraining. Hence, a greater proportion of younger women than older should be attracted to jobs in the new factory, and the full effect of its effect on completed fertility of younger women cannot be measured.

In one particular case, it is possible to establish whether a significant decrease in age-specific fertility for younger cohorts of women implies a significant reduction in completed fertility for those cohorts. Suppose it can be established that age-specific fertility is only slightly below the biological maximum for older cohorts with socioeconomic characteristics similar to the younger cohorts being observed in the experiment. Then, by assuming that the age-specific fertility of the younger cohorts will rise to these biological maxima later and calculating the implied total fertility, we have a strong test of the hypothesis that the experimental plant has a significant depressing effect on completed fertility. If, assuming that the age-specific fecundity schedule remains fixed, the reduction in the biological maximum completed fertility implied by the experiment falls below the actual number of children ever born, then this antinatalist hypothesis is supported.

Though it may be applicable during the initial stages of fertility decline in some countries, this approach will be inconclusive if age-specific fecundity is expected to rise in the future (because of improvements in health and nutrition) or actual intervals between births are well above the biological minima at present. In general, greater empirical study is required of the lagged impact of changes (ten or twenty years ago) in all relevant socioeconomic variables on the current age-specific fertility of women in their thirties. But such analysis has greater relevance in the case of socioeconomic variables influencing the composition of female employment, since they tend to influence significantly the numbers of children born to younger women, whereas many other socioeconomic changes (declines in infant mortality, for example) tend mainly to influence the fertility of older women.[15]

Appendix A: Notes on Sources of Data

Dependent Variables

URBAN CHILD–WOMAN RATIO. Data are drawn from UN *Demographic Yearbook* (1965 and 1969, table 8). The numbers represent the ratio of children under five years of age born to women fifteen to forty-nine years of age. Data for Zaïre, Iran, and Israel were computed on a denominator of women fifteen to fifty-four years of age.

CRUDE BIRTH RATE. Data represent our estimation of reasonable figures close to 1960 and are drawn from IBRD (January 1971, table 2), with the following exceptions.

Estimates for Ghana, Libya, and Nepal are based on data in the UN *Demographic Yearbook* (1965 and 1969); estimates for Angola, Botswana, Liberia, and Sudan are taken from H. J. Page and A. J. Coale, "Fertility and Child Mortality South of the Sahara," in *Population Growth and Economic Development in Africa,* edited by S. H. Ominde and C. N. Ejiogu; the estimate for Turkey is drawn from Ghazi Farooq and Baran Tuncer, "Fertility and Economic and Social Development in Turkey: A Cross-sectional Time Series Study," Yale Economic Growth Center Discussion Paper No. 175 (April 1973); and the estimate for

[15] Sidney Goldstein (1972) shows that the antinatalist effect of the labor-force participation of women in their twenties is at least offset by higher fertility in their thirties.

Syria was especially computed by the authors through the backward projection method from the 1960 aggregate proportion of the population under 5 [UN *Demographic Yearbook* (1970) table 6], using a survival ratio for the children 0–4 of .84 and the 1968 intercensal rate of natural increase of 2.9 percent [UN *Demographic Yearbook* (1969) table 3].

PROPORTION OF WOMEN IN THE NONAGRICULTURAL LABOR FORCE. Data are drawn from International Labour Organisation (ILO), *Yearbook of Labor Statistics* (1966 and 1969, table 2A). The nonagricultural labor force was computed as the total economically active population minus persons employed in agriculture.

RATIO OF FEMALE SERVICE WORKERS TO TOTAL FEMALE NONAGRICULTURAL LABOR FORCE. Data are taken from the appendix of Ester Boserup, *Woman's Role in Economic Development* (London: Allen and Unwin, 1973), with the exception of table 10-4. In this table, in order to obtain a larger sample, though with larger modern service representation, data are drawn from ILO, *Yearbook of Labor Statistics* (1966 and 1969, table 2A). ILO data for the number of women in the service sector and women in the nonagricultural labor force (including those under the age of fifteen) were used except for countries where comparable data from women fifteen years old and over are provided in UN *Demographic Yearbook* (1972, table 10).

Independent Variables

ADULT LITERACY. The data underlying this variable were drawn from UN *Demographic Yearbook* (1970, table 11), and supplemented with data drawn from IBRD, *World Tables* (January 1971, table 2).

FEMALE ADULT LITERACY RATE. The data underlying this variable were drawn from the UN *Demographic Yearbook* (1970, table 11).

PER CAPITA 1960 GNP AT FACTOR COST IN 1964 U.S. DOLLARS. All data were drawn from IBRD, *World Tables* (January 1971, table 4). The figure for Sierra Leone is for 1965, rather than 1960.

ADULT URBAN POPULATION–TOTAL INDUSTRIAL LABOR FORCE PER ADULT URBAN POPULATION. Adult urban population: the data underlying this variable were drawn from the UN *Demographic Yearbook* (1970, table 6), defining an adult as a person fifteen years of age or older. Where UN data were not available for urban areas, an estimate was constructed by applying an urbanization percentage taken from IBRD, *World Tables* (January 1971, table 2), to UN figures for the total adult population. Total industrial labor force: data were drawn from ILO, *Yearbook of Labor Statistics* (1966 and 1969, table 2A). We define the industrial labor force to include the following ILO categories: (1) mining and quarrying; (2–3) manufacturing; (4) construction; (5) electricity, gas, water, and sanitary services; and (6) transport, storage, and communication.

FEMALE PROPORTION OF TOTAL AGRICULTURAL LABOR FORCE. Data were drawn from ILO, *Yearbook of Labor Statistics* (1966 and 1969, table 2A).

DUMMY VARIABLE. A value of one was assigned to countries with strong Moslem cultural influence and a value of zero to other countries. The following countries in the sample were classified as having strong Moslem cultural influence: Algeria, Egypt, Libya, Sudan, Tunisia, Indonesia, Pakistan, Iran, Iraq, Jordan, Syria, Turkey.

RATIO OF FEMALE ADULT LITERACY TO TOTAL ADULT LITERACY. Data from the UN *Demographic Yearbook* (1970, table II) and IBRD, *World Tables* (January 1971, table 2).

Table A-1. Sample Base

Country	*Census date*	*Table and column numbers in which data from a given country are excluded (i.e., 4:(1) means table 4, column 1)*		*Equation numbers from which data from a given country are excluded*
Sub-Saharan Africa				
Angola	1960	10–4:(2)	10–5:(1–3)	10–8
Botswana	1964			10–8
Gabon	1960		10–5:(1–3)	10–8
Ghana	1960		10–5:(1–3)	
Liberia	1962	10–4:(2)	10–5:(1)	
Mauritius	1962	10–4:(2)	10–5:(1)	
Niger	1965	10–4:(2)	10–5:(1–3)	10–8
Sierra Leone	1963	10–4:(2)	10–5:(1–3)	10–8
South Africa	1960		10–5:(1–3)	10–8
Zaïre	1955–57			10–8
North Africa				
Algeria	1966			10–8
Egypt	1960			
Libya	1964			10–8
Morocco	1960			
Sudan	1956	10–4:(2)	10–5:(1)	10–8
Tunisia	1956	10–4:(2)	10–5:(1)	10–8
Middle East				
Iran	1956			
Iraq	1957			
Israel	1961			10–8
Jordan	1961			10–8
Syria	1960			
Turkey	1960			

(*continued*)

Table A-1 (*continued*).

Country	*Census date*	*Table and column numbers in which data from a given country are excluded (i.e., 4:(1) means table 4, column 1)*		*Equation numbers from which data from a given country are excluded*
Asia				
Hong Kong	1961	10–4:(2)	10–5:(1)	10–8
India	1961			
Indonesia	1961			10–8
Khmer Republic	1962			
Republic of Korea	1960			
Nepal	1961			10–8
Pakistan	1961			
Philippines	1960	10–4:(2)	10–5:(1)	
Singapore	1957	10–4:(2)	10–5:(1)	
Sri Lanka	1963			
Taiwan	1956	10–4:(2)	10–5:(1)	10–8
Thailand	1960	10–4:(2)	10–5:(1)	
Northern Latin America				
Barbados	1960			10–8
Belize	1960			10–8
Costa Rica	1963			
Dominican Republic	1960			
El Salvador	1961			
Guatemala	1964			10–8
Honduras	1961			
Jamaica	1960			10–8
Mexico	1960			
Nicaragua	1963			
Panama	1960			
Puerto Rico	1960			
Trinidad and Tobago	1960			10–8
Southern Latin America				
Argentina	1960	10–4:(2)	10–5:(1)	10–8
Brazil	1960			10–8
Chile	1960			
Colombia	1964			
Ecuador	1962			
Guyana	1960		10–5:(1–3)	10–8
Paraguay	1962			10–8
Peru	1961			10–8
Surinam	1964	10–4:(2)	10–5:(1–3)	10–8
Uruguay	1963			10–8
Venezuela	1961			

11.

Mass Media and Modern Consumer Goods: Their Suitability for Policy Interventions to Decrease Fertility

DEBORAH S. FREEDMAN

The fact that fertility fell in the West after the industrial revolution and without organized programs of family planning is often cited as evidence that profound social and economic changes are both necessary and sufficient to bring birth rates down to desired levels. Actually, we do not know what degree of change and modernization is required to alter fertility behavior. Recent historical studies of the demographic transition in the West find no evidence that changes in specific indicators of social change were systematically related to declines in fertility. Further, since the less developed countries today differ in significant ways from Europe before the demographic transition, the applicability of Western experience for developing countries is even more uncertain. In view of the difficulties in attaining large-scale industrialization and modernization, an important question is whether government efforts directed toward more limited and specific social and economic variables can lower fertility. For example, the recent history of Kerala and Sri Lanka illustrates that declines in fertility may follow advances in education and health without significant economic progress (Nair 1974, Fernando 1973, Nortman 1974).

The possibility of influencing fertility behavior by programmatic changes in two variables—exposure to mass media and consumption of

The empirical research in this chapter was made possible by a grant from the Population Council. The Population Studies Center of the University of Michigan made facilities available. The survey work was done by the Committee on Family Planning of Taiwan under the direction of Dr. Tom Sun. Valuable comments on earlier drafts were received from Ronald G. Ridker, Robert G. Repetto, T. Paul Schultz, Eva Mueller, Ronald Freedman, and Paul Demeny.

modern goods and services—will be explored in this chapter, in which the relationship of these two socioeconomic variables to two demographic measures—desired family size and current use of contraception—will be examined. The modernizing effect of changes either in exposure to mass media or in experience with modern consumer goods could alter attitudes about desired family size with an attendant change in the use of contraceptives for the purpose of attaining these new objectives. Though the ultimate goal of most programs is such a change in family-size norms, some decrease in fertility probably can be achieved before that goal is attained. Research in the behavioral sciences suggests that changes in behavior need not necessarily follow attitudinal change; they may precede and foster attitudinal change (Berelson and Steiner 1944). Thus programs to increase exposure to mass media or modern consumption aspirations could contribute to the use of contraceptives among couples who hold traditional family-size values but find them to be in conflict with the attainment of other goals. Couples who try using contraceptives and discover that they are thereby able to regulate their fertility may, as a result, decide to have fewer children.

I have developed a conceptual framework laying out possible links between these variables—exposure to the mass media and modern consumption—and fertility behavior. Then some evidence is presented on the nature and strength of these relationships. Finally, some policy implications are suggested.

Communication research suggests that use of the mass media could contribute in several ways to the reduction of fertility. Direct messages in the media can be used to make people aware of the nature of the population program and the advantages of fertility control to individual families. They also can provide information about specific methods of fertility control and the local availability of such services. The evidence from various studies shows, however, that direct messages in the media rarely persuade people to change deep-seated attitudes or behavior (Berelson, Lazarsfeld, and McPhee 1954). Communication research hypothesizes that the mass media can influence fertility attitudes and behavior, but they do so indirectly, by providing contact with the modern world and alternative life styles, one aspect of which is smaller families (Rogers 1973). This effect is not limited to the relatively few communications which concern population matters, since all media communications bring contact with a larger world and new ways of life.

There are a number of ways in which the mass media could influence fertility patterns. First of all, the mass media foster aspirations for new and different patterns of consumption, all more difficult to achieve if a couple has many children to support. Aspirations may be raised directly through advertising, but also indirectly by models of ordinary families enjoying new goods and services in their daily lives. The mass media also show women in new roles, ranging from participation in national affairs to those more likely to be available to the average wife, showing ordinary women working outside the home, becoming educated, and enjoying social contacts outside the immediate family. The mass media can acquaint couples with new opportunities that are available to children with sufficient education and at the same time provide models of ordinary families whose children have benefited from additional education. Thus, they can encourage a shift in preferences toward raising a few children of higher quality, in whom more can be invested, rather than providing fewer advantages to a larger number of children. The mass media also can illustrate some possibilities for economic advancement that are available to couples who have accumulated savings. Each of these new patterns conflicts with the raising of a large family.

The mass media also can influence fertility by publicizing the gains that have been achieved in mortality reduction. One reason couples in the less developed countries have wanted many births is to ensure the survival of the desired smaller number of children. Declining mortality in the less developed countries makes this hedge less necessary, but a substantial lag occurs before parents accept that fact and modify their behavior accordingly. This message, which probably needs continual reinforcement in many contexts to be effective, can be communicated in a variety of ways through the mass media.

Development requires the adoption of new modes of behavior, something that is never easy, particularly where deep-seated traditional beliefs are involved. Communication specialists stress that the mass media can create a climate favorable to the adoption of behavioral change, because continual exposure to new modes of behavior through the mass media develops empathy—the ability to envision oneself in others' roles (Lerner and Schramm 1967, Schramm 1964). Lerner (1958) and others hypothesize that the more a person is able to imagine himself in other roles, including those that are more modern, the greater his readiness for change. Everett Rogers (1969) reports that several pieces of research in less developed countries (in Colombia, India, and the Middle East) have found exposure to mass media to have a high correlation with empathy. Both the Indian and Colombian studies also found empathy related to such modernizing attributes as innovativeness and aspirations. Evidence of the positive relationship between exposure to mass media and modern behavior is not limited to studies by communication scientists. A recent cross-cultural study done by sociologists in six developing countries studied the process of modernization of individuals (Inkeles and Smith 1974). Inkeles and Smith report a regular association between exposure to mass communications and individual modernity. They conclude that "the mass media were in the front rank, along with the school and the factory, as inculcators of individual modernization" (p. 146). These relationships were equally strong in the rural areas in four out of six countries.

Turning to modern consumption, what are the possible theoretical linkages between consumption of modern goods and services and fertility behavior? The consumption pattern of a couple is a function of their income constraint, the relative prices they face on the market, including those for children and for all other goods, and their preferences. Given income and prices, any shift in preferences toward new consumer goods should increase the opportunity cost of children.

Undoubtedly, changes in tastes are one factor to account for the fact that couples have not increased family size in response to the rising incomes that have accompanied development in Western countries. Presumably, if both tastes and relative prices had remained constant, the relaxation of the income constraint would have increased demand for all consumer goods, including children. Instead, the secular increase in per capita income in developed countries has been accompanied by declining fertility, which stems in part from changes in tastes and changes in relative prices that have offset the positive effect that increasing incomes might have had on fertility. These changes in tastes are not limited to the desire for higher standards of consumption. One important change in tastes has been described as an increasing preference for children of higher quality requiring more inputs. Alternatively, one could regard this as an increase in the perceived relative price of children. Another taste trend is a growing preference among wives to spend time in pursuits other than child care. But certainly, one major factor is that couples have grown to enjoy and expect new modes of consumption that are more difficult to attain while supporting a large family.

Modern consumer goods and services are singled out in this discussion for several reasons. Since they are new and highly valued in developing countries, they should have considerably greater marginal utility than more conventional goods and services, and so more effectively decrease the demand for children. At the same time, the income elasticity of these goods is known to be considerably higher than that of more conventional goods, such as food (Shepherd 1963, Mueller 1958, D. S. Freedman 1972a). Additionally, studies in India show that couples in developing areas spend a smaller proportion of their income on food and more on manufactured goods than do couples with similar incomes residing in less developed areas.[1] Thus, the demand for new consumer

[1] National Council of Applied Economic Research (1962, 1967). The first study contrasted the consumption patterns of rural and urban groups. The latter,

goods should remain strong even after increases in income through development have permitted a rise in ownership levels.

Additionally, there are a number of externalities associated with modern consumption that may influence fertility behavior indirectly. This results partly from the impetus which the growth of modern consumption may give to the development effort. For example, persons may be motivated to greater or more innovative work effort by aspirations for new goods. Additionally, the creation of a strong market demand for consumer durables could spur the development of local manufacturing industries. Certainly it creates a demand for local marketing and servicing organizations which will have to be met by local businessmen. Another source of externalities is the modernizing influence of many modern goods on their users. For example, a bicycle or motorcycle increases mobility, both for social intercourse and work opportunities, while a watch makes it easier to conform to the time constraints of market activities. Radios and television sets are modern goods that play dual roles, since they increase their owners' exposure to the mass media, the other modernizing force discussed in this chapter.

Although aspirations for modern consumer goods could increase the opportunity cost of children, such aspirations may not be widespread in many developing countries because their inhabitants, having had little or no contact with such items, have not yet developed their "taste" or appreciation for these new goods. Even where the items were available, low-income levels may not have permitted such purchases, but in many areas distribution of modern goods has been limited, either through lack of enterprise or through market restrictions. Policy interventions to increase the visibility and availability of some modern goods could develop tastes for goods that might compete on the margin with children. Income constraints would undoubtedly still limit purchases. Some untapped purchasing power probably exists even in rural areas in the less developed countries, however, and in time these new wants may generate income through increases in work effort in addition to shifting consumption from children to goods.

Survey of Available Research Findings

Very little empirical work has been done on the effect of either modern consumption or exposure to the mass media on fertility behavior or

---

presumably more modern, had lower income elasticities for food-grain expenditures. The second study contrasted consumption patterns in developmental and nondevelopmental areas.

attitudes. The available literature, which will be reviewed, is scanty. Therefore, some data will be presented from a 1969 Taiwan survey in which measures of both modern consumption and exposure to the mass media were collected in addition to fertility data. These cross-sectional data permit some analysis of the relationship of exposure to the mass media and modern consumption to fertility behavior. Although causal relationships are difficult to substantiate with cross-sectional data, the data do show important relationships for both mass media and modern consumption with fertility behavior.

Exposure to the Mass Media

Most of the research on the relationship between exposure to the mass media and fertility has been concerned with the influence of programs using the media in direct attempts to influence fertility behavior. Since considerable use has been made of the mass media to promote family planning, a substantial interest exists in evaluating their effectiveness. Two fairly extensive surveys, one by John Ross and others (1972) and one by Wilbur Schramm (1971) have been made of the research in various countries on the effectiveness of messages offered through the mass media in altering fertility behavior. They report mixed results, reflecting in part the difficulties of evaluating the specific contribution of the mass media in field experiments with some uncontrolled inputs. The findings are that messages in the mass media may contribute both to awareness of the problem and to levels of information. In addition, messages in the media appear to improve the effectiveness of the personal contacts made by family-planning workers. There is no clear evidence that these messages by themselves motivate acceptance of family planning, however.

An analysis in some depth has been made of a specific mass media campaign mounted in Taiwan in 1972 to promote family planning. In this campaign a number of different media were used to promote family planning, including a slogan stressing the merits of the two-child family. Shortly after the campaign, a survey sample of both single and married women were asked about their contact with these family-planning messages in each of the media utilized. Carl Lin (1974) used these measures of exposure to media messages in an attempt to explain variation in desired family size. For married women, contact with media messages made no addition to variance explained, above that accounted for by age, education, income, and rural-urban status. For single women, contact with television, newspapers, or magazines increased explained variance by one percentage point (from 8 to 9 percent); contact with other media made no difference at all. Thus, basic attitudes about family size in Taiwan did not appear to be related in any appreciable degree to messages received through the mass media in this particular campaign.

Much less research has been done on the indirect effect of exposure to the mass media on fertility attitudes and behavior. Even where fairly large media campaigns have been directed specifically toward population problems, such as the recent Zero Population Growth (ZPG) efforts in the United States, little research has been done on their effectiveness. In several countries a large decline in survey measures of desired or expected family size has followed mass-media campaigns, but this cannot be accepted as proving a causal relationship. In the first place, there is some doubt about the extent to which the survey results measure a genuine decline in desired family size or how much they reflect only the respondent's feelings that he ought to respond in a way consistent with the message in the mass media. Even if the reported decline in expected family size is genuine, it may have been unaffected by the mass media campaigns and instead have been a response to other forces in the environment.

In assessing the effectiveness of the ZPG campaign in the United States, Judith Blake (1974) has suggested that the recent sharp decline in expected family size in the United States may be, at least in part, the respondents' verbal rather than real reactions to the extensive ZPG two-child campaign. She supports her view by citing what she regards as inconsistencies between the stated ideals for few children and other attitudes about family life.

In Taiwan also, a large mass media campaign conducted in 1971 for the two-child family coincided with a sharp drop in desired family size reported in successive surveys. It is possible that the mass media campaign influenced respondents to understate their desired family size. In Taiwan, however, as in the United States, the expressed desire for fewer children was accompanied by earlier and more effective use of contraception and a decrease in achieved fertility, lending credibility to the survey responses. This by no means establishes that the mass media campaigns made the difference, since there was rapid social change in both the United States and Taiwan during these periods.

These examples indicate some of the problems of measuring the effects of the mass media on attitudes through successive surveys. Assuming the measured change in attitude to be genuine, the extent to which it can be attributed to mass media efforts is problematic, since many other changes will be taking place in the environment at the same time. An additional problem is whether attitudes have really changed, or whether the change is only in what the respondents feel they must tell the interviewers. The argument can be made, however, that if respondents in a developing country have learned from the mass media what statements about fertility are considered acceptable, this is an important beginning of internalizing modern fertility norms.

Data that bear on the general relationship between exposure to the mass media and fertility behavior were collected in 1969 in a survey of 2,300 husbands in Taiwan whose wives were of child-bearing ages.[2] The survey was concentrated on the measurement of economic variables, both behavioral and attitudinal, while data on family characteristics, including fertility behavior, were also obtained. Since the wives had been interviewed previously in a knowledge, attitudes, and practice (KAP) survey and were reinterviewed shortly after the 1969 survey, a considerable body of additional data is available for these families. Among the data obtained in the economic survey were income from all sources for each family member, ownership of modern consumer durables, use of modern recreational services, aspirations for additional modern consumption, exposure to mass media, savings behavior, perceptions of the economic costs of children, and fear of child death. The husbands also were asked their desired number of children (assuming they could start over and have just the number wanted) and whether they were practicing contraception at the time. The last two measures are the dependent variables in this discussion.

The principal explanatory variables include income per adult and education of both husband and wife, which together give a rough measure of socioeconomic status. To measure exposure to the mass media, an index assigned weights to the frequency with which respondents read newspapers, read magazines, listened to the radio, and watched television.[3]

Other explanatory variables include modern consumption, measured by two variables—the number of different modern consumer durables owned out of a possible list of sixteen items and an index of the use of modern recreational services, based on the extent to which respondents

[2] The field work was carried out by the staff of the Committee on Family Planning in Taiwan. The work was financed by the Population Council. Eva Mueller collaborated on this project.

[3] The mass media index was constructed by assigning weights as follows: reads a newspaper at least several times a week (2); reads a newspaper occasionally (1); reads magazines often (2); reads magazines occasionally (1); listens to the radio at least several times a week (2); listens to the radio occasionally (1); watches television at least several times a week (2); watches television occasionally (1). Possible scores ranged from 0 to 8; the mean score was 2.95 and the distribution was as follows: 0–1 (32 percent), 2–3 (27 percent), 4–5 (23 percent), 6–8 (18 percent).

attended movies, dined in restaurants and took vacation trips. An index measure for consumption aspirations combines both hopes and plans to purchase consumer durables and to use more recreational services. The proportion of families who have accumulated savings since marriage measures savings behavior. An index of the husband's sensitivity to the cost of raising children measures the extent to which he cited the expenses of raising children spontaneously as an important consideration. A fear-of-child-death index combines awareness of decreasing child mortality with expressed fears of losing a child. The method of multivariate analysis used is multiple classification analysis (MCA).[4]

The analysis shows that, in Taiwan, husbands with greater exposure to the mass media are more likely than others to use contraceptives. The analysis separates the respondents into two groups, a "younger" group—those with wives under thirty years of age—and an "older" group—those with wives between the ages of thirty and forty-five. The incidence of contraceptive use differs markedly for these two groups, since couples in Taiwan use contraceptives mainly for limiting family size and not for spacing; only 27 percent of the younger couples used contraceptives as against 54 percent of the older couples. Among the older couples, 74 percent of the husbands in the group reporting the highest exposure to mass media were using contraceptives at the time as against 44 percent of the group with the lowest exposure (after adjusting for the effects of income and education), and the relationship is regular and monotonic (see adjusted mean percentages in table 11-1). This represents a difference of 30 percentage points in the use of contraceptives associated with exposure to the mass media. The relationship between mass media and the use of contraceptives is weaker and less regular for the younger group, with a net difference of 9 percentage points between the extremes of media use.

[4] MCA is a method of multiple classification analysis in which each of the subclasses of the independent variables is a predictor related to the dependent variable. Each subclass of the predicting variables converts into a "dummy variable," taking the value of either zero or one, depending on whether or not the case falls in that particular subclass. The advantage of this technique is that no assumption is made about either the linearity or the ordering of the subcategories of the independent variables. It derives the following statistical measures: (1) the mean value of the dependent variable for each subclass of the independent variable; (2) an adjusted mean for each subclass of the independent variables being considered; (3) a measure of the total variance explained by all the independent variables—the conventional R^2. Measures (1) and (2) enable us to see the pattern of variation of the dependent variable in the different subclasses of the independent variable and the extent to which the unadjusted deviations reflect the intercorrelations with the other explanatory factors being considered (Andrews, Morgan, and Sonquist 1973).

Table 11-1. Relationship of Exposure to the Mass Media to the Use of Contraceptives and Ideal Family Size by Age Groups

	Younger couples (wives under thirty) (grand mean = 27 percent)			*Older couples (wives over thirty) (grand mean = 54 percent)*		
Exposure to mass media	*No. of cases*	*Percentage currently using contraceptives*	*Adjusted percentage*[a]	*No. of cases*	*Percentage currently using contraceptives*	*Adjusted percentage*[a]
			Use of contraceptives			
Lowest	211	15	21	485	40	44
—	193	21	25	380	53	54
—	155	36	34	316	62	60
Highest	143	42	30	215	70	74
R^2 without mass media		0.091			0.055	
R^2 with mass media		0.094			0.074	
			Ideal family size			
Lowest	240	3.9	3.8	498	4.2	4.0
—	221	3.8	3.8	396	3.9	3.8
—	172	3.5	3.5	339	3.8	3.9
Highest	164	3.2	3.4	227	3.5	3.7
R^2 without mass media		0.089			0.068	
R^2 with mass media		0.104			0.077	

[a] Adjusted for income per adult, husband's education, and wife's education.

Exposure to the mass media also is related to lower family-size values. In this case the stronger and more regular relationships occur in the younger group, with a net difference of four-tenths of a child between the extremes of mass media exposure. The absence of large differentials in ideal family size reflect the strong consensus on families of three and four children in Taiwan (76 percent wanted either three or four children and only 6 percent wanted fewer than three). Still, a net difference of four-tenths of a child associated with mass media for the younger group is not unimportant, particularly since for them family-size goals probably represent significant, attainable goals, while for the older group they more often may be rationalizations of achieved size.

In assessing the importance of the relationship between exposure to the mass media and fertility, one important question is whether the mass media have an effectiveness over and above that contributed by education and ownership of modern objects (including radios and television sets) that largely control access to the mass media and are themselves strongly related to fertility. Of course, access to the mass media does not depend entirely on these factors; illiterate persons frequently have some access to the written media through listening to others read or discuss the news (Poffenberger 1971) while 46 percent of the women in Taiwan who watched television at least occasionally did not own a television set (D. S. Freedman 1973). Nevertheless, access to the written media depends primarily on literacy, and in a separate study owning a television set was singled out as the most important determinant of exposure to television in Taiwan (Cohen 1972). In a separate analysis an attempt was made to isolate the effects of the mass media from that of the variables governing access. Separate regressions related exposure to the mass media to the use of contraceptives, within age groups, by the literate and the illiterate, adjusting at the same time for ownership of a radio or a television set, or both. For each group the use of contraceptives remains positively related to exposure to the mass media, suggesting that neither education nor ownership of modern objects accounts for the total effects of exposure to the mass media. Mass media exposure contributes something over and above education and the ownership of modern objects to the explanation of the use of contraceptives.

The direct relationships between exposure to the mass media and fertility behavior shown above probably understate the total effect of the mass media, because exposure to the mass media affects a number of intervening variables which in turn influence fertility behavior. Table 11-2 shows the influence of exposure to the mass media on these intervening variables: Ownership of consumer durables, consumption of modern recreational services, consumption aspirations, the percentage who save, and fear of child death. In each case, high exposure to the mass media relates in the expected direction in a consistent monotonic pattern to each intervening variable; husbands with high exposure to the mass media have many modern durables, enjoy modern recreation, have high consumption aspirations, are likely to save, and worry relatively little about child mortality. Each of these variables in turn has a negative impact on fertility behavior. Consumption aspirations, in addition, are a major determinant of the awareness of the costs of children (the financial burden index) which in turn relates negatively to fertility. From Table 11-3 it can be seen that among younger couples, consumption aspirations, consumption of recreational services, and the financial burden index have substantial and fairly regular negative relationships to ideal family size. In addition, Shea Rutstein (1971) showed a differential in ideal family size of three-tenths to four-tenths of a child associated with fear of child mortality at each parity level. Mass media thus may influence couples to adopt smaller family-size ideals by raising their

Table 11-2. Relationship of Exposure to the Mass Media to Modern Consumption Measures and Other Socioeconomic Measures

Exposure to the mass media	*No. of cases*	*Sample mean*	*Adjusted mean*
		Ownership of durable goods *Grand mean = 5.3*	
Least	699	3.4	4.4[a]
—	581	5.0	5.3
—	486	6.6	6.0
Highest	356	7.9	6.2
		Consumption of modern recreational services *Grand mean = 1.7*	
Least	699	0.5	1.0[a]
—	581	1.4	1.5
—	486	2.4	2.1
Highest	356	3.6	2.8
		Consumption aspirations *Mean score = 2.1*	
Least	714	1.4	1.6[a]
—	591	2.0	2.1
—	496	2.5	2.4
Highest	371	2.8	2.7
		Percentage who have saved since marriage *Mean percentage = 38*	
Least	715	13	25[b]
—	591	33	36
—	492	52	45
Highest	363	77	58
		Fear of child death *Mean index score = 0.32*	
Least	382	0.45	0.43[c]
—	313	0.35	0.34
—	312	0.38	0.36
—	361	0.20	0.29
—	500	0.25	0.25
Highest	284	0.21	0.24

[a] Adjusted for husband's and wife's education, income per adult, and husband's occupation.

[b] Adjusted for income per adult, husband's education, husband's occupation and duration of marriage.

[c] Adjusted for date of first birth, number of child deaths, income per adult, and wife's education.

Table 11-3. Relationship Between Intervening Variables and Ideal Family Size for Younger Couples (with Wives Thirty Years of Age or Younger)
grand mean = 3.7

Intervening variable	*No. of cases*	*Mean ideal size*	*Adjusted mean[a] ideal size*
Aspiration to consume			
Lowest	115	4.1	4.0
—	127	3.6	3.6
—	172	3.8	3.8
—	149	3.5	3.6
Highest	138	3.3	3.5
Consumption of services			
Lowest	184	3.9	3.9
—	199	3.7	3.7
—	197	3.5	3.6
Highest	118	3.3	3.6
Financial burden index			
Lowest	40	4.4	4.3[b]
—	44	4.1	4.0
—	222	3.5	3.6
—	218	3.6	3.6
Highest	97	3.4	3.5

[a] Adjusted for wife's age, husband's education, wife's education, and income per adult.

[b] Adjusted for wife's age, husband's education, wife's education, income per adult, and all four consumption variables.

consumption goals, increasing their awareness of the financial costs of children, and lessening their fears of child mortality. The differences in ideal size associated with these intervening variables are modest but not unimportant, ranging from three-tenths to eight-tenths of a child, after adjusting for the effects of income and education. The intervening variables also influence the use of contraceptives (see table 11-4).

For younger couples, both consumption aspirations and consumption of services relate positively to contraceptive use, with consumption of services showing the largest net relationship. Perhaps couples who enjoy recreational activities outside the home begin the use of contraceptives earlier. For older couples, consumption of modern durables, aspirations, and the financial burden index show a substantial relationship to contraceptive use. In an additional analysis, a measure of saving since marriage also correlated positively with contraceptive use. For all the variables the differentials are substantial, with net differences of up to 19 per-

Table 11-4. Relationship Between Intervening Variables and Current Use of Contraception

Socio-economic variable	*No. of cases*	*Percentage currently using contraceptives*	*Adjusted percentage*[a]
		Wives under thirty (grand mean = 27 percent)	
Aspiration to consume			
None	115	17	22
—	127	26	27
—	172	25	26
—	149	28	32
Highest	138	37	32
Consumption of services			
None	184	18	24
—	199	21	24
—	197	27	26
Highest	118	50	38
		Wives thirty or over (grand mean = 54 percent)	
Aspiration to consume			
None	293	40	44
—	304	53	55
—	303	55	55
—	290	61	58
Highest	278	64	60
Modern objects owned			
3 or fewer	418	44	50
4–5	419	48	50
6–7	337	59	57
8 or more	298	72	63
Financial burden index[b]			
Low	94	35	40
—	217	47	51
—	429	54	53
—	409	57	54
High	280	66	59

[a] Adjusted for wife's age, wife's education, husband's education and income per adult.

[b] Adjusted for wife's age, wife's education, husband's education, income per adult, and all four consumption variables.

centage points in contraceptive use associated with the intervening variables.

The addition of the mass media variable (to education and income) increases explained variance for contraceptive use (for the older group) and for ideal family size (for the younger group)[5] by approximately 2 percentage points (see table 11-1). Since socioeconomic status, as indicated by education and income, explains only 9 percent of the variance in ideal size and 6 percent of the variance in contraceptive use, the net addition is not insignificant. The small R^2s, not atypical in cross-sectional analyses, here probably reflect the general consensus on ideal family size and the prevalence of contraceptive use in all strata in Taiwan, so that the myriad of individual factors, such as health, personality, and family relationships, obscure the effect of the general social and economic variables. The inclusion of all intervening variables in addition to mass media doubles the variance explained by income and education for ideal family size for younger couples and increases it to 9 percent for the use of contraceptives among older couples. More important, the pattern of relationships shows exposure to the mass media in Taiwan consistently associated with low-fertility behavior, both directly and through intervening variables. This makes the mass media promising candidates for policy programs designed to alter fertility behavior.

Modern Consumption

The research on modern consumption provides evidence of its possible indirect effects on fertility through promoting development (these are considered first) and on its more direct relationship to the opportunity cost of children.

Many discussions of the effects of consumption on development neglect its positive contributions, stressing only its possible negative effect on savings and investment. In the first place, the desire to enjoy modern consumer goods can motivate people to work harder. Ruth Mack, in a study of the causes of economic growth in the United States, attaches great importance to the "unusual force of the drive to consume and its effects in activating productive effort" (Mack 1956, p. 58). She cites particularly the unusually large demand for consumer durables. Arthur Cole (1962) also emphasizes the importance of the production of durable consumer goods in American economic growth, through main-

[5] For the other two groups, exposure to the mass media contributes much less. The following discussion concerns only the two groups cited.

taining a high level of effective demand, stimulating the development of auxiliary services industries, and engendering steady work habits (in order to manage the burden of installment debt). With regard to the less developed countries, Arthur Smithies (1961) has stressed the importance of feasible consumption goals for development efforts. A small body of empirical evidence supports the positive effect of aspirations on work efforts in less developed countries. Harry Oshima (1961) cites aspirations for consumer goods as a factor accounting for increased work participation by Japanese women. Levels of aspiration and high consumption have had a favorable impact on work effort in Puerto Rico; workers with installment debts are shown to work more responsibly and regularly than those without such debts (Rottenberg 1958). The Taiwan data showed high consumption aspirations positively correlated with high employment for wives (in nonfamilial occupations) and with the likelihood that the husband or wife holds an extra job (D. S. Freedman 1972a).

In addition, modern consumption aspirations can spur innovative behavior. Most economists agree that development "means change requiring broad innovations" (Harbison 1965). Some empirical evidence shows a positive relationship between both modern consumption aspirations and innovative behavior. Burkhard Strumpel (1965), in a study in British Honduras, found consumption aspirations positively related to the willingness to change, as measured by the acceptance of both spatial and occupational mobility, and to a rough measure of work effort. In a study made in Taiwan in 1965, the self-employed more often reported the use of modern productive methods and the adoption of new procedures if they owned a considerable number of modern durables (D. S. Freedman 1970). For farmers, the ownership of modern implements related positively to consumption of modern durables. For wage and salary workers, ownership of durables correlated positively with efforts to improve job performance. Owners of modern objects held attitudes that seem favorable to innovative behavior in that they made statements affirming the importance of individual effort for achievement. In each case, these relationships held within income classes.

Although modern consumption usually is considered a deterrent to saving, the 1969 Taiwan survey data do not support this. Consumption aspirations correlate positively with the percentage of couples who have accumulated savings. Also, families owning many modern durables have accumulated savings more often than others. In both cases, these relationships hold after adjusting for income, education, and duration of marriage. Undoubtedly, some families do use savings to purchase consumer durables, but families who have accumulated more durables are more likely than others to have savings, after adjusting for income. A longitudinal study measured the ownership of durables in 1962 and again in 1965 for a small group of Taiwanese families. Controlling level of ownership in 1962, families who made additional purchases during the intersurvey period were more likely to have savings in 1965 than those who made no such additions. When specifically questioned about reasons for saving, most respondents report purposes other than consumption: only 7 percent of the respondents spontaneously mentioned consumption goals as their purpose for saving, while 40 percent singled out the educational needs of children and 11 percent mentioned investment purposes. Since, within income classes, owners of modern durables manage to save more often than others, the question of possible sources of financing for such concurrent saving and consumption is relevant. Some might come from a decrease in expenditures for ceremonials and traditional entertainment, which accounted for 8 percent of the family budget in Taiwan in 1962 (Baker and Perlman 1968). Another source might be a decrease in the proportion of income spent on traditional cereals; a study of expenditure patterns in Taiwan found markedly lower income elasticities for food and particularly for cereals for urban families, presumably the more modern, than for rural families (Hsing 1960).

The purchase and use of modern durables can itself be a modernizing influence. These purchases usually require the acquisition of money, involving some contact with a market nexus beyond the local community. Since their price may be substantial, their purchase frequently requires a period of prior saving but they then yield gratification and services over a longer period. Thus, they provide a significant experience with planning and deferred gratification. Also, the use of modern durables provides a modernizing experience. An involvement with modern production or educational enterprises requires coordination with established time schedules; a watch facilitates this. A bicycle or motorcycle enlarges the circle of the owner's business and social contacts and may permit employment outside the village. A radio or television set brings the owner into contact with the mass media. A sewing machine can provide a means of self-employment. Household appliances provide experience with new ways of performing traditional tasks and free women's time for other pursuits, perhaps even for outside employment. Modern recreational activities, such as movies or trips, furnish opportunities for contacts outside the family and provide some knowledge of other ways of life, less of a possibility for couples with many children. It is significant that all these involve a pleasurable experience of change. They involve none of the trauma or uncertainty inherent in migration or experimentation with new productive techniques. Insofar as change from traditional ways makes subsequent change a little easier to accept, modern consumption may ease the way to new ways in production.

The establishment of a wide demand for consumer durables could provide the basis for the local manufacture of these items at an efficient scale of operation. Certainly these modern consumer durables are highly prized, many are not so expensive, and some purchasing power undoubtedly is available in most rural areas of the less developed countries. Rostow (1964) suggests that widespread vigorous marketing of modern goods in rural areas of the less developed countries might furnish the incentive needed to improve agricultural productivity while at the same time developing manufacturing and service industries for these products.

Evidence of the direct relationship between modern consumption and fertility behavior is found in the Taiwanese study. Couples with an interest in modern consumption tend to be educated, in touch with the mass media, and in modern occupations; they also are relatively well off, but differences in income account for less of the differentials in modern consumption than does education. Constrained as they were by income, couples with an interest in modern consumption had limited options for achieving it. We have already shown that they did not consume at the expense of saving. There is additional evidence that they do not buy consumption durables by restricting their long-range goals for the education of their children. Seventy-five percent of the husbands surveyed wanted to educate their children beyond the required junior high level, although they frequently had no clear conception of the magnitude of the costs involved. The higher the educational aspirations and the greater the awareness of the associated costs, the more modern durables the families owned. Thus it is not surprising that couples who value modern consumption are more likely than others to express small-family ideals and to use contraceptives.

The differences are quite substantial (see tables 11-3 and 11-4). For younger couples there is a net difference of three-tenths to five-tenths of a child in ideal family size and a difference of 10 to 14 percentage points in contraceptive use associated with consumption aspirations and consumption of services, after income and education have been taken into account. Consumption of services is particularly relevant for the fertility behavior of young couples; perhaps the burden of child care appears more onerous to those who enjoy recreation outside the home. For older couples, owning modern durables and aspirations has a sizable relationship to contraceptive use, both directly and through the financial burden index. Not only is the present relationship of modern consumption to fertility behavior fairly substantial, but the data suggests that the relationship will remain stable even after ownership levels rise. An additional analysis shows that the enjoyment of modern goods and services does not dampen aspirations for additional purchases. The level of ownership of modern durables has no effect, either positive or negative, on aspirations for additional durables; after adjusting for income and education, families with many durables were just as likely as families with few durables to say they wanted more. The level of enjoyment of modern recreational services has a strong positive association with wanting more. Apparently, a taste of modern recreation does not necessarily satiate, but instead may whet the appetite.

An alternative explanation for the positive relationship between modern consumption and the use of contraceptives must be considered. Inasmuch as couples using contraceptives have smaller families to support, this may account for their greater consumption of modern goods and services. Even aspiration levels, which tend to be oriented toward reality, could reflect the lesser budgetary constraints of smaller families. In fact, in a separate analysis of the effect of family size on the attained level of economic welfare it was shown that couples with smaller families in Taiwan were better off; they had higher levels of income per capita, higher levels of consumption of modern goods and services, and somewhat higher aspiration levels (D. S. Freedman 1972b). However, when an analysis is made separately for each family-size group (couples with three, four, or five or more children) the relationship between modern consumption and the use of contraceptives remains quite robust. For each parity group, contraceptive use is positively related to ownership of modern objects, to consumption of modern services, and to aspirations; the differences in the use of contraceptives between the extremes of each variable average about 11 percentage points and, with two exceptions, the relationships are quite regular. Since most couples in Taiwan at the time of this study wanted either three or four children, special interest is attached to the group with three children to see whether the data provide any clues as to what might influence their decisions to have an additional child. After adjusting for income, education, and age, couples with three children with no aspirations for additional modern goods are found to use contraceptives considerably less and want twice as many additional children as couples who have aspirations for increased consumption. Thus, the positive relationship between modern consumption and the use of contraceptives cannot be attributed solely to the lesser budgetary constraints of smaller families; instead high aspiration levels could be the motivation for the use of contraceptives.

Policy Implications

The third task of this chapter is the formulation of policy proposals with regard to the mass media and modern consumption for governments in the less developed countries and the design of experiments to test their efficacy. The evidence presented here has supported the viability of both modern consumption and the mass media as promising candidates for programs intended to decrease fertility. Before proceeding to a discussion of possible experiments, however, some reservations must be expressed.

Although the discussion of policy has been with reference to less developed countries in general, it is recognized that programs involving any particular variable will be appropriate for some countries but not for others. Furthermore, the specific variables dealt with in this chapter are likely to be of interest only as parts of general development programs in which they have been adapted to local needs, problems, and resource constraints. Governments in less developed countries would be unwise to mount intensive campaigns to extend exposure to the mass media or develop a consumer-goods industry solely for their possible effect on fertility, but they may want to initiate such programs as part of a general modernization effort. A point to stress here is the argument presented earlier that programs designed to increase exposure to the mass media or to develop consumption industries may contribute to development quite apart from any potential effect on fertility. Evidence that these programs also can contribute to a decline in fertility can make their use more advantageous. Where programs involving the mass media or modern consumption are deemed appropriate, they would have to be designed to fit the cultural and economic circumstances of the particular countries in question. For example, in very poor countries the marketing of consumption goods could stress simpler articles that poor people could buy more easily and that could be produced more readily under local conditions.

Although modern consumption and the mass media appear promising for policy programs, the data so far leave many questions unanswered. The available studies do not determine the level of modern consumption or exposure to the mass media necessary to influence fertility behavior, nor is there any indication of the period of time over which these variables may be able to influence fertility. A sizable policy effort over a considerable period would probably be necessary with regard to either mass media or modern consumption, if they were to influence anything so basic as fertility behavior. In addition, cultural and economic differences between countries would undoubtedly have an effect on the outcome, and it is by no means certain that these relationships would hold in a country less developed than Taiwan or in the most depressed rural communities of the less developed countries. Even though these relationships were found in Taiwan among the poorer rural strata, the rural poor in Taiwan undoubtedly enjoy higher levels of living than do those in some of the less developed countries. In addition, the general level of literacy and development is above that of many less developed countries, and this may result in more diffusion of modern behavior into the poor rural strata.

A common element in all development programs is the stimulation of aspirations for a different way of life. It may be that the specific ways of achieving this that I have presented in this chapter are inappropriate for the poorest strata in some less developed countries. However, experiments might help determine whether a certain threshold level of development is required for this effort to be effective. Such programs need not be universally applicable to all strata of all developing countries to be judged successful; high fertility exists in most strata of the less developed countries, so a program that failed to reach the poorest groups but did reach other groups of substantial numbers could still be worthwhile.

Finally, several relevant questions are beyond the scope of this chapter. One such question is whether governments in less developed countries possess the political and organizational ability to mount such programs. For example, one could fairly question whether a country lacking the entrepreneurial ability in the private sector to develop industries for production of durable consumer goods is likely to possess these needed talents in the government sector. However, the development of such entrepreneurial and managerial skills is a necessary element in any significant development effort. It also is true that programs to extend the mass media or develop consumption industries could be manipulated by inefficient or despotic governments to increase inequities in the distribution of income and foster inefficiencies; the resulting effect on fertility would then be problematic. However, it is difficult to imagine any government programs which could not be misused by a corrupt or irresponsible political organization. Another possible question involves value judgments about whether consumption-oriented programs are appropriate developmental goals for less developed countries. This judgment is best reserved for the governments of less developed countries but consumption goods are highly regarded by most inhabitants of less developed countries. I should like to emphasize that the kinds of consumer goods here being discussed—bicycles, radios, and sewing machines, for example—are part of development plans in a wide range of countries, irrespective of ideologies.

Tentative Research Proposals

The objective of further research is to determine in countries less developed than Taiwan what effect, if any, programmatic changes in either the mass media or modern consumption are likely to have on fertility. I will present the broad outline of several types of experiments to test the effect of such policies rather than attempt to design specific experiments. First, I will discuss experiments involving exposure to the mass media, then those concerning modern consumption.

Exposure to the Mass Media

The proposed plan is to make television readily available to the inhabitants of several hundred sites selected at random (including both villages and some urban areas), with a similar number selected as a control group. Both the sample and the control group should include areas encompassing a range of development levels, and all the inhabitants should have available to them the means of limiting the size of their families. The object of the experiment is to see whether and in what circumstances the modernizing stimuli afforded by television can motivate couples to use contraceptives and to want and have smaller families. In setting up the experiment, decisions will have to be made about the items which follow.

THE LENGTH OF TIME TO BE GIVEN TO THE EXPERIMENT. A minimum period of five years is suggested. I hypothesize that the modernizing effect of exposure to new ways of life through the mass media will motivate couples to have smaller families, but such changes cannot be expected in the short run. The results should be evaluated at regular shorter intervals, however, probably every twelve or eighteen months, to see whether they vary with the length of exposure.

CHOICE OF MEDIUM. Newspapers or other written media would not be appropriate for this experiment, since the medium chosen must be effective in areas with low literacy levels. Although both radio and television should be effective in these situations, television is selected for the experiment for two reasons: it should make it easier to prevent contamination of the control group, since one could more easily control access to television than to radios, and the combination of aural and visual stimuli seems most effective for exposing persons to modernizing influences. In Taiwan, where television has become increasingly popular and has reached all strata of the population, studies show that its use is related to all fertility variables. The reading of newspapers was also related to fertility in Taiwan, but the relationship became attenuated when a control was used for education. For television, the relationship held for all strata of the population, after controlling both education and rural-urban status. Thus, judging from the Taiwan experience, television appears an effective way to reach even illiterate and rural couples. Although most less developed countries do not at present have developed television networks available, a satellite communication system would make such mass media experiments feasible for rural areas. A number of less developed countries that are now investing in satellite systems would be possible locations for such experiments; India expects to have a system in operation in 1975 (UNESCO 1972); Brazil, in cooperation with Stanford University, is at present experimenting with satellite communication as a planned first step toward obtaining a domestic satellite system (Polcyn 1973); and both Iran and Indonesia are reported to be acquiring such systems.[6] New developments, such as electronic balloons, may make such experiments more feasible for other less developed countries.

PROGRAM CONTENT. Any government-sponsored satellite system would be used to project many developmental messages, both informational and educational. This should not conflict with the experiment, since a variety of programs—educational messages, soap operas, news broadcasts, even advertising—can all serve as modernizing forces. For the purposes of this experiment the programs should project pictures of life styles that are more modern than those of the viewers but still within the realm of possibility, all of which should include small-family norms as one important feature. Although the majority of the programs would not be so oriented, they should include some with an educational content focused on population matters. These could provide information on the local availability of family planning services as well as some reassuring facts about the safety of contraceptive devices. Also, an occasional discussion could be scheduled about the advantages of restricting family size. Most important, the programs should be interesting and entertaining. Many so-called educational programs are so dull that they defeat their own purpose by discouraging viewers. In a pilot television experiment (the Krishi Darshan project) in the Delhi region in 1967, a lack of interesting programs resulted in a steady erosion of the viewing audience. Chaman Lal (1970), in a report on this experiment, said, "With the introduction of the Krishi Darshan programmes in the television service of All-India Radio, a special 'signature tune' was devised [for the program's open and close]. . . . With the passage of time, this signature tune has acquired a notoriety which is now synonymous with boredom. As soon as this signature tune appears on the screen, the audience lets

[6] Information received in a conversation with Everett Rogers, 1973.

out a howl of dismay and this is the signal for them to leave" (p. 6). Obtaining an adequate supply of interesting programs which incorporate small-family norms among other modernizing messages will be one of the more difficult problems in mounting this particular experiment. Where programming for the mass media is already controlled by an established bureaucracy, this task may prove even more difficult.

Aside from these general guidelines about programs, any attempt at an elaborate content analysis to identify the most influential programs should probably be avoided. Such an analysis is unlikely to be successful and would unduly complicate an already difficult experiment. If the experiment proved successful, some moves in this direction could be made at a later time.

PROVIDING ACCESS TO THE MEDIUM. A more difficult problem is ensuring easy access to a television set for all inhabitants of the experimental villages. Ideally, the television would be placed in a community building open to all inhabitants with a responsible person in charge of both maintenance and of turning on the set during programming hours. Providing a suitable locus for the set would present problems in many villages; obtaining a satisfactory local caretaker may be even more difficult. Everett Rogers and Chris Ortloff (1975) discuss the difficulties encountered in the Krishi Darshan experiment, in which volunteers were recruited as caretakers. Although many were reasonably diligent, the difficulties of maintaining regular viewing hours suggests the advisability of offering some small return for the service. A related problem is the provision of prompt and effective maintenance of the sets so that reception is not interrupted. In this regard the experience of the Krishi Darshan experiment is encouraging; a UNESCO evaluation team found 90 percent of the sets in working condition. In this case the experimental area was within 50 miles of Delhi; more difficulties of maintenance would be encountered in remote villages. In fact, many communication projects have encountered considerably more difficulties; one communication experiment in a less developed country found a large percentage of the radio sets that had been placed in the villages inoperable by the end of the period of the experiment.[7] An imaginative administrator could undoubtedly provide mobile repair units which could check and repair the sets at frequent intervals. The difficulties of repair should not be underestimated, however, and adequate provision must be made, both in project plans and budget allocations.

POSSIBLE USE OF LISTENER FORUMS. Some consideration might be given to incorporating within the larger design a small-scale experiment

[7] Information received in a conversation with Everett Rogers, 1973.

with television forums as a possible means of increasing the impact of the medium. A number of experimenters in less developed countries have organized listener forums for educational radio programs which have incorporated a concerted effort to recruit a regular audience and to stimulate discussion among them of the program content (Roy Waisanen, and Rogers 1969; Rogers 1969). The hypothesis is that the combination of interpersonal and mass media communication can change attitudes and stimulate action more effectively than can the mass media alone. The evidence presented in these studies shows a higher gain in levels of knowledge about innovation in villages with organized radio forums than in those that had radios but no listener forums. A small experiment in a few locations could be worthwhile, but the results of existing experiments are too scanty and the difficulties in organizing such forums too great to warrant giving them much attention.

ESSENTIAL AUXILIARY SERVICES. Two complementary services are essential for the experiment. First, adequate family-planning services must be readily available. While the institution of such services is not the main thrust of this experiment, the effectiveness of the mass media in motivating couples to limit fertility cannot be assessed unless the means of family limitation are readily available to motivated couples. There must also be a program for measuring the relevant dependent variables—the practice of contraception and abortion; desired number of children, both total and additional; the number of pregnancies; and, most important, the number of births. This is a problem common to all the experiments being considered at this conference, since most of the experimental areas will lack adequate schemes for registration of vital statistics. An experiment must be implemented by a scheme, possibly a series of longitudinal surveys, to provide measures of the dependent variables, both initially and over a period of time since it would be impossible to assess any experimental program without adequate statistical monitoring.

SELECTION OF THE SAMPLE. Both technical and administrative problems are involved in choosing the sample. A fairly large sample—about four hundred villages and urban locations—is suggested, with an equal number of areas to be chosen as a control group. Given the long period of time of this experiment, it is inevitable that a number of the selected experimental sites will experience some exogenous developmental change, such as the construction of a new road or a new plant. There have been numerous examples of social change experiments conducted in only a few locations which have been vitiated because some major exogenous change has occurred at some of the sample sites. With four hundred locations in the sample, many may remain uncontaminated by major external events and the others will experience differing degrees of change. The use of a large random sample makes it possible to incorporate the degree of exogenous change as an independent variable in the analysis. Thus we can see the extent to which the relation between exposure to the mass media and fertility varies with the amount and kind of social change experienced during the experimental period. It is also important to take into account the initial development levels of the sampled areas. If possible, the experimental areas should be stratified by level of development, with the sampling done at random within these strata. Since one important question for this experiment is whether the relationship between exposure to the mass media and fertility found in some places is contingent on the prior attainment of a certain basic level of development, stratifying the sample by development level would help to answer this question. The use of a community level questionnaire (Ronald Freedman 1974) at the beginning of the experiment would provide information about the sampled areas for use in the analysis.

Selecting the sample also poses administrative problems. Attempts to select the villages at random and select a like control group may be frustrated by the desire of administrators to include favored villages. The continuity of a sympathetic administration throughout the life of the experiment is important if administrative tampering with the operation of the experiment is to be prevented.

Modern Consumption

Experiments to test the effectiveness of policy programs promoting modern consumption appear to be more difficult. The previous arguments in support of such policies were based on a number of points. First, it was assumed that the development of tastes for modern consumer goods could compete at the margin with the desire for additional children. To test this thesis, an experiment could be mounted to increase the availability of consumer goods in designated areas and see whether the development of tastes for these goods affected fertility behavior. Such experiments, which would of necessity be of long duration and expensive, are discussed briefly at the end of this chapter. Second, it was argued that the present low consumption of modern goods in the less developed countries is not due solely to low-income levels but also to the limited availability of such goods and that presumably many lower- and middle-income families could manage to purchase more modern goods if they were available on the market, even though income levels would limit the extent of such purchases. Research on this issue is recommended as an initial first step. Finally, some consideration was given to a number of externalities stemming from modern consumption that might promote development and thus indirectly affect fertility. In all projects attention should be given to measuring the spillover effects on development stemming from modern consumption. In plans for new experiments precedence should be given to consumption goods with which externalities favorable to development are associated.

One possible policy use of modern consumption goods which is not considered in this paper is their use as incentives in a fertility control program. Julian Simon's chapter includes a discussion of incentive programs. It is possible that attractive, well-displayed consumer goods might serve as more effective incentives than payments of money, but it is unlikely that the difference would be important. In addition, such an experiment could leave administrators open to charges of promoting frivolous consumption as a substitute for having children, a possibly difficult political issue.

Research on Existing Situations

First priority should be assigned to a research project to explore the possibilities for increasing consumption of modern goods among low- and middle-income families in less developed countries for two reasons. First, the feasibility of a policy program to develop tastes for modern goods through increasing their availability depends on the capacity of a reasonable proportion of the inhabitants to purchase some modern goods once the experiment makes them available at reasonable prices. Thus the consumption possibilities for modern goods in less developed countries should be thoroughly researched before more elaborate and expensive experiments are mounted. Second, some possibilities exist for exploring these questions without a contrived experiment in existing situations in less developed countries. If the findings are positive—that is, if a significant number of inhabitants could purchase some modern goods, then a field experiment could be undertaken to test the effect on fertility of direct policies to promote modern consumption.

Any location for effective research on the existence of latent purchasing power for modern goods in less developed countries must satisfy two criteria: The level of living must be low enough to be representative of a large group of less developed countries, and modern consumption goods must be reasonably available. This sharply limits the areas appropriate for this research, since the failure of most of the less developed countries to meet the second criterion is the rationale for our basic policy recommendation. There are some areas which do meet these criteria however. For example, some local areas in Indonesia might constitute an excellent location for such a research project. The low-income levels in Indonesia are representative of the income constraints in less developed countries, but modern goods are readily available on the market in some parts of Indonesia.[8] Undoubtedly a few additional locations that meet these criteria could be found in less developed countries.

A study of the feasibility of increasing modern consumption among lower- and middle-income groups in less developed countries would require, at a minimum, a survey to obtain data on ownership of modern goods, consumption aspirations, and income. However, the usefulness of the analysis for future planned experiments could be much enhanced by several additions. An effort should be made to integrate the survey with an ongoing KAP survey, either by incorporating it into the KAP survey or through a reinterview of a sample of the KAP families. Given the incidence of KAP surveys in less developed countries, including those under the auspices of the World Fertility Survey (WFS), the possibility of integrating a study of modern consumption with a KAP survey during the next few years appears promising.[9] A community area study (one collecting aggregate socioeconomic measures for each village and rural area in the sample district) should be undertaken and should include data on facilities for the manufacturing, servicing, and marketing of modern goods and on the availability and price of consumer credit (Ronald Freedman 1974). A longitudinal study, which obtained both the KAP data and the data on consumption and income from these families about three to five years after the original study would permit some analysis of behavioral change. This is likely to be most feasible if it could be integrated with a longitudinal KAP survey.

Some relevant questions include:

• Who buys modern objects? Is their purchase limited to the rich? To what extent do low- and middle-income families purchase these objects, and how do ownership levels relate to income?

• What is the pattern of ownership of different objects in relation to income? Any later experiments in promoting consumption must decide

[8] Modern consumer goods are freely available in the rural areas around Surabaya in Indonesia, where development is still at a low level, according to an oral report by Jeremiah Sullivan, who works in a Population Council project near Surabaya. Apparently, the long irregular coastline of Indonesia makes it difficult to control smuggling.

[9] At present a comprehensive family-planning research project is under way in the Surabaya area which would yield a rich body of data for these purposes if permission could be obtained for the addition of a small economic survey. The project is located in the Regency of Mojakarta near Surabaya, under the direction of the Minister of Health of Indonesia. Funding is through the International Development Authority (IDA) and the United Nations Fund for Population Activities (UNFPA), with technical assistance provided by the Population Council. This project, along with similar projects in other areas, is designed to determine the feasibility and effectiveness of providing family planning services in conjunction with maternal and child health services to large numbers of rural women in less developed countries. The plans are to collect over a five-year

which particular consumption items should be made available. These data could provide information as to which particular items are purchased by low- and middle-income couples.

• The relationships obtained above, together with data on desired and achieved family size obtained through a KAP survey, might provide some clues about which objects are most competitive with children. If longitudinal data were available, this would permit comparison, for couples of equal income, of the relationship of patterns of acquisition of modern objects to that of family growth. This should provide some evidence whether aspirations for modern consumption goods have any effect on fertility.

• The community-level survey could provide data on the externalities associated with modern consumption for the economy of the area. Has there been a development of local businesses to service these items or any development of new patterns of marketing? Are there any signs of the development of local plants either to assemble or to manufacture any of these modern goods?

• What are the individual externalities associated with the use of modern goods? Do users become more modern through experience with modern goods? If longitudinal data were available, measures of modernity could be obtained for the respondents, both in the initial and later survey; the change in modernity could then be related to patterns of ownership, both to the total number of objects owned and ownership of particular items. Another approach might be to include questions about the uses to which particular items are put by their owners.

• If adequate time-use and employment data could be obtained, we also could see whether couples who bought more modern goods exerted greater work effort.

The potential for research from such an economic survey, particularly if it could be coordinated with an ongoing KAP survey, appears promising. Undoubtedly, some of the resulting data could be utilized in connection with some of the other topics considered in this conference—the economic role of children in agriculture, for example.

New Experiments

If the research described above shows a potential market for modern consumption goods and a favorable effect of consumption on fertility, some experiments might be mounted involving deliberate government programs to increase the availability of consumer goods. Since these

---

period a large body of data, including KAP surveys, a community-variable survey, service statistics from the family planning program, and estimates of vital rates (Taylor and Lapham 1974).

programs would require a considerable input of resources for each experimental area, the large research design suggested for the mass media experiment does not appear feasible. In addition, the project for each area should be designed with reference to the area's production and marketing resources, the availability of raw materials, the import constraints, and the pattern of tastes. Therefore, such experiments should be confined to a limited number of areas. Even though an experiment in a few areas is less likely to obtain statistically conclusive results, if programmatic efforts to increase the availability of consumption goods were followed by an increase in the pace of development and lower fertility, the effort could be deemed a success even if the credit due the experiment is not precisely quantifiable.

Undoubtedly an initial research project, such as the one proposed above, would provide considerable guidance for such experiments. Some general guidelines follow:

- In choosing locations for the project, areas at different levels of development should be included. The success of the experiment may vary with the level of prior development, and the experiment should be designed to ascertain what it is.
- The choice of consumer goods must be carefully made so that those chosen are the ones that will have the greatest influence on consumers. They must be highly desirable, since it is hoped they will be competitive with having children. At the same time, they should exert a modernizing effect on the user. In addition, they should be useful items, so as to minimize charges that government officials are promoting "Western baubles." Goods which are useful, desirable, and modernizing might include bicycles, inexpensive clocks or watches, and small transistor radios (see earlier discussion of externalities). A fourth group might include objects which would simplify housework and so make more time available to the housewife for market work; such items might include small, automatic gas burners or rice cookers. Particularly important might be household goods which could furnish self-employment for the wives, such as sewing machines. One possibility would be to incorporate in the experimental design the promotion of cooperative workshops for women where mothers could use their sewing machines to produce and market simple clothing. Such a scheme was suggested by Aziz Bindary (1972) for Egypt as a program to influence fertility by changing women's roles.
- The consumption goods also should be chosen with a view toward their effect on production and employment. To maximize the backward linkages associated with modern consumption, the items ideally should lend themselves to production in simple workshops with a high labor component and a minimum of imported resources. Workshops need not

be limited to village sites but could be located in rural regional centers, where they could operate efficiently while still providing employment for village residents. What are the possibilities that increased consumption of modern goods in less developed countries would stimulate local production activities? Undoubtedly, the manufacture of many modern goods requires a technological and industrial capacity beyond that available in rural areas of less developed countries at present. Such items might be adaptable to local assembly, however, and the government might actively promote this activity. In Taiwan the development of the manufacture of durable consumer goods started with assembly plants using imported parts and only gradually shifted to locally produced components.

Research has been done on the growth of nonfarm employment in rural Gapan in the Philippines, stemming from increases in agricultural income and the associated growth of modern consumption (Gibbs 1974).[10] Sizable increases were reported in employment in carpentry, cement work, and other construction trades in response to new demands for modern housing. Associated with this was a threefold increase in craft industries producing furnishings or housing components, a large part of which was located in rural towns. Another growing industry with linkages to modern durables was dressmaking and tailoring, which more than doubled between 1967 and 1971. Some backward linkages would be established, even with respect to imported consumer goods, since there would be some development of marketing activities. In fact, an effort should be made to stimulate effective marketing schemes, inasmuch as the development of tastes for modern goods requires a reasonable degree of exposure. The Philippine data reported a fivefold increase in that rural area in retail establishments selling durables during a ten-year period. Additionally, there should be some forward linkages associated with modern consumption; shops to service these new goods undoubtedly would be established. In the Philippines there has been a fivefold growth in employment in repair and maintenance shops for light transport equipment, such as motorized tricycles, during the past decade.

One must admit that the data on modernizing externalities associated with modern consumption are scanty. One important research finding from experiments promoting modern consumption would be the extent to which increased consumption of modern goods generates backward and forward linkages creating modernizing production and employment opportunities. Attempts should be made to identify the particular consumer goods that appear most likely to make such a contribution to development.

[10] The Gapan area is in Central Luzon, with a population of about 107,000.

12.

Residential Location and Fertility

DAVID GOLDBERG

In a work committed to examining potential policy measures that may bear on fertility or fertility-related behavior, it would be difficult to avoid the topic of residential location. There is, after all, an immense literature pointing to the presence of an inverse relationship between urbanization and fertility across a wide range of the less developed countries.[1] However, several data sets do not show the expected relationships between community type or city size or agricultural versus nonagricultural occupations and fertility—for example, India (Robinson 1961, Das Gupta et al. 1955–56), Egypt (Abu-Lughod 1964, T. Paul Schultz and Da Vanzo 1970a, Omran 1973), Senegal (Lacombe 1972), and Zaïre (Romaniuc 1963). One need only open a Turkish census volume to discover that in the rural sections (population less than 10,000) of several western provinces the child–woman ratio (children under five per thousand, women between the ages of fifteen and forty-four) is about 600 or less but that Diyarbakir, an eastern city of over 100,000, has a ratio of 800 (Turkey, State Institute of Statistics 1969).

Even in the absence of these exceptions to the "rule," the central conceptual issue to be raised about the data is the decomposition of the fertility effects into those components attributed to the residual or undefined term *urbanization* and those components that are a function of the concomitant changes in social organization, *urban mentality* and *modernism*. Since this question is rarely attacked, though frequently posed, in the data we consume, it is entirely possible that most of the exceptions are not, in fact, exceptions. Where we do have answers, the data suggest that the bulk of the relationship is transmitted through

Funds for the field work were provided by the Population Council. A Ford–Rockefeller Population Policy grant supports the analysis.

[1] Several reviews of the literature on fertility, including its relationship to urbanization, have been published in the past five years. Included among the major efforts are William P. McGreevey et al. (1974), United Nations (1973), Karen Mason et al. (1971), and Geoffrey Hawthorn (1970).

correlated changes in structure or attitudes, though the direction of the original relationship, if there is any, remains in reduced form.[2]

Suppose that the residual urban effects were very large. What kinds of policy implications would follow? I presume that we would want to increase the access of villagers to the things we think of as being conducive to a decline in fertility—selected media, forms of female employment competitive with child rearing, modern objects that expand the horizon of the consumer beyond the boundaries of his home—but these are the precise subjects of other chapters.

None of these remarks implies that community effects are unimportant. On the contrary, I wish to argue that community imposes constraints on behavior that cannot be captured by the measurement of conventional individual characteristics. A recent paper dealing with data at the community level makes the point clearly: "Many people have recognized that the neighborhood, community, or social milieu in which the couples live may affect their reproductive behavior in interaction with the individual characteristics usually considered. The term 'ecological' is often used to designate supra-individual data about the social environment, delimited on an areal basis" (Ronald Freedman 1974, p. 5).

The topic I wish to pursue is population clustering and behavior that directly or indirectly affects fertility. In this pursuit, I choose to manipulate data sets rather than concentrating on a review of the literature. The research literature on the topic is totally dominated by single-variable analysis, with only an occasional multivariate analysis that corresponds to the way in which most writers conceptualize the problem. So that an effort other than a totally speculative one can be made in an examination of policy implications within the limits of the data available, the particular component of population clustering examined is residential location within cities.[3]

Population clustering was one of the chief components of a sociological style that is identified primarily with the University of Chicago through the period 1920–60. Its objective was to explain the fact of clustering and how it affected people's behavior. There was an intellectual tradition explicitly stating that segregated areas produce a set of

[2] For data analyzed for individuals, see Ronald Freedman et al. (1974). For data analyzed at an areal level, see Albert I. Hermalin (1972).

[3] I am not aware of published materials dealing with the relationship between population clustering and fertility in the less developed countries. However, in an unpublished dissertation, this relationship is examined for a sample of 2,700 women in Taichung, Taiwan. The author finds significant but small neighborhood (*lin*) effects on several measures of family planning. Neighborhood effects are neighborhood means, not population potentials (see Srikantan 1967).

behaviors and values that are not simply a function of the individual characteristics of the persons who live in the area. It is an emergent phenomenon following from the segregation of populations, partly as a result of selection based on competition, partly as a result of voluntary aggregation, and partly as a result of discrimination. In the language of the early period of the development of these ideas: "The ghetto, be it Chinese, Negro, Sicilian, or Jewish, can be completely understood only if it is viewed as a sociopsychological, as well as an ecological, phenomenon; for it is not merely a physical fact, but also a state of mind" (Wirth 1927, p. 71). This language emerged following the closing of the massive European migrations to the United States and the strong interests in ethnic groups. The hypothesis was extended to communities of any kind when it was fully realized that community was a consequence of territorial isolation. If clustering declined, the emergent effect declined (Hawley 1950). Unfortunately, what stands out as a result of these conceptual efforts can be summarized in a series of empirical density maps of the phenomenon under investigation. The efforts to explicate the causes and effects of clustering seem feeble in contrast to the efforts to describe clustering. Yet here is the richest of hypotheses. It does not predict a specific kind of behavior or attitude such as fertility. It predicts all behaviors and attitudes, including fertility.

Why deal with this topic now? In developing countries and in our own country, we act as if this area effect were known to exist. The concerns about the policy implications of population clustering are as great in the less developed countries as in our own. We would be foolish to ignore the fact that the growth of cities in Latin America, Asia, and Africa has been accompanied by burgeoning slums and shantytowns. The major population feeders of these *barriadas, colonias proletarias,* or *gecekondu* are rural migrants who, not infrequently, build their own houses, forming highly irregular clusters of settlement in the vacant and unserviced areas of the growing cities. Temporary housing in squatter settlements is gradually made permanent and eventually begins to receive services. But the density of the housing, the pathlike and almost random street pattern, the mode of construction, and the characteristics of the population serve as constant visual reminders of differences between these clusters and the indigenous urban neighborhoods. The language used to describe these settlements—"graveyards of overpopulation," "ghastly alleys," "slums of despair"—which are breeding grounds of a whole set of social ills, comes close to implying some special cultural stamp that results from the aggregation of population in uncontrolled settlements.[4]

[4] For an excellent review of the literature on less developed countries, see John Turner (1968).

The objective of the research would be to determine whether there are areal variations in fertility or fertility-related behavior and whether the areal differences function independent of several important personal characteristics that are also strongly related to fertility and fertility-related behavior.

The sources of my data are two probability samples of households containing married couples, one in Ankara, Turkey (1966), and one in Mexico City (1971). Each set of data is based on about eight hundred interviews with wives distributed across approximately two hundred blocks. The sets of questions are as close to identical as they could be in different cultural settings. The replication advantage is not trivial in the social sciences. How does one identify a characteristic of an area and bring it into the analysis? Most readers are familiar with the Burgess maps of Chicago subpopulations and are aware that these maps do not fit many European, Asian, African, or Latin American patterns of settlement. This "discovery" may have contributed significantly to the decline of human ecology. In the cities of developing countries, the squatter settlements are typically built on the fringes of the city, on the sides of hills, and on other forms of land that have low property values. Sometimes the result is one massive cluster; more frequently there are several large clusters. In Ankara, the name *gecekondu* is given to these areas. They are physically and visually different from the rest of the *planned* community. The categorization of blocks as *gecekondu* or non*gecekondu* was made by the Turkish State Institute of Statistics.

About 46 percent of the households in Ankara are in this area—clusters of squatter settlements not unlike settlements all over the less developed world. The inhabitants are likely to be of rural origin and to have little education and low incomes. In addition, the residents of the *gecekondu* are more traditional in a wide variety of behaviors and attitudes than are the residents of the planned parts of the city. The women are more restrained in their activities, the husbands have more power, and the wives believe in greater segregation of sex roles. At this point, we have the equivalent of the descriptive materials associated with Chicago-style ecology—a simple finding that there are geographically identifiable pockets of behavior and attitudes. The sociologists of the Chicago school could do little more, lacking the combination of data for individuals and areas.

To the best of my knowledge, there is no precise equivalent of *gecekondu* in Mexico City. There are massive slum areas as in Netzahualcoyotl and there are *vecindades,* clusters of shanties hidden behind a single door in a large wall located on a city block that could be called either slum or nonslum. I have not attempted to derive a classification scheme that resembles Ankara, for none exists. If we had restricted the classification to the "known" areas, we would have missed a substantial share of the entry gates used by the rural migrants to the city. This forced a healthy constraint on the data sets designed for replication. What was needed and is still needed to test the ecological hypothesis is a measure of location abstract enough to be free of descriptive spatial referents such as distance from city hall. For this purpose, an old friend and tool of anyone concerned with location theory was exploited—population potential (Isard 1960).

Population potential at point i is defined as the sum of X_j over D_j, where X_j is the number of persons with the characteristic being examined at point j and D_j is the distance between points i and j. If X_j were people, then $\Sigma X_j/D_j$ would represent people potential at point i. It seems to me that the concept of population clustering or segregation is better captured in this measure than in conventional segregation indexes (coefficients of dissimilarity) because it captures the scale of clustering. The measure of population potential can be generalized as an indicator of access to populations of any selected characteristics. Since each of the city blocks in these samples has measurable x and y coordinates that can be distributed among the eight hundred respondents, and since each respondent or husband can be classified as having high or low education, high or low income, high or low occupational status, or high or low anything, including attitudes and values, population potentials can then be computed for any desired characteristic. Each of these potentials can be interpreted as a measure of the access that persons from a local area have to other persons living in the community with the defined characteristic. A ratio of, say, population potential for high-school graduates to population potential for persons who have not completed primary school, can be interpreted as the extent to which persons living in a subarea have access to highly educated persons and are geographically segregated from those with little education. This measure of spatial location presumably identifies the more generalized environment of the respondent, with the weights being an inverse function of distance from the characteristic. I believe that this measure identifies the social space of the respondent—a "space" that several ecologists, referring to the urban environment, discuss. This social space is more highly differentiated in Ankara and Mexico City than it is in such places as Detroit. There is probably greater segregation in the cities of transitional countries. In this sense, if there is an emergent phenomenon, we should be able to locate it more easily in the types of cities represented in these samples. The procedure employed here overcomes the conventional map orientation to population clustering. Each person in the sample has his own measure of potential to selected characteristics. I do not care if Ankara does not look like Chicago. The substantive question is, Does one's location in relation to selected characteristics of others affect his behavior?

The transition from high fertility to low is typically seen as a process. The beginnings of the process are the instruments of change, the preconditions leading to a life style made up of components that form a loose system sometimes identified as modernism. This life style has implications for fertility simultaneously dependent on the preconditions and independent of them. In several studies part of the "modern" life style is defined as low fertility or the use of family-limitation techniques. In this study, the precondition equivalents, translated into individual characteristics, are three characteristics selected on the basis of their significant, known effect on fertility and other behavior: the wife's place of birth, the wife's education, and the husband's income. I will refer to these as background characteristics.

Since we wish to determine whether residential location has a potential effect on fertility, I have broadened the range of dependent variables to include a particular set of items of modernism known to have relatively high correlations with fertility behavior. Fertility-related behaviors or attitudes are a particular subset of the items frequently included among the dimensions of modernism.[5] I focus on variables that give us a fix on the breadth of the woman's horizon—power, segregation, and containment. Specifically, I choose to emphasize six fertility-related variables:

1. Husband's power index
2. Sex-segregation attitudes index
3. Containment: forbids index
4. Containment: restaurant, movies, parties index
5. Containment: nonhome-centered leisure index
6. Size-of-world index

In the list above we find overlapping references to the division of labor or activities between the nuclear family and the world outside the nuclear family, as well as the balance-of-power activity or interaction within the family. This short list of characteristics serves as a convenient reference point in dealing with an even longer list of values and behavior subsumed under the term *modernism*. I do not argue that one's relationship to the church or one's feeling about chance events and planned events

[5] One of the better statements about the process of modernization, its translation to individuals and its relationship to fertility—one on which I have drawn heavily—is Allan Schnaiberg (1970).

is irrelevant but rather that we can most efficiently capture the central themes of modernism which are relevant for fertility by focusing on the family. Whatever list we confront, the modern person is described as someone whose world is broader, whose sensitivities to that broader world are greater, whose identification, involvement, and attachment to the heterogeneity of a wider environment produce more *alternatives* to a traditionally defined existence. The most general underlying hypothesis is that the modern person will have lower fertility because of the potentially competing demands of alternatives. Many significant alternatives (or the freedom to have alternatives) are captured in the six fertility-related variables given above.

The first five indexes were constructed by dichotomizing three to eight individual items and taking the sum of the 0–1 collapsed coding. There are few surprises among the individual items that were combined to form the indexes. For example, in the sex-segregation-attitudes index, a couple of the questions included were:

> Most of the important decisions in the life of the family should be made by the man of the house.
>
> Strongly agree, agree, disagree, strongly disagree
>
> There is some work that is men's and some that is women's and they shouldn't be doing each other's.
>
> Strongly agree, agree, disagree, strongly disagree

The husband-power index items consisted of a relatively standard set of "Who decides?" questions. Whenever applicable, identical items were used in Ankara and Mexico City. The only item that is close to being unique is the one corresponding to the size-of-world index. The question was, What country in the world do you think is the farthest place in the world from Turkey [Mexico]?[6] A small world for Turkish wives was a response that fell in the Near East or among the countries of Europe other than England and Spain. For Mexican wives, a small-world response might have extended as far north as Canada and as far south as the northern countries of Latin America. A full listing of the questions is given in appendix A and in appendix tables A-1 through A-7.

If readers feel skeptical about the inclusion of such a set of "soft" variables in a discussion of fertility, then their attention should be drawn to the first six tables in the appendix. In these tables a pronounced re-

[6] This question was suggested by my colleague, Mubeccel Kiray, at Middle East Technical University in Ankara.

lationship can be seen between almost every question used in each of the six indexes and live births, expected total births, and use of family limitation techniques. The number of reversals in direction is so small that I have footnoted them. Appendix table A-8 contains the indexes built from the sets of individual questions. There are no sign reversals, and the relationships are rather strong for fertility data. For those who wish to argue that the modernism variables chosen are simply engaged in a spurious relationship with fertility, appendix tables A-9 and A-10 are included to show that a simple unmaximized combination of the six indexes has a strong *net* effect on fertility that cannot be attributed to the wife's place of birth, the wife's education, or the husband's income in either city. The index used in these tables simply employs the trichotomies shown in appendix table A-8, scores them 0, 1, or 2, and creates an arbitrary, poorly named "combined modernism index" (scored 0–12) that does an exceptional job of explaining fertility in Ankara and Mexico City. For example, the three background variables account for 29 percent of the variance in expected number of children in Ankara. The combined modernism index handles 27 percent by itself. There is a 1.7 child net difference in expected fertility between the least and most modern couples, which is substantial in relation to a mean of 4.6 children.[7] If location affects the fertility-related variables, we have good reason to suspect that it will ultimately have some effect on fertility.

We can now turn to a set of materials that will tell us whether or not we can begin to think about a realistic experiment or quasi experiment. Table 12-1 contains the gross and net relationships between the residential-location measures and the fertility and fertility-related measures for Ankara. The four measures of residential location are of two kinds—the simple dichotomy between *gecekondu* and non*gecekondu* areas and the ratios of population potential for individual persons on the basis of education, income, and the forbids index.

Since the concept of potentials may be new to some readers, let me repeat what is involved. For each person a potential is calculated on the basis only of X's defined as wives with more than a primary school education. Another potential is calculated, based only on X's defined as wives who are illiterate. There are 803 wives in the Ankara sample, so the computer is obtaining a summation of the term X/D 802 times for each of the 803 women. A ratio of two potentials for each woman is

[7] Net differences were obtained after adjustment for the categories of the wife's place of birth, her education, and the husband's income in a multiple-classification analysis. The procedure resembles a dummy-variable analysis for the categories of the variables. The method is explained by Frank Andrews, James Morgan, and John Sonquist (1967).

created. The highest ratios represent high access to other women of high education and low access to other women of low education. The lowest ratios are the reverse. High and low ratios represent the most segregated populations. These ratios may be treated like any other individual characteristic. In this case, the ratios were divided into quartiles and used as categories in the analysis.[8] Similar ratios were formed for high- and low-income *X*'s and high- and low-forbids index *X*'s.

At the gross level the relationships between the potential ratios and the dependent variables are very strong. Note the *eta* range of 0.32 to 0.63.[9] These values are typically lower than the *eta*s for the wives' education, but not by a wide margin. About half the time, predictions of the dependent variables are as accurate as or more accurate than predictions based on the wives' place of birth or the husbands' income. The unsophisticated but real *gecekondu*-non*gecekondu* classification has substantial effects on the dependent variables, perhaps reflecting the other activities and institutions in these areas that are not captured by obtaining characteristics of individuals in a household survey.

At the net-effects level (adjusted means), with the inclusion of the three background variables, the effect of the residential variables is, of course, reduced, but it has a consistent, and in some cases, strong effect on the dependent variables. It is clear that of the two fertility variables used, however, family limitation is better predicted from area than are statements of expectation. Net use of family planning is twice as high (48 percent) in the fourth quartile as in the first quartile (24 percent). It is not inconceivable to me that the use of contraceptives may fit a model that approximates ownership of durable consumer goods, for which contagion may be highly important.

The picture is fairly clear for Ankara: areal effects do not wash out in the presence of other variables. There are territorial effects across a wide variety of behaviors and attitudes. Net effects on use are almost shockingly large.

In table 12-2, I have used the same three background variables and two of the residential location variables *simultaneously*. This is of some interest because it can tell us whether or not potentials can help explain the *gecekondu*-non*gecekondu* effect in spite of the high correlation that

[8] Quartile cutting points were determined for the entire unweighted sample. Elimination of women over forty-five, the subfecund, and the use of weights results in a four-category system of potentials that does not quite correspond to quartiles for the women in the sample used in tables 12-1 to 12-5.

[9] *Eta* is the square root of the explained variance. For example, the four categories of the husbands' income potential account for 11.6 percent of the variance in the use of family-limitation methods, and *eta* is 0.34.

Table 12-1. Means and Adjusted Means for Selected Indexes of Fertility and Fertility-related Behavior or Attitudes by Residential Location Measures for Fecund Women Under Forty-five, Ankara, Turkey, 1966

	Husband power index (0–5)		*Sex-segregation attitudes index (0–5)*		*Containment: forbids index (0–8)*		*Containment: RMP[b] index (0–3)*	
Residential location measures	*Mean*	*Adjusted mean[a]*	*Mean*	*Adjusted mean*	*Mean*	*Adjusted mean*	*Mean*	*Adjusted mean*
Slum status								
Gecekondu	3.4	2.9	4.1	3.8	6.2	5.4	0.6	1.0
Non*gecekondu*	1.7	2.2	3.3	3.6	3.6	4.3	1.6	1.3
Wives' educational potential								
Low	3.6	3.0	4.4	4.0	6.3	5.4	0.5	0.9
Medium low	2.7	2.6	3.7	3.6	5.1	4.8	1.0	1.2
Medium high	2.3	2.4	3.5	3.5	4.5	4.6	1.1	1.1
High	1.3	2.1	3.0	3.5	3.2	4.5	2.0	1.4
Husbands' income potential								
Low	3.5	3.0	4.3	4.0	6.1	5.3	0.6	0.9
Medium low	2.8	2.5	3.8	3.7	5.2	4.8	0.8	1.0
Medium high	2.3	2.4	3.6	3.6	4.4	4.6	1.3	1.2
High	1.4	2.2	2.9	3.4	3.3	4.6	1.9	1.4
Forbids index potential								
High	3.6	3.0	4.4	4.0	6.5	5.6	0.5	0.9
Medium high	2.8	2.7	3.8	3.7	5.2	5.0	0.9	1.1
Medium low	2.1	2.2	3.4	3.5	4.2	4.3	1.2	1.2
Low	1.2	2.0	3.0	3.5	3.1	4.3	2.0	1.4
Total	2.5	2.5	3.7	3.7	4.8	4.8	1.1	1.1
Eta								
Wives' place of birth	0.43		0.36		0.52		0.49	
Wives' education	0.56		0.51		0.58		0.64	
Husbands' income	0.47		0.40		0.58		0.56	
Slum status	0.49		0.35		0.54		0.48	
Wives' educational potential	0.45		0.40		0.46		0.49	
Husbands' income potential	0.42		0.38		0.43		0.48	
Forbids index potential	0.48		0.40		0.52		0.49	

[a] Multiple classification analysis used to obtain the adjusted means. Adjusted means for the residential categories obtained *after* adjustment for the inclusion of wives' birthplace, education, husbands' income, and their net effects.

[b] The precise meaning of RMP (restaurants, movies, parties) and NHC (non-home-centered) is given by questions C8a–C8c in appendix A.

Containment: NHC[b] index (0–4)		*Size of world (percentage small)*		*Modernism index (0–12)*		*Expected number of children*		*Percentage ever used family planning*		*No. of re-spon-dents*
Mean	*Ad-justed mean*	*Mean*	*Ad-justed mean*	*Mean*	*Ad-justed mean*	*Mean*	*Ad-justed mean*	*Mean*	*Ad-justed mean*	
0.2	0.4	57	44	2.6	4.0	5.6	4.9	22	30	281
0.9	0.7	21	33	6.7	5.4	3.8	4.4	53	46	312
0.2	0.5	60	46	2.3	3.8	5.5	4.7	16	24	153
0.4	0.5	46	42	4.2	4.7	4.9	4.7	38	41	155
0.5	0.5	32	33	5.0	6.0	4.6	4.7	42	42	156
1.3	0.9	9	27	8.0	5.8	3.2	4.4	60	48	129
0.3	0.5	59	48	2.7	3.9	5.1	4.4	18	25	151
0.4	0.6	45	39	3.9	4.7	5.2	4.8	30	34	168
0.5	0.4	32	35	5.1	4.8	4.8	4.9	49	39	142
1.3	0.8	11	28	7.8	5.7	3.2	4.3	61	51	132
0.2	0.5	61	48	2.2	3.7	5.5	4.7	17	25	151
0.4	0.6	47	43	4.0	4.5	5.1	4.8	29	32	170
0.5	0.5	29	31	5.4	5.1	4.5	4.6	51	50	139
1.3	0.8	10	28	7.9	5.8	3.2	4.3	61	49	133
0.6	0.6	38	38	4.7	4.7	4.6	4.6	38	38	593
0.43		0.37		0.61		0.40		0.27		
0.59		0.45		0.77		0.51		0.31		
0.52		0.43		0.67		0.41		0.35		
0.46		0.38		0.63		0.37		0.33		
0.48		0.37		0.61		0.33		0.32		
0.44		0.36		0.57		0.32		0.34		
0.44		0.39		0.62		0.34		0.35		

necessarily exists between the two measures. One generally thinks of a ghetto effect as taking place through some kind of reinforcement derived from the homogeneity of the persons in the area. The potentials allow us

Table 12-2. Means and Adjusted Means for Selected Indexes of Fertility and Fertility-related Behavior or Attitudes by Slum Status and Wives' Educational Potential for Fecund Women Under Forty-five, Ankara, Turkey, 1966

Residential location measures	*Husband power index (0–5)* Mean	*Adjusted mean*[a]	*Sex-segregation attitudes index (0–5)* Mean	*Adjusted mean*	*Containment: forbids index (0–8)* Mean	*Adjusted mean*	*Containment: RMP*[b] *index (0–3)* Mean	*Adjusted mean*
Slum status								
Gecekondu	3.4	2.8	4.1	3.7	6.2	5.3	0.6	1.1
Non*gecekondu*	1.7	2.3	3.3	3.7	3.6	4.4	1.6	1.2
Wives' educational potential								
Low	3.6	2.8	4.4	4.1	6.3	5.0	0.5	0.9
Medium low	2.7	2.5	3.7	3.6	5.1	4.8	1.0	1.2
Medium high	2.3	2.5	3.5	3.6	4.5	4.6	1.1	1.1
High	1.3	2.3	3.0	3.5	3.2	4.8	2.0	1.4
Total	2.5	2.5	3.7	3.7	4.8	4.8	1.1	1.1

[a] Multiple classification analysis used to obtain the adjusted means. Adjusted means for the residential categories obtained after adjustment for five independent variables. For example, adjusted means for slum status (SS) are based on the inclusion of wives' birthplace (WBP), wives' education (WE), husbands' income (HI) and wives' educational potential (WEP), whereas adjusted means for WEP are based on the inclusion of WBP, WE, HI, and SS.

[b] The precise meaning of RMP (restaurants, movies, parties) and NHC (non-home-centered) is given by questions C8a–C8c and C1 contained in appendix A.

to make distinctions *within* areas. People at the center of a large ghetto have very different worlds of access from those of the people located at the periphery of the ghetto. In other words, the ecological measure (the potentials) may help us explain some of the variability that is unexplained otherwise. This table implies that both measures affect the dependent variables—sixteen of the eighteen net effects are in the "correct" direction, though these effects are frequently small, given the presence of the other four variables. In short, we gain some predictive power from each of the location variables.[10]

In table 12-3, I have provided the entire set of adjusted means for all five independent variables in relation to the use of family-planning methods. Use appears to be almost entirely a function of income and residential location. Place of birth and wives' education have collapsed

[10] A separate analysis of *gecekondu* and non*gecekondu* areas shows that potentials do have an effect on the dependent variables *within* areas.

Containment: NHC[b] index (0–4)		*Size o world (percentage small)*		*Modernism index (0–12)*		*Expected number of children*		*Percentage ever used family planning*		*No. of re-spon-dents*
Mean	*Ad-justed mean*	*Mean*	*Ad-justed mean*	*Mean*	*Ad-justed mean*	*Mean*	*Ad-justed mean*	*Mean*	*Ad-justed mean*	
0.2	0.4	57	41	2.6	4.3	5.6	4.9	22	33	281
0.9	0.7	21	35	6.7	5.2	3.8	4.4	53	43	312
0.2	0.6	60	44	2.3	4.1	5.5	4.5	16	28	153
0.4	0.5	46	43	4.2	4.7	4.9	4.7	38	41	155
0.5	0.5	32	34	5.0	4.8	4.6	4.8	42	41	156
1.3	0.8	9	30	8.0	5.5	3.2	4.5	60	44	129
0.6	0.6	38	38	4.7	4.7	4.6	4.6	38	38	593

as net predictors. Some might interpret this as a quirk of one set of data from Ankara in 1966 except that, in table 12-5, almost identical results are produced from Mexico City in 1971. The two cities share at least one important feature in relation to these results: Neither city had a public program of any magnitude in operation, so contraception was expensive in relation to income. Where costs are relatively low, the income effects might be smaller.

Table 12-4 is parallel to table 12-1, embodying the Mexico City data. The results are very similar, *eta*s ranging from 0.26 to 0.56 for the residential location variables, much stronger than those for place of birth, weaker than wife's education, and about the same as those for the income relationships. Once again, the net effects are fairly consistent.

The data, with respect to family planning, may be summarized for both settings by utilizing explained variance:

	Explained variance in use	
	Ankara (%)	*Mexico City (%)*
Gross background	14.6	23.0
Gross residential location	13.0	18.6
Explained by both	17.3	25.5

Table 12-3. Percentage Ever Used Family-planning Methods by Wives' Place of Birth, Wives' Education, Husbands' Income, Slum Status, and Wives' Educational Potential for Fecund Women Under Forty-five, Ankara, Turkey, 1966

	Percentage ever used family-planning methods		
Independent variable	*Mean*	*Adjusted mean*[a]	*No. of respondents*
Wives' place of birth			
City	50	39	243
Town	46	44	114
Village	22	34	236
Wives' education			
None, illiterate	21	35	203
None, literate	36	46	61
1–5 years	43	39	202
6–11 years	59	39	68
12 + years	63	39	59
Husbands' income			
Under $50 per month	19	29	181
$50–$69 per month	31	31	138
$70–$139 per month	47	42	182
$140 + per month	70	59	92
Slum status			
Gecekondu	22	33	281
Non*gecekondu*	53	43	312
Wives' educational potential			
Low	16	28	153
Medium low	38	41	155
Medium high	42	41	156
High	60	44	129
Total	38	38	593

[a] Means adjusted by multiple classification analysis.

	Explained variance in use	
	Ankara (%)	*Mexico City* (%)
Net background	4.3	6.9
Net residential location	2.7	2.5
Joint effect	10.3	16.1

This research represents an effort to put a fundamental ecological hypothesis to a rather demanding test, using some important "control" variables and a wide selection of dependent variables. The inclusion of a broad range of dependent variables (fertility and fertility-related behavior) is based on the following rationale:

• The fertility-related variables selected in this study are consistent with fertility "theory" insofar as such a thing exists, although several of the index names (forbids, size of world) may appear strange to economists. Interpretations of the relationship between the background variables and fertility typically invoke "explanations" involving the range of alternative life styles available to women of low education, high education, village background, city background, and so forth. For example, both economists and sociologists almost axiomatically include women's work in such explanations. But what is the axiom? Is it not that the time required by work makes it more difficult to have children or that exposure to roles other than that of homemaker has the potential for competing with the extensive demands of child rearing? If that is the case, work is only one of a variety of activities that drain time or expose women to competitive alternatives. Work or work potential (the "normal" variable used by economists) is a convenient and rather parochial variable, because it can be translated into dollars.

• Since evidence has been provided showing the relationship between the fertility-related variables and fertility, any relationship between the location variables and the fertility-related variables has the potential for affecting fertility.

• The so-called "modernism index" (that is simply a specific truncation of the concept, referring to the extensiveness of women's roles and attitudes) is included among the dependent variables because not all dimensions of modernism emerge simultaneously. Individuals "develop" unevenly. In that sense, the most appropriate test of the hypothesis that modernism leads to lower fertility is made by using an index that combines selected components. In this instance, I have tried to combine the dimensions of power, segregation, and containment.

• It is entirely possible that the policies of several countries could be directed at the development of female roles that approximate the "modern" for any number of reasons that may have nothing to do with fertility. Tables 12-1 and 12-4 indicate rather conclusively that any attempts to affect either the background variables or the location variables will have a considerable effect on "modernism."

• And the many dependent variables have been included to provide a broader base for evaluation of the results.

The idea that population clustering leads to distinctive behavioral patterns, independent of personal characteristics, holds up extremely well in these two research settings. This should be true for any city that has a substantial amount of residential segregation. It is my *impression* that residential segregation is more often characteristic of large cities in the less developed countries than of large cities in the more developed countries. I

Table 12-4. Means and Adjusted Means[a] for Selected Indexes of Fertility and Fertility-related Behavior or Attitudes by Residential Location Measures for Fecund Women Under Forty-five, Mexico City, 1971

Residential location measures	*Husband power index (0–5)* Mean	*Husband power index (0–5)* Adjusted mean	*Sex-segregation attitudes index (0–4)* Mean	*Sex-segregation attitudes index (0–4)* Adjusted mean	*Containment: strongly objects index (0–7)* Mean	*Containment: strongly objects index (0–7)* Adjusted mean	*Containment: RMP[b] index (0–3)* Mean	*Containment: RMP[b] index (0–3)* Adjusted mean
Wives' educational potential								
Low	2.8	2.4	2.8	2.6	5.7	5.2	0.5	0.9
Medium low	2.6	2.4	2.6	2.5	5.6	5.3	0.7	0.9
Medium high	2.3	2.4	2.3	2.4	4.6	4.8	1.1	1.0
High	1.4	2.1	1.9	2.3	4.0	4.9	1.7	1.0
Husbands' educational potential								
Low	2.9	2.6	2.8	2.6	5.9	5.5	0.6	0.9
Medium low	2.6	2.4	2.6	2.5	5.2	5.1	0.7	0.9
Medium high	2.3	2.2	2.5	2.5	4.2	4.7	0.9	0.9
High	1.3	2.0	1.9	2.3	3.4	4.3	1.8	1.1
Husbands' income potential								
Low	2.9	2.6	2.8	2.6	5.7	5.2	0.8	1.1
Medium low	2.7	2.4	2.8	2.7	5.6	5.2	0.5	0.7
Medium high	2.1	2.1	2.3	2.4	4.9	5.0	0.9	0.9
High	1.5	2.2	1.8	2.1	3.8	4.8	1.8	1.1
Total	2.3	2.3	2.5	2.5	5.1	5.1	1.0	1.0
Eta								
Wives' place of birth	0.21		0.08		0.17		0.21	
Wives' education	0.43		0.40		0.43		0.55	
Husbands' income	0.36		0.31		0.42		0.51	
Wives' educational potential	0.35		0.34		0.37		0.44	
Husbands' educational potential	0.38		0.33		0.39		0.43	
Husbands' income potential	0.35		0.36		0.37		0.46	

[a] Multiple classification analysis used to obtain the adjusted means. Adjusted means for the residential categories obtained *after* adjustment for the inclusion of wives' birthplace, education and husbands' income and their net effects.

[b] The precise meaning of RMP (restaurants, movies, parties) and NHC (non-home-centered) is given by questions C8a–C8c and C1 contained in appendix A.

[c] Total number of respondents may differ from the sum of those in individual categories by one or two cases because of fractional sample weights used in the Mexico City data.

Containment: NHC[b] *index (0–4)*		*Size of world (percentage small)*		*Modernism index (0–12)*		*Expected number of children*		*Percentage ever used family planning*		*No. of re-spon-dents*[c]
Mean	*Adjusted mean*	*Mean*	*Adjusted mean*	*Mean*	*Adjusted mean*	*Mean*	*Adjusted mean*	*Mean*	*Adjusted mean*	
0.6	0.8	46	36	3.5	4.8	7.2	6.2	14	23	190
0.6	0.8	29	27	4.3	5.0	6.3	6.0	19	24	113
0.8	0.8	14	20	6.0	5.5	6.1	6.5	39	36	101
1.4	1.0	12	24	7.8	5.7	4.9	6.3	58	43	133
0.6	0.8	43	33	3.6	4.8	7.2	6.5	12	20	158
0.5	0.7	28	24	4.4	5.0	6.6	6.2	24	30	139
0.8	0.9	26	30	5.3	5.2	6.2	6.3	29	28	119
1.4	1.0	10	25	8.2	6.0	4.6	6.0	65	49	122
0.6	0.8	45	36	3.9	5.0	7.2	6.5	10	19	155
0.5	0.6	29	23	3.8	4.6	6.7	6.2	23	29	142
0.9	0.9	22	27	5.7	5.5	5.9	6.1	33	30	119
1.4	1.1	11	25	8.1	5.9	4.8	6.2	64	48	122
0.8	0.8	28	28	5.2	5.2	6.3	6.3	31	31	537
0.24		0.13		0.28		0.27		0.21		
0.46		0.36		0.69		0.49		0.39		
0.35		0.30		0.57		0.36		0.45		
0.37		0.32		0.56		0.32		0.39		
0.39		0.26		0.56		0.34		0.43		
0.40		0.28		0.56		0.32		0.43		

believe that this contributes to the greater crystallization of population in the cities of the less developed countries. I can only *compare* Ankara and Mexico City data with American city data empirically. The two transitional cities are more segregated and their populations are more crystallized.

The major exception to the consistency of the data is found in Mexico City for the variable expected number of children. Although there are

Table 12-5. Percentage Ever Used Family-planning Methods by Wives' Place of Birth, Wives' Education, Husbands' Income, and Wives' Educational Potential for Fecund Women Under Forty-five, Mexico City, 1971

	Percentage ever used family-planning methods		
Independent variable	*Mean*	*Adjusted mean*[a]	*No. of respondents*[b]
Wives' place of birth			
City	39	34	305
Town	19	25	173
Smaller	24	32	59
Wives' education			
None	10	28	120
1–5 years	19	28	145
6 years	32	31	95
7–9 years	52	38	95
10 + years	57	30	81
Husbands' income			
Under $96 per month	12	18	196
$96–$159 per month	20	23	151
$160–$399 per month	55	49	137
$400 + per month	67	52	53
Wives' educational potential			
Low	14	23	190
Medium low	19	24	113
Medium high	39	36	101
High	58	43	133
Total	31	31	537

[a] Means adjusted by multiple classification analysis.

[b] Total number of respondents may differ from the sum of those in individual categories by one or two cases because of fractional sample weights used in the Mexico City data.

substantial differences among areas in the direction we normally anticipate, areal variations in expectations appear to be attributable entirely to the other characteristics of the people residing in the area. I am bothered by this because everything I know about expectations suggests that the responses are important conceptually and are oriented toward reality—which is not to say that it is the number of children these women will, in fact, have.[11]

The data from these studies are ex post facto and have all the typical problems of research in the social sciences. In this particular research,

[11] There has been considerable comment about the most appropriate form of the dependent variable for fertility studies. A review and contribution to these materials is contained in Namboodiri (1972).

the net areal effects on the dependent variables can be attributed to:

- A selective migration process within cities. The argument would go this way: People who live in the *gecekondu* or who live in areas having low potential to high education, high income, and the like, are different from those persons *with comparable background characteristics* who leave these areas to migrate to other parts of the city. Those who leave have more modern family structures, more modern attitudes and values, and lower fertility. It is not place of residence that affects these items but the reverse process that takes place.
- The aggregation of population into homogeneous clusters, which results in a reinforcement process that magnifies or extends the behaviors and attitudes associated with the background characteristics. Imitation may be the key social process involved. What is clear is that a structural effect takes place which results in differences in behavior that cannot be attributed to background.

The relative truth of these two positions cannot be untangled, no matter how much we jiggle the data at hand. I suspect that there is truth in both positions.

Most certainly these results are encouraging enough to make a strong case for additional research that would help clarify some important issues. Some of it can be done with the present data. Until now, the research has been concentrated on locational effects based on status. Several other kinds of personal characteristics could be examined—in fact, any of the 250–300 variables that exist on the tapes. If one were to include some of the dependent variables as a basis for making up the potentials, we would implicitly be testing some of the communication-diffusion hypotheses found in the literature on fertility and family planning. No attempt has been made to determine the most effective distance range for the potentials. This is roughly equivalent to determining the appropriate exponent for D_j. We may be grossly underestimating the importance of areal effects.

The data sets assembled here are consistent with the proposition that slum residence (*by itself*) leads to the conservation of traditional attitudes and behavior, some of which are anachronistic in the urban setting.

I think that this should be followed up in two ways: Additional ex post facto data should be examined using the kinds of tools and analysis employed in this research. We simply need more examples that could give us additional insight on the problem. All one needs are the X and Y coordinates for respondents and a programmer. Certainly these exist for dozens of data sets already collected. Second, a panel study should be conducted that would give us a base broad enough to compare movers and stayers over a five-year period. For this purpose, I would recommend Ankara, where there are people who are familiar with the problem already well trained.[12] Such a study could answer several questions about selectivity and change over a relatively short period. It would be no simple task, for it would require both commitment and sophistication.

Let us assume that the location effects do not result from selective migration. What are the policy implications, if the objective is to lower the fertility of a high-fertility group? To the extent that governments are involved in public housing, these results almost dictate the building of relatively small complexes rather than large ones. The block upon block of high-rise public housing strung out along South State Street in Chicago may have helped create the largest ghetto and largest ghetto effect the world has ever known. Any large, homogeneous complex is an instant ghetto. If it were not obvious already, these data illustrate quantitatively some of the problems associated with that sort of undertaking. Beyond that, policies are not as "obvious" to me as they might be to those who appear to be certain that moving people to various locations around the city will have a net beneficial effect for the entire population. Our results suggest the building of small clusters of housing spread across the community. This policy would undoubtedly encounter strong objections from the "moderns" as it has in this country. People are not chessmen who can be moved successfully from one square to another. Limits on the potential success of social engineering are imposed through a selective process, which is one of the conditions contributing to our own busing problems.

What can be offered from analysis of the kind employed here is greater intelligence in the selection of locations where several choices are possible. The options available and solutions offered open up a variety of experimental situations, some examples of which, together with the underlying potentials, are offered in Appendix B. We cannot do a double-blind study on this one, but it should be possible to obtain government cooperation in an experimental effort that would make available some areas that could be preselected (on the basis of potential measures) for squatter or "partly subsidized squatter" settlement in large or small settlements.

In the overwhelming majority of growing cities in the less developed countries there are several site options available for accommodating the increasing numbers of village migrants coming to these places and locating in squatter settlements. The particular sites available are a function of varying conditions from city to city; the location of municipally owned land; topography; private property the government does not wish to "protect" or on which it is willing to ignore law enforcement; zoning;

[12] A dissertation dealing with the effects of personal characteristics, friendship patterns, and population potentials on selected aspects of family structure has been written by Hasan Dogan (1974).

the present circumstances and plans for extension of services; and so on. Combinations of conditions create site options for the location of incoming populations. The research seems to indicate, in fairly strong terms, that measures of potential or access to selected populations has strong independent effects on behavior. If there is a choice of sites and if site affects behavior, then there are policy options. These experimental options would face serious problems of selectivity unless careful controls were exerted and would therefore run many of the same social and political risks as those associated with black public housing in white middle-class areas. Assuming that it was politically possible to engage in thoughtful social engineering, one could start panel studies among those "assigned" to the various locations.

A legitimate question could be raised about the overall level of fertility to be achieved within the community by manipulating sites. If fertility can be lowered by creating greater access to modern couples, won't the fertility of the modern couples be raised by giving them greater access to the higher-fertility population? The answer to this will depend largely on the way valued behavior filters through a population—and that answer is not completely obvious to me, though the "filtering down" hypothesis probably has some merit. At least, I find it easier to imagine the village migrant population beginning to model their fertility upon that of their indigenous urban neighbors, as former villagers are exposed to life styles that compete with child rearing, whereas I find it more difficult to imagine the converse taking place.

The questions raised by human ecology have regained their relevance in recent years as governments in countries at all levels of development are actively engaged in making plans affecting the redistribution of populations to achieved desired ends. While there are those who argue that such things as automobiles, television sets, and telephones have preempted the social significance of spatial location, at the same time, public policy becomes more directly involved in it. This is precisely the time when we should extend the efforts of a style of sociology that has almost been abandoned.

Appendix A

Table A-1. Questions Used in the Construction of Fertility-related Indexes

Index	*Ankara*		*Mexico City*	
Husband power	C13[a]	In most families, either the husband or the wife has the most say about some decisions, although they may talk it over first. I will read some items to you and I would like you to tell me whether your husband almost always decides, your husband usually decides, you usually decide, or you almost always decide.	C13.	Same as Ankara
	C13a.	For instance, who usually has the most say about which couples you see most often?	C13a.	Same
	C13b.	About which relatives you see?	C13b.	Same
	C13c.	About the purchase of major household items?	C13c.	Same
	C13d.	About how much money your family can afford to spend on food?	C13d.	Same
	C13e.	About how money saved or earned is to be spent?	C13e.	Same
Sex-segregation attitudes	C11.	Now I would like to get your opinion on some matters concerning family life. I will read you some statements and I would like you to tell me whether you strongly agree, agree, disagree, or strongly disagree. The first one is:	C11.	Same as Ankara
	C11a.	Most of the important decisions in the life of the family should be made by the man of the house.	C11a.	Same
	C11b.	There is some work that is men's and some that is women's and they shouldn't be doing each other's.	C11b.	Same
	C11c.	And how about the saying "If you leave a girl by herself she either marries a drummer or a piper."		

	C11d. A wife should not expect her husband to help around the house after he has come home from a hard day's work.	C11d. Same
	C11e. It is perfectly all right for men to go out alone about as often as they want.	C11e. Same
Containment: forbids or strongly objects	C12. Many husbands forbid their wives to do certain things. Does your husband forbid you to do any of these things?	C12. Many husbands strongly object to their wives doing certain things. Does your husband strongly object to any of these things?
	C12a. To wear short sleeve dresses	C12a. To talk to men your husband doesn't know
	C12b. To sit together with men during visits to your home	C12b. To visit women your husband doesn't know
	C12c. To go shopping by yourself	C12c. To go to the movies alone
	C12d. To talk to men your husband doesn't know	C12d. To go to fiestas by yourself
	C12e. To go without a scarf or head covering	C12e. To dance with other men at fiestas you both go to
	C12f. To visit women your husband doesn't know	C12f. To have a few drinks
	C12g. To go to the matinee at the movies alone	C12g. To wear clothes that catch the eye
	C12h. To go to parties by yourself	
Containment: restaurants, movies, and parties	C8. Now I would like to read you a list of activities and I would like you to tell me how often you and your husband do these things either alone or together:	C8. Same as Ankara
	C8a. Go to a restaurant	C8a. Same
	C8b. Go to movies	C8b. Same
	C8c. Go to parties	C8c. Go to reunions
Containment: nonhome-centered leisure	C1. Aside from visiting friends and relatives, what kinds of things do you do in the day or evening, when you have some free time?	C1. Same as Ankara
Size of world	C33. What country do you think is the farthest place in the world from Turkey?	C48. What country do you think is the farthest place in the world from Mexico?

[a] The index questions shown come from the middle portion of a one-hour interview. The numbers adjacent to the questions are the numbers used in the interview schedule and indicate their relative placement.

Table A-2. Live Births, Expected Births, and Percentage Ever Used Family Planning by Wives' Age and Decision-making Items for Ankara and Mexico City

		Wives under 30 years old			
City and question	*Decision made by*	*Live births*	*Expected births*	*Percentage ever used family planning*	*No. of respon-dents*
Ankara: Who has most say about:					
Which couples are seen?	Husband	2.7	4.4	26	234
	Both, Wife	1.8	3.5	42	90
Which relatives are seen?	Husband	2.7	4.5	22	199
	Both, Wife	2.0	3.6	45	125
Purchasing major goods?	Husband	2.8	4.6	19	124
	Both, Wife	2.2	3.9	39	200
Spending money on food?	Husband	2.9	4.8	20	129
	Both, Wife	2.1	3.8	38	195
Spending saved money?	Husband	2.8	4.6	19	173
	Both, Wife	2.1	3.7	44	151
Total		2.4	4.2	31	324
Mexico City: Who has most say about:					
Which couples are seen?	Husband	2.6	5.6	16	206
	Both, Wife	2.3	4.7	50	103
Which relatives are seen?	Husband	2.7	5.6	22	151
	Both, Wife	2.2	5.1	33	157
Purchasing major goods?	Husband	2.6	5.9	18	108
	Both, Wife	2.4	5.0	33	200
Spending money on food?	Husband	2.8	5.9	15	114
	Both, Wife	2.3	5.0	35	195
Spending saved money?	Husband	2.4[R]	5.5	17	155
	Both, Wife	2.5	5.1	39	153
Total		2.5	5.3	28	309

[R] = Direction reversal.

Note that in this table, and all subsequent tables, sampling weights may produce differences of one case between subtotals and totals.

Wives 30–44 years old				Wives 45 or older		
Live births	*Expected births*	*Percentage ever used family planning*	*No. of respondents*	*Live births*	*Percentage ever used family planning*	*No. of respondents*
4.2	5.0	33	230	4.7	22	79
3.1	3.6	59	114	3.7	45	56
4.5	5.4	28	170	4.6	20	60
3.3	3.7	55	174	4.0	40	75
4.7	5.5	27	132	5.2	15	41
3.3	3.9	50	212	3.8	38	94
4.4	5.2	29	122	4.7	15	47
3.6	4.6	48	222	4.0	40	88
4.5	5.3	33	178	4.8	17	64
3.2	3.7	51	166	3.7	44	71
3.9	4.5	41	344	4.3	31	135
5.4	6.8	24	204	6.8	6	85
5.2	6.1	41	107	5.5	17	92
5.7	7.0	20	153	6.7	7	73
5.1	6.1	39	159	5.6	15	104
5.5	6.9	18	113	6.4	8	60
5.3	6.3	36	199	5.9	14	117
5.4	6.6	29	99	7.3	10	57
5.4	6.5	30	213	5.5	13	121
5.4	6.7	28	143	6.8	9	82
5.4	6.4	31	169	5.5	15	95
5.4	6.5	30	312	6.1	12	178

Table A-3. Live Births, Expected Births, and Percentage Ever Used Family Planning by Wives' Age and Sex-segregation Attitudes for Ankara and Mexico City

City and question		Wives under 30 years old: Live births	Expected births	Percentage ever used family planning	No. of respondents
Ankara: Agree or disagree that					
Important decisions should	A	2.6	4.4	26	265
be made by the man.	D	1.8	3.3	51	59
Some work is men's.	A	2.6	4.3	29	272
	D	1.9	3.4	40	52
Wife should not expect her	A	2.5	4.3	29	284
husband to help.	D	1.9	3.1	43	40
It is all right for men to go out	A	2.8	4.6	23	141
alone as often as they wish.	D	2.2	3.8	37	183
A girl left by herself marries	A	2.6	4.4	26	247
a drummer or a piper.	D	1.9	3.4	47	77
Total		2.4	4.2	31	324
Mexico City: Agree or disagree that					
Important decisions should	A	2.6	5.6	22	224
be made by the man.	D	2.1	4.7	44	85
Some work is men's.	A	2.5	5.0	21	199
	D	2.5	5.0	40	110
Wife should not expect her	A	2.4[R]	5.4	23	240
husband to help.	D	2.7	5.1	44	69
It is all right for men to go out	A	2.5	5.7	27	98
alone as often as they wish.	D	2.4	5.2	28	211
Total		2.5	5.3	28	309

[a] Intermediate responses—those indicating neither agreement nor pronounced disagreement—are counted here as disagreement. There were only a few such responses.

[R] = Direction reversal.

Wives 30–44 years old				Wives 45 or older		
Live births	*Expected births*	*Percentage ever used family planning*	*No. of respondents*	*Live births*	*Percentage ever used family planning*	*No. of respondents*
4.2	4.9	35	261	4.5	27	102
2.8	3.3	60	83	3.6	42	33
4.2	4.9	37	265	4.2[R]	32[R]	111
2.8	3.3	56	79	4.3	29	24
4.0	4.7	39	300	4.2[R]	31[R]	118
3.0	3.7	55	44	4.4	29	17
4.7	5.5	27	141	4.4	24	59
3.3	3.9	51	203	4.2	37	76
4.2	4.9	38	264	4.5	27	112
2.7	3.2	52	80	3.3	52	23
3.9	4.5	42	344	4.3	31	135
5.5	6.7	24	239	6.3	8	132
5.2	6.0	49	72	5.6	25	45
5.7	6.9	28	175	6.7	6	108
5.0	6.1	32	136	5.1	21	69
5.5	6.6	25	240	6.1	12[R]	122
5.2	6.2	44	72	6.0	11	56
5.9	7.0	22	129	6.3	14[R]	108
5.0	6.2	35	183	5.7	9	69
5.4	6.5	30	312	6.1	12	178

Table A-4. Live Births, Expected Births, and Percentage Ever Used Family Planning by Wives' Age and Husband-Forbids Items (Ankara) or Husband-Strongly-Objects Items (Mexico City)

City and question		*Wives under 30 years old* Live births	Expected births	Percentage ever used family planning	No. of respondents
Ankara: Does husband forbid wife to:					
Talk to men?	F	2.5	4.3	29	280
	NF	1.8	3.3	45	44
Visit women?	F	2.7	4.5	26	196
	NF	2.1	3.6	39	128
Go to matinee alone?	F	2.5	4.3	27	244
	NF	2.2	3.7	43	80
Go to parties alone?	F	2.5	4.2	30	305
	NF	1.7	3.3	42	19
Sit with men?	F	2.8	4.8	22	105
	NF	2.3	3.9	35	219
Wear short-sleeved dresses?	F	2.9	4.8	24	189
	NF	1.8	3.3	40	135
Go shopping alone?	F	2.6	4.6	20	150
	NF	2.3	3.9	40	174
Go without scarf?	F	2.9	4.8	21	192
	NF	1.8	3.2	45	132
Total		2.4	4.2	31	324
Mexico City: Does husband strongly object to having wife:					
Talk to men?	SO	2.5	5.5	23	267
	NSO	2.4	4.3	55	42
Visit women?	SO	2.7	5.6	22	206
	NSO	2.1	4.7	38	103
Go to movies alone?	SO	2.5	5.6	23	254
	NSO	2.2	4.2	49	55
Go to fiestas alone?	SO	2.5	5.5	25	271
	NSO	2.0	3.9	47	37
Dance with other men?	SO	2.6	5.6	25	221
	NSO	2.2	4.7	34	88
Wear eye-catching clothes?	SO	2.5	5.5	23	186
	NSO	2.4	5.1	35	123
Have a few drinks?	SO	2.7	5.8	20	147
	NSO	2.3	4.9	35	162
Total		2.5	5.3	28	309

Wives 30–44 years old				Wives 45 or older		
Live births	*Expected births*	*Percentage ever used family planning*	*No. of respondents*	*Live births*	*Percentage ever used family planning*	*No. of respondents*
4.1	4.8	36	282	4.7	23	93
2.9	3.4	63	62	3.4	50	42
4.3	5.1	33	175	4.9	13	53
3.4	4.0	50	169	3.8	43	82
4.2	5.0	34	233	4.8	19	80
3.0	3.5	57	111	3.4	49	55
4.0	4.7	39	307	4.5	28	114
2.6	2.9	59	37	3.1	48	21
4.4	5.4	27	98	4.7	15	41
3.6	4.2	47	246	4.1	38	94
4.5	5.4	25	189	4.9	17	77
3.1	3.5	61	155	3.4	50	58
4.9	5.9	26	108	4.7	11	38
3.4	3.9	48	236	4.1	39	97
4.7	5.6	26	185	4.9	19	80
2.9	3.3	59	159	3.3	49	55
3.9	4.5	41	344	4.3	31	135
5.7	6.9	28	256	7.1	6	103
3.9	4.8	40	56	4.8	20	74
5.8	7.1	25	208	6.8	7	86
4.5	5.4	39	104	5.4	17	92
5.6	6.8	27	240	6.5	8	112
4.7	5.5	38	72	5.4	19	65
5.6	6.8	29	252	6.3	8	114
4.6	5.3	33	60	5.7	19	63
5.6	6.9	28	240	6.7	7	108
4.6	5.2	36	72	5.1	19	70
5.8	7.1	23	196	6.6	7	106
4.6	5.5	41	116	5.4	20	72
6.1	7.4	24	148	7.3	4	70
4.8	5.8	35	164	5.3	17	108
5.4	6.5	30	312	6.1	12	178

Table A-5. Live Births, Expected Births, and Percentage Ever Used Family Planning by Wives' Age and Restaurants, Movies, and Parties Items for Ankara and Mexico City

		Wives under 30 years old			
City and question	*Frequency*	*Live births*	*Expected births*	*Percentage ever used family planning*	*No. of respondents*
Ankara: How often wife goes to:					
Restaurants	Occasionally +	1.5	3.0	51	66
	Never	2.7	4.5	26	258
Movies	1–2 Times per month +	1.9	3.6	42	177
	<1–2 Times per month	3.1	4.9	17	147
Parties	Occasionally +	1.9	3.5	47	98
	Never	2.7	4.5	24	226
Total		2.4	4.2	31	324
Mexico City: How often wife goes to:					
Restaurants	1–2 Times per month +	2.1	4.5	50	114
	<1–2 Times per month	2.7	5.8	15	195
Movies	1–2 Times per month +	2.2	5.1	32	140
	<1–2 Times per month	2.7	5.5	24	169
Parties	1–2 Times per month +	2.0	4.7	34	77
	<1–2 Times per month	2.7	5.5	26	231
Total		2.5	5.3	28	309

Wives 30–44 years old				*Wives 45 or older*		
Live births	*Expected births*	*Percentage ever used family planning*	*No. of respondents*	*Live births*	*Percentage ever used family planning*	*No. of respondents*
2.6	3.0	63	97	3.1	48	29
4.3	5.1	33	247	4.6	26	106
3.1	3.6	54	189	3.8	51	61
4.7	5.6	26	155	4.6	15	74
3.1	3.7	54	141	4.1	40	40
4.4	5.2	32	203	4.3	27	95
3.9	4.5	41	344	4.3	31	135
4.4	5.2	45	101	4.6	26	47
5.8	7.2	22	211	6.6	7	130
4.4	5.2	45	94	4.8	20	51
5.8	7.1	23	218	6.6	9	126
3.9	4.8	46	53	4.7	39	29
5.7	6.9	26	259	6.4	7	148
5.4	6.5	30	312	6.1	12	178

Table A-6. Live Births, Expected Births, and Percentage Ever Used Family Planning by Wives' Age and Spare-time Activity Items for Ankara and Mexico City

City and question		Wives under 30 years old: Live births	Expected births	Percentage ever used family planning	No. of respondents
Ankara: Spare-time activities					
First	home-centered	2.6	4.4	28	281
activity:	mixed, nonhome-centered	1.3	2.8	49	43
Second	home-centered, none	2.7	4.4	26	263
activity:	mixed, nonhome-centered	1.5	3.1	52	61
Third	home-centered, none	2.5	4.2	30	289
activity:	mixed, nonhome-centered	1.9	3.6	34	35
Fourth	home-centered, none	2.5	4.2	29	296
activity:	mixed, nonhome-centered	1.8	3.5	46	28
Total		2.4	4.2	31	324
Mexico City: Spare-time activities					
First	home-centered	2.7	5.5	21	224
activity:	mixed, nonhome-centered	2.0	4.8	45	84
Second	home-centered, none	2.6	5.4	25	231
activity:	mixed, nonhome-centered	2.2	5.0	37	77
Third	home-centered, none	2.5	5.5	24	248
activity:	mixed, nonhome-centered	2.3	4.8	42	60
Fourth	home-centered, none	2.4	5.4	24	271
activity:	mixed, nonhome-centered	2.8[R]	5.0	51	38
Total		2.5	5.3	28	309

[R] = Direction reversal.

Wives 30–44 years old				Wives 45 or older		
Live births	*Expected births*	*Percentage ever used family planning*	*No. of respondents*	*Live births*	*Percentage ever used family planning*	*No. of respondents*
4.0	4.7	37	289	4.5	27	113
3.0	3.5	64	55	2.9	55	22
4.2	5.0	37	274	4.4	26	117
2.5	2.8	59	70	3.1	61	18
4.1	4.8	38	285	4.4	28	118
2.7	3.2	58	59	3.2	53	17
3.9	4.6	35	314	4.4	30	122
3.1	3.5	60	30	2.9	46	13
3.9	4.5	41	344	4.3	31	135
5.7	6.9	25	230	6.0	7	137
4.4	5.4	42	81	6.3[R]	28	40
5.7	6.9	27	240	6.6	9	137
4.3	5.3	40	72	4.6	24	41
5.6	6.8	28	264	6.4	10	149
4.5	5.1	40	48	4.7	21	28
5.5	6.6	28	276	6.6	12	153
4.7	5.8	46	35	3.2	11[R]	24
5.4	6.5	30	312	6.1	12	178

Table A-7. Live Births, Expected Births, and Percentage Ever Used Family Planning by Wives' Age and Size-of-World Question for Ankara and Mexico City

	Wives under 30 years old			
City and question	*Live births*	*Expected births*	*Percentage ever used family planning*	*No. of respondents*
Ankara: Size-of-world question				
Small[a]	3.1	5.1	18	136
Medium	2.1	3.8	39	127
Large	1.8	3.0	43	61
Total	2.4	4.2	31	324
Mexico City: Size-of-world question				
Small[b]	2.7	6.3	4	97
Medium	2.2[R]	5.2	27	70
Large	2.5	4.8	44	141
Total	2.5	5.3	28	309

[a] The responses grouped into perceptions of world size for Ankara were *small:* Don't know, ambiguous answers, Turkey, Near East, Western Europe except England and Spain; *medium:* Distant Europe, India, Africa, United States; *large:* Other Southeast and Central Asia, Latin America, Pacific Islands, Poles.

[b] The responses grouped into perceptions of world size for Mexico City were *small:* Don't know, Mexico, United States, northern Latin America; *medium:* Rest of Latin America, Europe except eastern portion; *large:* Eastern Europe, Asia, Africa.

[R] = Direction reversal.

Wives 30–44 years old				*Wives 45 or older*		
Live births	*Expected births*	*Percentage ever used family planning*	*No. of respondents*	*Live births*	*Percentage ever used family planning*	*No. of respondents*
4.5	5.3	26	123	5.0	17	47
3.8	4.5	42	145	4.0	32	72
2.9	3.3	64	76	2.9	69	16
3.9	4.5	41	344	4.3	31	135
6.6	7.8	21	71	7.2	4	47
5.6	6.9	23	97	6.5	7	38
4.6	5.7	38	144	5.4	18	93
5.4	6.5	30	312	6.1	12	178

Table A-8. Live Births, Expected Births, and Percentage Ever Used Family Planning by Selected Index for Fecund Women Under Forty-five for Ankara and Mexico City

Selected index	Criterion[a]		Ankara				Mexico City			
	Ankara	*Mexico City*	*Live births*	*Expected births*	*Percentage ever used family planning*	*No. of respondents*	*Live births*	*Expected births*	*Percentage ever used family planning*	*No. of respondents*
Husband's power										
Husband decides	0–1/5	0–1/5	2.5	3.5	56	202	3.6	5.5	51	178
	2–3/5	2/5	3.5	4.9	37	192	3.8	6.2	26	133
	4–5/5	3–5/5	3.9	5.4	21	199	4.3	6.9	17	225
Sex-segregation attitudes										
Wife agrees to	0–2/5	0–1/4	2.3	3.2	61	105	3.5	5.2	57	100
	3–4/5	2/4	3.1	4.5	40	306	3.7	6.1	30	163
	5/5	3–4/4	4.1	5.7	22	182	4.3	6.7	21	275
Forbids or strongly objects										
Husband forbids	0–2/8	0–3/7	2.5	3.5	60	120	3.2	4.9	54	111
	3–5/8	4–6/7	2.9	3.9	45	204	3.8	6.1	28	240
	6–8/8	7/7	3.9	5.7	24	269	4.6	7.2	21	186

Restaurants, movies, parties									
Wife goes occasionally/	0/3	4.1	5.6	21	249	4.7	7.1	22	247
frequently to	1/3	2.9	4.3	48	239	4.1	6.5	22	130
	2–3/3	2.1	3.0	56	105	2.7	4.8	51	159
Nonhome-centered leisure									
number of activities	0/4	3.8	5.3	27	368	4.6	7.0	21	241
	1/4	2.7	3.8	53	133	3.5	6.0	31	184
	2–4/4	2.0	3.0	60	92	3.2	5.1	52	112
Size of world									
	Small	3.9	5.6	23	225	4.3	7.1	11	151
	Medium	3.1	4.4	43	245	4.2	6.6	26	145
	Large	2.4	3.3	57	123	3.5	5.5	46	242
Total		3.3	4.6	38	593	3.9	6.3	31	537

[a] The meaning of the ratios listed under the criterion column is as follows:
0–1/5 = husband decides none or one of the five questions used.
2–3/5 = husband decides two or three of the five questions used, etc.

Table A-9. Expected Births and Percentage Ever Used Family Planning by Background Characteristics and Combined Modernism Index for Fecund Women Under Forty-five in Ankara

	Total expected births					*Percentage ever used family planning*					
Background characteristic	*Grand mean*	*Actual mean*	*Gross[a] deviation*	*Net effect*	*Residual effect*	*Grand mean*	*Actual mean*	*Gross[a] deviation*	*Net effect*	*Residual effect*	*No. of respon-dents*
Wives' place of birth											
City	4.6	3.6	−1.0	−0.2	−0.8	38	50	+12	−1	+13	243
Town	4.6	4.3	−0.3	−0.2	−0.1	38	46	+8	+7	+1	114
Village	4.6	5.8	+1.2	+0.3	+0.9	38	22	−16	−3	−13	236
Wives' education											
0, illiterate	4.6	6.1	+1.5	+0.8	+0.7	38	21	−17	+2	−19	203
0, literate	4.6	4.9	+0.3	−0.1	+0.4	38	36	−2	+10	−12	61
1–5 years	4.6	4.2	−0.4	−0.2	−0.2	38	43	+5	+1	+4	202
6–11 years	4.6	3.0	−1.6	−0.7	−0.9	38	59	+21	−6	+27	68
12+ years	4.6	2.5	−2.1	−1.1	−1.0	38	63	+25	−12	+37	59
Husbands' monthly income											
<$50	4.6	5.9	+1.3	+0.2	+1.1	38	19	−19	−8	−11	181
$50–69	4.6	4.7	+0.1	−0.1	+0.2	38	31	−7	−5	−2	138
$70–139	4.6	4.1	−0.5	0.0	−0.5	38	47	+9	+2	+7	182
$140+	4.6	2.9	−1.7	−0.3	−1.4	38	70	+32	+18	+14	92
Combined modernism index											
0–1 (traditional)	4.6	6.2	+1.6	+0.8	+0.8	38	14	−24	−19	−5	118
2–3	4.6	5.6	+0.8	+0.5	+0.3	38	25	−13	−11	−2	131
4–5	4.6	4.8	+0.2	+0.1	+0.1	38	35	−3	−4	+1	101
6–7	4.6	3.9	−0.7	−0.4	−0.3	38	47	+9	+6	+3	101
8–9	4.6	3.0	−1.6	−0.8	−0.8	38	62	+24	+20	+4	87
10–12 (modern)	4.6	2.7	−1.9	−0.9	−1.0	38	75	+37	+33	+4	55
Total	4.6	4.6	0	0	0	38	38	0	0	0	593

[a] The gross deviation (difference between category mean and the grand mean) is decomposed into net effect: the net contribution from being in the category, after adjustment for the distribution of the respondents in the category on all other independent variables in the system and residual effect: the difference between the gross deviation and the net effect, representing the contribution from the distribution of the category respondents on all other variables.

Table A-10. Expected Births and Percentage Ever Used Family Planning by Background Characteristics and Combined Modernism Index for Fecund Women Under Forty-five in Mexico City

Background characteristic	Total expected births					Percentage ever used family planning					No. of respondents
	Grand mean	Actual mean	Gross[a] deviation	Net effect	Residual effect	Grand mean	Actual mean	Gross[a] deviation	Net effect	Residual effect	
Wives' place of birth											
City	6.3	5.6	−0.7	−0.2	−0.5	31	39	+8	+2	+6	305
Town	6.3	7.0	+0.7	+0.3	+0.4	31	19	−12	−4	−8	173
Smaller	6.3	7.5	+1.2	+0.3	+0.9	31	24	−7	+2	−9	59
Wives' education											
0 years	6.3	7.9	+1.6	+1.1	+0.5	31	10	−21	−2	−19	120
1–5 years	6.3	7.3	+1.0	+0.8	+0.2	31	19	−12	−2	−10	145
6 years	6.3	5.9	−0.4	−0.4	0.0	31	32	+1	−1	+2	95
7–9 years	6.3	4.5	−1.8	−1.2	−0.6	31	52	+21	+7	+14	95
10+ years	6.3	4.4	−1.9	−1.1	−0.8	31	57	+26	−2	+28	81
Husbands' monthly income											
<$96	6.3	7.0	+0.7	−0.2	+0.9	31	12	−19	−12	−7	196
$96–159	6.3	7.0	+0.7	+0.5	+0.2	31	20	−11	−8	−3	151
$160–399	6.3	4.9	−1.4	−0.4	−1.0	31	55	+24	+16	+8	137
$400+	6.3	4.9	−1.4	−0.1	−1.3	31	67	+36	+24	+12	53
Combined modernism index											
0–2 (traditional)	6.3	7.5	+1.2	+0.3	+0.9	31	12	−19	−14	−5	120
3–4	6.3	7.2	+0.9	+0.5	+0.4	31	20	−11	−4	−7	129
5–6	6.3	6.3	0.0	0.0	0.0	31	27	−4	−1	−3	102
7–8	6.3	4.9	−1.4	−0.4	−1.0	31	51	+20	+8	+12	88
9–12 (modern)	6.3	4.6	−1.7	−0.7	−1.0	31	60	+29	+15	+14	98
Total	6.3	6.3	0	0	0	31	31	0	0	0	537

[a] The gross deviation (difference between category mean and the grand mean) is decomposed into net effect: the net contribution from being in the category, after adjustment for the distribution of the respondents in the category on all other independent variables in the system; and residual effect: the difference between the gross deviation and net effect, representing the contribution from the distribution of the category respondents on all other variables.

Appendix B. Population Potentials and Alternative Sites

Economists may not be familiar with the use of the population potential concept. It is a social science analogy to the gravity concept in physical sciences. Where we use X_j to represent number of persons having a given characteristic at point *j*, the physical scientist would use X_j to represent mass at point *j*. The symbol D_j has the same meaning for both—distance from *i* to *j*. The potential at point *i* becomes $\Sigma\frac{X_j}{D_j}$, the sum of gravitational forces at *i*.

Imagine a population of thirty village-migrant families living in the following areal pattern, where each subarea contains five village families in a unit square:

1	2
3	4
5	6

The village-migrant population potential for area 1 equals

$$P_{vi} = \Sigma X_j / D_j =$$
$$5/.35\sqrt{2} + 5/1 + 5/1 + 5/\sqrt{2} + 5/\sqrt{2} + 5/\sqrt{5} = 28.4.$$

All terms except the first should be obvious. For example, the contribution to potential for area 1 from area 4 is five families divided by their distance from area 1, the distance being $\sqrt{2}$, given unit squares. The first term is the contribution to potential in area 1 from area 1. This contribution is sometimes explicitly ignored and should be ignored if each observation is a point. Typically one has data for several observations within an area, say, a city block. If one wants to include the contribution from the local area, questions are usually raised about the appropriate distance factor. For squares and rectangles of almost any shape (the way most blocks look), the average distance between points is approximately $0.35 \times$ diagonal. In the example given, the distance would be about $0.35\sqrt{2}$. The data presented in this chapter include the contributions from the local area to the calculation of potential for the local area (block) based on measurements of actual diagonals. In the hypothetical configuration given above: $P_{v1} = P_{v2} = P_{v5} = P_{v6} = 28.4$ and $P_{v3} = P_{v4} = 32.2$. Blocks closer to the center of gravity have the highest potential.

Theoretically, villagelike behavior among village migrants to a city should be a function of access to other village migrants and access to the indigenous urban population. This is the basis of the argument made in the chapter that a series of small squatter settlements is likely to lead to a more rapid acculturation than would be the case given one large squatter settlement. This can be illustrated by using the potentials.

Imagine a city divided into thirty-unit subareas with five families in each area:

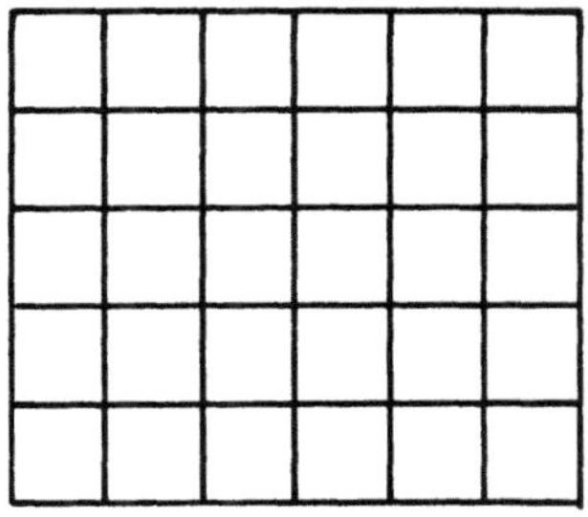

Now imagine three models of this city, each containing thirty village-migrant families (shaded) and 120 urban families:

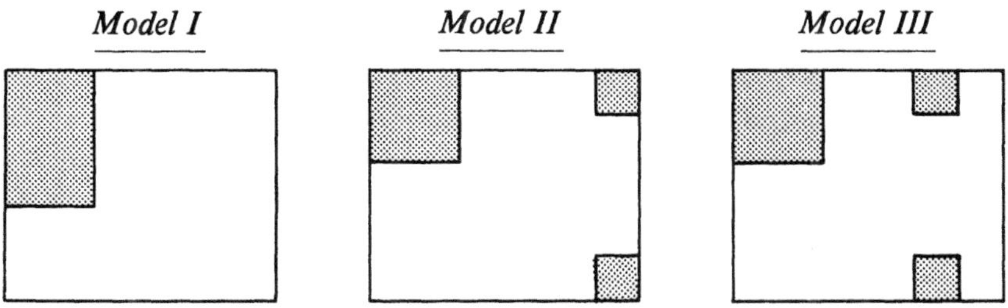

Let us define villager access as $VA = \Sigma N_{vi}P_{vi}$ and urbanite access as $UA = \Sigma N_{vi}P_{ui}$, where N_{vi} = number of village families in area i; P_{vi} = population potential for villagers in area i; and P_{ui} = population potential for urbanites in area i. VA is the aggregate access of villagers to themselves and UA is the aggregate access of villagers to urbanites. Using appropriate Ns and population potentials from the three models of the community, I obtain:

	Model I	*Model II*	*Model III*
Villager access (for villagers)	890	666	684
Urbanite access (for villagers)	1256	1315	1388

If villager fertility is directly related to villager access and inversely related to urbanite access, then Models II and III will produce lower fertility than Model I because there is lower-aggregate access to villagers and higher-aggregate access to urbanites in Models II and III. The distinction between Models II and III is a function of the relative sizes of the coefficients, not made explicit here.

Although the examples may be trivial and obvious, they do illustrate some possible effects where there is some degree of freedom in location of sites. The alternative locations set up the possibilities for experimental manipulation. This problem of the less developed countries should sound familiar to Americans living in the 1970s.

References

Abu-Lughod, Janet. 1964. "Urban–Rural Differences as a Function of the Demographic Transition," *American Journal of Sociology* 69(5):476–490 (March).

Acton, J. P. 1973. *Evaluating Public Programs to Save Lives: The Case of Heart Attacks.* Santa Monica, Calif.: The Rand Corporation, R-950-RC.

Adelman, Irma. 1963. "An Econometric Analysis of Population Growth," *American Economic Review* 53(3):314–339 (June).

———, and Cynthia Taft Morris. 1966. "A Quantitative Study of Social Political Determinants of Fertility," *Economic Development and Cultural Change* 1(2):129–157 (January).

———, and ———. 1968. "Performance Criteria for Evaluating Economic Development Potential: An Operational Approach," *Quarterly Journal of Economics* 82(2):260–280 (May).

Adlakha, Arjun. 1972. "Model Life Tables: An Empirical Test of Their Applicability to Less Developed Countries," *Demography* 9(4):589–601 (November).

Afzal, Mohammad, Lee L. Bean, and Imtiazuddin Husain. 1973. "Muslim Marriages: Age, *Mehr,* and Social Status," *Pakistan Development Review* 12(1):48–61 (Spring).

Amemiya, T. 1973. "Regression Analysis When the Dependent Variable Is Truncated Normal," *Econometrica* 41:997–1016 (November).

American Technical Assistance Corporation (ATAC). 1971. *AID-Supported Programs to Improve Primary Education in Northeast Brazil.* Washington, D.C.

Anderson, C. A., and M. J. Bowman, eds. 1965. *Education and Economic Development.* Chicago: Aldine.

Anderson, J. E. 1975. "The Relationship Between Change in Educational Attainment and Fertility Rates in Taiwan," *Studies in Family Planning* 6(3):72–81 (March).

Andrews, Frank, James Morgan, and John Sonquist. 1967. *Multiple Classification Analysis.* Ann Arbor: Survey Research Center, University of Michigan.

Anker, Richard Bruce. 1973. "Socio-Economic Determinants of Reproductive Behavior in Households of Rural Gujarat, India." Ph.D. dissertation, University of Michigan.

———. 1974. *An Analysis of International Variations in Birth Rates: Preliminary Results.* World Employment Program working paper no. 3. Geneva: International Labour Organisation.

Antonovsky, Anton. 1967. "Social Class, Life Expectancy, and Overall Mortality," *Milbank Memorial Fund Quarterly* 45(2):31–73 (April, pt. 1).

Arensberg, Conrad M. 1937. *The Irish Countryman.* New York: Macmillan.

Arriaga, E. E. 1967a. "Rural–Urban Mortality in Developing Countries: An Index for Detecting Rural Underregistration," *Demography* 4(1):98–107.

———. 1967b. "The Effects of a Decline in Mortality on the Gross Reproduction Rate," *Milbank Memorial Fund Quarterly* 46(3):333–352 (July).

———. 1970. *Mortality Decline and Its Demographic Effects in Latin America.* Berkeley: University of California Population Monograph Series, no. 6.

———, and Kingsley Davis. 1969. "The Pattern of Mortality Change in Latin America," *Demography* 6(3):223–242 (August).

Ashenfelter, Orley. 1973. "Comment," *Journal of Political Economy* 81(2):S96–98 (March/April, pt. 2).

Austin, J. E., and F. J. Levinson. 1974. "Population and Nutrition: A Case for Integration," *Milbank Memorial Fund Quarterly* 52(2):169–184 (Spring).

Baird, Dugald. 1965. "Variations in Fertility Associated with Changes in Health Status." In *Public Health and Population Change.* Pittsburgh: University of Pittsburgh Press.

Baker, Timothy, and Mark Perlman. 1968. *Health Manpower in a Developing Economy in Taiwan, A Case Study in Planning.* Baltimore: Johns Hopkins University Press.

Balassa, Bela. 1964. "The Purchasing Power Parity Doctrine: A Reappraisal," *Journal of Political Economy* 72(6):584–596 (December).

Balfour, Marshall C. 1962. "A Scheme for Rewarding Successful Family Planners." Mimeographed.

Banfield, Edward. 1958. *The Moral Basis of a Backward Society.* Chicago: Free Press.

Banks, Joseph A. 1954. *Prosperity and Parenthood.* London: Routledge and Kegan Paul.

Barlow, Robin. 1967. "The Economic Effects of Malaria Eradication," *American Economic Review* 57(2):130–148 (May).

Barnett, L. D. 1969. "Population Policy: Payments for Fertility Limitation in the United States?" *Social Biology* 16(4):239-248 (December).

Beaver, M. W. 1973. "Population, Infant Mortality, and Milk," *Population Studies* 27(2):242–254 (July).

Becker, Gary S. 1960. "An Economic Analysis of Fertility." In *Demographic and Economic Change in Developed Countries,* pp. 209–231. Universities National Bureau Conference Series 11. Princeton, N.J.: Princeton University Press for the National Bureau of Economic Research.

———. 1965. "A Theory of the Allocation of Time," *Economic Journal* 75(299):493–517 (September).

———. 1973. "A Theory of Marriage: Part I," *Journal of Political Economy* 81(4):813–846 (July/August).

———. 1974. "A Theory of Marriage: Part II," *Journal of Political Economy* 82(2):S11–26 (March/April, pt. 2).

Becker, G. S., and H. G. Lewis. 1973. "On the Interaction Between the Quantity and Quality of Children," *Journal of Political Economy* 81(2):S279–288 (March/April, pt. 2).

Behrman, Jere. 1968. *Supply Response in Underdeveloped Agriculture: A Case Study of Four Major Annual Crops in Thailand, 1937–1963*. Amsterdam: North-Holland.

———. 1969. "Supply Response and Modernization in Peasant Agriculture." In *Subsistence Agriculture and Economic Development*, edited by C. R. Wharton, Jr. Chicago: Aldine.

Belmont, L., and F. A. Marolla. 1973. "Birth Order, Family Size, and Intelligence," *Science* 182(4117):1096–1101 (December 14).

Ben-Porath, Yoram. 1970. "Fertility in Israel, An Economist's Interpretation: Differentials and Trends, 1950–1970." Santa Monica, Calif.: The Rand Corporation, RM-5981-FF. Reprinted in Cooper, C. A., and S. S. Alexander, eds. 1972. *Economic Development and Population Growth in the Middle East*. New York: American Elsevier.

———. 1973a. "Economic Analysis for Fertility in Israel: Point and Counterpoint," *Journal of Political Economy* 81(2):S202–233 (March/April, supplement 2).

———. 1973b. "Short-term Fluctuations in Fertility and Economic Activity in Israel," *Demography* 10(2):185–204 (May).

———. 1973c. "Labor-Force Participation and the Supply of Labor," *Journal of Political Economy* 81(3):697–704 (May/June).

———. 1974a. "Child Mortality and Fertility." Mimeographed.

———. 1974b. "Notes on the Micro Economics of Fertility," *International Social Science Journal* 26(2):302–314.

———. 1975. "Fertility in Israel: A Mini Survey and Some New Findings." In *Economic Aspects of Population Growth*, edited by A. J. Coale. International Economics Association Conference. New York: Halsted Press.

———, and Finis Welch. 1972. *Chance, Child Traits, and the Choice of Family Size*. Santa Monica, Calif.: The Rand Corporation, R-1117-NIH/RF.

Berelson, Bernard. 1966. "KAP Studies on Fertility." In *Family Planning and Population Programs: A Review of World Developments*. Proceedings of the International Conference on Family Planning Programs, Geneva, 1965. Chicago: University of Chicago Press.

———. 1969. "Beyond Family Planning," *Studies in Family Planning,* no. 38 (February).

———. 1973. "Status Report on Population Developments." Paper presented at the Third Population Conference, Bellagio, Italy (May).

———. 1974. "An Evaluation of the Effects of Population Control Programs," *Studies in Family Planning* 5(1):2–12 (January).

———, Paul Lazarsfeld, and William McPhee. 1954. *Voting.* Chicago: University of Chicago Press.

———, and Gary Steiner. 1944. *Human Behavior: An Inventory of Scientific Findings.* New York: Harcourt, Brace and World.

Berg, Alan (with Robert Muscat). 1973. *The Nutrition Factor: Its Role in National Development.* Washington, D.C.: Brookings Institution.

Bhutnagar, Shri. 1972. "Status of Women and Family Planning in India," *The Journal of Family Welfare* 18(3):21–29 (April).

Billings, Martin H., and A. Singh. 1970. "Mechanization and Rural Employment," *Economic and Political Weekly* 5(26):1–10 (June).

Bilsborrow, Richard. 1973a. "Fertility, Savings Rates, and Economic Development in Less Developed Countries." In *Proceedings of the International Population Conference,* pp. 445–458. Liège: International Union for the Scientific Study of Population.

———. 1973b. "Effects of Economic Dependency on Labor Force Participation Rates in Less Developed Countries." Chapel Hill: University of North Carolina. Mimeographed.

Bindary, Aziz. 1972. "New Approaches to Rural Population Problems." Paper prepared for the United Nations FAO/UNFPA Seminar on Population Problems as Related to Food and Rural Development in the Near East, Cairo.

———. 1975. "The Women's Employment Action Research Project." Processed. Cairo: Family Planning Board.

———, Colin B. Baxter, and T. H. Hollingsworth. 1973. "Urban–Rural Differences in the Relationship Between Women's Employment and Fertility: A Preliminary Study," *Journal of Biosocial Science* 5(2):159–167 (April).

Bjork, Robert M. 1971. "Population Education and Modernization." In *Education in National Development,* edited by Don Adams. London: Routledge and Kegan Paul.

Blake, Judith. 1965. "Demographic Science and the Redirection of Population Policy," *Journal of Chronic Diseases* 18:1181–2000.

———. 1967. "Parental Control, Delayed Marriage and Population Policy." In United Nations, *Proceedings of the World Population Conference,* vol. 2.

———. 1968. "Are Babies Consumer Durables? A Critique of the Economic Theory of Reproduction Motivation," *Population Studies* 22:5–25 (March).

———. 1974. "Can We Believe Recent Data on Birth Expectations in the U.S.?" *Demography* 2(1):25–44 (February).

Blalock, H. M. 1969. *Theory Construction: From Verbal to Mathematical Formulations*. Englewood Cliffs, N.J.: Prentice-Hall.
———. 1971. *Causal Models in the Social Sciences*. Chicago: Aldine.
Blandy, Richard J. 1974. "The Welfare Analysis of Fertility Reduction," *Economic Journal* 84(333):109–129 (March).
Blau, P. M., and O. D. Duncan. 1967. *The American Occupational Structure*. New York: John Wiley and Sons.
Bogue, Donald J. 1969. *Principles of Demography*. New York: John Wiley and Sons.
Bonte, M., and H. Vanbalen. 1969. "Prolonged Lactation and Family Spacing in Rwanda," *Journal of Biological Science* 1:97–100.
Boserup, Ester. 1965. *The Conditions of Agricultural Growth*. Chicago: Aldine.
———. 1970. *Women's Role in Economic Development*. New York: St. Martin's Press; London: George Allen & Unwin.
Branson, William H. 1968. "Social Legislation and the Birth Rate in Nineteenth-century Britain," *Western Economic Journal* 6:134–144 (March).
Brass, William, ed. 1971. *Biological Aspects of Demography*. New York: Barnes and Noble.
Browning, H. L. 1968. "Life Expectancy and the Life Cycle—Some Interrelations." In *World Population—The View Ahead,* edited by R. N. Farmer, Long, and Stolnitz. Bloomington: Bureau of Business Research, Indiana University.
Bureau of Labor Statistics. 1960. "Estimating Equivalent Incomes or Budget Costs by Family Types," *Monthly Labor Review* 83:1197–1200 (November).
Burleson, Noel-David. 1969. "The Time Is Now: Population Education." Mimeographed. Cambridge, Mass.: Graduate School of Business, Center for Studies on Education and Development, Harvard University.
Butz, William P. 1972. *Research and Information Strategies to Improve Population Policy in Less Developed Countries*. Santa Monica, Calif.: The Rand Corporation, R-952-AID.
Cain, Glen G. 1973. "The Effect of Income Maintenance Laws on Fertility: Preliminary Results from the New Jersey-Pennsylvania Experiment." Paper presented at the annual meeting of the Population Association of America.
———, and Adriana Weininger. 1973. "Economic Determinants of Fertility: Results from Cross-sectional Aggregate Data," *Demography* 10(2):205–223 (May).
Caldwell, John C. 1967. "Fertility Attitudes in Three Economically Contrasting Rural Regions of Ghana," *Economic Development and Cultural Change* 15(2):217–238 (January).
———. 1968a. "The Control of Family Size in Tropical Africa," *Demography* 5(2):598–619 (January).
———. 1968b. "The Demographic Implications of the Extension of Education in a Developing Country: Ghana." Paper presented at the meeting of the Population Association of America, Seminar 6.

———. 1968c. *Population Growth and Family Change in Africa: The New Urban Elite in Ghana.* New York: Humanities Press.

Cantrelle, Pierre, and Henri Leridon. 1971. "Breast Feeding, Mortality in Childhood, and Fertility in a Rural Zone of Senegal," *Population Studies* 25(3):505–533 (November).

Carleton, Robert O. 1965. "Labor Force Participation: A Stimulus to Fertility in Puerto Rico?" *Demography* 2:233–239.

———. 1967. "The Effect of Educational Improvement on Fertility Trends in Latin America." In *Proceedings of the World Population Conference, Belgrade, 1965*, vol. 4, pp. 141–145. New York: UN.

Carr-Saunders, A. M. 1922. *The Population Problem: A Study in Human Evolution.* Oxford, England: Oxford University Press.

Cernada, George, and Laura Lu. 1972. "The Kaoshiung Study," *Studies in Family Planning* 3(8):198–203.

Chandrasekhar, Sripati. 1972. *Infant Mortality, Population Growth and Family Planning in India.* Chapel Hill: University of North Carolina Press; London: George Allen and Unwin.

Chase, H. C. "Registration Completeness and International Comparisons of Infant Mortality," *Demography* 6(4):425–433.

Chayanov, A. V. 1966. *The Theory of Peasant Economy*, edited by Daniel Thorner, Basile Kerblay, and R. E. F. Smith. Homewood, Ill.: Richard D. Irwin.

Chen, L. C., and W. H. Mosley. 1974. "Population Control: What Is the Impact and Role of Health Programs?" Unpublished. Baltimore: The Johns Hopkins University.

Cheung, S. N. S. 1972. "Enforcement of Property Rights in Children and the Marriage Contract," *Economic Journal* 82(326):641–657 (June).

Chou, L. P. 1971. A "Positive" Incentive Scheme Encouraging Family Planning Practice in Rural Areas—Draft Proposal. Baltimore: The Johns Hopkins University, Department of Population Dynamics. Mimeographed.

———. 1972. "Study on the Feasibility of a Monetary Incentive Scheme to Encourage Fertility Control Practices." Baltimore: The Johns Hopkins University, Department of Population Dynamics. Mimeographed.

Chung, Bo Mo, J. A. Palmore, and S. J. Lee. 1972. *Psychological Perspectives: Family Planning in Korea.* Seoul: Hullym Corporation.

Clark, Colin. 1967. *Population Growth and Land Use.* New York: St. Martin's Press.

Cleave, John H. 1970. "Labor in the Development of African Agriculture." Ph.D. dissertation, Stanford University.

Coale, A. J. 1965. "Birth Rates, Death Rates, and Rates of Growth of Human Populations." In *Public Health and Population Change*, edited by M. C. Sheps and J. C. Ridley. Pittsburgh: University of Pittsburgh Press.

———. 1972. *The Growth and Structure of Human Population.* Princeton, N.J.: Princeton University Press.

———. 1973. "The Demographic Transition Reconsidered." Paper presented at the International Population Conference of the International Union for the Scientific Study of Population, Liège, Belgium.

———, and P. Demeny. 1966. *Regional Modal Life Tables and Stable Populations*. Princeton, N.J.: Princeton University Press.

———, and E. M. Hoover. 1958. *Population Growth and Economic Development in Low-Income Countries*. Princeton, N.J.: Princeton University Press.

Cogan, J. F. 1975. *Labor Supply and the Value of the Housewife's Time*. Santa Monica, Calif.: The Rand Corporation, R-1461-OEO/EDA/RF.

Cohen, J. E. 1975. "Childhood Mortality, Family Size, and Birth Order in Pre-Industrial Europe," *Demography* 12(1):35–55 (February).

Cohen, Richard. 1972. "The Relationship of Ownership of Television and Radio to Use of the Mass Media in Taiwan." Unpublished. Ann Arbor: Population Studies Center, University of Michigan.

Cole, Arthur. 1962. "Durable Consumer Goods and American Economic Growth," *Quarterly Journal of Economics* 76(3):415–423.

Coleman, James S. et al. 1966. *Equality of Educational Opportunity*. Washington, D.C.: U.S. Gov. Print. Off.

Collier, Frances. 1964. *The Family Economy of the Working Classes in the Cotton Industry*. Manchester, England: Manchester University Press.

Collver, Andrew, and Eleanor Langlois. 1967. "The Female Labor Force in Metropolitan Areas: An International Comparison," *Economic Development and Cultural Change* 10(4):367–385.

Commission on Population Growth and the American Future. 1972. *Aspects of Population Growth Policy*. Research Papers, vol. 6. Washington, D.C.

Correa, Hector, and Gaylord Cummins. 1970. "Contribution of Nutrition to Economic Growth," *The American Journal of Clinical Nutrition* 23(5):500–565 (May).

Crawford, Thomas J. 1971. "Beliefs about Birth Control and Their Relationship to Attitudes and Reported Behavior." In *Conference Proceedings: Psychological Measurement in the Study of Population Problems*. Berkeley: Institute of Personality Assessment and Research, University of California.

Cromwell, Ronald E., Ramon Corrales, and Peter M. Torsiello. 1973. "Normative Patterns of Marital Decision Making Power and Influence in Mexico and the United States: A Partial Test of Resource and Ideology Theory," *Journal of Comparative Family Studies* 4(2):177–196 (Autumn).

Dandekar, Kumundi. 1967. "Effect of Education on Fertility." In *Proceedings of the World Population Conference, Belgunda 1965*, pp. 146–149. New York: UN.

Das Gupta, Ajit, Ranjan Kumar Som, Murari Majumdar, and Shri Asok Mitra. 1955–56. "Couple Fertility. National Sample Survey No. 7," *Sankhya: The Indian Journal of Statistics* 16:230–434.

DaVanzo, Julie. 1972. *The Determinants of Family Formation in Chile, 1960*. Santa Monica, Calif.: The Rand Corporation, R-830-AID.

Davis, Kingsley. 1963. "The Theory of Change and Response in Modern Demographic History," *Population Index* 29(4):345–369 (October).

———. 1967. "Population Policy: Will Current Programs Succeed?" *Science* 158:730–739 (November 10).

———, and Judith Blake. 1956. "Social Structure and Fertility: An Analytical Framework," *Economic Development and Cultural Change* 4:211–235.

Demeny, Paul. 1961. "The Economics of Government Payments to Limit Population: A Comment," *Economic Development and Cultural Change* 9(2):641-644 (July).

———. 1965. "Investment Allocation and Population Growth," *Demography* 2:203–232.

De Tray, Dennis N. 1970. *An Economic Analysis of Quantity-Quality Substitution in Household Fertility Decisions.* Santa Monica, Calif.: The Rand Corporation, P-4449.

———. 1972. *The Interaction Between Parent Investment in Children and Family Size: An Economic Analysis.* Santa Monica, Calif.: The Rand Corporation, R-1003-RF.

———. 1973. "Child Quality and the Demand for Children," *Journal of Political Economy* 81(2):S70–95 (March/April, Supplement 2).

———. Forthcoming. *Education and Nonmarket Productivity.* Santa Monica, Calif.: The Rand Corporation, R-1838-HEW.

———. Forthcoming. "Child Schooling and Family Size: An Economic Interpretation." Santa Monica, Calif.: The Rand Corporation.

Dixon, Ruth B. 1971. "Explaining Cross-Cultural Variations in Age at Marriage and Proportions Never Marrying," *Population Studies* 25(2): 215–233 (July).

———. 1975. *Women's Rights and Fertility.* Reports on Population/Family Planning, no. 17 (January).

Dogan, Hasan. 1974. "Social Consequences of Residential Segregation in Ankara, Turkey." Ph.D. dissertation, University of Michigan.

Dorn, H. 1959. "Mortality." In *The Study of Population,* edited by P. M. Hauser and O. D. Duncan. Chicago: University of Chicago Press.

Dowie, J. A. 1970. "Valuing the Benefits of Health Improvement," *Australian Economic Papers,* pp. 21–41 (June).

Drake, Michael, ed. 1969. *Population in Industrialization.* London: Methuen & Company.

Driver, P. N., and D. K. Desai. 1962. *Studies in the Economics of Farm Management in Bombay State, 1954–55 to 1956–57.* New Delhi: Ministry of Food and Agriculture, Government of India.

Dube, S. C. 1963. "Men's and Women's Roles in India: A Sociological Review." In *Women in the New Asia,* edited by Barbara E. Ward. Amsterdam: UNESCO.

Dublin, L. I., and A. J. Lotka. 1946. *The Money Value of a Man.* New York: Ronald Press.

Duesenberry, James. 1960. Commentary on "An Economic Analysis of

Fertility," by Gary S. Becker. In *Demographic and Economic Change in Developed Countries.* Universities National Bureau Conference Series 11. Princeton, N.J.: Princeton University Press.

Duncan, Beverly. 1967. "Education and Social Background," *American Journal of Sociology* 72(4):363–372 (January).

Duncan, Otis Dudley. 1964. "Residential Areas and Differential Fertility," *Eugenics Quarterly* 2(2):82–89 (June).

———. 1966. "Path Analysis: Sociological Examples," *American Journal of Sociology* 72(1):1–16 (July).

———, D. L. Featherman, and Beverly Duncan. 1972. *Socioeconomic Background and Achievement.* New York: Seminar Press.

Durand, John D. 1973. "Economic Development and Dimensions of the Labor Force: Some Results of a Comparative International Study." In *Proceedings of the International Population Conference,* pp. 397–408. Liège: International Union for the Scientific Study of Population.

———. 1975. *The Labor Force in Economic Development: A Comparison of International Census Statistics: 1946–66.* Princeton, N.J.: Princeton University Press.

Easterlin, Richard A. 1968. *Population, Labor Force, and Long Swings in Economic Growth: The American Experience.* General Series 86. New York: National Bureau of Economic Research.

———. 1969. Towards a Socio-Economic Theory of Fertility: Survey of Recent Research on Economic Factors in American Fertility." In *Fertility and Family Planning: A World View,* edited by S. J. Behrman, pp. 127–150. Ann Arbor: University of Michigan Press.

———. 1971. "Does Fertility Adjust to the Environment?" *American Economic Review* 61:399–407 (May).

———. 1973. "The Economics and Sociology of Fertility: A Synthesis." Philadelphia: The University of Pennsylvania. Mimeographed.

———. Forthcoming. "The Economics and Sociology of Fertility: A Synthesis." In *Historical Studies of Changing Fertility,* edited by Charles Tilly. Princeton, N.J.: Princeton University Press.

Eaton, J. W., and A. J. Mayer. 1954. *Man's Capacity to Reproduce: The Demography of a Unique Population.* Glencoe, Ill.: Free Press.

Encarnacion, Jose. 1972. "Family Income, Educational Level, Labor Force Participation, and Fertility." Mimeographed.

Enke, Stephen. 1960a. "The Gains to India from Population Control: Some Money Measures and Incentive Schemes," *Review of Economics and Statistics* 42:175–180 (May).

———. 1960b. "The Economics of Government Payments to Limit Population," *Economic Development and Cultural Change* 8(4):339–348 (July).

———. 1961. "A Rejoinder to Comments on the Superior Effectiveness of Vasectomy-Bonus Schemes," *Economic Development and Cultural Change* 9(3):645–647 (July).

———. 1962. "Some Misconceptions of Krueger and Sjaastad Regarding the Vasectomy-Bonus Plan to Reduce Births in Overpopulated and Poor Countries," *Economic Development and Cultural Change* 10(3):427–431 (July).

———. 1963. *Economics for Development.* Englewood Cliffs, N.J.: Prentice-Hall.

———. 1966. "The Economic Aspects of Slowing Population Growth," *Economic Journal* 76:44–56 (March).

Ensign, Forest C. 1969. *Compulsory School Attendance and Child Labor.* American Education: Its Men, Institutions, and Ideas series. New York: Arno Press, reprint of 1921 edition.

Epstein, T. S. 1967. "The Data of Economics in Anthropological Analysis." In *The Craft of Social Anthropology,* edited by A. L. Epstein, pp. 153–180. London: Social Science Paperbacks.

Espenshade, T. J. 1973. *The Cost of Children in the United States.* Population Monograph Series no. 14. Berkeley: Institute of International Studies, University of California.

Ettore, Denti. 1968. "Sex-age Patterns of Labor Force Participation by Urban and Rural Populations," *International Labour Review* 98(6):525–550 (December).

Fawcett, James T. 1971. "Attitude Measures in KAP Studies: An Overview and Critique." In *Conference Proceedings: Psychological Measurement in the Study of Population Problems,* pp. 11–18. Berkeley: Institute of Personality Assessment and Research, University of California.

———, F. Arnold, R. A. Bulato et al. 1974. "The Value of Children in Asia and the United States: Comparative Perspectives." Paper presented at the annual meeting of the Population Association of America, New York, April.

Feldstein, Martin. 1966. "A Binary Variable Multiple Regression Method of Analyzing Factors Affecting Perinatal Mortality and Other Outcomes of Pregnancy," *Journal of the Royal Statistical Society* A 129.

Felson, Marcus, and Mauricio Solaun. 1974. "The Effect of Crowded Apartments on Fertility in a Colombian Public Housing Project." Mimeographed. Urbana-Champaign: University of Illinois, Workshop Papers in Applied Social Statistics.

Fernando, D. F. S. 1973. "Female Educational Attainments and Fertility."

Finnigan, Oliver D. III. 1972. "Testing Incentive Plans for Moving Beyond Family Planning." Mimeographed. Manila.

———, and T. H. Sun. 1972. "Planning, Starting, and Operating an Educational Incentives Project," *Studies in Family Planning* 3(1):1–7 (January).

Firth, Raymond. 1936. *We, the Tikopia.* London: Allen and Unwin.

———. 1939, 1965. *Primitive Polynesian Economy.* London: Routledge and Kegan Paul.

Flinn, M. W. 1970. *British Population Growth, 1700–1850.* London: Macmillan.

Fogel, R. W., and S. L. Engerman. 1974. *Time on the Cross.* 2 vols. Boston: Little, Brown.

Ford, Clellan S. 1952. "Control of Contraception in Cross-Cultural Perspective." In *World Population Problems and Birth Control. Annals of the New York Academy of Sciences* 54:763–768 (May).

Frankel, Richard. 1973. "A System Approach to Assessment of Rural Water Supply Program Effectiveness." Lucerne: Paper presented at the International Development Research Seminar, June.

Frederiksen, Harold. 1960. "Malaria Control and Population Pressure in Ceylon," *Public Health Reports* 75(10):865–868 (October). Reprinted in *Readings in Population,* edited by David Heer. Englewood Cliffs, N.J.: Prentice-Hall.

———. 1961. "Determinants and Consequences of Mortality Trends in Ceylon," *Public Health Reports* 76(8):659–663 (August).

Freedman, Deborah S. 1963. "The Relation of Economic Status to Fertility," *American Economic Review* 53(3):414–426 (June).

———. 1970. "The Role of Consumption of Modern Durables in Economic Development," *Economic Development and Cultural Change* 19(1):25–48 (October).

———. 1972a. "Consumption Aspirations as Economic Incentives in a Developing Country—Taiwan." In *Human Behavior in Economic Affairs,* edited by Burkhard Strumpel, James Morgan, and Ernest Zahn. Amsterdam: Elsevier.

———. 1972b. "Family Size and Economic Welfare." *Proceedings of the American Statistical Association,* pp. 240–244.

———. Unpublished tables. 1973. Ann Arbor: Population Studies Center, University of Michigan.

Freedman, Ronald. 1963. "Norms for Family Size in Underdeveloped Countries," *Proceedings of the Royal Statistical Society* B 159:220–245.

———. 1974. *Community-Level Data in Fertility Surveys.* Occasional papers, no. 8. London: World Fertility Survey, International Statistical Institute.

———. 1975a. *The Sociology of Human Fertility.* New York: John Wiley and Sons.

———. 1975b. Personal communication to Robert G. Repetto, March.

———, and Lolagene C. Coombs. 1974. "Cross-cultural Comparisons: Data on Two Factors in Fertility Behavior." Occasional Paper. New York: Population Council.

———, ———, Ming-Cheng Chang, and Te-Hsiung Sun. 1974. "Trends in Fertility, Family Size Preference, and Practice of Family Planning: Taiwan, 1965–1973," *Studies in Family Planning* 5(9):270–288 (September).

———, ———, and J. Friedman. 1966. "Social Correlates of Foetal Mortality," *Milbank Memorial Fund Quarterly* 44:327–344.

———, P. K. Whelpton, and A. A. Campbell. 1959. *Family Planning, Sterility, and Population Growth.* New York: McGraw-Hill.

Frejka, Tomas. 1971. "Demographic Aspects of Women's Employment," *International Population Conference, London, 1969,* vol. 3. Liège: International Union for the Scientific Study of Population.

Frieden, Alan. 1974. "The U.S. Marriage Market," *Journal of Political Economy* 82(2):S34–53 (March/April, pt. 2).

Friedlander, Stanley, and Morris Silver. 1967. "A Quantitative Study of the Determinants of Fertility Behavior," *Demography* 4(1):30–70.

Frisch, R. E. 1974. "The Critical Weight at Menarche and the Initiation of the Adolescent Growth Spurt, and the Control of Puberty." In *The Control of the Onset of Puberty,* edited by M. M. Grumback, G. Grave, and F. Mayer. New York: John Wiley and Sons.

Fuchs, Victor. 1973. "Some Aspects of Mortality in Developed Countries." Paper presented at a conference of the International Economics Association, April.

Gaisie, S. K. 1975. "Levels and Patterns of Infant and Child Mortality in Ghana," *Demography* 12(1):21–34 (February).

Galenson, Walter, and Graham Pyatt. 1964. *The Quality of Labor and Economic Development in Certain Countries.* Geneva: International Labour Office.

Garcia, E., and A. Ramirez. 1971. *Informe final del estudio de los niveles de vida en la Republica Dominicana.* Santo Domingo: Research Center of the National University, Pedro Henriquez Urena.

Gardner, Bruce. 1973. "Economics of the Size of North Carolina Rural Families," *Journal of Political Economy* 81(2):S99–122 (March/April, pt. 2).

Geissler, A. 1885. "Über den Einfluss der Säuglingssterblichkeit auf die eheliche Fruchtbarkeit," *Zeitschrift des Sächsishen statistischen Bureaus* 31:23–27.

Gendell, Murray. 1967. "The Influence of Family-Building Activity on Woman's Rate of Economic Activity." In *United Nations World Population Conference,* vol. 4. New York: UN.

———, Maria Nydia Maraviglia, and Philip C. Kreitner. 1970. "Fertility and Economic Activity of Women in Guatemala City, 1964," *Demography* 7(3): 273–286.

Gibbs, Arthur. 1974. "Agricultural Modernization and Low-level Urbanization." Ph.D. dissertation, University of Michigan.

Gille, Halvor. 1949. "The Demographic History of the Northern European Countries in the Eighteenth Century," *Population Studies* 3:3–70 (June).

———. 1971. "Summary Review of Fertility Differentials in Developed Countries." In *International Population Conference, London, 1969.* Liège: International Union for the Scientific Study of Population.

Gillespie, Robert. n.d. "Economic Incentives in Family Planning Programs." New York: Population Council. Mimeographed.

———. 1969. *Second Five-Year Plan for Economic and Social Development, United Republic of Tanzania.* Dar-es-Salaam: Gov. Print. Off.

Glass, D. V. 1940. *Population Policies and Movements in Europe.* Oxford, England: Clarendon Press.

———, and E. Grebenik. 1966. "World Population, 1800–1950." In *The Industrial Revolutions and After,* edited by H. J. Havakkuk and M. Postan. Cambridge Economic History of Europe, vol. 6. Cambridge, England: Cambridge University Press.

Goldberg, David. 1974. *Modernism: The Extensiveness of Women's Roles and Attitudes.* Occasional paper no. 14. World Fertility Survey.

Goldstein, Sidney. 1972. "The Influence of Labour Force Participation and Education on Fertility in Thailand," *Population Studies* 26(3):419–436 (November).

Goode, William J. 1963. *World Revolution and Family Patterns.* New York: Free Press.

Goodman, Leo A. 1971. "The Analysis of Multidimensional Contingency Tables: Step-wise Procedures and Direct Estimation Methods for Building Models for Multiple Classifications," *Technometrics* 13:33–61 (February).

———. 1972a. "A Modified Multiple Regression Approach to the Analysis of Dichotomous Variables," *American Sociological Review* 33:28–46 (February).

———. 1972b. "A General Model for the Analysis of Surveys," *American Journal of Sociology* 77:1035–1086 (May).

———. 1973. "Causal Analysis of Data from Panel Studies and Other Kinds of Surveys," *American Journal of Sociology* 78:1135–1191 (March).

Gopalan, C., and A. Nadamuni Naidu. 1972. "Nutrition and Fertility," *Lancet,* November 18, 1972.

Gordon, J. E., M. A. Guzman, W. Ascoli, and N. S. Scrimshaw. 1964. "Acute Diarrheal Disease in Less Developed Countries," *Bulletin of the World Health Organization* 31:1–28.

Gore, M. S. 1968. *Urbanization and Family Change.* Bombay: Popular Prakashan.

Gray, R. H. 1974. "The Decline of Mortality in Ceylon and the Demographic Effects of Malaria Control," *Population Studies* 28(2):205–229 (July).

Griffith, D. H., D. V. Ramana, and H. Mashaal. 1971. "Contribution of Health to Development," *International Journal of Health Services* 1:253–270 (August).

Griliches, Zvi. 1974. "Comment," *Journal of Political Economy* 82(2): S219–221 (March/April, pt. 2).

Gronau, Reuben. 1973a. "The Effect of Children on the Housewife's Value of Time," *Journal of Political Economy* 81(2):S168–199 (March/April, pt. 2).

———. 1973b. "The Intra-Family Allocation of Time: The Value of Housewives' Time," *American Economic Review* 63(4):634–651 (September).

Grossman, M. 1972. "On the Concept of Health Capital and the Demand for Health," *Journal of Political Economy* 80(2):223–255 (March/April).

Habicht, Jean-Pierre, and Moises Behar. 1974. "Nutrición, planificación familiar y salud en la madre y en el niño," *Revista social pediatria El Salvador* 4(2):48–60.

———, and Hernan Delgado. 1973. Unpublished data. Institute for Nutrition of Central America and Panama (INCAP).

———, ———, Charles Yarbrough, and R. E. Klein. 1973. "Repercussions of Lactation on Nutritional Status of the Mother and the Infant." In *Nutrition,* edited by A. Chavez, H. Bourges, and S. Basta, vol. 2, pp. 101–108. Basel: S. Karger.

———, and Robert Klein. 1972. "Possible Factors Affecting Acceptability of Fertility Regulation Methods in Four Guatemalan Ladino Villages." Paper presented at the WHO Task Force Symposium on Contraceptive Acceptability, Geneva, June 21–23.

———, Aaron Lechtig, Charles Yarbrough, and R. E. Klein. "The Timing of the Effect of Supplementation Feeding on the Growth of Rural Preschool Children."

———, ———, R. M. Malina, and Reynolds Martorell. 1972. "Height and Weight in Rural Guatemalan Ladino Children, Birth to Seven Years of Age." Manuscript in progress. Division of Human Development, Institute for Nutrition of Central America and Panama (INCAP).

———, Reynolds Martorell, Charles Yarbrough, R. M. Malina, and R. E. Klein. 1974. "Height and Weight Standards for Preschool Children: Are There Really Ethnic Differences in Growth Potential?" *Lancet* 1:611–615.

———, Charles Yarbrough, Aaron Lechtig, and R. E. Klein. 1973. "Relationships of Birthweight, Maternal Nutrition, and Infant Mortality," *Nutrition Reports International* 7(5):533–546.

Hajnal, John. 1953. "Age at Marriage and Proportions Marrying," *Population Studies* 7:130 (November).

Hanock, Giora. Forthcoming. *Theory and Estimation of a Complete Labor Supply Model.* Santa Monica, Calif.: The Rand Corporation, R-1869-HEW.

Hansen, Bent. 1969. "Employment and Wages in Rural Egypt," *American Economic Review* 59(3):298–313 (June).

Hansen, W. L. 1957. "A Note on the Cost of Children's Mortality," *Journal of Political Economy* 65(3) (June).

Harbison, Fred. 1965. "The Prime Movers of Innovation." In *Education and Economic Development,* edited by C. A. Anderson and M. J. Bowman. Chicago: Aldine.

Harbison, Frederick H. 1973. *Human Resources as the Wealth of Nations.* New York: Oxford.

Harman, A. J. 1970. *Fertility and Economic Behavior of Families in the Philippines.* Santa Monica, Calif.: The Rand Corporation, RM-6385-AID.

Hartwell, R. M. 1971. *The Industrial Revolution and Economic Growth.* London: Methuen.

Hashimoto, Masanori. 1974. "Economic Interpretations of Japanese Fertility Behavior," *Journal of Political Economy* 82(2):S170–194 (March/April, supplement).

Hass, Paula H. 1972. "Maternal Role Incompatibility and Fertility in Urban Latin America," *Journal of Social Issues* 28(2):111–127.

Hassan, S. 1966. "Influence of Child Mortality on Fertility." Paper presented at the annual meetings of the Population of Association of America, New York, April.

Hauser, Philip M. 1962. "Population-Gap in the Curriculum," *Teachers College Record* 63:425–433 (March).

Hawley, Amos. 1950. *Human Ecology*. New York: Ronald Press.

Hawthorn, Geoffrey. 1970. *The Sociology of Fertility*. London: Collier-Macmillan.

Heckman, James J. 1974. "Shadow Prices, Market Wages, and Labor Supply." *Econometrica* 42(4):679–694 (July).

———, and R. J. Willis. 1974. "Estimation of a Stochastic Model of Reproduction: An Econometric Approach." In *Household Production and Consumption,* edited by Nectos Terleckyj. New York: Columbia University Press.

Heer, David M. 1966. "Economic Development and Fertility," *Demography* 3(2):423–444.

———. 1972. "Determinants of Family Planning Attitudes and Practices." A report on contract AID/scd 2478 covering field study conducted in Taiwan during 1968–72.

———, and D. O. Smith. 1968. "Mortality Level, Desired Family Size and Population Increase," *Demography* 5:104–121.

Henry, Louis. 1972. *The Measurement of Fertility*. Translated by M. C. Sheps. New York: American Elsevier.

Hermalin, Albert I. 1972. "Taiwan: Appraising the Effect of a Family Planning Program through an Areal Analysis," *Population Papers* 2:1–39 (June). London: The Institute of Economic Academica Sinica.

———. 1975. "Empirical Research in Taiwan on Factors Underlying Differences in Fertility." In *Economic Aspects of Population Growth,* edited by A. J. Coale. New York: Halsted Press.

Hickman, Bryan D. 1972. *Economic Incentives: A Strategy for Family Planning Programs.* Santa Barbara, Calif.: G. E. Tempo.

Hicks, J. R. 1965. *Value and Capital.* Oxford, England: Clarendon Press (1939; reprinted 1965).

Hill, C. R., and F. P. Stafford. 1972. "Allocation of Time to Preschool Children and Educational Opportunity." Discussion paper. Ann Arbor: Institute of Public Policy Studies, University of Michigan.

Hill, Reuben, J. Mayone Stycos, and K. W. Back. 1959. *The Family and Population Control: A Puerto Rican Experiment in Social Change.* Chapel Hill: University of North Carolina Press.

Hinshaw, Robert, Patrick Pyaett, and Jean-Pierre Habicht. 1972. "Environmental Effects on Child-Spacing and Population Increase in Highland Guatemala," *Current Anthropology* 13(2):216–230 (April).

Holsinger, Donald B. 1974. "The Elementary School as a Modernizer." In *Education and Individual Modernity in Developing Countries,* edited by Alex Inkeles and Donald B. Holsinger. Leiden: E. J. Brill.

———. 1976. "The Schooling Environment as a Context for Individual Modernization."

Houthakker, H. S. 1952. "Compensated Changes in Quantities and Qualities Consumed," *Review of Economic Studies* 19(3):55–61.

Hsing, Mo-huan. 1960. "Relationships Between Agricultural and Industrial Development in Taiwan during 1950–59." Report prepared for the Economic Commission for Asia and the Far East (ECAFE) under the auspices of the Joint Commission for Rural Reconstruction (JCRR) of Taiwan.

Husain. 1970a. "Education Status and Differential Fertility in India," *Social Biology* 17(2):132–139.

———. 1970b. *An Urban Fertility Field: A Report on the City of Lucknow.* Lucknow: Demographic Research Center, Lucknow University.

Inayatullah, Attiya. 1963. "Impact of Culture on Fertility in Pakistan." In *Proceedings of the Seventh Conference of the IPPF*. Singapore.

Inkeles, Alex. 1969. "Making Men Modern: On the Causes and Consequences of Individual Change in Six Developing Countries," *American Journal of Sociology* 75:208–225 (September).

———. 1974. "The School as a Context for Modernization." In *Education and Individual Modernity in Developing Countries,* edited by Alex Inkeles and Donald B. Holsinger. Leiden: E. J. Brill.

———, and Donald B. Holsinger, eds. 1974. *Education and Individual Modernity in Developing Countries*. Leiden: E. J. Brill.

———, and David H. Smith. 1974. *Becoming Modern: Individual Change in Six Developing Countries.* Cambridge, Mass.: Harvard University Press.

Institute of National Planning. 1965. *Research Report on Employment Problems in Rural Areas*. Cairo.

International Bank for Reconstruction and Development (IBRD). 1974. *Population Policies and Economic Development*. Report no. 481. Baltimore: Johns Hopkins University Press.

———. 1973. "World Tables." Washington, D.C. Mimeographed.

International Labour Office. 1969. *Rural Employment Problems in the United Arab Republic*. Geneva.

———. n.d. *The Yearbook of Labour Statistics.*

International Labour Organisation. 1971, 1972, 1973. *Yearbook of Labour Statistics*.

Isard, Walter. 1960. *Methods of Regional Analysis: An Introduction to Regional Science*. Cambridge, Mass.: Massachusetts Institute of Technology Press.

Jaffe, A. J. 1959. *People, Jobs, and Economic Development*. Glencoe, Ill.: Free Press.

———, and K. Azumi. 1960. "The Birth Rate and Cottage Industries in Underdeveloped Countries," *Economic Development and Cultural Change* 9(1):52–63 (October).

Jahan, Rounaq. 1973. "Women in Bangladesh." Unpublished. Dacca: The Ford Foundation.

Jain, Anrudh K. 1968. "Fecundity Components in Taiwan: Application of a Stochastic Model of Human Reproduction." Ph.D. dissertation, University of Michigan.

———. 1969. "Socio-Economic Correlates of Fecundability in a Sample of Taiwanese Women," *Demography* 6(1):75–90 (February).

———, T. C. Hsu, Ronald Freedman, and M. C. Chang. 1970. "Demographic Aspects of Lactation and Postpartum Amenorrhea," *Demography* 7(2):255–271 (May).

Jain, Shail, and Arthur E. Tiemann. 1973. "Size Distribution of Income: Computation of Data." Discussion paper no. 4. Washington, D.C.: Development Research Center, International Bank for Reconstruction and Development (IBRD).

Jayasuriya, J. E. 1972. *Some Guidelines for Training Population Educators.* Bangkok: Asian Regional Office, UNESCO.

Johnson, D. G. 1974. "Population, Food and Economic Development," *American Statistician* 28(3):89–93 (August).

Johnson, G. Z. 1964. "Health Conditions in Rural and Urban Areas of Developing Countries," *Population Studies* 17(3):293–309 (March).

Johnson, Harry. 1968. "Economic Approaches to Social Questions," *Economica* n.s.35(137):1–21 (February).

Jones, Gavin. 1971. "Effect of Population Change on the Attainment of Educational Goals in the Developing Countries." In *Rapid Population Growth,* edited by the Committee of the National Academy of Sciences. Baltimore: The Johns Hopkins University Press.

Kallen, D. J., ed. 1972. *Nutrition, Development, and Social Behavior.* Washington, D.C.: U.S. Gov. Print. Off.

Kalvalsky, Basil. 1973. "An Experimental Program for Population Control and Social Security in Bangladesh." Washington, D.C.: World Bank. Mimeographed.

Kangas, L. W. 1970. "Integrated Incentives for Fertility Control," *Science* 169:1278–1283 (September).

Kankalil, M. S. 1973. "The Odds are Changing for Women in Nepal," *UNICEF News* 76:18–21.

Kasarda, John D. 1971. "Economic Structure and Fertility: A Comparative Analysis," *Demography* 8(3):307–317 (August).

Kelley, Allen C. 1973. "Population Growth, the Dependency Rate, and the Pace of Economic Development," *Population Studies* 27(3):405–414 (November).

Kershaw, David N. 1972. "A Negative Income Tax Experiment," *Scientific American* 227(4):19–25 (October).

———, and Jerilyn Fair. 1975. *Final Report on the New Jersey Experiment: Operations, Administration, and Surveys.* New York: Academic Press.

Khalifa, A. 1973. "The Status of Women and Family Planning in Egypt." Cairo: National Center of Social and Criminological Research.

Kirk, Dudley. 1969. "Natality in the Developing Countries: Recent Trends and Prospects." In *Fertility and Family Planning: A World View,* edited by S. J. Behrman, Leslie Corsa, and Ronald Freedman. Ann Arbor: University of Michigan Press.

———. 1971. "Some Reflections of a Sociologist Demographer on the Need for Psychological Skills in Family Planning Research." In *Conference Proceedings: Psychological Development Measurement in the Study of Population Problems*. Berkeley: Institute of Personality Assessment and Research, University of California.

Kitagawa, E. M., and P. M. Hauser. 1968. "Education Differentials in Mortality by Cause of Death, U.S. 1960," *Demography* 5(1):318–353.

———. 1973. *Differential Mortality in the United States*. Cambridge, Mass.: Harvard University Press.

Kleiman, E. 1967. "A Standardized Dependency Ratio," *Demography* 4(2):876–893.

Kleinman, David. 1973. "Fertility Variation and Resources in Rural India," *Economic Development and Cultural Change* 21(4):679–696 (July).

Kmenta, Jan. 1971. *Elements of Econometrics*. New York: Macmillan.

Knodel, J. E. 1968. "Infant Mortality and Fertility in Three Bavarian Villages—An Analysis of Family Histories from the Nineteenth Century," *Population Studies* 22(3):297–318 (November).

———. 1970. "Two and a Half Centuries of Demographic History in a Bavarian Village," *Population Studies* 24(3):353–376 (November).

———. 1974. *The Decline of Fertility in Germany, 1871–1939*. Princeton, N.J.: Princeton University Press.

———, and Etienne van de Walle. 1967. "Breast Feeding, Fertility, and Infant Mortality," *Population Studies* 21(2) (July).

Knowles, James C. 1970. "The Economic Effects of Health and Disease in an Underdeveloped Country." Ph.D. dissertation, University of Wisconsin.

Kocher, James E. 1973. *Rural Development, Income Distribution, and Fertility Decline*. Occasional paper. New York: Population Council.

Krueger, A. O., and L. A. Sjaastad. 1962. "Some Limitations of Enke's Economics of Population," *Economic Development and Cultural Change* 10(3):423–426.

Kripalani, Gul, P. Maitra, and T. Bose. 1971. "Education and Its Relation to Family Planning," *Journal of Family Welfare* 18(2):3–8 (December).

Krzywicki, Ludwik. 1934. *Primitive Society and Its Vital Statistics*. London: Macmillan.

Kuznets, Simon. 1965. "Demographic Aspects of Modern Economic Growth." Paper presented at the World Population Conference, September.

———. 1973. "Population Trends and Modern Economic Growth." Economic Growth Center Discussion Paper no. 191. New Haven, Conn.: Yale University.

———. 1974. "Rural-Urban Differences in Fertility: An International Comparison," *Proceedings of the American Philosophical Society* 118(1):1–29 (February).

Labour Bureau, Government of India. 1960. *Report on the Second Agricultural Labour Enquiry, 1956–57* (7 volumes). Vol. 1, All India. Simla.

Lacombe, B. 1972. "Fertility and Development in Senegal." In *Population Growth and Economic Development in Africa,* edited by S. H. Ominde and Charles Ejiougu, pp. 123–124. London: Heinemann.

Lal, Chaman. 1970. *A Review of the Delhi Pilot Rural Television Project and its Lessons.* Ahmadabad: India Space Research Organization.

Lancaster, K. J. 1966. "A New Approach to Consumer Theory," *Journal of Political Economy* 74(2):132–157 (April).

Land, K. C. 1969. "Principles of Path Analysis," In *Sociological Methodology 1969,* edited by Edgar Borgatta, pp. 3–37. San Francisco: Jossey-Bass.

Latham, Michael C., and Francisco Cobos. 1971. "The Effects of Malnutrition on Intellectual Development and Learning," *American Journal of Public Health* 61:1307–1324 (July).

Lave, L. B., and E. P. Seskin. 1973. "An Analysis of the Association Between U.S. Mortality and Air Pollution," *Journal of the American Statistical Association* 68(342):284–290 (June).

Lebergott, Stanley. 1960. "Population Change and the Supply of Labor." In *Demographic and Economic Change in Developed Countries.* Princeton, N.J.: Princeton University Press for the National Bureau of Economic Research.

Lechtig, Aaron. 1973. "Nutritional Status and Fertility." Mimeographed. Institute for Nutrition of Central America and Panama (INCAP).

Lee, Hoon K. 1936. *Land Utilization and Rural Economy in Korea.* New York: Greenwood Press.

Lee, Ronald. 1971. "Population in Pre-Industrial England: An Econometric Analysis." Mimeographed. Ann Arbor: Department of Economics and Population Studies Center, University of Michigan.

———. 1973. "Population in Pre-Industrial England," *Quarterly Journal of Economics* 87(4): 581–607 (November).

Lee, T. H. 1971. *Intersectoral Capital Flows in the Economic Development of Taiwan, 1895–1960.* Ithaca, N.Y.: Cornell University Press.

Leff, Nathaniel. 1969. "Dependency Rates and Savings Rates," *American Economic Review* 59(5):886–896 (December).

Leibenstein, Harvey. 1954. *A Theory of Economic-Demographic Development.* Princeton, N.J.: Princeton University Press.

———. 1957. *Economic Backwardness and Economic Growth: Studies in the Theory of Economic Development.* New York: John Wiley and Sons.

———. 1974. "An Interpretation of the Economic Theory of Fertility: Promising Path or Blind Alley?" *Journal of Economic Literature* 12(2): 457–479 (June).

Leibowitz, Arleen. 1974. "Home Investments in Children," *Journal of Political Economy* 82(2):S111–131 (March/April, pt. 2).

Lerner, Daniel. 1958. *The Passing of Traditional Society: Modernizing the Middle East.* New York: Free Press.

———, and Wilbur Schramm. 1967. *Communication and Change in Developing Countries*. Honolulu: East-West Center Press.

Levy, Marion, Jr. 1972. *Modernization: Latecomers and Survivors*. New York: Basic Books.

Lewis, Anthony. 1970. "How Pointless it all Seems Now," *New York Times Magazine,* February 8.

Lin, Carl. 1974. Master's thesis, Brown University.

Lindenbaum, Shirley. 1974. "The Social and Economic Status of Women in Bangladesh." Dacca: The Ford Foundation.

Lindert, Peter H. 1973. *The Relative Cost of American Children*. Economic History Discussion Papers. Madison: University of Wisconsin.

———. 1974. *Family Inputs and Inequality among Children*. Discussion Paper 218–74. Madison, Wis.: Institute for Research on Poverty.

———. Forthcoming. *Fertility and Scarcity in America*. Princeton, N.J.: Princeton University Press.

Lloyd, Cynthia. 1972. "The Effect of Child Subsidies on Fertility." Ph.D. dissertation, Columbia University.

Lorimer, Frank. 1954. *Culture and Human Fertility*. Paris: UNESCO.

———. 1965. "The Economics of Family Formation Under Different Conditions." In *World Population Conference,* vol. 2, pp. 92–95. New York: UN Department of Economic and Social Affairs.

McCabe, James L. 1974. "Economic Determinants of Fertility in Kinshasa Zaïre: An Analysis of the Published Data." Discussion paper no. 206. New Haven, Conn.: Economic Growth Center, Yale University.

———, and Mark R. Rosenzweig. 1976. "Female Labor Force Participation, Occupational Choice, and Fertility in Developing Countries," *Journal of Development Economics* 3:1–20 (June).

———, and David S. Sibley. 1974. "Two-Period Models of Savings and Fertility." Unpublished. Paper presented at meetings of the Econometric Society, San Francisco, December.

McDermott, Walsch. 1966. "Modern Medicine and the Demograph-Disease Pattern of Overly Traditional Societies: A Technological Misfit," *Journal of Medical Education* 41(9):137–162 (September).

McGreevey, William P., Nancy Birdsall, James Creager, Anne McCook, and Bernice Slutsky. 1974. *The Policy Relevance of Recent Social Research on Fertility*. Occasional monograph series no 2. Washington, D.C.: Interdisciplinary Communications Program, Smithsonian Institution.

McInnis, R. Marvin. 1972. "Birth Rates and Land Availability in Nineteenth Century Canada." Population Association of America paper.

McIntyre, Robert J. 1974. "Pronatalist Programs in Eastern Europe." Paper presented at the annual meetings of the Population Association of America, New York, April.

Macisco, J. J., L. F. Bouvier, and M. J. Renzi. 1969. "Migration Status, Education and Fertility in Puerto Rico," *Milbank Memorial Fund Quarterly* 47(2):167–187 (April).

Mack, Ruth. 1956. "Trends in American Consumption and the Aspiration to Consume," *American Economic Review* 46(2):55–68.

Malenbaum, Wilfred. 1970. "Health and Productivity in Poor Areas." In *Empirical Studies in Health Economics,* edited by Herbert E. Klarman, pp. 31–54. Baltimore: Johns Hopkins University Press.

Mamdani, Mahmoud. 1972. *The Myth of Population Control: Family, Caste and Class in an Indian Village.* New York: Monthly Review Press.

Mandelbaum, David. 1974. *Human Fertility in India.* Berkeley and Los Angeles: University of California Press.

Marshall, T. H. 1929. "The Population Problem during the Industrial Revolution," *Economic History* 1(4):429–456 (January).

Mason, Karen, David Abraham, Eva Gerstel, Quentin Lindsey, and Michael Rulison. n.d. *Social and Economic Correlates of Family Fertility: A Survey of the Evidence.* Research Triangle Institute.

Massialis, Byron. 1972. "Population Education as Exploration of Alternatives," *Social Education* (April) pp. 347–356.

Matras, Judah. 1973. *Population and Societies.* Englewood Cliffs, N.J.: Prentice-Hall.

Mauldin, W. Parker. 1975. "Assessment of National Family Planning Programs in Developing Countries," *Studies in Family Planning* 6(2): 30–36 (February).

———, Nazli Choucri, Frank W. Notestein, and Michael Teitelbaum. 1974. "A Report on Bucharest," *Studies in Family Planning* 5(12):357–396 (December).

Maurer, K. M., Rosalinda Ratajczak, and T. Paul Schultz. 1973. *Marriage, Fertility, and Labor Force Participation of Thai Women: An Econometric Study.* Santa Monica, Calif.: The Rand Corporation, R-829-AID.

May, D. A., and D. M. Heer. 1968. "Son Survivorship and Family Size in India: A Computer Simulation," *Population Studies* 22(2):199–210.

Mayer, A. J., and P. M. Hauser. 1953. "Class Differentials in Expectation of Life at Birth." In *Class Status and Power,* edited by Reinhardt Bendix and S. M. Lipset, pp. 281–284. Glencoe, Ill.: Free Press.

Meegama, S. A. 1967. "Malaria Eradication and Its Effects on Mortality Levels," *Population Studies* 21(3):207–237 (November).

Mendels, Franklin. 1970. "Industry and Marriages in Flanders Before the Industrial Revolution." In *Population and Economics,* edited by Paul Deprez. Winnipeg: University of Manitoba Press.

Michael, Robert T. 1971. "Education and Fertility." New York: National Bureau of Economic Research. Mimeographed.

———. 1972. "The Effect of Education on Efficiency in Consumption." Occasional paper no. 116. New York: National Bureau of Economic Research.

———. 1973a. "Education and the Derived Demand for Children," *Journal of Political Economy* 81(2):S128–164 (March/April, Supplement 2).

———. 1973b. "Education and Non-Market Production," *Journal of Political Economy* 81(2):306–327. (March/April).

———, and Gary S. Becker. 1973. "On the New Theory of Consumer Behavior," *Swedish Journal of Economics* 75(4):378–396 (December).
———, and R. J. Willis. 1976. "Contraception and Fertility: Household Production Under Uncertainty." In *Household Production and Consumption, Studies of Income and Wealth,* vol. 40. New York: National Bureau of Economic Research.
Miller, Karen A., and Alex Inkeles. 1974. "Modernity and Acceptance of Family Limitation in Four Developing Countries," *Journal of Social Issues* 30(4):167–188.
Mincer, Jacob. 1962. "Labor Force Participation of Married Women: A Study of Labor Supply." In *Aspects of Labor Economics.* Princeton, N.J.: Princeton University Press.
———. 1963. "Market Prices, Opportunity Costs, and Income Effects." In *Measurement in Economics: Studies in Mathematical Economics and Econometrics in Memory of Yehuda Grunfeld,* edited by Carl Christ et al., pp. 67–82. Stanford, Calif.: Stanford University Press.
———. 1974. *Schooling Experience and Earnings.* New York: Columbia University Press.
———, and Solomon Polachek. 1974. "Family Investments in Human Capital: Earnings of Women," *Journal of Political Economy* 82(2): S76–108 (March/April, pt. 2).
Minkler, Meredith. 1970. "Fertility and Female Labour Force Participation in India: A Survey of Workers in Old Delhi Area," *Journal of Family Welfare* 17(1):31–43 (September).
Miró, Carmen A., and Walter Mertens. 1968. "Influences Affecting Fertility in Urban and Rural Latin America," *Milbank Memorial Fund Quarterly* 46:89–117 (July, pt. 2).
———, and Ferdinand Rath. 1965. "Preliminary Findings of Comparative Fertility Surveys in Three Latin American Cities," *Milbank Memorial Fund Quarterly* 43(4):36–68 (October, pt. 2).
Mishan, E. J. 1971. "Evaluation of Life and Limb: A Theoretical Approach," *Journal of Political Economy* 79(4):687–705 (July/August).
Mitchell, Robert E. 1971. "Changes in Fertility Rates and Family Size in Response to Changes in Age at Marriage, the Trend Away from Arranged Marriages, and Increasing Urbanization," *Population Studies* 25(3):481–489 (November).
———. 1972. "Husband-Wife Relations and Family-Planning Practices in Urban Hong Kong," *Journal of Marriage and the Family* 34(1):139–146 (February).
Momeni, Djamchid, A. 1972. "The Difficulties of Changing the Age at Marriage in Iran," *Journal of Marriage and the Family* 34(3):545–551 (August).
Moos, Rudolph. 1974. *Evaluating Treatment Environments: A Social Ecological Approach.* New York: John Wiley and Sons.
Morris, J., and J. Heady. 1955. "Social and Biological Factors of Infant Mortality," *Lancet* (February 12, pt. 1 through March 12, pt. 5).

Reprinted in *Uses of Epidemiology,* edited by J. Morris. Edinburgh and London: Livingstone, 2d ed., 1964.

Mueller, Eva. 1958. "The Desire for Innovations in Household Goods." In *Consumer Behavior,* vol. 3, edited by L. H. Clark, pp. 13–37. New York: Harper & Row.

———. 1972a. "Economic Cost and Value of Children: Conceptualization and Measurement." In *The Satisfactions and Costs of Children,* edited by J. T. Fawcett. Honolulu: East-West Center Press.

———. 1972b. "Economic Motives for Family Limitation: A Study Conducted in Taiwan." *Population Studies* 27(3):383–403 (November).

———. 1975. "The Impact of Agricultural Change on Demographic Development in the Third World." In *Population Growth and Economic Development in the Third World.* Dolhain, Belgium: International Union for the Scientific Study of Population.

Mukherjee, Bishwa Nath. 1973. *Condensed Report on the Survey of Women and Family Planning in India, Part II.* Unpublished. New Delhi: Council for Social Development.

Mushkin, S. J. 1962. "Health as an Investment," *Journal of Political Economy* 70(2):129–157 (October, pt. 2).

Muth, R. F. 1966. "Household Production and Consumer Demand Function," *Econometrica* 34:699–708 (July).

Myrdal, Gunnar. 1968. *Asian Drama.* New York: Pantheon Books.

Mysore. 1961. *The Mysore Population Study: A Cooperative Project of the United Nations and the Government of India.* New York: UN Department of Economic and Social Affairs.

Nag, Moni. 1968. *Factors Affecting Human Fertility in Nonindustrial Societies: A Cross-Cultural Study.* New Haven: Yale University Press.

———. 1972. "Economic Value of Children in Agricultural Societies: Evaluation of Existing Knowledge and an Anthropological Approach." In *The Satisfactions and Costs of Children: Theories, Concepts, Methods,* edited by James Fawcett. Honolulu: East-West Center Press.

Nair, P. R. G. 1974. "Decline in Birth Rate in Kerala," *Economic and Political Weekly* 9(6,7,8,):324–336.

Namboodiri, N. K. 1972. "Some Observations on the Economic Framework for Fertility Analysis," *Population Studies* 26(2):185–206 (July).

National Academy of Sciences. 1970. *Maternal Nutrition and the Course of Pregnancy.* Washington, D.C.

———. 1966. *Pre-School Child Malnutrition.* Publication No. 1282. Washington, D.C.

———. 1975. *Nutrition and Fertility Interrelationships: Implications for Policy and Action.* Washington, D.C.

National Board of Bangladesh Women's Rehabilitation Programme. 1974. *Women's Work.* Dacca: Bangladesh Co-operative Book Society.

National Council of Applied Economic Research. 1962. *Long-term Projections of Demand and Supply of Selected Agricultural Commodities, 1960–61 to 1976.* Bombay: Commercial Printing Press.

———. 1963. *Contractual Saving in Urban India*. New Delhi.

———. 1967. *All India Consumer Expenditure Survey*, vol. 2. New Delhi.

———. 1974. "Additional Rural Income Survey." New Delhi. Mimeographed.

Neher, Philip. 1971. "Peasants, Procreation, and Pensions," *American Economic Review* 61(3):380–389 (June).

Nelson, Richard R. 1956. "A Theory of the Low Level Equilibrium Trap in Underdeveloped Economies," *American Economic Review* 46:894–908 (December).

———. 1974. *The Effects of Income on Fertility*. Chapel Hill: Carolina Population Center, University of North Carolina.

———, T. Paul Schultz, and R. L. Slighton. 1971. *Structural Change in a Developing Economy*. Princeton, N.J.: Princeton University Press.

Nerlove, Marc. 1974. "Household and Economy: Toward a New Theory of Population and Economic Growth," *Journal of Political Economy* 82(2):S200–218 (March/April, pt. 2).

———, and S. James Press. 1973. "Univariate and Multivariate Log-Linear and Logistic Models." Santa Monica, Calif.: The Rand Corporation, R-1306-EDAINIH.

———, and T. Paul Schultz. 1970. *Love and Life Between the Censuses: A Model of Family Decision-making in Puerto Rico, 1950–1960*. Santa Monica, Calif.: The Rand Corporation, RM-6322-AID.

Nerlove, Sara B. 1974. "Women's Workload and Infant Feeding Practices: A Relationship with Demographic Implications." *Ethnology* 13(2):207–214 (April).

Newell, Elizabeth. 1972. "Sources of Mortality Change in Italy Since Unification," Ph.D. dissertation, University of Pennsylvania.

Newman, Peter. 1965. *Malaria Eradication and Population Growth with Special Reference to Ceylon and British Guiana*. Bureau of Public Health Economics, Research Series no. 10. Ann Arbor: School of Public Health, University of Michigan.

———. 1970. "Malaria Control and Population Growth," *Journal of Development Studies* 6(2):133–158.

———, and S. A. Meegama. 1969. "Discussion," *Population Studies* 23:2 (July).

Nordhaus, W. D., and James Tobin. 1973. "Is Growth Obsolete?" In *The Measurement of Economic and Social Performance*, edited by Milton Moss. Studies in Income and Wealth, no. 38. New York: Columbia University Press for the National Bureau of Economic Research.

North, Douglass C., and Robert Paul Thomas. 1973. *The Rise of the Western World*. Cambridge, England: Cambridge University Press.

Nortman, Dorothy. 1974. "Population and Family Planning Programs: A Factbook." In *Reports on Population/Family Planning* no. 2, 6th ed., p. 12.

Oelhaf, Robert C. 1971. "Interaction between Nutrition and Family Planning."

O'Hara, Donald J. 1972a. *Changes in Mortality Levels and Family Decisions Regarding Children.* Santa Monica, Calif.: The Rand Corporation. R-914-RF.

———. 1972b. "Mortality Risks, Sequential Decisions on Births, and Population Growth," *Demography* 9(3):285–298 (August).

———. 1974. "Microeconomic Aspects of the Demographic Transition," Discussion paper. University of Rochester.

Ohlin, Goran. 1967. *Population Control and Economic Development.* Paris: Development Centre, Organisation for Economic Co-operation and Development.

———. 1969. "Population Pressure and Alternative Investments." In *World Population Conference Proceedings,* vol. 3, pp. 1703–1728. London: International Union for the Scientific Study of Population.

Olusanya, P. O. 1971. "Status Differentials in the Fertility Attitudes of Married Women in Two Countries in Western Nigeria," *Economic Development and Cultural Change* 19(4):641–651 (July).

Omran, Abdel R. 1971. "The Epidemiologic Transition: A Theory of the Epidemiology of Population Change," *Milbank Memorial Fund Quarterly* 49(4):509–538 (October, pt. 1).

———. 1973. *Egypt: Population, Problems, and Prospects.* Chapel Hill: Carolina Population Center, University of North Carolina.

Oppong, Christine. 1970. "Conjugal Power and Resources: An Urban African Example," *Journal of Marriage and the Family* 32(4):676–680 (November).

Oshima, Harry. 1961. "Consumer Asset Formation and the Future of Capitalism," *Economic Journal* 71:20–35 (March).

Paik, Hyun Ki. 1973. "A Field Try-out of Population Education Curriculum Materials for Teacher Education Programmes—An Experimental Study: A Case of the Philippines." Bangkok: Asian Regional Office, UNESCO.

Pan American Health Organization. 1970. *Maternal Nutrition and Family Planning in the Americas.* Scientific Publication No. 204. Washington, D.C.

Papanek, Hanna. 1971. "Purdah in Pakistan: Seclusion and Modern Occupations for Women," *Journal of Marriage and the Family* 33(3):517–530 (August).

———. 1973. "Purdah: Separate Worlds and Symbolic Shelter," *Comparative Studies in Society and History* 15(3):289–325 (June).

Peled, Tsiyona. 1969. *Problems and Attitudes in Family Planning* (in Hebrew, with summary in English). Israel Institute of Applied Social Research.

Perez, Alfredo, Patricio Vela, R. G. Potter, and G. S. Masnick. 1971. "Timing and Sequence of Resuming Ovulation and Menstruation after Childbirth," *Population Studies* 25(3):491–503 (November).

———. 1972. "First Ovulation After Childbirth: The Effect of Breastfeeding," *American Journal of Obstetrics and Gynecology* 114(8):1041–1047 (December).

Piepmeier, K. B., and T. S. Adkins. 1973. "The Status of Women and Fertility," *Journal of Biosocial Science* 4(4):507–520 (October).

Pinnelli, Antonella. 1971. "Female Labour and Fertility in Relationship to Contrasting Social and Economic Conditions," *Human Relations* 24(6):603-610 (December).

Pirie, Peter. 1972. "The Effect of Treponemators and Gonorrhea on the Populations of the Pacific Islands," *Human Biology in Oceania* 1(3): 187–206 (February).

Poffenberger, D. S. 1971. *Reaction to World News Events and the Influence of Mass Media in an Indian Village*. Michigan Papers on South and Southeast Asia, no. 1.

Poffenberger, Thomas, and Shirley B. Poffenberger. 1973. "The Social Psychology of Fertility in a Village in India." In *Psychological Perspectives on Population,* edited by James T. Fawcett, pp. 135–162. New York: Basic Books.

Pohlman, Edward. 1971. *Incentives and Compensations in Birth Planning*. Monograph No. 11. Chapel Hill: Carolina Population Center, University of North Carolina.

Polcyn, Kenneth. 1973. *An Educator's Guide to Communication Technology*. Washington, D.C.: Information Center on Instructional Technology.

Popkin, Barry M. 1972. "Report: Research Priorities. Unpublished. Methodologies Conference on Economics of Malnutrition, Office of Nutrition, Agency for International Development, Washington, D.C.

Population Council. 1970. *A Manual for Surveys of Fertility and Family Planning: Knowledge, Attitudes, and Practice*. New York.

Potter, R. G., M. L. New, J. B. Wyon, and J. E. Gordon. 1965. "Application of Field Studies to Research on the Physiology of Human Reproduction: Lactation and Its Effects Upon Birth Intervals in Eleven Punjab Villages, India." In *Public Health and Population Change,* edited by M. C. Sheps and J. C. Ridley. Pittsburgh: University of Pittsburgh Press.

Preston, Sam, Nathan Keyfitz, and R. Schoen. 1972. *Causes of Death: Life Tables for National Populations*. New York: Seminar Press.

Preston, S. H., and V. E. Nelson. 1974. "Structure and Change in Cause of Death: An International Summary," *Population Studies* 28(1):19–52 (March).

Puffer, R. R., and C. V. Serrano. 1973. *Patterns of Mortality in Childhood*. Scientific Publication no. 262. Washington, D.C.: Pan American Health Organization, WHO.

Rainwater, Lee. 1965. *Family Design: Marital Sexuality, Family Size, and Contraception*. Chicago. Aldine.

Ramakumar, R., and Y. S. Gopal. 1972. "Husband–Wife Communication and Fertility in a Suburban Community Exposed to Family Planning," *Journal of Family Welfare* 18(3):30–36 (March).

Reid, M. G. 1975. "Income, Health and Disability," ch. 4. University of Chicago. Mimeographed.

Reiss, A., ed. 1964. *Louis Wirth: On Cities and Social Life*. University of Chicago Press.

Repetto, Robert G. 1968. "India: A Case Study of the Madras Vasectomy Program," *Studies in Family Planning* 31:8–16 (May).

———. 1972. "Son Preference and Fertility Behavior in Developing Countries," *Studies in Family Planning* 3(4):74–76 (April).

———. 1974. "The Interaction of Fertility and the Size Distribution of Income." Mimeographed. Cambridge, Mass.: Harvard University Population Center.

Research and Marketing Services. 1971. "A Study in the Evaluation of the Effectiveness of the Tata Incentive Program for Sterilization." Bombay.

Reutlinger, Schlomo, and Marcelo Selowsky. 1975. "Malnutrition and Poverty: Magnitude and Target Group-oriented Policies." Working paper. Washington, D.C.: International Bank for Reconstruction and Development (IBRD).

Rich, William. 1973. *Smaller Families Through Social and Economic Progress*. Washington, D.C.: Overseas Development Council.

Ridker, Ronald G. 1967. *The Economic Costs of Air Pollution*. New York: Praeger.

———. 1969. "Synopsis of a Proposal for a Family Planning Bond," *Studies in Family Planning* 43:11–16 (June).

———. 1971. "Savings Accounts for Family Planning: An Illustration from the Tea Estates of India," *Studies in Family Planning* 2(7):150–152 (July).

———. 1974. "Incentives and Disincentives for Fertility Reduction," *Population Policies and Economic Development* (Report no. 481). Washington, D.C.: International Bank for Reconstruction and Development (IBRD).

———, and Robert Muscat. 1973. "Incentives for Family Welfare and Fertility Reduction: An Illustration for Malaysia," *Studies in Family Planning* 4(1):1–11 (January).

Ridley, J. C., M. C. Sheps, J. W. Lingner, and J. A. Menken. 1967. "The Effects of Changing Mortality on Natality," *Milbank Memorial Fund Quarterly* 45(1):77–93 (January).

Robinson, Warren C. 1961. "Urban–Rural Differences in Indian Fertility," *Population Studies* 14(3):218–234 (March).

———. 1963. "Urbanization and Fertility: The Nonwestern Experience," *Milbank Memorial Fund Quarterly* 41(3):291–308 (July).

———. 1972. "Peasants, Procreation, and Pensions: Comment," *American Economic Review* 62(5):977–978 (December).

———, and D. E. Horlacher. 1971. "Population Growth and Economic Welfare," *Reports on Population/Family Planning* 6:1–39 (February).

Rodgers, G. B. 1974. "An International Cross-Section Analysis of Mortality." Mimeographed. Geneva: International Labour Office.

Rogers, Everett M. 1969. *Modernization Among Peasants: The Impact of Communication*. New York: Holt, Rinehart and Winston.

———. 1971. "Incentives in the Diffusion of Family Planning Observation,"

Studies in Family Planning 2:241–248.

———. 1972. "Field Experiments on Family Planning Incentives." East Lansing: Department of Communication, Michigan State University. Mimeographed.

———. 1973. *Communication Strategies for Family Planning.* New York: The Free Press.

———, and Chris Ortloff. 1975. "The India Satellite Experiment." In *The Educational Uses of Broadcast Satellites: Status, Applications, Costs, and Issues,* edited by Kenneth Polcyn. Educational Technology Publications.

Romaniuc, Anatol. 1963. "Fecunditê et sterilitê des femmes congolaises." In *Proceedings of the International Population Conference, 1961,* vol. 2, pp. 109–122.

Rosario, Florangel Z. 1970. "Husband-Wife Interaction and Family Planning Acceptance: A Survey of the Literature." Working paper no 3. Honolulu: Population Institute, East-West Center.

Rosen, Bernard C., and Alan B. Simmons. 1971. "Industrialization, Family, and Fertility: A Structural-Psychological Analysis of the Brazilian Case," *Demography* 8(1):49–69 (February).

Rosen, Sherwin. 1974. "Hedonic Prices and Implicit Markets," *Journal of Political Economy* 82(1):34–35 (January/February).

Ross, John, Adrienne Germain, Jacqueline Forrest, and Jeroen Van Ginneken. 1972. "Findings from Family Planning Research," *Reports on Population/Family Planning* (October). New York: The Population Council.

Rostow, Walter. 1964. *A View From the Seventh Floor.* New York: Harper & Row.

Rottenberg, Simon. 1958. "Consumption Choices and Change: Puerto Rico." In *Consumer Behavior,* edited by L. H. Clark. New York: Harper & Row.

Roy, Prodipto, Frederick Waisanen, and Everett Rogers. 1969. *The Impact of Communication on Rural Development.* Paris: UNESCO.

Russell, L. B., and C. S. Burke. 1974. *Determinants of Infant and Child Mortality: Report of a Feasibility Study,* pts. 1 and 2. Washington, D.C.: National Planning Association.

———. 1975. *Determinants of Infant and Child Mortality: Econometric Analysis of Survey Data for San Juan, Argentina.* Washington, D.C.: National Planning Association.

Rutstein, Shea O. 1970. "The Relation of Child Mortality to Fertility in Taiwan." In *Social Statistics Proceedings of the American Statistical Association,* pp. 348–353.

———. 1971. "The Influence of Child Mortality on Fertility in Taiwan." Ph.D. dissertation, University of Michigan.

———. 1974. "The Influence of Child Mortality on Fertility in Taiwan," *Studies in Family Planning* 5(6):182–189 (June).

Ryan, Bryce. 1952. "Institutional Factors in Sinhalese Fertility," *Milbank Memorial Fund Quarterly* 30:359-381 (October).

Ryder, N. B. 1967. "The Character of Modern Fertility," *Annals of the American Academy of Political and Social Sciences* 369:26–36 (January).

———. 1973. "Comment," *Journal of Political Economy* 81(2):S65–69 (March/April, pt. 2).

———, and C. F. Westoff. 1971. *Reproduction in the United States, 1965.* Princeton, N.J.: Princeton University Press.

Safilios-Rothschild, Constantina. 1969. "Sociopsychological Factors Affecting Fertility in Urban Greece: A Preliminary Report," *Journal of Marriage and the Family* 31(3):595–606 (August).

———. 1970. "The Study of Family Power Structure: A Review 1960–1969," *Journal of Marriage and the Family* 32(4)539–552.

———. 1972. "The Relationship Between Work Commitment and Fertility," *International Journal of Sociology of the Family,* vol. 2. Lucknow, India: Lucknow Publishing House.

Said, S., E. D. B. Johansson, and C. Gemzell. 1974. "Return of Ovulation During the Postpartum Period," *Acta Obstetrica et Gynecologica Scandinavica* 53:63–67.

Saiyidain, K. G., Naik, J. P., and Husain, S. A. (1952). 1966. *Compulsory Education in India.* Paris: UNESCO.

Salaff, Janet W. 1971. " 'Tilling the Land for the Revolution': The Implications of the Ideology of Equality for Women's Fertility Goals in China." Paper presented at the annual meetings of the Population Association of America, Washington, D.C.

———. 1972a. "Institutionalized Motivation for Fertility Limitation in China," *Population Studies* 26(2):233–262 (July).

———. 1972b. "Social and Demographic Determinants of Marriage Age in Hong Kong." Working paper no 2. Vancouver: Institute of Asian and Slavonic Research, University of British Columbia.

Salber, E. J., Manning Feinleib, and Brian MacMahon. 1966. "The Duration of Postpartum Amenorrhea," *American Journal of Epidemiology* 82(3):347–358.

———, J. J. Feldman, and M. Hannigan. 1968. "Duration of Postpartum Amenorrhea in Successive Pregnancies," *American Journal of Obstetrics and Gynecology* 100(1):24–29 (January 1).

Sanders, J. 1931. *The Declining Birthrate in Rotterdam.* The Hague: Martinus Nijhoff.

Sanderson, W. C. 1974. "Economic Theories of Fertility: What Do They Explain?" Working paper no. 36. New York: National Bureau of Economic Research.

Schelling, T. C. 1968. "The Life You Save May Be Your Own." In *Problems in Public Expenditure,* edited by S. B. Chase, Jr. Washington, D.C.: Brookings Institution.

Schnaiberg, Allan. 1970. "Measuring Modernism: Theoretical and Empirical Explorations," *American Journal of Sociology* 76(3):399–425 (November).

Schramm, Wilbur. 1964. *Mass Media and National Development.* Stanford, Calif.: Stanford University Press.

———. 1971. "Communication in Family Planning," *Reports on Population/Family Planning* (April). New York: The Population Council.

Schultz, T. Paul. 1967. *A Family Planning Hypothesis: Some Empirical Evidence from Puerto Rico.* Santa Monica, Calif.: The Rand Corporation, RM-5405-RC/AID.

———. 1969a. An Economic Model of Family Planning and Fertility," *Journal of Political Economy* 77(2):153–180 (March/April).

———. 1969b. "An Economic Perspective on Population Growth." Mimeographed.

———. 1971. *Evaluation of Population Policies: A Framework for Analysis and Its Application to Taiwan's Family Planning Program.* Santa Monica, Calif.: The Rand Corporation, R-643-AID.

———. 1972a. "Retrospective Evidence of a Decline in Fertility and Child Mortality in Bangladesh," *Demography* 9(3):415–430 (August).

———. 1972b. *Explanations of Birth Rate Changes over Space and Time: A Study of Taiwan.* Santa Monica, Calif.: The Rand Corporation, RM-1079-RF. For a less detailed account, see Schultz, T. Paul (1973). *Journal of Political Economy* 81(2):S238–274 (March/April, supplement 2).

———. 1974. *Fertility Determinants: A Theory, Evidence, and an Application to Policy Evaluation.* Santa Monica, Calif.: The Rand Corporation, R-1016/RF/AID.

———, and Julie DaVanzo. 1970a. *Fertility Patterns and Their Determinants in the Arab Middle East.* Santa Monica, Calif.: The Rand Corporation, RM-5978-FF. Reprinted in *Economic Development and Population Growth in the Middle East,* edited by C. A. Cooper and S. S. Alexander, pp. 401–500. New York: American Elsevier, 1972.

———, ———. 1970b. *Analysis of Demographic Change in East Pakistan: A Study of Retrospective Survey Data.* Santa Monica, Calif.: The Rand Corporation, R-564-AID.

Schultz, Theodore W. 1964. *Transforming Traditional Agriculture.* New Haven, Conn.: Yale University Press.

———. 1973. "The Value of Children: An Economic Perspective," *Journal of Political Economy* 81(2):S2–13 (March/April, pt. 2).

———, ed. 1962. *Investments in Human Beings.* A supplement to *Journal of Political Economy* 60(5) (October, pt. 2).

Scrimshaw, Nevin S., and J. E. Gordon, eds. 1968. *Malnutrition, Learning and Behavior.* Cambridge, Mass.: Massachusetts Institute of Technology Press.

———, C. E. Taylor, and J. E. Gordon. 1968. *Interactions of Nutrition and Infection,* World Health Organization Monograph Series, no. 57. Geneva: WHO.

Selowsky, Marcelo. 1971. "An Attempt to Estimate Rates of Return to Investment in Infant Nutrition Programs." Discussion paper no. 209. Cambridge, Mass.: Institute of Economic Research, Harvard University.

———, and Lance Taylor. 1971. "The Economics of Malnourished Children: A Study of Disinvestment in Human Capital." Discussion paper no. 13. Minneapolis: University of Minnesota.

———. 1973. "The Economics of Malnourished Children: An Example of Disinvestment in Human Capital," *Economic Development and Cultural Change* 22(1):17–30 (October).

Sen, Jukta, and D. K. Sen. 1967. "Family Planning Practice of Couples of Reproduction Age Group in a Selected Locality in Calcutta," *Journal of Family Welfare* 14(1):13–24 (September).

Sethuramen, S. V. 1972. "Underemployment in Rural India." New Delhi: U.S. Agency for International Development. Mimeographed.

Shah, F. K., and Helen Abbey. 1971. "Effects of Some Factors on Neonatal and Post-neonatal Mortality," *Milbank Memorial Fund Quarterly* 49(1) (January, pt. 1).

Shanas, Ethel, et al. 1968. *Old People in Three Industrial Societies*. New York: Atherton Press.

Shepherd, Geoffrey. 1963. *Agricultural Price Analysis*. Ames, Iowa: University of Iowa Press.

Sheps, M. C. 1964. "On the Time Required for Conception," *Population Studies* 18(1):85–87 (July).

———. 1965. "Applications of Probability Models to the Study of Patterns of Human Reproduction." In *Public Health and Population Change*, edited by M. C. Sheps and J. C. Ridley, pp. 307–332. Pittsburgh: University of Pittsburgh Press.

———, J. A. Menken, J. C. Ridley, and J. W. Lingner. 1970. "The Truncation Effect in Closed and Open Birth Interval Data," *Journal of the American Statistical Association* 65:678–693.

———, and J. A. Menken. 1973. "On Estimating the Risk of Conception from Censored Data," In *Population Dynamics*, edited by T. N. E. Granville, pp. 167–200. New York: Academic Press.

Shorter, F. C. 1968. "Information on Fertility, Mortality, and Population Growth in Turkey," *Population Index* 34(1):3–21 (January/March).

Siegel, Earl, and Naomi Morris. 1970. "Epidemiology of Human Reproductive Casualties, with Emphasis on Role of Nutrition." In *Maternal Nutrition and the Course of Pregnancy*, pp. 5–40. Washington, D.C.: National Academy of Sciences.

Simmons, G. B. 1971. *The Indian Investment in Family Planning*. New York: The Population Council.

Simon, Julian L. 1968. "The Role of Bonuses and Persuasive Propaganda in the Reduction of Birth Rates," *Economic Development and Cultural Change* 16(3):404–411 (April).

———. 1969. "Money Incentives to Reduce Birth Rates in Low Income Countries. A Proposal to Determine the Effect Experimentally." Urbana: University of Illinois. Mimeographed.

———. 1974a. *The Effects of Income on Fertility*. Monograph 19. Chapel Hill: Carolina Population Center, University of North Carolina.

———. 1974b. "Segmentation and Market Strategy in Birth-control Campaigns," *Studies in Family Planning* 5(3):90–97 (March).

Simon, Rita J., and Julian L. Simon. 1974–75. "The Effect of Money

Incentives on Family Size: A Hypothetical Question Study," *Public Opinion Quarterly* 38:585–595 (Winter).

Sirageldin, I., and S. Hopkins. 1972. "Family Planning Programs: An Economic Approach," *Studies in Family Planning* 3:2:17–23.

Sloan, Frank. 1971. *Survival of Progeny in Developing Countries: An Evidence from Costa Rica, Mexico, East Pakistan and Puerto Rico.* Santa Monica, Calif.: The Rand Corporation, R-773-AID.

Smith, David H., and Alex Inkeles. 1966. "The OM Scale: A Comparative Socio-Psychological Measure of Individual Modernity," *Sociometry* 29: 353–388 (December).

Smith, T. E. 1960. "The Cocos-Keeling Islands: A Demographic Laboratory," *Population Studies* 14(2):94–130 (September).

Smithies, Arthur. 1961. "Rising Expectations and Economic Development," *Economic Journal* 71 (282)255–272 (June).

Snyder, D. W. 1974. "Economic Determinants of Family Size in West Africa," *Demography* 11(4):613–627 (November).

Spengler, J. J. 1966. "Values in Fertility Analysis," *Demography* 3(1): 109–130.

Srikantan, Kodaganallur S. 1967. "Effects of Neighborhood and Individual Factors on Family Planning in Taichung." Ph.D. dissertation, University of Michigan.

———. 1973. "Economic Activity and Labour Force Participation Rates." In *Population Papers,* February, pp. 189–207. Taiwan: The Institute of Economics, Academica Sinica.

Stettler, L. H. III. 1968. "The New England Throat Distemper and Family Size." Paper presented at the Second Conference on the Economics of Health, Baltimore, December.

Stigler, George. 1950. *Employment and Compensation in Education.* Occasional paper no. 23. New York: National Bureau of Economic Research.

Stolnitz, G. J. 1955. "A Century of International Mortality Trends," *Population Studies* 9(1):24–55 (July).

———. 1956. "A Century of International Mortality Trends," *Population Studies* 10(1):17–43 (July).

———. 1965. "Recent Mortality Trends in Latin America, Asia, and Africa," *Population Studies* 19(2):117–138 (November).

Strumpel, Burkhard. 1965. "Consumption Aspirations: Incentives for Economic Change," *Social and Economic Studies* 14(2):183–193 (June).

Stycos, J. Mayone. 1955. *The Family and Fertility in Puerto Rico.* Ithaca, N.Y.: Cornell University Press.

———. 1967. "Education and Fertility in Puerto Rico." In *Proceedings of the World Population Conference, Belgrade 1965,* vol. 4, pp. 177–180. New York: United Nations.

———, K. W. Back, and Reuben Hill. 1956. "Problems of Communication Between Husband and Wife on Matters Relating to Family Limitation," *Human Relations* 9:207–215.

———, and R. N. Weller. 1967. "Female Working Roles and Fertility," *Demography* 4(1):210–217.

Stys, W. 1957. "The Influence of Economic Conditions on the Fertility of Peasant Women," *Population Studies* 11:136–148 (November).

Sullivan, J. M. 1972. "Models for the Estimation of the Probability of Dying between Birth and Exact Ages of Early Childhood," *Population Studies* 26(1):79–97 (March).

———. 1973. "The Influence of Cause-Specific Mortality Conditions on the Age Pattern of Mortality with Special Reference to Taiwan," *Population Studies* 27(1):135–158 (March).

Tabbarah, Riad B. 1971. "Toward a Theory of Demographic Development," *Economic Development and Cultural Change* 19(2):257–276 (January).

Taylor, Carl E. 1965. "Health and Population," *Foreign Affairs* 43(3):475–486 (April).

———, and Marie-Françoise Hall. 1967. "Health, Population, and Economic Development," *Science* 157:651–657 (August).

———, J. S. Newman, and N. U. Kelly. 1974. "Health Aspects of Population Increase." Working Paper no. 8. World Population Conference, Baltimore.

Taylor, Howard C., and Robert J. Lapham. 1974. "A Program for Family Planning Based on Maternal/Child Health Services," *Studies in Family Planning* 5(3):71–82 (March).

Teitelbaum, Michael S. 1975. "Relevance of Demographic Transition Theory for Developing Countries," *Science* 188(4187): 420–425 (May 2).

Thaler, Richard, and Sherwin Rosen. 1974. "The Value of Saving a Life: Evidence from the Labor Market." Discussion paper 74–2. Rochester, N.Y.: University of Rochester.

Tharpar, Romila. 1963. "The History of Female Emancipation in Southern Asia." In *Women in the New Asia*, edited by Barbara E. Ward. Amsterdam: UNESCO.

Theil, Henri. 1952. "Qualities, Prices, and Budget Inquiries," *Review of Economic Studies* 19(3):129–147.

———. 1971. *Principles of Econometrics*. New York: John Wiley and Sons.

Thomas, Dorothy S. 1941. *Social and Economic Aspects of Swedish Population Movements*. New York: Macmillan.

Turkey. State Institute of Statistics. 1969. Census of Population, 1965. Social and Economic Characteristics of Population, pp. 52–65. Ankara, Turkey.

Turner, John. 1968. "Uncontrolled Urban Settlement: Problems and Policies." In *Urbanization: Development Policies and Planning*. New York: United Nations.

United Nations, Department of Economic and Social Affairs. 1953. *The Determinants and Consequences of Population Trends*. Population Studies, no. 17.

———. 1956. *The Aging of Populations and Its Economic and Social Implications*. Population Studies, no. 26.

———. 1962. *Demographic Aspects of Manpower: Sex and Age Patterns of Participation in Economic Activities*. Population Studies, no. 33.

———. 1963. *Population Bulletin of the United Nations, 1962.*

United Nations, Economic Commission for Asia and the Far East (ECAFE). 1973. "The Status of Women and Family Planning." Paper prepared for the United Nations Seminar on the Status of Women and Family Planning. Jogjakarta, Indonesia, June 20–30.

United Nations, Economic and Social Council (ECOSOC). 1973. *Status of Rural Women, Especially Agricultural Workers.* Report prepared by the International Labour Organisation for the Commission on the Status of Women (E/CN.6/583/Add.1, December 17, and E/CN.6/583/Add.2, December 27).

UNESCO. 1954. *Studies on Compulsory Education.* New York: United Nations.

———. 1970. *Proceedings: Asian Regional Workshop on Population and Family Life Education.* Bangkok: UNESCO, Asian Regional Office.

———. 1972. *A Guide to Satellite Communication.* Reports and Papers on Mass Communication, no. 66.

University of California at Los Angeles, School of Public Health, and University of Ghana Medical School, Department of Preventive and Social Medicine. 1972. "Danfa Comprehensive Rural Health and Family Planning Project: Ghana—Research Design."

Usher, Dan. 1973. "An Imputation to the Measure of Economic Growth for Changes in Life-Expectancy." In *The Measurement of Economic and Social Performance,* edited by M. Moss. National Bureau of Economic Research Conference on Research in Income and Wealth, pp. 193–226. New York: Columbia University Press.

Vaizey, John. 1962. *The Economics of Education.* London: Faber and Faber.

Vance, R. B., and F. C. Madigan, S.J. 1956. "Differential Mortality and the 'Style of Life' of Man and Woman: A Research Design." In *Trends and Differentials in Mortality.* New York: Milbank Memorial Fund.

van de Walle, Etienne. 1974. *The Female Population of France in the Nineteenth Century.* Princeton, N.J.: Princeton University Press.

Van Ginneken, Jeroen K. 1974. "Prolonged Breastfeeding as a Birth Spacing Method," *Studies in Family Planning* 5(6):201–206 (June).

Verijn-Stuart, C. A. 1902. "Natalité, morinatalité et mortalité infantile selon le degré d'assistance dans quelques villes et un nombre de communes rurales dans les Pays-Bas," *Bulletin de L'Institute International de statistique* (Hungary) 13:357–368.

Viederman, Stephen. 1971. "Population Education in the United States." Report to the Commission on Population Growth and the American Future.

———. 1972. "Population Education in Elementary and Secondary Schools in the United States." In *Aspects of Population Growth Policy,* edited by R. Parke, Jr., and C. F. Westoff, pp. 429–458. U.S. Commission on Population Growth and the American Future Research Reports, vol. 6. Washington, D.C.: U.S. Govt. Print. Off.

———. 1974. "Towards a Broader Definition of Population Education," *International Social Science Journal* 16:319.

———, and Sloan Wayland. 1972. "In-School Population Education." In *Population Communications: Overview and Outlook,* edited by Wilder Johnson et al.

Visaria, Pravin. 1973. "The Level and Nature of Work Participation by Sex, Age, and Marital Status in India, 1961." Mimeographed.

Walberg, Herbert J. 1971. "Models for Optimizing and Individualizing School Learning," *Interchange* 2(3):15–27.

Wang, D. M., and S. Y. Chen. 1973. "Evaluation of the First Year of the Educational Savings Program in Taiwan," *Studies in Family Planning,* 4(7):157–161 (July).

Ward, Barbara E., ed. 1963. *Women in the New Asia.* Amsterdam: UNESCO.

Warriner, Doreen. 1957. *Land Reform and Development in the Middle East.* New York: Royal Institute of International Affairs.

Wayland, Sloan. 1971a. "Issues and Problems in Introducing Population Education." Unpublished.

———. 1971b. "Population Education as It Exists Today: A Global Perspective." Paper presented at the Population Education Conference, Chapel Hill: Carolina Population Center, University of North Carolina.

Weintraub, Robert. 1962. "The Birth Rate and Economic Development," *Econometrica* 40(4):812–817 (October).

Weisbrod, B. A., R. L. Andreano, R. E. Baldwin, E. H. Epstein, and A. C. Kelley. 1973. *Disease and Economic Development: The Impact of Parasite Diseases in St Lucia.* Madison: University of Wisconsin Press.

Welch, Finis. 1970. "Education in Production," *Journal of Political Economy* 78(1):35–59 (January/February).

———. 1974. *Sex of Children: Prior Uncertainty and Subsequent Fertility Behavior.* Santa Monica, Calif.: The Rand Corporation, R-1510-RF.

Weller, Robert H. 1968. "The Employment of Wives, Role Incompatibility, and Fertility: A Study Among Lower and Middle Class Residents of San Juan, Puerto Rico," *Milbank Memorial Fund Quarterly* 46(4):507–526 (October).

———. 1973. "Female Labor Force Participation, Fertility, and Population Policy." Paper presented at the General Conference of the International Union for the Scientific Study of Population, Liège, Belgium.

West, E. G. 1968. "Social Legislation and the Demand for Children: Comment," *Western Economic Journal* 6:419–424 (December).

Westoff, Charles, Robert G. Potter, Jr., and Philip C. Sagi. 1973. *The Third Child.* Princeton, N.J.: Princeton University Press.

White, Benjamin. 1973. "The Economic Importance of Children in a Javanese Village." Mimeographed. New York: International Institute for the Study of Human Reproduction, Columbia University.

Wiley, David. 1976. "Another Hour, Another Day: Quantity of Schooling, a Potent Path for Policy." In *Schooling and Achievement in American*

Society, edited by W. H. Sewell, R. M. Hauser, and D. L. Featherman. New York: Academic Press.

———, and Annegret Harnischfeger. 1974. "Explosion of a Myth: Quantity of Schooling and Exposure to Instruction, Major Educational Vehicles," *Educational Researcher* 3:7–12 (April).

Wilkinson, Maurice. 1973. "An Econometric Analysis of Fertility in Sweden, 1870–1965," *Econometrica* 41:633–642 (July).

Williams, A. D. 1974. "Fertility and Child Mortality: Interactions in the 1965 National Fertility Study." Applications Workshop, Department of Economics, University of Chicago.

Willis, Robert J. 1969. "A New Approach to the Economic Theory of Fertility Behavior." Mimeographed. Middletown, Conn.: Wesleyan University.

———. 1973. "A New Approach to the Economic Theory of Fertility Behavior," *Journal of Political Economy* 81(2):S14–69 (March/April, Supplement 2).

Wirth, Louis. 1927. "The Ghetto," *American Journal of Sociology* 32(1): 57–71 (July).

Wishik, Samuel M. 1972. "Nutrition, Family Planning, and Fertility." Paper presented at the Twenty-first Meeting of the Protein Advisory Group, United Nations, Paris, April.

———, Angus Thomson, and Jean-Pierre Habicht. 1972. "Drafts of Nutrition-Interaction Working Group." Geneva: WHO.

———, and Susan Van der Vynckt. 1973. "Uncontrolled Fertility and Malnutrition." Washington, D.C.: Committee on International Nutrition Programs, National Academy of Sciences.

Wold, C. H. 1953. *Demand Analysis.* New York: Wiley.

Wolf, Margery. 1974. "Chinese Women: Old Skills in a New Context." In *Woman, Culture, and Society,* edited by Michelle Zimbalist Rosaldo and Louise Lamphere. Stanford, Calif.: Stanford University Press.

Woodbury, Robert (1944). "Economic Consumption Scales and Their Uses," *Journal of the American Statistical Association* 39:445–468.

World Health Organization. 1950. *Epidemiological and Vital Statistics Reports* 3 (June 6).

———. 1972. "Drafts of Nutrition-Reproduction Working Group."

Wray, Joe D. 1971a. "The Malnutrition-Morbidity-Mortality (Triple-M) Complex in Pre-School Children." Working draft. New York: The Rockefeller Foundation.

———. 1971b. "Population Pressure on Families: Family Size and Child Spacing." In *Rapid Population Growth: Consequences and Policy Implications,* edited by Roger Revelle. Baltimore: The Johns Hopkins University Press.

———. 1975. "Does Better Nutrition Increase Fertility?" In Proceedings of the Ninth International Congress on Nutrition, Mexico. *Nutrition* 2:16–31.

Wright, Sewell. 1934. "The Method of Path Coefficients," *Annals of Mathematical Statistics* 5(3):161–215 (September).

———. 1960. "Path Coefficients and Path Regressions: Alternative or Complementary Concepts?" *Biometrics* 16:189–202.

Wrigley, E. A. 1969. *Population and History*. New York: McGraw-Hill.

Wyon, John B., and John E. Gordon. 1971. *The Khanna Study: Population Problems in the Rural Punjab*. Cambridge, Mass.: Harvard University Press.

Yasuba, Yasukichi. 1962. *Birth Rates of the White Population in the United States, 1800–1860: An Economic Study*. Baltimore: The Johns Hopkins University Press.

Yaukey, David. 1961. *Fertility Differences in a Mediating Country: A Survey of Lebanese Couples*. Princeton, N.J.: Princeton University Press.

———, T. Thorsen, and A. Onaka. 1973. "Marriage at an Earlier Age than Ideal Age in Six Latin American Capital Cities," *Population Studies* 27: 263–272.

Yi Hun-Gu. 1936. *Land Utilization and Rural Economy in Korea*. Westport, Conn.: Greenwood Press, reprinted 1968.

Youssef, Nadia Haggag. 1974. *Women and Work in Developing Societies*. Population monograph series no. 15. Berkeley: Institute of International Studies, University of California.

Zacharias, C. W. B. 1960. *Ministry of Food and Agriculture, Government of India, Studies in the Economics of Farm Management in Madras, 1956–57*. New Delhi.

Zarata, A. O. 1967. "Differential Fertility in Monterrey, Mexico: Prelude to Transition?" *Milbank Memorial Fund Quarterly* 45(2):93–108 (April).

Conference Participants

C. STEPHEN BALDWIN, Population Council, New York, New York
WILLIAM P. BUTZ, Rand Corporation, Santa Monica, California
PAUL DEMENY, Population Council, New York, New York
DENNIS N. DE TRAY, Rand Corporation, Santa Monica, California
RUTH B. DIXON, Department of Sociology, University of California, Davis, California
M. BADRUD DUZA, Population Council, New York, New York
SCARLETT EPSTEIN, Institute for Development Studies, University of Sussex, Brighton, England
DEBORAH S. FREEDMAN, Department of Economics, University of Michigan, Ann Arbor, Michigan
RONALD FREEDMAN, Population Studies Center, University of Michigan, Ann Arbor, Michigan
DAVID GOLDBERG, Population Studies Center, University of Michigan, Ann Arbor, Michigan
JOHN-PIERRE HABICHT, The National Center for Health Statistics, Bethesda, Maryland
JAMES HECKMAN, Department of Economics, University of Chicago, Chicago, Illinois
DONALD B. HOLSINGER, Comparative Education Center, University of Chicago, Chicago, Illinois
JOHN KANTNER, Department of Population Dynamics, The Johns Hopkins University, Baltimore, Maryland
JOHN D. KASARDA, Department of Sociology, University of North Carolina, Chapel Hill, North Carolina
TIMOTHY KING, International Bank for Reconstruction and Development, Washington, D.C.
JAMES L. MCCABE, Economic Growth Center, Yale University, New Haven, Connecticut

EVA MUELLER, Population Studies Center, University of Michigan, Ann Arbor, Michigan

KRISHNAN NAMBOODIRI, Department of Sociology, University of North Carolina, Chapel Hill, North Carolina

HANNA PAPANEK, Department of Sociology, Boston University, Boston, Massachusetts

ROBERT G. REPETTO, Center for Population Studies, Harvard University, Cambridge, Massachusetts

RONALD G. RIDKER, Resources for the Future, Washington, D.C.

MARK R. ROSENZWEIG, Economic Growth Center, Yale University, New Haven, Connecticut

T. PAUL SCHULTZ, Economic Growth Center, Yale University, New Haven, Connecticut

MARCELO SELOWSKY, International Bank for Reconstruction and Development, Washington, D.C.

JULIAN L. SIMON, Department of Economics, University of Illinois, Urbana, Illinois

ISMAIL SIRAGELDIN, Department of Population Dynamics, The Johns Hopkins University, Baltimore, Maryland

CARL TAYLOR, International Health, School of Hygiene, The Johns Hopkins University, Baltimore, Maryland

Library of Congress Cataloging in Publication Data

Main entry under title:

Population and development.

Includes bibliographical references and index.
1. Fertility, Human—Addresses, essays, lectures.
2. Population policy—Addresses, essays, lectures.
I. Ridker, Ronald Gene, 1931– II. Resources for the Future.
HB903.F4P66 301.31 76-16806
ISBN 0-8018-1884-2

For Product Safety Concerns and Information please contact our EU
representative GPSR@taylorandfrancis.com
Taylor & Francis Verlag GmbH, Kaufingerstraße 24, 80331 München, Germany

www.ingramcontent.com/pod-product-compliance
Ingram Content Group UK Ltd.
Pitfield, Milton Keynes, MK11 3LW, UK
UKHW022212190926
475702UK00003B/322
* 9 7 8 1 6 1 7 2 6 0 4 6 9 *